Sweepingly ambitious, *The Oxford History of Western Music* sets close examination of representative works within a socially and culturally oriented narrative to illuminate the themes, styles, and currents that gave shape and direction to the literate or "art" tradition of Western music. Taking a critical perspective that challenges the received wisdom of the field, Richard Taruskin treats the conventional narrative of music history as a historical artifact in its own right, within a new approach that gives critical discourse and reception equal billing with composition and performance.

Written by a towering and often provocative figure in musicology, *The Oxford History of Western Music* provides a critical esthetic position with respect to individual works, and a context in which each composition may be evaluated and remembered. This landmark set considers individual works both with respect to the esthetic and critical paradigms of their own contemporaries and as entities that have ever since been weathering the flux of time and taste. The flux is as much a part of the story as the original context. *The Oxford History of Western Music* is a first attempt at a twenty-first-century view of its subject. Taruskin provides greater attention to the full range of twentieth-century art music, including American music, than any previous music historian, devoting fully a third of the text to the relatively recent past, and concluding with some informed speculation on the future.

THE OXFORD HISTORY OF

WESTERN MUSIC

THE OXFORD HISTORY OF WESTERN MUSIC

THE OXFORD HISTORY OF

WESTERN
MUSIC

Richard Taruskin

Volume 1

THE EARLIEST NOTATIONS TO THE
SIXTEENTH CENTURY

OXFORD
UNIVERSITY PRESS
2005

OXFORD

UNIVERSITY PRESS

Oxford   New York

Auckland   Bangkok   Buenos Aires   Cape Town   Chennai
Dar es Salaam   Delhi   Hong Kong   Istanbul   Karachi   Kolkata
Kuala Lumpur   Madrid   Melbourne   Mexico City   Mumbai   Nairobi
São Paulo   Shanghai   Taipei   Tokyo   Toronto

Copyright © 2005 by Oxford University Press, Inc.

Published by Oxford University Press, Inc.
198 Madison Avenue, New York, New York 10016
http://www.oup.com/us

Oxford is a registered trademark of Oxford University Press

Library of Congress Cataloging-in-Publication Data
Taruskin, Richard.
The Oxford history of western music / by Richard Taruskin.
p. cm.
Includes bibliographical references and index.
ISBN 0-19-516979-4
1. Music — History and criticism. I. Title.
ML160.T18 2004
780′.9 — dc22
2004017897
ISBN Vol. 1   0-19-522270-9
ISBN Vol. 2   0-19-522271-7
ISBN Vol. 3   0-19-522272-5
ISBN Vol. 4   0-19-522273-3
ISBN Vol. 5   0-19-522274-1
ISBN Vol. 6   0-19-522275-X
1   3   5   7   9   8   6   4   2
Printed in the United States of America

To my mother, Beatrice Filler Taruskin,

My first music teacher

Contents of Volume 1

VOLUME 1: The Earliest Notations to the Sixteenth Century

Contents of Other Volumes

VOLUME 2: The Seventeenth and Eighteenth Centuries

Introduction: The History of What?

The argument is no other than to inquire and collect out of the records of all time what particular kinds of learning and arts have flourished in what ages and regions of the world, their antiquities, their progresses, their migrations (for sciences migrate like nations) over the different parts of the globe; and again their decays, disappearances, and revivals; [and also] an account of the principal authors, books, schools, successions, academies, societies, colleges, orders—in a word, everything which relates to the state of learning. Above all things, I wish events to be coupled with their causes. All this I would have handled in a historical way, not wasting time, after the manner of critics, in praise and blame, but simply narrating the fact historically, with but slight intermixture of private judgment. For the manner of compiling such a history I particularly advise that the matter and provision of it be not drawn from histories and commentaries alone; but that the principal books written in each century, or perhaps in shorter periods, proceeding in regular order from the earliest ages, be themselves taken into consultation; that so (I do not say by a complete perusal, for that would be an endless labour, but) by tasting them here and there, and observing their argument, style, and method, the Literary Spirit of each age may be charmed as it were from the dead.

—Francis Bacon, *De dignitate et augmentis scientiarum libri IX* (1623)[1]

Mutatis mutandis, Bacon's task was mine. He never lived to complete it; I have—but only by dint of a drastic narrowing of scope. My *mutandes* are stated in my title (one not chosen but granted; and for that honor I extend my thanks to the Delegates of the Oxford University Press). For "learning and the arts" substitute music. For "the different parts of the globe" substitute Europe, joined in Volume 3 by America. (That is what we still casually mean by "the West," although the concept is undergoing sometimes curious change: a Soviet music magazine I once subscribed to gave news of the pianist Yevgeny Kissin's "Western debut"—in Tokyo.) And as for antiquities, they hardly exist for music. (Jacques Chailley's magnificently titled conspectus, *40,000 ans de musique*, got through the first 39,000 years—I exaggerate only slightly—on its first page.[2])

Still, as the sheer bulk of this offering attests, a lot was left, because I took seriously Bacon's stipulations that causes be investigated, that original documents be not only cited but analyzed (for their "argument, style, and method") and that the approach should be catholic and as near exhaustive as possible, based not on my preferences but on my estimation of what needed to be included in order to satisfy the dual requirement of causal explanation and technical explication. Most books that call themselves histories of Western music, or of any of its traditional "style periods," are in fact surveys, which cover—and celebrate—the relevant repertoire, but make little effort truly to explain why and how things happened as they did. This set of books is an attempt at a true history.

Paradoxically, that means it does not take "coverage" as its primary task. A lot of famous music goes unmentioned in these pages, and even some famous composers (Ralph Vaughan Williams for one, as the compiler of the Chronology noticed; and Conlon Nancarrow for another, as I noticed in responding to a query from the art editor; not to mention practically all the composers—Marin Marais, Antoine Forqueray, Louis de Caix d'Hervelois, Johann Schenk, John Jenkins, *i tutti quanti*—whose music I used so lovingly to perform on the viola da gamba in a different phase of my life; and now they've all been mentioned). Inclusion and omission imply no judgment of value here. For the record, I listen often and with delight to many of Vaughan Williams's works, and as my students can confirm, I admire Nancarrow's tremendously. I never asked myself whether this or that composition or musician was "worth mentioning," and I hope readers will agree that I have sought neither to advocate nor to denigrate what I did include.

But there is something more fundamental yet to explain, given my claim of catholicity. Coverage of all the musics that have been made in Europe and America is obviously neither the aim of this book nor its achievement. A glance at the table of contents will instantly confirm, to the inevitable disappointment and perhaps consternation of some, that "Western music" here means what it has always meant in general academic histories: it means what is usually called "art music" or "classical music," and looks suspiciously like the traditional "high canon" that has come under so much justified fire for its long-unquestioned dominance of the academic curriculum (a dominance that is now in irreversible process of decline). A very challenging example of that fire is a fusillade by Robert Walser, a scholar of popular music, who characterizes the repertoire treated here in terms borrowed from the writings of the Marxist historian Eric Hobsbawm. "Classical music," writes Walser,

> is the sort of thing Eric Hobsbawm calls an "invented tradition," whereby present interests construct a cohesive past to establish or legitimize present-day institutions or social relations. The hodgepodge of the classical canon—aristocratic and bourgeois music; academic, sacred and secular; music for public concerts, private soirées and dancing—achieves its coherence through its function as the most prestigious musical culture of the twentieth century.[3]

Why in the world would one want to continue propagating such a hodgepodge in the twenty-first century?

The heterogeneity of the classical canon is undeniable. Indeed, that is one of its main attractions. And while I reject Walser's conspiracy-theorizing, I definitely sympathize with the social and political implications of his argument, as will be evident (for some—a different some—all too evident) in the many pages that follow. But that very sympathy is what impelled me to subject that impossibly heterogeneous body of music to one more (perhaps the last) comprehensive examination—under a revised definition that supplies the coherence that Walser impugns. All of the genres he mentions, and all of the genres that are treated in this book, are literate genres. That is, they are genres that have been disseminated primarily through the medium of writing. The sheer abundance and the generic heterogeneity of the music so disseminated in "the West" is a truly distinguishing feature—perhaps the West's signal musical distinction. It is deserving of critical study.

By critical study I mean a study that does not take literacy for granted, or simply celebrate it as a unique Western achievement, but rather "interrogates" it (as our hermeneutics of suspicion now demands) for its consequences. The first chapter of this book makes a fairly detailed attempt to assess the specific consequences for music of a literate culture, and that theme remains a constant factor—always implicit, often explicit—in every chapter that follows, right up to (and especially) the concluding ones. For it is the basic claim of this multivolumed book—its number-one postulate—that the literate tradition of Western music is coherent at least insofar as it has a completed shape. Its beginnings are known and explicable, and its end is now foreseeable (and also explicable). And just as the early chapters of this book are dominated by the interplay of literate and preliterate modes of thinking and transmission (and the middle chapters try to cite enough examples to keep the interplay of literate and nonliterate alive in the reader's consciousness), so the concluding chapters are dominated by the interplay of literate and postliterate modes, which have been discernable at least since the middle of the twentieth century, and which sent the literate tradition (in the form of a backlash) into its culminating phase.

This is by no means to imply that everything within the covers of these volumes constitutes a single story. I am as suspicious as the next scholar of what we now call metanarratives (or worse, "master narratives"). Indeed, one of the main tasks of this telling will be to account for the rise of our reigning narratives, and show that they too have histories with beginnings and (implicitly) with ends. The main ones, for music, have been, first, an esthetic narrative—recounting the achievement of "art for art's sake," or (in the present instance) of "absolute music"—that asserts the autonomy of artworks (often tautologically insulated by adding "insofar as they are artworks") as an indispensable and retroactive criterion of value and, second, a historical narrative—call it "neo-Hegelian"—that celebrates progressive (or "revolutionary") emancipation and values artworks according to their contribution to that project. Both are shopworn heirlooms of German romanticism. The first of these romantic tales is "historicized" in chapters 30 to 34, and the second in chapter 40, one of the key chapters in this text, for it furnishes our intellectual present with a past. This is done in the fervent belief that no claim of universality can survive situation in intellectual history. Each of the genres that Walser names has its own history, moreover, as do the many that he does not name, and it will be evident to all readers that this book devotes as much attention to a congeries of "petits récits"—individual accounts of this and that—as it does to the epic sketched in the foregoing paragraphs. But the overarching trajectory of musical literacy is nevertheless a part of all the stories, and a particularly revealing one.

* * * * *

The first thing that it reveals is that the history narrated within these covers is the history of elite genres. For until very recent times, and in some ways even up to the present, literacy and its fruits have been the possession — the closely guarded and privileging (even life-saving) possession — of social elites: ecclesiastical, political, military, hereditary, meritocratic, economic, educational, academic, fashionable, even criminal. What else, after all, makes high art high? The casting of the story as the story of the literate culture of music turns it willy-nilly into a social history — a contradictory social history in which progressive broadening of access to literacy and its attendant cultural perquisites (the history, as it has sometimes been called, of the democratization of taste), is accompanied at every turn by a counterthrust that seeks to redefine elite status (and its attendant genres) ever upward. As most comprehensively documented by Pierre Bourdieu, consumption of cultural goods (and music, on Bourdieu's showing, above all) is one of the primary means of social classification (including self- classification) — hence, social division — and (familiar proverbs notwithstanding) one of the liveliest sites of dispute in Western culture.[4] Most broadly, contestations of taste occur across lines of class division, and are easiest to discern between proponents of literate genres and nonliterate ones; but within and among elites they are no less potent, no less heated, and no less decisively influential on the course of events. Taste is one of the sites of contention to which this book gives extensive, and, I would claim, unprecedented coverage, beginning with chapter 4 and lasting to the bitter end.

Indeed, if one had to be nominated, I would single out social contention as embodied in words and deeds — what cultural theorists call "discourse" (and others call "buzz" or "spin") — as the paramount force driving this narrative. It has many arenas. Perhaps the most conspicuous is that of meaning, an area that was for a long time considered virtually off limits to professional scholarly investigation, since it was naively assumed to be a nonfactual domain inasmuch as music lacks the semantic (or "propositional") specificity of literature or even painting. But musical meaning is no more confinable to matters of simple semantic paraphrase than any other sort of meaning. Utterances are deemed meaningful (or not) insofar as they trigger associations, and in the absence of association no utterance is intelligible. Meaning in this book is taken to represent the full range of associations encompassed by locutions such as "If that is true, it means that . . . ," or "that's what M-O-T-H-E-R means to me," or, simply, "know what I mean?" It covers implications, consequences, metaphors, emotional attachments, social attitudes, proprietary interests, suggested possibilities, motives, significance (as distinguished from signification). . . and simple semantic paraphrase, too, when that is relevant.

And while it is perfectly true that semantic paraphrases of music are never "factual," their assertion is indeed a social fact — one that belongs to a category of historical fact of the most vital importance, since such facts are among the clearest connectors of musical history to the history of everything else. Take for example the current impassioned debate over the meaning of Dmitry Shostakovich's music, with all of its insistent claims and counterclaims. The assertion that Shostakovich's music reveals him to be a political dissident is only an opinion, as is the opposite claim, that his music shows him to have been a "loyal musical son of the Soviet Union"—as, for that matter, is the alternative claim that his music has no light to shed on the question of his personal political allegiances. And yet the fact that such assertions are advanced with passion is a powerful testimony to the social and political role Shostakovich's music has played in the world, both during his lifetime and (especially) after his death, when the Cold War was playing itself out. Espousing a particular position in the debate is no business of the historian. (Some readers may know that I have espoused one as a critic; I would like to think that readers who do not know my position will not discover it here.) But to report the debate in its full range, and draw relevant implications from it, is the historian's ineluctable duty. That report includes the designation of what elements within the sounding composition have triggered the associations—a properly historical sort of analysis that is particularly abundant in the present narrative. Call it semiotics if you will.

But of course semiotics has been much abused. It is an old vice of criticism, and lately of scholarship, to assume that the meaning of artworks is fully vested in them by their creators, and is simply "there" to be decoded by a specially gifted interpreter. That assumption can lead to gross errors. It is what vitiated the preposterously overrated work of Theodor Wiesengrund Adorno, and what has caused the work of the "new musicologists" of the 1980s and 1990s—Adornians to a man and woman—to age with such stunning rapidity. It is, all pretenses aside, still an authoritarian discourse and an asocial one. It still grants oracular privilege to the creative genius and his prophets, the gifted interpreters. It is altogether unacceptable as a historical method, although it is part of history and, like everything else, deserving of report. The historian's trick is to shift the question from "What does it mean?" to "What has it meant?" That move is what transforms futile speculation and dogmatic polemic into historical illumination. What it illuminates, in a word, are the *stakes*, both "theirs" and "ours."

Not that all meaningful discourse about music is semiotic. Much of it is evaluative. And value judgments, too, have a place of honor in historical narratives, so long as they are not merely the historian's judgment (as Francis Bacon was already presciently aware). Beethoven's greatness is an excellent case in point because it will come in for so much discussion throughout the second half of this book. As such, the notion of Beethoven's greatness is "only" an opinion. To assert it as a fact would be the sort of historians' transgression on which master narratives are built. (And because historians' transgressions so often make history, they will be given a lot of attention in the pages that follow.) But to say this much is already to observe that such assertions, precisely insofar as they are not factual, often have enormous performative import. Statements and actions predicated on Beethoven's perceived greatness are what constitute Beethoven's authority, which certainly is a historical fact—one that practically determined the course of late-nineteenth-century music history. Without taking it into account one can explain little of what went on in the world of literate music-making during that time—and even up to the present. Whether the historian agrees with the perception on which Beethoven's authority has been based is of no consequence to the tale, and has no bearing on the historian's obligation to report it. That report constitutes "reception history"—a relatively new thing in musicology, but (many scholars now agree) of equal importance to the production history that used to count as the whole story. I have made a great effort to give the two equal time, since both are necessary ingredients of any account that claims fairly to represent history.

* * * *

Statements and actions in response to real or perceived conditions: these are the essential facts of human history. The discourse, so often slighted in the past, is in fact the story. It creates new social and intellectual conditions to which more statements and actions will respond, in an endless chain of agency. The historian needs to be on guard against the tendency, or the temptation, to simplify the story by neglecting this most basic fact of all. No historical event or change can be meaningfully asserted unless its agents can be specified; and *agents can only be people.* Attributions of agency unmediated by human action are, in effect, lies—or at the very least, evasions. They occur inadvertently in careless historiography (or historiography that has submitted unawares to a master narrative), and are invoked deliberately in propaganda (i.e., historiography that consciously colludes with a master narrative). I adduce what I consider to be an example of each (and leave it to the reader to decide which, if any, is the honorable blunder and which the propaganda). The first comes from Pieter C. Van den Toorn's *Music, Politics, and the Academy,* a rebuttal of the so-called New Musicology of the 1980s.

> The question of an engaging context is an aesthetic as well as an historical and analytic-theoretical one. And once individual works begin to prevail for what they are in and of themselves and not for what they represent, then context itself, as a reflection of this transcendence, becomes less dependent on matters of historical placement. A great variety of contexts can suggest themselves as attention is focused on the works, on the nature of both their immediacy and the relationship that is struck with the contemporary listener.[5]

The second is from the most recent narrative history of music published in America as of this writing, Mark Evan Bonds's *A History of Music in Western Culture.*

> By the early 16th century, the rondeau, the last of the surviving *formes fixes* from the medieval era, had largely disappeared, replaced by more freely structured chansons based on the principle of pervading imitation. What emerged during the 1520s and 1530s were new approaches to setting vernacular texts: the Parisian chanson in France and the madrigal in Italy.
>   During the 1520s, a new genre of song, now known as the Parisian chanson emerged in the French capital. Among its most notable composers were Claudin de Sermisy (ca. 1490–1562) and Clément Jannequin (ca. 1485–ca. 1560), whose works were widely disseminated by the Parisian music publisher Pierre Attingnant. Reflecting the influence of the Italian frottola, the Parisian chanson is lighter and more chordally oriented than earlier chansons.[6]

This sort of writing gives everybody an alibi. All the active verbs have ideas or inanimate objects as subjects, and all human acts are described in the passive voice. Nobody is seen as *doing* (or deciding) anything. Even the composers in the second extract are not described in the act, but only as an impersonal medium or passive vehicle of "emergence." Because nobody is doing anything, the authors never have to deal with motives or values, with choices or responsibilities, and that is their alibi. The second extract is a kind of shorthand historiography that inevitably devolves into inert survey, since it does nothing more than describe objects, thinking, perhaps, that is how one safeguards "objectivity." The first extract commits a far more serious transgression, for it is ideologically committed to its impersonality. Its elimination of human agency is calculated to protect the autonomy of the work-object and actually prevent historical thinking, which the author evidently regards as a threat to the universality (in his thinking, the validity) of the values he upholds. It is an attempt, caught as it were in the act, to enforce what I call the Great Either/Or, the great bane of contemporary musicology.

The Great Either/Or is the seemingly inescapable debate, familiar to all academically trained musicologists (who have had to endure it in their fledgling proseminars), epitomized in the question made famous by Carl Dahlhaus (1928–89), the most prestigious German music scholar of his generation: Is art history the *history* of art, or is it the history of *art*? What a senseless distinction! What seemed to make it necessary was the pseudo-dialectical "method" that cast all thought in rigidly — and artificially — binarized terms: "Does music mirror the reality surrounding a composer, OR does it propose an alternative reality? Does it have common roots with political events and philosophical ideas; OR is music written simply because music has always been written and not, or only incidentally, because a composer is seeking to respond with music to the world he lives in?" These questions all come from the second chapter of Dahlhaus's *Foundations of Music History*, the title of which — "The significance of art: historical or aesthetic?" — is yet another forced dichotomy. The whole chapter, which has achieved in its way the status of a classic, consists, throughout, of a veritable salad of empty binarisms.[7]

This sort of thinking has long been seen through — except, it seems, by musicologists. A scurrilous little tract — David Hackett Fischer's *Historians' Fallacies* — that graduate students of my generation liked to read (often aloud, to one another) behind our professors' backs includes it under the rubric "Fallacies of Question-Framing," and gives an unforgettable example: "Basil of Byzantium: Rat or Fink?" ("Maybe," the author comments, "Basil was the very model of a modern ratfink."[8]) There is nothing *a priori* to rule out both/and rather than either/or. Indeed, if it is true that production and reception history are of equal and interdependent importance to an understanding of cultural products, then it must follow that types of analysis usually conceived in mutually exclusive "internal" and "external" categories can and must function symbiotically. That is the assumption on which this book has been written, reflecting its author's refusal to choose between *this* and *that*, but rather to embrace this, that, and the other.

Reasons for the long if lately embattled dominance of internalist models for music history in the West (a dominance that in large part accounts for Dahlhaus's otherwise inexplicable prestige) have more than two centuries of intellectual history behind them, and this book will attempt to illuminate them at appropriate points. But a comment is required up front about the special reasons for their dominance in the recent history of the discipline — reasons having to do with the Cold War, when the general intellectual atmosphere was excessively polarized (hence binarized) around a pair of seemingly exhaustive and totalized alternatives. The only alternative to strict internalist thinking, it then seemed, was a discourse that was utterly corrupted by totalitarian cooption. Admit a social purview, it then seemed, and you were part of the Communist threat to the integrity (and the freedom) of the creative individual. In Germany, Dahlhaus was cast as the dialectical antithesis to Georg Knepler, his equally magisterial East German counterpart.[9] Within his own geographical and political milieu, then, his ideological commitments were acknowledged.[10] In the English-speaking countries, where Knepler was practically unknown, Dahlhaus's influence was more pernicious because he was assimilated, quite erroneously, to an indigenous scholarly pragmatism that thought itself ideologically uncommitted, free of theoretical preconceptions, and therefore capable of seeing things as they actually are. That, too, was of course a fallacy (Fischer calls it, perhaps unfairly, the "Baconian fallacy"). We all acknowledge now that our methods are grounded in and guided by theory, even if our theories are not consciously preformulated.

And so this narrative has been guided. Its theoretical assumptions and consequent methodology — the cards I am in process of laying on the table — were, as it happens, not preformulated; but that did not make them any less real, or lessen their potency as enablers and constraints. By the end of writing I was sufficiently self-aware to recognize the kinship between the methods I had arrived at and those advocated in *Art Worlds*, a methodological conspectus by Howard Becker, a sociologist of art. Celebrated among sociologists, the book has not been widely read by musicologists, and I discovered it after my own work was finished in first draft.[11] But a short description of its tenets will round out the picture I am attempting to draw of the premises on which this book rests, and a reading of Becker's book will, I think, be of conceptual benefit not only to the readers of this book, but also to the writers of others.

An "art world," as Becker conceives it, is the ensemble of agents and social relations that it takes to produce works of art (or maintain artistic activity) in various media. To study art worlds is to study processes of collective action and mediation, the very things that are most often missing in conventional musical historiography. Such a study tries to answer in all their complexity questions like "What did it take to produce Beethoven's Fifth?" Anyone who thinks that the answer to that question can be given in one word — "Beethoven" — needs to read Becker (or, if one has the time, this book). But of course no one who has reflected on the matter at all would give the one-word answer. Bartók gave a valuable clue to the kind of account that truly explains when he commented dryly that Kodály's *Psalmus Hungaricus* "could not have been written without Hungarian peasant music. (Neither, of course, could it have been written without Kodály.)"[12]

An explanatory account describes the dynamic (and, in the true sense, dialectical) relationship that obtains between powerful agents and mediating factors: institutions and their gatekeepers, ideologies, patterns of consumption and dissemination involving patrons, audiences, publishers and publicists, critics, chroniclers, commentators, and so on practically indefinitely until one chooses to draw the line.

Where shall it be drawn? Becker begins his book with a piquant epigraph that engages the question head-on, leading him directly to his first, most crucial theoretical point: namely, that "all artistic work, like all human activity, involves the joint activity of a number, often a large number, of people, through whose cooperation the art work we eventually see or hear comes to be and continues to be." The epigraph comes from the autobiography of Anthony Trollope:

> It was my practice to be at my table every morning at 5:30 A.M.; and it was also my practice to allow myself no mercy. An old groom, whose business it was to call me, and to whom I paid £5 a year extra for the duty, allowed himself no mercy. During all those years at Waltham Cross he was never once late with the coffee which it was his duty to bring me. I do not know that I ought not to feel that I owe more to him than to any one else for the success I have had. By beginning at that hour I could complete my literary work before I dressed for breakfast.[13]

Quite a few coffee porters, so to speak, will figure in the pages that follow, as will agents who enforce conventions (and, occasionally, the law), mobilize resources, disseminate products (often altering them in the process), and create reputations. All of them are at once potential enablers and potential constrainers, and create the conditions within which creative agents act. Composers will inevitably loom largest in the discussion despite all caveats, because theirs are the names on the artifacts that will be most closely analyzed. But the act of naming is itself an instrument of power, and a propagator of master narratives (now in a second, more literal, meaning), and it too must receive its meed of interrogation. The first chapter of the book can stand as a model, in a sense, for the more realistic assessment of the place composers and compositions occupy in the general historical scheme: first, because it names no composers at all; and second, because before any musical artifacts are discussed, the story of their enabling is told at considerable length — a story whose cast of characters includes kings, popes, teachers, painters, scribes and chroniclers, the latter furnishing a *Rashomon* choir of contradiction, disagreement and contention.

Another advantage of focusing on discourse and contention is that such a view prevents the lazy depiction of monoliths. The familiar "Frankfurt School" paradigm that casts the history of twentieth-century music as a simple two-sided battle between an avant-garde of heroic resisters and the homogenizing commercial juggernaut known as the Culture Industry is one of the most conspicuous and deserving victims of the kind of close observation encouraged here of the actual statements and actions of human agents ("real people"). Historians of popular music have shown over and over again that the Culture Industry has never been a monolith, and all it takes is the reading of a couple of memoirs — as witnesses, never as oracles — to make it obvious that neither was the avant-garde. Both imagined entities were in themselves sites of sometimes furious social contention, their discord breeding diversity; and paying due attention to their intramural dissensions will vastly complicate the depiction of their mutual relations.

If nothing else, this brief account of premises and methods, with its insistence on an eclectic multiplicity of approaches to observed phenomena and on greatly expanding the purview of what is observed, should help account for the extravagant length of this submission. As justification, I can offer only my conviction that the same factors that have increased its length have also, and in equal measure, increased its interest and its usefulness.

R. T. El Cerrito, California
5 August 2004

Acknowledgments

Not every book has a clearcut moment of conception. This one does. I will never forget the day in May 1991 when Maribeth Anderson Payne — then an editor at Schirmer Books, with which firm I had already published a collection of source readings (*Music in the Western World: A History in Documents*, coauthored with Piero Weiss) — approached me during a break at the Lincoln Center conference "Performing Mozart's Music" with the terrifying and irresistible proposal that I write, solo, a soup-to-nuts narrative history of a kind that, it had long become conventional to say, no one author could reasonably undertake. The book came to Oxford along with Maribeth; and although she has since moved on to yet another place, she is the one "without whom, etc." I thank her for keeping me off the streets for thirteen years.

One of her many favors to me was keeping her counterparts in other Oxford divisions informed about my project, especially when it became clear that she would not be there to see it through the press. That is how it found its happy home in the reference division, where Nancy Toff became its good shepherd. In the enormously complicated task of production I have been the fortunate beneficiary of a wonderfully smart, efficient, and generous team of editors. To name them all would be impossible (I'm sure I don't even know them all, just as I don't know the identities of the small army of proofreaders, copyeditors, and factcheckers — perhaps as many as forty people, I'm told — who have helped so much with the project), but the ones with whom I have had frequent (ultimately daily) contact are Timothy DeWerff, Tanya Laplante, Gabriel Caplan, and Timothy Sachs. By now I have worked with enough editors to know how exceptionally well this book has been served.

As a publisher-instigated project, then, this book has had a well-defined and lucky history: it was commissioned, written, and produced in a manner that lends itself to easy recounting. In a larger sense, of course, it is the product of a professional education and subsequent career *in toto*. Unlike my previous books, it had no designated period of research before writing, although one of the great pleasures of the task was the chance it afforded me to read all the books and articles I had never had the time to read when I was engaged in specific and specialized research. The preparation for it was a lifetime of analysis and synthesis, looking and listening, reading and reflecting, attendance and participation at concerts and conferences, lectures and seminars and discussions and debates, table talk and meetings and parties and jokes. And so when it comes to acknowledgments I think back to those to whose example I owe the life I have chosen and led.

Two of my teachers deserve my greatest gratitude. Joel Newman taught music history to the Columbia and Barnard music majors during my undergraduate years. He was a close associate of Noah Greenberg of the New York Pro Musica, and lived the life of a performing scholar in a way that inspired me to emulate it. He was my role model in all phases of my professional career — as instrumentalist, as choral director, and as musicologist — since the day I met him during freshman orientation week in 1961. It delights me that he is still alive and well and likely to read this tribute.

Paul Henry Lang is no longer among the living, but his immortality among musicologists has long been assured by the generations of pupils he trained, among whom I am proud to have been one of the last. He was an apostle of *Geistesgeschichte* in an age of positivism; and it amuses those of us who imbibed his old-world scholarship in the 1960s (like Rose Rosengard Subotnik, my dear friend from those days, with whom I have often giggled about it) that so much of what was touted as radical in the musicology of the 1980s and 1990s was in so many ways — *on revient toujours!* — a circle (or spiral) back to the older, intellectually more generous Langian outlook. It was not exactly a return. Today's musicology is, at its best, far more informed by social science than Lang's was (and knowledgeable readers of this book will not miss its many points of difference with Lang, some of them quite explicit). But however differently I may see things now, I received many gifts from my old professor; and this offering, which obviously stands in the tradition of Lang's *Music in Western Civilization*, can be viewed as an attempt to repay them. Lang, who served for nine years as chief music critic for a daily newspaper, was another role model for an interestingly divided life. But the most valuable thing Lang gave his pupils was joy in work. Like Otto Luening, my beloved composition teacher, he had the knack of opening the floodgates. Some teachers notoriously impart constipation; Lang imparted . . . well, the opposite. One wrote reams for him, and his seminars were jolly sharing sessions.

That is the atmosphere I have tried to cultivate in my own classroom, and being a member of the Berkeley music department has vouchsafed me the chance to train many wonderfully gifted graduate students, with whom I have enjoyed endless cordial and fruitful exchanges over the years, a teacher's best reward. I want to acknowledge by name those of my pupils whose scholarly work has directly influenced the content of this book. What follows is anything but a list of research assistants. I am the worst delegator that ever lived, and have never had a research assistant. The list that follows (and it is inevitably the lamentably incomplete product of a fallible memory) is of students who have actually taught me as a result of their independent research, often helping me at the most basic conceptual level, and whose contribution to the present work is in many cases acknowledged in the footnotes. To the best of my recollection, the ones who have contributed to my project in this concrete way have been Laura Basini, Gregory Bloch, Thomas Brothers, Gregory Dubinsky, Robert Fink, Danielle Fosler-Lussier, A. Nalini Gwynne, Elisabeth LeGuin, Beth Levy, Klára Móricz, David Paul, Stephen Rumph, Peter Schmelz, David Schneider, Leslie Sprout, Anya Suschitzky, Benjamin Walton, Holly Watkins, Heather Wiebe, and Christopher Williams. Danielle Fosler-Lussier and Klára Móricz deserve thanks as well for use-testing portions of this book in the classroom (Danielle at Princeton, Klára at Amherst) and for giving me detailed critiques based on their experience. But nearly all my graduate students have left a trace, through their written texts and their verbal acts, on my thinking, and the distinction I have just been forced to draw has been excruciatingly invidious.

My colleague Kate van Orden was also kind enough to give chapters of this book a use test in her undergraduate course on medieval and Renaissance music at Berkeley. Other colleagues from whom I have received obliging feedback include Richard L. Crocker, Daniel Heartz, Wendy Allanbrook, Katherine Bergeron, John Roberts, and Mary Ann Smart. I am likewise indebted to the reviewers to whom the publisher sent portions of this book for critique. Musicology being a small world, I recognized most of them from what they wrote, and can therefore thank Anna Maria Busse Berger, Leeman L. Perkins, Julie E. Cumming, Douglas Johnson, Elaine R. Sisman, and Richard Crawford by name for their great generosity, not just in praise (though that is pleasant) but in offering constructive suggestions, some of them directly incorporated into the text. The four constructive reviewers whose identities I did not divine are no less deserving of thanks. And even the Bach scholar who reacted to my work with phobic revulsion helped assure me that I was on the right track. He, too, has my sincere gratitude.

Benevolent colleagues and friends who responded to queries over the course of my labors are of course too numerous to list. But I would like to thank a few who were able to answer some particularly urgent last-minute requests for assistance: Michael Beckerman, J. Peter Burkholder, Michael Hicks, Kim H. Kowalke, Peter Lefferts, Barry Millington, James Parakilas, Roger Parker (who also read some chapters during his stay as Bloch lecturer at Berkeley), W. Anthony Sheppard, László Somfai, and Pieter C. Van den Toorn. Amy Beal, Karol Berger, Anna Maria Busse Berger, Fred Lerdahl, Hendrik van der Werf, and especially Michael Long generously shared their unpublished work with me. Finally, Eric Salzman kindly furnished the score page shown in chapter 61 from his unpublished *Nude Paper Sermon*, and La Monte Young and Marian Zazeela provided authoritative corrections to the musical examples in chapter 67.

One always finishes writing a set of acknowledgments with a cheering sense that one is not friendless in the world, and with a heightened consciousness of the interdependence of the communities to which one belongs. Since that interdependence — or, to put it more strongly, one's dependence on social relations of all kinds in all one's endeavors — is one of the major themes of this book, I feel as though I have just supplied some introspective or confessional evidence in support of my scholarly claims. That feeling enhances the optimism I felt at reaching the conclusion of my narrative. I commend this work to the readers of the twenty-first century in that spirit, in hopes that their musical experience will confirm my happy hunches.

THE OXFORD HISTORY OF
WESTERN MUSIC

The Curtain Goes Up

"Gregorian" Chant, the First Literate Repertory, and How It Got That Way

LITERACY

Our story begins, as it must, in the middle of things. The beginning of music writing in the West—which not only made history possible, but in large part determined its course—coincided with no musical event. Still less did it mark the origin of music, or of any musical repertory.

Something over a thousand years ago music in the West stopped being (with negligible exceptions) an exclusively oral tradition and became a partly literate one. This was, from our perspective, an enormously important change. The beginning of music writing gives us access through actual musical documents to the repertories of the past and suddenly raises the curtain, so to speak, on developments that had been going on for centuries. All at once we are witnesses of a sort, able to trace the evolution of music with our own eyes and ears. The development of musical literacy also made possible all kinds of new ideas about music. Music became visual as well as aural. It could occupy space as well as time. All of this had a decisive impact on the styles and forms music would later assume. It would be hard for us to imagine a greater watershed in musical development.

At the time, however, it did not seem terribly important. There is not a single contemporary witness to the introduction of music writing in the West, and so we have only a rough idea of when it took place. Nobody thought of it then as an event worth recording, and that is because this innovation—momentous though it may appear in retrospect—was the entirely fortuitous by-product of political and military circumstances. These circumstances caused the music sung in the cathedral churches of Rome, the westernmost "see" or jurisdictional center of early Christendom, to migrate northward into areas that are now parts of France, Germany, Switzerland, and Austria. Musical notation arose in the wake of that migration.

The music thus imported during the eighth and ninth centuries—the first Western repertory to be notated as a coherent *corpus* or body of work—was not only sacred but liturgical. That is, it was set to the official Latin texts of Western Christian worship. It was not only vocal but monophonic, which is to say that it was sung by soloists or by chorus in unison, without accompaniment. From these facts it is easy to draw various false conclusions. It is easy to assume that in the West there was sacred music before there was secular, liturgical music before there was nonliturgical, vocal music before there was instrumental, and monophonic (single-voiced) music before there was polyphonic (multivoiced).

But Roman church chant was only one of many musical repertories that coexisted in Europe a thousand years ago. It is the first repertory that, thanks to notation, we can study in detail, and so our story must inevitably begin with it. And yet we know from literary and pictorial sources that there was plenty of secular and instrumental music at the time, as well as non-Christian worship music, and that these repertories had long histories going back long before the beginnings of Christian worship. We have every reason to assume, moreover, that much of the music sung and played in Europe had for centuries been polyphonic — that is, employing some sort of harmony or counterpoint or accompanied melody.

The fact that eighth-century Roman liturgical song — *cantus* in Latin, from which we get the word "chant" — was singled out for preservation in written form had nothing to do with musical primacy, or even with musical quality. The privilege came about, as already implied, for reasons having nothing to do with music at all. It will not be the last time such "extramusical" factors will play a decisive role in our account of musical history. That history, like the history of any art, is the story of a complex and fascinating interaction of internal and external influences.

THE ROMANS AND THE FRANKS

Late in the year 753, Pope Stephen II, accompanied by a large retinue of cardinals and bishops, did something no previous Roman pope had done. He crossed the Alps and paid a visit to Pepin III, known as Pepin the Short, the king of the Franks. They met on 6 January 754 at Pepin's royal estate, located at Ponthion, near the present-day city of Vitry-le-François on the river Marne, some 95 miles from Paris in what is now northeastern France. (France, then the western part of the Frankish kingdom, went in those days by the Roman name of Gaul; the country's modern name is derived from that of the people Pepin ruled.)

The pope was coming as a supplicant. The Lombards, a Germanic tribe whose territories reached from what is now Hungary into northern Italy, had conquered Ravenna, the capital of the Western Byzantine (Greek Christian) Empire, and were threatening Rome. Stephen asked Pepin, who three years earlier had concluded a mutual assistance pact with his predecessor Zacharias, to intercede on his behalf. When Pepin agreed to honor his earlier commitment, Stephen went with him to the cathedral city of Saint-Denis, just north of Paris, and cemented their covenant by officially declaring Pepin and his heirs to be honorary "Roman patricians" and recognizing them as the legitimate hereditary rulers of the united kingdom of the Franks, which encompassed (in addition to France) most of present-day Germany, Switzerland, and Austria, in addition to smaller territories now belonging to Italy, Slovenia, Croatia, and the Czech Republic. This ceremony inaugurated the Carolingian dynasty, which for the next two centuries would remain the most powerful ruling house in Europe.

Pepin duly invaded Italy. He not only successfully defended Rome but also wrested Ravenna and its surrounding territories back from Aistulf, the Lombard king. Ignoring the claims of the Byzantine emperor, Pepin made a gift of these territories to the pope; they became the so-called "Papal States," which were administered by the Roman see

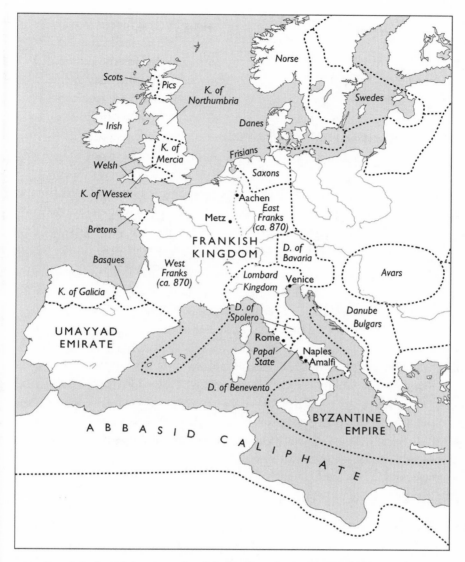

FIG. I-I   Europe in the eighth century, shortly before the earliest notations of Christian chant.

as an independent country, with the pope as temporal ruler, until the unification of Italy in the nineteenth century. (The immediate territory around St. Peter's Church in Rome—a few city blocks known as Vatican City—is still recognized internationally as a temporal state, the world's smallest.) The Carolingian king and the Roman pope thus became political and military allies, pledged to mutual long-term support.

Thus, when in 773 Desiderius, a later Lombard king, made renewed forays against Adrian I, a later pope, it was a foregone conclusion that Pepin's son and successor Charles I, known as Charlemagne ("Charles the Great"), would intervene. Charlemagne did even better than his father, defeating the Lombards in Italy on their own ground and incorporating their kingdom into his own. After yet another intervention, this time on behalf of Adrian's successor, Pope (later Saint) Leo III, Charlemagne entered Rome in triumph and was crowned by Leo on Christmas Day, 800 CE, as temporal ruler (with Leo as spiritual ruler) of the reconstituted Western Roman Empire. This date is traditionally said to inaugurate the so-called "Holy Roman Empire," which lasted—in name, anyway—until the First World War. (The actual title Holy Roman Emperor was first assumed by Otto I, crowned in 962.)

THE CAROLINGIAN RENAISSANCE

The nexus of imperial and papal authority thus achieved ushered in a short period comparable to the *pax romana* ("Roman peace") of late antiquity, in which the existence of an invincible and unchallengeable state brought about an era of relative political stability in Europe. Until the partition of Charlemagne's Empire in 843, the only significant changes in the map of Europe were those that marked the Empire's expansion, which reached a peak around 830. The period from the 780s, when Charlemagne finally gained the upper hand in a protracted, savage war with the pagan Saxons to the east, into the reign of his son and successor Louis I (known as Louis the Pious, reigned 814–840), was devoted to the consolidation of centralized power within the Carolingian domains. In 812, two years before his death, Charlemagne had the satisfaction of being formally recognized as an equal by the Byzantine Emperor Michael I, whose imperial lineage, unlike Charlemagne's, reached back into antiquity.

This interval of stability enabled a spectacular rebirth of the arts of peace, particularly at Charlemagne's courts at Aachen (or Aix-la-Chapelle), now in westernmost Germany, and Metz (or Messins), in northeastern France. This happy period for learning and creativity, purchased by a period of endless battles, forced migrations and conversions, and genocidal massacres, is known as the Carolingian Renaissance.

THE CHANT COMES NORTH

The importing of the Roman chant to the Frankish lands was one of the many facets of that Renaissance, during which all kinds of art products and techniques, from Ravenna-style architecture to manuscript illumination, were brought north from Italy to France and the British Isles, and all kinds of administrative, legal, and canonical practices were standardized. The central figure in this process was an English scholar, Alcuin or Albinus of York (ca. 735–804), whom Charlemagne invited to Aachen around 781 to set up a cathedral school.

A great proponent of literacy, Alcuin instituted one of the earliest systems of elementary education in Europe. He also devised a curriculum for higher education based on the seven "liberal arts" of the ancients, so named because they were the arts practiced by "free men" (men of leisure, which is to say the rich and the well-born). They consisted of two basic courses: the three arts of language (grammar, logic, and rhetoric), known as the *trivium*, which led to the Bachelor of Arts degree, and the four arts of measurement (arithmetic, geometry, astronomy, and music), known as the *quadrivium*, which led to the Master of Arts. (Doctoral studies were devoted to canon law and theology.) Within the quadrivium, music was conceived in entirely theoretical terms as an art of measurement:

measurement of harmonic ratios (tunings and intervals) and of rhythmic quantities (the classical poetic meters). This made possible its academic study in the absence of any form of practical musical notation. As a university subject music continued for centuries to be studied in that generalized and speculative way, quite unrelated to actual singing or playing. And yet Alcuin's zealous emphasis on writing things down became a Carolingian obsession that was eventually extended to practical music as well.

The reason the Roman chant needed to be imported had to do with the stress the Carolingians laid on centralization of authority, both worldly and ecclesiastical. The Carolingian territories were vast, incorporating peoples speaking many languages and a large assortment of local legal systems and liturgies. With the establishing of the Roman pope as spiritual patron of the Carolingian Empire, the liturgical unification of the whole broad realm according to the practices of the Roman See became imperative. It would symbolize the eternal order that undergirded the temporal authority of the Carolingian rulers and established their divine mandate.

This meant suppressing the so-called Gallican rite, the indigenous liturgy of the northern churches, and replacing it with Roman liturgical texts and tunes. "As King Pepin, our parent of blessed memory, once decreed that the Gallican be abolished," Charlemagne ordered the Frankish clergy on 23 March 789, in a document known as the *Admonitio generalis* ("General advisory"), "be sure to emend carefully in every monastery and bishop's house the psalms, notes, chants, calendar material, grammars, and the Epistles and Gospels. For often enough there are those who want to call upon God well, but because of poor texts they do it poorly." The texts in question, of course, were texts to be sung, as all liturgical texts are sung (for one does not "call upon God" in the kind of voice one uses to converse with one's neighbor). The words of the Roman liturgy could be imported easily enough in books, but in the absence of a way of writing down the tunes, the only means of accomplishing the required "emendation" was to import cantors (ecclesiastical singers) from Rome who could teach their chant by laborious rote to their Frankish counterparts. Difficulty was compounded by resistance. Each side blamed the other for failure. John the Deacon, an English monk writing on behalf of the Romans in 875, attributed it to northern baseness and barbarity. Notker Balbulus ("Notker the Stammerer"), the Frankish monk who wrote Charlemagne's first biography around the same time, attributed it to southern pride and chicanery.

THE LEGEND OF ST. GREGORY

From these squabbles we can guess at the reason for a venerable legend that became attached to the Roman chant around the time of its advent into written history. It was then widely asserted that the entire musical legacy of the Roman church was the inspired creation of a single man, the sainted Pope Gregory I, who had reigned from 590 until his death in 604. John the Deacon's complaint about Frankish barbarism actually comes from his biography of the presumed author of the chant. "St. Gregory compiled a book of antiphons," John wrote, using the contemporary term for a kind of liturgical singing. "He founded a *schola*," the chronicler continued, using the contemporary term for a choir, "which to this day performs the chant in the Church of Rome according to his instructions; he also erected two dwellings for it, at St. Peter's and at the Lateran palace, where are venerated the couch from which he gave lessons in chant, the whip with which he threatened the boys, and the authentic antiphoner," the latter being the great book containing the music for the whole liturgical calendar.

That book could not have existed in St. Gregory's day, because there would have been no way of putting music into it. As Gregory's contemporary St. Isidore, Bishop of Seville (ca. 560–636), put it in his great encyclopedia called *Etymologiae* (or "Origins", "Unless sounds are held in the memory by man they perish, because they cannot be written down." By the ninth century, however, the legend of Pope Gregory as composer of what has been known ever since as "Gregorian chant" was firmly in place. It was propagated not only in literary accounts like that of John the Deacon but also in an iconographic or pictorial tradition that adapted a motif already established in Roman illuminated manuscripts containing Gregory's famous Homilies, or sermons, on the biblical books of Job and Ezekiel. According to this tradition, the pope, while dictating his commentary, often paused for a long time. His silences puzzled the scribe, who was separated from Gregory by a screen. Peeping through, the scribe beheld the dove of the Holy Spirit hovering at the head of St. Gregory, who resumed his dictation only when the dove removed its beak from his mouth. (It is from such representations of divine inspiration that we get our expression, "A little bird told me.")

(a)   (b)

FIG. I-2   Two Carolingian manuscript illustrations showing divinely inspired authors at work. (a) In this illustration, from the so-called Gospel Book of Ebbo (first quarter of the ninth century), St. John is receiving the Gospel from the Holy Spirit in the guise of a dove. (b) This illustration, dating from about half a century later, is one of the earliest representations of Pope Gregory I (Saint Gregory the Great), who is receiving the chant from the same source. It comes from a sacramentary, a book containing the prayers recited by the celebrant at a solemn Mass. Charlemagne is known to have requested and received just such a book from Pope Hadrian I in 785.

These pictures are again found in early written antiphoners, or chant books, which began appearing in the Carolingian territories during the eighth century. Such books were generally headed by a prologue, which in the ninth century was occasionally even set to music to be sung as a "trope" or preface to the first chant in the book. *Gregorius Praesul*, it read in part, *composuit hunc libellum musicae artis scholae cantorum*: "Gregory, presiding [over the Church], composed [or, possibly, just 'put together'] this little book of musical art of the singers' choir." Thus the legend of St. Gregory's authorship was closely bound up with the earliest notation of the chant, suggesting that the two phenomena were related.

In fact both inventions, that of the legend and that of musical notation in the Christian west, were mothered by the process of musical migration decreed by the Carolingian kings. The legend was a propaganda ploy contrived to persuade the northern churches that the Roman chant was better than theirs. As a divine creation, mediated through an inspired, canonized human vessel, the Roman chant would have the prestige it needed to triumph eventually over all local opposition.

Gregory I was chosen as the mythical author of the chant, it is now thought, because many of the leading intellectual lights of the Carolingian court—like Alcuin and his predecessor St. Boniface (675–754), the reformer, under Pepin, of the Frankish church—were English monks who venerated St. Gregory as the greatest Christian missionary to England. (It was Alcuin's teacher, Bishop Egbert of York, who first referred to the Roman liturgy as "Gregory's antiphoner.") To this great figure, already reputed to be a divinely inspired author, these English writers may have attributed the work of his successor Pope Gregory II (reigned 715–731), who, it seems, really did have something to do with drawing up the standard Roman liturgical books some decades before their export north.

THE ORIGINS OF GREGORIAN CHANT

But of course neither did Gregory II actually compose the "Gregorian" chants. No one person did. It was a huge collective and anonymous enterprise that seems to have achieved standardization in Rome by the end of the eighth century. But what were its origins? Until very recently it was assumed as a matter of course that the origins of Christian liturgical music went back, like the rest of Christian practice and belief, to the "sacred bridge" connecting the Christian religion with Judaism, out of which it had originated as a heresy. The textual contents of the Gregorian antiphoner consisted overwhelmingly of psalm verses, and the recitation of psalms, along with other scriptural readings, is to this day a common element of Jewish and Christian worship.

It turns out, however, that neither the psalmody of the Christian liturgy nor that of today's synagogue service can be traced back to pre-Christian Jewish worship, let alone to Old Testament times. Pre-Christian Jewish psalmody centered around temple rites that came to an end when the temple itself was destroyed by the Romans in 70 CE. One has only to read some famous passages from the psalms themselves, as well as other biblical texts, to become aware of this disjuncture. Psalm 150, the climax of the Psalter, or Book of Psalms, is in fact a description of ancient temple psalmody — singing God's praises — in fullest swing. It reads, in part:

> Praise him with fanfares on the trumpet,
>   praise him upon the lute and harp;
> praise him with tambourines and dancing,
>   praise him with flute and strings;
> praise him with the clash of cymbals,
>   praise him with triumphant cymbals;
> let everything that has breath praise the LORD!

One will not find such goings-on in any contemporary Catholic church or synagogue; nor were they ever part of pre-Reformation Christian worship. (The Eastern Orthodox church, in fact, expressly bans the ritual use of instruments, and does so on the basis of the last line of this very psalm, for instruments do not have "breath," that is, a soul.) Nor can one find today much reflection of the "antiphonal" manner of psalmody described in the Bible, despite the later Christian appropriation (in modified form and with modified meaning) of the word "antiphon."

In its original meaning, antiphonal psalmody implied the use of two choirs answering each to each, as most famously described in the high priest Nehemiah's account of the dedication of the Jerusalem walls in 445 BCE, when vast choirs (and orchestras!) mounted the walls on opposite sides of the city gates and made a joyful noise unto the Lord. The verse structure of the psalms themselves, consisting of paired *hemistichs*, half-lines that state a single thought in different words (as in the extract above), suggests that antiphony was their original mode of performance.

And yet, although it was (and remains) the central musical activity in Jewish worship services, psalmody was — perhaps surprisingly — not immediately transferred from Jewish worship to Christian. It does not figure in the earliest accounts of Christian worship, such as Justin Martyr's description of the Sunday Eucharist (ritual of blessings) or Lord's Supper, later known as the communion service or Mass, at Rome sometime around the middle of the second century. Justin mentions readings from the prophets and apostles, sermons, prayers, and acclamations, but no psalms. In short, there is nothing in the earliest descriptions of Christian worship to correspond with the later repertory of Gregorian chant. That repertory was not a direct inheritance from Christianity's parent religion. It originated elsewhere, and later.

Exactly when cannot be pinpointed, but psalmody had entered the Christian worship service by the beginning of the fifth century, when the Spanish nun Egeria sent a letter back home from Jerusalem describing the services she had witnessed in the oldest and holiest Christian see. "Before cockcrow," she wrote, "all the doors of the church are opened and all the monks and nuns come down, and not only they, but also those lay people, men and women, who wish to keep vigil at so early an hour. From that time until it is light, hymns are sung and psalms responded to, and likewise antiphons; and with every hymn there is a prayer."

The important points to note are two: it is a night service (or office) that is being described, and it is primarily a monastic gathering, even though the laity has been admitted. The origins of Christian psalmody, hence the earliest intimations of Gregorian chant, lie not in the very public worship of the Jewish temple, but in the secluded vigils of the early Christian ascetics.[1]

MONASTIC PSALMODY

Christian monasticism arose in the fourth century in reaction to the church's worldly success following its establishment as the official religion of the late Roman empire. Whereas earlier the Christians were persecuted in Rome for their pacificism and their contempt for temporal authority, now, as the custodian of an imperial state religion, the Christian church itself took on the attributes of an imperium. Its clergy was organized into a steep hierarchy. That clerical hierarchy, in turn, put forth an elaborate theology and an enforceable canon law, and modified the church's teachings so as to support the needs of the temporal state that supported it, needs that included the condoning of legal executions and military violence. The state Christian church could no longer afford the pure pacificism it had espoused when it was a persecuted minority. Indeed, it now became itself a persecutor of heretics.

In the face of this increasingly pompous and official ecclesiastical presence in the world, an increasing number of Christian enthusiasts advocated flight from the city, retreating into a solitary and simple life more consonant, in their view, with the original teachings of Christ. Some, like the Egyptian hermit St. Anthony the Abbot (ca. 250–350), established colonies of anchorites devoted to solitary prayer and mortification of the flesh. Others, like St. Basil (ca. 330–379), the Bishop of Caesarea, the Roman capital of Palestine (now Kayseri in central Turkey), conceived of monastic life not in

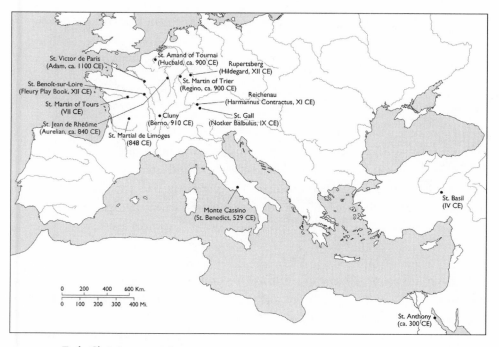

FIG. 1-3 Early Christian monastic centers.

eremitic terms but in terms of *koinobios*—ascetic communal living devoted to pious, meditative fellowship and productive work.

It was in such a communal context that the psalmodic practices arose that would eventually produce the Gregorian chant. An important aspect of the monastic regimen was staying up at night, a discipline known as the vigil. To help them keep awake and to assist their meditations, monks would read and recite constantly, chiefly from the Bible, and particularly from the Psalter. The standard practice, eventually turned into a rule, was to recite the Psalter in an endless cycle, somewhat in the manner of a mantra, to distract the mind from physical appetites, to fill the back of the mind with spiritually edifying concepts so as to free the higher levels of consciousness (the *intellectus*, as it was called) for mystical enlightenment. In the words of St. Basil himself:

> A psalm implies serenity of soul; it is the author of peace, which calms bewildering and seething thoughts. For it softens the wrath of the soul, and what is unbridled it chastens. A psalm forms friendships, unites those separated, conciliates those at enmity. Who, indeed, can still consider him an enemy with whom he has uttered the same prayer to God? So that psalmody, bringing about choral singing, a bond, as it were, toward unity, and joining the people into a harmonious union of one choir, produces also the greatest of blessings, charity.[2]

Half a century after St. Basil wrote these words, St. John Chrysostom, an eminent Greek church father, confirmed the triumph of psalmody, the musical legacy of David, the biblical Orpheus, who like his Greek mythological counterpart could miraculously affect the soul with his singing:

> In church when vigils are observed David is first, middle and last. At the singing of the morning canticles David is first, middle, and last. At funerals and burials of the dead again David is first, middle, and last. O wondrous thing! Many who have no knowledge of letters at all nonetheless know all of David and can recite him from beginning to end.[3]

Christian psalmody emphasized not metaphors of wealth and exuberance (the orchestras, dancers, and multiple choirs of the Temple) but metaphors of community and discipline, both symbolized at once by unaccompanied singing in unison. That remained the Gregorian ideal, although the community of worshipers was replaced in the more public repertory of the Mass by the specially trained and eventually professional *schola*. Monophony was thus a choice, not a necessity. It reflects not the primitive origins of music (as the chant's status as oldest surviving repertory might all too easily suggest) but the actual rejection of earlier practices, both Judaic and pagan, that were far more elaborate and presumably polyphonic.

THE DEVELOPMENT OF THE LITURGY

One of the first steps toward organizing the ceaseless cyclic psalm-chanting of early monastic vigils into a liturgy—that is, a prescribed order—was taken by St. Benedict of Nursia in his famous *Regula monachorum*, the book of rules that governed the lives of the monks in the monastery Benedict founded at Monte Cassino in 529. With apologies for the laxity of his ordinance, he required that the Psalter be recited not in a single marathon bout but in a weekly round or *cursus* of monastic Offices, eight each day. The greatest single portion went to the Night Office (now called *matins*, literally "wee hours"), in which twelve or more full psalms were performed, grouped by threes or fours (together with prayers and readings from scripture) in large subdivisions known as "nocturns."

The Night Office, traditionally the primary site of psalmodic chanting, thus accounted for roughly half of the weekly round of psalms. It being the most spacious of the monastic services (since there was nothing else to do at night but sing or sleep), many psalms were sung, and the lessons were framed by lengthy *responsoria* (responsories)—chants sung in a more expansive style in which individual syllables could be sung to two, three, four, or more notes, even whole cascades called melismas.

Melismatic singing was held by Christian mystics to be the highest form of religious utterance: "It is a certain sound of joy without words," St. Augustine wrote of melismatic chanting in the fourth century, "the expression of a mind poured forth in joy."[4] It came to be called jubilated singing, after *jubilus*, Latin for a "call" upon God (as in Charlemagne's *Admonitio*, quoted earlier; compare the root *ju-*, pronounced "yoo," as in "yoo-hoo!"). This musical jubilation, in fact, was the means through which the Latin word took on its secondary (in English borrowings, primary) association with joy.

The jubilated singing at matins was a lusher version of the refrains that were added to psalms—together with a concluding *doxology* (from the Greek for "words of praise") to the Holy Trinity—in their other Christian uses. These simpler refrains were called antiphons, possibly because they alternated with the psalm verses in a manner that recalled biblical multichoral antiphony.

The shorter services were the day offices. They began with the dawn office of praise (*Lauds*) and continued with four "minor hours" named after the clock hours in medieval parlance: *prime* (the first hour; in present-day terms, 6 A.M.), *terce* (the third hour, or 9 A.M.), *sext* (the sixth hour, or 12 noon), and *none* (the ninth hour, or 3 P.M.; the fact that our word noon derives from none is just one of those things). At these tiny services (often combined in pairs so that there would be more uninterrupted time for work), we can observe the liturgy in microcosm. At a minimum an office included a psalm, a scripture reading ("chapter" or *capitulum*), and a hymn, which was a metrical song of praise derived from Greek pagan practice, showing again how eclectic were the sources of the Christian liturgy that was once thought to descend in simple fashion from that of the temple and synagogue. St. Augustine's definition of a hymn is neat:

> A hymn is song with praise of God. If you praise God and do not sing, you do not utter a hymn. If you sing and do not praise God, you do not utter a hymn. If you praise anything other than God, and if you sing these praises, still you do not utter a hymn. A hymn therefore has these three things: song, and praise, and God.[5]

The public liturgical day ended with evensong or Vespers, consisting of several full psalms with antiphons, along with the psalm like "Canticle of Mary" (known as the *Magnificat* after its first word). There was a bedtime service for monks called *Compline* (completion), at which special elaborate antiphons (or "anthems," to use the English cognate) came to be sung, in the later middle ages, to the Blessed Virgin as a plea for her intercession. (Compline and Lauds are the other services that contain canticles — texts from the New Testament that are sung in the same manner as psalms, with antiphons and doxology.)

Just as the liturgical day was a cycle of services, and the monastic week was a cycle of psalms, so the whole church calendar was organized in a yearly cycle of commemorations, known as feasts, that became ever more copious and diverse over time — wheels within wheels within wheels, within which Christian monastics lived out their lives, fulfilling the prophet's mystical vision (see Ezekiel 1:15–21). The basic framework was provided by the Proper of the Time, or *temporale*, commemorating events in the life of Christ, organized in two great cycles surrounding the two biggest feasts, Christmas and Easter.

Their complicated relationship epitomizes the eclecticism of Christian worship. The Christmas cycle, beginning with four solemn weeks of preparation called Advent and ending with the feast of Epiphany, is reckoned by the Roman pagan (secular and solar) calendar. The Easter cycle, beginning with the forty-day fast called Lent and ending with the feast of Pentecost, is reckoned by the Jewish lunar calendar, as modified by councils of Christian bishops to insure that Easter fell on Sunday (*Dominica* — "the Lord's Day" — in Latin). Since the date of Easter can vary by as much as a month relative to that of Christmas, the calendar allows for a variable number of Sundays after Epiphany (on one side of Easter) and Sundays after Pentecost (on the other) to take up the slack.

The church calendar also came to include a cycle of Saints' commemorations (the *sanctorale*), a cycle of feasts of the Virgin Mary, and many other occasions as well, including special (so-called votive) occasions where prayers and offerings are made, such as weddings, funerals, or the dedication of a church. As official occasions were added to the calendar — and they continue, in a small way, to be added and deleted to this day — they had to be provided with appropriate texts and tunes. The actual book of psalms was fixed, of course, but the antiphons and responds drawn from it could vary; indeed they had to, for this was the primary means of differentiating the feasts. Antiphons and responds, then, became the primary site of new musical composition during the centuries in which the evolution of the chant was hidden behind the curtain of "oral tradition." Antiphons remain, by and large, settings of psalm verses; but they are composites, made up of individual, freely selected verses that have some reference to the occasion. Selecting individual verses for setting as antiphons and responds is called the "stichic" principle (from the Greek for "verse") as opposed to the "cursive" principle of complete cyclic readings. The stichic chants are not merely sung to a monotonous recitation "tone," as in cursive psalmody, but are set as real melodies, the glory of the Gregorian repertory.

THE MASS AND ITS MUSIC

The greatest flowering of such liturgical "arias" came toward the end of the period of Gregorian oral composition, with the selection and completion of formularies — full sets of antiphons and responds — for the yearly round of Mass services.

The Mass is a public adaptation of the Christian counterpart, known as *agape* or "love feast," of the Jewish Passover seder, the occasion of Christ's last supper. It has two parts. The first, called the *synaxis* ("synagogue," after the Greek for a meeting or assembly) or the Mass of the Catechumens, consists, like the synagogue service, of prayers and readings. It is an exoteric service, open to those who have not yet completed their religious instruction (known as *catechism*, whence *catechumen*, one undergoing indoctrination). The second, an esoteric service known as the Eucharist or the Mass of the Faithful, is closed to all who have not yet been baptized and consists of a reenactment of the last supper in which the congregation mystically ingests the blood and body of Christ in the form of miraculously transubstantiated wine and bread.

Mass was at first celebrated only on the Dominica and the Christian holidays, between the hours of terce and sext (i.e., around 10 A.M.). Later on, it came to be celebrated also on weekdays (*feriae* in Latin, whence "ferial" as opposed to "festal" Mass). Being a public service that incorporated a great deal of action, the Mass did not contain full cursive psalmody or hymns with their many *strophes* or stanzas. Instead, it featured short, stichic texts set to elaborate music; these short texts, assembled in large repertories, articulated the "proper" identity of each occasion at which Mass was celebrated — feast, Sunday, or saint's day.

An antiphon plus a verse or two accompanies the entrance of the celebrants, called the *Introit*. Between the two main synaxis readings or "lessons" (from Paul's Epistles and from the Gospels, respectively) come the *Gradual*, named for the stairs by which the celebrants ascend to the pulpit from which the Gospel is read, and the *Alleluia*. These are the most ornate responds of all, with elaborately set verses for virtuoso soloists. Probably the oldest psalmodic chants specifically designed for the Mass, the lesson chants are said to have been introduced by Pope Celestine I, who reigned from 422 to 432. Antiphons then accompany the collection (Offertory) and the consummation of the Eucharist (Communion).

NEUMES

It is this special body of psalmodic chants for the Mass, consisting of about five hundred antiphons and responds, that is in strictest terms the repertory designated by the phrase "Gregorian chant." It was this corpus that was imported by the Carolingian Franks under Pepin and Charlemagne and thus became the earliest music in the European tradition to be written down. The interesting thing, as we have already observed, is that this writing down, which seems to us such a momentous event, seems to have occasioned so little notice at the time.

There is not a single literary reference to document the invention of the so-called *neumes* that tracked the relative rise and fall of the tunes, and the placement within them of the text syllables, in the earliest musically notated ("neumated") manuscripts. Etymologically, the word "neume," which comes to us by way of medieval Latin from the Greek word *pneuma* ("breath," whence vital spirit or soul), referred to a characteristic melodic turn such as may be sung on one breath. By now, however, the word more commonly denotes the written sign that represented such a turn. Since surviving antiphoners with neumes do not seem to date before the beginning of the tenth century, several generations after the Carolingian chant reform had been undertaken, scholarly speculation about the actual origins of the neumes and the date of their first employment has enjoyed a very wide latitude.

Traditionally, scholars assumed that the Carolingian neumes were an outgrowth of the "prosodic accents," the signs — acute, grave, circumflex, etc. — that represented the inflection of poetry-recitation in late classical antiquity, and that still survive vestigially in the orthography of modern French. (As originally conceived, the acute accent meant a raising of the vocal pitch, the grave a lowering, the circumflex a raising-plus-lowering.) Others have proposed that the neumes were *cheironomic*: that is, graphic representations of the hand-signaling (*cheironomy*) by which choirmasters indicated to their singers the rise and fall of a melody. A more recent theory associates the neumes with a system of punctuation signs that the Franks seem to have developed by around 780 — functional equivalents of commas, colons, question marks, and so on, which break up (parse) a written text into easily comprehended bits by governing the reader's vocal inflections. All of these explanations assume that the neumes were parasitic on some earlier sign-system, and yet we have no actual basis in evidence to rule out the possibility that the neumes were independently invented in response to the immediate musical purpose at hand.

There were other early schemes for graphically representing music, some of them much older than the Carolingian neumes. Some did not even reflect melodic contour but were entirely arbitrary written signs that represented melodic formulas by convention, the way alphabet letters represent speech sounds. The ancient Greeks used actual alphabetic signs as musical notation. Alphabetic notation survived to a small extent in medieval music treatises, like that of the sixth-century encyclopedist Boethius, which formed the basis for music study within the *quadrivium* curriculum.

More familiar examples of special formula-signs for music, called *ecphonetic* neumes, include the so-called Masoretic accents (*ta'amim*) of Jewish biblical cantillation, which Jewish children are taught to this day in preparation for their rite of passage to adulthood (*bar* or *bat mitzvah*), when they are called to the pulpit to read from scripture. To learn to read *ta'amim* one must have a teacher to instruct one orally in the matching of sign and sound. Such matching, being arbitrary, can vary widely from place to place, and also varies according to the occasion, or according to what kind of text is being read. The same signs, for example, will be musically realized one way in readings from the prophets and another, usually more ornate, in readings from the Pentateuch; the very same portion of Scripture, moreover, will be variously realized on weekdays, Sabbaths, or holidays.

The contour-based Carolingian neumes follow an entirely different principle of representation. It is the only system that has direct relevance to the history of Western music, because out of it developed the notation that is familiar to every reader of this book, the one that has served as graphic medium for practically all music composed in what we consider to be our own continuous (or at least traceable) musical tradition.

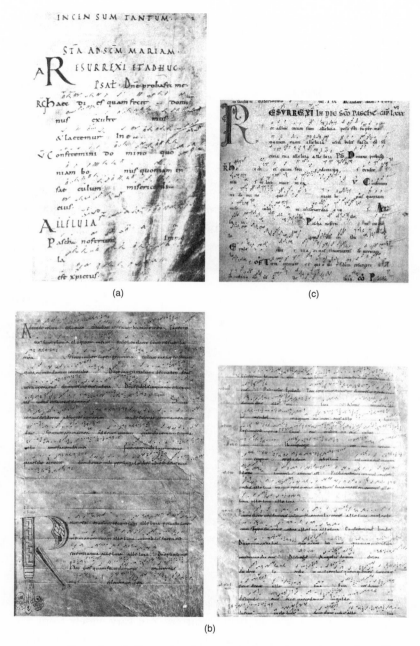

FIG. 1-4 Easter Introit, *Resurrexi*, as it appears in three neumated manuscripts from the Frankish territories. (a) From a cantatorium, or soloist's chant book, prepared at the Swiss monastery of St. Gallen early in the tenth century (before 920). (b) This may be the oldest version of the chant to have survived into modern times; it comes from a graduale, or book of chants for the Mass, prepared in Brittany in the late ninth or early tenth century and kept at the municipal library of Chartres, near Paris. It was destroyed toward the end of World War II. (c) From a graduale prepared perhaps 250 years later (early twelfth century) in the cathedral town of Noyon in northern France and kept today at the British Library in London. By this time the neumes might have been written on a staff to fix their pitches precisely, but the scribe did not avail himself of this notational innovation — indicating that the notation still served as a reminder to the singer of a melody learned orally and memorized.

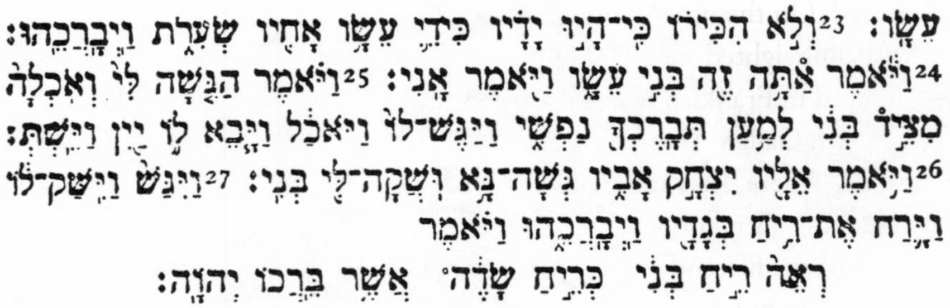

עֵשָׂו: 23וְלֹא הִכִּירוֹ כִּי־הָיוּ יָדָיו כִּידֵי עֵשָׂו אָחִיו שְׂעִרֹת וַיְבָרֲכֵהוּ:
24וַיֹּאמֶר אַתָּה זֶה בְּנִי עֵשָׂו וַיֹּאמֶר אָנִי: 25וַיֹּאמֶר הַגִּשָׁה לִּי וְאֹכְלָה
מִצֵּיד בְּנִי לְמַעַן תְּבָרֶכְךָ נַפְשִׁי וַיַּגֶּשׁ־לוֹ וַיֹּאכַל וַיָּבֵא לוֹ יַיִן וַיֵּשְׁתְּ:
26וַיֹּאמֶר אֵלָיו יִצְחָק אָבִיו גְּשָׁה־נָּא וּשְׁקָה־לִּי בְּנִי: 27וַיִּגַּשׁ וַיִּשַּׁק־לוֹ
וַיָּרַח אֶת־רֵיחַ בְּגָדָיו וַיְבָרֲכֵהוּ וַיֹּאמֶר
רְאֵה רֵיחַ בְּנִי כְּרֵיחַ שָׂדֶה אֲשֶׁר בֵּרֲכוֹ יְהֹוָה:

FIG. I-5   Passage from the Book of Genesis showing *ta'amim*, ecphonetic neumes entered above or below each word in the Torah along with the vowels. Starting at the number 23 (remember that Hebrew is written from right to left), in the first word the neume is the right-angled corner below the middle letter; in the second word it is the dot above the last letter. In the hyphenated word that follows there are two neumes: the vertical dash below the first letter and the right angle under the penultimate word. Unlike Gregorian neumes, *ta'amim* do not show melodic contour and must be learned orally by rote according to an arbitrary system that can vary from place to place, book to book, or occasion to occasion.

Some scholars think that the Carolingian neumes, in their very earliest application, were used not to notate the imported, sacrosanct Gregorian repertory, which was learned entirely by heart, but to notate lesser, newer, or local musical accessories to the canonical chant such as recitation formulas (known as "lection tones") for scriptural readings, as well as the explanatory appendages and interpolations to the chant, including polyphonic ones, about which there will be more to say in the next chapter. (It is true that the earliest neumated sources for such "extra" items do predate the earliest surviving neumated antiphoners.) Other scholars assume that prototypes for the surviving Carolingian antiphoners once existed, perhaps dating from as early as the time of Charlemagne's coronation as Emperor at the end of the eighth century, more than a century before the earliest surviving manuscripts were produced.[6]

Whenever the Carolingian neumes first appeared, whether before 800 or after 900, the fact remains that they shared the limitation of all the early neumatic systems: one cannot actually read a melody from them unless one knows it already. To read a previously unknown melody at sight, one needs at a minimum a means of precise intervallic (or relative-pitch) measurement. It was not until the early eleventh century that neumes were "heighted," or arranged *diastematically*, on the lines and spaces of a cleffed staff (invented, according to tradition, by the monk Guido of Arezzo, whose treatise *Micrologus*, completed around 1028, included the earliest guide to staff notation). Only thereafter was it possible to record melodies in a way that could actually transmit them soundlessly.

PERSISTENCE OF ORAL TRADITION

As scholars are beginning to recognize, the fact that the earliest notations of the canonized liturgy did not communicate actual pitch content shows that no one expected or needed them to do so. In some theoretical treatises of the ninth century, when pitch content needed to be shown, alphabetic notation adapted from the quadrivium treatises was employed. On the other hand, manuscripts with unheighted neumes went on being produced in Frankish monastic centers—even St. Gallen (now in eastern Switzerland), where the earliest surviving neumated antiphoners were inscribed—until the fifteenth century. This shows that the communication of the actual pitch and interval content of liturgical melodies went right on being accomplished by age-old oral/aural methods, that is, by listening, repeating, and memorizing. Most monks (and regular churchgoers, too, until

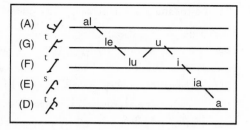

FIG. I-6 Greek-derived alphabetic notation from *Musica enchiriadis* (ca. 850). Such notation (used by Boethius in the sixth century) did fix pitch precisely; this suggests that Gregorian chant might have been notated that way from the beginning, had anyone seen the need for it.

the chant was largely abandoned by the church in the 1960s) still learn their chants that way. Notation did not supersede memory, and never has.

After a thousand years of diastematic notation, five hundred years of printing, and a generation of cheap photocopying, Western "art-musicians" and music students (especially those with academic educations) have become so dependent on texts that they (or rather, we) can hardly imagine minds that could really use their memories—not just to store melodies by the thousand, but to create them as well. By now, we have all to some degree fallen prey to the danger about which Plato was already warning his contemporaries some two and a half millennia ago: "If men learn writing, it will implant forgetfulness in their souls" (*Phaedrus*, 275a). So it is no wonder that "classical" musicians habitually—and very wrongly—tend to equate musical composition in an oral context with improvisation.

Improvisation—making things up as you go along in "real time"—is a performance art. It implies an ephemeral, impermanent product. But while some forms of orally transmitted music (jazz, for example) do enlist the spontaneous creative faculty in real time, there have always been musicians (today's rock bands, for example) who work out compositions without notation yet meticulously, in detail, and in advance. They fix their work in memory in the very act of creating it, so that it will be permanent. Every performance is expected to resemble every other one (which of course need not preclude retouching or improvement over time, or even spontaneously). Their work, while "oral," is not improvisatory. The creative and re-creative acts have been differentiated.

And that is how Gregorian chant seems to have been created over a period spanning half a millennium at least. It was the exigencies of migration northward that made notation desirable as a fixative, but the nature of the early written sources (tiny books, for the most part) suggests that notation was at first not the primary means of transmission but only a mnemonic device (that is, a reference tool to refresh memory), or an arbiter of disputes, or even a status symbol. (If the Mass celebrants—the priests and deacons—had their little books, why not the cantors?) So it is important to remember that literacy did not suddenly replace "orality" as a means of musical transmission but gradually joined it. Since the time of the earliest Carolingian neumated antiphoners, the two means of transmission have coexisted in the West in a complex, ever-evolving symbiosis. There are plenty of familiar tunes that are still transmitted within our culture almost exclusively by oral means: national anthems, patriotic and holiday songs ("America," "Jingle Bells"), songs for occasional use ("Take Me Out to the Ballgame," "Happy Birthday to You"), folk songs ("Home on the Range," "Swanee River"), as well as a vast repertory of children's songs — or songs that have become children's songs — in transmitting which adults rarely play a part ("It's raining, it's pouring," "Oh they don't wear pants in the sunny south of France").

Almost all of these songs, many of them composed by literate musicians (like Stephen Foster, author of "Swanee River" and many other songs that now live mainly in oral tradition), have been published and even copyrighted in written form. Yet while almost every reader of this book will be able to sing them by heart, very few will have ever seen their "sheet music." They are generally encountered "in situ" — in the places and on the appropriate occasions of their use. Some of them, especially patriotic and religious songs, are formally taught by rote in schools or churches or synagogues; many others, perhaps most, are simply "picked up" the way a language is by its native speakers.

At the same time, the Western music most likely to be thought of as belonging exclusively to the literate tradition — sonatas, symphonies, "classical music" generally — actually relies for its transmission on a great deal of oral mediation. Teachers demonstrate to their pupils by aural example many crucial aspects of performance — nuances of dynamics, articulation, phrasing, even rhythmic execution — that are not conveyed, or are inadequately conveyed, by even the most detailed notation; and the pupils learn directly to imitate what they have been shown (or better, to emulate it, which implies an effort to surpass). Conductors communicate their "interpretations" to orchestras and choruses by singing, shouting, grunting, gesticulating. Earlier, the composer may have sung, shouted, grunted, and gesticulated at the conductor. Not only jazz performers, but classical ones, too, copy the performances of famous artists from recordings as part of their learning process (or as part of a less openly admitted process of appropriation). All of this is just as "oral" a means of transmission as anything that may have happened in Rome to produce the Gregorian chant before its migration northward.

The great difference, of course, is that when a work within a partly literate tradition is completed, it need not be committed to memory in order to go on in some sense existing. It is the sense that an art work may exist independently of those who make it up and remember it that is distinctive of literate cultures. (As we shall see, it is that sense that allows us even to have the notion of a "work of art.") And another difference is that having works of music, however large their scale, in written form encourages us to imagine or conceptualize them as objects, which is to say as "wholes," with an overall shape that is more than the sum of its parts. Concepts of artistic unity in works of performing art, and, conversely, an awareness of the function of the parts within the whole in such works (what we call an *analytical* awareness), is thus distinctive of literate cultures. Since the performance of such works must unfold in time, but the written artifacts that represent them are objects that occupy space, one can think of

FIG. 1-7 Original sheet music for the chorus of "Take Me Out to the Ball Game," a waltz song composed in 1908 by Albert Von Tilzer to words by Jack Norworth. Very few people remember these facts about the song's provenance, and virtually nobody learns it from the printed page. Its utterly forgotten lead-in verse puts the famous chorus in the mouth of a young girl: "Katie Casey was baseball mad,/Had the fever and had it bad;/Just to root for the hometown crew,/Ev'ry sou Katie blew./On a Saturday, her young beau/Called to see if she'd like to go/To see a show, but Miss Kate said, 'No,/I'll tell you what you can do.'" The chorus has flourished by itself in oral tradition for almost a century. As always, the oral tradition has modified what it transmits, here only in small ways, but irrevocably. The tune has survived the mouth-to-mouth process unchanged, but many people now sing "Take me out to the crowd," and everyone sings "For it's root, root, root."

literate cultures as cultures that tend conceptually to substitute space for time—that is, to spatialize the temporal. This is an important idea, one that we shall have many occasions to refer to in the course of our survey of Western music in history.

PSALMODY IN PRACTICE: THE OFFICE

It is time now for some music. Many of the points in the foregoing account of the history and prehistory of Gregorian psalmody, and also something of its many genres and styles, may be illustrated by tracing settings of a single psalm verse through its various liturgical habitats. The twelfth verse of Psalm 91 (according to the numbering in the standard Latin Bible, known as the Vulgate, translated by St. Jerome in the late fourth century) was especially favored in the liturgy, perhaps owing to its vivid similes. It crops up time and again in many contexts, running the full stylistic gamut of Gregorian chant from the barest "liturgical recitative" to the most flamboyant jubilation.

In the "original" Latin the verse reads, *Justus ut palma florebit, et sicut cedrus Libani multiplicabitur.* In the Authorized (King James) Version of 1611, long the standard English translation (in which the parent psalm carries the number 92), it reads, "The righteous shall flourish like the palm tree: he shall grow like a cedar in Lebanon." In its simplest musical form, the verse takes its place in the cursive recitation of the psalm from which it comes, within the weekly monastic office round. In such contexts it is sung to an elementary reciting formula or "tone," each verse alternating in historical practice with an antiphon. In modern, somewhat streamlined practice the refrain sandwiches the entire psalm rather than alternating with every verse. In Ex. 1-1, the psalm is paired with an antiphon consisting of its own twelfth verse, the *Justus ut palma* verse, extracted according to the stichic principle for use in a service commemorating a martyr saint, to whom the sentiments expressed in the text are especially pertinent.

A psalm tone like the one given here is music stripped to its minimum functional requirements as a medium for the exaltation of a sacred utterance. In the example, the tone formula is analyzed into its constituent parts, which function very much like punctuation marks. First there is the intonation (in Latin, initium or beginning), given the first time by a soloist (called the precentor) to establish the pitch. As in a declarative sentence, the intonation formula always ascends to a repeated pitch, called the reciting tone or tenor (because it is held, for which the Latin is tenere; other names for it include repercussa, because it is repeated, and tuba, because it is "trumpeted"). The tenor is repeated as often as necessary to accommodate the syllables of the text: since psalms are prose texts, the number of syllables varies considerably from verse to verse. In a long verse there will be many repetitions of the tenor, lending the whole the "monotone" quality often associated with the idea of "chanting." The longest verses (here, verses 2, 4, and 5) have a "bend" (flexus) as additional punctuation.

The end of the first hemistich is sung to a formula known as the mediant (in Latin, mediatio), which functions as a divider, like the comma or colon in the text. The second hemistich again begins on the tenor, and the whole verse ends with the termination (in Latin, terminatio), often called the cadence because, again as in a declarative sentence, it entails a lowering (or "falling," for which the Latin is cadere) of pitch. Note that at the

EX. 1-1   *Justus ut palma* as antiphon to Psalm 91

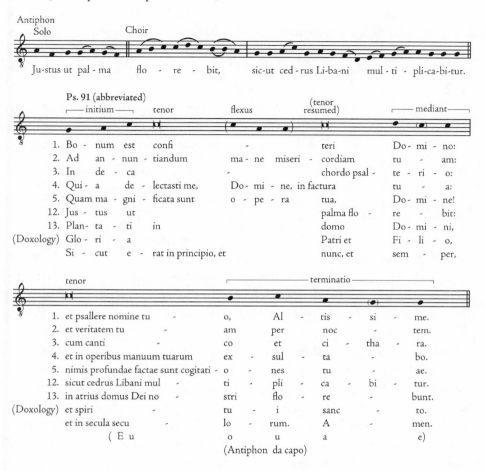

end of the psalm, the doxology—the Christianizing tag invoking the Holy Trinity (a notion assuredly unfamiliar to the Old Testament authors of the Psalter)—has been appended. It is treated simply as an extra pair of psalm verses.

Psalm and lection tones like these are very ancient. They carry a whiff of the origins of music, at least in its cultish uses. Singing, however minimal, is numinous; it elevates words out of the context of the everyday. Like the biblical readings themselves, the use of lection tones is a definite point of kinship between Christian and Jewish worship. The Roman psalm tones are mentioned and described in Carolingian service books as early as the eighth century. They were not actually notated until the early tenth century, however, and are not found in the early antiphoners, for which reason they are not part of the "Gregorian" repertory in what we have identified as the strictest, most authentic sense of the term. But the term "Gregorian" is used by now to cover the whole medieval repertory of the Roman church.

Eight psalm tones (of which the one given in the example is listed last in the standard books) are used in the Latin liturgy, plus one called the tonus peregrinus ("migrating tone") because the tenor of the second hemistich is different from that of the first. The eight-tone system seems to have been borrowed in concept (though not in actual musical content) from that of the Greek (Byzantine) church. Because the music of a psalm tone is so obviously related in its function to that of punctuation, the Gregorian tones (incorporating those used for prayers, as well as psalms and scriptural readings) are often collectively characterized by the word accentus, or "accent," already associated with chant notation in one hypothesis of its origin.

Although the designation accentus seems to have been used in this sense no earlier than the sixteenth century, it is nevertheless very apt, because a psalm sung to a tone is in fact an accentuated or heightened recitation. Sixteenth-century and later writers who use the word accentus in this way contrast it with the word concentus, a Latin word associated with the pleasures of music (it may be translated as "harmony," or "concert," or "choir," or "concord," depending on the context), which denotes the more distinctive and decorative melodies found in antiphons, responds, or hymns.

The antiphon in Ex. 1-1 is a modest example of concentus melody. Where the relationship between the text and music in the psalm tone is straightforwardly syllabic (one note to each syllable, the reciting tone accommodating most of them), the antiphon is a moderately neumatic chant, in which nine of the twenty-one syllables in the text carry what were known as "simple" (two- or three-note) neumes. In the figure accompanying Ex. 1-1, the antiphon is printed exactly as it is found in the *Liber responsorialis*, a book of Office chants published in 1895 by the monks of the Benedictine Abbey of Solesmes, who carried out a vast restorative project during the late nineteenth century in which the corpus of Gregorian chant was reedited from its original manuscript sources. The notation they used, called "square" or "quadratic" after the shape of the note-heads, was adapted from a calligraphic style that became prevalent in twelfth-century manuscripts, especially those containing polyphonic music, in which (as will be seen in due course) the various neume shapes often assumed specific — eventually measured — rhythmic values.

As early as the tenth century, neumes were learned from tables in which each shape was given a distinctive name. The two-note ascent over pal-, for example, was called the pes (or podatus), meaning "foot." Its descending counterpart, over -ma, was called the clivis (meaning "sloped"; compare "declivity"). The three-note neumes (grouped, appropriately enough, over a word meaning "flourish") were known respectively as the scandicus (from scandere, "to climb"), the torculus ("a little turn"), and the trigon ("a toss"). The motion opposite to the torculus (i.e., down-and-up) is shown by the porrectus ("stretched"), with its striking oblique stroke: ◣. The pes, clivis, torculus, and porrectus were the basic shapes, corresponding to the acute, grave, circumflex, and anticircumflex accents. They were retained in later notational schemes, where we will encounter them again.

The group of six notes following the antiphon verse, set over the letters E u o u a e (sometimes informally combined into a mnemonic, pronounced "e-VO-vay") shows the ending of the psalm — or rather the doxology, for the letters are the vowels in ". . . seculorum. Amen." The six-note formula is called the differentia, because it tells you which of the different available endings of the psalm tone to employ in order to achieve a smooth transition into the repetition of the antiphon. The differentiae are now given in books, but even today's practicing monks have them down cold and need only glance at the required "evovay" formula in order to sing the psalm from memory (or at most from the written text).

Justus ut palma appears twice more in the Office of Martyrs. At Vespers it also functions as a psalm antiphon, but is sung to a different melody requiring a different psalm tone (Ex. 1-2). And a really minimal setting of the verse functions as a concluding versicle (from the Latin versiculum, "little verse"), sung by the officiant and answered by a congregational response at the end of one of the "lesser hours." The one on *Justus ut palma* comes at the end of none (Ex. 1-3). The extreme simplicity of the versicle illustrates the direct connection between the importance of an occasion and the elaborateness of the music that enhances it.

EX. 1-2 *Justus ut palma* as a Vespers antiphon

Ju-stus ut pal - ma flo - re-bit, sic-ut ce-drus Li - ba-ni mul - ti-pli - ca-bi - tur.

EX. 1-3 *Justus ut palma* as a versicle

Justus ut palma flo - re - bit: sicut cedrus Libani multipli- ca - bi - tur.

PSALMODY IN PRACTICE: THE MASS

No fewer than four stichic settings of the *Justus ut palma* verse are found in the original Gregorian corpus of "Mass propers," the psalmodic chants for the yearly round of feasts, recorded formulary by formulary in the early Carolingian antiphoners. Like the Office chants, they are more or less elaborate depending on the occasion and the liturgical function they accompany. All of the examples from the Mass are given in square notation, as they are found in the *Liber usualis*, an anthology of the basic chants for Mass and Office, issued by the Benedictine monks of Solesmes for the use of Catholic congregations following the official adoption of their restored version by Papal decree in 1903.

The *Justus ut palma* verse, being an encomium (that is, an expression of praise), is particularly suitable for Mass formularies honoring saints. As an Introit antiphon (Ex. 1-4) it is sung in tandem with the next verse in its parent psalm at Masses commemorating saints who were priests but not bishops (or confessors but not martyrs). Then comes "Bonum est," the opening verse of Psalm 91 (plus the obligatory doxology, given in a space-saving abbreviation), sung to an accentus tone — the vestigial remains of full cursive psalmody such as now survives only in the Office. Being Mass chants, though, both the antiphon and the vestigial verse are considerably more elaborate, indeed rhetorical, than their Office counterparts.

The antiphon has a few compound neumes verging on the melismatic style. The very first syllable is set to a seven-note complex that ends with a long drawn-out, throbbing triple note (*tristropha*). Over *palma* there is a three-note ascent (*salicus*), immediately followed by a *climacus* (cf. "climax"), a three-note descent from a high note (*virga*, meaning "staff" or "walking stick" after its shape), the latter being sung twice for additional emphasis (*bivirga*). The highest note, a full octave above the lowest note (on *ut*), is reached in the middle of a torculus on -*ca*-, which is then coupled with a clivis to produce a five-note complex. The final phrase of the antiphon, *Dei nostri*, returns three times to the lowest note before cadencing on D. Overall, the antiphon thus describes the same graceful, characteristic arclike shape we have already observed in microcosm in the Office psalm tones. Meanwhile, the psalm tone used here, in a festal Mass, is almost as pneumatically ornate as the Office antiphons already examined.

The pair of "alleluia" exclamations that comes between the antiphon and the verse is sung when the saint's commemoration happens to fall during the fifty-day period after Easter known as Paschal Time, the gladdest season of the church year.

E X. 1-4   *Justus ut palma* as Introit

The Offertory and the Communion, the psalmodic chants of the Eucharist, have by now been entirely shorn of their psalm verses, which in the case of the Offertory were once very elaborate indeed. They are sung as free-standing antiphons amounting to autonomous stichic "arias" for the choir. The Offertory on *Justus ut palma* is sung at a Mass commemorating a saint who was a "Doctor of the Church," especially distinguished for wisdom and learning. (Many of the early Church Fathers whose pronouncements have been quoted in this chapter belong to this category.)

The setting (Ex. 1-5) is even more ornate than the foregoing example: each of the words set to compound neumes in the Introit (*justus*, *palma*, *multiplicabitur*, plus the Paschal alleluia) now carry full-fledged melismas. In addition, the use of what are called ornamental or liquescent neumes implies a particularly expressive manner of singing, though its exact nature is uncertain. The third note over *justus*, for example, as well as the second note over *cedrus*, has a "trembling" shape called *quilisma* (from the Greek *kylio*, "to roll"), which may denote a trilling effect or a vibrato. The word *in* is set to a *clivis liquescens* or *cephalicus*, which involved an exaggerated pronunciation of the "liquid" consonant *n*.

EX. I-5 *Justus ut palma* as Offertory

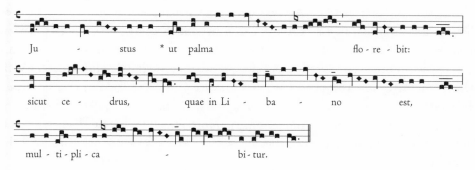

Ju - stus * ut palma flo - re - bit:

sicut ce - drus, quae in Li - ba - no est,

mul - ti - pli - ca - bi - tur.

Finally, settings of the *Justus ut palma* verse function as "lesson chants," sung between the scripture readings that cap the Synaxis portion of the Mass, at a time when there is little or no liturgical action going on. Of all the chants in the Mass, these are the most florid, because more than any other they are meant as listener's music, filling the mind with the inexpressible joy of which St. Augustine wrote so eloquently. *Justus ut palma* is found both as a Gradual, following the Epistle, and as an Alleluia verse (Ex. 1-6), preceding the Gospel. The rhapsodic, essentially textless, fifty-one-note *jubilus* that follows the word "alleluia" in the latter setting (sung at a Mass commemorating a saint who was an abbot, or head of a monastery) is repeated note for note at the end of the verse, showing an apparent concern for ideal musical shaping that is mirrored on a smaller scale by the internal repetitions (representable as **aabb**) that make up the internal melisma on the word *cedrus*. The lesson chants are responsorial chants, in which a soloist (*precentor*) alternates with the choir (*schola*). At the beginning, the precentor sings the word "alleluia" up to the asterisk, following which the choir begins again and continues into the jubilus. The same precentor/schola alternation is indicated in the verse (given mainly to the soloist) by the asterisk before *multiplicabitur*. The choral alleluia is repeated like an antiphon after the verse, giving the whole a rounded (ABA) form.

EX. I-6 *Justus ut palma* as Alleluia

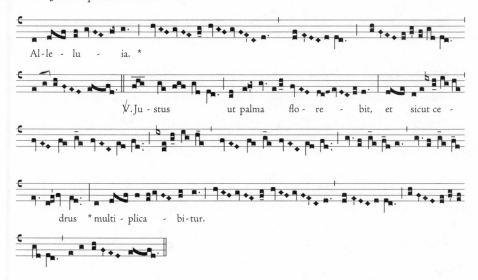

Al - le - lu - ia. *

℣. Ju - stus ut palma flo - re - bit, et sicut ce -

drus *multi - plica - bi - tur.

EVIDENCE OF "ORAL COMPOSITION"

The repetitions that give the Alleluia setting its striking shape are memorable not just for the listener, but also for the performer. Such things were, in fact, a vital memory aid in an age of oral composition and show the relationship between this extraordinarily ornate, mystically evocative composition and the simple psalm tone with which our survey of chant genres began. However protracted and however beautiful, the jubilation-melismas served a practical, syntactical purpose as well as a spiritual or esthetic one. Like the mediant and termination formulas in the tones, albeit at a much higher level of expressive artistry, they mark endings and give the precentor and the schola their cues.

Repetitions of this type not only link the parts of individual chants, they link whole chant families as well. Ex. 1-7 contains two Graduals, each consisting of a melismatic respond and an even more melismatic verse for a virtuoso cantor. The respond in the first of these Graduals, from a formulary assigned in Carolingian times to the commemorative feast of St. John the Baptist, is a setting of the *Justus ut palma* verse. The second (Ex. 1-7b) is the very famous Easter Gradual, in which the text consists of two verses from Psalm 117, one functioning as respond, the other as soloist's verse:

> R: *Haec dies, quam fecit Dominus: exsultemus, et laetemur in ea.*
> V: *Confitemini Domino, quoniam bonus: quoniam in saeculum misericordia ejus.*
> [Ps. 117, 24: This is the day which the Lord hath made: we will rejoice and be glad in it.
> Ps. 117, 1: O give thanks unto the Lord, for He is good: because his mercy endureth for ever.]

EX. I-7A   *Justus ut palma* as Gradual

EX. I-7B   *Haec dies* (Easter Gradual)

It is easy to show (here, by bracketing them) that these two chants draw heavily upon a shared fund of melodic turns. In fact a whole family of Graduals, numbering more than twenty in all, have these formulas in common: besides the two given here, they include the Graduals for the Christmas Midnight Mass (to the words *Tecum principium*, "With Thee in the day of Thy power") and the funeral Mass, called the Requiem after the opening word of its Introit, which happens to recur in the Gradual (*Requiem aeternam*, "Eternal rest"). Again, what is striking is that the shared formulas are found most frequently at initial and (especially) cadential points, and that internal repetitions regularly occur to accommodate lengthier texts. In other words, these extremely elaborate chants still behave, under their flowing melismatic raiment, very much like the psalm tones they may once have been.

How did the one evolve into the other? While we will never find a contemporary witness to musical developments that took place before there were any means of documenting them, an answer to this question is nevertheless suggested by recent research into the practices of more recent, in some cases still active, oral traditions of church music. Nicholas Temperley, investigating the history of what has sometimes been called "the Old Way of Singing" in English parish churches of the seventeenth century and New England Congregational churches of the eighteenth, and the "surge songs" of black churches in the American south, noted a pattern.[7] Musically unlettered or semilettered congregations that sing without professional direction over long periods of time tend to develop a characteristic style: "the tempo becomes extremely slow, the sense of rhythm is weakened; extraneous pitches appear, sometimes coinciding with those of the hymn tune, sometimes inserted between them." Wesley Berg, a Canadian scholar working with Mennonite communities in Western Canada, has corroborated the process by direct observation.[8]

What both scholars describe is the transformation, over time, of simple syllabic melodies into ornate, melismatic ones. (And the point about rhythmic weakening jibes tellingly with the notorious nonmetrical rhythm of the chant, about which little is known and about which, therefore, many strong opinions are maintained.) In New England, the process was thought to be one of corruption. Professional singing masters, armed with notated hymnbooks, sought to counteract the tendency by training their congregations to be not only literate but literal-minded in their attitude toward written texts. In a wholly oral age, when alternative methods of transmission were not available, the process of transformation was more likely seen as desirable, since it produced an ever more artistic, "skilled" product. In the context of the evolving Christian liturgy, degrees of melismatic elaboration served as a means of differentiating types of chants as well as liturgical occasions on the basis of their relative "solemnity." As we will see in the next chapter, moreover, there is evidence that the Gregorian chant itself continued to develop melismatic embellishments in parts of Europe where a relatively fluid oral culture seems to have continued, perhaps for centuries, after the Franks had begun relying on notation as a fixative.

It used to be thought that the large amount of shared material within chant families reflected a "patchwork" process of composition, called *centonization* (after the Latin *cento*, "quilt"). Peter Wagner, one of the pioneering historians of early Christian music, compared centonized chants to articles of jewelry in which prized gems have been selected to receive "a splendid mounting, an ingenious combination, and a tasteful arrangement."[9] Today, scholars prefer a different analogy or model: instead of a fund of individual memorized formulas from which chants are assembled on the basis of artistic ingenuity and taste, one imagines a process of elaboration from a repertory of simple prototypes for various liturgical genres and classes.

The shared formulas found in the Graduals we have been comparing, for example, are found only in Graduals. Another type of chant that is comparably formulaic in its melodic content is the *Tract*, a long, sometimes highly melismatic psalm setting that is sung in place of the Alleluia during penitential seasons such as Advent and Lent, when the joyous ejaculation *alleluia* — Hebrew for "Praise God!" — is suppressed. Tracts come in two mutually exclusive formula-families, and their characteristic turns are not found in any other chant genre.[10]

A fund of shared melodic turns characterizing the chants of a given functional type, or those proper to a certain category of ritual observance, is exactly how the term *mode* is defined in its earliest usages. The concept of mode as formula-family is still prevalent in the Greek Orthodox (Byzantine) church, where the liturgical singing follows what is known as the *oktoechos*, an eight-week cycle of formulaic "modes" (*echoi* in Greek).

Our more recent concept of mode, based on that of a scale, and defined mainly in terms of its final note, fits the Gregorian repertory poorly. (We have already seen, in fact, that Gregorian psalm tones often have a variety of potential final notes, the *differentiae* — see Ex. 1-8.) The concept of mode as a function of scale and final was originally the product of Frankish and Italian music theory of the tenth and eleventh centuries, in which an attempt was made to organize the chants of the Roman church according to the categories of ancient Greek music theory, which was well known from treatises, even if practical examples of ancient Greek music are virtually nonexistent. (As we shall see, the chants composed by later Frankish musicians who had been trained according to this theory conform much more closely to our accustomed idea of what a mode is.)

EX. 1-8 *Differentiae* of the first psalm tone

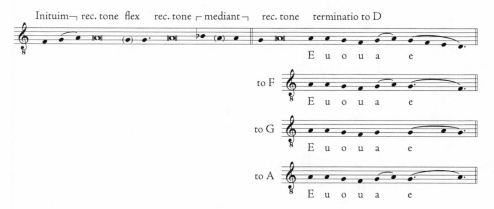

WHY WE WILL NEVER KNOW HOW IT ALL BEGAN

Yet even if the ancient Greek catalogue of lyre tunings was conceptually foreign, hence irrelevant, to the modal structure of Gregorian chant, the attempt to codify medieval modal theory according to Greek ideas of order was not wholly misplaced. The Greek system and the Gregorian corpus did have one thing self-evidently in common. They both employed what some scholars now call the "diatonic pitch set," the field of pitches and pitch relationships reducible to a specific arrangement of tones and semitones ("whole steps" and "half steps"), of which the familiar major and minor scales are among the possible representations.

When staff notation was introduced in the eleventh century, it made tacit yet explicit provision for that arrangement. There is no way of telling the diatonic half steps (between B and C and between E and F) from the whole steps on the basis of their appearance on the staff; from its very beginning, in other words, the staff was "prejudiced" to accommodate the two different sizes of step-interval as musicians had from time immemorial habitually "heard" and deployed them.

Thus there is no point in inquiring about the historical origins of the diatonic pitch set, our most fundamental musical possession. We will never know them. We can do no better than the legends by which the Greeks sought to explain the origins of their musical practice. In one of these, related by Nicomachus in the second century CE, Pythagoras, the reputed inventor of music, heard beautiful sounds coming unexpectedly out of a blacksmith's shop. Weighing the anvils the smiths were striking, he discovered the harmonic ratios governing the perfect ("Pythagorean") consonances, as well as the whole step. Laying these intervals out on a staff, and adding the two extra tones that are obtained when the Pythagorean complex is transposed to begin on each

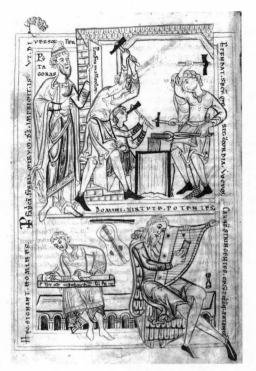

FIG. I-8 Illustration from a thirteenth-century manuscript of a famous music treatise by John of Cotton, now housed at the Bavarian State Library in Munich, which shows Pythagoras in the blacksmith shop, measuring the harmonic consonances. The inscriptions read, *Per fabricam ferri mirum deus imprimit* ("By means of a smithy God has imparted a wonder") and *Is Pythagoras ut diversorum/per pondera malleorum/perpendebat secum quae sit concordia vocum* ("It was this Pythagoras who, by the weights of the various hammers, worked out the consonances for himself"). The lower panel shows a monochord, a more "modern" device for tone measurement, and a harp, laterally strung like a lyre, which represents music's power of *ethos* or moral influence.

of its own constituent pitches, we may arrive at a primitive five-note ("pentatonic") scale. Plugging the "gaps," we find that we have "discovered" the half steps (see Ex. 1-9a).

Another way of deducing the diatonic pitch set from properties of acoustic resonance is to generate it by fifths radiating outward from a central tone. (If D is chosen for this demonstration the whole complex may be represented on the staff without the use of accidentals.) A trace of this deduction survives in the names of our scale degrees, "dominant" being the name of the tone produced by the first fifth "up," and *sub*dominant ("underdominant") being the name of the tone produced by the first fifth "down" (see Ex. 1-9b).

But these deductions are all long after the fact and have nothing to do with history. They are rationalizations, designed to show that our familiar musical system is "natural." (Efforts to deduce the diatonic pitch set from the so-called natural harmonics, or "overtones," are especially ahistorical, because the overtone series was not discovered and described until the eighteenth century.) Yet if the immemorial diatonic pitch set is to be understood as "natural," it must be understood in terms not only of physical but of human nature.

The historical evidence suggests that our diatonically apportioned musical "space," while grounded in acoustic resonance, may also be the product (or one of the possible products) of a physiological predisposition governing "musical hearing," that is, our discrimination of meaningful pitch differences and pitch relationships.

Where actual musical practice is concerned, the relevant historical fact is that people have evidently internalized the diatonic pitch set—carried it around in their heads as a means of organizing, receiving, and reproducing meaningful sound patterns—as far back as what is as of now the very beginning of recorded musical history, some three and a half millennia ago.

EX. 1-9A   Deduction of the diatonic pitch set from the Pythagorean consonances

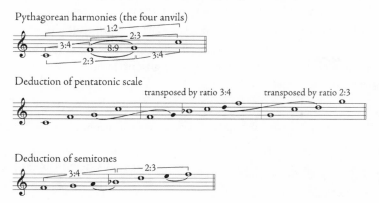

Pythagorean harmonies (the four anvils)

Deduction of pentatonic scale

transposed by ratio 3:4   transposed by ratio 2:3

Deduction of semitones

EX. 1-9B   Deduction of the diatonic pitch set by fifths

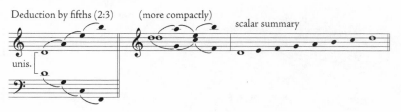

Deduction by fifths (2:3)   (more compactly)   scalar summary

unis.

BEGINNINGS, AS FAR AS WE KNOW THEM

This new "beginning" was established in 1974 when a team of Assyriologists and musicologists at the University of California at Berkeley managed to decode and transcribe the musical notation on a cuneiform tablet dating from around 1200 BCE that had been unearthed on the site of the ancient Babylonian city of Ugarit, near Ras-Shamra in modern Syria.[11] The tablet contained a hymn, composed in Hurrian, a dialect of the Sumerian language, to the goddess Nikkal, the wife of the moon god. The music can be read as being set for a solo voice accompanied homorhythmically by a harp or lyre, thus testifying to a practice of polyphonic composition many centuries before the rise of Christian chant. Most remarkable is how unremarkable this earliest preserved piece of music now seems: it consists of harmonic

FIG. 1-9   Harpist in the garden of Sennacherib, shown in a neo-Assyrian bas-relief from the palace at Niniveh, seventh century B.C.E., 500 years later than the earliest musical notation, of similar geographical provenance, to have been successfully transcribed in modern times. That piece, described in the text, could have been performed by one or both of the figures represented here.

intervals recognized as consonant in most Western practice, and is easily notated on the normal Western staff because it conforms to the same disposition of diatonic whole and half steps used in Western music since the start of its continuous written tradition (Ex. 1-10). Like the Gregorian chant, the Babylonian melody conforms to the basic contents of the familiar diatonic pitch set, though not to any of our modern ways of patterning it.

EX. 1-10   First phrase of Hurrian cult song from ancient Ugarit, transcribed by Anne Draffkorn Kilmer

(Fragmentary and untranslatable text omitted.)

Pretty much the same may be said about the handful of ancient (if relatively "late") Greek melodies that happen to survive in decipherable practical sources, as well as the earliest Greek Christian music that grew more or less directly out of prior pagan practice.[12] The earliest such Greek remnant, the first of two surviving Delphic Hymns, or paeans to Apollo sung by a priestess at the Delphic oracle's abode, was set down around 130 BCE on a now only partly legible stone tablet that is kept at the National Archaeological Museum in Delphi. It employs a learned and artificial style, called the "chromatic [i.e., colorful] genus" by the Greeks, in which some of the strings of the lyre were tuned low in order to provide two semitones in direct succession. (Hence the adaptation of the word "chromatic" to denote the much later Western practice of inflecting scale degrees by semitones; Greek theorists also describe an "enharmonic" genus in which the semitones could

FIG. 1-10   Attic Greek amphora (jar), ca. 490 B.C.E., showing someone singing to a lyre. Greek music theory was mainly confined to prescribing tunings for the lyre, in three *genera*, or types: diatonic, chromatic, and enharmonic. These words have survived in modern musical terminology, although not with precisely the same meanings.

be replaced by quarter tones.) Ex. 1-11a shows the second half of the melody, in which the embellishing "chromatic semitones" are most prevalent, adapted from a somewhat speculative transcription made about eighty years ago by the French archaeologist Théodore Reinach: it reproduces the melodic pitches exactly as "alphabetically" notated in the source but infers the meter and rhythm from that of the text.

Ex. 1-11b contains the earliest surviving artifact of actual Christian service music, a fragment from the close of a Greek hymn to the Holy Trinity, notated on a papyrus strip during the fourth century CE and discovered in 1918. The hymn is probably a translated extract from the liturgy of the Syriac Christian church. Although we cannot be certain (since it is our only example), it seems to be built up out of a diatonic formula-family. It is the earliest surviving representative, by six or seven centuries, of the Greek-texted music of the Orthodox (that is, official) church of the Eastern Roman Empire, known as the Byzantine Empire after Byzantium (or Constantinople), its capital until 1453.

EX. 1-11A   Second stanza of the First Delphic Hymn, transcribed by Egert Pöhlmann and Martin L. West

Behold Attica's great city, which by the prayers of the warrior maiden Tritonic dwells in a plain inviolate! On the holy altars Hephaistos the fire god burns the thighs of young bulls, while the fragrance of Arabia is wafted to Olympus; and the flute in clear, shrill notes pipes its song with varied tunes; and the sweet-voiced lyre of gold strikes up the hymns.

Unlike the Western Roman church, which came to cultivate the traditional prose-poetry of the Psalter as its main sphere of musical creativity, the Eastern Orthodox church emphasized hymnody, newly composed "songs with praise of God" in metrical verse. This repertory, known as Byzantine chant, consists of hymns in many liturgical genres or categories ranging from the single-stanza *troparion* (for the Vigil, or Night Office) and *sticheron* (for the day services), which attach themselves to psalms in a

EX. I-IIB Fourth verse of a proto-Byzantine Hymn to the Trinity, transcribed by E. Pöhlmann and M. West

Hym-noun-ton d' hy-mon pa-te-ra hui-on ha-gi-on pneu-ma Pa-sai dy-na-meis

e-pi-pho-noun-ton a-min a-min. Kra-tos ai-nos a ei hai do-xa The-o

do-ti-ri mo-noi pan-ton a-ga-thon A-min a-min.

manner matching that of the Gregorian antiphon—through the *kontakion* (from the Greek for "scroll"), an elaborate metrical sermon in as many as 30 stanzas—to the *kanon* (from the Greek for "rule"), a magnificent cycle of nine *odes*, each based on a different metrical prototype or model stanza called a *hiermos*.

One of the oldest melodies still in active liturgical use is the one called "Credo I" in modern chant books (Ex. I-I2). It is a setting of the Nicene Creed: a recitation of articles of Christian faith that was adopted in the fourth century, originally for use in the baptism ceremony. The Creed eventually joined the Eucharistic liturgy, sung first in the Eastern churches, later (sixth century CE) in Spain and in Ireland. It was adopted by the Franks in 798 and was formally incorporated into the "universal" (or "Catholic") Latin Mass by Pope Benedict VIII in 1014, positioned between the Gospel reading and the Offertory as the divider between the synaxis and Eucharist services.

Despite its late adoption, the formulas to which this venerable text is most often sung are demonstrably archaic and demonstrably Greek. Its formula-family, with its

EX. I-I2 Beginning of "Credo I"

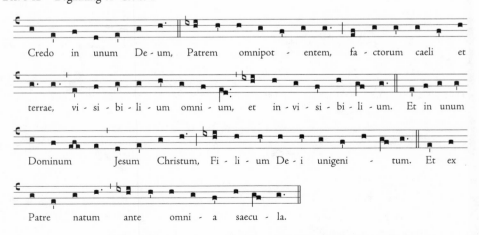

Credo in unum De-um, Patrem omnipot-entem, fa-ctorum caeli et

terrae, vi-si-bi-li-um omni-um, et in-vi-si-bi-li-um. Et in unum

Dominum Jesum Christum, Fi-li-um De-i unigeni-tum. Et ex

Patre natum ante omni-a saecu-la.

I believe in one God, Father almighty, maker of heaven and earth
and of all things visible and invisible. And in one Lord Jesus Christ,
the only begotten Son of God, born of the Father before all ages.

regular use of B-flat and E to surround the reciting tone on G, and its final cadence on E, is a rather exotic specimen within the Gregorian corpus. (But compare the Offertory on *Justus ut palma* in Ex. 1-5.) Yet although it seems to emphasize the odd interval of a diminished fifth, the melody nevertheless fully conforms to the intervallic structure of the diatonic pitch set. Transposed up a fifth or down a fourth it could be accommodated on the staff without accidentals. (The reason why it is not notated at that pitch level in the Gregorian sources will become clear in the next chapter.)

As these very old melodies suggest, there are many ways of patterning and embellishing the diatonic pitch set, giving rise to any number of historical, culture-bound musical styles. Tracing their development will be one of this book's primary tasks. Yet history also suggests that the pitch set as such — the raw material, so to speak, that precedes patterning — may be a natural "datum," given to a degree in external nature (the physics of sound) but, more relevantly, in human nature (call it the physiology of sound cognition). Within the tradition of Western music, there may be cognitive universals that, as in language, underlie and undergird all cultural practices, and (the downside, some may feel) set limits to them.

New Styles and Forms

FRANKISH ADDITIONS TO THE ORIGINAL CHANT REPERTORY

LONGISSIMAE MELODIAE

A malar (or Amalarius) of Metz, an urban cleric and a disciple of Alcuin, served Charlemagne and his successor Louis as both churchman and statesman. He was one of the supervisors of the Carolingian chant and liturgy reform, and virtually our sole witness to it. After a diplomatic sojourn in Rome in 831, Amalar spent the remaining decades of his life compiling liturgical books, to which he added commentaries replete with information about the church singing he had heard, which he wished to see transplanted to Frankish soil. Although Amalar did not use neumes (possibly because he lived just too early to have had the option of using them), his descriptions of the ways in which the Roman chant was adapted to the use of the Franks are uniquely detailed and vivid.

One thing we learn from Amalar is that the Roman cantors he observed had taken one of their real showpieces — a *neuma triplex*, a huge threefold melisma from a matins responsory commemorating St. John the Baptist's day (December 27) — and transferred it back to Christmas, where its festive jubilation seemed even more appropriate. This practice was part of a general trend, which Amalar wanted to abet, toward adorning the liturgy with special music. Christmas, liturgically the most elaborate of days (on which, for example, not one but three Masses were sung: at midnight and at dawn as well as at the usual hour between terce and sext), was of course especially favored. The *neuma triplex* was available for insertion, however, wherever it was wanted. In different sources it is found associated with the feast of the Holy Innocents and with the feasts of various saints as celebrated, with special pomp, in their home diocese.

The third and most sumptuous of the *neuma triplex* melismas, with its seventy-eight notes, may be the longest *melodia*, or stretch of textless vocalizing, in the entire repertory of medieval chant. In Example 2-1, the concluding words (*fabricae mundi*, "of the structure of the world") from *Descendit de caelis* ("He descended from Heaven"), the crowning responsory from Christmas matins, are given first in their "normal" form, then with the *neuma triplex* melisma as eventually written down in staff notation about three centuries after Amalar described it. (We can assume that it still pretty much resembles the eighth-century melody Amalar described because it concords well with unheighted neumes in much older manuscripts.)

Amalar enthusiastically endorses the practice of interpolating such *neumae* or melismas into festive chants, in keeping with the old idea of "jubilated" singing. Noting that in its original context (the feast of St. John the Baptist) the triple melisma fell on the word *intellectus*, which he interprets to mean an ecstatic or mystical kind of "understanding" beyond the power of words to convey, Amalar exhorts monastic musicians that "if you ever come to the 'understanding' in which divinity and eternity are beheld, you must tarry in that 'understanding,' rejoicing in song without words which pass away."[1]

EX. 2-1   *Neuma triplex*

End of original respond

And the light, the glory of the universal structure of the world, will go out through the golden gate.

The three melismas (inserted into the respond on its three repetitions)
a. (on the first repetition)

b. (on the second repetition)

c. (on the concluding repetition)

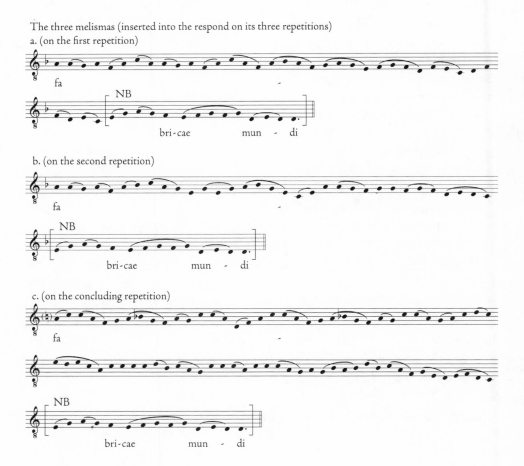

This passage from Amalar recalls the famous words in which St. Augustine, five hundred years earlier, had extolled the "jubilated" singing of his day, associated by the time of Amalar chiefly with the Mass Alleluia. And sure enough, Amalar writes enthusiastically of another Roman practice, that of replacing the traditional *jubilus*, the melisma on the "-ia" of "Alleluia," with an even longer melody, which he describes as "a jubilation that the singers call a *sequentia*," presumably because of the way it followed after the Alleluia chant.[2]

That the Franks enthusiastically adopted the practice of adorning their service music with ever lengthier *melodiae* we learn from Agobard of Lyons, another ninth-century ecclesiastical observer, who condemned what Amalar endorsed. From childhood to old age, Agobard complained, the singers in the schola spent all their time improving their voices instead of their souls, boasted of their virtuosity and their memories, and vied with one another in melismatic contest. The *sequentia* repertoire was the tamed and scripted issue of these frantic oral engagements.

PROSA

Like the jubilus itself, the early *sequentia* vocalises — sung on the word "Alleluia" but so melismatic as to be virtually textless — had many internal phrase repetitions designed to make them easier to memorize. Another memory aid employed by Frankish singers was of far-reaching artistic significance: they added words to melismatic chants that turned them, perhaps paradoxically, into syllabic hymns. This led to a fantastic flowering of new devotional song that developed over three centuries and reached its peak in twelfth-century France.

Its beginnings are what concern us now. Amalar's *neuma triplex* can serve as our starting point. As its surviving sources attest, it begat several little prose poems, or *prosulae*; compare the pair in Example 2-2 with the climactic third melisma in Ex. 2-1.

The texts are in prose (or "art-prose" as it has been called, since its diction is very high-flown) because the original melody, like most melismatic chants, is rhythmically rhapsodic and irregular. (The use of prose was nothing new, of course; the psalms themselves are examples of art-prose.) But the melody's one regularizing feature — the use of a repeated phrase at the outset (disguised by the interpolation of a pair of low notes) — lends the texted version a slight suggestion of strophic or "couplet" form. (In strophic form every line of text is set to the same melody; in couplet form the melody changes after every pair of lines.) Also note parenthetically the interpolated "key signature" of one flat in Ex. 2-2a. This was not part of the original notation, but reflects the way we assume any medieval singer would have sung a melody in which B immediately preceded or followed an F, or in which F and B described the outer limits of a melodic "turn." (The augmented fourth, not recognized by the Frankish music theory we will shortly be investigating, was adjusted to the perfect fourth in practice long before it was "prohibited" in theory.)

A similar underlaying of a prose text or *prosula* to a preexisting melisma adorns a famous chant we met in the previous chapter. The eleventh-century Gradual of St. Yrieux, which contains elaborated versions of the Mass propers, has what looks like

EX. 2-2A   *Prosulae* to the *neuma triplex, Facture tue*

EX. 2-2B   *Prosulae* to the *neuma triplex, Rex regum*

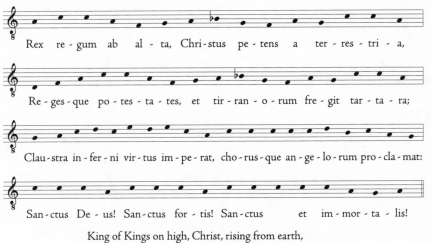

King of Kings on high, Christ, rising from earth,
overcomes princes and potentates, and the powers of Hell;
Good conquers the infernal regions, and the choirs of angels sing:
Holy God! Holy and Mighty! Holy and immortal!
(Trans. Richard L. Crocker)

a syllabic version of the Alleluia *Justus ut palma*: an entire poem is interpolated into the text of its verse to correspond with the notes of the long melisma on "cedrus." As we may recall from Ex. 1-6, that melisma is distinguished by regularizing internal repetitions that can be represented as **aabb**. When the prose text is underlaid to the melisma, the resulting prosula has the appearance of a poem in couplets (pairs of lines set to the same tune). As we shall see, paired verses are characteristic of many medieval chants. We may be witnessing the procedure in its embryo (compare Ex. 2-3 with Ex. 1-6).

E X. 2-3   Prosulated version of Alleluia, *Justus ut palma*

An early witness to the practice of "prosulation" — as good a term as any for the interpolation of syllabic texts into melismatic tunes — is Notker Balbulus (Notker the Stammerer, d. 912), a monk at the East Frankish monastery of St. Gallen, already known to us as Charlemagne's first biographer. In the introduction to his Book of Hymns (*Liber hymnorum*), which dates from about 880, Notker recalls that in his youth he learned the practice from a monk who had escaped from the West Frankish abbey of Jumièges (near Rouen in northwestern France), after it had been laid waste by marauding "Normans" (that is, Vikings).[3] This would have been in 852, about twenty years after Amalar had first described the sequentia and promoted it among the Franks. This monk, Notker tells us, had with him an antiphoner in which some *sequentia* melismas had been "prosulated." Notker, so he tells us, leapt at this device for making extra-long vocalises (*longissimae melodiae*, he calls them) memorable, and went on, so he boasts, to invent what we now call the *sequence*.

SEQUENCES

We now use the English word "sequence," derived from the Latin *sequentia* (or, sometimes, "prose," derived from the Latin *prosa*) to denote not the jubilus-replacing melisma itself but the syllabic hymn that (as Notker tells us) was originally derived from it by matching prose syllables to its constituent notes. The sequence eventually became a canonical part of the Mass, on a par with the Alleluia that it followed and the Gospel reading that it preceded. It is one of the indigenous Frankish contributions to the evolving "Roman" liturgy, and Notker (despite the studied modesty of his diction) may have exaggerated his role in its creation.

Also evidently exaggerated in his telling is the dependency of the sequence, as Notker and others actually practiced it in the late ninth century, on the earlier *sequentia* described by Amalar. Only a handful of surviving sequences (out of the thirty-three in Notker's book, only eight) can be linked up with a known *sequentia* melisma. By the time Notker completed his book, the sequence had already matured into a substantial composition, fresh in both words and music and novel in style, that was sometimes (but far from always) modeled on a liturgical Alleluia melody. It is of course possible that a lost or unrecorded *sequentia* lurks behind each of Notker's "hymns." But

FIG. 2-1 Notker Balbulus, a ninth-century monk from the Swiss monastery of St. Gallen, shown in an illumination from a manuscript probably prepared there some 200 years later. He looks as though he is cudgeling his brain to recall a *longissima melodia*, as he tells us he did in the preface to his *Liber hymnorum* (Book of hymns), which contains some early examples of prosulated melismas known as sequences.

to assume that this is the case would be to confuse the origin of the genre with the origin of each individual specimen (as if every symphony were assumed to be an operatic overture because, as we will learn later, the earliest ones were). That kind of false assumption about origins is known as the "genetic fallacy." To illustrate the early sequence we can examine two specimens from Notker's own *Liber hymnorum*, reminding ourselves that Notker himself was able to notate only the texts of his sequences; the melodies come from later manuscripts that may or may not transmit them exactly as Notker composed or adapted them in the ninth century. *Angelorum ordo* (Ex. 2-4a) represents the earliest stage, a simple prosulated *sequentia* melisma that belongs to the Alleluia *Excita Domine* (third Sunday in Advent). It conforms to Notker's description of how the sequence was born. The little melodic repetitions are of the kind we have already encountered in many melismatic chants.

Altogether different is *Rex regum* (Ex. 2-4b), a mature sequence that happens to share its text incipit with one of the items in Ex. 2-2. Its opening melodic phrase is artfully derived from the Alleluia *Justus ut palma* (Ex. 1-6); there are other similarities between the two melodies as well. The sequence may thus have been meant to link up with that particular Alleluia (sung at St. Gallen, Notker's monastery, at the Mass commemorating St. John the Baptist), but there is no reason to suppose it would have been limited to that use. The melodic resemblance being approximate rather than exact, it has effect of an allusion: an honorific, like those in the text, that might compliment any distinguished churchman. In any case, the reference to *Justus ut palma* is not in this case the automatic result of an adaptive process but a deliberate artistic touch, replete with a couple of neumes that in this context suggest flourishes.

Thereafter, the sequence proceeds in strictly syllabic couplets, successive pairs of lines sung to repeated portions of the melody. (In sequences of a later date, when texts in rhymed verse replaced the earlier "prosa" type, the couplets are often called "paired versicles.") There is no preexisting *sequentia* melisma with such a regular structure, but it would remain standard for sequences for the next three hundred years. That structure, which begins to suggest strophic repetitions, may be the reason why Notker called his compositions "hymns."

HOW THEY WERE PERFORMED

Even greater regularity, and even greater independence from preexistent models, can be seen in *Rex caeli* (Fig. 2-2; its first five lines are transcribed in Ex. 2-5), a composition

EX. 2-4A   Sequence by Notker Balbulus, *Angelorum ordo*

EX. 2-4B   Sequence by Notker Balbulus, *Rex regum*

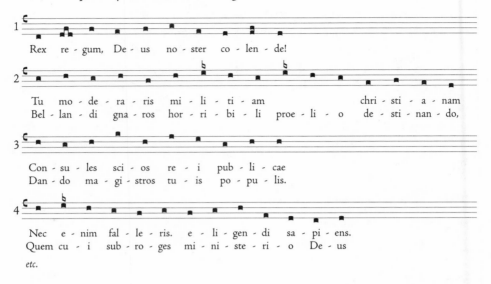

1 Rex re - gum, De - us no - ster co - len - de!

2 Tu mo - de - ra - ris mi - li - ti - am   chri - sti - a - nam
   Bel - lan - di gna - ros hor - ri - bi - li proe - li - o de - sti - nan - do,

3 Con - su - les sci - os re - i pub - li - cae
   Dan - do ma - gi - stros tu - is po - pu - lis.

4 Nec e - nim fal - le - ris. e - li - gen - di sa - pi - ens.
   Quem cu - i sub - ro - ges mi - ni - ste - ri - o De - us

etc.

of such sophisticated, artful shape that its status as a sequence has been questioned. (So let's call it a sequence-type hymn.) Unlike most early sequences, it is structurally "rounded" on several levels. It lines are arranged not only in couplets but occasionally in quatrains—groups of four successive lines sung to the same melody. The melody of the first couplet recurs in the fourth, and the whole series of seven melodic strains then repeats (in a so-called double cursus or "double run-through") to provide the next seven. The last pair of melodic units recapitulates the opening and closing strains of the cursus. Line lengths are almost uniformly in multiples of four syllables (eight, twelve, sixteen), giving an impression of regular meter. Not only that, but the words of many of the couplets are linked by such a strong use of assonance—similarity of vowel placement—as to approach rhyme.

This was not only a remarkable composition but a famous one. It is found complete on a French manuscript leaf dating from the tenth century, but we know that it was a ninth-century composition—and already famous in the ninth century—because its first two couplets were chosen as a didactic illustration in *Musica enchiriadis* ("Handbook of music"), the earliest surviving Frankish treatise about practical music-making, which is thought to date from some time between 860 and 900. The illustration is reproduced in Fig. 2-2. It is one of several examples in the treatise of polyphonic singing, and can serve us as a forceful reminder that polyphony was routinely practiced among the Franks as early as we have any evidence of their musical practice at all.

In this arrangement (transcribed in Ex. 2-6), the upper voice sings the original *Rex caeli* melody, for which reason it is called the "principal voice" (*vox principalis*). The lower voice, called the *vox organalis* because it produces the harmony or counterpoint (called *organum* at the time), begins at the unison and holds on to its initial pitch as a drone until the principal voice has reached the interval of a fourth above it, the smallest interval considered consonant according to the theory of the time. At this point, the two voices move in parallel until the cadence (or *occursus*, as it was called, meaning

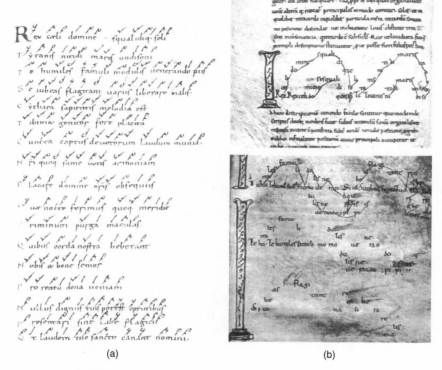

(a)   (b)

FIG. 2-2 *Rex caeli Domine*, a sequence-like hymn probably dating from the ninth century. (a) Its most complete source, a French manuscript from the tenth century written in an alphabetic notation that specifies pitch precisely. (b) Its earliest source, the ninth-century treatise *Musica enchiriadis*, which shows a fragment of it, in a similar notational style, adapted to illustrate a common practice whereby monophonic chants were amplified polyphonically in performance. This provides evidence of polyphony as early as any evidence of the chant itself.

EX. 2-5 *Rex caeli Domine* (Fig. 2-2a) transcribed

1. Rex cae - li, Do - mi - ne ma - ris un - di - so - ni, Ti - ta - nis ni - ti - di squa - li - di - que so - li,
King of heaven, Lord of the sounding sea, of the shining Titan sun and the gloomy earth,
8. Mor - ta - lis o - cu - lus vi - det in fa - ci - e, Tu au - tem la - te - bras a - ni - mi per a - gras.
The mortal eye sees the external form; Thou, however, dost search through the hiding places of the soul.

2. Te hu - mi - les fa - mu - li mo - du - lis ve - ne - ran - do pi - is,
Thy humble servants, worshiping Thee with devout song as Thou has bidden,
9.   So - no - ris fi - di - bus fa - mu - li ti - bi - met de - vo - ti
With sounding strings, we servants devoted to Thee

Se, ju - be - as, fla - gi - tant va - ri - is li - be - ra - re ma - lis
earnestly entreat Thee to order them freed from their various ills.
       Da - vi - dis se - qui - mur hu - mi - lem re - gis pre - cum ho - sti - am.
attend the humble offering of the prayers of King David.

EX. 2-5 (continued)

3. Ci - tha - ra sa - pi - en - tis me - lo - di - a est Ti - bi - met, ge - ni - tor, for - te pla - ci - ta;
The cithara is the song of the wise; to Thee, Creator, may it be pleasing.
10. Hoc Sa - ul lu - di - cro mi - ti - ga - ve - rat, Spi - ri - tu cum si - bi for - te de - bi - lem
With this entertainment he had soothed Saul when from his soul, made feeble by chance,

Cun - cta ca - ptus de - vo - to - rum lau - dum mu - ni - a No - stri quo - que su - me vo - ti har - mo - ni - am.
Having obtained the whole service of praise of the devoted, receive also the harmony of our prayer.
Spi - ri - ta - lem a - bo - le - bat ju - sti - ti - am Ip - so jo - co tu - a can - tans prae - co - ni - a.
he was blotting out righteous justice; in this pastime singing your praises.

4. Pla - ca - re, Do - mi - ne, no - stris ob - se - qui - is, Quae noc - te fer - i - mus, quo - que me - ri - di - e,
May Thou be appeased by our services, which we offer by night and also by day . . .
11. Haec si - bi cae - li - tus mu - ne - ra ve - ne - rant, Ut i - ram dul - ci - bus pre - me - ret mo - du - lis.
These gifts had come to him from heaven, that he might check anger with pleasant melodies.

Trans. Richard H. Hoppin

EX. 2-6 Polyphonic example from *Musica enchiriadis* (Fig. 2-2b) transcribed

a. Rex cae - li, do - mi - ne ma - ris un - di - so - ni,
b. Ti - ta - nis ni - ti - di squa - li - di - que so - li,

a. Te hu - mi - les fa - mu - li mo - du - lis ve - ne - ran - do pi - is.
b. Se, iu - be - as, fla - gi - tant va - ri - is li - be - ra - re ma - lis.

the coming-together), which restores the unison. In the second phrase, the augmented fourth against B is avoided first by sustaining the "organal" G, and then by leaping to E. Once again unison is restored at the end.

This is *not* a polyphonic "composition." Rather, it is an example of how Frankish cantors harmonized the chants they sang "by ear." How did that style of harmony get into their ears? The answer to that question is lost among the unnotated musical repertories that existed alongside the privileged repertory of notated Roman and Frankish chant. Literate musicians have always been much affected by the music in their aural environment, and the performance of all music, whether written down or not, is governed in part by unwritten conventions. (Otherwise, one could learn to compose or to play the piano simply by reading books.) We can assume that the monks who recorded our first examples of polyphony were not inventing it but adapting it from oral (probably secular) practice, and that the early examples were meant as models for application to other melodies.

Which melodies? More likely the new Frankish repertory of proses, hymns, and suchlike than the canonical Roman chant. That chant, being largely psalmodic, had (as we have seen) an exceptional "ethical" tradition demanding unison performance. The other, simpler examples given in *Musica enchiriadis* of polyphonic "performance practice" (strictly parallel doubling at the fourth, the fifth, and the octave) are based, like the one shown in Fig. 2-2, on syllabic Frankish compositions in the new style. But we do not really know what restrictions or preferences there may have been at this time; and it is tantalizingly possible that polyphonic singing was not the exception but the rule, at least in certain monastic communities.

The other remarkable feature of the *Rex caeli* hymn, both in its complete source and as quoted in *Musica enchiriadis*, is its notation. It is called Daseian notation after the Greek *prosodia daseia*, the "sign of rough breathing" used in various modified forms by Greek music theorists to indicate pitches, and it is found mainly in didactic treatises. In Fig. 2-1, Daseian signs showing the pitches from *c* to *a* are written in ascending order inside the column preceding the first phrase of *Rex caeli*, and those from *c* to *c'* precede the wider-ranging second phrase. Here is proof that the Franks had at their disposal a notation that showed exact pitches. They could have used it in their chant manuscripts, too, if they had wanted to do so. Again we must confront the fact that music was still primarily an art of memory, and that in practical sources all that was required was enough notation to bring a melody forward, so to speak, from the back of the mind. "Sight-reading," as we know it today, was not yet thought a useful skill.

HYMNS

The sequence, although it was the most elaborate, was only one of many new musical forms with which the Franks adorned and amplified the imported Roman chant, and made it their own. The strophic office hymn was another genre that they cultivated avidly. The Latin liturgy had known hymnody since at least the fourth century, but for doctrinal reasons it was rejected in Rome (and so it was not part of the repertory brought north under the Carolingians). St. Augustine recounts that his teacher St. Ambrose, the fourth-century bishop of Milan, had adapted hymns from Greek practice for full congregational singing during vigils. The greatest Latin hymnographer after Ambrose was a contemporary of Pope Gregory named Venantius Fortunatus (d. ca. 600), an Italian who served as bishop of Poitiers in west-central France. His most famous composition, *Pange lingua gloriosi* ("Sing, O my tongue"), used a metrical scheme (trochaic tetrameter) that would be widely imitated by later hymn composers.

Both Ambrose's fourth-century Milanese texts and Venantius's sixth-century "Gallican" ones remained current into the twentieth century, but no melodies can be documented before the year 1000, and once they begin appearing in monastic manuscripts, they appear in such profusion that most of the oldest texts are provided with as many as a dozen or more tunes. There is no telling which or how many of them date from before the ninth century, but the overwhelming majority conform so much better with the tonal criteria established by the ninth-century Frankish music theorists (whose work we will shortly be investigating) than they do with the tonal types of the Roman chant, that their Frankish origin seems virtually certain.

Hymnody is the apparent antithesis (or rather, the calculated complement) of psalmody. Where psalms and their stichic appendages are lofty and numinous, conducive to spiritual repose and contemplation, hymns are the liturgy's popular songs: markedly rhythmical (whether their rhythms are organized by syllable count or by actual meter), strongly profiled in melody, conducive to enthusiasm. The first verses of three of the most famous ones are given in Ex. 2-7. At this point they may be regarded primarily as illustrations of the genre, but later they will serve as examples of contrasting tonalities within the Frankish "mode" system (and later still, we will see them embodied in polyphonic settings by famous composers).

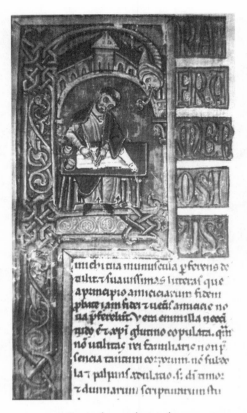

FIG. 2-3   St. Ambrose, the ninth-century governor and bishop of Milan who introduced Byzantine-style hymn-singing to the Western church. He is shown writing, in an illumination — initial F (Frater Ambrosius) — from the Bible of Pedro de Pamplona, Seville, MS 56-5-1, fol. 2.

Ave maris stella ("Hail, Star of the sea") is an acclamation to the Blessed Virgin Mary intended for one of the many offices devoted to her that burgeoned in the Franco-Roman liturgy around the time of the early neumated manuscripts. The text is securely dated to the ninth century. The rather decoratively neumatic tune, the most famous of several associated with the poem, makes its appearance in the extant manuscripts somewhat later. In a still primarily oral age, however, the date of a melody's earliest written source bears no reliable witness to the date of its creation.

The version of *Pange lingua* that follows is not Venantius's original but a reworking — called "parody," but without any connotation of satire — by St. Thomas Aquinas (d. 1274), composed for the office of Corpus Christi (veneration of the body of Christ). Like our contemporary satirical parodies, medieval sacred parodies (also called *contrafacta*) were meant to be sung to traditional tunes, so that in this case the melody is far older than the words. Both this example and the preceding one testify in their opposite ways to the fluidity of the text-music relationship in this and many other medieval sung repertories.

Veni creator spiritus, the great Pentecost hymn and something of a Carolingian anthem, has been attributed honorifically to many famous Franks, including Hrabanus Maurus (d. 856), the archbishop of Mainz, and even Charlemagne himself. The poem employs the so-called Ambrosian stanza (four lines of eight syllables each), established by the original Latin hymnodist five centuries before; but the dynamically arching melody, its successive phrases marking cadences on what we still identify as "primary" scale degrees, is of exemplary Frankish design.

EX. 2-7   Three Frankish hymns

a. *Ave maris stella*

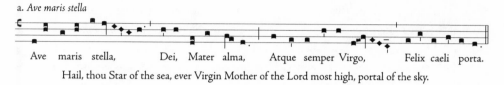

Ave   maris stella,   Dei, Mater alma,   Atque semper Virgo,   Felix caeli porta.

Hail, thou Star of the sea, ever Virgin Mother of the Lord most high, portal of the sky.

EX. 2-7B   *Pange lingua gloriosi*

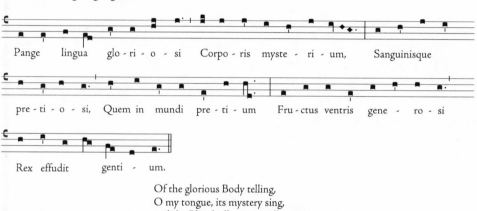

Pange   lingua   glo - ri - o - si   Corpo - ris   myste - ri - um,   Sanguinisque

pre - ti - o - si, Quem in mundi pre - ti - um   Fru - ctus ventris   gene - ro - si

Rex effudit   genti - um.

Of the glorious Body telling,
O my tongue, its mystery sing,
and the Blood, all price excelling,
which for this world's ransoming
in a noble womb once dwelling
he shed forth, the Gentiles' king.

EX. 2-7C   *Veni creator spiritus*

Veni Cre - a - tor Spi - ri - tus, Mentes tu - orum   vi - si - ta: Imple su - perna

gra - ti - a Quae tu cre - asti   pecto - ra.

Thou, Holy Ghost, Creator, come,
and make thy people's souls thy home:
with grace celestial animate
the hearts thou didst thyself create.

TROPES

Sequences and hymns were complete compositions in their own right—freestanding songs, so to speak, on a par (but contrasting in style) with the psalmodic chants of the inherited Roman chant. Another large category of Frankish compositions consisted of chants that did not stand alone but were attached in various ways and for various reasons to other—usually older, canonical—chants. One of the commonest ways of attaching new musical settings to older ones was by casting the new one as a preface, to amplify and interpret the old one for the benefit of contemporary worshipers. Although the practice, like most Frankish musical innovations, can be dated to the ninth century, it was cultivated most intensely beginning in the tenth, reflecting (if only indirectly) the spiritual and creative ideals of the so-called Cluniac reform of monastic life.

The Benedictine monastery of Cluny, in east-central France, was founded by the Abbot Berno in 910 under the patronage of Guillaume (William) the Pious, the first duke of Aquitaine. It was established on land recently won by William from the duke of Burgundy and deeded to the monastery outright so as to free it from lay interference. There, Berno sought to reestablish the original Benedictine discipline that had seriously eroded during two centuries of Norse invasion. The chief means of purifying monastic life was vastly to increase the amount of time and energy devoted to liturgical observances. That meant not only expanding the duration and gravity of services but also educating the monks in devotion. This was a possible purpose of the newly composed prefaces, called tropes (from the Latin *tropus*, possibly related to the Byzantine-Greek *troparion*, or nonscriptural hymn stanza in art-prose).

The primary sites of troping were the antiphons of the Mass proper. Attached most characteristically to the Introit, the trope became a comment on the Mass as a whole, as if to say, "We are celebrating Mass today, and this is the reason." Tropes were also attached to the other Gregorian antiphons that accompanied ritual action, especially the Offertory ("we are offering gifts, and this is the reason") and the Communion ("we are tasting the wine and the wafer, and this is the reason"). While troping became a very widespread practice as the Cluniac reform spread over large areas of France, Germany, and northern Italy, the individual tropes were a more local and discretionary genre than the canonical chant. A given antiphon can be found with many different prefaces in various sources, reflecting local liturgical customs.

At their most elaborate, tropes could function not only as preface to a complete Introit, say, but also as prefaces to each stichic psalm-verse in the antiphon, or to the cursive verse or verses that followed, or even to the doxology formula. Thus, in practice, tropes could take the form of interpolations as well as prefaces. Unlike the syllabic sequence, which contrasted starkly with the melismatic alleluia that it followed, tropes imitated the neumatic style of the antiphons to which they were appended, to all intents and purposes becoming part of them. Because the first words of chants are always sung by the precentor to set the pitch, it is thought that the tropes may have been differentiated from the choral antiphons by being assigned to soloists.

Manuscripts containing tropes, called "tropers," are preeminently associated with two monasteries. One is the East Frankish monastery of St. Gallen, where Notker played his part in the development of the sequence, and where the monk Tuotilo (d. 915) may have had a similar hand in the development of the trope. The other is the West Frankish monastery of St. Martial at Limoges in southwestern France, which in the tenth century belonged, like Cluny, to the Duchy of Aquitaine. The four tropes or sets of tropes in Ex. 2-8 and Ex. 2-9 are all found in tenth-century St. Martial tropers (but with later concordances in staff notation), and all meant to enlarge upon the same canonical item—the Introit of the Easter Sunday Mass, the most copiously troped item in the entire liturgy.

The canonical text of the Introit consists of excerpts from three verses—18, 5, and 6 respectively—of Psalm 138, words that by the ninth century already had a long tradition of Christian *exegesis*, or doctrinal interpretation. Within the original Psalm, the verse excerpt that opens the Introit—*Resurrexi, et adhuc tecum sum* ("I arose, and am still with thee")—refers to an awakening from sleep. Amalar of Metz was one of the many Christian commentators who construed these words as having been addressed by the eternal Christ to his Father through the unwitting agency of the psalmist David, and thus to refer prophetically to the event the Easter Mass commemorates: Christ's resurrection from the dead on the third day after his crucifixion. It was one of the functions of the tropes to confirm this interpretation and render it explicit.

The first and simplest trope in the sample (Ex. 2-8a) consists of a single exhortation or invitation to the choir to sing, strengthening the assumption that the trope would have been performed by a precentor or cantor. Despite its brevity, it manages most economically to accomplish the task of an exegetical trope, identifying the psalmist's words with the victory of Christ. Ex. 2-8b contains what might be called a full set of tropes to the Introit, introducing not only the first stich but each of the other two as well. An even more elaborate set has a fourth line to set off the concluding "alleluia." Like the one in Ex. 2-6b, it amplifies the psalm verses with a patchwork of texts freely mined and adapted from the Bible and meant in this context, like the Introit verses themselves, to represent the words of Christ. Yet another set of Introit tropes from St. Martial embeds the Introit text within a narrative that imitates the style of the Gospels, and attaches *neumes* or interpolated melismas to each stich in the antiphon as a further embellishment.

EX. 2-8A   Prefatory trope to the Easter Introit, *Resurrexi*

Make music in honor of our great King who defeated death's dominion, saying "Eya":
I rose again, and am still with you . . .

EX. 2-8B   The Easter Introit, larded with two sets of tropes from the monastery of St. Martial

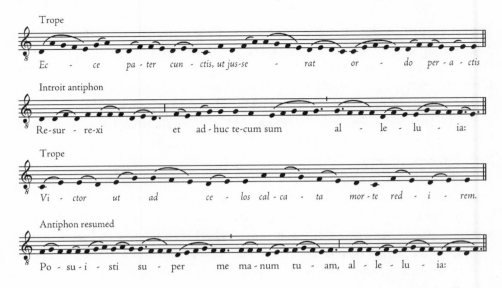

Trope

Ec - ce pa - ter cun - ctis, ut jus-se - rat or - do per - a - ctis

Introit antiphon

Re-sur - re-xi et ad - huc te-cum sum al - le - lu - ia:

Trope

Vi - ctor ut ad ce - los cal - ca - ta mor-te red - i - rem.

Antiphon resumed

Po - su - i - sti su - per me ma-num tu - am, al - le - lu - ia:

By all odds the most famous of the *Resurrexi* tropes, probably the most famous of all tropes, are the ones that recount the *visitatio sepulchri* — the visit of the three Marys to Christ's tomb on the morning after his burial — in the form of a dialogue between them and the angel who announces the Resurrection, thus furnishing a very neat transition into the Introit text. In Ex. 2-9, which gives an early version of this trope from a St. Gallen manuscript dating around 950, the text carries special directions (known in liturgical books as *rubrics*, since they were often entered in red ink made from *rubrica*, Latin for "red earth") somewhat needlessly specifying what is a "question" (*interrogatio*) and what an "answer" (*responsorium*). These rubrics seem to be an indication that two (or several) singers were to act out the dialogue in parts. Tropes like this one were the earliest and simplest of what became a large repertory of Latin church plays (sometimes called "liturgical dramas") with music. More elaborate ones will be described in the next chapter.

Like many favorite chants, the Easter dialogue trope gave rise to parodies. An eleventh-century manuscript at St. Martial contains a dialogue trope for Christmas that mimics the Easter prototype in entertaining detail, beginning with the famous incipit *Quem quaeritis* ("Whom do you seek?"), then substituting the manger for the tomb and the shepherds for the Marys. Once again, the object is to justify an Old Testament reading as a prophecy of Christ's coming, in this case the famous lines from the book of Isaiah ("Unto us a child is born") on which the Christmas Introit is based. Christmas, too, became a fertile site of church dramas ("manger plays") in centuries to come. Scholars used to think that the eventual medieval church plays, enacted not at Mass but after matins, were amplifications of actual Introit tropes (tropes on tropes, so to speak). The relationship has turned out to be far less direct than that, but the general practice of acting out the liturgy did nevertheless originate in the dialogue tropes for Easter and Christmas.

EX. 2-9   Easter dialogue trope (*Quem quaeritis in sepulchro*)

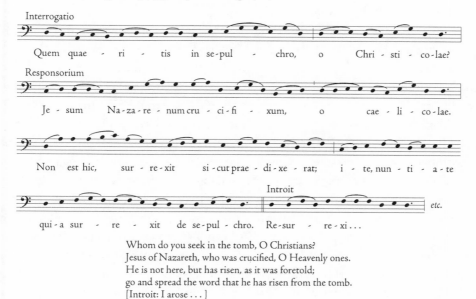

Interrogatio

Quem quae - ri - tis   in se-pul - chro,   o   Chri - sti - co-lae?

Responsorium

Je - sum   Na-za-re - num cru - ci-fi - xum,   o   cae - li - co-lae.

Non   est hic,   sur - re - xit   si - cut prae - di - xe - rat;   i - te, nun - ti - a - te

Introit

qui - a sur - re - xit   de se - pul - chro. Re-sur - re - xi . . .   *etc.*

> Whom do you seek in the tomb, O Christians?
> Jesus of Nazareth, who was crucified, O Heavenly ones.
> He is not here, but has risen, as it was foretold;
> go and spread the word that he has risen from the tomb.
> [Introit: I arose . . .]

THE MASS ORDINARY

Finally, Frankish composers were responsible for creating fancy melodies for the invariant texts of the Mass liturgy, the ones recited at every Mass regardless of the occasion. There had not been any need for such settings in pre-Carolingian times, because these texts—acclamations all—had not yet been assigned stable liturgical positions. Their adoption by the Franks reflects a love of pomp, most likely transferred from civic ceremonial (like the *laudes regiae*, the "royal acclamations," with which Charlemagne was greeted after his Roman coronation). Once these texts became fixed, they could be written down as part of the Mass *ordo* (Latin for "order of events"), which listed things to do at a given service.

The texts (and chants) proper to the unique occasion were collected in their own books (antiphoners, graduals, and the like). Those that were sung at every Mass were included in the ordo itself. Hence to musicians the term "Mass Ordinary" (from *ordinarium missae*) has come to mean, precisely, the five invariant texts sung by the choir: Kyrie, Gloria,

FIG. 2-4 Ivory book cover, probably of a sacramentary or a graduale, from the court of Charles the Bald, Charlemagne's grandson, who ruled the kingdom of the West Franks from 843 to 877. It shows the Eucharist service—the second part of the solemn Mass, in which the wine and host are miraculously transformed.

Credo, Sanctus, and Agnus Dei. These began to receive significant musical attention in the Carolingian period; much later they began to get set as a unified polyphonic cycle, spawning a tradition of Mass composition that lasted into the twentieth century, to which many famous composers of the standard concert repertory (Bach, Mozart, Beethoven, to name a few) made contributions. Another text that was often included in the early ordinary formularies was the dismissal versicle (*Ite, missa est*—from which the term Missa, for Mass, was adopted) and its response, *Deo gratias* ("Thanks be to God").

The Gloria, also known as the "Gloria in excelsis" or Greater Doxology (to distinguish it from the "Gloria patri" formula or Lesser Doxology, inserted at the end of psalms and canticles), was the first to be cultivated. Its text begins with two verses or stichs from the Gospel of St. Luke, quoting the angels' greeting to the shepherds on the night of the Nativity. For this reason, before it was assigned to its fixed position in the Mass, the *Gloria in excelsis* was often used as a Christmas processional hymn, forming the culmination of the celebrants' entrance. (It was also used this way at Easter; and after it joined the Mass, it was not sung during the penitential weeks preceding those two feasts so that its reappearance would express seasonal gladness.) Following the angelic hymn are a series of *laudes* that may actually have originated in the context of ruler worship. Next come a series of litanies, or petitions, and finally a concluding praise-song. While its earliest use seems to have been congregational, implying a simple, formulaic style, the Glorias preserved in Frankish manuscripts are neumatic chants with occasional melismas, and (once past the celebrant's intonation) are clearly intended for the clerical or monastic *schola*. Ex. 2-10 is a ninth-century Gloria melody, one of the earliest of the forty or so surviving Frankish settings. (Its number, IV, is the one assigned to it in modern chant books.)

The Sanctus is a biblical acclamation (from the book of Isaiah). Under its Hebrew name, *Kedusha*, it has been part of the Jewish worship service since ancient times, whence it was taken over by the earliest Christians as the congregation's part of the "eucharistic" (thanksgiving) prayer. Even in its Latin form, the text retains a pair of Hebrew words: *Sabaoth* ("hosts") and *Hosanna* ("save us"). The earliest Frankish settings, like Ex. 2-11, date from the tenth century. By then, like the Gloria, it was sung not by the entire congregation but by the trained *schola*.

The Agnus Dei has a much shorter history in the liturgy than the Sanctus, having been introduced to the Mass only in the seventh century, to accompany the breaking of bread before communion. At first it was cast as litanies, with an unspecified number of repetitions of the acclamation to the Lamb of God, answered by the congregational prayer, "have mercy on us." Later the chant was standardized and abbreviated, limited to three acclamations, and with the third response changed to "grant us peace." This happened right around the time the Franks were busy composing their "ordinary" chants, and so the early melodies were in this case coeval with the text. Of the two following examples, the first (Ex. 2-12a) probably represents a survival from the older litany practice, while the second (Ex. 2-12b), a Frankish arrangement and abridgment of the earliest (Greek) surviving melody for the Agnus Dei, is cast in a rounded "ternary form" (ABA) to match the adapted text. Its neumatic antiphon-like style makes it suitable for performance by the *schola*.

Since the ordinary chants were composed precisely when the practice of antiphon-troping was at its height, they too played host to sometimes very extended tropes. Particularly rich is the repertory of Gloria tropes, many of which were proper to specific feasts or classes of feast (such as those in honor of the Blessed Virgin). These tropes often took the form of additional *laudes* or acclamations, inserted in between the

EX. 2-10 Gloria IV

Glory to God on high.
And on earth peace to men of good will.
We praise thee, we bless thee, we adore thee, we glorify thee.
We give thee thanks for thy great glory.
O Lord God, King of heaven,
God the Father almighty.
O Lord, the only begotten Son, Jesus Christ.
O Lord God, Lamb of God, Son of the Father.
Thou who takest away the sins of the world, have mercy on us.

Thou who takest away the sins of the world, receive our prayer.
thou who sittest at the right hand of the Father, have mercy on us.
For thou only art holy,
Thou only art Lord.
Thou only art most high, O Jesus Christ,
With the Holy Ghost,
In the glory of God the Father.
Amen.

standard ones. One such verse that seemed to live a life of its own in the manuscripts went *Regnum tuum solidum permanebit in aeternum* ("Your abiding reign will endure forever"). It is found following "Tu solus altissimus, Jesu Christe" in many sources, associated with many different Gloria melodies.

What is especially fascinating is the way in which *Regnum tuum solidum* itself became a site for embellishment. In some sources, an impressive *neuma* (as Amalar would have called it) has been grafted in to coincide with the first syllable of the word *permanebit* ("will endure"). This seems to be an example of what would later be called "tone

EX. 2-11 Sanctus I

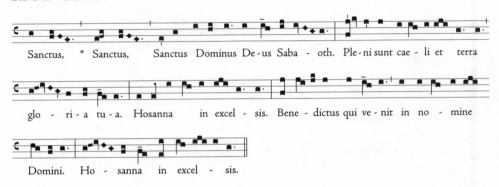

Sanctus, * Sanctus, Sanctus Dominus De-us Saba - oth. Ple-ni sunt cae - li et terra glo - ri - a tu - a. Hosanna in excel - sis. Bene - dictus qui ve - nit in no - mine Domini. Ho - sanna in excel - sis.

Holy, holy, holy, Lord God of Hosts.
The heavens and earth are full of thy glory.
Hosanna in the highest.
Blessed is he who comes in the name of the Lord.
Hosanna in the highest.

EX. 2-12A Agnus XVIII

Agnus De - i, * qui tollis pecca - ta mundi: mi - se - re - re no - bis. Agnus De - i, * qui tollis pecca - ta mundi: mi - se - re - re no - bis. Agnus De - i, * qui tollis pecca - ta mundi: dona nobis pa - cem.

Lamb of God,
who takest away the sins of the world,
have mercy on us.

Lamb of God,
who takest away the sins of the world,
have mercy on us.

Lamb of God,
who takest away the sins of the world,
give us peace.

painting," since the melisma, by stretching the word out, in effect illustrates its meaning. And then, in other sources, the melisma is subjected in turn to syllabic texting in the form of a *prosula*. Thus two types of liturgical embroidery — melodic (*neuma*) and textual (*prosula*) — have been combined with a melodic/textual interpolation (*trope*) in one magnificent clump (Ex. 2-13).

EX. 2-12B   Agnus II

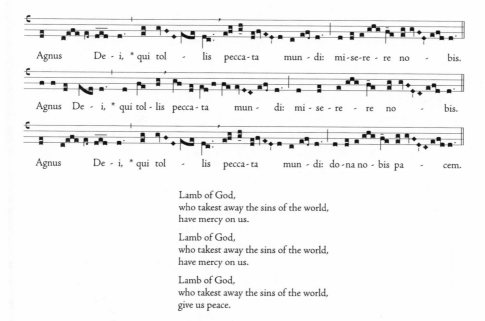

Lamb of God,
who takest away the sins of the world,
have mercy on us.

Lamb of God,
who takest away the sins of the world,
have mercy on us.

Lamb of God,
who takest away the sins of the world,
give us peace.

EX. 2-13   A *prosula* within a *neuma* within a *laus* within a Gloria

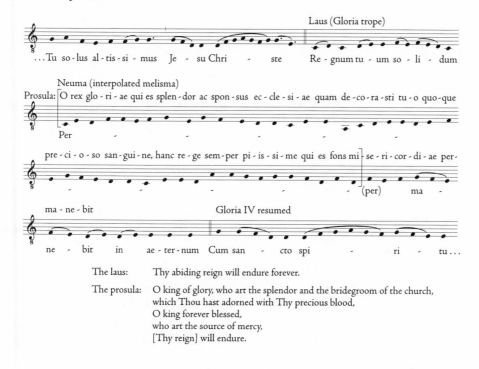

The laus: Thy abiding reign will endure forever.

The prosula: O king of glory, who art the splendor and the bridegroom of the church,
                which Thou hast adorned with Thy precious blood,
                O king forever blessed,
                who art the source of mercy,
                [Thy reign] will endure.

KYRIES

The remaining "ordinary" chant, the *Kyrie eleison*, has a more complex—indeed, a somewhat puzzling—history. Its special status is evident first of all from its language: the one Greek survival in the Latin Mass. *Kyrie eleison* means the same thing as *Domine, miserere nobis*: namely, "Lord, have mercy on us" (compare the middle part of the Gloria in Excelsis and the Agnus Dei refrain). It used to be a common liturgical response, especially appropriate for use in the long series of petitions known as litanies, which often accompanied processions. Pope Gregory the Great, in one of the few musically or liturgically significant acts that may be firmly associated with his name, decreed in a letter that the formula *Kyrie eleison* should alternate with *Christe eleison* ("Christ [that is, Savior], have mercy on us"). By the ninth century, when the Frankish musicians went to work on the chant, the Kyrie had been established as a ninefold acclamation: thrice Kyrie eleison, thrice Christe eleison, thrice Kyrie eleison.

As in the case of the other "ordinary" chants, there are simple Kyries that probably reflect early congregational singing, and more decorative melodies that were probably produced at the Frankish monasteries, beginning in the tenth century, for performance by the *schola*. These more artful Kyrie tunes often reflect the shape of the litany they adorn, matching its ninefold elaboration of a three-part idea with patterns of repetition like AAA BBB AAA' or AAA BBB CCC'. (In both cases the last invocation—the A' or C'—is usually rendered more emphatic than the rest, most typically by inserting or repeating a melisma.) Ex. 2-14a is one of these tenth-century tunes; note that while the words *Kyrie – Christe – Kyrie* are set to a non-repeating (ABC) pattern, the word *eleison* has an AA'B pattern. The retention of the same formula for *eleison* while *Kyrie* changes to *Christe* and back seems to be a vestige of an old congregational litany refrain.

EX. 2-14A   Kyrie IV

The earliest sources for ordinary chants were little books called *Kyriale*, by analogy with *Graduale*, the much bigger book that contained the Mass propers. Most Kyriales date from the tenth and eleventh centuries. One of their curious features is the way Kyrie melodies are recorded in them. They are entered twice, first in melismatic form as shown in Ex. 2-14a, and then in syllabically texted form as shown in Ex. 2-14b.

The easy explanation would be that the melismatic Kyrie is the canonical version, and the syllabically texted one has been enhanced (or corrupted) by a prosula. That, at any rate, was the assumption made by the sixteenth-century editors of the chant who, in the purifying spirit of the Counter Reformation, purged all Kyries of their syllabic texts. (Even so, their old incipits are still used to identify the Kyrie melodies in modern liturgical books: Ex. 2-14a is now called "Kyrie IV, *Cunctipotens Genitor Deus*.") There are several reasons to question that assumption. For one thing there is no evidence that the melismatic Kyries are any older than the texted ones. They appear side by side in the sources from the beginning. Indeed, the earliest text we have for a Mass Kyrie, from Amalar of Metz himself, writing around 830, is "texted," as follows: *Kyrie eleison, Domine*

EX. 2-14B   Kyrie, *Cunctipotens Genitor Deus*

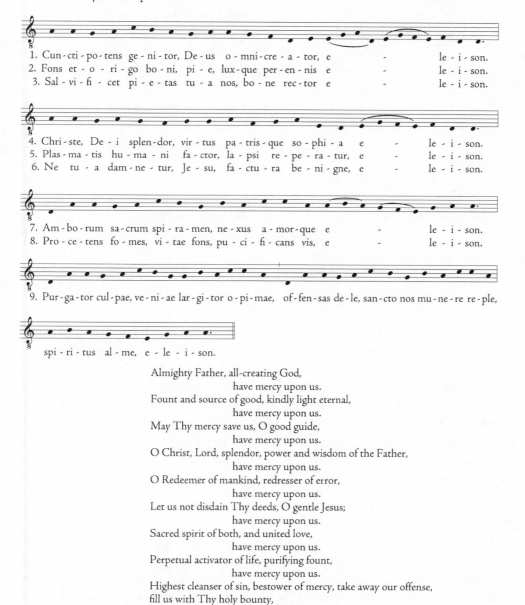

1. Cun-cti-po-tens ge-ni-tor, De-us o-mni-cre-a-tor, e - le-i-son.
2. Fons et-o-ri-go bo-ni, pi-e, lux-que per-en-nis e - le-i-son.
3. Sal-vi-fi-cet pi-e-tas tu-a nos, bo-ne rec-tor e - le-i-son.

4. Chri-ste, De-i splen-dor, vir-tus pa-tris-que so-phi-a e - le-i-son.
5. Plas-ma-tis hu-ma-ni fa-ctor, la-psi re-pe-ra-tur, e - le-i-son.
6. Ne tu-a dam-ne-tur, Je-su, fa-ctu-ra be-ni-gne, e - le-i-son.

7. Am-bo-rum sa-crum spi-ra-men, ne-xus a-mor-que e - le-i-son.
8. Pro-ce-tens fo-mes, vi-tae fons, pu-ci-fi-cans vis, e - le-i-son.

9. Pur-ga-tor cul-pae, ve-ni-ae lar-gi-tor o-pi-mae, of-fen-sas de-le, san-cto nos mu-ne-re re-ple,

spi-ri-tus al-me, e-le-i-son.

Almighty Father, all-creating God,
    have mercy upon us.
Fount and source of good, kindly light eternal,
    have mercy upon us.
May Thy mercy save us, O good guide,
    have mercy upon us.
O Christ, Lord, splendor, power and wisdom of the Father,
    have mercy upon us.
O Redeemer of mankind, redresser of error,
    have mercy upon us.
Let us not disdain Thy deeds, O gentle Jesus;
    have mercy upon us.
Sacred spirit of both, and united love,
    have mercy upon us.
Perpetual activator of life, purifying fount,
    have mercy upon us.
Highest cleanser of sin, bestower of mercy, take away our offense,
fill us with Thy holy bounty,
O nourishing spirit, have mercy upon us.

pater, miserere; Christe eleison, miserere, qui nos redemisti sanguine tuo; et iterum Kyrie eleison, Domine Spiritus Sancte, miserere. [Lord have mercy on us; O Lord our father, have mercy on us; Christ, have mercy on us, O Thou who hast redeemed us with Thy blood; and again, Lord, have mercy on us; O Lord, Holy Spirit, have mercy on us.]

This, then, was a Kyrie that to a ninth-century writer looked normal, consisting as it did of a traditional Greek acclamation amplified with newer and more specific Latin ones.

Evidence concerning chronology—the age of sources, the testimony of early witnesses—counts as "external" evidence. There is "internal" evidence, too, on behalf of the primacy of texted Kyries—that is, evidence based on observation of the musical artifacts themselves (or rather, their appearance in the manuscripts we have). If the texts in the texted Kyries are indeed prosulas—that is, words added to a preexisting melismatic chant—then why is the short neuma on *eleison* left "unprosulated" every time? Would it not be more plausible to assume that the regular alternation of syllabic and neumatic prosody was part of the original conception? In the case of *Cunctipotens genitor*, the texted form must have come first for the additional reason that the text is in verse, not prose. What is not prose is no prosula. Less tautologically, there is little likelihood that the notes of a preexisting melisma will by chance accommodate the strict requirements of poetic scansion.

It has been suggested that the reason for the appearance of texted and melismatic Kyrie melodies side by side has to do with the state of notation in the tenth century, when the neumes had been well established, but the staff had yet to be invented. The syllabic notation was necessary in order to show which syllables were sung to which notes; but the melismatic notation, in which the various neume shapes indicated rise and fall much better than single notes could do, was necessary in order to record the melodies' contour accurately enough to serve even a rudimentary mnemonic purpose. The same double-entry procedure is found in early sequence manuscripts. Both the syllabic sequence melody and a melismatic counterpart, conventionally texted *Alleluia*, are frequently found side by side, or else in consecutive sections of the book. The assumption that these melismatic tunes were in every case preexisting *sequentia* melismas, to which the words of the sequence were later added, has been questioned on the same grounds of chronology as in the case of the Kyries, and this has led to a thorough revision of the history of the sequence.[4] It was probably cases like these, where double notation was necessary in order to convey all the needed information, that made it urgent to find a way of conveying all the information at once. This, in short, may have been the necessity that mothered the invention of the staff.

THE FULL FRANKO-ROMAN MASS

With the standardization of the "ordinary" chants, the Franks completed a musical enhancement of the sixth-century *ordo* (or agenda) of the western Mass that established its form for the next millennium. Their version, which was reimported back to Rome in the eleventh century and became standard almost everywhere in Europe and the British Isles, is given in Table 2-1.

TABLE 2-1 Ordo of the Western Mass

SUNG (concentus)		SPOKEN OR RECITED TO A TONE (accentus)	
Proper	Ordinary	Proper	Ordinary
SYNAXIS			
1. Introit			
	2. Kyrie		
	3. Gloria (omitted during Lent and Advent)		
		4. Collect (call to prayer)	
		5. Epistle reading	
6. Gradual (replaced between Easter and Pentecost by an Alleluia)			
7. Alleluia (replaced during Lent and Advent by the Tract)			
8. Sequence (ubiquitous and fully canonical from the tenth to the sixteenth centuries; only four survived the Counter Reformation*)			
		9. Gospel reading	
		(Sermon)	
EUCHARIST			
	10. Credo		
11. Offertory			
			12. Offertory prayers
		13. Secret (Celebrant's silent prayer)	
		14. Preface to the Sanctus	
	15. Sanctus		
			16. Canon (Celebrant's Prayer consecrating wine and bread)
			17. Lord's Prayer (congregation)
	18. Agnus Dei		
19. Communion			
		20. Postcommunion prayer	
	21. Dismissal (Ite, missa est, replaced during Lent and Advent by Benedicamus Domino, "Let us bless the Lord")		

*The fortunate four were the sequences for Easter (*Victimae paschali laudes*), Pentecost (*Veni sancte spiritus*), Corpus Christi (*Lauda Sion*, by St. Thomas Aquinas), and the funeral or Requiem Mass (*Dies Irae*). During the eighteenth century a new one (*Stabat mater dolorosa*) was added upon the creation of a new feast, the "Seven Sorrows of the Blessed Virgin Mary." Its text is by the fourteenth-century Italian poet Jacopone de Todi; the music in modern chant books was composed in the nineteenth century by a choirmaster from the Benedictine abbey of Solesmes.

"OLD ROMAN" AND OTHER CHANT DIALECTS

The reintroduction of the Frankish redaction, or adaptation, of the Roman chant back to Rome was to have marked the final stage in the musical unification of Western

Christendom. It also entailed the importation of the Frankish neumes, which were soon adapted to the staff and became a universal European system of notation. Once neumatic chant manuscripts began to be produced in Rome, however, some surprising anomalies appeared. The most surprising consists of a small group of graduales and antiphoners, produced in Rome between the eleventh and the thirteenth centuries, containing a repertory of chants for the Mass and Office that, while clearly related to it, differs significantly from the standard Franco-Roman "Gregorian" chant. It is, generally speaking, both more formulaic and more ornamental than the standard redaction.

Most scholars agree that this variant repertory, which has been nicknamed the "Old Roman" chant, shares with Gregorian chant a common origin in the Roman church singing of the eighth century. The basic, as yet unanswered, question is whether the Old Roman chant, despite the late date of its sources, represents this original tradition, which later Roman singers (perhaps under Pope Vitalian, who reigned from 657 to 672) or even the Franks themselves radically edited and streamlined; or whether the Old Roman chant is the evolutionary result of three hundred years of oral tradition in Rome itself that took place after the original eighth-century version had gone north.

To put these matters in terms of a bald "either/or" is very much to oversimplify a complicated situation. Yet of the two alternatives just described, the second seems to accord better with what is known of the nature of oral transmission. Repertories, even those available in written form, are never wholly stable but are in a constant, indeed daily state of gradual incremental flux that comes about inescapably with use. Any living tradition, whatever its ostensible aims, is an engine of change.

Thus, although it is much more common, and certainly appropriate, to pay tribute to the Carolingians' centralizing achievement by remarking on the high degree of uniformity among the earliest Frankish manuscripts containing the Gregorian chant, the fact remains that there are also many small discrepancies among them—indeed, between any two of them. There are also distinct, recognized local or geographical "dialects" within the tradition of Gregorian chant. East Frankish (that is, German) sources often turn the semitones in West Frankish (that is, French) sources into minor thirds, possibly reflecting the habits of ears and throats accustomed to a pentatonic (or, more precisely, an *anhemitonic*—that is, semitoneless) folk idiom (see Ex. 2-15).

EX. 2-15 Incipit of the *Gaudeamus* Introit and the climactic phrase of the *Haec dies* gradual in West Frankish and East Frankish versions

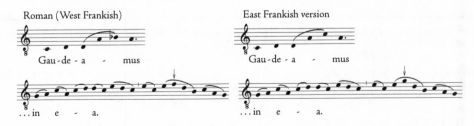

To ignore these differences in favor of the uniformity (or, contrariwise, to de-emphasize the uniformity in favor of the differences) is a decision one makes depending

on the kind of story one wants to tell. Stories that emphasize sameness are, in the first place, shorter and more manageable than stories that emphasize difference. The tendency in a book like this is to minimize exceptions and get on with things. But one pays a price for the space or the time one saves. One can form the mental habit of looking for sameness instead of difference, which can lead to an actual (perhaps unconscious) preference for simplifying sameness, and a concomitant (equally unconscious) antagonism toward complicating difference.

In the case of the history of Gregorian chant, such an antagonism toward difference recapitulates on the apparently innocuous plane of historiography the ruthless political program of the Carolingians and the papacy. (This seems to be one reason why the Old Roman chant, whose existence — or persistence — makes for a pesky complication of an otherwise simple and triumphant narrative, has received from many scholars a very negative "aesthetic" assessment.[5]) To generalize even further, antagonism toward difference implies sympathy with the interests of elites. This tendency is particularly characteristic of histories of the fine arts, for the fine arts have always depended upon political, social, and religious elites for support.

That is why it seems appropriate, as a way of ending a chapter about the propitious musical achievements of the ninth- and tenth-century Franks who succeeded in establishing and canonizing one particular repertory of plainchant, briefly to cast an eye at some pockets of resistance — chant repertories that, like the Old Roman, managed to hold out (at least for a while) against the Gregorian tide.

The most successful of these was (or is) the liturgical chant of the archdiocese of Milan, which has lasted to this day, although, like the Gregorian chant, it is falling out of use (or where still used, sung in Italian translation) in the wake of the liturgical reforms instigated by the Second Vatican Council in the 1960s. Milan, as we know, was the fourth-century seat of St. Ambrose, a figure with a legend and an authority equal to St. Gregory's; and so the myth of Ambrose has legitimized the survival of the Milanese (or "Ambrosian") rite and sustained it even as the myth of Gregory legitimized the ascendency almost everywhere else of the Franco-Roman.

Like the Old Roman chant, the Ambrosian entered the written tradition later than the Gregorian; most manuscripts containing it were notated in the twelfth century or later. Whether because of its actual age or because of its longer preliterate tradition, the Ambrosian chant tends to be more melismatic than the Gregorian and, in the Mass propers, more given to responsorial psalmody, in which a soloist sings verses in alternation with melismatic choral refrains, a practice largely confined to the Office in Gregorian psalmody. Since they were never mediated by Frankish editors, the Ambrosian melodies conform only vaguely with the familiar system of medieval "church modes" (the subject of our next chapter).

Also notated in the tenth and eleventh centuries was the chant sung on the Iberian peninsula, sung at least since the seventh century, but called Mozarabic (a term referring to Christians living under Islamic domination) because it continued to be sung after the Moorish invasion of 711, which ushered in a period of Muslim political rule that lasted almost until the end of the fifteenth century. The Mozarabic chant was officially suppressed in favor of the Gregorian in 1085 following the Christian reconquest of Toledo, the seat of the Spanish church. Hence almost all of the Mozarabic sources are notated in nondiastematic neumes that cannot now be read for their precise pitch content. But even so, the makeup of the liturgy, the style of its constituent melodies (whether syllabic or melismatic, etc.), and hence its relationship to other rites can be assessed; and because they are the largest body of liturgical manuscripts to preserve an authenticated pre-Carolingian Latin rite, the Mozarabic sources have attracted a good deal of scholarly attention, if not as much as they deserve. The rite underwent a spurious nationalistic revival in the late fifteenth century, when the Moors were expelled from Spain. Printed books of "Mozarabic chant" were then prepared, but the melodies they contain (some of them still sung at the Cathedral of Toledo) bear no discernible relation to the neumes in the authentic Mozarabic sources.

The so-called Beneventan chant, a repertory sung at various locales in southern Italy (Benevento, Monte Cassino, etc.) was another rite that lasted just long enough alongside the Gregorian to make it into neumatic notation. Beneventan manuscripts dating from the tenth to the thirteenth centuries survive, but only the oldest layer (mainly consisting of chants for Easter and Holy Week) is free of Gregorian infiltration. Judging from what little remains of it, it is possible that the Beneventan repertory was largely a Latinized import from the Byzantine church. The same may be said for the rite of Ravenna, the ex-Byzantine city that Pepin conquered and bestowed on Pope Stephen II. It survived into the manuscript age in shreds and was mostly extinct by the end of the eleventh century.

WHAT IS ART?

As has been observed frequently and well, the forms of Frankish musical composition, the earliest composition in the literate tradition we habitually call our own, often contradict the assumptions that we habitually make about musical compositions — assumptions we do not usually even know we are making, precisely because they are habitual. We normally neither reflect upon them nor consider alternatives. Very old music often asks us to consider alternatives, and to reflect.

Regarding tropes to the Introit, for example, one might well ask in what sense a series of interpolations into a preexisting piece can itself be considered "a piece." It is neither continuous nor coherent nor unitary nor independent, all of these adjectives naming qualities that we tacitly expect pieces of music to exemplify. Indeed, the Introit itself, once it plays host to the trope, loses its continuity, its coherence, its unity, and its independence. Does it lose its piecehood when invaded by the other? And if its piecehood is so easily lost, how genuine was it to begin with?

Rather than judge the trope or its host on the basis of their conformity with our casual expectations (for such a judgment can only be invidious), we might take the opportunity the trope affords us to critique those expectations. For it would indeed be surprising if musical expectations had not changed over a period of a thousand years.

The first criterion that might be questioned is the notion from which all the others stem — namely, that a piece of music worthy of consideration as such ought to be able to stand timelessly on its own two feet. What is demanded is that it have an existence independent of its context, its observers, and particularly its users. This is called the principle of autonomy, and it is pretty universally regarded today as a requirement for aesthetic appreciation — that is, for evaluation as a work of art. A trope certainly fails this test, but then so do all the other musical artifacts of its time.

For music only became autonomous when it stopped being useful; and this did not happen until conditions allowed such a thing to happen. Some of those conditions were beginning to exist a thousand years ago. The potential for autonomy existed as soon as the means of recording music in writing existed. Until then, music was only an activity — something you did (or that others did while you did something else). All of the music we have been considering thus far falls into that category. It is both literally and figuratively service music: music for the divine service and music that serves a divine purpose. And yet the divine service was after all a human activity, and the music that both accompanied this activity and gave it shape was a music that functioned in symbiosis with a social framework as yet undivorced from daily life. A lot of music is still like that; we call it "folk." But some music has since been objectified as "art." It happened in stages, of which the first, as we know, was writing. In written form music at last possessed (or could possess) some sort of physical reality independent of the people who made it up and repeated it. It could outlive those who remembered it. (And it could reach us, who no longer have a use for it.) It could be silently reproduced and transmitted from composer to performer, thus for the first time completely distinguishing their roles. With the advent of printing, almost exactly five hundred years ago (and also almost exactly five hundred years after the introduction of music writing), reproduction became easy and cheap. Music could be disseminated much more widely than before, and much more impersonally. In the form of a printed book, music could be all the more readily thought of not as an act but as a thing. Philosophers have a word for this conceptual transformation: they call it *reification* (from *res*, Latin for "thing"). The durable music-thing could begin to seem more important than ephemeral music-makers. The idea of a classic — a timeless aesthetic object — was waiting to be born.

For reasons that we will later need to consider in detail, its birth had to await the birth of "aesthetics," which was a by-product of romanticism, an intellectual and artistic movement of the late eighteenth century. Only then do we encounter notions of transcendent and autonomous art — art that was primarily for contemplation, not for use, and for the ages, not for you or me. Since then the reification of music has reached new heights (and depths) with the advent of actual sound recording, leading to new sorts of music-things like compact discs and digital audiotapes. Thanks to these, music was commercialized in the twentieth century to an extent previously unimaginable, yet it has also been more completely classicalized than ever before. A recording of a piece of music is more of a thing than ever before, and our notion of what "a piece" is has been correspondingly (and literally) solidified.

So if a set of interpolated tropes — or a vagrant melisma, or a now-you-see-it-now-you-don't prosula — challenges or "problematizes" the notion of a piece of music as an autonomous work of art, we should realize that the problem thus created is entirely our problem, and that it arises out of an anachronism. Our casual assumptions about music and art are no longer congruent with those that motivated the Frankish musicians of a thousand years ago. Realizing this can help us approach more realistically not only the art products of the distant past but also the ones with which we are most familiar — precisely because, in a context of alternative views, the familiar is no longer quite so familiar. When things are no longer taken for granted they can be more clearly and meaningfully observed; when we allow our values to be challenged by different ones, they can be more fully and discerningly understood. They are in fact more our own once we have reflected on them.

None of this should imply that the musicians of a thousand years ago, and the people who heard them, could not enjoy their work sensuously. Indeed, Saint Augustine admits to just such an enjoyment of liturgical singing in his *Confessions*. And yet although he admits *to* it, he does not admit it. Recognizing that "there are particular modes in song and in the voice, corresponding to my various emotions and able to stimulate them because of some mysterious relationship between the two," he maintains a special guard "not to allow my mind to be paralyzed by the gratification of my senses, which often leads it astray."[6] That ambivalence, expressed by Saint Augustine in the fourth century, has remained a characteristic of Western religious thinking about music.

But if the early medieval Christians did not recognize our category of the "aesthetic," which anachronistically implies a "pure" (that is, disinterested) contemplation of beauty, that does not mean that we cannot now apprehend a musical product of the ancient church — say, a troped Introit — with aesthetic appreciation. (Indeed, if we did not know how the process of troping worked, we would never have had an aesthetic problem with a troped Introit; it would just be a longer Introit.) As Saint Augustine implies, and as a hackneyed proverb confirms, the religious or sensuous or aesthetic "content" of works of art (or, to be careful, works capable of being regarded as art) is not an inherent property of such works but the result of a decision taken by the beholder, and defines a relationship between the observer and the observed. When such decisions are not consciously taken but are the result of cultural predisposition, they can easily seem to be attributes of works, not of observers.

By now, the aesthetic reception of ancient service music is well established. Gregorian and medieval chants can be for us (and, indeed, have definitely become) a form of concert music, which we now experience in new surroundings (concert halls, our homes, our cars) and for new purposes. In 1994, the year this chapter was first drafted, a compact disc of Gregorian chants sung by a *schola* of Spanish monks unexpectedly rose to the top of the popular music sales charts, betokening a wholly new way of apprehending (and using) them. Or maybe not so new: the pop reception of chant may not be so much an aesthetic phenomenon as a renewed form, mediated and modified by the pacifying objectives of "New Age" meditation, of the *intellectus* Amalar celebrated at the very beginning of our story.

Be that as it may, putting ourselves imaginatively in the position of the chant's contemporaries gives us access to meanings we might otherwise never experience. And perhaps even more important, it gives us a distanced perspective on our own contemporary world, a form of critical awareness we would otherwise never gain. These are among the most potent reasons for studying history.

Retheorizing Music

New Frankish Concepts of Musical Organization and Their Effect on Composition

MUSICA

When musicians thought "theoretically" about music — that is, made systematic generalizations about it — before the tenth century, they usually did so in terms of the *quadrivium*, the late-classical postgraduate curriculum, in which music counted as one of the arts of measurement. What was measurable was what was studied: abstract pitch ratios (we call them intervals) and abstract durational ratios (we call them rhythms, organized into meters). Reducing music to abstract number was a way of emphasizing what was truly "real" about it, for late-classical philosophy was strongly influenced by Plato's doctrine of forms. A Neoplatonist believed, first, that the world perceived by our sense organs was only a grosser reflection of a realer world, God's world, that we perceive with our God-given capacity for reasoning; and, second, that the purest form of reasoning was numerical reasoning, because it was least limited to what our senses tell us. Education meant the development of one's capacity to transcend the limitations of sense and achieve comprehension of "essences," purely rational, quantitative concepts untouched by any "stain of the corporeal."[1] A medieval treatise on music theory, then, emphasized *musica speculativa* (we may call it Musica for short), "music as reflection of the real" (from *speculum*, Latin for looking glass or mirror).[2] Such a treatise had as little to do as possible with actual "pieces of music," or ways of making them, for such music was merely music for the senses——unreal and (since real meant divine) unholy. The two most-studied late-classical texts on Musica were *De musica* ("About Musica") by none other than St. Augustine (Aurelius Augustinus, 354–430), the greatest of the Fathers of the Christian Church, and *De institutione musica* ("On the organization of musica") by Anicius Manlius Severinus Boethius (ca. 480–ca. 524), the Roman statesman and educational reformer who first proposed the division of the liberal arts curriculum into the trivium and the quadrivium. Both of these books, but especially the one by Boethius (which was virtually rediscovered by the Franks), were mainstays of the Carolingian academic curriculum instituted by Alcuin.

St. Augustine's treatise, completed in 391, is the sole survivor from an enormous projected set of treatises that would have encompassed the whole liberal arts curriculum. It covers nothing but rhythmic proportions (quantitative metrics) and contains a famous definition of music——as *bene modulandi scientia*, "the art of measuring well—"—that

FIG. 3-1 St. Augustine, depicted in an eleventh-century French manuscript of his treatise "On Baptism," disputing in 411 with Felicianus of Musti, a Donatist bishop, who represented a schismatic sect that practiced rebaptism of the righteous (comparable to the "rebirth" of Protestant fundamentalists in later periods).

was quoted as official doctrine by practically every later medieval writer. The treatise ends with a meditation, reminiscent of Plato's dialogue *Timaeus*, on the theological significance of the harmonious proportions with which it deals, and the way in which they reflect the essential nature of the universe. (The *Timaeus*, translated by Cicero, was the only Platonic text known to late-classical Latin writers.) Boethius's treatise covers much more ground than Augustine's. It consists largely of translations from the Hellenistic writers Nicomachus and Ptolemy. (The term "Hellenistic" refers to the Greek-influenced culture that flourished in the non-Greek territories conquered by Alexander the Great.) It thus became the sole source of medieval knowledge of Greek music theory, which included the Greater Perfect System, a scale constructed out of four-note segments called tetrachords; and also the Pythagorean classification of consonances (simultaneous intervals). The treatise also contained directions for representing pitch intervals in terms of spatial ratios, which made possible the construction of "laboratory instruments" called monochords (later to be described in more detail) for demonstrating number audibly, as sound.

While Greek music theory still involved practical music for Nicomachus and Ptolemy (who lived in the second century CE in Arabia and Egypt, respectively), by the time of Boethius the actual music practiced by the ancient Greeks had fallen into oblivion, along with its notation. Accordingly, Boethius's treatise concerns not practical music but abstract Musica, as the author declares quite explicitly.

Boethius inherited two transcendent ideas from the Neoplatonists: first, that Musica mirrored the essential harmony of the cosmos (an idea we have already encountered in Augustine); and, second, that owing to this divine reflection it had a decisive influence on human health and behavior. This was known as the doctrine of *ethos*, from which the word "ethics" is derived. Audible music (*musica instrumentalis*, "music such as instruments produce") is thus only a gross metaphor for the two higher and "realer" levels of Musica, perhaps best translated in this context as "harmony." At the top there was the harmony of the cosmos (*musica mundana*), and in the intermediate position there was the harmony of the human constitution (*musica humana*), which *musica instrumentalis* — depending on its relationship to *musica mundana* — could either uplift or put awry. All of this is most effectively expressed not in words but in a famous manuscript illumination of the thirteenth century, fully seven hundred years after Boethius (Fig. 3-2). In each of the three panels of this illumination, "Musica"points to a different level of her manifestation. In the top panel Musica points to a representation of the universe with its four elements: earth, air, fire (the sun), and water. The sun and moon further represent the periodic movements of the heavens, an aspect of measurable "harmony." In the middle panel Musica points to four men representing the four "humors," temperaments, or basic personality types[[em dash]]that is, the four types of "human harmony." The proportions of these humors were thought to determine a person's physical and spiritual constitution: the "choleric" temperament was ruled by bile, the "sanguine" by blood, the "phlegmatic" by phlegm, and the "melancholic" by black bile. The four humors mirror the four elements; thus, human harmony is a function of the celestial. In the bottom panel we find musica instrumentalis, the music that we actually hear. Musica is reluctant to point; instead, she raises an admonishing finger at the fiddle player, obviously no disciple of hers but a mere sensory titillator. Whatever its relation to actual sounding music, the idea of Musica had remarkable staying power.

One who has mastered Musica, Boethius concluded, and only such a one, can truly judge the work of a musician, whether composer or performer. The composer and performer are after all concerned only with music, a subrational art, while the philosopher alone knows Musica, a rational science. The stringent differentiation between music and Musica, and their relative evaluation, were easily translatable from Platonist into Christian terms and remained standard in music treatises until the fourteenth century and even beyond. The idea that music was ideally a representation of Musica remained current in certain circles of musicians, and in certain genres of music, even longer than that.

At the height of the Carolingian renaissance, the liberal arts were studied at the great Benedictine abbeys, such as St. Gallen (where the Irish monk Moengal instructed the likes of Notker and Tuotilo), St. Martin at Tours (where Alcuin himself taught beginning in 796), St. Amand at Tournai (now in the southern, French-speaking part of Belgium), and Reichenau (on an island in Lake Constance, Switzerland). The libraries of all of these monasteries contained copies of Boethius's treatise on

FIG. 3-2 Frontispiece of a mid-thirteenth-century manuscript — Florence, Biblioteca Medicea Laurenziana, MS Pluteo 29.I — representing the musical cosmology described by Boethius in *De institutione musica.*

music, and Neoplatonist ideas about Musica were incorporated as theological under-pinning into liturgical music study. At the same time, however, the pressures of liturgical reorganization and chant reform created the need for a new kind of theoretical study, one that served the purposes not of theological or ethical indoctrination but of practical music making and memorization. Beginning very modestly, this new theoretical enter-prise, and the documents it generated, led to a complete rethinking of the principles not of Musica but of actual music, as we understand the term today. Its repercussions were nothing short of foundational to the tradition of "Western music," however we choose to define that slippery term.

TONARIES

Among the earliest documents we have for the Carolingian reorganization of the liturgy and the institutionalization of Gregorian chant are the manuscripts, which begin to appear soon after Pepin's time, that group antiphons (represented by their incipits or opening words) according to the psalm tones with which they best accord melodically. These lists, which began to appear long before the Franks had invented any sort of neumatic notation, at first took the form of prefaces and appendices to the early Frankish graduals and antiphoners that contained the texts to be sung at Mass and Office. (The earliest appendix of this kind is found in a gradual dated 795.) By the middle of the tenth century, these lists had grown large enough to fill separate books for which the term *tonarius* or "tonary" was coined.

These books served an eminently practical purpose, since in every service newly learned antiphons had to be attached appropriately to their full cursive psalms (in the Office) or at least to selected stichs (in the Mass) as a matter of basic operating procedure. In the Vespers service, for example, there were for any given day of the week five unchanging "ordinary" psalms and literally hundreds of ever-changing "proper" antiphons that had to be matched up with them in daily worship. To achieve this practical goal, large stylistic generalizations had to be made about the antiphons on the basis of observation. Classifying the Gregorian antiphons was thus the earliest European exercise in "musical analysis," analysis being (literally and etymologically) the breaking down of an observed whole (here, a chant) into its functionally significant parts. The generalizations thus produced constituted a new branch of "music theory."

The earliest analysts and theorists, like the earliest composers of medieval chant, were Frankish monks. The most extensive early tonary was the one compiled around 901 by Regino of Prüm, the abbot of the Benedictine monastery of St. Martin near the German town of Trier. It contains the incipits of some thirteen hundred antiphons as well as five hundred introits and offertories (performed in those days with psalm verses), all keyed to the ending formulas (*differentiae*) of the eight psalm tones. To achieve this abstract classification of melody types, the compiler had to compare the beginnings and endings of the antiphons with those of the psalm tones.

In effect, a corpus of actual melodies inherited from one tradition (presumed to be that of Rome, the seat of Western Christianity) was being compared with, and assimilated to, an abstract classification of melodic turns and functions imported from another tradition (the *oktoechos*, or eight-mode system, of the Byzantine church). The result was something neither Roman nor Greek but specifically Frankish—and tremendously fertile, a triumph of imaginative synthesis. What was actually abstracted through this process of analysis by observation and assimilation was the intervallic and scalar structure of the chant.

Specifically, antiphons were compared with psalm tones to see how the interval was filled in between their ending note (*finalis*) and the pitch corresponding to the psalm tone's reciting tone (*tuba*), normally a fifth above. (Since most often the last note of a Gregorian chant is the same as the first, Regino actually classified antiphons—or so he said—by their first notes; the concept was refined slightly later.) There are four ways a fifth can be filled in within the aurally internalized diatonic pitch set, with its preset arrangement of tones (T) and semitones (S). In the order of the tonaries these were (1) **TSTT**, (2) **STTT**, (3) **TTTS**, and (4) **TTST**. What is identified in this way are scale degrees. The notion of scale degrees, and their identification, thus constitutes from the very beginning—and, one is tempted to add, to the very end—the crucial "theoretical" generalization on which the concept of tonality in Western music rests.

These intervallic "species," as they came to be called, could be demonstrated in various ways. One method was by the use of the monochord, the medieval theorist's laboratory instrument, which consisted of a sound-box surmounted by a single string, under which there was a movable bridge. The surface of the box was calibrated, showing bridge placements vis-à-vis one end of the string or the other, by means of which one could exactly measure off (or "deduce") the various intervals. Another, more abstract, way of demonstrating the species was notation—at first by means of Daseian signs as illustrated in the previous chapter (see Fig. 2-2), later (from the eleventh century) by means of the staff. When one writes things down, one can demonstrate or discover that the diatonic scale segment descending from A to D (or ascending from A to E) corresponds with the first species of fifth listed above; that the segment descending from B to E corresponds to the second species; that the segment descending from C to F corresponds to the third species; and that the segment descending from D to G corresponds with the fourth (Ex. 3-1).

EX. 3-1   The four species of fifth and the "four finals"

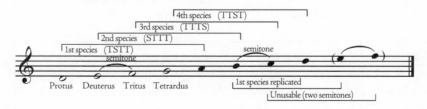

The ending notes of these four species-defining segments—D, E, F, and G—were dubbed "the four finals" in Frankish tonal theory and named (in keeping with the Byzantine derivation of the mode system) according to their Greek ordinal numbers: *protus* (first), *deuterus* (second), *tritus* (third), and *tetrardus* (fourth) respectively. (The fifth A–E was considered a doubling, or transposition, of the first segment; hence

A was functionally equivalent to D as a final.) Full correspondence between the chant-classification and the preexisting eightfold system of psalm tones was achieved by invoking the category of *ambitus*, or range. Chants ending on each of the four finals were further broken down into two classes. Those with the final at the bottom of their range were said to be in "authentic" tonalities or modes, while those that extended lower than their finals, so that the final occurred in the middle of their range, were called "plagal," from the Greek *plagios*, a word derived directly from the vocabulary of the *oktoechos*, where it referred to the four lower-lying scales.

Thus the four finals each governed two modes (*protus authenticus, protus plagalis, deuterus authenticus*, and so on), for a total of eight, in exact accordance with the configuration (but only in vague accordance with the content) of the eightfold system of psalm tones. In elaborating this system, the basic fifth (or modal *pentachord*, from the Greek) whose diatonic species defined the final's domain was complemented with a fourth (or *tetrachord*) to complete the octave. (According to the terminology of the day, the tetrachord was said to be *conjunct*—rather than disjunct—with the pentachord because its first pitch coincided with the last one in the pentachord rather than occupying the next scale degree.) The authentic scales were those in which the pentachord was placed below its conjunct tetrachord, so that the final was the lowest note. In the plagal scales the tetrachord was placed below the pentachord, so that the final came in mid-range. The result was a series of seven distinct *octave species* or scales with particular orderings of the diatonic tones and semitones. There are only seven possible octave species but eight modes; hence the last scale in Table 3-1 (tetrardus, plagal) has the same order of intervals as the first (protus, authentic), but they are split differently into their component pentachord and tetrachord. Although their octave species coincide, the modes do not, for they have different finals: D and G, respectively.

TABLE 3-1   Modes and Octave Species

		TETRACHORD — PENTACHORD — TETRACHORD				
Protus (D)	Authentic			T–S–T–T	—	T–S–T
	Plagal	T–S–T	—	T–S–T–T		
Deuterus (E)	Authentic			S–T–T–T	—	S–T–T
	Plagal	S–T–T	—	S–T–T–T	—	
Tritus (F)	Authentic			T–T–T–S	—	T–T–S
	Plagal	T–T–S	—	T–T–T–S		
Tetrardus (G)	Authentic			T–T–S–T	—	T–S–T
	Plagal	T–S–T	—	T–T–S–T		

In Ex. 3-2 this table is translated into modern staff notation, giving the full array of so-called "medieval church modes." They will henceforth be numbered from one to eight, as they are in the later Frankish treatises, and they will be given the Greek geographical names that the Frankish theorists borrowed from Boethius, the authority of authorities. Boethius had adopted these names from late Greek (Hellenistic) sources, where they had referred not to what we would call modes but to what the Greeks called *tonoi*, transpositions of a single scale rather than different diatonic scales. Thus the familiar Greek nomenclature of the medieval modes was actually a misnomer, first perpetrated by an anonymous ninth-century treatise called *Alia musica* (literally, "More about Music"); but there is not much point in trying to rectify that now. (Note that the Greek prefix *hypo-*, attached to the names of the plagal scales, is roughly synonymous with the word plagal itself: both mean "lower.") Ex. 3-2 also includes the *tubae* of the corresponding psalm tones, for these were sometimes claimed by contemporary theorists to pertain to the church modes as well. The tuba of an authentic mode lies a fifth above the final, as already observed in chapter 1. The tuba of a plagal mode lies a third below that of its authentic counterpart. Note that wherever, according to these rules, the tuba would fall on B, it is changed to C. This was evidently because of an aversion to reciting on the lower note of a semitone pair. Note, too, that the tuba of the fourth tone is A rather than G by the regular application of the rules: it is a third lower than its adjusted counterpart (C in place of B transposes to A in place of G).

EX. 3-2   The eight medieval modes

Perhaps the most important thing to bear in mind regarding this array of medieval modal scales is that the staff positions and their corresponding "letter names" *do not* specify actual pitch frequencies, the way they do in our modern practice. Thus one must try to avoid the common assumption that the Dorian scale represents the piano's white keys from D to D, the Phrygian from E to E, and so on. Rather, the "four finals" and their concomitant scales represent nothing more than the most convenient way of notating intervallic patterns, relationships between pitches that can be realized at any actual pitch level, the way singers (unless cursed with "perfect pitch") can at sight — or rather, by ear — transpose the music they are reading, wherever it happens to be notated, to a comfortable *tessitura* or "placement" within their individual vocal ranges. What we are now conditioned to regard as fixed pitch associations (e.g., "A-440") were at first no more than notational conventions.

If this is a hard idea to get used to, imagine a situation in which all pieces in the major were written "in C" and all pieces in the minor "in A," regardless of the key in which they would actually be performed. Only instrumentalists, whose physical movements are coordinated with specific pitches, or singers with perfect pitch, who have memorized and internalized the relationship between specific frequencies and the appearance of notated music, would be seriously discommoded by such an arrangement. Such musicians can only transpose by mentally changing clefs and signatures. And as we shall see, it was the rise of an extensive independent repertory of instrumental music in the seventeenth century that brought about our modern "key system," in which actual pitches were specified by notation and in which key signatures mandated specific transpositions of the standard scales.

A NEW CONCEPT OF MODE

Thanks to the work of the "tonarists" who coordinated the Roman antiphons with the psalm tones, and the theorists who drew general conclusions from the tonarists' practical observations, a new concept of mode arose. Instead of being a formula-family, a set of concrete, characteristic turns and cadences arising out of long oral tradition, a mode was now conceived abstractly in terms of a scale, and analytically in terms of functional relationships (chiefly range and finishing note or final). We owe this change, on which all our own theoretical notions of musical "structure" ultimately depend, and the classifications and terminology outlined above, primarily to the work of two Frankish theorists of the ninth century.

Aurelian of Réôme, the earlier of them, was a member of the Benedictine abbey of St. Jean de Réôme in what is now the Burgundy region of France, southeast of Paris. His treatise, *Musica disciplina* ("The discipline of music"), was completed sometime around 843. Beginning with its eighth chapter, subtitled "De octo tonis," it consists of the earliest description (or at least the earliest naming, for it is impressionistic and nontechnical) of the eight church modes with their pseudo-Greeky tribal names. Aurelian changed the order of the tones from what it was in Byzantine theory. Instead of grouping the four authentic modes together and following them with the four plagal modes, Aurelian paired authentic modes with plagal ones that shared the same finals, thus enhancing the role of what we now call the "tonic" in establishing a tonality. Aurelian's chapter on psalm recitation contains the oldest extant notations in early Frankish neumes.

Hucbald (d. 930), a monk from the abbey of St. Amand, was the real genius of medieval modal theory. His treatise, *De harmonica institutione* ("On the principles of music"), thought to have been completed around 880, is a far more original work than Aurelian's and far less dependent on the received academic tradition. It was the earliest treatise to number the modes, following the order established by Aurelian, straight through from one to eight. It is also the earliest treatise we have that replaces the relative-pitch or interval/degree nomenclature of ancient Greek music — the so-called Greater Perfect System, transmitted by Boethius — with the alphabet letter names still in use. The name of the lowest note of the Greek system, *proslambanomenos*, was mercifully shortened to "A," and the rest of the letters were assigned from there. Hucbald did not, however, recognize what we now call "octave equivalency," but continued the series of letters through the full two-octave compass of the Greeks, all the way to P. Modern usage, in which A recurs after G and so on, was established by an anonymous Milanese treatise of ca. 1000 called *Dialogus de musica*, once attributed erroneously to Abbot Odo of Cluny.

Hucbald sought to ground his theory as far as possible in the chant itself. He grasped that the "four finals" used in actual singing formed a tetrachord in their own right (T–S–T), and he showed how the scale of the first mode could be built up from it by means of disjunct replication: TST–(T)–TST. He defined the four finals in a manner that resonates fully with our modern notion of a tonic: "Every song," he wrote, "whatever it may be, however it may be twisted this way and that, necessarily may be led back to one of these four; and thence they are termed 'final,' because all things which are sung may take an ending in them." By relocating the tetrachord of the four finals (D–E–F–G) on its fourth note rather than its first (or, to speak technically, by conjunctly replicating it: T–S–T/T–S–T), he deduced the tetrachord G–A–B♭–C.

FIG. 3-3   The Abbey of St. Amand, where Hucbald lived and worked, as it looked in the eighteenth century. This painting was made by J. F. Neyts shortly before the abbey was destroyed, an early casualty of the French Revolution.

Thus he was able to rationalize within the new modal system the old singer's practice of adjusting the note B to avoid the tritone with F. In effect he admitted two versions of B (the hard and the soft, as they came to be known) into the system (Ex. 3-3) to account for the pitches actually called for by the Gregorian melodies.

EX. 3-3   Disjunct and conjunct replication of the T-S-T tetrachord (the tetrachord of the four finals) as described by Hucbald

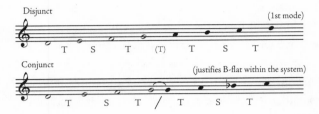

MODE CLASSIFICATION IN PRACTICE

As continually emphasized in this discussion, modal theory arose out of an attempt at classifying the existing Gregorian chant, particularly the antiphons, as an aid to mastering an enormous body of material that had somehow to be committed to melodic memory. Modal theory was thus one of the very many aspects of medieval music-making that originated, very humbly, as *mnemotechnics* (memory aids). Every chant was eventually assigned a modal classification in the tonaries, and eventually in the graduals and antiphoners themselves, including the modern chant books from which some of the examples in the previous chapters were taken. Let us now cast an eye back over some of those examples and see how modal classification worked in practice.

In Ex. 1-1 an actual pairing of antiphon and psalm tone was given. Even though the psalm tone covers no more than the modal pentachord (D descending to G, as it was first theoretically abstracted), the use of C as the tuba identifies the tone as plagal, not authentic (Ex. 3-1). The antiphon is even easier to identify as being in the eighth mode, the Hypomixolydian: its final is G, but the range extends down as far as the D below (and exactly as far up as the D above), establishing the octave species as D to D with cadence in the middle, on G.

Approaching the antiphon in Ex. 1-2 with a tonarist's eye, we notice that it basically outlines the pentachord A-down-to-D, and dips down one note below the final into the lower tetrachord. We have no hesitation, therefore, in assigning it to the second mode, the Hypodorian. And yet the Introit antiphon in Ex. 1-4 is unequivocally assignable to mode 1, the authentic Dorian, even though it, too, frequently makes use of the lower neighbor to the same final. That is because the melody extends above the limits of the modal pentachord as well, reaching the C above. The final is thus clearly located near the bottom of the total range. The psalm verse, chosen expressly to conform to the antiphon, confirms the modal classification. Besides the tuba on A, note the similar approaches to the high C. Here we have a case of modal affinity of the older kind (involving turns of actual phrase) working in harness with the newer classification: the very thing the tonarists and theorists sought to ensure.

As a matter of fact the compilers of the tonaries, and the theorists who followed them, made special allowance for the lower neighbor to the final (called *subtonium modi*), especially in the *protus* or Dorian tonality. As the anonymous author of *Alia musica* put it, "and if a note is added on to some song, above or below the species of the octave, it will not be out of place to include this as being in the tune, not out of it." Thus we are to regard the low C in Ex. 1-4 to be a "note added on below" rather than a full-fledged member of the modal tetrachord. This seeming exception to the rule about mode classification was based on the observed behavior of mode 1 antiphons, as they existed in Pope Gregory's inspired (and therefore not-to-be-tampered-with) chant. Again we see the influence, even within the characteristically rationalistic Frankish mode theory, of the older concept of mode as formula-family.

The Offertory antiphon in Ex. 1-5, although it ends on E, is only arbitrarily assigned to mode 4 (rather than 3) by the tonarists. Clearly, it was (orally) composed with no awareness of the eventual criteria of modal propriety, for its range partakes of tetrachords both below and above the tetrachord that descends to the final, and it "repercusses" more on F than on either of the "Phrygian" reciting tones. Many of its phrases, moreover, seem to belong to a different octave species altogether. Consider the second ("ut palma florebit"), for example: it begins and ends on D, and it introduces B-flat as upper neighbor to A, emphasizing the A as an apparent upper limit to a pentachord. This phrase by itself would unequivocally be assigned to the first mode. Thus, where the Introit in Ex. 1-4 was a case of close correspondence between the old Roman melody and the new Frankish theory, Ex. 1-5 shows a poor fit between the two. Both hits and misses are equally fortuitous, for the chant evolved long in advance of the theory and quite without premonition of it.

Proof of that fortuity comes in Ex. 1-6, the Alleluia. Phrases that closely resemble that second phrase of Ex. 1-1d abound here (for example, the famous melisma on *cedrus*). Since there is no contradiction between the internal phrases and the final cadence, it is easy to assign the melody to mode 1. (Here is the reasoning: the lower neighbor to the final counts less as a representative of a complementary tetrachord than does the upper neighbor to the fifth above; hence we may conceptualize the octave species with the pentachord below the tetrachord; and in additional confirmation, the vast preponderance of melody notes lie above the final, establishing the mode as authentic.) With the two Graduals in Ex. 1-7, we are back in ambiguous territory. The final, A, is accommodated to the theory of the four finals by the back door, as we have seen, on the basis of the congruence between its modal pentachord (TSTT) and that of the protus final, D. Its complementary tetrachord (STT) differs from that of the protus modes, however, resembling the deuterus instead. So the assignment of these melodies to the second mode is more or less arbitrary, especially in view of that pesky B-flat — over *cedrus* in Ex. 1-7a, and over the very opening word, *Haec*, in Ex. 1-7b — preceding a cadence on A that would seem to invoke (if anything) a transposed deuterus or Phrygian scale. There is a considerable gap here between the reality of the chant and the theoretical abstraction of a modal system.

It was noted in chapter 1 that these Graduals come from an old, distinguished formula-family that is suspected of being among the most ancient on record. Thus it is really no surprise that its melody conforms so little with a body of generalizations (that is, a theory) that arose many centuries later — the more so as Graduals, not being antiphons, were not much taken into account by the tonarists. The Frankish mode theory did have a way of accounting for melodies that were wayward by its standards: they were classified as being of "mixed mode" (*modus mixtus*), meaning that some of their constituent phrases departed from the basic octave species of the melody as a whole. But that is just another effort to dispel an anomaly by giving it a name — something on the order of an exorcism.

MODE AS A GUIDE TO COMPOSITION

What a difference we will observe when we look at melodies written after the Frankish chant theory had been formulated! For that theory, modest in its intention, was huge in its effect. While it may have begun as a way of improving the efficiency with which a body of ancient music was mastered and memorized, it quickly metamorphosed into a guide to new composition, achieving a significance its early exponents may never have envisioned for it. From a description of existing music it became a prescription for the music of the future.

The first composer whom the chant theory "influenced" may have been Hucbald himself, its chief early exponent. His surviving compositions include a set of antiphons for the Office of St. Peter, as well as the famous set of *laudes* or Gloria tropes. They are all modally systematic in a way that earlier chant had never been. The Office antiphons, for example, are arranged in a cycle progressing through the whole array of church modes in numerical order — Hucbald's own numerical order! The trope, *Quem vere pia laus*, does not employ the common melodic formulae of the existing Gloria chants — in other words, it eschews the old concept of mode as a formula-family — but instead exemplifies the more abstract features of scalar construction.

In Ex. 3-4, Hucbald's set of laudes is embedded in a Gloria that shares its mode (the sixth, or Hypolydian) and seems, on the basis of its sources as well as its style, to date from within, or shortly after, Hucbald's lifetime. In both, the tonal focus is sharp, with the final, F, located in the middle of the melody's range, providing a clear line of demarcation between the modal pentachord and the plagal tetrachord below. Hucbald uses three pitches to end the constituent (and, remember, nonconsecutive) phrases of his laudes. Only the last ends, as might be expected, on the final. A plurality, five, end on the reciting tone, namely A. The other four, which end on G, seem to have picked up the influence of some secular genres, especially dance songs, which, as we will see in the next chapter, frequently use the "supertonic" degree to create half (or "open") cadences, to be fully closed by the final at the end of the next phrase of the original chant. That is what happens in Hucbald's second, third, and fourth phrases, all of which end on G. The second phrase is answered and "closed" by the full cadence on "Benedicimus te"; the fourth by the close on "Glorificamus te." The one in between (*Qui dominator . . .*) is answered strategically by "Adoramus te" with a cadence on D, so that a tonally closed ABA pattern sets off the three parallel acclamations from the rest of the Gloria. This kind of tonally articulated formal structure was the great Frankish innovation.

The same regular features can be discerned in many of the trope melodies discussed in chapter 2. That is because the authors of tropes had to be music analysts as well as poets and composers. They had to determine and reproduce the mode of the chant to which they were setting their prefaces and interpolations, whether or not they actually intended to imitate the style of the earlier chant. (In practice, it seems, some did so intend and some evidently preferred their new melodies to stand out from the old;

EX. 3-4   Gloria in mode 6, with laudes by Hucbald of St. Amand (texted in italics)

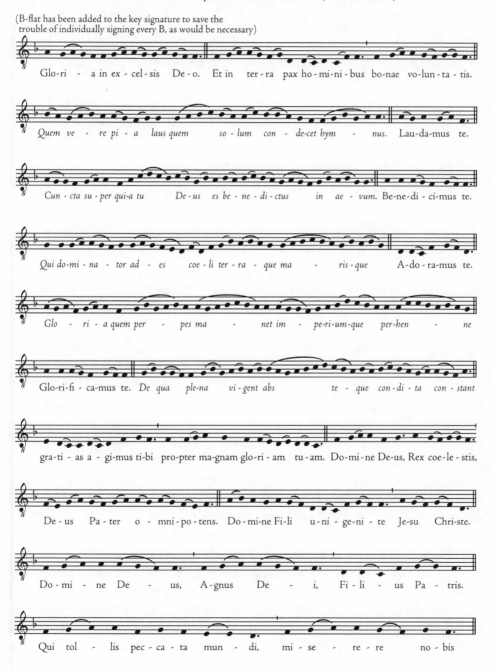

(B-flat has been added to the key signature to save the trouble of individually signing every B, as would be necessary)

EX. 3-4 *(continued)*

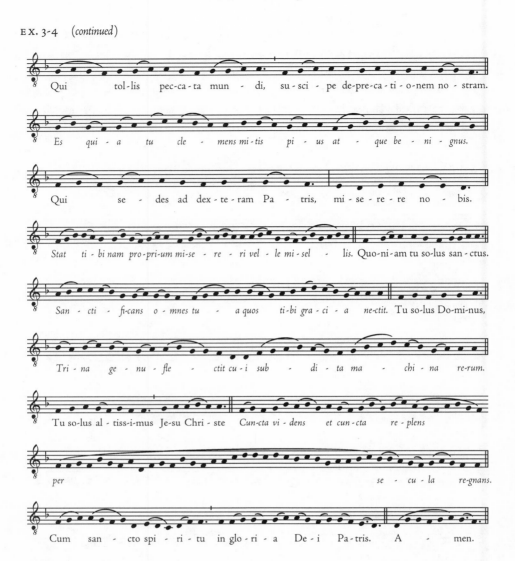

all, however, understood the requirement of modal conformity.) Consider the preface
to the Easter Introit in Ex. 2-8a. The mode of the Introit antiphon itself is given as
the fourth (*Deuterus plagalis* or Hypophrygian), and one can immediately see why: it
begins with D, a note in the lower tetrachord (and the first phrase, "Resurrexi," actually
cadences there); the range will later touch bottom on the C below that. The highest
note in the melody is A, which means that the full modal pentachord above E is never
expressed at all. Only the final cadence on E (something that could hardly be predicted
at the outset) justifies the assignment of the melody to the Phrygian tribe. The gap
between the reality of the chant and the utopia of mode theory yawns.

"Psallite regi," the little prefatory trope shown in Ex. 2-8a, resolutely closes the gap.
It begins on E, precisely so that the beginning of the newly augmented antiphon will
conform to the end (and so that the end, so to speak, can now fulfill the implications
of the beginning). It sounds the B above the final so that the full modal pentachord of
mode 4 is represented. It expressly avoids a modal cadence at the end, of course, so that

it will flow imperceptibly into the antiphon it is introducing. But it has very perceptibly enhanced the conformity of the actual Gregorian antiphon with the Frankish definition of its mode.

Although it is the shorter and the simpler of the introit tropes for Easter shown in chapter 2, "Psallite regi" is by far the most radical in its transformation of the melody to which it is appended. Ex. 2-8b is more obviously an imitation of the Gregorian antiphon. Its prefacing phrase begins, like the antiphon, with a feint toward D, and ends, again like the antiphon, with a cadence on the final. It even mimics the Introit's ambitus (C up to A) instead of, like Ex. 2-8a, completing the modal pentachord with a B.

The *Quem quaeritis* trope (Ex. 2-9) is modally whimsical. It actually takes the initial feint to D at its word, so to speak, and prepares it with an actual melody in mode 2 (Hypodorian). It is the descent to the bottom of the lower tetrachord at the very beginning of the "Interrogatio" that establishes the melody as plagal, even though the "Responsorium," as befits the heavenly voice that sings it, ascends into the upper tetrachord (though not all the way to the top of it). Melodies that encompass more than two primary scale segments (or that have ranges of more than an octave) exemplify what medieval theorists called *commixtio*, or *modus commixtus*. The term is often "translated" into a nonexistent English cognate: "commixture" or "commixed mode." In any case, it needs to be distinguished from the *modus mixtus* defined above. "Mixed mode" denotes a mixture of different octave species. "Commixture" refers to the extension of a melody so as to encompass both authentic and plagal scales.

The hymn melodies in Ex. 2-7 were chosen, among other reasons, to exemplify "modern" Frankish melodies in various modes. *Ave maris stella* (Ex. 2-7a) is a wonderfully clear example of post-Gregorian Dorian melody. Its composer most assuredly knew all about abstract modal syntax, and about the relationship between antiphon modes and psalm tones as laid out in the tonaries. Note how the first phrase leaps up from the final to the upper tetrachord, which it fully describes, meanwhile emphasizing the note dividing the pentachord and tetrachord (the tuba, so to speak) with a turn figure. The second phrase completely describes the pentachord. The third phrase cadences on the "note added on below," introducing it with a veritable flourish. And the fourth phrase returns to the uncluttered pentachord for the final cadence. This kind of clearly delineated structure can hardly be found in the original corpus of Gregorian chant. It is the product of "theory," and of a single composer's shaping hand. For the first time, it seems, we are looking at a piece not merely maintained but composed within the literate tradition—composed, that is, in the sense we usually have in mind when we use the word.

Pange lingua (Ex. 2-7b), in the third mode (authentic Phrygian), also gives its "modernity" away, this time by giving cadential emphasis to the note C, high above the final. (Third mode melodies in the original Gregorian corpus often emphasize this C, but not as a cadence.) By the time *Pange lingua* was composed, theoretical rationalization had made such emphasis common. The same point may be made, even more emphatically, about *Veni creator spiritus* (Ex. 2-7c). It is assigned to the eighth mode (rather than the seventh), but not for any reason having to do with its ambitus or final. The final, G, is common to all *tetrardus* melodies. The range could be described as the modal pentachord with a "note added on" either above or below, again suggesting that the authentic and the plagal scales have an equal claim on the tune's allegiance. What clinches things for the plagal is the cadential emphasis on C, the tuba of the corresponding psalm tone. (The authentic tuba, D, also gets a cadence, but C gets two.)

Thus these hymn melodies graphically illustrate the synthesis of Roman and Byzantine elements that made up Frankish mode theory and its perhaps unforeseen compositional influence. (The regularity of structure in the hymns may of course also reflect the influence of popular genres that have left no written trace and are consequently beyond our historical ken.) The style and the effect of these tunes is altogether different from those of the true Gregorian corpus. Where the older melodies were discursive, elusive, and ecstatic, these are dynamic, strongly etched, and therefore highly memorable (as congregational songs need to be). The influence of "theory" on them was in no way an inhibition. Quite the contrary; it seems to have been an enormous spur to the Frankish musical imagination, leading to a great burst of indigenous musical composition in the north of Europe, contributing a new (and lasting) kind of musical beauty.

To savor this new Frankish style at its best and most characteristic, let us have a look at a melody composed around 1100, after mode theory had a century or more in which to establish itself in singers' consciousness: Kyrie IX, which bears the subtitle *Cum jubilo* ("with a shout") after its perhaps original texted form (Ex. 3-5). Never yet have we seen a melody that, by so clearly parsing itself into the "principal parts" of its mode, advertises the fact that the mode, as a concept, preceded and conditioned the composition of the melody.

EX. 3-5   Kyrie IX, *Cum jubilo*

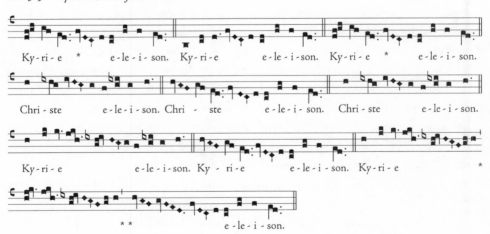

Consider first the opening threefold acclamation. The first eight notes of the opening "Kyrie" exactly stake out the modal pentachord. The rest of the phrase decorates the final with the characteristic "Dorian" lower neighbor. The second acclamation begins by staking out the lower tetrachord just as the first had staked out the pentachord. It then proceeds like the first. The third is a full repetition of the first. Summing up the pattern of repetitions, we find that the opening threefold litany mirrors in melodic microcosm the shape of the entire ninefold text: a melodic ABA or "sandwich" form nested within a textual ABA (threefold Kyrie/threefold Christe/threefold Kyrie). At the same time, the melisma on "-e," plus the "eleison" (into which the melisma flows smoothly by vowel elision), are the same every time, reflecting the old practice of choral refrains. Hence, the overall shape of the opening threefold acclamation could be represented as A(x) B(x) A(x). So far the melody conforms closely to the principal parts of mode 2, the Hypodorian (with the refrain dwelling significantly on F, the tuba).

The first "Christe," consisting for the most part of turn figures around A, substitutes the tuba of the authentic Dorian for that of the plagal and similarly emphasizes it; this gives us an inkling that the chant is going to encompass a mixed mode. As to overall shape, the threefold Christe is also cast, like the previous threefold acclamation, in an ABA design that mirrors in melodic microcosm the overall form of the text. But note one playful detail: what fills the Christe sandwich is a variant of what was the "bread" in the Kyrie sandwich.

The concluding threefold acclamation begins by confirming the impression that this will be a mixed-mode chant. Compare the new intonation on "Kyrie" with the "filling" of the first Kyrie sandwich. It is the same motive an octave higher, now staking out the upper tetrachord and completing the authentic Dorian scale. (Because of the many repetitions this motive will receive in the higher octave, the complete melody is classified as a mode 1 chant.) And now notice that the continuation on "eleison" is a variant of the continuations of the first and last "Christe" phrases. This brings about another playful switch of functions between "filling" and "bread," and it also means that the "eleison" phrases following the first and last "Christe" phrases were another detachable refrain, alternating with the first. Wheels within wheels!

The last threefold acclamation, like the others, is a sandwich; its filling is the same as that of the second sandwich (namely a variant of the bread in the first). The final acclamation is augmented by an internal melisma that repeats the melody of the entire first Kyrie; but then, in order to end on the final rather than the tuba, the second Kyrie is recapitulated, too, so that the last word is sung to the original "eleison" refrain. The entire subtly interwoven and integrated formal scheme looks like Table 3-2.

Thus a sort of "rondo" scheme (**AbAcAcdAdA**) crosscuts the trio of sandwiches, and a single dynamic pitch trajectory, from the bottom of the Hypodorian tetrachord

TABLE 3-2   Structure of Kyrie IX

A.	Kyrie eleison	A(x)		
	Kyrie eleison	B(x)		
	Kyrie eleison	A(x)		
B.	Christe eleison	C(y)	=	A
	Christe eleison	A'(x)		B
	Christe eleison	C(y)		A
A.	Kyrie eleison	D(y')	=	A
	Kyrie eleison	A'(x)		B
	Kyrie eleison	D(y') – D(y') – A'(x)		A

to the top of the authentic Dorian tetrachord, seems to describe a progression from darkness to light (or, in terms of mood, from abjection to rejoicing) that accords with the implied (or hoped-for) answer to the prayer, the more so as the peak of the melodic range coincides with the peak of melismatic "jubilation." Finally, the melody's tonal regularity, with its alternation of cadences on final and tuba a fifth apart, was a permanent "Western" acquisition. It would outlast the modal system that gave rise to it.

For a final indication of the Frankish passion for formal rounding and regularity, compare the concluding item in the Ordinary formulary initiated by Kyrie IX, the dismissal formula (Ex. 3-6). It is set to the same melody as the opening "Kyrie eleison" in Ex. 3-4, the phrase designated "A(x)" in Table 3-2, which recurred throughout the litany and came back out of retirement to conclude it. The whole Mass service is thus effectively rounded off the same way the Kyrie was, with a significant melodic refrain. The Frankish ambition to use music as a shaping and a unifying force is exercised here at the highest possible level.

EX. 3-6 *Ite/deo gratias* from Mass IX

I - te, missa est.
De- o gra-ti- as.

VERSUS

The same urge to regularize tonally and formally, and to use the two stabilizing dimensions to reinforce one another, can be seen in late Frankish sequences as well, together with the additional regularizing element of metrical verse, eventually replete with rhyme. Settings of such texts, especially rhymed metrical sequences, are often called *versus* to distinguish them from the older *prosa*. Ex. 3-7 contains two of the sequences that have survived into the modern liturgy. The Easter sequence, *Victimae paschali laudes* ("Praises to the Paschal victim"), is attributed in both words and music to the German monk Wipo, chaplain to the Holy Roman Emperor Conrad II (reigned 1024–39). It has the paired versicle structure common to the form: A, BB, CC, DD. The constituent phrases describe the principal parts of the modal scale with great regularity. The two phrases of verse A describe the modal pentachord, with the first phrase darkened by the Dorian lower neighbor, and the second compensating by adding the previously withheld top note. Verse B makes a steady descent from the authentic tetrachord (cadencing on the tuba) through the pentachord, through the darkened pentachord with lower neighbor and no tuba. Verse C extends downward, like the second Kyrie in Ex. 3-5, to describe the plagal tetrachord, proceeding through the "darkened" pentachord to the full pentachord. Phrase D, which resembles phrase B, begins like it with the authentic tetrachord at the top of the modal ambitus, and again gradually descends to the final, with the final phrase (and also the paschal alleluia) colored dark by the use of the *subtonium* (the lower neighbor).

Ex. 3-7 gives the musical text of *Victimae paschali laudes* exactly as it is found in the *Liber usualis*, a practical edition of Gregorian chant first published in 1934 for the use of modern Catholic congregations. It lacks a repetition of the D phrase because the text has been officially expurgated. The omitted verse, the first of the pair sung to phrase D, had read: *Credendum est magis soli Mariae veraci/quam Judeorum turbe fallaci* ("More trust is

EX. 3-7   Two sequences in modern use

a. *Victimae paschali laudes* (Easter)

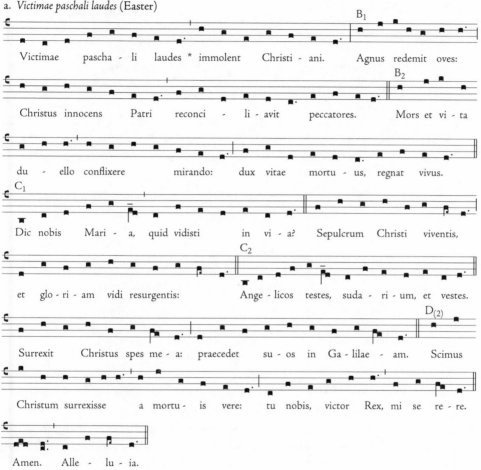

To the Paschal Victim, hymns of praise, come, ye Christians, joyous raise:
Lamb unstained, unmeasured price hath paid, ransom for the sheep that strayed.
To a father kind, rebellious men sinless Son hath led again.
Life and death in combat fierce engage, marvel dazzling every age.
Price of life by hellish monster slain living now shall ever reign.
Tell us, Mary, thou our herald be, what in passing thou didst see?
Empty tomb, where Christ, now living, lay.
Angels saw I in bright array: shroud and vesture loosely cast aside
Prove he's risen glorified.
Yea! my Hope hath snapped the fatal chain, smiting Death hath risen again:
quick before you, sped to Galilee.
Know we now that Christ hath truly risen.
Glorious King, help us while we sing:
Amen. Alleluia.

EX. 3-7B   *Dies irae* (Requiem)

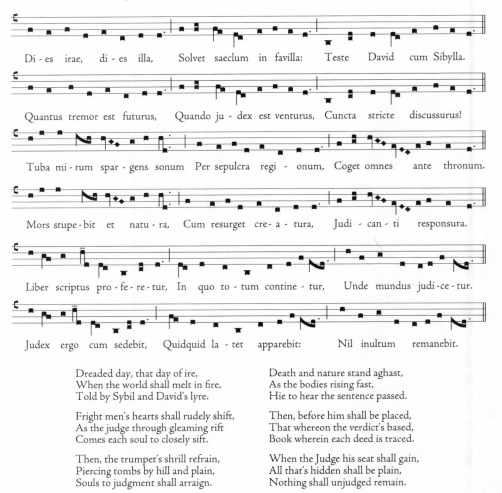

Di - es irae, di - es illa,   Solvet saeclum in favilla: Teste   David   cum Sibylla.

Quantus tremor est futurus,   Quando ju - dex est venturus,   Cuncta   stricte   discussurus!

Tuba mi - rum spar - gens sonum Per sepulcra regi - onum, Coget omnes   ante   thronum.

Mors stupe - bit et   natu - ra,   Cum resurget cre - a - tura,   Judi - can - ti   responsura.

Liber scriptus pro - fe - re - tur, In quo to - tum contine - tur,   Unde mundus judi - ce - tur.

Judex ergo cum sedebit,   Quidquid la - tet apparebit: Nil inultum   remanebit.

Dreaded day, that day of ire,	Death and nature stand aghast,
When the world shall melt in fire,	As the bodies rising fast,
Told by Sybil and David's lyre.	Hie to hear the sentence passed.
Fright men's hearts shall rudely shift,	Then, before him shall be placed,
As the judge through gleaming rift	That whereon the verdict's based,
Comes each soul to closely sift.	Book wherein each deed is traced.
Then, the trumpet's shrill refrain,	When the Judge his seat shall gain,
Piercing tombs by hill and plain,	All that's hidden shall be plain,
Souls to judgment shall arraign.	Nothing shall unjudged remain.

to be put in honest Mary [Magdalen] alone than in the lying crowd of Jews"). Sensible to its nastiness, and aware of its bearing on a history of persecutions, the Council of Trent, the mid-sixteenth century congress of church reform that evicted almost all the other sequences from the liturgy, pruned the offending verse from *Victimae paschali* as a gesture of reconciliation with the Jews.

Dies irae ("Day of wrath"), from the Requiem Mass (Ex. 3-7b), is probably the most famous of all medieval liturgical songs, and a very late one. It may even be a thirteenth-century composition, for the text is attributed to Thomas of Celano (d. ca. 1255), a disciple and biographer of St. Francis of Assisi. Thomas's poem is a kind of meditation or gloss in rhymed three-line stanzas (tercets) on the second verse — "Dies illa, dies irae" — of the responsory *Libera me, Domine, de morte aeterna* ("Deliver me, O Lord, from eternal death"), which is sung at the graveside service that follows the Requiem Mass. Even the melody begins as a parody (or gloss, or takeoff—but not a trope, except in the loosest possible use of the term) on that of the responsory verse (Ex. 3-8).

E X. 3-8   *Libera me* (responsory verse)

Di - es il - la, di - es   i - rae,   ca - la - mi - ta - tis   et   mi - se - ri - - ae,   di - es ma - gna

et   a - ma - ra val - de.

O that day, that day of wrath, of sore distress and of all wretchedness, that great and exceeding bitter day.

Like *Rex caeli* (Ex. 2-1), in its full form the *Dies irae* has a melodic repetition scheme that exceeds the normal allotment of a sequence. (There can be no doubt about its status, though, because within the actual liturgy it occupies the place and accomplishes the business of a sequence.) Its three paired versicles go through a triple cursus—a threefold repetition like that of a litany: AABBCC/AABBCC/AABBC, with the last C replaced by a final couplet, to which an additional unrhymed couplet and an Amen were added by an anonymous reviser. (Ex. 3-7b contains only the first cursus.) The various constituent phrases have many internal repetitions as well: the second phrase of B, for example, is an embellished variant of the responsory-derived opening phrase of A, which (like the opening acclamation in Kyrie "Cum jubilo") thus assumes the role of a refrain.

Once again, as by now we may expect to find in a late medieval Dorian chant, the melody delineates the principal parts of the mode with great clarity. The A phrase occupies the Hypodorian ambitus, minus the highest note; the B phrase stakes out the upper tetrachord (but again minus the highest note); and the C phrase sinks back into Hypodorian space (this is, after all, a funereal chant). Only the final couplet (on "judicandus . . . .") manages to reach the top of the authentic octave, vouchsafing a mode 1 classification for the melody. Until the "coda," moreover, with a pair of half cadences on A (the mode 1 tuba), every one of the melody's frequent cadences has been to the final, imparting an additional, very heavy-treaded, dimension of repetition.

Despite its formal peculiarities, the *Dies irae* is a very typical late sequence in its verse structure. By the middle of the twelfth century, rhymed tercets composed of eight-syllable lines with regularly alternated accent patterns were very much the norm, not only for sequences but for new Office formularies as well. This verse pattern (especially in a modified tercet with syllable count 8+8+7) is often associated with Adam Precentor, alias Adam of St. Victor (d. 1146) a much-venerated Parisian churchman and an "outstanding versifier" (*egregius versificator*) who is credited with churning out between forty and seventy sequences of this type, most of them set to a small repertory of stereotyped and interchangeable tunes. These sequences were composed not only for the Augustinian abbey of St. Victor, where Adam was resident, but also for the newly consecrated Cathedral of Notre Dame, where he served as cantor. The most famous melody associated with Adam is the Mixolydian tune to which St. Thomas Aquinas's sequence *Lauda Sion Salvatorem* ("Praise the Savior, O Zion") is still sung at traditional Catholic churches on the feast of Corpus Christi. In Ex. 3-9 the first two melodic phrases are given both with St. Thomas Aquinas's words and with Adam's original poem, *Laudes crucis attollamus* ("Praises to the cross we bear"), composed about a hundred years earlier. Mixing and matching texts and tunes (especially new texts and familiar tunes) was a common practice, called *contrafactum*, that throve especially in genres that exhibited the kind of rigorous regularity of form and meter that we find in the late Parisian (or "Victorine") sequence.

EX. 3-9 *Lauda Sion Salvatorem/Laudes crucis attolamus*

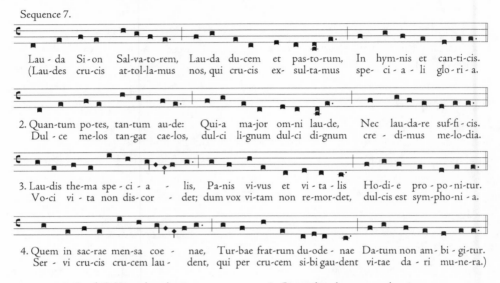

Sequence 7.

1. Laud, O Zion, thy salvation,
   laud with hymn and exaltation,
   Christ, thy king and shepherd, too.

2. Spend thyself, honor raising,
   who surpasseth all thy praising;
   never canst thou reach his due.

3. Sing today, the mystery showing
   of the living, life-bestowing
   Bread from heaven before Thee set.

4. Even the same of old provided,
   where the Twelve, divinely guided,
   at the holy table met . . .

Altogether different were the contemporaneous sequences of Hildegard of Bingen (1098–1179), Abbess of the Benedictine convent of Rupertsberg in the Rhine valley near the German city of Trier. In its formal, modal, and metrical clarity, the Parisian sequence accorded with the scholastic tradition of Augustine and Boethius; scholastic thinkers sought, through orderly and cogent argument, to make faith intelligible to reason. Hildegard, by contrast, used poetry and music to express a visionary "symphony of the harmony of heavenly revelations" (*symphonia armonie celestium revelationum*), as she called her collected poetical works, assembled by the late 1150s. Besides her famous sequences, the book contains antiphons, responsories, hymns, and Kyries.

Hildegard's melodies often have an extraordinary ambitus (up to two and a half octaves!), and they are not easily parsed into abstract modal functions. Rather, they exhibit the older formula-family notion of modal identity, just as their verbal patterns, avoiding both rhyme and regular accentuation, revert to the older, Notker-style notion of *prosa*. Her fantastic diction and imagery are all her own.

In the sequence *Columba aspexit* ("The dove looked in") for the commemoration feast of St. Maximinus, a local saint of Trier, the versicles are paired in the traditional way, but loosely. (Ex. 3-10 shows the first two pairs.) The members of a pair do not always correspond exactly in syllable count. Compared with the literal strophic repetition we have become used to in the late medieval sequence, Hildegard's melodic parallelism seems more to resemble a process of variation. (Some of her sequences avoid parallelism altogether, something unheard of since the ninth century and probably unknown to Hildegard as a precedent.) The result of all these irregularities is a relatively difficult melody to comprehend rationally or memorize. That lack of easy grasp, which induces a passivity of mind, combined with a flamboyant imagery, much of it derived from the Song of Songs, that evokes strong sensory impres-

FIG. 3-4 Hildegard of Bingen, the twelfth-century abbess of Rupertsberg, writing down her visions (or, possibly, her chants). The illustration comes from a manuscript of her treatise *Scivias* ("Know the ways of the Lord") called the Codex Rupertsberg. It disappeared during World War II.

sions (specially implicating the sense of smell), conspire to produce an immensity of feeling one associates with revelation rather than reflection. Unlike the elegant, urbane creations of the Victorines, Hildegard's is a lyricism of mystical immediacy. (Nor is this the last time French and German "schools" will be so differentiated.)

EX. 3-10   Hildegard of Bingen, *Columba aspexit*

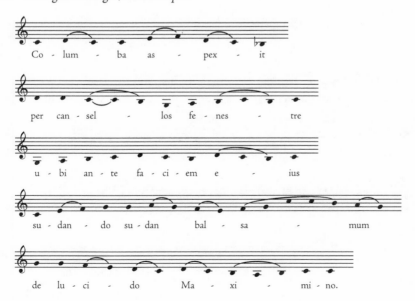

EX. 3-10   (*continued*)

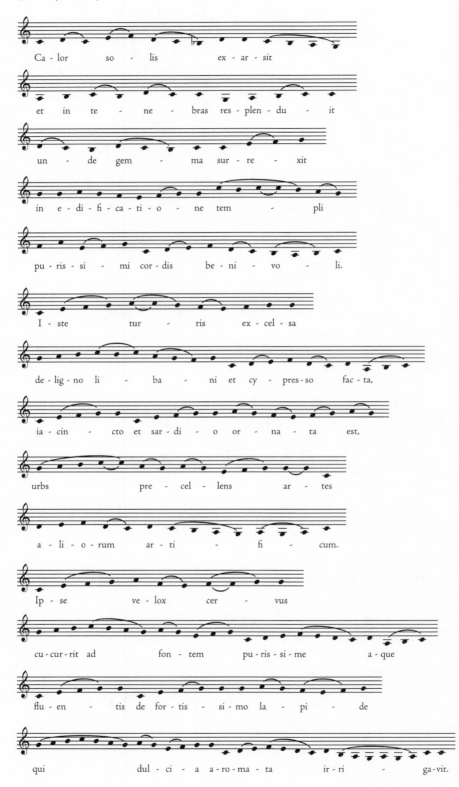

LITURGICAL DRAMA

Hildegard's largest work is a play with music called *Ordo virtutum* ("The enactment of the virtues"). In it, the Devil and the sixteen virtues do battle for the possession of a Christian soul. It is by far the oldest extant example of what is now called the "morality play," a form of allegorical drama (chiefly popular between the fourteenth and the sixteenth centuries) in which the actors personify virtues and vices. In terms of content, then, Hildegard's play was unusual and, it could be said, prophetic. In terms of its genre, however, it was not unusual at all.

By Hildegard's twelfth century, the sung verse play in Latin was a veritable craze in northern Europe and England, and church space was increasingly given over on major festivals to dramatic representations of various kinds. Such plays begin to appear in written sources in the tenth century, and it is probably no accident that the earliest ones of all enact the same episode — the visit of the women (or the Magi) to Christ's tomb (or the manger) and their meeting with an angel — that we encountered in the previous chapter in the form of tropes to the Easter and Christmas Introits. While it would be misleading to allege (as scholars once believed) that the so-called liturgical drama (performed at matins) grew directly or "organically" out of the earlier tropes (performed at Mass), it is clear that the church plays were a part — the crowning part, it is fair to say — of the same impulse to adorn and amplify the liturgy that produced the trope, the sequence, and all the other specifically Frankish liturgical genres that we surveyed in the previous chapter.

One of the most fully worked out of these early plays, with detailed directions for the costumes and the movements of the actors, is found in the *Regularis concordia* of 973, a code of monastic law produced by a council of bishops under Ethelwold (ca. 908–984) at the cathedral of Winchester. Its music is preserved in the famous Winchester Tropers, two great books of liturgical supplements, the earlier of them roughly contemporaneous with the council. (Unfortunately the Winchester Tropers are both notated in staffless neumes, and their contents cannot be reliably transcribed for performance.)

Like the tropes and sequences, the church plays evolved — between the tenth and twelfth centuries — from a prose into a verse genre. Twelfth-century liturgical dramas were elaborate composites of newly composed *versus* (music set to verse texts in the latest Frankish style), older hymns and sequences, and Gregorian antiphons, these last being retained as a kind of scriptural allusion or invocation. Their subjects included *Peregrinus* plays (dramatizations of the risen Christ's appearances to his disciples), shepherds' plays for Christmas, the Slaughter of the Holy Innocents (sometimes called the "Play of Herod"), the Wise and Foolish Virgins, the Raising of Lazarus, the miracles of St. Nicholas, and the so-called *Ludus Danielis*, the "Play of Daniel."

The largest single source of these twelfth-century verse plays is the so-called Fleury Play-book, a manuscript copied at the Benedictine monastery of St. Benoit at Fleury-sur- Loire near Orleans, the burial place of King Philip I of France (d. 1108). The best-known single item in the repertory is the Play of Daniel, thanks to its spectacular revival in 1958 by Noah Greenberg's New York Pro Musica ensemble, a milestone in the "early music" performance movement (a recording was still in print as of 2001).

It was composed by students at the Cathedral school of Beauvais for the Feast of the Circumcision (January 1): "In your honor, Christ, this Daniel play was written at Beauvais, the product of our youth," the first words proclaim. In this treatment, the Old Testament story of the prophet Daniel and his deliverance from the lion's den (vividly evoked in prescribed sets and costumes) is turned at the end into a prophecy of the coming of Christ: *Ecce venit sanctus ille, / sanctorum sanctissimus*, Daniel sings: "Behold, he comes, the Holy One, the Holiest of Holies," followed by a traditional Christmas hymn and the ancient hymn of thanksgiving, *Te Deum laudamus*, the concluding chant at matins, to which the whole foregoing complement of dramatic verses, processional songs, and expressive lyrics could be interpreted as a huge explanatory preface or trope.

The processional songs that accompany the entrances and exits of the *dramatis personae* in the Play of Daniel are labeled *conductus* (escorting-song) in the manuscript rubrics, one of the earliest uses of a term that later became synonymous with *versus*, or freely composed Latin song in verse. Ex. 3-11 gives the first of these *conducti*, to the verse *Astra tenenti / cunctipotenti*, which accompanies the entrance of King Belshazzar at the very beginning of the play, and then Daniel's lyrical petition after King Darius sentences him to die in the lions' den. (In order to accompany the actual procession of actors more effectively in performance, Noah Greenberg decided on the basis of the word-accents to impose a regular compound-triple meter on the five-syllable lines of text in the conductus; there is no evidence to gainsay him.) Between them, these two samples will give an idea of the extraordinary range of poetic and musical style encompassed by post-Gregorian *versus* settings.

MARIAN ANTIPHONS

The very latest genre of medieval chant to be incorporated (in some part) into the canonical liturgy was the votive antiphon. Votive antiphons were psalmless antiphons — that is, independent Latin songs — attached as riders onto the ends of Office services to honor or appeal to local saints or (increasingly) to the Virgin Mary. As a human chosen by God to bear His son, Mary was thought to mediate between the human and the divine. One fanciful image casts her as the neck connecting the Godhead and the body of the Christian congregation. As such she was the natural recipient of personal prayers or devotional vows (and it is from "vow" that the word "votive" is derived). From the cult of Mary arose the Marian antiphon or "anthem to the Blessed Virgin Mary." Our English word "anthem," meaning a song of praise or devotion by now as often patriotic as religious, descends (by way of the Old English *antefne*) from "antiphon." These ample songs of salutation to the Mother of God appear in great numbers in written sources beginning early in the eleventh century. By the middle of the thirteenth, a few had been adopted for ordinary use in monasteries to conclude the Compline service (hence the liturgical day itself). At English cathedrals they enhanced the Evensong service, which lay worshipers attended. It was to keep these prayers for intercession going in perpetuity that the "choral foundations" — endowments to fund the training of choristers — were set up at English cathedrals and university chapels. They have lasted to this day.

EX. 3-11A   The Play of Daniel, *Astra tenenti* (conductus)

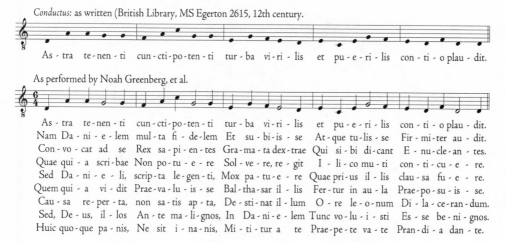

Conductus: as written (British Library, MS Egerton 2615, 12th century.

As - tra te - nen - ti cun - cti - po - ten - ti tur - ba vi - ri - lis et pu - e - ri - lis con - ti - o plau - dit.

As performed by Noah Greenberg, et al.

As - tra te - nen - ti cun - cti - po - ten - ti tur - ba vi - ri - lis et pu - e - ri - lis con - ti - o plau - dit.
Nam Da - ni - e - lem mul - ta fi - de - lem Et su - bi - is - se At - que tu - lis - se Fir - mi - ter au - dit.
Con - vo - cat ad se Rex sa - pi - en - tes Gra - ma - ta dex - trae Qui si - bi di - cant E - nu - cle - an - tes.
Quae qui - a scri - bae Non po - tu - e - re Sol - ve - re, re - git I - li - co mu - ti con - ti - cu - e - re.
Sed Da - ni - e - li, scrip - ta le - gen - ti, Mox pa - tu - e - re Quae pri - us il - lis clau - sa fu - e - re.
Quem qui - a vi - dit Prae - va - lu - is - se Bal - tha - sar il - lis Fer - tur in au - la Prae - po - su - is - se.
Cau - sa re - per - ta, non sa - tis ap - ta, De - sti - nat il - lum O - re le - o - num Di - la - ce - ran - dum.
Sed, De - us, il - los An - te ma - li - gnos, In Da - ni - e - lem Tunc vo - lu - i - sti Es - se be - ni - gnos.
Huic quo - que pa - nis, Ne sit i - na - nis, Mi - ti - tur a   te Prae - pe - te va - te Pran - di - a dan - te.

To the almighty holder of the firmament
This throng of men and boys
    Assembled gives praise.
	But to Daniel, upon reading the writing,
	It became clear at once
	    What had been hidden to them.

For it listens attentively
To the many things faithful Daniel
    Underwent and suffered.
	When Belshazzar saw how he excelled the others
	He placed him above them in the hall,
	    So it is related.

The King calls before him the wise men
To explain the meaning of the letters
    Written by that hand.
	A case, not very solid, found against him,
	And sentenced him to be torn
	    By the teeth of the lions.

Since the wise men were not able to solve them,
Silent before the King
    They held their tongues.
	But, O God, it was then your wish
	That those who had been cruel to Daniel
	    should become kind.

And to him, lest he fall faint,
You sent bread by the angel-borne prophet,
Bringing him food.

EX. 3-11B   The Play of Daniel, *Heu heu* (Daniel's lament)

He - u, he - u, he - u quo ca - su, sor - tis
ve - nit hec damp - na - ti - o mor - tis?
He - u, he - u, he - u sce - lus in - fan - dum
cur me da - bit ad la - ce - ran - dum
hec fe - ra tur - ba fe - ris?

EX. 3-11B (*continued*)

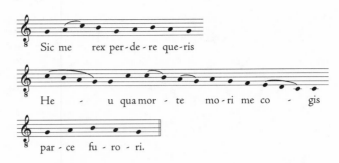

Sic me   rex per-de-re que-ris

He - u qua mor - te mo-ri me co - gis

par - ce fu - ro - ri.

Alas, Alas, Alas!
By what fate am I condemned to death?
Alas, Alas, Alas!
O unspeakable crime!
Why does this crowd of cruel men
Give me to be torn in the wild beasts' den?
Is it thus, O King, that you wish me to perish?
Alas! By what death do you doom me to die?
Spare your anger.

At first the Marian antiphons were sung, like the psalms, in a weekly cursus. In the modern liturgy, only four have been retained, and they follow a seasonal round. In winter (that is, from Advent until the Feast of the Purification on February 2), the seasonal anthem to the Blessed Virgin Mary is the penitential *Alma Redemptoris Mater* ("Sweet Mother of the Redeemer . . . have pity on us sinners"). In spring (from Purification until Holy Week), it is the panegyric *Ave Regina coelorum* ("Hail, O Queen of the heavens"). For the exultant fifty-day period between Easter and Pentecost, known as Paschal Time, *Regina caeli, laetare* ("O Queen of heaven, rejoice") is the prescribed antiphon (Ex. 3-12a); and during the remaining (biggest) portion of the year, encompassing late summer and fall, it is *Salve, Regina* ("Hail, O Queen"), the most popular of the Marian antiphons (Ex. 3-12b) and the only one for which a plausible author has been proposed: Adhémar, Bishop of Le Puy and a leader of the First Crusade (d. at Antioch, 1098).

These eleventh-century melodies, the one exultant and the other penitent, exemplify in their contrast of modes the persistence of the doctrine of *ethos*, alive even today

EX. 3-12A Marian antiphon, *Regina caeli, laetare*

Regina caeli * laeta - re, alle - lu - ia: Qui-a quem me-ru - isti

por - ta - re, alle - lu - ia: Resurre - xit,

sic - ut dixit, alle - lu - ia: O - ra pro no - bis De - um, alle - *

EX. 3-12A (*continued*)

* * lu - ia.

O Queen of heaven, rejoice, alleluia.
For He whom thou didst merit to bear, alleluia,
has risen, as He said, alleluia.
Pray for us to God, alleluia.

EX. 3-12B Marian antiphon, *Salve, Regina*

Sal - ve, * Re - gi - na, mater mi - se - ricordi - ae: Vi - ta, dulce - do,

et spes nostra, sal - ve. Ad te clama - mus, exsu - les, fi - li - i Hevae. Ad te suspi - ra -

mus. gementes et flen - tes in hac lacrima - rum valle. E - ia ergo, Advoca - ta nostra,

illos tu - os mi - se - ri cordes ocu - los ad nos conver - te, Et Jesum, benedi - ctum fructum

ventris tu - i, no - bis post hoc exsi - li - um os - tende. O cle - mens: O pi - a:

O dulcis * virgo Ma - ri - a.

Hail, holy Queen, Mother of mercy;
hail, our life, our sweetness, our hope!
To thee do we cry, poor banished children of Eve;
to thee do we send up our sighs,
mourning and weeping in this vale of tears.
Turn then, most gracious advocate,
thine eyes of mercy towards us;
and after this our exile,
show unto us the blessed fruit of thy womb, Jesus.
O clement, O loving, O sweet Virgin Mary.

in our conventional assignment of contrasting moods to the major and the minor. *Regina caeli*, in fact, *is* in the major mode to all intents and purposes. Its final, F (tritus), became ever more prevalent in the later Frankish genres; and when it appeared, it was usually given a "signature" of one flat to "soften" progressions from B to F (of which *Regina caeli* is especially full). The resulting "Lydian" octave species, TTST–TTS, is identical to what we would call the major scale. (Its "natural" diatonic occurrence, beginning on C, was not recognized as a mode in its own right until the middle of the sixteenth century, but it was obviously in practical use for centuries before its theoretical description.) The mode here works in tandem with other traditional earmarks of rejoicing, notably "jubilation" (melismas on *portare* and, especially, *alleluia*, replete with internal repeats clearly modeled on those of the Mass Alleluia).

Salve Regina is dark. Like so many late Dorian chants it covers the combined (or "commixed") plagal-authentic ambitus, but its tessitura favors the lower end. (Its official assignment to mode 1 was due, most likely, to the repeated cadences of the concluding acclamations — *O clemens: O pia: O dulcis* — on A.) Although there are no real melismas, there is a great deal of melodic parallelism; indeed, the first two main phrases ("Salve Regina..." and "Vita dulcedo...") are nearly identical. This last, it turns out, is a common feature of many medieval songs, although it is not found in many chants. (It should not be confused with the paired versicles of a sequence, because the first line of a sequence was the one line that was not usually paired.) Compare the melody in Ex. 3-13. This is a *canso*, a song of "courtly love." Its language is Provençal, then the language of what is now central and southern France. The composer, Raimon de Miraval (d. ca. 1215), was a troubadour, that is, a member of the first school of European poets to use for creative purposes one of the then "modern" languages of Europe. Their line began with Guillaume IX, Duke of Aquitaine and Count of Poitiers (1071–1127), a younger contemporary of Adhemar, the putative author of the *Salve Regina*. Like Adhemar, Guillaume took part in the Crusades, as did many other troubadours.

E X. 3-13   Raimon de Miraval, *Aissi cum es genser pascors*

For from the one who is the essence of all virtues
I wish to seek mercy,
And not on account of the first difficulty,
That causes me many sighs and many tears,
Do I despair of the noble succor
That I have long awaited.
And if it pleases her to aid me,
Above all loyal lovers
I shall be blessed with joy.

Raimon's *canso* begins, like the *Salve Regina*, with a repeated melodic phrase. Like the *Salve Regina*, it is a song of devotional praise to a remote, idealized lady. Like the *Salve Regina*, it is a Dorian tune in a lightly neumatic style. The *Salve Regina*, in effect, may thus be looked upon as a canso to the Blessed Virgin. There is no inherent or intrinsic difference between the idioms of sacred and of "secular" devotion, and no stylistic difference between the sacred verse-music of the eleventh and twelfth centuries and such "secular" verse-music as was deemed worthy, beginning in the twelfth century, of preservation in writing.

THEORY AND THE ART OF TEACHING

Before exploring the implications of these statements, though, or taking a closer look at music set to vernacular poetry, or discussing the reasons why the word "secular" is being set off in this context by quotation marks, let us return briefly to the original subject of this chapter, the formulation of new theoretical concepts and their influence on musical practice. There is one more tale to tell.

For a long time, two of the Marian antiphons, *Alma Redemptoris mater* and *Salve Regina*, were attributed to Hermannus Contractus (Hermann the Lame, 1013–1054), a monk at the Swiss abbey of Reichenau. That attribution is no longer credited, but Hermann was a notable poet-composer (of sequences and Offices for local saints) and a major theorist. In his treatise, *Musica*, Hermann proposed surrounding the tetrachord of four finals (D, E, F, G) with a tone on either end, thus producing a six-note diatonic segment or hexachord from C to A, and with symmetrical intervallic content TTSTT.[3] This module, Hermann implied, sums up with the greatest possible economy the tonal range of Gregorian chant. The tetrachord beginning with the first note, C, gives the beginning of the Mixolydian scale as well as that of the adjusted Lydian with B-flat: TTS. (In view of what we have observed about the F mode with B-flat, we could call this the major tetrachord.) If one begins on the second note of the hexachord, one gets the beginning of the Dorian scale, TST (we can call it the minor tetrachord). And by beginning on the third note one derives the essence of the Phrygian, STT. For all practical purposes, this model implies, there are only three finals — not four — and their scales are best thought of as beginning on C, D, and E. It was a step in the direction of what we call major-minor tonality.

Hermann appears to have been unaware of the fact, but his conceptual module had already been abstracted from the chant itself as part of a great pedagogical breakthrough — perhaps the greatest in the history of the literate tradition of music in the West. For it was precisely this breakthrough that at last made "sight-singing" possible and put Western music on a literate footing in truly practical terms. Its importance would be hard to overestimate.

The man responsible for this signal achievement was the same Italian monk, Guido of Arezzo, who around 1030 (in the prologue to an antiphoner) first proposed placing neumes on the lines and spaces of a ruled staff to define their precise pitch content. Guido used special colors, later replaced by alphabet signs, to denote the C and F, "key" lines — *claves* in Latin — that have semitones below them; these letters survive as our

FIG. 3-5   Guido of Arezzo instructing his pupil Theodal at the monochord, from a twelfth-century manuscript in the Austrian National Library, Vienna.

modern "clefs." We, who still rely on his inventions nearly a thousand years later, owe him a lot, as did all the generations of Western musicians preceding us. No wonder he was a legend in his own time, and by now is something of a myth, a musical Prometheus.

The actual Guido lived from about 990 to about 1033 and specialized for most of his fairly brief life in the training of choirboys. Like many teachers of ear training, he was ever on the lookout for melodies (in his case, chiefly chant antiphons) with which to exemplify the various intervals. Imagine his excitement, then, when (as he tells us) he chanced upon a tune that could exemplify all of them. This was the hymn *Ut queant laxis* ("So that tongues might loosen"), composed in the late eighth century by Paul the Deacon, a monk at the Benedictine abbey of Monte Cassino, in honor of the abbey's patron saint, John the Baptist. This hymn tune is so constructed that the first syllable in each half-line is one scale degree higher than the one that precedes it, the whole series exactly tracing out the basic hexachord from C to A (Ex. 3-14). So well does it fit the pedagogical bill that scholars now suspect that Guido actually wrote the melody himself on the familiar words of the hymn.

EX. 3-14   Hymn, *Ut queant laxis*; words by Paul the Deacon, music possibly by Guido d'Arezzo

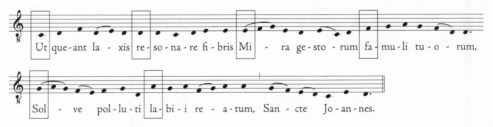

That thy servants may freely proclaim the wonders of thy deeds, absolve the sins of their unclean lips, O holy John.

This module gave a syllable-name (or *vox*, "voice") to each degree (or *locus*, "place") in the hexachord. Once internalized, the set of "musical voices" (*voces musicales*) served a double purpose for ear training. In the first place any interval, ascending or descending, could be demonstrated in terms of a *vox* combination (thus: ut–re, the tone; ut–mi, the major third; ut–fa the perfect fourth; re–fa the minor third; etc.). And, second, the difference between the tone and the semitone, the all-important definer of mode quality, could be mastered by drilling the interval mi–fa.

Around the beginning of the seventeenth century, the syllable *si*, derived from the initials of "Sancte Ioannes," was added by some singing teachers to the Guidonian module so that a full major scale could be sung with model ("solmization") syllables. (In modern practice, as every music student knows, *si* has been replaced by *ti*, and the closed syllable *ut* has been replaced by the open syllable *do*, sometimes spelled "doh" in English speaking countries to avoid confusion with the verb "to do.") Guido, however, who did not as yet have or need the concept of the major scale, managed to complete the octave by transposing the basic module so that it began on G, the hexachord G–E being intervallically identical (or "affined," to use Guido's vocabulary) with C–A. In this new placement, the progression mi–fa corresponds with the semitone B–C. To solmize the full scale from C to c, one "mutates" at some convenient point (either on sol–ut or la–re) from one location of the module to the other, thus (dashes denoting semitones):

```
C   D   E — F G A B — C . . . . . .
ut  re  mi — fa sol la
             ut re mi — fa sol  la
```

To take care of the F-with-B-flat situation, later theorists recognized another transposition of the module, beginning on F, that would place the mi–fa pair on A and B-flat. The whole range of hexachord transpositions thus achieved, mapping out the whole musical space within which Gregorian chant was habitually sung, finally looked like Ex. 3-15.

EX. 3-15   The gamut, or full range of pitches represented on the Guidonian hand, together with the seven hexachords that are required for its solmization. The recurrent pitch names across the bottom of the diagram are called claves in medieval music theory; the recurrent solmization syllables are the voces. An individual pitch, or locus ("place" within the gamut), is specified by a combination of clavis and vox, from Gamma ut (whence "gamut") to E la. What we now call "middle C" was C sol-fa-ut to medieval singers

In order to gain an *ut* at the bottom on which to begin the first set of *voces*, Guido placed a G below the A that normally marked the lower end of the modal system. This extra G was represented by its Greek equivalent, gamma. Its full name within the array

of voces was "Gamma ut," which (shortened to *gamut*) became the name of the array itself. (The word "gamut," of course, has entered the common English vocabulary to denote the full range of anything.) The two versions of B (the one sung as *mi* over G, corresponding to our B natural, and the one sung as *fa* over F, corresponding to B-flat), were assigned to a single mutable space, whose actual pitch realization would depend on the context. The higher B was known as the hard one (*durus*), and was represented by a square-shaped letter that eventually evolved into the modern natural sign. The hexachord containing it was also known as the "hard" hexachord (*hexachordum durum*). The lower one, which softened augmented fourths into perfect ones, was known accordingly as soft (*mollis*) and was represented by a rounded letter that eventually evolved into the modern flat sign. The hexachord containing B-flat (*B-mollis*) was known as the "soft" hexachord (*hexachordum molle*; the original module, derived from the hymn, was called the "natural" hexachord.)

Eventually, the use to which Guido put the C–A hexachord module and the concepts that arose from it, began to influence the more theoretical notion of the hexachord as expounded by Hermann. One now could distinguish pieces ending "on ut" (*Regina caeli*, for example) from pieces ending "on re" (like *Salve Regina*). A whole interval-species could be summoned up by a single syllable. This, too, reinforced the tendency to simplify the concept of mode and reduce it all the more to our familiar major-minor dualism. Eventually the "ut" modes (like G with a B natural) were called *durus*, and "re" modes (like G with a B flat, a "transposed" Dorian) were called *mollis*. This terminology survives to this day in some languages, like German and Russian, as equivalents for major and minor (thus in German G-*dur* means "G major" and g-*moll* means "G minor.") In French and Russian, the word *bémol* (from "B-mollis") denotes the flat sign.

As an aid toward internalizing the whole set of *voces* and applying them to the actual notes written on Guido's other invention, the staff, Guido — or, more likely, later theorists acting in his name — adopted a mnemonic device long used by calendar makers and public speakers, whereby items to be memorized were mapped spiralwise onto the joints of the left palm (Fig. 3-6). (The once widespread use of such devices is still reflected in our daily language by expressions like "rule of thumb" and "at one's fingertips.") In its fully developed musical form (not actually reached until the thirteenth century, two hundred years after Guido), each location on the "Guidonian hand" (and one in space, above the middle finger) represented a musical *locus*, defined by the conjunction of two overlapping cycles: the octave-cycle naming the notes as written (the *claves*, or letter names), and the series of hexachord placements that assigned *voces* to each of the *claves*. A specific locus, then, represents the product of a *clavis* and a *vox*. C *fa ut* (lowest joint of index finger), for example, is the C below middle C (C), and only that C: it can be solmized only in the hard hexachord (in which it is *fa*) and the natural (in which it is *ut*); there is no F below it in the gamut, so it cannot be solmized as sol. Middle C (c, top joint of ring finger) is C *sol fa ut*: it can be solmized in all three hexachords. The C above middle C (cc, second joint of ring finger), and only that C, is C *sol fa*, for it can only be solmized in the soft and hard hexachords. To sing it as *ut* would imply that the gamut (or "hand," as it was fondly called) continued past its upper limit.

Armed with the memorized and internalized gamut, a singer could parse a written melody into its constituent intervals without hearing it or hunting for it on a monochord. The first phrase of *Salve Regina* (Ex. 3-10b), for example, could be seen at a glance to lie exactly within the compass of the natural hexachord, in which it would be solmized with these *voces*: /la sol la re/ (Salve); /la sol fa mi fa sol fa mi re/ (Regina); /ut re re ut re mi fa sol re mi ut re / (mater misericordiae). All of *Regina caeli* (Ex. 3-10a) lies within a single soft hexachord. The beginning of the second phrase ("Quia quem meruisti"), the first that encompasses the entire range of the chant, would take

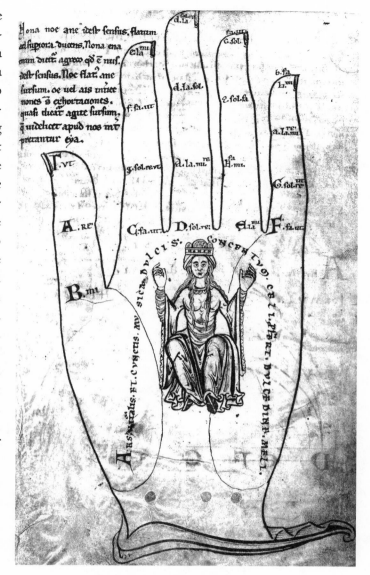

FIG. 3-6   The "Guidonian hand" as represented in a thirteenth-century Bavarian manuscript.

these *voces*: /ut sol sol la la sol fa mi re ut re mi mi/. Finally, here are the *voces* for the first "Kyrie" acclamation and the first "Christe" in Kyrie IX (Ex. 3-4):

Kyrie: /re fa sol la sol fa mi re fa re ut re ut re fa sol fa mi re/(natural hexachord).
Christe: /mi mi re fa mi re re ut re fa re mi/(soft hexachord).

Except for the beginning of the second "Kyrie" invocation, which extends down into the first hard (or "gamma") hexachord (syllables: re fa sol sol), the whole of Kyrie IX can be solmized using one natural and one soft hexachord. It would be a good exercise for the reader. Another good exercise would be to seek out phrases in the chants used as examples in this book so far that exceed the interval of a sixth, and that therefore require a mutation for their proper solmization. *Salve Regina* contains a number of interesting examples of this type. The phrase "Ad te suspiramus, gementes et flentes" requires a mutation from natural to soft and back again, thus: /re fa la (think *mi*) sol re re ut re mi (think *la*), re fa sol sol re fa mi re ut/. The phrase "Eia ergo, Advocata nostra, illos tuos misericordes oculos" is tricky: it begins in the soft hexachord, and descends into the natural; but when the upper range is regained, mutation must be not to the soft hexachord but to the hard, since the melody (as the alert singer will have scanned ahead to notice) has a B-natural, not a B-flat, thus: /ut ut re ut re mi mi, sol re mi re ut (think *fa*) re sol la (think *re*), sol sol fa mi fa sol re sol fa re ut (think *fa*) la sol fa mi fa mi re ut/. At "nobis," however, where the B-flat is called for, so is the soft hexachord: /re la (think *mi*) fa mi/.

Armed with these techniques, and with Guido's hand stored in memory for ready reference, a singer could truly sing at sight, or (as Guido put it in the title of his famous epistle of 1032) "sing an unknown melody." Reinforced over centuries of practice, this pedagogical aid wrought enormous changes in the way music was disseminated and thought about. When transmission from composer to performer could take place impersonally, without direct oral/aural contact, music became that much less a process or a social act, and that much more a tangible, autonomous thing. The notion of a "piece" of music could only arise when music began to be thought of in terms of actual pieces of paper or parchment. For these far-reaching conceptual changes, we have the legendary Guido, the greatest ear trainer of them all, to thank. He turned out to be even more a trainer of eyes and minds than of ears.

Music of Feudalism and *Fin' Amors*

THE EARLIEST LITERATE SECULAR REPERTORIES: AQUITAINE, FRANCE, IBERIA, ITALY, GERMANY

BINARISMS

One of the lessons the study of history can teach us is to appreciate the futility of rigidly oppositional distinctions and to resist them. Hard and fast antitheses, often called binarisms, are conceptual rather than empirical: that is, they are more likely to be found in the clean laboratories of our minds than in the messy world our bodies inhabit. (And even to say this much is to commit several errors of arbitrary opposition.) One can hardly avoid categories; they simplify experience and, above all, simplify the stories we tell. They make things intelligible. Without them, writing a book like this—let alone reading it!—would be virtually impossible. And yet they involve sacrifice as well as gain.

The invention of staff notation, placed at the climax of the previous chapter and presented as a great victory, is a case in point. The gain in (apparent) precision was accompanied by a definite loss in variety. The staff is nothing if not an instrument for imposing hard distinctions: between A and B, between B and C, and so forth. These distinctions are gross as well as hard; singing from a staff is like putting frets on one's vocal cords. One has only to compare the staffless neumes of early chant manuscripts with the staved notations of the "post-Guidonian" era to see how much more stylized notation had to become—and how much farther, one must conclude, from the oral practice it purported to transcribe—in order to furnish the precise information about pitch that we now prize. A whole category of ornamental neumes (called *liquescent*, implying fluidity, flexibility of voice, and, most likely, intonation "in the cracks") was sacrificed, and eventually lost from practice. No one knows today just what they once signified. The precision of staff notation, like the precision of the modal theory that preceded and preconditioned it, regularized certain aspects of music and made many developments possible. Yet at the same time they foreclosed other aspects and potential developments that other musical cultures have continued to prize and to cultivate. Anyone who has heard the classical music of Iran or India will have an idea of what may have been lost from the European tradition.

On a more conceptual plane, consider the distinction between sacred and secular. Up to now only the former has figured in our story, simply because only it was available for description. Now we are about to encounter the earliest available secular repertories—the first musical repertories that were not intended for use in divine worship but were nevertheless deemed worthy of preservation in writing. On the basis of the firm distinction between the sacred and the secular on which, for example, our present-day institutions of government depend, we may tend to assume that secular music will contrast radically with sacred. Perhaps some did; the writings of the early Church Fathers abound in condemnations of "licentious songs" that express and arouse "passions sprung of lack of breeding and baseness,"[1] or that call forth "the Devil's great heap of garbage."[2] But we don't know these songs. We will never know exactly how they differed from the music of which the Fathers approved, and we may even suspect that what made them objectionable had less to do with their essential nature or "style" than with the occasions at which they were sung, or with the people who sang them. "Sacred" and "secular" are not so much styles as uses. The distinction between them is at least as much a social as a generic one.

AQUITAINE

TROUBADOURS

The earliest secular repertories of which we have direct knowledge consist of songs by knightly poets of courtly love and feudal service. Stylistically, they are remarkably like the sacred repertories with which we have been dealing so far. Not that this should surprise us: if these secular songs were thought worthy of commemoration and permanence (that is, worthy of writing down), they must have had some transcendent or elevating purpose like that of the sacred. And as surely as style follows function, a like purpose should entail a like manner.

The earliest such written-down knightly songs in a European vernacular (that is, a currently and locally spoken language) originated in Aquitaine, a duchy whose territory occupied parts of what is now southern and south-central France. It had been conquered by Charlemagne in the late eighth century and incorporated into the Carolingian Empire; but with the weakening of the Empire as a result of invasions by Normans on one side and Muslims on the other, royal influence over Aquitaine gave way over the course of the ninth and tenth centuries to several independent noble families who established local jurisdictions and maintained networks of patronage and protection among themselves. Eventually the counts of Poitou emerged as the most powerful among these clans and, from 973, asserted dominion over the whole territory and took the title of Duke. (Later, the marriage of the duchess Aliénor or Eleanor of Aquitaine to the French king in 1137 joined Aquitaine to France; and her second marriage, to the Norman duke who later became King Henry II of England, led to a long struggle over the territory that would not be ended until the fifteenth century.)

It was during the period of Aquitaine's relative independence that its courtly poetic and musical traditions arose. William (Guillaume), seventh count of Poitiers and ninth duke of Aquitaine (1071–ca. 1127), was the first European vernacular poet whose work has come down to us. The tradition, socially speaking, thus began right at the top, with all that that implies as to "highness" of style, tone, and diction. The language William used was Provençal, alias Occitan or *langue d'oc*, from the local word for "yes." (Old French, spoken to the north, was called *langue d'oïl* for the same reason.) In Provençal, poetry was called *trobar*, meaning words "found," and a poet was called a *trobador*, a "finder" of words. In English we use the Frenchified form, troubadour.

A troubadour's subject matter was the life he led, viewed in terms of his social relations, which were ceremonial, idealized, and ritualized to the point of virtual sacralization. In keeping with the rarefied subject matter, the genres and styles of troubadour verse were also highly formalized and ceremonious, to the point of virtuosic complexity of design and occasional, sometimes deliberate, obscurity of meaning.

The genres reflected social relations directly. Feudalism, arising in unsettled conditions of weak central power and frequent ruinous invasion, was based on land grants and on contractual, consensual exchanges of service and protection on which everyone's welfare depended. The bonds of honor thus pledged were taken very seriously indeed. The utopian ideal — never realized except (more or less theoretically) in the tiny, short-lived "Latin Kingdom of Jerusalem" established by the Crusaders in 1099 — was a wholly hierarchical — and therefore, theoretically, a wholly harmonious — society. Under feudalism, all land was legally owned by an elected (rather than a hereditary) king, who deeded and parceled it out to the greatest nobles in the form of "fiefs" (from the Latin *feodum*, whence "feudal"), who deeded it in turn to lesser nobles, and so on down to the manorial barons and their serfs, who actually worked it.

The granting of a fief created the relationship of lord (or suzerain) and vassal. The bond thus created was solemnized downright liturgically, in a ritual of homage whereby the vassal, placing his hands in the lord's, swore an oath of fealty that obliged him to perform certain specified acts and services, including military service. The suzerain, in turn, bound himself to protect the vassal from incursions. The feudal nobility was thus primarily a military caste system, a hierarchy of knights or warriors-in-service. These military bonds were at first envisioned as a system of mutual defense (although in reality disruptive conflict among lords was common), but in the period of the Crusades the knightly armies went on the offensive. William IX of Aquitaine, our first troubadour, led a Crusade himself in 1101; his unlucky army never reached the Holy Land.

Several genres of troubadour verse celebrated feudal ideals. A *sirventes* was a song from vassal to lord about knightly service or about some theme of political alliance; such a song could be either serious or satirical. An *enueg* (compare the French *ennui*) was a complaint about infractions of knightly decorum. A *gap* (compare *jape* or *gibe*) was a bluster-song, glorifying one's own exploits or issuing a challenge. The most serious of such types was the *planh* (compare the French *plainte*), a eulogy on the death of a lord. There were also many songs about crusading zeal.

The true heart of the troubadour legacy, however, was the *canso*, which means a love poem — or better, perhaps, a poem about love. For the love celebrated by knightly singers was just as "high," just as formalized and ritualized, as any other publicly enunciated theme. And the poems of the troubadours were always meant for public performance—hence the music!—not for private reading; theirs was still an eminently oral tradition. Modern scholars have christened the subject of the *canso* "courtly love" (*amour courtoise*); the troubadours themselves called it *fin' amors*, "refined love," defined by one modern authority as "a great imaginative and spiritual superstructure built on the foundation of sexual attraction."

It is widely thought that Arabic sung poetry—known in southern Europe from the ninth century, and also emphasizing secret love and the spiritualization of the erotic (including the homoerotic)—had a formative influence on the concept of *fin' amors*. Its main genre is the *nawba* (or *nuba*), a lengthy vocal performance accompanied by the *oud* (literally "wood"), a gourd-shaped plucked-string instrument from which the European lute had been adapted by the thirteenth century. It consisted of several stanzas (some in Arabic and some in Persian), connected with improvisatory instrumental interludes. No musical relationship between the *nawba* and the troubadour repertory has as yet been definitely established, but some modern performers of early music have experimented effectively with performance practices derived from those of present-day Arab musicians.

The love songs of the troubadours were like their knightly songs in that they emphasized service and the idolization of those above, as the lady was invariably held to be. The style was self-consciously lofty, as exemplified by the imagery of the most famous of all cansos, *Can vei la lauzeta mover* by Bernart de Ventadorn (d. ca. 1200), which begins with an unforgettable metaphor comparing the joy of love to the soaring and swooping of a lark in flight. This is contrasted with the lovesick poet's unhappy state, condemned to adore a cold and unresponsive lady from afar.

Fin' amors was furtive and hopeless as a matter of course, because the lady was always held to outrank her lover. She was married into the bargain, as a rule, though often left alone for long periods while her husband was out on campaigns or Crusades. At such times she was the effective ruler of his domain, as the Occitan word for lady—*domna*—already suggests (compare the Latin *domina* and the Italian *donna*). Her identity is always concealed behind a code name (*senhal*; in Bernart's song it is Tristan), supposedly known only to the lady and her lover.

FIG. 4-1 Medieval lutenist, from an illumination in a thirteenth-century manuscript now at the Biblioteca Nazionale in Florence, Italy. The instrument he is playing entered Europe as war booty from the Crusades.

But secrecy and illegitimacy should not be confused with licentiousness. The conventions of *fin' amors* heightened the unavailability of the lady as actual lover and made her an object not of lust but of veneration. The *canso* was thus essentially a devotional song, a song of worship—another link with the sacred sphere, especially with the burgeoning liturgy of the Blessed Virgin. Veneration of the lady, like veneration of Mary, promoted not license or sensuality but rather the sublimation of amorous desire in charity, self-mortification, and acts of virtue. It was another bond of honor, hence a quintessentially feudal attitude.

MINSTRELS

In Bernart's case it was easy enough to feel outranked by the lady: like many of the later troubadours, he was a commoner — according to various traditions the son of the baker or the furnace stoker in the castle of Ventadorn, near Poitiers — who rose to prominence, and received noble patronage, strictly on his merits as a poet. (Bernart's patron was Eleanor of Aquitaine herself, with whom he traveled to France after her first marriage, and to England after her second, thus spreading his art abroad.) While the art of the troubadours was a quintessentially aristocratic art, an art of the castle, it was not an art practiced only by aristocrats. Rather, whoever the actual practitioner may have been, it was an art cultivated and patronized by aristocrats and expressive of their outlook.

Indeed, the actual practice — the actual performance, that is, of the noble song-

FIG. 4-2 Bernart de Ventadorn, from an illumination accompanying his *vida*, the biographical preface to his collected song texts without melodies, in a manuscript copied in Italy in the late thirteenth or early fourteenth century, by which time the Occitan culture of southern France had already been destroyed. (Only five of the thirty-seven manuscripts known to have contained troubadour songs had musical notations.) The manuscript found its way to the Bibliothèque Nationale in Paris as war booty, having been confiscated from the Vatican Library by Napoleon's army. The portrait of Bernart, dating from at least a century after his death, is obviously fanciful.

product — was usually left to what we now call minstrels: professionals of a lower caste, singer-entertainers called *joglars* in Provençal (*jongleurs* in French, both from the Latin *joculatores*, "jokers"); the derivation of our English word "juggler" from *joglar* should leave no doubt about its subartistic connotation. Most of the commoner-troubadours like Bernart started out as minstrels who learned the work of the noble poets by rote and who later developed creative facility in their own right. The relationship of troubadour to minstrel, and particularly the means of transmission from the one to the other, attest that the art of the troubadours remained an oral art. A noble poet would compose a song and teach it to a minstrel, thus sending it out into the oral tradition from which it might be transcribed, with luck, a hundred years later.

For written documentation of the troubadour art began only when the tradition was already moribund. The manuscripts containing troubadour songs, called *chansonniers*, are retrospective anthologies prepared in the middle of the thirteenth century. (Any song found in multiple copies in these late sources exists in multiple variants, thus precluding the restoration of a definitive "text," assuming there ever was such a thing.) Besides the songs themselves, chansonniers contain fanciful portraits and biographies (*vidas*) of the poets. Their purpose was commemorative and decorative; they had nothing to do with practice or performance. They were "art objects," rich "collectibles."

That the composition of troubadour songs was just as much an oral practice as their transmission and performance is shown by a very revealing anecdote in the *vida* of Arnaut Daniel, one of the greatest knightly poets, known for his exceptional virtuosity in rhyme. It supposedly happened at the court of Richard I (Lion-Heart), Eleanor's son. Another troubadour had boasted that he could compose a better poem than Arnaut and challenged him to a contest. The king confined the two poets to different rooms in his castle, stipulating that at the end of the day they were to appear before him and recite their new poems, whereupon Richard would determine the winner of the bet. Arnaut's inspiration failed him; but from his room he could hear his rival singing as he composed his song, and learned it by heart. When the time of the trial came he asked to perform first and sang his rival's song, leaving the latter to look like the copycat.

Like many of the anecdotes in the vidas, this one probably never happened. (There is no corroborating evidence that Arnaut, himself a nobleman, was ever in anyone's employ, or that he knew Richard, or that he went to England.) But, as the Italian proverb has it, *se non è vero, è ben trovato*: "even if it isn't true, it's very apt (literally, well made-up)" — and note how the Italian for "making up" comes from the same root stock as *trobar*. What is so apt about it, and revealing, are the points the author of the vida took for granted: first, that a troubadour in the act of composition did not write but sang aloud; and second, that a troubadour could memorize a song at an aural glance. These are the assumptions of an oral culture.

It was that congruence of creating and performing as oral acts, and that ease of memorization, that made the minstrel an apt and necessary accessory to the troubadour. Yet because the creation of poetry, as opposed to its performance, was nevertheless viewed as a noble pastime rather than a profession, it could be practiced by lords — and by ladies, too. The vidas tell us of at least twenty lady troubadours (for which the Provençal word was *trobairitz*) who created courtly songs but never sang them, at least in public.

HIGH (LATINATE) AND LOW ("POPULAR") STYLE

The only type of troubadour love song that emphasized the joy of consummation was the thrilling genre known as the *alba*, or "dawn-song." The lovers, having passed a clandestine night together in oblivious bliss, are aroused — by the sun, by singing birds, by a watchman's cry, or by a confidant — to the breaking day and to the peril of discovery. The most famous alba was *Reis glorios* by Guiraut de Bornelh, a contemporary of Bernart and, like him, a commoner whose skill found favor with the noble audiences (Ex. 4-1). Where Bernart's stanza (or *cobla*, to use the Occitan word) had consisted, in *Can vei la lauzeta*, of eight different phrases, each corresponding to a line of poetry, Guiraut's is regularized by an initial melodic repetition (or *pes*) — as in the *Salve Regina* melody discussed in the previous chapter—and by a concluding refrain as in, say, a Frankish Kyrie. The resemblance of Guiraut's melody to that of the Kyrie verse *Cunctipotens genitor* (Ex. 2-14b) has been noted.

EX. 4-1   Guiraut de Bornelh, *Reis glorios* (first verse)

Reis glo-ri-os ve - rais lums _ e clar - tatz _ Deus po-de-ros, Se - nher, si ____ a vos __ platz, _

Al ___ meu com-panh si-atz fi-zels a-iu - da _ Qu'eu non lo vi __ pos __ la nochs _ fo ven-gu - da

Et a-des se - ra ____ l'al - ba. _

Glorious king, true light and clarity,
Powerful God, Lord, if it please You,
To my companion be a faithful aid,
For I have not seen him since the night came,
And soon it will be dawn.

The higher the style of a troubadour melody, the more likely were its chant affinities. Comparison of Bernart's or Guiraut's melodies with those of the late Frankish chant discloses a great similarity of style. Like *Salve Regina* or Kyrie IX, they are exemplary "first mode" melodies according to the rationalized concept of mode studied in chapter 3. (The composers probably picked up the style by ear on the basis of the chants they heard sung.) There are even instances that show the influence of late chant poetry on troubadour diction and sentiment. A familiar Provençal dictum—*fin' amors, fons de bontat*, "courteous love is the source of all goodness"—echoes in close cognates the tenth-century Kyrie verse *Fons bonitatis*. (Its third-mode melody, shorn of the verse but still sporting the incipit as a title, can be found in modern chant books as "Kyrie II.") The hypothesis that the music of troubadour song—the performance medium of a liturgy of aristocratic mores—aped the actual liturgical music of its time has been gaining strength as more is learned about actual twelfth-century chant. Quite near William the Ninth's seat at Poitiers was Limoges, another Aquitanian town and the site of the Benedictine abbey of St. Martial, the greatest center for the production of Latin *versus* on which the troubadours modeled their *vers* (to use the Provençal word for poetry-with-music).

Rhythmically and formally, Latin *versus* (or *conductus* as it was called in northern France) was just as various and almost as virtuosic as troubadour songs. Actual Provençal words occasionally appear in *versus* from St. Martial. Most striking of all, there are subgenres of *versus* that, like the most elevated troubadour genres, straddle the nebulous line between the sacred and the secular. Some of them have actual troubadour parallels, for example the *planctus* (=*planh*). St. Martial manuscripts contain a celebrated planctus for Charlemagne and an even more illustrious song called *planctus cigni* ("The

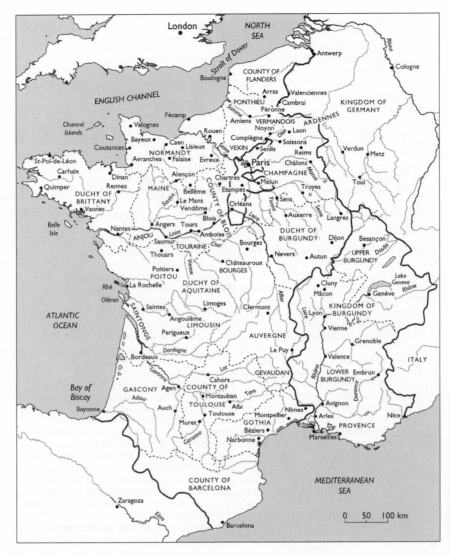

FIG. 4-3   The Languedoc region in the twelfth century. Note the close proximity of Limoges, the monastic center, where Latin liturgical poetry to music was composed in profusion; and Poitiers, the center of troubadour activity.

lament of the swan"), a moving metaphor of exile, in which a swan, caught in a storm over the sea, laments the loss of its verdant homeland. The famous theologian Pierre Abelard (1079–1142), an exact contemporary of William of Aquitaine, wrote six *planctus* on biblical themes, two of which exist in staff notation. A large collection of *versus* in an early thirteenth-century French manuscript best known for polyphonic music includes *planctus* commemorating a whole honor roll of recently deceased aristocrats and churchmen, and what may be described as Latin *sirventes* (one of them concerning Pope Innocent III's excommunication of Otto IV, the Holy Roman Emperor, in 1210 and the ensuing war of succession). Many *planctus* settings (including the *planctus cigni*) are in a form resembling the older (pre-"Victorine") liturgical sequence, with its melodically paired verses of differing lengths. This form, too, had its Provençal counterpart, called the *descort*. The name, translated literally, means "discordant," the idea being that its component stanzas are in varying (disagreeing) rhyme and meter schemes, requiring new melodies for each. Such a structure particularly suited narrative poems.

Other troubadour genres or individual melodies affected a mock-popular style that may have drawn stylistically not on chant but on otherwise unrecorded folk idioms. *A chantar m'er de so gu'en no volria* ("I must sing of that which I would rather not"), the one poem with surviving tune attributed to the late twelfth-century *trobairitz* Beatriz, Countess of Dia, departs markedly from the chant idiom. Its overall structure is that of the regularized or "rounded" canso with its repeated couplet and final refrain (AB AB CD B), but the tune alternates cadences on E and D in a fashion never encountered in first-mode chants but common in the dances and dance songs of a slightly later period. (Such endings would be designated *ouvert* and *clos* — "open" and "shut" — in thirteenth century dance manuscripts; they correspond to, and prefigure, what we would now call half and full cadences.) One genre that always affected a mock-popular tone was the *pastorela*, in which a knight seduces (or tries to seduce) a shepherdess. The best-known survivor of this genre is *L'autrier jost' una sebissa* ("The other day by a hedge row") by Marcabru (or Marcabrun), one of the early troubadours, who served in his youth at the court of William of Aquitaine and who memorialized his patron in a Crusader song (*Pax! In nomine Domini*, "Peace! In the name of the Lord") that actually mixes Latin verses with vernacular ones. Texts that do this are called *macaronic* ("jumbled" like macaroni).

Another mock-popular genre was the *balada*, or dance-song, of which a rare surviving example is the anonymous *A l'entrada del tens clar* (Ex. 4-2). This melody, of an altogether different character from the preceding ones, seems to be a sophisticated imitation folk song with its call-and-response verses (ending with "Eya," Occitan for "Hey!"), its half and full cadences, and its lengthy refrain.

EX. 4-2   *A l'entrada del tens clar* (balada)

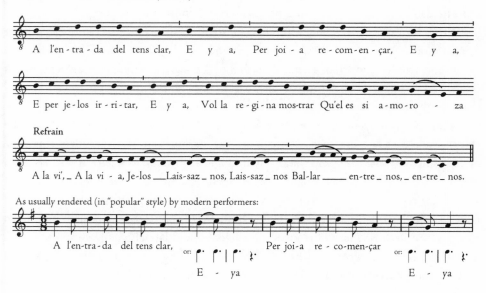

113

EX. 4-2   (continued)

E - per je - los ir - ri - tar   E - ya,   Vol - la re - gi - na mo-strar Qu'el es si a - mo-

ro - za   A la vi',___   A la vi',___   Je - los   Lais - saz ___ nos   Lais - saz ___ nos

Bal - ler _____   en - tre ___ nos, ___   en - tre ___ nos.

When sunny days begin,
To renew joy
And provoke the jealous
The queen decides to show
That she is madly in love.
Be on your way, jealous folk,
Leave us to our dance.

RHYTHM AND METER

If, as the text suggests, this song is meant to accompany a *carole*, an actual public dance, then its rhythm has got to be metrical. No such information is conveyed by the actual notation, which like that of the other troubadour melodies is indistinguishable from the "quadratic notation" (notation with square note-heads) used in contemporary chant manuscripts. ("Contemporary" here means thirteenth-century, the period of the retrospective *chansonniers*.) Meter has to be supplied conjecturally, on the basis of the words. In the case of a dance, no one is likely to object to such a conjecture; but the question of the proper rhythmic style for troubadour songs — indeed, for verse-music in general before the thirteenth century — is one of the most hotly contested issues in musical scholarship.

The poetry is of course metered; indeed, metrical design (along with rhyme scheme) was a field in which the troubadours vied to excel one another in virtuosity. The question is whether the metric patterning was reflected in the music in patterns of note lengths or by means of stress patterns. Or, as some maintain, were the troubadour songs performed in a supple rhythm modeled, perhaps, on that of the sacred chant? Such an attribute of "high" style would free the troubadour art from any taint of the "popular" — if indeed that was thought desirable.

This is certainly not the place to adjudicate such a question; but it should be emphasized that we are just as much in the dark about the intended rhythmic performance of *versus* (or even Frankish hymns and sequences) as we are about *vers*. And it should be noted that the scholarly consensus has lately been swinging, in the case of all of these repertories, away from the a position (now regarded as anachronistic) that favored applying quantitative meters wherever possible. This theory, which dominated editions and performances of troubadour melodies and late chants alike in the earlier part of the twentieth century, was based on a misreading of treatises on the rhythmic performance of late medieval polyphonic music (to be described in chapter 6).

The approach most favored now is the so-called "isosyllabic" approach, whereby all syllables, whether sung to a single note or to a group or two or three notes, are given roughly equal length. Another possibility, which also has its adherents, is the "equalist" approach that makes precisely the opposite assumption. It gives all notes the same length, regardless of how many of them are given to a syllable. This fairly radical "solution" to the problem of rhythmic interpretation is the one recommended by the editors of modern chant books (officially adopted by the Catholic church in 1904 and in general Catholic use until 1963), and is therefore the one most widely practiced today wherever the Gregorian chant is still sung as service music.

TROBAR CLUS

There is one more important genre of troubadour poetry with music: the *tenso* (or *joc-partit*), an often jesting debate-song that involves two or more interlocutors, and that was sometimes, but not necessarily, actually a joint composition by two or more poets. The subject matter could be some fine point of love or feudal service (like, "if you love a lady, would it be better to be married to her or to have her love you back?"), or it could be — and most often was — about poetry itself. Here the troubadour addressed his craft directly and with marvelous self-consciousness. The tenso was thus a sort of school for poets and can be extremely instructive for us.

One of the favorite themes for debate was the eternal conflict between *trobar clus* and *trobar clar*, between "closed" or difficult poetry for connoisseurs and "clear" poetry designed for immediate pleasure and easy communication. The virtues claimed for the first were its technical prowess, its density of meaning, and the exclusive nature of its appeal, which lent it an ability to create an elite occasion and foster solidarity among a coterie of insiders. It promoted social division and hierarchy, and was therefore an art quintessentially expressive of aristocratic values. The virtues claimed for the second were its *greater* technical prowess (or so it was argued, since as the Roman poet Horace famously remarked, the greatest art is the art that conceals art) and its power to create a sense of community and shared values. Within the narrow social context of troubadour culture this is hardly to be looked upon as a "democratic" ideal. It might better be regarded as a feudal piety.

These arguments were given an early, classic exposition in a tenso by Guiraut de Bornelh, a recent convert to *trobar clar*, in mock debate with a fellow troubadour, Raimbaut d'Aurenga (called Linhaure), who remained loyal to *trobar clus*. The melody, unfortunately, has not survived. In somewhat abridged translation, the dispute runs as follows:

> 1. I should like to know, G. de Bornelh, why you keep blaming the obscure style. Tell me if you prize so highly that which is common to all? For then would all be equal.
> 2. Sir Linhaure, I do not take it to heart if each man composes as he pleases; but judge that song is more loved and prized which is made easy and simple, and do not be vexed at my opinion.
> 3. Guiraut, I do not like my songs to be so confused, that the base and good, the small and great be appraised alike; my poetry will never be praised by fools, for they have no understanding nor care for what is more precious and valuable.

4. Linhaure, if I work late and turn my rest into weariness to make my songs simple, does it seem that I am afraid of work? Why compose if you do not want all to understand? Song brings no other advantage.

5. Guiraut, provided that I produce what is best at all times, I care not if it be not so widespread; commonplaces are no good for the appreciative—that is why gold is more valued than salt, and with song it is just the same.[3]

For the troubadours, these opposing sentiments were not so much passionately held convictions as postures; many poets cultivated both styles depending on the occasion and saw no compelling reason to choose between them. And yet the debate continues. It will run through this book like a red thread, steadily gathering force and urgency as the audience for art changes (and inexorably widens) over time. For one of the enduring characteristics of "high art," and a perennial source of contention, is the fact that it is produced by and for political and social elites. That, after all, is what makes it "high." But then there can be many reasons for hiding meaning, and not all of them are proud.

Nor is original purpose an inherent limitation on meaning or value. Art devised to serve the interests or the needs of a feudal aristocracy must be serving other interests now, if it is serving any interests at all. And yet *trobar clus* and *trobar clar*, by other names and in other forms, are with us still. Each still has its ardent defenders and its adamant detractors. Their subtexts and agendas are many. There is no more consequential theme in the history of art.

The art of the troubadours lasted about two hundred years. It declined together with the Provençal culture that sustained it. Many of the later troubadours fled southward, into present-day Spain and Italy, at the time of the so-called Albigensian Crusade (from 1208). This was a drawn-out, devastating war of aggression waged by the northern French against the courts of Languedoc under pretext of a religious campaign. (The ostensible targets were the so-called Cathari or Albigenses, adherents of an old philosophical tradition called Manicheism that had been declared a heresy by the Catholic Church.) Guiraut Riquier (ca. 1230–ca. 1300), the last of the troubadours, found employment at the court of Alfonso X of Castile, which became a major center of vernacular courtly and devotional song in the later thirteenth century, but no longer in Provençal. Nor was Guiraut the only troubadour who stimulated the spread of vernacular poetry into other languages. As we will see, the nobleman Arnaut Daniel (by common consent the preeminent master of *trobar clus*) had a formative, if posthumous, influence on the art of Dante and Petrarch, as well as their fourteenth-century Italian musical contemporaries. But long before that, indeed by the end of the thirteenth century, the art of the troubadour was at an end.

FRANCE

TROUVÈRES

By that time, however, it had spawned a hardy successor in northern France itself, despite hostilities between the northern courts and those of Languedoc. The earliest

French imitations of Provençal lyrics, by poet-musicians who called themselves *trouvères* (in direct translation from the Occitan), were composed something less than a century after the Provençal tradition had its start, and gathered strength all through the thirteenth century while the art of the troubadours declined.

One of the main brokers of this northward migration was Eleanor of Aquitaine herself. She was the granddaughter of the first troubadour, the patron of a great troubadour (Bernart de Ventadorn), whom she brought with her up to France, and both mother and great-grandmother of notable trouvères. Eleanor's trouvère son, Richard I (Lion-Heart), though born in England and eventually his father's successor as king (1189–99), had succeeded first to the titles of his great-grandfather William and lived most of his life in Aquitaine. He never learned English. His poems are found in both Provençal and French sources; the only one to survive with its melody (or, at any rate, with a melody) is found only in French.

That song, *Ja nun hons pris* (Ex. 4-3), while cast in a form resembling the *canso* (or, in French, *chanson courtoise*), is not about love but about honor. It is a lament on his famous captivity (1192–94) following the Third Crusade, when his enemy Leopold V of Austria held him for the proverbial "king's ransom," a ruinous levy that was eventually raised by Richard's English subjects. (Apocryphal though it almost surely is, one cannot omit the "well-found" legend that Richard's squire and fellow trouvère Blondel de Nesle succeeded in learning the captured king's whereabouts by singing one of Richard's songs within the royal earshot and hearing the King come back in turn with the refrain. The tale goes back to the thirteenth century and in 1784 was turned into an opera by the French composer André Grétry, in which Richard's "romance," as imagined by

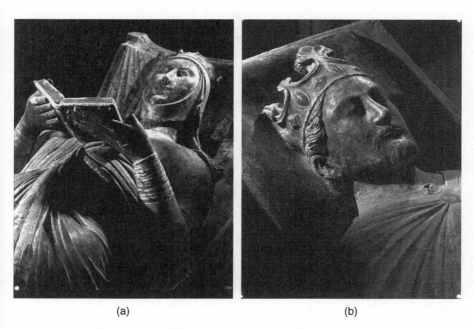

(a)   (b)

FIG. 4-4   Tomb effigies of (a) Eleanor of Aquitaine and (b) her son, Richard I (Lion-Heart), in the crypt of the Plantagenet kings at the Abbey of Fontevrault, France.

Grétry, is a dramatically recurring "leitmotif." True or false, the story certainly shows the importance the knight-crusaders attached to their musical activity.)

EX. 4-3   Richard Coeur-de-Lion (Lion-Heart), *Ja nun hons pris* (first verse)

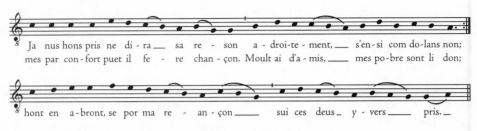

Ja nus hons pris ne di - ra __ sa re - son a - droi-te-ment, __ s'en-si com do-lans non;
mes par con-fort puet il fe - re chan - çon. Moult ai d'a - mis, __ mes po-bre sont li don;

hont en a-bront, se por ma re - an - çon ___ sui ces deus _ y - vers ___ pris. _

> No prisoner will ever speak his mind
>   fittingly unless he speaks in grief.
> But he can, for consolation, make a song.
>   I have many friends, but their gifts are poor.
> It will be their shame if, for want of ransom,
>   I stay these two winters prisoner.

In its thirteenth-century sources Richard's song is classified as a *rotrouenge*, a term modern scholars have not yet succeeded in defining. It may mean no more than a song in the vernacular rather than Latin, but it probably has to do with the use of a concluding tag line or refrain. The form of the song will be familiar with its initial melodic repetition or *pes*, producing the stanzaic pattern *aab*. We first encountered it in the *Salve Regina* (it can be traced further back yet, all the way to the classical Greek ode), and we will re-encounter it again and again in later repertories. The German guild poets called *Meistersinger* ("master singers"; about them see below) finally gave it a name — "bar form" — in the fifteenth century, and we might as well borrow it back from them to describe their forgotten model. (The term came from the jargon of fencing, in which a *bar* or *barat* meant a well-aimed thrust.)

Eleanor's trouvère great-grandson was Thibaut IV (1201–53), Count of Champagne and King of Navarre in what are now the Spanish Pyrenees. He was one of the most prolific of the French noble poets at the very height of their activity. His grandmother, Countess Marie of Champagne, Eleanor's daughter by her first marriage, was the patron of Gace Brulé (ca. 1160–sometime after 1213), the first great trouvère, from whom Thibaut may have begun to learn his craft. Between them Gace and Thibaut turned out 110 songs with surviving music (62 and 48 respectively; of course these numbers reflect the much higher general survival rate among trouvère songs compared with those of the troubadours). Thibaut's *De bone amour vient seance et bonté* ("From love all wisdom and goodness come") expresses the conventional, by now somewhat hackneyed if elegant sentiments of *fine amours* (to use the French variant of the phrase) in the equally stereotyped ode or bar form, by now the stock formal mold for channeling lofty expression (Ex. 4-4).

The foregoing pair of songs, by a pair of kings, shows how closely the early trouvère repertory was modeled on its Provençal progenitor. As long as the art of the trouvère remained an art of the castle, it seemed to differ little, except in language, from the art

E X. 4-4   Thibaut IV de Champagne, *De bone amour vient seance et bonté* (first verse)

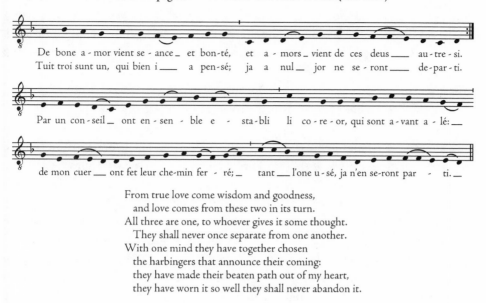

De bone a - mor vient se - ance — et bon-té, et a - mors — vient de ces deus —— au-tre - si.
Tuit troi sunt un, qui bien i — a pen-sé; ja a nul — jor ne se - ront —— de-par-ti.

Par un con-seil — ont en - sen - ble e - sta-bli li co - re - or, qui sont a-vant a - lé: —

de mon cuer — ont fet leur che-min fer - ré; — tant — l'one u - sé, ja n'en se-ront par - ti. —

> From true love come wisdom and goodness,
>   and love comes from these two in its turn.
> All three are one, to whoever gives it some thought.
>   They shall never once separate from one another.
> With one mind they have together chosen
>   the harbingers that announce their coming:
> they have made their beaten path out of my heart,
>   they have worn it so well they shall never abandon it.

of the troubadour. And yet from the very beginning there were in fact some subtle but significant differences, both on the level of form and style and on that of social attitude and practice; and they became more pronounced with the passage of time.

SOCIAL TRANSFORMATION

To begin with, narrative genres loomed much larger in the trouvère repertory and vied more seriously with the lyric genres for pride of place. The *lai*, a sequence-like series of changing stanzas held together by a story line, was much more important to the trouvères than its Provençal counterpart, the *descort*, had ever been to the troubadours. This reflects the longstanding popularity of narrative poetry (romances and *chansons de geste*, "songs of deeds") in the north. It was a Celtic rather than a Mediterranean inheritance. One of the earliest trouvères, Chrétien de Troyes, who was active at the court of Marie of Champagne from the 1160s to the 1190s, was much better known for his epic romances, including the original Arthurian legends of Perceval and Lancelot, than for his handful of lyrics.

New genres of narrative song based on the folklike *pastorela* (*pastourelle*) idiom became popular in thirteenth-century France. One of these, the *chanson de toile*, always reflected the woman's point of view, whatever the sex of the singer. The name of the genre, literally "picture-song" (from *toile*, "a canvas"), referred to the opening device of setting a domestic scene (what in painting is called a "genre scene"), usually of a lovely maiden (Bele Doette, Bele Ysabiauz, Bele Yolanz, etc.) spinning, weaving, or reading a book — but mainly pining for her lover. Each stanza ended with an exclamatory refrain to underscore the maiden's tender feelings.

Most *chansons de toile* have come down to us without attribution. The name of only one poet is primarily associated with this genre: Audefroi le Bastart, to whom are attributed six out of the two dozen or more specimens that survive. Like the songs of Thibaut IV, Audefroi's *Bele Ydoine* is found in the so-called *Manuscrit du Roi*, prepared for Charles d'Anjou, the brother of King Louis IX of France (and himself a trouvère), between 1246 and 1254. With over five hundred songs (fifty by troubadours, the rest by trouvères in descending order of social rank), it is the largest and most sumptuous of all chansonniers.

Refrains lived a life of their own in the works of the trouvères. Detached from their original contexts—in pastourelles, in chansons de geste, in otherwise unrecorded dance songs (*caroles*) and popular ditties—they circulated like proverbs from song to song, and it became a mark of skill for a trouvère to contrive new settings for familiar tags. *Ier mains pensis chevauchai* by Ernoul Caupain, an especially elaborate *chanson avec des refrains*, incorporates no fewer than eight of them, one into each stanza.

Narratives and migrating refrains were both popularizing touches, and so was the general lack of concern among the trouvères for the values of *trobar clus*, so beloved of the troubadours. *Chançon legiere à entendre ferai*, wrote Conon de Béthune (d. 1220), one of the noblest trouvères by birth and a knight-crusader to boot: "I will make a song that is light upon the ear, for it matters to me that all may learn it and willingly sing it." Few among his northern counterparts were inclined to contradict him, and Conon's sentiment would only gain in force as the courtly art he practiced underwent a phenomenal social transformation.

For past the middle of the thirteenth century, the main site of musico-literary activity among the French shifts from castle to town, mirroring the general movement of society. Urbanization, on the rise since the eleventh century, had begun to gallop. Over the century ending around 1250, the city of Paris doubled in size. Its streets were paved and its walls expanded. The first Louvre (a fortress) and several major churches including Notre Dame were built, and the city's schools were organized into a university. The episcopal town of Arras to the north was granted a commercial charter in 1180 and soon became an international center of banking and trade, the bastion of France's emerging class of town-dwelling freemen—*bourgeoisie*, in the original meaning of the term. It was at Paris and (especially) Arras that musical activity burgeoned among this capacious class and came to be organized along lines comparable in some respects to crafts guilds.

This tendency was epitomized in the Confrérie des Jongleurs et des Bourgeois d'Arras (Brotherhood of Minstrels and Townspeople of Arras), nominally a lay religious guild founded near the beginning of the thirteenth century, which became a leading sponsor of musico-poetic pursuits. Audefroi le Bastart, the specialist in *chansons de toile*, was a member, as were the three most important trouvères of the late thirteenth century: Moniot d'Arras (d. 1239), Jehan Bretel (d. 1272), and Adam de la Halle, the last of the line (d. ca. 1307).

To the first of this trio, whose pseudonym means "The Little Monk of Arras," belongs the most famous *pastourelle* in the repertory, *Ce fut en mai* ("It happened in May"; Ex. 4-5). Its text contains a valuable bit of testimony, corroborated by other witnesses, about how such songs were performed: it describes a dance accompanied by a fiddle (*viele*). On the assumption that it is itself a dance song, it is transcribed in a regular alternation of long and short syllables yielding a sort of iambic meter. The musical structure approximates the "binary" form of later dance styles: two phrases of equal length, each repeated with contrasting "open" and "shut" cadences. That plus the use of the major mode (Lydian with B-flat) makes this a consummate imitation folk song. There is little left here of the Latinate.

EX. 4-5   Moniot d'Arras, *Ce fut en mai* (pastourelle)

It happened in May,
when the heavens laugh,
a lovely time of year.
I got up early
to play at the fountain.
In a garden
surrounded by wild roses
I heard a fiddle playing;
and there I saw a knight
and a girl dancing.

Jehan Bretel was the great master of the *jeu-parti* ("mock-debate"), the trouvère equivalent of the troubadour *tenso*. These jousts-in-song were performed and judged before the so-called Arras Puy, a branch of the Confrérie that held regular competitions at which songs were "crowned." At least one manuscript from the period actually indicates with little cartoon crowns the *chansons couronées* that were so honored by the Puy. Jehan Bretel, not a nobleman but a wealthy burgher of the town, won these contests so often with his *jeux-partis* that he was elected "Prince" or presiding judge of the Puy, thus putting him out of contention. His elevation was a formal assertion of artistic "meritocracy" — aristocracy achieved by merit, not birth.

ADAM DE LA HALLE AND THE *FORMES FIXES*

Jehan's musical debating partner at the Arras Puy was often Adam de la Halle, called "Adam le Bossu" — Adam the Hunchback — by his contemporaries ("although I am not one," he complained in one of his poems). At the time of their jointly composed jeux-partis, Adam was a young man, just back from his studies in Paris. His advanced studies had acquainted Adam with the various forms of "university music" that we will take up in later chapters. They equipped him to compose polyphonic music, and he became the only trouvère to do so. His skills made him famous, and he had an international career that ranged from Italy, which he visited in the retinue of Charles d'Anjou, to England, where he is reputed to have performed, as an old man, at the coronation of Edward II in 1307. An entire chansonnier, evidently compiled late in the thirteenth century, is given over almost wholly to a retrospective collection of his works, grouped by genres: first traditional *chansons courtoises*, then the jeux-partis, and finally the polyphonic works.

Of these last there are two groups. The first consists of French verses, harmonized the way Latin *versus* (or, up north, *conductus*) were often harmonized at the time, in a fairly strict homorhythmic (note-against-note or "chordal") texture, and notated in score. (The second group consists of more complicated polyphonic compositions called motets; we will deal with them in chapter 7.) Like all polyphonic music of the period, Adam's used a new type of notation that fixed the rhythms exactly. (We will deal with that in chapter 7, too.) Polyphonic writing was a very "learned" style for a trouvère, so what is especially interesting — even curious — about Adam's polyphonically set verses is that they are cast in the folksiest (or rather, the most mock-naive) of all quasi-pastoral genres, the dance-song called *rondel*.

Mock-naive, because for all its rustic pretension the rondel (or *rondeau*, as it is more commonly called by musicians) is actually a quite sophisticated kind of poem. The name ("round" or "circular") may originally have stemmed from the nature of the dance it accompanied; but it also well describes the "rounded" form of the poem, in which a "contained refrain" both frames the verse and appears, truncated, within it. A contained refrain is one that uses the same melody as the verse itself; thus the form of a rondeau can be represented with letters as follows: AB a A ab AB, where the capital letters stand for the refrain text, and the lower case letters for new text, all sung to the same tune. The trick was to contrive a poem in which the refrains both rounded the verse and also made linear sense when the whole verse was sung or recited in sequence. The clever effect that can be achieved in this way, even without music, has kept the "rondel" (as it is still called by poets) popular with makers of "light verse" into recent times. Here is an example by Austin Dobson (1840–1921):

A KISS

[A] Rose kissed me today
[B] Will she kiss
me tomorrow?
[a] Let it be as it may,
[A] Rose kissed me today,
[a] But the pleasure gives way
[b] To a savour of sorrow; —
[A] Rose kissed me today, —
[B] *Will* she kiss me tomorrow?

And here is an example by Adam de la Halle, perfect for memorization even in this hopelessly literate day and age because the "A" and the "B" have each been whimsically held down to a single measure (Ex. 4-6).

EX. 4-6   Adam de la Halle, *Bone amourete*

1. Bon' a - mou - re - te   2. Me   tient gai;
3. Ma com - pai - gne - te,
4. Bon' a - mou - re - te,
5. Ma' chan - ço - ne - te   6. Vous   di - rai.
7. Bon' a - mou - re - te   8. Me   tient gai.

My kind mistress
Keeps me gay;
My sweet companion,
My kind mistress,
I will sing you
my little song:
My kind mistress
Keeps me gay.

The first written rondeaux (texts only) are "found objects," popular songs interpolated into old narrative romances to "illustrate" dance scenes. (The first such usage is in a manuscript dated 1228.) Rondeaux were the source of many of the popular refrains in the store from which thirteenth-century composers of *chansons avec des refrains* would draw. In fact, the word "rondeau" may have originally meant a song framed (sur-rounded) by a quoted refrain. No rondeau with surviving music seems to be any older than Adam's polyphonic ones, however. There are ten monophonic rondeaux by Adam's contemporary Guillaume d'Amiens, who was a famous manuscript illuminator besides being a trouvère, and another dozen by a Parisian cleric named Jehannot de l'Escurel (hanged for debauchery in 1304). There is no reason to think these pieces any earlier than Adam's, though, just because they are written in a simpler texture.

The rondeau was one of three types of dance-song (*carole*) with refrain that came into widespread use as models for composed music beginning with Adam in the late thirteenth

EX. 4-7   Adam de la Halle, *Dieus soit en cheste maison* (ballade)

Dieus soit en _ ches - te mai - son, _ Et biens e goie a _ fui - son!

EX. 4-7 *(continued)*

century. They differed from one another chiefly in the deployment of the refrains. What they had in common was more significant. Take away the refrains from a rondeau — that is, simply take away the capital letters from the alphabet scheme up above — and we are left with the long-familiar *canso*, the basic stanza in ode or bar form, thus:

[AB] a [A] ab [AB] → aab.

Add a refrain (not a "contained" refrain but one with different music) on either side of the basic stanza, and we get the form of Adam's *Dieus soit en cheste maison* ("God be in this house"):

R aab R [aab R aab R aab R, etc.].

It was called a *ballade* (Ex. 4-7). Give the refrain the same music as the "tail" (*cauda*) or nonrepeating line of the stanza, so that it is "contained," and we get the form of Adam's

Fines amouretes ai ("Many fine lovers have I"):

B **aab** B [**aab** B **aab** B **aab** B, etc.].

It was called a *chanson balladé*, "danced song," or more commonly, *virelai*, from the Old French verb *virer*, "to turn around" (Ex. 4-8; since it is conventional and commonsensical to begin an alphabet scheme with the letter A, the virelai form is almost always given as A **bba** A, which unfortunately disguises the basic stanza within it). These three genres—ballade, virelai, rondeau—encompass the whole repertoire of what would be called the *formes fixes*, the "fixed forms" in which lyric poetry, no longer associated with the dance, would continue to be written and set to increasingly elaborate music over the next two centuries. Rather quickly, moreover, the ballade shed its refrain when set as a fancy polyphonic composition; in doing so, of course, it merely reverted to the basic *canso* shape.

EX. 4-8A   Adam de la Halle, *Fines amouretes ai* (virelai)

Back to refrain

EX. 4-8A (*continued*)

> I have had fancy love affairs, God knows!
> Such that I don't know when I will see the like again.
>
> Now I will send for my little friend,
> who is pretty and refined
> and so tasty a dish
> that I won't be able to hold myself in!
> I have had fancy, etc.
>
> But if she should become pregnant by me,
> and gets pale and sickly,
> and should a scandal and an outcry ensue,
> then I shall have dishonored her.
> I have had fancy, etc.
>
> It would be better if I abstained,
> and, for the pretty one's sake,
> contented myself with merely remembering her.
> Thus does her honor protect her.
> I have had fancy, etc.

EX. 4-8B Adam de la Halle, *Fines amouretes ai* (Rondeau)

> I die, I die of love, ah weary, ah me,
> it is my beloved's want of all mercy!
>
> At first she was demure and attractively docile;
> I die, I die of love, ah weary, ah me,
>
> With that catching little way she has, I saw her then;
> but since I've found her so proud when I beg for loving.
>
> I die, I die of love, ah weary, ah me,
> it is my beloved's want of all mercy!

THE FIRST OPERA?

It was during his sojourn in Italy that Adam wrote what has become his best known work, *Le jeu de Robin et de Marion*, best translated as "Robin and Marion, a play with music." It was a sort of offering from his employer, the Count of Anjou (based in Sicily), to the king of Naples, before whom it was performed in 1283. With its alternation of dialogue and sixteen diminutive monophonic dance-songs and duets, this work has often been anachronistically compared with the later "singspiel" or comic opera. More appropriately, it can be described as an acted-out *pastourelle*, for that is the narrative tradition to which its dramatized plot belongs. Marion, a shepherdess, loves the shepherd Robin (as she tells us in the opening song, a modified virelai; Ex. 4-9); accosted by Sir Aubert, a knight out hunting, she resists; Robin goes to town in search of protection for her; while he is gone Sir Aubert comes back, abducts Marion; Robin, warned by his friend Gautier, pursues, is beaten back; Marion escapes anyway; the lovers, reunited, celebrate.

EX. 4-9   Adam de la Halle, *Robins m'aime* (from *Le jeu de Robin et de Marion*)

Robin loves me; I belong to Robin; Robin has asked for my hand; he will have me.
Robin bought me a dress of scarlet silk, lovely and fine, gown and girdle, tra-la-la!
Robin loves me, *etc.*

Because Adam's collected work is so readily available in the retrospective manuscript described above, it was published in an edition by the French musical antiquarian Charles-Edmond-Henri de Coussemaker as early as 1872. "Le trouvère de la Halle," as he was called there, thus became the earliest medieval musician whose work was comprehensively recovered in modern times. Performances of *Le jeu de Robin et Marion* (usually harmonized in a contemporary fake-medieval style), billed as "the world's first opera," enjoyed a big vogue in all the capitals of Europe. There was a particularly successful revival in St. Petersburg's "Antique Theater" in 1907, with harmonizations by the local conservatory musicologist, an Italian named Liberio Sacchetti. It was produced by the same team that later brought "Russian ballet" to Paris and made musical and theatrical history. Thus it is a striking instance of the interest musical modernists have often shown in "early music" and the inspiration they have drawn from it — another theme to be pursued in later chapters.

GEOGRAPHICAL DIFFUSION

The earliest written vernacular repertories in several other European countries are traceable to the influence, both artistic and ideological, of the troubadours and trouvères. The troubadour influence went south, as we have seen, into the Iberian peninsula and Italy. That of the trouvères went east into Germany.

CANTIGAS

In some parts of what is now Spain, especially the eastern part (then Aragon, now Catalonia), the presence of troubadours stimulated the rise of a latter-day Provençal school, of little interest to music history. On the western side, however, and especially at the northwestern court of Castile and León, the troubadours were emulated in the local literary vernacular, Galician-Portuguese. This brief efflorescence left a major musical monument in its wake, the *Cantigas de Santa Maria*, compiled over a period of as much as thirty years (1250–80) under the supervision of King Alfonso X (*el Sabio*, "The Wise").

The word *cantiga* (or *cantica*) is the equivalent of *canso*: a courtly song in the vernacular. Alfonso's collection of courtly songs expressed loving devotion to the Virgin Mary, and once again blurred the line we now insist on drawing between the sacred and the secular. (Sometimes the blur is finessed by using the word "paraliturgical" — "outside the liturgy" yet still somehow sacred — to cover it up; the belief that demons and fractious categories can be exorcised by naming them is indeed an old superstition.) In its most comprehensive sources, Alfonso's book of cantigas comprises over four hundred pious love lyrics, organized into decades (groups of ten) consisting of nine strophic narrative songs relating miracles performed by the Virgin (often in the mundane context of contemporary daily life), followed by a hymn of praise to her in a more exalted style.

FIG. 4-5 *Le jeu de Robin et Marion* as staged at St. Petersburg's "Antique Theater" in 1907 (costumes and set design by Mstislav Doboujinsky).

The opening song in the collection (the *prologo*), following the most venerable troubadour traditions, is a poem about poetry, with a characteristic pious twist (Ex. 4-10). It is cast in the first person, which implies (but certainly does not prove) that it was composed by Alfonso himself, who is known to have been a poet. The melody takes the form of a very grace-fully modified "bar," in which the *pes* is given dancelike open and shut cadences before opening out on the *cauda*. Most of the narrative cantigas are dance songs with refrains, combining a verse structure similar to the Arabic *zajal* (though it is an open question whether the cantigas were modeled on zajals or the zajals on cantigas) with music following a modified *virelai* pattern, in which the refrain borrows its music from the "tail" (*cauda*) of the strophe. In Spanish this form would be known as the *villancico*.

EX. 4-10   *Porque trobar* (canso)

(notation interpreted as semi-mensural)

Since writing verse entails
understanding, the troubadour must have
knowledge sufficient for
perceiving and expressing
what he feels and wishes to say.
In this way good verse is made.

Though I do not understand as much
as I ought, yet will I try to show
the little I do perceive,
trusting in God, the source of all we know,
from Whom I possess whatever I may reveal
of the troubadour's art.

A NOTE ON INSTRUMENTS

Even if the rich thirteenth- and fourteenth-century cantiga manuscripts contained no actual music, they would still be prize documents for music history on account of the dozens of colored miniatures that decorate them. These little paintings are so detailed and precisely drawn that they are believed in some cases to be portraits of actual people. They show courtiers and minstrels of every stripe—Spanish, Moorish,

Jewish, male and female—all rubbing shoulders at Alfonso's Toledo court and playing an encyclopedic assortment of instruments (more than forty, from the ubiquitous minstrel's fiddle to Moorish exotica, encompassing zithers, bladder pipes, castanets, and hurdy-gurdies).

These illustrations inevitably raise more questions than they answer. They stimulate the performer's imagination (and the cantigas have been well and colorfully served by early music ensembles, especially in recordings), but as historical evidence they must be approached with caution, despite their evident realism. The encyclopedic impulse—the urge to include everything (here, every instrument and costume known to the artist)—serves the purposes of rich decoration and con-

FIG. 4-6   Miniatures from the cantiga manuscript at the Escorial Palace, Madrid, showing various contemporary instruments.

spicuous consumption, not those of accurate depiction. One cannot merely assume that all the instruments so marvelously depicted in the cantiga manuscripts ever played together, or that they played cantigas.

And yet the opposite assumption, that the notation of monophonic ("unaccompanied") medieval songs reflects their actual performance practice, would be equally unfounded. As we have observed more than once, the written sources of medieval music were more often prestige items—"collectibles"—than performance materials. And, as we may recall from the first chapter, the strictly unaccompanied unison style of Gregorian chant was regarded as something of a special effect. So there is really no reason to allow the stark appearance of early written music in itself to influence or limit our notion of what it may have sounded like in performance.

If a team of Martian musicologists were to visit the desolate earth after World War III and discover a "fake-book" (a big compilation—often produced illicitly, in violation of copyright—of pop tunes with shorthand chord symbols for the use of nightclub or "cocktail" pianists), would they know they were seeing a blueprint for elaborate impromptu arrangements, or might they draw false conclusions about the "monophonic" musical culture of twentieth-century America?[4] And yet even the fake-book is more closely allied with actual performance, and gives far more performance information, than the average medieval manuscript, especially retrospective anthologies containing "monophonic" vernacular songs that were performed by nonliterate professionals (joglars or minstrels).

On the basis of all the available evidence—contemporary pictures, literary descriptions of musical performances, the writings of music pedagogues and theorists, archival documents—historians now believe that the use of instruments to accompany the written repertories of medieval song depended a great deal on genres and their social connotations. The higher the style and the closer its alliance with the ethos of liturgical chant, the more likely was performance by solo voice alone. (Among the troubadours, instrumentalists are known to have participated only in the marginal genres—*descorts* and dance songs.) With the lowering of the social standing of trouvère song and its urbanization in the thirteenth century came a greater participation in it by minstrel instrumentalists, especially fiddlers (*viellatores*), who had their own professional guild in Paris. Such musicians regularly took part in *pastourelles*, in Latin *conductus*, in church plays, and the like.

As Moniot d'Arras's *Ce fut en mai* explicitly informs us, fiddlers had a repertory of their own in the form of dances. The most elaborate dance form was variously called *estampie*, which suggests a heavy, vigorous step, and *danse royale*. Its form was a little like that of the lai or sequence: a series of paired strains called *puncta* (singular *punctum*) with alternately open and shut cadences. The earliest estampies preserved in writing are those in the mid-thirteenth-century *Manuscrit du roi* (Fig. 4-8). Their notation is very advanced for the time and completely encodes their rhythm (according to principles to be discussed in chapter 7), as untexted dance notation needs to do.

So far the evidence seems to suggest that instrumentalists performed such pieces and accompanied singers where appropriate, predominantly as

FIG. 4-7A Notation of Ex. 4-10 (*Porque trobar*) in the cantiga manuscript. Compare this with Fig. 4-7b.

FIG. 4-7B Page from a mid-twentieth-century fake book, to be compared with Fig. 4-7a.

soloists rather than in "bands"—which is not to say that such accompaniments were necessarily modest or primitive. Both historical evidence and observation of contemporary instrumentalists who mostly work without notation suggest that medieval fiddlers and harpers were often prodigious technicians, and that they cultivated techniques of self-accompaniment (drones, heterophonic doubling, even counterpoint). Evidence of ensemble performance is rare, ambiguous, and often (like the cantiga miniatures) questionable. But it cannot be discounted.

One genre that is espe-
cially well documented as a site
of instrumental performance is
the *carole*, the public springtime dance-festivity. Its musical
component remained for the
most part an unwritten tradition—but some of the music,
transformed, may have survived
in the *formes fixes*, the villancico, and all the other genres
that descend from ring-dances
with refrains. The relationship
between the forms and practices that survive in written form
and those that came and went
without a paper trail has been
aptly characterized as "the iceberg problem." The written elite
dominates our view, but it accounts for only the smallest fraction of what existed at the time.
The great vanished mass is what
dominated the view—that is,
formed the assumptions and
the expectations—of contemporaries, even (or especially)
those who performed the elite

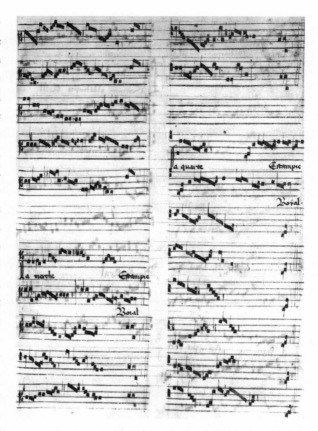

FIG. 4-8   Dances from the *Manuscrit du Roi*, a huge codex,
copied in the mid-thirteenth century, that contains songs of the
troubadours alongside those of the trouvères, and even a few
items, like these dances, in mensural notation (that is, notation
prescribing rhythm).

fraction. Vague references to "instruments," in the plural, can be found in many
descriptions of the carole. And with that we circle back to the cantigas, many of which,
as virelai types, can trace their lineage back to the carole. All the questions raised by
those lovely, pesky miniatures remain open after all.

LAUDE AND RELATED GENRES

The earliest surviving genre of Italian vernacular song was cultivated by a very different
sort of musician from those we have examined thus far. The thirteenth-century *lauda
spirituale* ("devotional [song of] praise") was not a courtly genre but a frankly religious
one, sung in congregational unison by lay fraternities who called themselves *laudesi*, by
Franciscan street missionaries who called themselves "God's minstrels" (*joculatores Dei*),
and by ardent penitents, called *disciplinati* or *flagellanti*, who sang them while walking
naked through the streets and lashing themselves with whips. Many *laude* were sung as
contrafacta to familiar melodies and could thus be characterized as pious pop songs.
Others, particularly those used by the Franciscans, were the work of skilled and highly

educated poets from the urban upper classes like the Florentine Jacopone da Todi (ca. 1230–1306), a jurist turned monastic ascetic, two of whose *laude* survive with music. Jacopone is also credited in the Vatican chant books, however dubiously, with the Marian sequence *Stabat mater dolorosa* ("The mother stood by sorrowfully"), one of the latest additions to the canonical liturgy.

Like most genres of medieval vernacular song, *laude* were written down somewhat after the fact, in large "gift-shop" manuscripts that had little to do with their performance occasions. (Flagellants, even if they could read, had their hands full.) Like many of the *cantigas*, to which they were contemporary, *laude* were apt to be cast in the popular form of the *virelai* (stanza plus contained refrain: A bba A bba A, etc.). In Italy, beginning in the fourteenth century, such songs would be called *ballate*, betraying their descent from the dance.

The flagellant movement was international. From northern Italy it spread into Germany and thence as far east as Poland, as far west as Britain, and as far north as Scandinavia, becoming especially intense in the mid-fourteenth century, when the population of Europe was devastated by epidemics. It was then that the German variants, known as *Geisslerlieder* (from *Geißel*, German for whip) were written down by clerics who found the spontaneous fervor of the flagellants both inspiring and frightening.

Geisslerlieder borrowed their form not only from the *laude spirituale* but also from indigenous pilgrimage and processional folk hymns known as *Rufe* ("calls") or *Leisen*. In these, the refrain is whittled down to a single call—often *Kyrioleis!* (from *Kyrie eleison*)—in the manner of a litany. These are in fact actual folksongs, noted down (not for perpetuation in singing but as documentation) from actual popular performance, chiefly by a Swabian priest named Hugo Spechtshart von Reutlingen in his chronicle of the plague of 1349. Nowadays we would call such a transcriber an ethnomusicologist.

EX. 4-11 Flagellants' song: *Nu ist diu Betfart so here* (Geisslerlied, transcribed by Hugo Spechtshart von Reutlingen)

MINNESANG

By that date, however, there was already a large body of German courtly song. Originating as an imported luxury item, it soon took on a distinctive coloration and underwent a vigorous indigenous development in which many social classes participated. The eastward migration of the art of *fine amours* is often said to begin with the wedding, in 1156, of Frederick I (known as Barbarossa, "Redbeard"), the Holy Roman Emperor and German king, to the duchess Beatrice of Burgundy. A notable early trouvère, Guyot de Provins, was a member of Beatrice's retinue, and some of the earliest German *Minnelieder*, like the one in Ex. 4-12, were set as *contrafacta* to melodies by Guyot.

EX. 4-12 Guyot de Provins, *Ma joie premeraine*, with German text (*Ich denke under wilen*) by Friedrich von Hausen

Minnelieder were songs composed by *Minnesinger* — singers of *Minne*, German for courtly love. The earliest Minnesinger assumed to have made up their own melodies were those who, in the early thirteenth century, began composing in new and specifically German meters that required them. The important name in this generation was that of the Austrian Walther von der Vogelweide (d. ca. 1230), regarded both by his contemporaries and by his successors as the preeminent master of *Minnesang*, the German medieval lyric. His poetry survives abundantly in many manuscripts, but only one contemporaneous source contains a complete melody attributed to him — the famous crusader song *Allererst lebe ich mir werde* ("Only now do I live in dignity"), called the *Palästinalied* ("Palestine song;" Ex. 4-13). It was evidently composed in 1224 or 1225, when the Holy Roman Emperor Frederick II, of the German house of Hohenstaufen, was conscripting an army to lead on a much-postponed Crusade.

EX. 4-13 Walther von der Vogelweide, *Palästinalied*

EX. 4-13 (*continued*)

Mirst ge-sche-hen des ich ie bat Ich bin ko-men an die stat

Dâ got mensch-lî - chen trat.

Only now I live in dignity,
now that my sinful eyes have seen
that pure land and earth as well
which have been given such great honor.
To me has happened what I always hoped,
for I am come unto that place
where God once trod the earth as man.

Its melody, a "rounded bar" in which the last line is set to the ending phrase of the initial pair, has been compared both to a melody by the troubadour Jaufre Rudel and to the Gregorian hymn *Te Joseph celebrent* (for the feast of St. Joseph the Workman, Mary's husband). One does not have to call it a contrafactum of either of these in order to recognize its derivation from the common fund of "Dorian" melody on which anyone who heard and sang chant in church, and who aspired to a lofty style, would surely have drawn.

The knightly Minnesinger cultivated three main genres, all more or less directly adapted from the Romance vernacular tradition. The narrative *Leich* derived directly from the French lai. The *Lied* was the equivalent of the *canso* or *chanson courtoise*, and like its Romance counterparts it encompassed an important subgenre, the *Tagelied* (daybreak song), equivalent to the troubadour *alba* (*aube* in French). Finally, there was the *Spruch*. The word means a "saying," and the genre encompassed many of the same topics as did the Provençal *sirventes* and *tenso* and their French equivalents (though the Minnesinger did not use dialogue form): praise of patron, complaint at base behavior, political commentary and satire, moral precept, poetic craft. Many moralizing *Sprüche* are in single stanzas and have the character of sung proverbs. These seem to go back to an indigenous German tradition not directly related to Romance models.

As with the work of the trouvères, the art of Minnesang underwent a "popularization" over the course of the thirteenth century, involving what looks like assimilation of unwritten folk models (though one can never be sure). The first signs can be detected in the work of the knight and crusader Neidhardt von Reuenthal (d. ca. 1250), who despite his lofty social standing specialized in dance songs, divided into two subgenres: *Sumerlieder* (summer songs) for outdoor dancing and *Winderlieder* (winter songs) for indoor dancing. Like the French *chansons de toile*, they begin by setting a scene: in Neidhardt's case (as perhaps in some folk tradition on which he may have drawn) the scenes they set invariably had to do with nature and with seasonal weather. The ensuing narrative poem often departs from courtly subject matter, and very much departs from courtly tone and diction, lapsing into a sort of dialect and using blunt or even downright coarse language.

Neidhardt's work was exceedingly popular. He had legions of imitators. Some are known by name, and at least one of these names, that of a thirteenth-century Bavarian poet-singer who called himself *der Tannhäuser*, was restored to fame in the nineteenth century thanks to Richard Wagner, who made him the title character of an opera. Many more are anonymous; their works have been collected by modern scholars under the charming rubric "Pseudo-Neidhardt." The folksy and hilarious *Meienzit* ("In Maytime"; Ex. 4-14) is a work by a latter-day (early fourteenth-century) Pseudo-Neidhardter. Its melody, like many folk melodies, is "gapped." By diatonic reckoning it lacks a sixth degree (and the second degree is clearly an auxiliary degree, used only in the Dorian cadence formula). The tune is so simple, in fact, that it is more to be looked upon as a "tone" (*Ton* in German), a reciting formula in which every third phrase is varied to give a whiff of the old courtly *aab* stanza. But the melody itself seems no more courtly than does the gross behavior of "hairy Hildemar," a boorish knight who, as the poem goes on to relate, plays an embarrassing practical joke on the poet's lady.

EX. 4-14   Anon. ("Pseudo-Neidhardt"), *Meienzit*

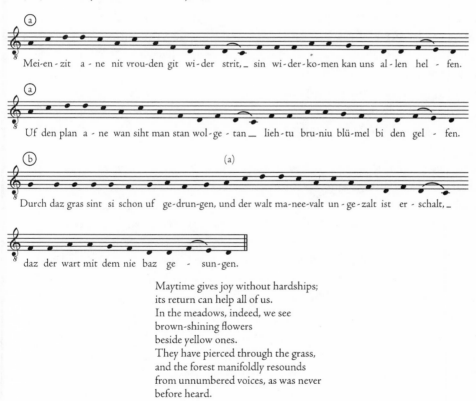

Maytime gives joy without hardships;
its return can help all of us.
In the meadows, indeed, we see
brown-shining flowers
beside yellow ones.
They have pierced through the grass,
and the forest manifoldly resounds
from unnumbered voices, as was never
before heard.

POPULARIZATION, THEN AND SINCE

The other way in which we know Neidhardt's songs were popular is that some of them have actually become folk songs. That is, they have rejoined the oral tradition, and were unwittingly collected (in considerably altered form, of course, but still recognizable) by the early folklorists of the German Romantic movement in the eighteenth and nineteenth centuries. Along with this, Neidhardt himself became a folk hero, acclaimed in legend (by storytellers unaware of his noble rank) as the leader of peasant revolts. Tannhäuser, too, became a figure of legend; the tall tale about his dalliance with Venus and his pilgrimage to Rome, traceable to the fourteenth century, was memorialized as a major plot ingredient of Wagner's opera of 1845. (Walther von der Vogelweide makes an appearance in the opera too, as does Wolfram von Eschenbach, more an epic poet than a Minnesinger, from whose *Parzival* Wagner would draw plot ingredients for his next opera, *Lohengrin*, and for *Parsifal*, his last one.)

As these references to Wagner and to early folklore collectors suggest, the art of the Minnesingers greatly appealed to the German artists and art historians of the nineteenth century, a time when progressive thinkers were striving to unite the German nation. The earliest German vernacular poetry and its music became an important symbol of German nationhood, and a rallying point for German nationalists.

So, too, a bit later, did the Latin *versus* settings by the wandering poet-musicians who called themselves *goliards*. (The name may derive from the Latin *gula*, "gullet," suggesting gluttony; or from the biblical Goliath, suggesting brawn). These were impecunious, unattached monks and scholars, learned mendicants and itinerant teachers, who loved using the language of the Roman classics and the church to entertain themselves not just with serious religious or mythological poems but also with hymns to the pleasures of youthful flesh — drinking, feasting, gambling, roistering, and (especially) lechery, the best theme of all with which to satirize the lofty motifs of *Minnesang*.

An especially large collection of some two hundred goliardic poems (about one-quarter with old-fashioned staffless neumes) is found in an early thirteenth-century manuscript from the environs of Munich. Long housed in a Benedictine abbey called Benediktbeuren, it was published in 1847 under the title *Carmina burana* ("Songs of Beuren"). Even though much of the manuscript's contents can be traced back to French sources (and a few concordances with French manuscripts with staff notation enable the deciphering of a few of its melodies), and although it contains much serious religious poetry (including two impressive "liturgical dramas"), the bawdy Latin songs in the *Carmina burana* became for romantic nationalists of a later age another trophy of native German genius, flaunted especially during the period of the Third Reich (1933–45), when German nationalism, under the by-name of National Socialism, achieved its most extreme manifestation. A cantata called *Carmina burana* (1937), with rousing music set to boisterous verses from the Benediktbeuren manuscript by Carl Orff (1895–1982), was heavily promoted by the National Socialist regime at a time when it was engaged in a strenuous propaganda battle with the Christian churches of Germany. The *Carmina burana* verses, with their glorification of youth culture and their neo-paganism, effectively epitomized the "New Germany." This was a blatant case of appropriation after the fact, of course, but it is now part of the history of the *Carmina burana*, and therefore part of its meaning. No appropriation, however, is ever complete or conclusive. Since the fall of the Third Reich, Orff's *Carmina burana* has retained a place in the standard choral-orchestral repertory. Audiences now respond more directly, and perhaps more innocently, to its message of springtime pleasures and renewal.

MEISTERSINGER

The original romantic nationalist view of medieval German art music reached its peak in another Wagner opera, *Die Meistersinger von Nürnberg* ("The master singers of Nuremberg," 1868), of which the first libretto sketches were made in 1845, the same year as *Tannhäuser* reached the stage. The Meistersinger were guild musicians who flourished in southern German towns between the fourteenth and the seventeenth centuries (but chiefly in the fifteenth and sixteenth). Like the very late trouvères, on whose *confréries* their guilds were evidently modeled, the Meistersinger were burghers, not nobles. Their chief activity consisted in convening assemblies, like the *puys* of northern France, at which song contests were held and prizes awarded. A *Meisterlied* (master-song) was the musical equivalent

FIG. 4-9 Opening page of the so called *Carmina burana* manuscript, showing Dame Fortune and her fateful wheel, a favorite topic of Goliard verse.

of a *Meisterstück* (master-piece, from which we get our English term masterpiece), the culminating offering by which an apprentice graduated to the rank of master artisan in a medieval guild. Like a master-piece, a master-song was judged on the success with which its maker demonstrated his *mastery*—that is, his command of established rules and practices. These rules—ostensibly derived from the practices of the Minnesinger, whom they venerated—were strictly codified by the Meistersinger in books called *Tabulaturen*. This is where the old "bar form" was actually christened and described in terms of its constituent parts: two *Stollen* (pillars) followed by an *Abgesang* ("sing-off") corresponding to the *pedes* and *cauda* of the troubadour *canso* (first described, incidentally, by Dante in the fourteenth century, also long after the fact). One can hear this lore actually being imparted in the third act of Wagner's opera, when the shoemaker Hans Sachs, the leader of the Nuremberg master singers (an actual historical personage who lived from 1494 to 1576, and whose musical works survive) instructs the entirely fictional Walther von Stolzing in the making of a prize-song.

The *Tabulaturen* also contained what were said to be exemplary melodies by the leading Minnesinger, especially Walther von der Vogelweide. Modern scholars strongly doubt the authenticity of these melodies, as well as the Meistersinger's claim to have inherited their art as a direct legacy from the noble poet-singers of the earlier tradition. The art of the Meistersinger consisted mainly of the fashioning of *Töne*, song-formulas à la Pseudo-Neidhardt, which they then decorated with melismas called *Blumen* or "flowers" that had no counterpart in the Minnesinger tradition. By the sixteenth century, their literary themes were fairly remote from those of the original Minnesinger. *Minne* itself had disappeared as a subject in favor of *Spruchdichtung*, the moralizing poetry of the later German poet-singers, notably Heinrich von Meissen (d. 1318), called Frauenlob (Lady's Praise) because of his many songs in honor of the Virgin Mary. By Hans Sachs's time, the Virgin had been replaced as a subject, under pressure of the Reformation, by Bible stories and pious proverbs, and especially by verses celebrating the theory and practice of *Meistergesang* itself. Such a song is Hans Sachs's own Meisterlied, called *Silberweise* ("The Silver Tune"), composed in 1513.

EX. 4-15   Hans Sachs, *Silberweise*

I praise a cool, fresh brook
with its own bubbling source,
far higher than a water hole
which has no source
but is dependent on the water
of streams that may flow into it
and keep it filled; I tell you true;
the water hole will not last long,
for with the great heat of the sun
on fine, long summer days,
it soon becomes useless and quite fouled,
and evil smelling, too;
it dries up, becomes green and yellow;
the brook, however, is always refreshed
by its clear source,
the sunshine's heat
does not affect it,
it never becomes foul or stagnant.

PEOPLES AND NATIONS

Wagner, of course, accepted the Meistersin ger's claims implicitly, and even projected the attributes of *Meistergesang* back onto the Minnesinger with the enormous (and enor- mously anachronistic) scene in *Tannhäuser* of the song contest at Wartburg. So for Wag- ner (as earlier, it should be added, for the eighteenth-century poet Goethe), the Meis- tersinger, too, stood for a united German nation and a rallying point for nationalism, the more so since the Meistersinger were "democratic" burghers, not nobles, there- fore progressive from the nineteenth-century point of view.

Just how anachronistic this view really was can be seen at the end of Wagner's opera, when Hans Sachs sings his famous, thrilling (and for some by now perhaps somewhat chilling) hymn to *die heil'ge deutsche Kunst* (holy German art) with its call to keep it *deutsch und echt* (German and pure) against the threat of "base alien domination" (*falscher wälscher Majestät*). The notion of a German nation — and, by extension, of a German art — was foreign to the thinking of the Meistersinger, let alone the Minnesinger. Both Germany and (as we have already seen) France were many nations, not one. Larger political entities — the Holy Roman Empire or its Carolingian predecessor, to say

FIG. 4-10   The Minnesinger Heinrich von Meissen, known as Frauenlob ("praiser of women"), one of the many magnificent illumi- nations in the Grosse Heidelberger Liederhand- schrift ("Great Heidelberg Song Manuscript"), an early fourteenth-century collection of Ger- man song texts. The noble courtly singer is shown directing or admonishing from on high a group of plebeian *Spielleute* ("player folk"), play- ing or holding a variety of recognizable instru- ments like the fiddle, the shawm (the conical oboe-like instrument being raised aloft), and drums. Whether such an orchestra ever accom- panied *Minnesang* is debatable. The depiction might rather imply the relative social standing of musicians and musical genres.

nothing of the earlier Roman empire on which both were modeled — were multinational abstractions. They were not nations at all by any modern definition (and nations, as we now conceive of them, have only a modern definition).

Political and social allegiance, under conditions of feudalism, was dynastic and personal, not national or collective. When Western Europe did act collectively, as in the Crusades, it was in the name of religious, not political, unity. The major European division by this time was likewise religious, not political: the schism between the Eastern and Western Christian churches, brewing since the ninth century, became formal and final in 1054, with the excommunication of the patriarch of Constantinople by Pope Leo IX. The followers of Eastern Orthodoxy, cut off from Western Europe not only by their allegiance to Constantinople but, later, by centuries of Turkish and Mongol political domination, will not rejoin our narrative of literate art music in the West until the eighteenth century — that is, not until the modern notion of the secular nation state was born.

Thus, while kings and their vassals went to war against one another frequently, nations (as we think of them) never fought with or resisted other nations. Most literate Europeans were polyglot and owed no primary allegiance to a mother tongue. (If they had a linguistic allegiance, it was, as Christians or as scholars, to Latin; and local dialects — mother tongues — were often scorned by the literate as "low.") When Wagner's Sachs warns against *wälscher Majestät*, "foreign domination," the nation he (that is, Wagner) had above all in mind was France, the nation against which Germany was about to fight a war in 1868, and against which the German Romantics had been waging esthetic war for a century. How far this attitude applied in medieval Germany can be judged from the fact that the whole "holy German art" of the Minnesinger was knowingly and cheerfully borrowed from the French. The meaning of the French artistic legacy to the Germans had to do with its courtliness, not its nationality. That courtliness, at the outset at least, was indeed next to godliness, and it encompassed all nations that valued it.

WHAT IS AN ANACHRONISM?

The point to ponder about *Minnesang* and *Meistergesang* is their longevity, not their putative national character. The original appropriation from France was made not very long after the French had appropriated the art of Languedoc. By the end of the twelfth century all three linguistic branches of the courtly song tradition were thriving side by side and did not differ greatly from one another. By the end of the thirteenth century, the troubadours were a memory, and the trouvères, having been absorbed into the urban *confréries*, were singing pop songs at *puys* and (in the person of Adam de la Halle) making contact with the clerical and university arts of polyphonic composition.

FIG. 4-11 Oswald von Wolkenstein, as depicted in a manuscript at the University Library of Innsbruck, Austria, one of two fifteenth-century collections of his works.

Adam de la Halle, as it happened, had a close German counterpart in the latter-day Minnesinger Oswald von Wolkenstein, a knight and imperial emissary from the Tyrol region in the Austrian Alps. Like Adam, he is regarded as the last of his line. Like Adam, he composed in a wide range of genres, both narrative (including the autobiographical masterpiece *Es fuegt sich*, "It so befell me . . .") and lyric. Again like Adam, Oswald supervised the collection of his complete works, grouped by genres, into valuable retrospective manuscripts. Yet again like Adam, Oswald (alone among his breed) dabbled in polyphonic composition, mainly in the dance-derived *formes fixes*, and in so doing proclaimed his knowledgeable love of French song: many of his polyphonic settings (like many of the earliest Minnelieder) were contrafacta of French originals. (The best known of these is Oswald's *Der May*, a summer-song with imitation bird calls, modeled on a virelai with bird calls by a French contemporary named Vaillant.)

The only thing that separated Adam and Oswald was time. They were not contemporaries at all. Oswald was born around 1376, at least seventy years after Adam's death, when the monophonic art of the trouvères was long since superseded. He died in 1445, by which time the Meistersinger were already well established (and, in Western Europe, monophonic song was hardly practiced any longer as a literate art). Oswald himself cannot be classified as a guild musician, though. Both his social class and his subject matter preclude that, and his poetic and musical style was remote from that prescribed by the *Tabulaturen*.

Persistence, like Oswald's, in old ways is often represented by historians as anachronism — in this case, as a pocket of "the Middle Ages" surviving like a fossil into "the Renaissance," or as resolute "conservatism," resistance to change. What is anachronistic, however, is the modern linear view of history that produces such an evaluation, and the implicit isolation of artistic practices or styles from the historical conditions that enabled them.

Feudal society and "castle culture" retained their currency longer in Germany than they did in France. The rise of towns and, consequently, of urbanized mores happened later there. The institution of serfdom, for example, the sine qua non of feudal economy, which bound the lower classes of society to the land and retarded urbanization, made a sort of eastward migration over the course of time covered by this chapter: from the Romance countries (France, Italy, Spain) to Germany, and finally (during the fifteenth century) to the Slavic countries. (Essentially "feudal" conditions persisted in Russia until the Emancipation Act of 1861; were Russia not culturally cut off from the West during its long period of Mongol occupation, it would probably have developed an art of courtly song last of all, and kept it latest.) The growth of towns and the beginnings of a mercantile (money-based) economy came later to Germany than they did to France and arrived along with the Meistersinger — or rather, obviously, the art of the Meistersinger guild was made possible by the growth of the urban and mercantile society that supported it and to which it gave expression.

To regard an Oswald von Wolkenstein or a Hans Sachs as an artistic anachronism, then, is to regard their societies as historical anachronisms. And one has to ask by what premises — indeed, by what right — and from what vantage point one can make such a judgment. When things become truly anachronistic, they disappear (as did the Meistersinger guild when it officially disbanded in 1774). As long as they thrive, they are *ipso facto* — by that very fact — relevant to their time, and it is the historian's job to understand how. Judging cultures by the standards of other cultures (most often, by the standards of one's own culture) is called ethnocentrism, and it has been the source of many fallacious historical verdicts, to say nothing of ethnic, religious, or racial intolerance.

Another premise that can lead to the illusory notion of historical anachronism is the premise that history is teleological — that it has a purpose or an end (*telos* in Greek). This kind of thinking leads to determinism: the explanation of events in terms of inevitable movement toward the perceived goal, and the assignment of value to phenomena (or to artifacts, like works of art) depending on their nearness to it.

PHILOSOPHY OF HISTORY

An argument like the one made here, which seeks to account for the circumstances of art history (here, its nonsynchronicity) by appealing to factors deemed external to "art itself," is often mistaken for a determinist argument. (In this case, some balance of historical, social, and economic determinisms would appear to be invoked.) That is a misnomer, engendered by the confusion of causes or purposes with enabling conditions. To say that certain conditions made a development — say, the art of the Meistersinger — possible is not the same as predicting the nature of that development from a knowledge of those conditions, or ascribing a value to it on that basis.

And yet even this much appeal to "external" factors is often avoided. Until recently it was not customary in books like this. That is because the historiography of art in the West has long been dominated by a view of art that arose in the wake of the social emancipation (or, perhaps, the social abandonment) of the artist in the nineteenth century. The concept of "the emancipated and abandoned artist," the artist-loner, is thus the product of nineteenth-century aesthetics — in a word, of Romanticism. Since the nineteenth century it has been, and still often is, the custom to view art romantically, which means viewing it as being *autonomous*. An autonomous entity is one that follows an independent course and a self-determined one. To regard art as autonomous is to regard its history as being determined solely by those who produce it.

Yet the "autonomist" position, as already implied, was itself called forth by social and economic conditions. It does a poor job of explaining the work even of its own adherents, let alone that of much earlier artists who functioned in harmony with their society (indeed, at the very top of it) at a time when all art served a well-defined social purpose. To regard the art of the troubadours or the Meistersinger — however it may still delight or move us, and however we may still treasure it — as if it were no different from the autonomous output of the emancipated and abandoned artists of our own time, and therefore subject to similar "laws of evolution," is the very height of anachronism.

That may seem obvious enough, but the view of history that arises from that basic anachronism is still the prevailing one. The only model of change the autonomist view of art history can recognize is strictly linear stylistic evolution, often described using biological or otherwise "organic" metaphors (styles being born, reaching maturity, declining, dying). Art history is viewed as a procession of styles in a single file, along which different artists occupy positions either ahead or behind one another, depending on the style they employ.

From such a vantage point an artist's style defines the artist in essential terms. (Recall the old French saying, *Le style, c'est l'homme* — "the style is the man.") Depending on his or her style, an artist is judged either "advanced" ("forward-looking," "progressive") or "regressive" ("backward-looking," "conservative"). To make such a judgment, of course, is unwittingly to turn style into politics, for politics is the primary point of reference for terms like "progressive" or "conservative." And these terms, whether in politics or in style-politics, are never value-free, though the valuation will vary depending on the evaluator's political outlook.

In any case, style-politics engendered by autonomist esthetics, paradoxically enough, turns out to be an especially deterministic view of history. It is from that standpoint, especially when concepts of style are allowed to congeal into hard-and-fast categories of "period style" ("medieval," "Renaissance"), that one is most apt to regard artists and whole artistic movements as "ahead of their time" or as "lagging behind" it. These are invidious judgments, and (except as historical events in their own right) irrelevant to history. Everything possible will be done in this book to avoid them.

Which, alas, makes our story even harder to tell, since it militates against the construction of a single linear narrative. If all times are plural even within a single ostensible tradition (just think of the European scene in the twelfth century, when sacred chants and Latin *versus* and courtly song in three vernaculars were all being composed side by side, not to mention the massive, unprecedented cultivation of written polyphony that will be the subject of the next chapter), then so are all histories. Our story will have to keep moving back and forth, tracing beginnings and endings, showing not only how beginnings lead to endings, but also how endings lead to beginnings. Having in this chapter traced one strand — or rather, one complex of strands — from the eleventh to the fourteenth centuries (with many glances backward as far as antiquity and forward as far as the present), we will now return to square one and trace another.)

Polyphony in Practice and Theory

EARLY POLYPHONIC PERFORMANCE PRACTICES AND THE TWELFTH-CENTURY BLOSSOMING OF POLYPHONIC COMPOSITION

ANOTHER RENAISSANCE

As we have seen, and as it is important to remember, there has never been a time in the recorded history of European music — or of any music, it seems — when polyphony was unknown. Descriptions of music-making in classical Greece and Rome are full of tantalizing suggestions about harmonic and contrapuntal practices, and music theory, all the way back to "Pythagoras," is full of elaborate accounts of harmonic consonances. As soon as they were in possession of the means for writing their liturgical music down, moreover, the Franks illustrated sundry methods of harmonically amplifying that music. We have evidence of polyphonic performance practice for medieval chant as early as we have written evidence of the chant itself.

Polyphonic performance practices, even if we have only a sketchy idea of them, were surely applied (or at least available for application) to all the early genres of courtly and urban music encountered in the previous chapter as well. Reports of rustic part-singing are likewise tantalizing. Gerald de Barri, a Welsh churchman and historian who wrote under the name Giraldus Cambrensis, made a famous description of his countrymen's singing in a volume completed in 1194:

> They sing their tunes not in unison, but in parts with many simultaneous modes and phrases. Therefore, in a group of singers you will hear as many melodies as there you will see heads, yet they all accord in one consonant and properly constituted composition.[1]

Giraldus also commented with enthusiasm on the virtuosity of unlettered instrumentalists, harpers who played "with such smooth rapidity, such unequaled evenness, such mellifluous harmony throughout the varied tunes and the many intricacies of the part music" — harmony and polyphonic intricacies of which actual musical documents disclose nothing.

Since there is no period in which the known practices of European music did not include polyphony, polyphony cannot be said to have an origin in the European tradition. Written or not, it was always there. As with any other kind of music, its entry into written sources was not any sort of "event" in its history. (The event, as such, was in *our* history, the history of what we are able to know.) And by the same token, there is no point at which polyphony completely supplanted "monophony" in the history of Western music, especially if we recognize that monophony is only a style of notation, not necessarily a style of music.

Even if we take the strictest view of monophony, the view that equates it with liturgical chant that is unharmonized in accord with the preference of the Roman Catholic church, the history of its composition continues for centuries beyond the point at which we can afford the time in a book like this to go on tracking it. (Still, when a young researcher named Barbara Haggh discovered in the early 1980s that Guillaume Dufay, a major "Renaissance" composer, had composed elaborate chant offices in the middle of the fifteenth century, her findings made scholarly headlines — and rightly so, for it served as a forcible reminder that the march of musical genres and styles down through the ages in single file is something historians, not composers, have created.)[2]

Yet even granting all of this, we can still identify the extraordinary twelfth century as the one in which European musical practice took a decisive turn toward polyphonic composition. And if we are interested in isolating the fundamental distinguishing feature of what may be called "Western" music, this might as well be it. After this turning point, polyphonic composition in the West (not just polyphonic performance practice) would be indisputably, increasingly, and uniquely the norm. From now on, stylistic development and change would essentially mean the development and refinement of techniques for polyphonic composition.

Training in composition would henceforth be basically training in polyphony — in "harmony and counterpoint," the controlled combination of different pitches in time — and such training would become increasingly "learned" or sophisticated. *Combination*, the creation of order and expressivity out of diversity or even clash, became the very definition of music (or, to be more precise, the primary musical metaphor). During the later Middle Ages, the early polyphonic age, music was often called the *ars combinatoria* or the *discordia concors*: the "art of combining things" or the "concord of discord." The terms go back to the *Musica enchiriadis*. They not only underscore the new preoccupation with polyphony but also reconcile it with older notions of *Musica* as an all-embracing cosmic harmony. The word "harmony" was given a new context and a new meaning — the one that is still primary for us.

So the "polyphonic revolution," while real, should not be mistaken for the beginning, or the invention, or the "discovery" of polyphony. It was, rather, the coalescing into compositional procedure of what had always been a performance option and its intensive cultivation. The great spur to this vastly accelerated development of compositional technique was not so much a change in taste or "aesthetics" as it was a change in educational philosophy. The twelfth century was the century in which the primary locus of education shifted first from monasteries to urban cathedral schools and thence to something new: secular universities. In the course of this shift, Paris emerged as the undisputed intellectual center of Europe.

The burgeoning of polyphonic composition followed exactly the same trajectory. Beginning in monasteries, it reached its first great, transfiguring culmination in the cathedral schools of Paris, and in a new form it radiated from that cosmopolitan center throughout Western Christendom, receiving a special ancillary cultivation in the universities. It was all a part of what cultural historians call the "renaissance of the twelfth century."

"SYMPHONIA" AND ITS MODIFICATIONS

To trace this trajectory we need to begin by reviewing some earlier, more or less scattered manifestations of written polyphony. As a performance practice associated with plainchant, polyphony makes its documentary debut (as noted briefly, with an example, in chapter 2) in the ninth-century treatise *Musica enchiriadis*. A contemporary commentary to it, called the *Scolica* (or *Scholia*) *enchiriadis*, describes two basic techniques of embellishing a melody harmonically. One consists of simply accompanying a melody in bagpipe fashion, with a drone on the final of the mode. That method—under the name of *"ison* chanting" after the Greek word for "the same note"—still survives as a traditional way of performing the so-called Byzantine chant of the Greek Orthodox church. The other technique consisted of "parallel doubling"—that is, accompanying melody with a transposition of itself at a constant consonant interval (for which the Greek term, used in the treatise, was *symphonia*). Three intervals were considered eligible as *symphoniae* for this purpose; they are the ones we still call "perfect" (fourth, fifth, and octave).

These methods are easy to describe and to illustrate (Ex. 5-1), and they seem eminently practical. In actual fact they were entirely "theoretical" and, in the case of the second, impracticable. As the examples in the *Musica enchiriadis* itself suffice to prove, these simple devices were actually practiced in a complex synthesis requiring considerable artistry—which, of course, is why a treatise needed to be written about them in the first place. That artistic synthesis—not (as often assumed) mere parallel doubling—was what the author of the treatise called *organum*.

The reason why parallel doubling is not acceptable without modification can be expressed in a single word: *tritones*. If a given diatonic melody is doubled at a constant fourth or fifth below, then tritones will emerge whenever the note B has to

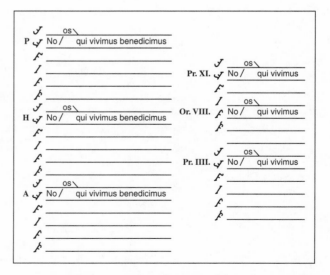

FIG. 5-1 Polyphonic or organal settings of the sequence *Nos qui vivimus* (We the living) in *Scolica enchiriadis*, ca. 850.

be doubled at the fourth or the note F at the fifth. Adjustment of the doubling-voice (called the *vox organalis*) at these places produces a built-in discrepancy between its mode species and that of the original chant (*vox principalis*). The result is "polytonality" — quite literally so, given that parallel lines by definition never meet, and so two voices in strict parallel motion at any interval except the octave will appear to end on different finals.

Consider Ex. 5-1b, the demonstration of "the symphonia of the diapente" (parallel doubling at the perfect fifth) in the *Scolica enchiriadis*. The ending note of the *vox organalis* (G) contradicts the Dorian final, and the B-natural in the *vox principalis* (a psalm tone) is answered in the *vox organalis* by a B-flat. If the *vox principalis* is modified with a B-flat to agree with the *vox organalis* (and to smooth the contour between its highest note and the F of its own medial cadence), then an E-flat (a note not present in the normal diatonic system) must be introduced beneath it, which creates a new discrepancy between the voices. (It can never be erased; if the *vox principalis* takes over the E-flat, the *vox organalis* will need an A-flat, and so it will go on forever.)

EX. 5-1A   Transcriptions of *Scolica enchiriadis* examples (Fig. 5-1), Double diapason

EX. 5-1B   Diapente

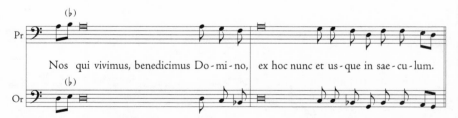

EX. 5-1C   Diatessaron

EX. 5-1D   Composite

Nos qui vivimus, benedicimus Do-mi-no,   ex hoc nunc et us-que in sae-cu-lum.

To "hear" (that is, aurally conceptualize) strict parallelism at the fifth without any sense of "polytonal" contradiction, one must be able to imagine "fifth equivalency" on a par with the octave equivalency we have all learned to take for granted as a listening norm. The author of the *Musica enchiriadis* recognized as much and even constructed a scale that exhibits fifth equivalency as the basis for "the symphonia of the diapente" (Ex. 5-2a). Instead of reproducing interval species at the octave, this scale duplicates interval sequences at the fifth. Just as one encounters discrepancies in fifth-size (perfect vs. diminished) when harmonizing within the "normal" diatonic scale, so in the *Musica enchiriadis* scale there will be uniform fifths but discrepancies in octave-size (perfect vs. augmented).

EX. 5-2A   Disjunct tetrachord scale from *Musica enchiriadis*

EX. 5-2B   Hypothetical conjunct tetrachord scale

Unlike the octave system, with a scale constructed (as we saw in chapter 3) out of alternately conjunct and disjunct tetrachords, the *Musica enchiriadis* scale is constructed entirely out of disjunct tetrachords. Beginning with the familiar tetrachord of the four finals, *d–e–f–g*, you add a disjunct tetrachord below, and thus obtain the B-flat in Example 5-1b. Add a disjunct tetrachord above and you get the B-natural as part of the same scale. Add another tetrachord above that and F-sharp appears. Above that there will be a C-sharp. (This much is actually demonstrated in the treatise. If one were to extend the scale at the bottom, of course, one would keep adding flats, beginning with the E-flat hypothetically added to Ex. 5-1b.) The result is a scale altogether without diminished fifths. An analogous hypothetical scale composed of nothing but conjunct tetrachords would eliminate augmented fourths; it is not given in the treatise but can be easily deduced: see Ex. 5-2b.

These scales produce perfect parallel counterpoint in theory but bear no relationship to normal oral (that is, aural) practice. And that is why strict parallel doubling, though conceptually as simple as can be, is literally utopian. It occurs nowhere in the "real world" of musical practice. Polyphonic music actually composed according to the *Musica enchiriadis* scales (to quote a wry comment of Claude Debussy on a piece the young Igor Stravinsky showed him in 1913) "is probably Plato's 'harmony of the eternal spheres' (but don't ask me on which page); and, except on Sirius or Aldebaran or some other star, I do not foresee performances . . . especially not on our more modest Earth."[3]

On our modest Earth, in other words, compromise with theory — that is, with imagined perfection — is usually required. The author of the *Scolica enchiriadis* tacitly recognized this crucial point when constructing an example to illustrate "the symphonia of the diatessaron" (parallel doubling at the perfect fourth). The counterpoint in this case has been "cooked," precisely so as to avoid the "polytonal" situation encountered in the case of fifths. The two lines end on the same final; that is to say, they end on a unison. In order to meet, of course, they must stop being parallel. Instead, they approach the final note in contrary motion. Such an approach is called an *occursus*, literally "a meeting."

In order to smooth the way to the *occursus* (and also to avoid the B-flat from the Musica enchiriadis scale, which would produce an augmented fourth against the E in the *vox principalis*), the *vox organalis* behaves, in the second half of the example, like a drone — or like a sequence of drones. Instead of following the contour of the *vox principalis*, the *vox organalis* hugs first the D and then the C, moving from the one to the other when the opportunity presents itself to recover the correct *symphonia* (perfect fourth) against a repeated note in the *vox principalis*. The *voces organales* above and below the *vox principalis* in Ex. 5-1d, a composite organum simultaneously demonstrating octaves, fifths, and fourths, behave similarly.

Curiously (and rather characteristically), the author of the *Scolica enchiriadis* does not actually explain the modifications — the drones, the occursus — by which the purely conceptual idea of parallel doubling is transformed into the actual practice of organum. Acknowledging that the case is not as straightforward as the other examples, the author refers the discrepancy to "a certain natural law about which we shall speak later" (but of course "we" never get around to it), meanwhile counseling the student not to ask questions but just to perform the example and learn to imitate its "smoothness of harmony." This deferral of explication should perhaps be viewed not as mere dogmatism ("'Shut up,' he explained,"[4] in the immortal words of Ring Lardner). Rather, it reflects the author's reliance on time-honored oral/aural methods — hearing, repeating, imitating, applying, as opposed to "analysis" — in training musicians. It also suggests that the technique being imparted was no recent invention but already a tradition, "oral" by definition.

When the *vox organalis* moves in this modified, somewhat independent (though still entirely rule-bound) way, using not just parallel motion vis-à-vis the *vox principalis* but oblique and contrary motion as well, a variety of harmonic intervals are introduced into the texture, and the resulting line or voice-part can be described as a true "counterpoint." The intervals are still ordered hierarchically. In addition to the actual *symphonia* (perfect consonance) of the fourth, Ex. 5-1c contains thirds and unisons. The organum setting of the sequence *Rex caeli* from *Musica enchiriadis*, discussed in chapter 2 and shown in Fig. 2-2, contains actual dissonances. The *vox organalis* begins with a dronelike stretch against which the *vox principalis* rises by step from unison until the *symphonia* is reached. Its second note, then, forms a "passing" dissonant second against the accompanying voice.

The thirds, "imperfect" consonances, are contrapuntally subordinate in Exx. 5-1c and 5-1d: a *vox organalis* can *move* only to a perfect consonance; the thirds (like the second in Fig. 2-2) can occur only over a stationary accompaniment. Thus the fourth, being unrestricted in its possible occurrences, is "functionally consonant" according to the style-determining rules here in force, while the third is "functionally dissonant."

It has been worth our while to take a very close look at these primordial specimens of written counterpoint because the principles we have observed in them will remain the bedrock principles of Western polyphonic practice for centuries. The art of counterpoint (and of harmony as well, which is just counterpoint slowed down) is most economically defined as the art of balancing normative harmonies ("consonances") and subordinate ones ("dissonances"), and elaborating rules for "handling" the latter. The quotes around the terms are a reminder that criteria of consonance and dissonance are culture-bound, hence relative and changeable, and are best described not on the basis of their sound as such but on the basis of how they function within a style. The styles we all assimilate today in the process of acculturation (otherwise known as "growing up") teach us to hear — hence use — intervals a different way. We have all been trained to "hear" thirds as consonances and fourths as dissonances.

The chief distinguishing characteristics of any contrapuntal or harmonic style, including those used today, come down to two: the ways in which voices move with respect to one another (in terms of rhythm as well as pitch direction), and the ways in which dissonance functions vis-à-vis consonance. To assess any contrapuntal or harmonic style we need to make the same sorts of observations that we have been making with regard to our primordial specimens.

GUIDO, JOHN, AND DISCANT

As if the achievements with which he has already been credited — the invention of the staff, the operational rules of sight-singing — were not enough, Guido of Arezzo also made a decisive contribution to the development of contrapuntal technique. It was yet another of that brilliant monk's many impressive contributions to the early rationalization of literate musical practice and its transformation into transmissible technique. In his *Micrologus* ("Little treatise"), a guide to the rudiments of music theory, Guido devoted one section to a very influential discussion of organum. The main emphasis was on obtaining maximum variety in interval succession (though the fourth is still recognized as the primary *symphonia*) and on fashioning a good *occursus* (a term Guido was in fact the first to use in connection with musical cadences).

The main innovation in Guido's discussion — and it was crucial — was attitudinal rather than substantive, something that seeped from between the lines. Like the author of the *Enchiriadis* treatises, Guido illustrated his points with examples; but unlike the earlier writer he gave more than one solution to contrapuntal problems, between which the student was invited to choose *ad libitum*, "at pleasure." Here, for example (Ex. 5-3), are two counterpoints to a psalm that produce the same *occursus*: in one case by direct leap to the final (*occursus simplex*), in the other by the use of a passing tone to smooth the way (*occursus per intermissas*).

EX. 5-3 Guido d'Arezzo, *Micrologus*; Two counterpoints to *Jherusalem*

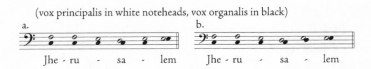

(vox principalis in white noteheads, vox organalis in black)

a. Jhe - ru - sa - lem b. Jhe - ru - sa - lem

Note that for Guido the major second can be used as a secondary consonance (it was, after all, a "Pythagorean" interval), whereas, as he tells us, the perfect fifth was to be avoided as "hard-sounding." So much for the "natural" basis of counterpoint! And Guido makes the rejection of the "natural" explicit. He does not claim that his methods follow "a certain natural law," only that they are pleasing. And by allowing the reader to choose between his two cadences on the basis of personal preference ("taste"), and implicitly allowing that there may be other solutions for the student to discover (or invent), Guido is in fact taking an important step in the direction of what we would call an "art," rather than a mere mechanical or technical procedure.

Another point Guido did not make explicit, but which was extremely influential nevertheless, was the fact that the pursuit of maximum variety of interval content implied a "parsimony principle," a minimum of motion in the *vox organalis*. (Today's counterpoint teachers still grade on the basis of "smoothness" of voice-leading, in fact.) Some of Guido's examples resemble drones, though he never says as much. One example (Ex. 5-4), ostensibly intended as an illustration of the desirability of occasional voice-crossing, yields an actual drone that is maintained throughout the chant.

EX. 5-4 Guido d'Arezzo, *Micrologus*; Counterpoint to *Sexta hora*

Sex - ta ho - ra se - dit su - per pu - te - um

Guido's *Micrologus* was the most frequently copied-out and widely disseminated book on music theory before the age of printing. Every monastery or cathedral library had a copy, and it was used in primary music instruction as late as the fifteenth century. We should not be surprised to discover its influence in the early centers of polyphonic composition that begin to leave documentary traces at about the same time, but which really flowered about a century later.

The earliest such trace is actually pre-Guidonian: a huge collection of polyphonic tropes from Winchester in a manuscript (one of the so-called Winchester Tropers) copied over a ten-year period ending in 1006. The Winchester Tropers are notated in staffless neumes, showing that the Winchester cantors (or the monks of the nearby Abbey of St. Swithin, including the celebrated Wulfstan to whom the whole corpus has been attributed) sang their counterpoints by heart. We cannot decipher them with much precision, but their contours definitely accord with Guidonian preferences regarding voice-crossing and *occursus*. In fact, the implicit Guidonian predilection for contrary motion at cadences now begins to spread to other parts of the setting, so that the older concept of *symphonia*—parallel doubling—survives only sporadically. The contents of the Winchester organum manuscript mix the monastic repertory of St. Swithin (Responsories, processional antiphons) with the public repertory of the cathedral Mass (Kyries, Gloria tropes, tracts, sequences, and no fewer than fifty-three Alleluias).

The earliest fully legible practical source of composed polyphonic music is a late eleventh-century fragment from Chartres containing Alleluia verses and processional antiphons set in two-part, note-against-note (homorhythmic) counterpoint. There is virtually no parallel doubling; nor is there much note-repetition in the *vox organalis*, even when the original chant has a repeated note. Instead, there is pervasive contrary motion and ceaseless intervallic variety; this, or what we would call an "independent" voice line, was what the composer of the *vox organalis* was clearly striving for. (The word "independent," of course, should be understood in relative terms: no line constructed in a style that is subject to so many harmonic constraints can ever be truly independent of the given melody—but this is just as true of later contrapuntal styles, including those still academically taught).

Most often cited from the Chartres fragment is the verse "Dicant nunc judei" from the Easter processional *Christus resurgens* ("Christ rising again"), an especially bold setting in which every interval from the unison to the octave except the seventh is employed, including both major and minor sixths (unrecognized as concords by theorists), and in which voice-crossing gives the *vox organalis* almost equal prominence with the *vox princpalis* (Ex. 5-5a). In another verse, "Angelus Domini" from the Easter Alleluia *Pascha nostrum immolatus est Christus* ("Christ our paschal lamb is sacrificed"), different counterpoints are added to a repeated phrase in the *vox principalis*, and the occursus is made not to the unison but to the octave (Ex. 5-5b).

EX. 5-5A   From the Chartres fragment. "Dicant nunc judei"

Now the Jews said, "How did the soldiers guarding the tomb lose [the risen Christ]?"

EX. 5-5B   "Angelus Domini"

An - ge - lus Do - mi - ni de-scen - dit

de   coe - lo:

The Angel of the Lord descended from heaven . . .

The style of counterpoint exemplified in the Chartres fragment strikingly resembles the one described (or prescribed) by John of Afflighem, a Flemish theorist of the early twelfth century whose treatise *De musica* was the only one to rival Guido's *Micrologus* in distribution and authority. In the later twelfth century this style would become known as *discantus* or "descant." The Latin word means literally "singing apart," whence "singing in parts." Music historians generally prefer "discant" to "descant" as an English equivalent; not being standard English, it can be more easily restricted in meaning to refer specifically and technically to medieval polyphony.

POLYPHONY IN AQUITANIAN MONASTIC CENTERS

By the time the word discant became current, a new style of organum had arisen in contrast to it. This new style resembles some of Guido's examples (which may have helped inspire it) in that one voice is relatively stationary while the other moves freely, creating a variety of intervals against the first. The great difference is that in the new style the dronelike voice is the *vox principalis*, and the *vox organalis* is the moving voice — or, as we now should call it, the melismatic voice, since it sings several notes against each syllable-carrying note of the original chant. Hand in hand with this difference went another just as big: the *vox principalis* is now the lower, not the upper voice.

What brought about these momentous practical departures? They amount virtually to standing the older polyphonic texture on its head: what was top is now bottom; what was mobile is now stationary, and vice versa. And perhaps most important from the listener's perspective, what had been subordinate (namely, the added voice) is now dominant. In the new melismatic organum, the chant seems paradoxically to accompany its accompaniment.

In keeping with this changed perspective, a new terminology is warranted, one that will remove the apparent paradox. Instead of *vox principalis*, let us simply call the voice that sustains the long-held notes of the original chant the "holding part." Since the Latin infinitive "to hold" is *tenere*, the chant-bearing part will henceforth be known as the *tenor*. The word actually begins appearing in this sense in the treatises of the thirteenth century, and though its meaning has varied over the years, it is still an important musical term today. This was its first meaning for polyphonic music — the voice that holds a preexistent melody out in long notes over which another voice sings a florid counterpoint. It was the relegation of the chant melody to the tenor that was the new event, for it inaugurated a texture — and a procedure — that would last for centuries. Indeed it is still practiced (or at least administered), under the thirteenth-century name *cantus firmus* or "fixed tune," in academic counterpoint studies today. For a sample of the new texture see Fig. 5-2.

This composition is from a manuscript that dates from around 1100 and was long kept in the library of the biggest Aquitanian monastery, the Abbey of St. Martial at Limoges. Its Aquitanian origin and its association with St. Martial is already a clue to the new style's why and wherefore, for we have encountered St. Martial before, as a center of trope and *versus* composition. The tenor in Fig. 5-2 is in fact a metrical *versus* composed to adorn the end of Christmas matins. What

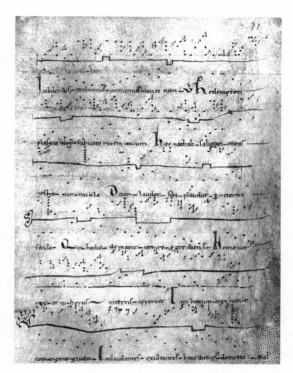

FIG. 5-2 Melismatic organum on the versus *Jubilemus, exultemus* from one of the twelfth-century "St. Martial" manuscripts (Paris, Bibliothèque Nationale, Fonds Latins MS 1139, fol. 41).

is melismatic organum then but an adornment of an adornment, a polyphonic gloss? It is a *longissima melodia* (to recall some terminology from chapter 2) sung not in place of an older chant, or in between its phrases, but (imagining two singers now) literally alongside it. "St. Martial"-style polyphony is thus a new kind of trope, simultaneous rather than prefatory, and a literal (that is, sonic) amplification of the liturgy.

"St. Martial" polyphony is found in four bound volumes comprising nine separate manuscripts, compiled between ca. 1100 and ca. 1150. (The quotes here are a reminder that the music was kept and used at St. Martial but not necessarily composed there.) The notation, like that of the contemporary chant, is specific as to pitch but not as to rhythm, reminding us once again that the music was composed, learned, and performed by oral methods. We, who must read these texts in order to sing the music the twelfth-century monks knew by heart, are more seriously handicapped by their rhythmic indeterminacy than we are in the case of chant, and for a fairly obvious reason. When two parts are sung simultaneously, the singers have to know how they "line up." In particular, the singer of the holding part has to know when to change to the next note — or else the singer of the moving part has to know when to cue his colleague on the tenor.

All we have to go on today in guessing at what contemporary singers knew cold is the rough — the *very* rough — vertical alignment of the parts in the manuscript "score," and the rule (already implied as far back as *Musica enchiriadis*) that the sustained part can move only when its motion will create a consonance against the faster-moving part. Applying these rules is not enough to arrive at a definitive text, assuming there was such a thing (which is a great deal to assume). Nor do we know if it is the tenor's notes that are meant to be "equipollent" (that is, roughly equal in length, like spoken syllables), or those of the melismatic part, or neither.

Thus the notation in Fig. 5-2 is (by the standards today's literate musicians are taught to demand) vague and insufficient for performance. The transcription of the beginning of the piece in Ex. 5-6 is entirely speculative. The transcriber, Carl Parrish, sums up the problem:

> The number of notes in the upper part to those in the lower varies considerably — from one to fifteen, actually — so that an effort to keep the lower part [i.e., the original chant] uniform in pace would cause a great variety of speeds in the upper note groups. On the other hand, a uniform pace in the upper part would cause as much variety in the notes of the slower-moving tenor.[5]

Citing mutually exclusive solutions favored by equally respected specialists, Parrish comments that "both interpretations produce satisfactory musical results, although there is no way of knowing which, if either, corresponds to the manner originally intended." In addition to the one to which Parrish called attention, there is the further problem of guessing exactly which notes of the tenor coincide with which notes of the melismatic voice at moments of change in the slower-moving part. For assured transcription or performance of this music, then, we would need to hear it sung by its "native" singers, and that is something we will never hear.

That has not stopped imaginative early-music performers from conjecturing a performance practice for this music, often very persuasively. As Leo Treitler, a specialist

EX. 5-6 Transcription of the beginning of *Jubilemus, exultemus* (Fig. 5-2)

in early notation and polyphony, has justly observed, "the question for us is not 'how must they have sung this music?' but rather 'how can we sing it?'" In seeking an answer to "our" question, Prof. Treitler goes on, "it may be that analysis and performance can teach us what exact methods have so far withheld about the problems confronting the musicians of the twelfth century."[6]

But whatever we learn from our own analyses and our own performances must obviously go far beyond the evidence of the sources into a realm where only artists dare tread, not historians. The speculative or conjectural performance of early music to delight modern audiences has provided an arena where artists and historians have been collaborating fruitfully, sometimes within the heads of a new breed of scholarly or musicologically-minded performer. But such performers know best of all that the historian cannot always helpfully advise the artist, and that the artist's successes, though they may convince an audience that includes the historian, still cannot provide the latter with evidence.

Not all the polyphonic pieces in the St. Martial manuscripts present modern performers with such difficulties. Along with sustained-note organum settings like the one in Fig. 5-2, the St. Martial sources contain numerous *versus* and hymn settings in discant style, in which the two frequently crossing voices, if not precisely note-against-note, are at least rhythmically similar. In such settings it is not often possible to identify a preexisting tune or cantus firmus in either part; thus there is nothing in them to distinguish a *vox principalis* from a *vox organalis*. In such cases the two parts were in all likelihood conceived as a pair.

To say this is not necessarily to imply that the two-part texture was actually conceived as a unit, even if it was composed in one sitting. One voice might have been written first and then treated as an ersatz cantus firmus for the second; some theoretical discussions seem to imply as much. But in some settings the two voices are so intricately (and playfully!) interrelated that simultaneous conception of the whole texture seems a virtual certainty. One such is given in Ex. 5-7.

The texture here is "neume-against-neume" rather than note-against-note. (The slurs in the example show how the notes in the original notation were joined into neumatic groups or *ligatures* — literally, "bindings" — of two, three, four, or more.) The transcription, by Leo Treitler, follows the "isosyllabic" principle we encountered as an option in transcribing troubadour songs; every neume is assumed to last the same amount of time, represented in the transcription as a quarter note's duration. At the beginning of the piece this duration also corresponds to the syllables, but the neumes in the decorative melismas that come at the ends of verses are treated in the same way.

Notice the way the melismas "accelerate" through the piece from two-note to four-note to five-note patterns. (This seems to argue in favor of the isosyllabic scheme, in which ligatures actually gather speed as they grow in size.) Notice, too, the repetitive or sequential patterns into which the melismas are organized, and the way the voices complement one another's contour by the use of contrary motion. This complementary relationship definitely betokens "whole-texture conception": the individual lines have meaning only in terms of their complementation. For a third thing, notice the way

EX. 5-7 Versus sung as a prosulated *Benedicamus Domino* response at St. Martial and elsewhere (Paris, BN, LAT. 1139)

EX. 5-7   (continued)

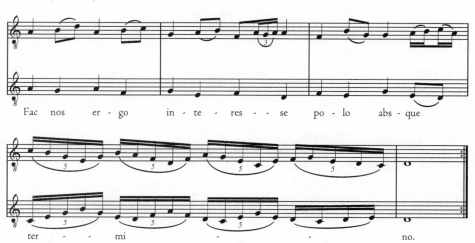

in which the two voices exchange roles in the first two measures (=lines of the poem), but also notice the slight differences between them (ligature G – F in the first measure, upper part, answered in the second measure by a single G in the lower; the two-note ligature F – E in the first measure, lower part, answered in the second measure by a three-noter, E – F – E, in the upper) that insure variation within repetition, small irregularities within a larger regularity. Fascination with abstract patterning here produces a fascinating result.

Even though it uses a texture that was described by earlier writers such as Guido and John, while the cantus-firmus settings seem to be unprecedented, this composition is in fact a much more "modern" piece — and a much more "artistically" shaped product, as we understand the word — than the one in Fig. 5-2. Where a cantus firmus may happen to show up in the texture is less of a defining trait than its sheer presence or absence, and here we have a composition that seems to have been elaborated musically from scratch, out of sheer joy in pattern-making. "The spirit" of such music, Prof. Treitler has written, "is that of the magic square and the palindrome."[7] Such a spirit of playful creativity is more in keeping with modern understanding of the word "art" than are the functional amplifications of plainchant that we have been encountering up to now. All at once we seem to behold a planned and finished "artwork" — a fully shaped *res facta*, a "made thing," as musicians would later call such works to distinguish them from ephemeral improvisations.

Yet we should resist the temptation to imagine that such works, because they are so meticulously worked out, had to be literally worked out on paper in advance. We are still dealing with the products of a predominantly oral culture, of which only a few specimens — the cream, presumably — ever found their way into writing. A piece like the one in Ex. 5-7 was in all likelihood composed by a singer — or more likely, by two singers — in the act of singing.

The regularities and symmetries — the voice exchanges, the complementation of contour, the melodic repetitions and sequences — may appear to us to suggest the shaping hand of an "author," as "classical" musicians have come to understand the term. (That is to say, a creator who works apart from performers, out of "real time.") But they are more likely just the opposite. Patterns like these are not abstract ideas but memory aids—which is why we use the word "catchy" to describe them. They bear witness to the process (and the fun) of creativity within an oral culture. *Homo ludens* and *homo faber*—"humanity at play" and "creative humanity"—were close allies in such a culture.

THE CODEX CALIXTINUS

What the rare written-down specimens could do was travel. The *versus* in Ex. 5-7 was a great favorite. It is found in three of the four "St. Martial" manuscripts containing polyphony, and it is found as a conductus in the other main source of early-to-mid-twelfth-century polyphonic composition. This other source is a magnificent copy of the Codex Calixtinus, more accurately known as the "Book of St. James" (*Liber sancti Jacobi*), a huge memorial potpourri dedicated to the apostle James the Greater, commissioned by Pope Callistus (Calixtus) II, who reigned from 1119 to 1124.

According to tradition, the body of St. James was miraculously translated, after his martyrdom in Judea, to Spain, where he had preached and where he is now venerated (under the name Sant' Iago or Santiago) as patron saint. His relics are said to be housed in the Cathedral of Santiago de Compostela, an Atlantic coastal town in the extreme northwest corner of Spain (above Portugal), built over his reputed gravesite in 1078. The copy of the Codex Calixtinus at Saint James's own shrine, one of the great pilgrimage spots in late-medieval Europe, is of course an especially lavish one, and it is fitted out with many special features. One of these is an appendix of a dozen parchment leaves containing some two dozen polyphonic compositions, some specially written for the Office of St. James, others (like the one given in Ex. 5-7) borrowed from the common monastic repertory of southern and central France.

The appendix is now thought to have been compiled in the cathedral town of Vézelay by around 1170 and shipped or carried down as a gift to the shrine at Compostela. One of the reasons for associating the manuscript with a fairly northern point of origin is its use of the word *conductus* in place of *versus* for pieces like the one in Ex. 5-7. Another is the inclusion of standard Mass and Office items in polyphonic elaborations along with the more usual tropes and *versus*. These settings consist of six responsorial chants—four matins Responsories, a Gradual, and an Alleluia—from the special local liturgy of St. James, as given in chant form in an earlier part of the Codex. The polyphonic versions are in the sustained-tone organum style, with the original chant as the tenor and an especially florid counterpoint above it. As we shall see, this is cathedral, not monastic, polyphony.

The most florid of all the settings in the Codex Calixtinus is the Kyrie *Cunctipotens genitor*, familiar to us already as a chant. It was something of a favorite for polyphonic treatment in the twelfth century. An anonymous treatise of ca. 1100 called *Ad organum faciendum* ("How to do organum") had already used it to demonstrate note-against-note discant in a rather dogged contrary motion (Ex. 5-8a). The example has its own historical significance because it is one of the earliest settings to give the *vox organalis* a higher tessitura than the original melody.

The placement of the counterpoint above the chant makes comparison with the melismatic setting of the same item in the Codex Calixtinus (Ex. 5-8b) particularly apt. Putting them side by side, one can easily imagine the one, or something like it, turning into the other over time (especially if one recalls the observations in chapter 1 about the gradual elaboration of "the old way of singing"), and finally getting written down as a "keeper." Proceeding on the assumption that we are dealing with an embellished discant, the transcription in Ex. 5-8b has been spatially laid out so that the notes in the tenor come beneath notes in the *vox organalis* that form perfect consonances with it. This arrangement corresponds only loosely with the way in which the parts line up in the manuscript, it is true (see Fig. 5-3). But since the notation still conveys no specific information about duration, the manuscript alignment may not seem as reliable a guide to the actual counterpoint as the theoretical principles on which all writers agree. (Particularly important to the theorists, of course, is the principle of *occursus*, which the transcription does its bit to reinforce.)

Of course it could be argued just as logically that in the absence of a precise rhythmic notation, the manuscript alignment was the only possible—and therefore an indispensable—guide to the counterpoint. Yet a glance at Fig. 5-3 will suffice to

EX. 5-8A   *Cunctipotens genitor* setting, from *Ad organum faciendum*

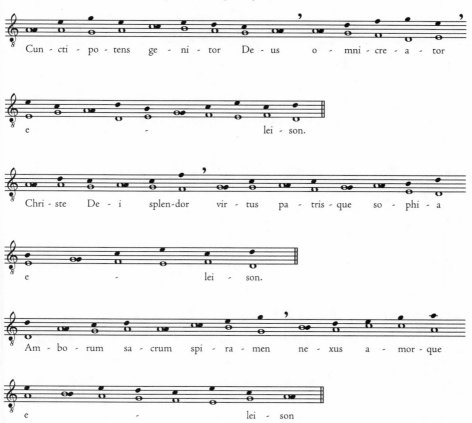

EX. 5-8B   *Cunctipotens genitor setting, from Codex Calixtinus*

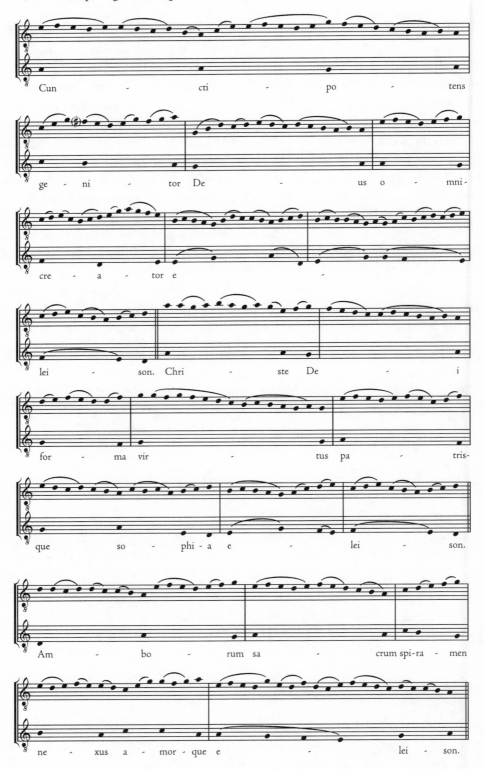

show that the alignment was not a matter of great concern to the copyist. Even more basically, to argue that the alignment was meant to guide performance is to assume that the piece was transmitted primarily in writing, and that its performers read it off the page. The opposite assumption, that the piece was transmitted orally and performed from memory (with the notation having little more than the status of a souvenir or an art-object), accords better with what we know of medieval practice.

The most famous piece in the Codex Calixtinus appendix is famous for the wrong reason. It is a conductus, *Congaudeant catholici* ("Let all Catholics rejoice together"), that is furnished with two counterpoints, one in a fairly florid "organal" style, the other a simple discant. Although it is quite obvious that the two counterpoints were entered separately (the moderately fancy organal voice occupies a staff of its own,

FIG. 5-3 *Cunctipotens genitor*, as set melismatically in the Codex Calixtinus, a late twelfth-century French manuscript now kept at the cathedral of Santiago de Compostela in Spain. The setting begins halfway through the second system and ends at the beginning of the fifth system.

above the tenor; the note-against-note discant is entered, in red ink for contrast, directly on the staff containing the tenor), the piece was long taken to be a unique three-part polyphonic setting, supposedly the first of its kind (Fig. 5-4; Ex. 5-9). (*Congaudeant catholici*'s "rightful" claim to fame is the fact that it may be the earliest polyphonic piece to carry an attribution in its source; the Codex names "Magister Albertus Parisiensis" as composer, identifiable by his title as the Albertus who served as cantor at the cathedral of Notre Dame from around 1140 to 1177.)

The extremely high level of dissonance that resulted from performing the two settings simultaneously was not at first considered a deterrent. Careless reading of the medieval music theorists, together with equally incautious assumptions about the relationship of writing to composition, encouraged the belief that the harmonic style of early polyphony was entirely rationalistic, based on speculative numerology, and, from a practical — that is, aural — point of view, virtually haphazard. (It was thought, to be specific, that voices written in succession against a cantus firmus had to accord

FIG. 5-4   The conductus *Congaudeant catholici* as it appears in the Codex Calixtinus (fol. 214, the bottom half of the page).

harmonically only with it, not with each other; both "written" and "in succession" are now acknowledged to be anachronistically limiting terms.)

What may in fact be the earliest surviving three-part polyphonic composition is a Christmas conductus, *Verbum patris humanatur* ("The word of the Father is made man"). It is found as a two-part discant setting in one of the Aquitanian manuscripts, and in three parts (of which one, the tenor of course, is common to both settings) in a small French manuscript of the late twelfth century now kept in the library of Cambridge University. The notation is still noncommittal with respect to rhythm. The transcription in Ex. 5-10 is "isosyllabic," resulting in an implicit duple meter based on the accentual scansion of the text. The longer values on the exclamatory O's and elsewhere are conjectural; they arise out of the same implicit (or perhaps it would be more honest to say "presumed") musical pulse.

The basic "harmony of three voices" emerges here as octave (or unison) plus fifth. The octave-filled-by-fifth sonority includes every perfect consonance (or *symphonia*, to

EX. 5-9   *Congaudeant catholici* transcribed as two separate two-part pieces, but aligned

EX. 5-9   (continued)

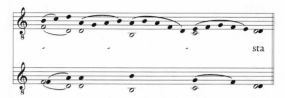

Let catholics rejoice together, let the denizens of heaven be glad this day.

EX. 5-10   *Verbum patris humanatur* (twelfth-century conductus setting in three parts)

The Word of the Father becometh man,
For a maiden was greeted,
Was greeted, impregnated,
Without knowing any man;
Hey, Hey, receive the joyous news.

Beyond the natural the generation,
Beyond the natural the conception,
Joining Lord of all creation
And created soul!
Hey, Hey receive the joyous news.

With the mother of the Savior,
It is not as it is with humans;
A virgin gives birth without shame,
A spotless lily she remains!
Hey, hey, receive the joyous news.

recall the old organum terminology). In places where imperfect consonances had been common before (especially the "precadential" position), we are now apt to find triads, or else a combination of fourth or fifth plus a seventh over the lowest voice that is justified by its characteristic approach to the concluding consonance by contrary motion — a harmonically amplified occursus.

The strategic placement of dissonance (or imperfect consonance) immediately before perfect consonance, and its "resolution" to the latter by contrary voice-leading, was henceforth regarded as the essential "function" of discant harmony and the definer of musical "motion." It became the primary signal of "closure," or phrase-ending in polyphonic music, the necessary determiner of cadences, and eventually the primary shaper of musical form. As befits something so important to musical structure and perception — to musical "language," in effect — it was eventually standardized in practice, and particularly in teaching, as "laws of counterpoint."

Still and all, the note-against-note harmony of the earliest surviving three-part discants, like *Verbum patris humanatur*, is the kind of harmony that is easily worked out in the act of "harmonizing" — that is, by ear — and depicts in writing, like a kind of snapshot, an informal oral practice of evident long standing, and with many descendants in today's world. There is no telling how far back in time such practices may extend.

Notre Dame de Paris

PARISIAN CATHEDRAL MUSIC IN THE TWELFTH AND THIRTEENTH CENTURIES AND ITS MAKERS

THE CATHEDRAL-UNIVERSITY COMPLEX

Many circumstances conspired to make Paris the undisputed intellectual capital of Europe by the end of the twelfth century. The process of urbanization, traced to some degree in chapter 4, brought about a decline in the importance of monasteries as centers of learning and a swift rise in the prestige of cathedral schools. These schools were learning centers attached to cathedral churches, the large urban churches that were the seats (*cathedrae*) of bishops and that served as administrative centers for a surrounding ecclesiastical territory called a diocese.

The enhanced importance of the cathedral beginning in the twelfth century, especially in northern Europe, was underscored by the gigantism of cathedral architecture. The Gothic style (so called since the nineteenth century to emphasize its northern European provenance), with its soaring lines and huge interior spaces, had its start precisely at this time. Paris and the surrounding area (including the northern suburb of Saint-Denis, site of the royal crypt) was one of its earliest sites. The abbey and basilica of Saint-Denis were constructed between 1140 and 1144. The cornerstone of the present-day cathedral of Paris, dedicated to the Virgin Mary and affectionately known therefore as *Notre-Dame de Paris* ("Our Lady of Paris"), or simply as Notre Dame, was laid in 1163 by Pope Alexander III himself. The altar was consecrated twenty years later, and the building began to function, although the whole enormous structure was not finished until the beginning of the fourteenth century.

Within and around the great Gothic cathedrals, the clergy was organized into a community modeled in many of its aspects on the feudal ideal. The resident staff or faculty was sworn to a quasi-monastic regime defined by a *canon* or consensual law. From this word they derived their title: a full member of the community was a "canon regular," or simply canon. The canons elected the bishop who ruled them, and who parceled out the church lands and their incomes to the canons in the form of *prebends* (from *praebenda*, that which is to be granted), much as a lord would deed land to his vassals. The community of canons, known as the college or chapter, was organized into a hierarchy of ranks and offices overseen by the chancellor or dean, the bishop's chief of staff. They included the *scolasticus* (school director) and the *precentor* (musical director).

Much of this vocabulary, as the reader has surely noticed, is now used to designate the ranks and offices in a university, and that is no coincidence. The university as we

FIG. 6-1 Interior of the cathedral of Notre Dame, Paris.

know it—or as it was originally called, the *universitas societas magistrorum discipulorumque* (universal association of masters and disciples, i.e., teachers and pupils)—was a twelfth-century innovation, formed initially by consolidating and augmenting the faculties of cathedral schools. The University of Paris, the first great northern European university, was by far the largest. It was preceded only by the University of Bologna, originally endowed in the eleventh century as the pope's own vocational school of "canon law" for training church administrators.

Its instructional and administrative staff was formed out of the faculties of three large existing schools: that of Notre Dame, that of the canons regular at the abbey of St. Victor (known to us already as a center of sequence composition), and that of the collegiate church of St. Geneviève. (A collegiate church was the next lower rank after cathedral: it had a dean and chapter but no resident bishop.) As a physical plant the University of Paris grew up alongside the new cathedral. It was fully functioning by around 1170 with the cathedral's chancellor as its ecclesiastical superintendent" charged with granting its faculty the *licentia docendi* (license to teach), known to us as the doctor's degree. It was formally chartered by a papal bull—a letter carrying the pope's *bulla* or seal—in 1215. Since the sixteenth century it has been known as the Sorbonne, after its largest constituent college, an elite doctoral school of theology founded—that is, funded—by Robert de Sorbon, the royal chaplain, in 1253.

This unprecedented royal/papal

FIG. 6-2 Philip II of France (Philip Augustus, r. 1180–1223), handing the royal privilege to the masters and students of the University of Paris in 1200. Illumination from a mid-fourteenth-century Latin chronicle known as the Book of Procurors, now kept at the Bibliothèque Nationale, Paris.

ecclesiastical/educational establishment was the environment in which an equally unprecedented musical establishment thrived. Our knowledge of it, while extensive, is curiously indirect, pieced together by collating evidence from two or three skimpy descriptive accounts, four immense musical manuscripts, and half a dozen more or less detailed theoretical treatises. What we now call the "Notre Dame School" of polyphonic composition, and are accustomed to regarding as the first great "classical" flowering of Western art music, is actually a sort of grand historiographical fiction. Constructing it was one of the earliest triumphs of modern musicology — and still one of the most impressive.

The musical documents, three service books compiled in Paris in the mid-to-late thirteenth century and one compiled in Britain somewhat later (but seemingly containing a somewhat earlier version of the repertory), house an imposing body of polyphonic chant settings that stands in relation to the modest repertories of the "St. Martial" and Compostela manuscripts in more or less the same way that the great central cathedral-university complex itself stood in relation to the outlying monasteries and shrines of an earlier age.

The earlier repertories had been local ones in the main, emphasizing patron saints and intramural observances, and concentrating on recent chants like sequences and *versus*. The new one emphasized the general ("catholic") liturgy, the great yearly feasts, and the largest, musically most elaborate liturgical items. The Parisian or Parisian-style music books consisted mainly of settings of the Great Responsories for matins and the highly melismatic "lesson chants" (Gradual and Alleluia) of the Mass, arranged in the order of the church calendar, with particular concentrations around Christmas, Easter, and Pentecost (along with the Feast of the Assumption, in recognition of the Virgin Mary's status as patron at Notre Dame; but even so, she was hardly a local figure).

Where the earlier repertories had consisted, with only the rarest (and oft-times dubious) exceptions, of two-part settings that paired the original chant tenor with one added voice, there is a whole cycle of Notre Dame settings with two added parts for a total texture of three voices, and even a few especially grandiose items with three added parts for an unheard-of complement of four. The earlier repertories had favored two styles: a note-against-note style called discant, and a somewhat more florid style called organum, with the tenor sustained against short melismatic flights in the added voice. A typical Notre Dame composition alternated the two styles and took them both to extremes. In "organal" sections, each tenor note could literally last minutes, furnishing a series of protracted drones supporting tremendous melismatic outpourings; the discant sections, by contrast, were driven by besetting rhythms that (for the first time anywhere) were precisely fixed in the notation.

The chant settings associated with Notre Dame, in short, were as ambitious as the cathedral for which they were composed. They took their stylistic bearings from existing polyphonic repertories but vastly outstripped their predecessors in every dimension — length, range, number of voices. They set the world (well, the Western-world) record for "intrasyllabic melodic expansion,"[1] to use a wonderfully precise term a Russian folklorist once coined to describe melismatic proliferation and the way it eats up a text. (That record still stands, by the way, after eight hundred years.)

To find the motivation for this astonishing copiousness, one might look no further than St. Augustine's metaphor of "a mind poured forth in joy." But there may be more to it. The overwhelming dimensions these composers achieved may not only have accorded with the size of the reverberant spaces their works had to fill, but may also have carried a message of institutional triumph at a time notable for its triumphant institutionalism.

In any case, the Notre Dame composers aspired to an unprecedented universality. Their works, unlike those created at previous polyphonic centers, could be used anywhere the Latin liturgy of the western Christian church was used. And they aspired to encyclopedic completeness: it is evident that the surviving codices reflect an attempt — indeed, multiple attempts — to outfit the entire calendar of feasts with polyphony. (A codex, plural *codices*, is a large manuscript consisting of several smaller component "fascicles" collected and bound together.) Thus, with their works, the musicians of Notre Dame symbolized the strong, united church they served, and promoted catholicism in the literal and original sense of the word. As we know from the dispersion of their works in the extant sources, their program was successful. The central Parisian repertory was copied far and wide and sung well beyond its home territory. Either as such or as the basis for further elaboration, moreover, the repertory lasted for generations after its creators' lives had ended.

PIECING THE EVIDENCE TOGETHER

Those who copied and sang these works for generations did not, however, know their authors' names. Like most manuscripts containing music for ecclesiastical use, the Notre Dame sources carried no attributions. (Only "secular" works like courtly songs could carry an author's name without taint of pride, a deadly sin.) We do think we know the identities of some of the authors, though, and we think we know something about the history of the repertory and its development. And we know what we know (or what we think we know) precisely thanks to the alliance of the cathedral church of Notre Dame with the University of Paris.

From the very beginning, the student body at the university had comprised a strong English contingent. Even earlier, it had been the rule for English theologians to go to Paris for their doctoral training. An example was John of Salisbury (ca. 1115–80), the great neo-Platonic (or "realist") philosopher and biographer of Thomas à Becket, who traveled to Paris in his youth to study with Pierre Abélard. His first important work, a treatise on good government called *Policraticus*, was written around 1147, when he had just returned from Paris, and contains a notorious complaint about the gaudy music he heard in churches there. We don't know what music he heard; maybe it was something like *Congaudeant catholici* (Ex. 5-9), whose composer, Albertus, was the cantor at Notre Dame around the time of John's visit. More likely it was never written down at all. But the fact that the dour English clergyman found so much to condemn is already an indication that Paris was a special place for music.

Something over a hundred years later, around 1270 or 1280, we get another Englishman's testimony—in this case entirely approving, even reverent—about music in Paris. This second Englishman was the author of a treatise called *De mensuris et discantu* ("On Rhythmic Notation and Discant") that was published as the fourth item in a batch of anonymous medieval writings on music brought out by the great music bibliographer Charles-Edmond-Henri de Coussemaker in 1864, when musicology was in its infancy. The treatise was headed *Anonymus IV* in this celebrated publication, and the name, anglicized by the insertion of an "o," has unfortunately come since to be associated, thanks to popular writers and textbook authors, with the writer instead of the text. The poor fellow, whatever his name may have been, is irrevocably known to music history students as "Anonymous Four." We can surmise that he was English since the treatise survives in English manuscript copies and makes reference to local English saints (and even to the "Westcuntrie," the author's immediate neighborhood). We assume that he learned the contents of his treatise as a student in Paris, since he based most of his discussion slavishly (at times verbatim) on the known writings of Paris University *magistri* (lecturers), which he may have first encountered in the lecture hall.

If, as seems evident, the treatise is something like a set of university lecture notes, we may imagine the lecturer pausing amid the technical complexities he was laboriously imparting to reminisce briefly about the traditions of Parisian polyphony and the men who made it. This brief memoir—it is without doubt the most famous passage in any medieval treatise on music—begins with an obeisance to "Leoninus magister" (Master Leonin, short for Leo), who, "it is said," was the best *organista* (composer of organum). He made a *magnus liber*, a "great book" of organa *de gradali et de antiphonario*, "from the Gradual and the Antiphoner"; that is, he made organa on chants from the Mass and the Office books. That is all we are told about Master Leonin.

Next, Anonymus IV reports what the lecturer said about *Perotinus magnus* (the great Perotin or Pierrot, short for Pierre), who was the best *discantor* (composer of discant) and "better than Leoninus." Perotin is identified first as the reviser of Leonin's work. He *abbreviavit* the great book (let the translation of that word wait for now) and inserted many *clausulae* ("little discant sections") of his own devising into Leonin's compositions.

Then comes a list of Perotin's original works, beginning with the real newsmakers, the *quadrupla*, organa in four parts (that is, three parts added to the Gregorian tenor). Two titles are given: *Viderunt* and *Sederunt*. Both, it turns out, are graduals: *Viderunt omnes fines terrae* ("All the ends of the earth have seen"), for Christmas, was reserved at Notre Dame for the newly instituted Feast of the Lord's Circumcision (January 1); *Sederunt principes et adversum me loquebantur* ("Princes sat and plotted against me") was the gradual for the Feast of St. Stephen the Martyr (December 26).

Next some famous *organa tripla* by Perotin are listed, including an Alleluia for the Mass commemorating the birth of the Virgin Mary. Finally, Perotin is credited with continuing the already venerable tradition of composing music to new Latin religious lyrics in the form of conductus, both polyphonic and monophonic. Three titles are mentioned, of which one—*Beata viscera* ("O blessed womb") in honor of the

Virgin — was set to a poem by Philip the Chancellor (of Notre Dame), head of the University of Paris from 1218 to his death in 1236.

The link between Philip and the work attributed to Perotin is choice evidence for the close creative relationship that obtained between the cathedral clergy and the university faculty. Philip's death, moreover, marks what is known as the *terminus ante quem*, the latest possible date (literally, "the end point before which" something happens) for Perotin's compositional activity. (It also marks the virtual end of the Latin *versus* tradition, for Philip was one of the last of that line.)

There is no telling, of course, exactly how Perotin's lifetime overlapped with Philip's, and good reason to believe that he did most of his work considerably before 1236. For there is another category of historical document that can be linked with him — or rather, with the works attributed to him in Anonymus IV. In 1198 and again in 1199, the Bishop of Paris, Eudes (or Odo) de Sully, issued letters cautioning against excessively boisterous holiday celebrations in the cathedral.[2] Keep the bell-ringing down, they instruct; keep the mummers and maskers out of the sanctuary; no fools' processions, please. Instead, let there be good music, and let it be lavish.

In both letters, the bishop promises payment for *organum quadruplum*: in 1198 he requests it for the Feast of the Circumcision; in 1199, for the Feast of St. Stephen. Comparison with the list of Perotin's works in Anonymus IV shows a remarkable correspondence; for these feasts are precisely the ones at which the two *quadrupla* enumerated there would have been sung. So again we have a probable *terminus ante quem*: the largest of the works attributed to Perotin must have been composed by — or, most likely, just at — the end of the twelfth century. One or both of the famous *quadrupla*, moreover, can be found in every one of the four big "Notre Dame" manuscripts mentioned above, as well as other manuscripts of the time or shortly after. And that observation holds as well for every other piece named in Anonymus IV. On the basis of that list, Perotin's "complete works" have been collected and published.

So we appear to have a remarkable convergence of prose description, archival document, and actual musical source, each corroborating the content of the others. It is owing to Anonymus IV and the bishop's letters that we can identify the four manuscripts as containing a repertory specifically and officially associated with Notre Dame. And the musical sources corroborate the specifics of the documentary accounts.

The only uncorroborated information, frustratingly enough, is the identity (or indeed, the existence) of the musicians named in Anonymus IV. Three are named in all: besides Leonin and Perotin, there is one Robert de Sabilone, who is lavishly praised but otherwise unidentified and whose name is found nowhere else. But neither is the name of Perotin! About the greatest musician of his time, as the author of Anonymus IV emphatically insists he was, we have no evidence at all except a chance mention in a set of lecture notes taken down by a nameless Englishman at least fifty and possibly as many as seventy years after Perotin's death. (There did happen to be a cantor at Notre Dame named Petrus, who was born Pierre Hosdenc near Beauvais and served at the Paris cathedral from 1184 to 1197; needless to say, strenuous efforts have been made to identify him with Anonymus IV's Perotin, but the facts and the chronology do not add up.) The situation is more promising in the case of Leonin. Two candidates have been more or less plausibly identified. One is a certain Henricus Leonellus, who owned a house near Notre Dame and was a lay member of the abbey of St. Victor. According to the available documents, he died some time between 1187 and 1192, which would place him in the generation of Anonymus IV's "Leoninus." There is nothing in the documents to connect him with music, though.

The other candidate, recently put forward by the music historian Craig Wright, is especially appealing: a canon and priest at Notre Dame and St. Victor whose name was Leonius but who was sometimes referred to in official documents by the same affectionate diminutive—Leoninus, "old man Leo"—used in Anonymus IV.[3] The peak of his documented activity was reached in the 1180s and 1190s, and he died in 1201 or 1202. This Leonius is not identified as a musician, but he was a poet of considerable renown, best known for his *Hystorie sacre gestas ab origine mundi* ("Acts of sacred history since the beginning of the world"), a paraphrase of the first eight books of the Old Testament in verse—some 14,000 lines of it! Anyone who could write that, it seems, could also write "a great book of organa from the Gradual and the Antiphoner to adorn the Divine Service." But this still does not constitute factual corroboration of Anonymus IV's terse report, and we ought to proceed with utmost caution when it comes to identifying the composers of the "Notre Dame school" with actual persons. For the unconfirmed account in Anonymus IV, written long after the fact, has all the earmarks of a "creation myth"—that is, a story that seeks to account for the existence of something wonderful (here, the matchless repertory of polyphonic music at Notre Dame) by supplying it with an origin and an originator. (Compare the way the Bible accounts for the existence of music by naming its inventor—Jubal, son of Lamech, "the forerunner of all who play the harp and flute"—in Genesis 4:21. Or the way Haydn has been named the "father of the symphony" or the string quartet, to say nothing of Saint Gregory and his dove.)

MEASURED MUSIC

Even if the poet Leonius *was* Anonymus IV's (or rather, the Paris university lecturer's) Leoninus, that still would not guarantee the story's status as fact. A famous church poet would in fact be the ideal mythological creator of Notre Dame polyphony, for the great glory of that repertory in the eyes of its latter-day practitioners was the fact that it was *metrical*. That is to say, it managed to incorporate precise time-measurement into musical composition and notation, and it did so by adapting to musical purposes the principles of "quantitative" poetic meter.

This, too, shows the connection between musical practice at Notre Dame and the University of Paris curriculum. By the twelfth century, quantitative meter—defined by syllable-length rather than by "accent" or stress—was no longer used by contemporary poets, even when writing in Latin. But it was studied academically as part of the quadrivium, often from the famous textbook by St. Augustine suggestively titled *De musica* ("About music"—that is, the "music" or sonic organization of verse). The rhythmic practice at Notre Dame was based on similar principles of versification.

In a quantitative meter, one assumes at least two abstract durations — one "long," the other "short" — that are related to each other by some simple arithmetic proportion. The simplest proportion is a factor of two: a long equals two shorts. That already gives the gist of the earliest abstractly conceived musical meter, as practiced at Notre Dame. Two note-lengths were assumed: a *nota longa* (shortened in normal parlance to *longa*, or in English, a "long") and a *nota brevis* (shortened to *brevis*, or in English, a "breve"). A long was assumed to equal two breves, and the simplest way of turning their relationship into a metrical pattern (called an *ordo*, plural *ordines*) was simply to alternate them: LBLBLBLBLBL . . . ; in effect "tum-ta-tum-ta-tum-ta-tum-ta-tum-ta-tum . . . ," and so on. This was the basic *modus* (or "rhythmic mode," or "way of doing rhythm") in use at the time of the "Leonin" generation.

So the standard musical "foot" (*pes*) was like the classical "trochee": a long followed by a short. The difference between a *pes* (mere building-material) and an *ordo* (an actual "line" of musical poetry) was that the ordo ended with a "cadence" on the long, after which a pause (for the sake of scansion or simply for a breath) could take place. The basic pattern, then, was not LB but LBL, "tum-ta-tum." The shortest finished "line" of rhythmicized melody, consisting of one of these patterns, was called the "first perfect ordo." (Thus LBLBL, or "tum-ta-tum-ta-tum," was the "second perfect ordo," the third was LBLBLBL, or "tum-ta-tum-ta-tum-ta-tum," etc.)

The beautifully elegant thing about this abstractly conceived "modal" meter was that its notation did not require the invention of any new signs or shapes. The old "quadratic" chant neumes could be adapted directly to the new purpose. There was no special sign for a long or for a breve. There was no need for one, because the unit of notation was not the note but the ordo, the pattern. And the most efficient way of representing such a pattern of measured sounds was by a pattern of familiar neume shapes — that is, "ligatures," in which two, three, or more pitches were "bound together" in a single sign.

Generically, a ligature of two notes (whether ascending or descending) was called a *binaria*, one of three notes a *ternaria*, of four notes a *quaternaria*. An ordo was represented by a particular sequence of these shapes. The basic modus, described above as "trochaic" meter, was shown by an initial ternaria followed by any number of binariae, as in Ex. 6-1a. If one wanted the opposite metrical arrangement ("iambic" rather than trochaic meter), in which the basic foot is BL and the first perfect ordo is BLB, all one had to do was reverse the pattern of ligatures. Now there will be a series of binariae followed by a ternaria, as in Ex. 6-1b.

EX. 6-1A   Trochaic pattern notated with "modal" ligatures

LBL BL BL BL BL BL BL BL BL BL BL BL

EX. 6-1B   Iambic pattern notated with "modal" ligatures

BL BL BL BL BL BL BL BLB L BL BL BL BLB

Comparing Ex. 6-1a with Ex. 6-1b, one readily sees that the rhythmic significance of a given neume shape is not stable or immanent, but depends on the context. The ternaria in Ex. 6-1a is read LBL, while the ternaria in Ex. 6-1b has exactly the opposite meaning: BLB. The fact that the binariae in both are read BL should not be regarded as an inherent property of the sign, but as the coincidence or overlap of two different contexts. Later, as the result of a new notational refinement, shapes—both of single notes and of ligatures—did acquire inherent meanings. At that time the binaria did finally assume the "proper" meaning BL. But the invention of that refinement, like all inventions, had to await its necessity.

To observe Notre Dame polyphony in action, rhythm and all, we can begin with a two-part setting (*organum duplum*; or, as some theorists called it, *organum per se*) of the kind associated in Anonymus IV with the original "great book" of Leonin. The obvious choice for this purpose is the original two-part setting of the Gradual *Viderunt omnes*, used variously, as we have seen, at Christmas and at the Feast of the Circumcision (January 1), and eventually recomposed as a *quadruplum*.

The two-part *Viderunt* is the great book's opening piece as preserved in all its extant sources, since they are all organized according to the church calendar, which begins with Advent, the lead-up to the Christmas season. Fig. 6-3a reproduces the original chant from the *Liber usualis*, until 1963 the official modern chant book of the Roman Catholic church. Fig. 6-3b shows the organum, as found in its most lavish source, a codex copied in Paris during the 1240s, now kept in the Medici library in Florence. (It is usually called the "Florence manuscript," and is known to its friends as **Flo** or simply as **F**.) As befits its pride of place, the organum is decorated with an impressive "illuminated" capital *V* containing a three-part illustration or trip-tych. Reading from the top down, the three panels illustrate three successive phases of the Christmas story: the Adoration of the Magi, the Flight into Egypt, and the Slaughter of the Innocents. The tenor corresponds to the chant, and it is evident at a glance that the Notre Dame style gave new meaning to the word "melisma." The first syllable of text ("Vi-") carries an outpouring of more than forty notes of duplum. That's "intrasyllabic melodic expansion" with a vengeance!

A second glance discloses something that may seem puzzling. The organum set-ting is drastically incomplete. After the opening pair of words, "Viderunt omnes," the organum skips all the way to "Notum fecit," the beginning of the verse. The verse is set almost complete but is missing just the final pair of words, "justitiam suam." What

FIG. 6-3A The Christmas gradual *Viderunt omnes* as it appears in *Liber usualis*, the standard modern chant book of the Catholic church (in use from 1903 to 1963). Translation: "All the ends of the earth have seen the salvation of our God; sing joyfully to God, all the earth. The Lord hath made known his salvation; he hath revealed his justice in the sight of the Gentiles" (Psalm 97).

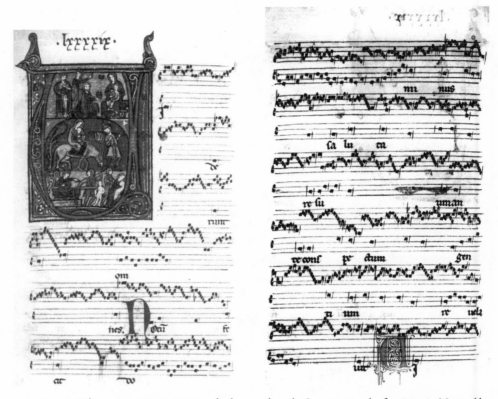

FIG. 6-3B *Viderunt omnes* set as organum duplum, perhaps by Leoninus, as the first item in *Magnus liber de gradali et antefonario* (Florence, Biblioteca Medicea Laurenziana, Plut.29.I, fols. 99-99v; this source will be abbreviated *Flo* in subsequent references).

happened to the rest? The asterisks in the chant text as given in the *Liber usualis* are our clue. They are the cues that show how the soloist and choir divide up the text in this responsorial chant. The opening respond, once past the *incipit* (the opening pair of words), belongs to the choir. The verse, excepting the final melisma, belongs to the soloist.

Putting that information together with the polyphonic setting reveals that the composer set as organum only the soloist's portion of the chant. The two-voice polyphony thus represents a multiplied soloist, so to speak. The parts sung by the choir are not set but were supplied in performance from memory. Since the choristers did not need to learn their part from the book, the book does not contain their part. Materials were expensive and space was at the highest premium.

From all of this we learn that polyphony at Notre Dame was the art of virtuoso soloists — the cantor and his assistant, the succentor. (And that is why only responsorial chants — matins responsories, Graduals, Alleluias — were set as organum there.) The astonishingly expansive treatment of the incipit is something of a counterpart to the illuminated capital: a rich decoration.

Again comparing the chant in Fig. 6-3a with the organum in Fig. 6-3b, we notice that when the soloist's portion of the chant has its own melismas (at "om-" of *omnes* and especially at "Do-" of *Dominus* in the verse), the organum tenor notes are written in clumps, taking up far less space (=time). The primary motivation for hurrying the tenor along at such spots was undoubtedly practical: just imagine how long the music would have to last if every tenor note were held out like the first few! But what begins in necessity often ends in play — that is, in "art." It was precisely these hurried-along sections of the organum, where the tenor is melismatic, that evoked from the composers what we would call the greatest artfulness or creativity. We will be tracing the repercussions of that creative response for the next three chapters.

The ratio of notes in the duplum to notes in the tenor in such sections becomes much closer; we are now obviously dealing with a type of discant. It is here, too, that we are most apt to find the clear organization of ligatures in the *duplum* voice into "modal" patterns, invoking the abstract metrical schemes described above.

From this we learn that in *organum duplum* or *organum per se*, the kind associated in Anonymus IV with the name of Leonin, measured rhythm is essentially an aspect of discant. In sections where the tenor is held long, called *organum purum* — "pure (or plain) organum" — to distinguish it from the discant, the rhythm is not organized in this way. The notes are sung "freely," as in chant. But not entirely freely, of course. Guides to organum emphasize that notes forming consonances with the tenor were or could be sung longer than those forming dissonances. This habit, or rule, was probably what prompted the adoption of trochaic (long-short) patterns as the rhythmic norm: the note that in the added voice intervenes between two harmonic consonances is often dissonant (a "passing" or "neighbor" tone, as we now call such things), hence sung short.

In a style where "organal" and discant sections are so radically contrasted in rhythm, meter, and (consequently) tempo, it is not surprising that there is an intermediate texture as well, called *copula* (from the Latin for "something that binds," like a string). In a copula, the duplum sings (usually) two phrases in regular modal patterns over sustained tenor notes. In *Viderunt omnes* this happens most clearly over "-de-" and "-runt." In Ex. 6-2 you can see the two *copulae* in transcription, following the notation in a manuscript roughly contemporaneous with **Flo** but copied in England or Scotland for the Augustinian abbey of St. Andrews. (It is now the older of two Notre-Dame

EX. 6-2   Transcription of *-derunt* from organum setting shown in Fig. 6-3b

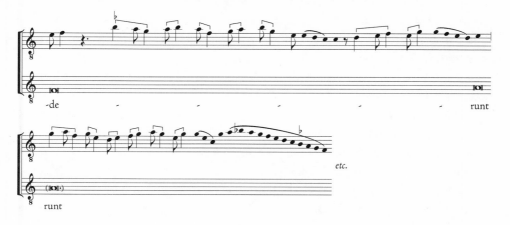

codices kept at the former ducal library in the German town of Wolfenbüttel, for which reason it is known to its adepts as W_1.) The modal ligatures are somewhat clearer in W_1 than in **Flo**.

In discant sections or *clausulae*, where the tenor moves rapidly against the "modal" rhythms of the duplum, it too must be organized into notes of determinate length. The usual method was to have each note of the tenor equal a metrical foot in the duplum. Such a note would equal the sum of a long and a breve. So now we are dealing with three durations: a breve consisting of one *tempus* or time unit, a long consisting of two *tempora*, and a tenor note consisting of three tempora, which defines the length of a foot.

Different theorists called this longest value by different names. The varying nomenclature reveals a change in attitude. Some writers were content to call the three-tempora length a *longa ultra mensuram*, which simply means "a long beyond (normal) measure." Others, however, called it a "perfect" (that is, completed) long, recognizing it as the primary unit, of which the shorter values were now both regarded as subdivisions. Theorists began to speak abstractly of "perfections" — time units measured out in advance, as it were, waiting to be filled. Such a concept corresponds in some ways to our modern idea of a "measure." Ex. 6-3a is a transcription of the big discant *clausula* on the chant melisma "Do-" as shown in Fig. 6-3b, from the Florence manuscript. Note that the perfect longs in the tenor group the notes of the chant melisma irregularly: 6, 4, 4, 6, 4, 4, 4, 6, 5, etc. (The barring of the transcription follows this grouping, set off in the manuscript by vertical lines called *tractus*, which look like bars and eventually developed into bars, but which are actually rests at this point.) But also note that the opening pattern of 6+4+4, when repeated, corresponds to a melodic repetition in the tenor. The overall organization of the discant section is clearly being "modeled" on that of the chant melody. And yet the most conspicuous component of the clausula, the duplum melody, does not participate in the repetition. The cantor, in other words, sings a continuously evolving, quasi-improvisatory string of ordines over the highly organized tenor.

Ex. 6-3b shows the same "Do-" clausula as it is found in a different manuscript, also copied in Paris but about two or three decades later than **Flo**. (This is the later of the two now kept in Wolfenbüttel, known as W_2.) Although the *Viderunt* organum as a whole is more or less the same in the two sources, this particular clausula is altogether different. It is a later insert, much more tightly organized into short ordines than its predecessor, and the tenor participates fully in the modal rhythm with a mode of its own that is based on groups of perfect and "duplex" or double-measure longs (the latter designated D).

These tenor notes are organized according to a pattern reminiscent of the classical "spondee." The spondaic foot consists of two long syllables, and the tenor's rhythmic mode organizes the spondaic foot into two alternating perfect ordines: the first consists of a single spondaic foot with a cadential long (LLL+rest); the other ties the initial foot into a duplex (DL+rest). This modal pattern is now allowed to override the melodic repetition in the original chant. The repeated phrase is still discernible, but its notes now have different metrical placements: as the rhythm becomes more abstract and independent as an organizing factor, pitch and rhythmic organization are somewhat dichotomized. The more abstract the organization, one might say, the more "artificial" (in the sense of "artful") the resulting musical shape. This clausula, with its regular tenor patterns of four "perfections" each, can be conveniently transcribed into our modern compound-duple meter.

The same clausula is found in **Flo** as well, but in a special section that contains no fewer than ten clausulae on the "Do-" melisma: a set of spare parts, so to speak, for insertion into the organum at pleasure. Just about anything can happen in these playfully ("artfully") imaginative discants. One of them (Ex. 6-3c) puts the tenor through a double cursus in strict LLL ordines while the duplum carols away ever more decoratively, its notes "broken up" into extra breves by a process called *fractio modi*, literally "breaking the rhythmic pattern." (One of the easiest ways of doing this was to add a little stroke called a *plica* or "fold" to a neume. The stroke usually stood for a breve on the next higher or lower note in the scale, its duration "folded" into that of the long to which it is attached. In the transcription, *plicae* are indicated by little strokes through the note stems.) There is even an especially souped-up clausula (Ex. 6-3d) in which both duplum and tenor contain longs and breves in ordines similar to the "iambs" shown in Ex. 6-1b.

EX. 6-3A   "Do-" clausulae transcribed from **Flo**, f. 99', with barring following the tractus in the tenor

EX. 6-3B   "Do-" clausulae transcribed from **W₂**, f. 63–63', in 6/8 meter

EX. 6-3C   "Do-" clausulae transcribed from **Flo**, f. 150' (with double cursus)

EX. 6-3C (*continued*)

EX. 6-3D "Do-" clausulae transcribed from **Flo**, f. 149' (both parts in iambic patterns)

WHYS AND WHEREFORES

There are large sections devoted to spare parts like these, sometimes called "substitute clausulas" or "ersatz clausulas," in all four major Notre Dame codices. (In addition to **Flo**, W_1, and W_2, there is a slightly smaller one called **Ma**, roughly contemporaneous with W_2, copied in Spain for the cathedral at Toledo, and now kept at the National Library in Madrid.) They raise tantalizing questions about the nature of this music, its transmission, and its history.

Every piece in the so-called Magnus Liber — the "great book" attributed to Leonin by Anonymus IV — exists, as we have observed in the case of *Viderunt omnes*, in significantly different versions in its various sources, and since all the extant written sources were copied at least two or three generations, and in some cases as much as a century, after the purported time of Leonin, it is impossible to determine what the original form of any of these pieces was. And every piece in the Magnus Liber is equipped with a multitude of interchangeable parts like the clausulae we have observed on "Do-." Besides the ones on "Do-," the Notre Dame codices contain interchangeable *Viderunt* clausulas on the tenor fragments "om-" (from *omnes*), "su-" (from *suum*) in the verse, and even on "conspectum gentium" from the verse, which is not a melisma.

One can only conclude that the identity of a "piece of music" was a far more fluid concept for the Notre Dame cantors than it is for us. An organum as actually performed was essentially a patchwork created more or less on the spot, or after a brief consultation, from the many available parts in the manuscripts we have (and who knows how many others that were never entered in those lucky survivors or — now here's a thought — that were never written down at all).

Even if we limit the choice to what is written and what is extant, it is nevertheless hard to imagine the Notre Dame cantors furiously leafing forward and back through their books during the service to find the clausulas they wished to perform on a given day. And as we have already observed about the earliest chant books, the Notre Dame codices, while "immense" (as noted above) in terms of their total contents, were tiny in actual physical dimensions. The actual written area of a page from W_1 measures approximately 5 1/2 × 2 1/2 inches, while **Flo**, the largest, measures approximately 6 1/4 by 4. A musicologist in her study, working at leisure, has to squint at W_1 to make its bitsy flyspecks out; one can hardly assume that such a book could have been used in the act of performing. The assumption has to be, rather, that the Notre Dame cantors, and anyone else who sang their music in the dark confines of a medieval church, performed from memory.

The question of memory once again opens out quickly onto a much larger, more critical terrain. There are absolutely no written sources of Notre Dame polyphony from the period from the 1170s to the 1190s, when Anonymus IV's Leonin supposedly lived and worked (or, for that matter, when Professor Wright's Leonius actually lived and worked). All the extant sources postdate the lifetime of Anonymus IV's Perotin as well, even if we grant Perotin the longest conceivable life span (say, to the time of Philip the Chancellor's death in 1236). The sources were all written between the 1240s and the 1280s, and the author of Anonymus IV, as well as all the other theorists of "modal rhythm" and its notation, lived and worked around the same time.

A strong suspicion arises from these circumstances that the organa dupla of the so-called Magnus Liber were not part of a *liber* at all during their period of greatest use, but were created, sung, and transmitted from singer to singer within what was, yes, still predominantly an oral culture. Far from adding to the mystery of this music, however, the assumption of an oral tradition actually suggests the best answer to the riddle of how Notre Dame polyphony came to be the epoch-making thing it was — namely, the first "measured music" in the West.

Now it is time to pose explicitly the questions that have been stalking our discussion of modal rhythm from the beginning: What was its purpose? What did it accomplish? Often it is claimed that the Notre Dame composers, whoever they were, finally managed to "solve" a longstanding "problem," namely that of notating rhythm precisely, thereby making it possible for precisely measured music to be composed. But that puts the cart before the horse, in fact several carts before several horses.

If we know one thing for certain from the history of medieval music to the point where we have traced it, it is that notation follows rather than precedes practice. In the case of Gregorian chant, it followed by a matter of centuries, not to say millennia. In the case of chant-based polyphony it also followed, perhaps by centuries, as we know from the implicit testimony of the *Scolica enchiriadis*. So if the theorists of the thirteenth century finally took up and "solved" the problem of notating a metrically organized melismatic polyphony, our assumption should be that they were finding a notation for something that was already well established in oral practice.

Furthermore, to say that rhythmic notation was a "problem" to be solved before there could be rhythmic composition is to assume that without such notation music was perceived as lacking something. We easily imagine such an absence as a lack, because the absence of a method for notating precise rhythms would be a crippling lack for making our music. To assume that the composers of twelfth-century Paris felt such a lack is to assume that they wanted to make our music, too. Only the assumption that it is up to "them" to become "us" — in other words, the ethnocentric assumption — can sanction the notion that discovering modal rhythm was a progressive evolutionary step (from "themness" to "usness").

So, if it was not the solution to an obvious notational problem, what was the motivation for developing the patterning techniques collectively known as modal rhythm? The best theory so far, recently advanced by the medievalist Anna Maria Busse Berger, is that modeling musical rhythm on classical versification served the same purpose that versification itself originally served — namely, a mnemonic (or more precisely, a "mnemotechnic") purpose.[4] It enhanced memory skills, an essential function in an oral culture.

Rhythm has always been an imprinting device, and remains one to this day. That is why so many rules and aphorisms are cast as jingles. (*Cross at the green,/Not in between*; or *Red sky at morning:/Sailor, take warning!*; or *Early to bed and early to rise/Makes a man healthy, wealthy, and wise.*) It is why no medieval treatise on anything from shipbuilding to organum-singing was without rhyming rules. It is why the poet Leonius, who may or may not have been Leonin, gave as his reason for writing his 14,000 lines of biblical verse that it helped "the mind, which, delighted by the brevity of the poetry and by the song, may hold it more firmly."[5]

Here is a catchy Latin rhyme, attributed to Guido of Arezzo, that every literate or academic musician from the eleventh to the fifteenth century learned at the beginning of his training since is a popularization of one of Boethius's main ideas:

> Musicorum et cantorum magna est distancia.
> Isti dicunt, illi sciunt, quae componit Musica.
> Nam qui facit, quod non sapit, diffinitur bestia. It's a long way from a musician
> to a singer. The one knows what music is made of, the other just talks about it.
> And he who performs what he knows nothing about is considered an animal.

So "Guido well puts it in his *Micrologus*," wrote John of Afflighem.[6] But the rhyme is not found in the *Micrologus* at all; and John surely heard it, and memorized it, years before he ever read it, which is why he forgot where he actually came across it. It is found in Guido's *Regulae rhythmicae*, a brief digest of Guido's teachings on the gamut, intervals, staff notation, modes, and finals, all cast for easy retention (as the title, "Rhyming Rules," already indicates) in verse.

And that is why the composers of Notre Dame, who were creating a music of unheard-of melismatic profusion, found it advantageous to cast their enormously long melodies in an untexted musical counterpart to verse. In this form it evidently went from mouth to mouth for a generation or two before a notation for it was invented. And when the notation for it was invented, it was not really for it, but for something else. Again, and even more spectacularly, what was prompted by practical need became the stimulus for luxuriant artistic play.

Here is where the generation of Anonymus IV's "Perotin the Great" comes in. As you may recall, the treatise credits the great discantor with having *abbreviavit* the Magnus Liber. The translation has been put off until now because the word has an ambiguous range of meaning in Latin. The closest English cognate, "abbreviated," though followed by many writers, does not seem to fit the facts of the case, since so many "substitute clausulas" (like the one on "Do-" in Ex. 6-3c) so clearly lengthen rather than shorten the pieces into which they are inserted.

Another possible translation of *abbreviavit* is "edited." This fits better, since the differing versions of the *organum duplum* repertory in the four Notre Dame sources obviously show the hand of a reviser — or likelier, of many revisers. And yet, to cite a case we have already seen, the presence of the same revised "Do-" clausula within the body of the organum in W_2 and in the section containing the "substitute clausulas" in **Flo** would seem to indicate that whoever revised the Magnus Liber did not have in mind the goals of a modern editor. That is, he (or they) aimed not at establishing an improved, corrected, or definitive text. The aim, rather, seems to have been just to make a wealth of interchangeable material available.

And so we are left with the third and most general possible translation of *abbreviavit* — simply, "written down." This one not only fits but explains a great deal. If we assume that the "Perotin" generation finally wrote down the music of the "Leonin" generation (in the process devising a notational method that opened up a whole new world of musical possibilities that they were quick to exploit), then we can not only account for the gap between the twelfth-century repertory and its thirteenth-century sources, but also make sense of the fact that the theoretical descriptions of modal rhythm come as late as they do. As a fully elaborated *system* of metrics and notation, modal rhythm pertains not to the orally created and rhythmically transmitted music of the Leonin generation, but to the very intricate and stylized output of the Perotin generation, which is found in all its many sources in essentially one version, and which may have been the first musical style in the West that actually depended on notation for its composition.

ORGANUM CUM ALIO

The major works of the Perotin generation differ from those of the previous generation in one fundamental respect. They are written for more than two parts — or, to make the point in most essential terms, they are written for more than one part against the Gregorian tenor. That is why contemporary theorists called their style *organum cum alio* ("organum with another [voice]") to distinguish it from *organum per se* ("organum by itself").

The presence of the added voice or voices changed everything. They moved at the rate of the duplum, not the tenor (so they were called the *triplum* and, when present, the *quadruplum*). Two or three parts moving at a similar rate are in effect in discant with one another, regardless of whether there is a long-held tenor note, and so they had to be notated throughout in strict modal rhythm (*modus rectus*, as it was called). Everything now had to move in countable perfections; there could be no spontaneous coordination in performance, the way there could be with a single cantor in the driver's seat, ad-libbing "freely" and giving all necessary signals to his subordinates on the tenor line.

For an example of *organum cum alio* at its most luxuriant, we can examine the four-part setting (*organum quadruplum*), attributed to Perotin in Anonymus IV and requested by Bishop Eudes de Sully for performance at the Feast of the Circumcision, 1 January 1198 (we would say 1199, but the New Year was celebrated in those days on 1 March). This was the recognized jewel in the Notre Dame crown, the opening work both in **Flo** (where it faces the famous Boethian allegory we have already encountered in Fig. 3-2) and in **W₂** (according to its table of contents; the pages containing it have unfortunately been lost). The setting of the incipit is shown in the original notation (from **Flo**) in Fig. 6-4; Ex. 6-4 is a transcription of the part corresponding to the opening syllable.

This composition moves throughout in an especially stately version of the trochaic meter we first observed in "Leonine" discant and copula. What makes it "stately" is the liberal admixture into the rhythms of the upper parts of perfect and duplex longs. The basic modal pattern, established by a repeated phrase in the quadruplum, consists of a ternaria plus a binaria, establishing tum-ta-tum-ta-tum ("second perfect ordo"), but followed by a *nota simplex*, a freestanding note. That freestanding note, a long (since it follows a long), forces the preceding note to be perfect. (It is itself "imperfected" by the tractus, the breath mark, which takes the time of a breve and separates one ordo from the next.)

The first note in the duplum, triplum, and quadruplum alike is a duplex, indicated by the literal elongation of the note's oblong shape. The chord thus created (and no doubt held extra long for dramatic effect) is a composite of all the *symphoniae*. There is an octave between the tenor and the triplum, a fifth between the tenor and the duplum (or the quadruplum), a fourth between the duplum and the triplum, and a prime or unison between the duplum and the quadruplum. This harmony (a sort of Pythagorean summary) would be the normative consonance for polyphony in three or more parts until the sixteenth century. Not every piece made such a spectacular opening display of it as this one, but every piece had to end with it. From its original signification—harmoniousness, fitting-in, "*e pluribus unum*"—it came to signify completion, consummation, achievement.

Notice now how at the outset every successive ordo re-achieves that normative perfect consonance. And notice, too, how in every ordo the perfect long preceding the final consonance makes a calculated maximum dissonance (*asymphonia*), both with respect to the tenor and within the upper parts themselves. In the first ordo the next-to-last note (penult) in the quadruplum is D, a major sixth from the tenor (the least consonant of the imperfect consonances as then classified). The penult in the triplum is E, a major seventh from the tenor and a major second from the quadruplum;

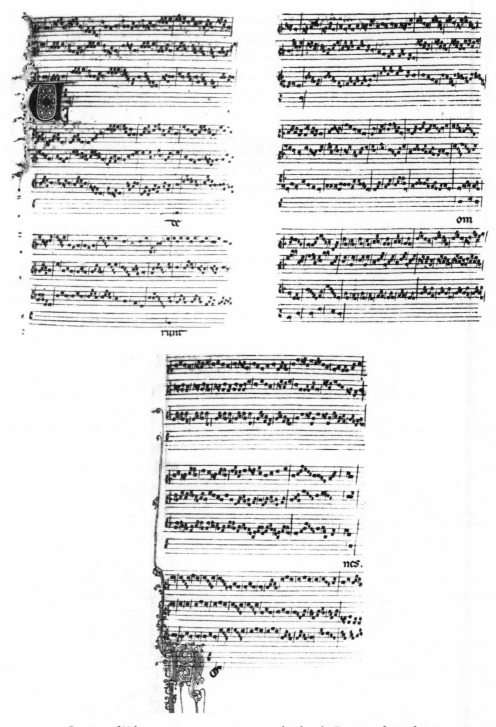

FIG. 6-4 Opening of *Viderunt omnes*, set as organum quadruplum by Perotinus for performance in 1198 (**Flo**, fols. 1–2).

its dissonance speaks for itself. The duplum's penult is B-flat, a tritone from the triplum's E. If isolated from its context and banged out at the keyboard, the chord would startle even a twenty-first-century ear.

In context, of course, the chord is heard as implying its resolution to the normative consonance. Note that in making the resolution, every voice proceeds by step. The dissonant second between the triplum and quadruplum arises not out of some "non-harmonic" medieval way of hearing (as we are sometimes tempted to imagine it), but out of the implied voice-leading rule that dissonance proceeds to consonance by step. We have, in short, the beginnings of a cadential practice here, in which the motions of the individual parts are subordinated to an overall harmonic function (maximum

EX. 6-4   *Viderunt omnes* a 4 (attributed to Perotin), first syllable of setting

EX. 6-4 *(continued)*

dissonance resolving to maximum consonance). This is the beginning of harmonic tonality (or, if you prefer, of tonal harmony). It exemplifies textural integration, control, and planning.

To see textural integration, control, and planning from another perspective, compare the triplum in the first ordo with the duplum in the second ordo, the triplum in the third ordo, the duplum in the fourth ordo, the triplum in the sixth, and finally the quadruplum in the seventh. Now compare the triplum in the second ordo with the duplum in the third, the triplum in the fourth, and the quadruplum in the fifth and sixth. Elaborate voice exchanges of this kind, the most conspicuous of integrative devices, can be traced throughout the piece.

For yet another, look at the third system of the first manuscript page in Fig. 6-4, halfway through the syllable "-DE-" (in "Viderunt") in the tenor, and find the analogous spot in Ex. 6-4. Now the motion has slowed down to an alternation between "spondaic" perfect longs and the normative trochees. The figure C–D–C in longs, and its trochaic variant C–D–E–D–C, are tossed back and forth between the duplum and triplum. Their exchanges are now dovetailed so that the first note in one voice coincides with the third note in the other. In between, a note in one voice coincides with a rest in the other. This kind of exchange between notes and rests (done slowly here, but sometimes done with lightning speed, as we shall see) was a specialty of *organum cum alio* and its derivative genres. For the singers this kind of controlled textural fragmentation was great fun, as we can tell by the name they gave it: *hoquetus* — "hocket" in English — from the Latin for "hiccup," no doubt because of the way the rests interrupt the melodic lines like spasms. An even more radically fragmented "hocket" texture comes over the first tenor note of "-RUNT."

The spirit of creative exuberance, of delight in construction, so evident in this and every other Notre Dame quadruplum led inevitably to an expansion of the repertory of rhythmic "modal" figures. The obvious choice for a new metric foot to apply to music was the dactyl, the most widely cultivated foot for contemporary Latin poetry. (It was the foot adopted by the poet Leonius, for example, in his *Hystorie sacre gestas*.)

A dactylic foot consists of a long and two shorts. In contrast to the trochee (LB), which contains three tempora (2+1), the normal dactyl (LBB) contains four (2+1+1), which would make it longer than a "perfection." To accommodate the dactylic foot to what had become the *de facto* ternary meter of modal rhythm, it was stretched out over two perfections, becoming inherently a *modus ultra mensuram*, a "mode beyond (normal) measure." The first perfection was entirely occupied by the long, now perfect by definition. The remaining perfection was divided unequally between the two breves, one of them becoming a so-called *brevis altera* ("altered" or "alternate" breve) containing two tempora. Thus the six tempora occupied by the LBB of the dactylic foot was apportioned 3+2+1 or 3+1+2, with the latter much more frequently described (or prescribed, which amounts to the same thing) by mid-thirteenth century theorists, and that is the pattern commonly employed in modern transcriptions, though the other is not by any means precluded.

One of the most widely circulated dactylic pieces is the *Alleluia Nativitas*, an *organum triplum* for the Mass of the Feast of Mary's

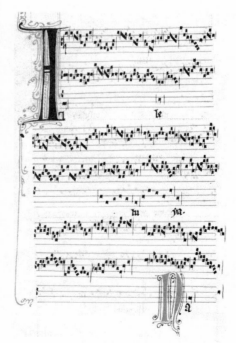

FIG. 6-5   Opening of *Alleluia Nativitas*, set as organum triplum by Perotinus (W₁, f. 16).

Nativity (an especially important feast at "Our Lady's" own church, Notre Dame), attributed to Perotin in Anonymus IV. Its first page, as given in **W**₂, is shown in Fig. 6-5; Ex. 6-5 is a transcription of three significant excerpts, beginning with the word "Alleluya" (Ex. 6-5a).

The basic ligature pattern for this rhythmic mode consists of a *nota simplex*, representing the first perfect long, followed by a series of ternariae. This pattern is very clearly set out at the beginning of the *Alleluia Nativitas*, but gives way at various points, particularly near the ends of sections, to the more fluid trochaic pattern. (Look, for example, at "-YA," the concluding portion in Fig. 6-4.) Remarkable in this composition is the sheer number of rhythmically active clausulae in the verse. There are half a dozen

EX. 6-5A   *Alleluia Nativitas* (attributed to Perotin), mm. 1–63

EX. 6-5A   (*continued*)

EX. 6-5A   (*continued*)

EX. 6-5B   *Alleluia Nativitas,* mm. 72–104

EX. 6-5B (*continued*)

EX. 6-5C *Alleluia Nativitas,* mm. 168–89

of them, including one (on *Ex semine*) that is of great historical significance for a reason we will discover in the next chapter (Ex. 6-5b). The last clausula, on "*IU-*" (Ex. 6-5c), is also of special interest for the way the 12-note tenor is put through a second cursus in diminution: irregular ordines of duplex and perfect longs give way to an uninterrupted and self-evidently climactic run of perfect longs that end the composition on a note of maximum excitement.

But while this remarkable run ends the composition, very narrowly defined, it does not end the Alleluia, or even the verse. The chorus must sing its brief response (including the melisma on the name of "David" that recapitulates the melody of the jubilus, the enormous melisma at the end of the choral repetition of the word "Alleluia"; it, too, will figure again in a later chapter). And then the whole Alleluia with jubilus must be repeated, either with polyphony (as some of the sources direct) or without. A polyphonically outfitted liturgical chant as sung at Notre Dame, though far more elaborately composed than any other polyphonic music of its time, is still not a composition in our modern sense. It is not solely the product of an author's shaping hand but the complex response to a variety of ceremonial and artistic demands, some seemingly in mutual contradiction.

THEORY OR PRACTICE?

The most authoritative source for our knowledge of the epochal rhythmic practices of the Notre Dame School is the treatise *De mensurabili musica*, written around 1240 by Johannes de Garlandia. He was a lecturer (*magister*) at the University of Paris, possibly the very one from whom the author of Anonymus IV learned what he passed on to us. His name derives from his university affiliation: the *clos de Garlande* was a colony on the left bank of the Seine where many members of the university arts faculty made their homes.

De mensurabili musica ("On measured music") was one of two textbooks Johannes wrote for the university music curriculum to supplement the venerable treatise of Boethius. (The other one was called *De plana musica*, "On plainchant.") Its method of organization and instruction vividly exemplifies the approach known as "scholasticism" (because it was practiced by *scholastici*, "schoolmen"). This approach was thought of as descending not from Plato, the "idea man," but from Aristotle, the great observer of things as they are. It purported to be empirical (that is, based on observation) and descriptive rather than speculative.

The first task in any scholastic description was analysis and classification, and the establishment of clear conceptual relations between larger divisions (*genera*) and smaller divisions (*species*), proceeding, as we still say, from the "general" to the "specific." Thus Johannes begins by dividing the consonances (a genus) into three classes (species): perfect (prime and octave), intermediate (fourth and fifth), and imperfect (thirds). He also makes a tripartite division of dissonances, with the "perfect" ones being the most dissonant, etc. He then proceeds to a similarly tripartite division of measured music into three species: organum, copula, and discant. And finally, he divides discant into six, or twice-three, "manners" (*maneries*) or rhythmic modes.

Garlandia's classification was extremely influential in its time, as we can tell by how many other theorists copied it. And it has been equally influential in our time, as we can tell by the way modern musicology has adopted the Garlandian classification scheme and terminology. Our own discussion has accepted Garlandia's classification of polyphonic genres, including the somewhat slippery category of copula "between discant and organum," as Garlandia defined it long after the fact. Up to now, however, we have avoided the classic and ubiquitous Garlandian classification of the rhythmic modes.

The reason is that, like many scholastic classification schemes, Garlandia's discussion of the rhythmic modes is not really descriptive—not entirely, at any rate. Its descriptive content has clearly been supplemented by a notional component so that the resulting system will satisfy *a priori* (that is, preconceived) standards of completeness and, above all, of symmetry.

Garlandia's idea of completeness was evidently formed not on the basis of observed contemporary musical practice but on a list of meters taken over from another authoritative scholastic classification, a grammar textbook called *Doctrinale* ("Book of teachings"), written more than a generation earlier (in 1199) by another famous schoolman, Alexandre de Villedieu (or Villa-Dei). In this textbook, six classical poetic meters are defined in terms of long and short syllables, which are defined in exactly the same terms employed by contemporary musicians when speaking of note values. Villedieu even refers to singing the syllables, perhaps (though not necessarily) in recognition of the analogous musical meters of Notre Dame polyphony: "the syllable which is short holds one beat (*tempus*) in which it is sung; you must double that length for the long."[7] In terms of our accustomed symbols for longs (L) and breves (B), Villedieu's enumeration is as follows: dactyl (LBB), spondee (LL), trochee (LB), anapest (BBL), iamb (BL), and tribrach (BBB).

Garlandia took this list over directly and asserted that there were six rhythmic modes in use in Notre Dame polyphony. Then he went Villedieu one better by arranging the modes in three symmetrical pairs. Modes 1 and 2, according to Garlandia, were the trochee (LB) and its reverse, the iamb (BL). Modes 3 and 4 were the dactyl (LBB) and its reverse, the anapest (BBL). Modes 5 and 6 were the spondee (LL), confined to longs, and its conceptual opposite the tribrach (BBB), confined to breves.

At least one of these modes, the fourth, was pure fiction, included in deference to authority and for the sake of a symmetry that would justify the inclusion of the dactyl. There is not a single practical source that contains music in Garlandia's fourth mode. It exists only in his didactic example of it, and the ones contrived by subsequent theorists on the basis of his authority. And yet in the thirteenth and fourteenth centuries—and again in the nineteenth and twentieth—countless students have memorized its pattern and its notation. (The latter is easy enough to guess, being the exact reverse of the dactyl or third mode: a series of ternariae followed by a *nota simplex*.)

Garlandia's sixth mode, too, is more or less notional, included on Villedieu's authority as a complement or balance to the fifth, which of course has a long history in practice. Brief passages in uniform breves are found in many compositions of the "Notre Dame school." They can be just as easily notated (with plicas, for example) without any special mode. There is one famous passage in an Alleluia attributed in Anonymus IV to Perotin that has a few ordines ostensibly in Garlandia's sixth mode and using the notation he assigns to it. But the passage could as easily have been written in "fractured" trochees (first mode), and might very well have actually been written that way in its earliest sources.

That would mean that Garlandia's treatise, which purported to describe a musical practice, ended up prescribing one instead. The same possibility, that the theorist influenced the composition style he ostensibly reported involves the second mode (iambic) as counterpart to the ubiquitous first. We have seen an example of the second mode in practice, in one of the spare "DO-" clausulas from the Florence manuscript (Ex. 6-3d). But that manuscript was compiled after Garlandia's treatise had become a standard text, and there is little or no evidence for the use of Garlandia's second mode at any earlier time.

What we seem to have in Garlandia, then, is a summary of an actual rhythmic practice that was more or less confined to three patterns (trochaic, dactylic, and spondaic), corresponding to Garlandia's odd-numbered modes. And then there is a supplementary, even-numbered, trio (iambic, anapestic, tribrachic) that were there for the sake of the theory—but that were later incorporated to some extent into practice under the influence of the theory. It is an excellent paradigm or instructive model for considering the complex relationship that usually obtains between theory and practice.

Theory is almost never pure description. It is usually a representation not of the world the theorist sees but of a more orderly, more easily described world the theorist would like to see. A persuasive theory, particularly one of suggestible human behavior or practice, can often to some extent reshape the world to conform, for better or worse, to the utopian image. But an attractive theory uncritically accepted can also blind the believer to existing conditions, and lessen rather than enhance comprehension. Uncritical acceptance of Garlandia's six-mode scheme can obscure the actual history of musical practice at Notre Dame, and that is why it should be regarded as a secondary rather than a primary source of knowledge.

CONDUCTUS AT NOTRE DAME

The remaining polyphonic genre practiced at Notre Dame was the conductus. Its status there was far more modest than at previous monastic polyphonic centers, but well over a hundred conductus nevertheless survive, in two, three, and four voices.

Conductus was exceptional among Notre Dame genres in that it was not based on a preexisting chant, but was a setting of a contemporary poem, potentially composed from scratch. Contemporary theorists described the method of composing a conductus in terms as close as possible to those governing discant composition, however. Franco of Cologne, with whom we will become better acquainted in the next chapter, wrote that anyone wishing to compose a conductus should first "invent as beautiful a melody as he can," and then "use it as a tenor for writing the rest."[8] Sometimes, indeed, conductus are found in both monophonic and polyphonic versions; and when this is the case, the melody that exists alone is almost always the tenor in the polyphonic variant, confirming Franco's prescription. But the texture of a conductus, while basically homorhythmic (note-against-note) can also be well enough integrated by means of hockets and voice exchanges to suggest that not all composers relied on the "write-your-own-cantus-firmus" method.

There was another way in which the conductus was an exceptional genre. It was the only type of polyphonic composition that was syllabically texted. In contemporary parlance it was *musica cum littera* ("music with letters," i.e., words). And that meant it had to be notated in *notae simplices* rather than in ligatures, because ligatures functioned in Notre Dame notation just as they did in plainchant. They were used only to carry melismas, which means music without text (*musica sine littera*). There was no standard method for applying text to notation in ligatures.

The conductus thus exposed the chief shortcoming of the system or practice of "modal" rhythm. The four-voice Christmas conductus *Vetus abit littera* from the Florence manuscript (Fig. 6-6) shows how, and also shows a possible attempt to remedy the situation. (It also has a very interesting, quasi-modulatory tonal shape, but we'll let that aspect of the piece speak for itself.)

Until the penultimate syllable of text, the notation consists almost entirely of single notes. If read strictly according to the rules of modal rhythm, they are all perfect longs, casting the setting in a very heavy spondaic meter throughout. But that penultimate syllable has a sizable melisma in all voices. A melisma at the tail end is a standard feature

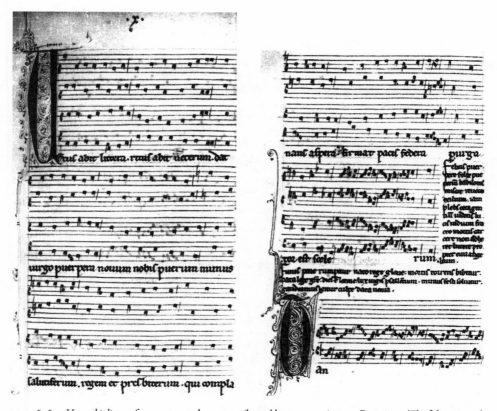

FIG. 6-6 *Vetus abit littera*, four-part conductus attributed by some writers to Perotinus (*Flo*, fols. 10–10v).

in Notre Dame conductus settings, common enough to have a generic name. It is called the *cauda*, which literally means the tail, as in tail end. (The term was re-introduced into musical terminology centuries later, when Latin had been replaced by Italian as musical *lingua franca*: we all know what a coda is and can see how it relates conceptually to the medieval cauda.)

Being a melisma, the cauda is written in ligatures. As a second glance at them will show, the ligatures in question could hardly form a clearer trochaic ("first mode") pattern. No question, then, that the cauda is supposed to go tum-ta-tum-ta-tum-ta-tum in good "modal" fashion. And so the question arises: Is the "first mode" cauda supposed to contrast with the "fifth mode" of the rest of the piece? Or, perhaps, is the cauda there not simply for the sake of embellishment but also to convey the otherwise unconveyable information that the whole piece is to be sung in "first mode"? Ex. 6-6a

EX. 6-6A   *Vetus abit littera*, transcribed in first mode

EX. 6-6A   (*continued*)

> The old word has passed away,
> The ancient rite is gone,
> The child-bearing virgin gives
> To us a new son,
> A life-giving gift,
> A king and priest,
> Who smoothes the rough places
> And strengthens the pacts of peace:
> He is the cleanser of sin.
> (Trans. Alexander Blachly)

is a transcription of the whole piece in "first mode," which turns the accentual pattern of the entire poem quite convincingly into a quantitative musical meter. But there is no authority to back that decision up; it is simply a preference. To give the other side its due, Ex. 6-6b shows another hypothetical transcription cast in fifth mode up to the cauda.

One cannot solve the rhythmic riddle this piece poses on the basis of the notation itself, because the notation has to be as it is regardless of the answer. But at least it is clear that the "fifth mode" or spondaic appearance of the syllabic notation does not tell us what the composer's intention may have been with respect to rhythm. It is a default notation, and therefore an ambiguous one.

Consider another example. *Dic, Christi veritas* ("Say, O truth of Christ"), an angry screed against clerical hypocrisy, was one of the most famous poems by Philip the Chancellor, the old rector of the University of Paris. As a conductus it is found in the *Carmina burana* manuscript in a monophonic version, and in all the main Notre Dame sources in an elaborate three-voice setting. The tenor in this version is clearly related to

EX. 6-6B   *Vetus abit littera*, transcribed in fifth mode

EX. 6-7   Final cauda from *Dic, Christi veritas* (text by Philip the Chancellor), transcribed from **Flo**, f. 204

EX. 6-7 (continued)

FIG. 6-7A Last line of *Dic, Christi veritas*, beginning at bottom left and continuing at top right; from **Flo**, fol. 203v–204 (cf. final tenor melisma in Ex. 6-7).

the monophonic *Carmina burana* tune, but like the other voices it is decorated with lots of *caudae*, with an especially lavish one at the end. The caudae, as usual, are in a clearly notated first mode. The meter of the verse, however, is not straightforwardly trochaic. The final cauda is given in Ex. 6-7.

The last line of the tenor part from the Florence version of *Dic, Christi veritas*, including the big first-mode cauda, is shown in Fig. 6-7a. But now look at Fig. 6-7b. It contains a monophonic conductus, *Veste nuptiali*, found in the last fascicle of the Florence manuscript, far away from *Dic, Christi veritas*. It is written, as music *cum littera* has to be, in what look like perfect longs. Compare it with Fig. 6-7a. Although the notation differs radically, it is the same melody exactly. Is *Veste nuptiali* a "prosulated"

FIG. 6-7B *Veste nuptiali* (monophonic conductus), beginning with the ornamental V; from *Flo*, f. 450v.

version of the cauda? Perhaps; but then again, perhaps not: the first two phrases of the melody are an ouvert/clos pair, suggesting that it may be a disguised love song. By now the fluidity of medieval genres should be no surprise to us. This is one of the most piquant instances in the repertory.

Whatever the case, one thing is certain. The singer of *Veste nuptiali* would not have been able to guess its rhythm from the notation in Fig. 6-7b, but (unless, quite fortuitously, he recognized the cauda of *Dic, Christi veritas* as notated elsewhere) he would have had to know the song already from the oral tradition (as reconstructed, hypothetically, in Ex. 6-8) in order to sing it correctly in its written guise. A singer who did not know the song in advance would thus have been keenly aware of the notation's limits. Such a singer would have felt a lack and would have wished for a more explicit way of notating the rhythm of measured music. In other words, the problem of *musica cum littera*, more and more acutely felt as texted genres (including some new ones) became more and more prevalent,

EX. 6-8 Transcription of *Veste nuptiali* (Fig. 6-7b) in rhythm of Fig. 6-7a

created the necessity that mothered the invention of an explicit rhythmic notation, in which individual notes carried rhythmic information. First described in full around 1260, it sustained three centuries of development and continues, in a more remote way, to underlie the rhythmic notation we use today. Those genres, and that notation, will be the subject of the next chapter.

Music for an Intellectual and Political Elite

THE THIRTEENTH-CENTURY MOTET

A NEW CLASS

The rise of the university produced a new class, emanating from Paris, of *literati*: urban clerics with secular educations who were put to work as administrators on behalf of the universities themselves, on behalf of the increasingly feudalized church hierarchy (sometimes called the "cathedral nobility"), and above all on behalf of the burgeoning *civitas*, the secular state. The University of Paris, as one historian has put it, became "the training-ground for Europe's bureaucrats." This class found a musical spokesman in a university *magister* named Johannes de Grocheio (sometimes gallicized informally as "Jean de Grouchy"), the author, around 1300, of a remarkable treatise variously called *Ars musicae* ("The art of music") or *De musica* ("About music").[1]

What makes this treatise remarkable is its worldly bent. It contains neither cosmic speculation nor nuts-and-bolts theory nor guide to notation. Instead, it offers a survey of "the music which men in Paris use," classified according to "how men in Paris use it." It is, in effect, the first sociological treatise on music, in which musical genres are defined primarily in terms of their "class" affiliations. It is a potential goldmine of information for students of music history.

But it can only serve us in that way if its ore is properly refined. Like any theoretical treatise, it should be handled with care and with a certain skepticism. Its ostensibly descriptive content should be scrutinized with an eye out for covert prescription, and its explicit social content should be considered in relation to its implicit social content—namely, its author's own tacit but all-important social perspective.

The first of these interpretive tasks is not all that difficult in the case of Grocheio's survey, because many of his social classifications are quite plainly prescriptive, and his prescriptions all serve a purpose he specifies without any undue reticence. That purpose is "leading all things to a good order" in the interests of

FIG. 7-1 Professor lecturing at the University of Paris (from "Les Grandes Chroniques," an early fifteenth-century historical manuscript now at the Bibliothèque Nationale, Paris).

social stability. His description of how various types of music are used, then, is really a description of how various types of music ought to be used. All the genres of music that we have encountered thus far are given not so much an actual as an ideal place in what is less a realistic than a utopian depiction of social harmony.

Thus epic songs (*chansons de geste*), for example, *ought to be* provided, Grocheio says, "for old men, working citizens, and for average people when they rest from their accustomed labor, so that, having heard the miseries and calamities of others, they may more easily bear up under their own, and go about their tasks more gladly," and without threatening the peace with any newfangled notions about social justice.[2] "By these means," Grocheio adds, "this kind of music has the power to protect the whole state." The philologist and music historian Christopher Page has found some striking parallels for this passage in sermons by Parisian churchmen who, while basically rejecting the music of minstrels as a "low" or sensual pleasure, nevertheless conceded its utility in mitigating the sadness of human life and enabling men to bear their lot without protest.[3] (For the same reason, he notes, some medieval churchmen were even "prepared to countenance prostitution within the *civitas* as a measure to preserve public order.")

For an example at the other end of the social spectrum, Grocheio says that *cantus coronatus* (by which he means the kind of trouvère songs that competed for prizes) are ordained among kings and nobles in order to "move their souls to audacity and bravery, to magnanimity and liberality,"[4] qualities that also keep society running smoothly. Lower types of secular song, namely those with refrains, are meant for "the feasts of the vulgar," where they serve a similar edifying purpose, but more artlessly.

The chant, and its polyphonic offspring, the organum, "is sung in churches or holy places for the praise of God and reverence of His high place." Even dance music has its assigned place in a well-ordered polity, for it "excites the soul of man to move ornately" and in its more artful forms it "makes the soul of the performer and also the soul of the listener pay close attention and frequently turns the soul of the wealthy from depraved thinking."

So despite Grocheio's disavowal of all interest in metaphysics and his insistence that he meant only to describe music in the world he knew, his account of it is quite consistent with that of Plato, the greatest of all utopians and idealists. For both of them, music was above all a social regulator, a means for organizing and controlling society. As Page emphasizes, "Grocheio belonged to the class which supplied princes with their advisers and provided the whole of France with the principal agents and beneficiaries of bureaucratic power."[5] Indeed, his treatise reads like nothing so much as musical advice to a prince, of a kind that we now (after the greatest and most cynical of princely advisers) call "Machiavellian."

The one part of Grocheio's treatise that does have a realistic ring, and which can be taken as truly descriptive, is the part devoted to the music of Grocheio's own class, the music he knew best and valued most. It was a new sort of music, one that we have not encountered as yet. Johannes de Grocheio was the preeminent social theorist of the medieval *motet*.

THE NASCENT MOTET

The simplest definition of a motet, in its earliest form, would simply be a texted bit of discant. In its origins, as we may surmise from the genre's earliest sources, the motet was actually a *prosulated* bit of discant — discant (by definition melismatic in tenor as well as added voices) to which a syllabic text has been grafted onto the added voice or voices in the manner of a prosula. We can trace the process by returning to a piece already familiar from the previous chapter: the "Ex semine" clausula from the *Alleluia Nativitas* attributed by Anonymus IV to Perotin.

A transcription of the clausula was included in Ex. 6-5. Figure 7-2a shows the clausula in its original notation, from the Notre Dame manuscript W_2. Fig. 7-2b shows the duplum from the same clausula in prosulated form, as it is found in a different fascicle of W_2. The syllabic text it now carries is a Latin poem honoring both the Virgin Mary's birth and that of her son. It opens with a quotation from the text of the Marian Alleluia verse *Nativitas* at the very point where the clausula begins (*Ex semine Abrahe*, "from the seed of Abraham"), and closes with a repetition of the word *semine*. These, along with yet an additional allusion to the Alleluia text, are italicized in the following transcription of the prosula-poem:

Ex semine	*From the seed*
Abrahe, divino	*of Abraham,* by divine
Moderamine,	control,
Igne pio numine	in the holy fire of your presence,
producis domine,	Lord, you bring forth
Hominis salutem,	the salvation of mankind
Paupertate nuda,	from stark poverty,
Virginis nativitate	by the birth of a Virgin
de tribu Iuda.	from the tribe of Judah.
Iam propinas ovum	And now you proffer an egg
Per natale novum,	for an additional birth,
Piscem, panem dabis,	by which you will give fish and bread
Partu sine *semine.*	all delivered without *seed.*

Thus the prosula-poem is a textual interpolation into the canonical chant as well as a potentially self-contained song. It is a gloss on the text of the Alleluia in the manner of a trope, and was probably meant for insertion directly into a performance of the organum. (But note that Fig. 7-2b also contains the tenor, so that the texted clausula can also be performed independently of the chant and its other polyphony.)

Since it is now notated *cum littera* like the conductus studied at the end of the previous chapter, the duplum can no longer use the first-mode ligatures of the clausula. It is now a *motellus* (later, and more standardly, a *motetus*), a "texting" or a "wording" or a "part with words." The term itself is a curious Latin back-borrowing from French, in which *mot* is the word for "word." Anyone actually inserting the motetus into the organum would have to know the rhythms of the clausula by heart. So at this stage a prosulated discant or motet has to be notated twice: once for the tune, again for the text.

Indeed, when motets, freshly weaned from their incubator within the organum, began to be written as new, freestanding pieces of texted music rather than mere textual grafts on existing discants, they still needed at first to be notated twice, syllabically for the words and melismatically for the rhythm. The only reasonable explanation for the extravagant excess of discant clausulae one finds in the Notre Dame sources — as many as two dozen or more for a tenor that might only be sung liturgically once a year — is that many or most of these "clausulae" were actually rhythmic templates to guide the performance of already-composed motets. What this also shows is that one must take care to distinguish between the chronology of genres and that of individual pieces. The fact that the clausula as a genre precedes the motet as a genre in no way implies that any given untexted clausula must have preceded its texted counterpart or counterparts. The latter may indeed be prosulated versions of the former, but the former may just as easily be an aid to assist in performing the latter.

Now compare Fig. 7-3, a page from a later manuscript that contains nothing but motets. It is the same clausula on *Ex semine*, now given complete, in all three parts. The motetus, or texted duplum shown in Fig. 7-2b occupies the right hand column. Under it is the familiar tenor. Opposite it, in the left column, is the triplum from the clausula (compare Fig. 7-2a), now also outfitted with a text — another text! It is another gloss on the text of the same Alleluia, reflecting and enlarging, like its counterpart, on the marvel of the Virgin's birth and the miracle of the actual "virgin birth," that is, her son's.

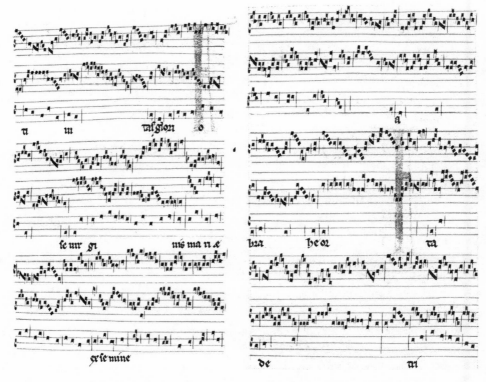

FIG. 7-2A   *Ex semine* clausula (W₂, fols. 16v–17). It begins halfway through the bottom system on the left.

FIG. 7-2B   Motetus on the same clausula (W₂, fol. 146v–147) as in Fig. 7-2a. It begins with the ornate capital E halfway down the left side and ends halfway down the right.

This triplum text, which begins and ends with the same verbal allusions as the motetus, was explicitly fashioned as a sort of rhetorical double or echo to it:

Ex semine	*From the seed*
Rosa prodit spine;	of a thorn, a rose comes forth.
Fructus olee	The olive fruit
Oleastro legitur;	Is plucked from the olive tree.
Virgo propagine	A Virgin comes forth
Nascitur Judee.	From Judah's line.
Stelle matutine	The morning star's
Radius exoritur	radiance shines forth
Nubis caligine;	from the cloudy gloom;
Radio sol stelle;	The sun, from the star's ray;
Petra fluit melle	A stone flows with honey;
Parit flos puelle	A flower of maidenhood gives birth
Verbum sine *semine.*	to the Word, without *seed.*

Our piece is now a doubly prosulated clausula, more commonly known as a double motet. (Ex. 7-1 is a transcription of it.) And that is both the fascination and the enigma of the medieval motet. In its developed form, the one Grocheio knew and loved, the

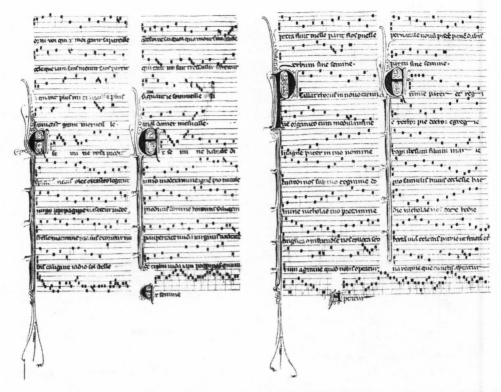

FIG. 7-3 Double motet on *Ex semine* (Bamberg, Staatliche Bibliothek, Lit. 115, fols. 15v–16). The triplum and motetus voices are notated side by side (note the capital initial E's). The tenor is beneath the motetus (to its left is the end of the tenor for the preceding motet).

genre was "polytextual," which is to say it had as many texts as it had voices over the Gregorian tenor. Before we get any deeper into the question of polytextuality, however, there is another matter, also well illustrated in Fig. 7-3, to investigate.

"FRANCONIAN" NOTATION

As one can see at a glance, the manuscript from which Fig. 7-3 has been reproduced uses a different kind of notation from the one that had been devised at and for Notre

EX. 7-1 Double motet on *Ex semine* (transcription of Fig. 7-3)

EX. 7-1 (continued)

Dame. It is a notation specially tailored to the requirements of motets, that is *musica cum littera*. (It would have served nicely for conductus, too; but by mid-century the conductus was moribund.) It supplies the very thing that Notre Dame notation lacked, namely a means of specifying the rhythmic significance of individual "graphemes," or written shapes. Notation that does this is called "mensural" notation, from *mensura*, Latin for measurement. Its invention was a watershed, not only in the history of notation but in the wider history of musical style. The new resources of mensural notation greatly lessened the dependency of "literate" music (here, literally, the music of the *literati*) on oral supplements. From now on, literate genres could pursue a relatively autonomous line of development. We will never finish discussing the consequences of this turning point—some foreseen, others not; some indubitably "progressive," others more equivocal. Their repercussions continue to affect musical composition, musical practice, musical attitudes, and musical controversies right up to the present day.

Like the melismatic notation that was developed to specify the rhythms of Notre Dame organum, the syllabic notation that was developed later in the thirteenth century to specify the rhythms of the motet was very efficiently fashioned out of the existing fund of "quadratic" plainchant neumes. The first prerequisite was to come up with single note-shapes to represent the longa and the brevis. The solution will seem obvious to us, who have lived with its consequences since birth, but at the time it was a considerable feat of imagination.

As we have known since chapter 1, chant notation already possessed two different *notae simplices* or single-note shapes: the point or *punctum* (simple square) and the rod or *virga* (square with tail at right). The distinction between them had to do with pitch: the *virga* represented a melodic peak. What some audacious soul had to do was re-imagine the distinction in rhythmic terms: the *virga* would henceforth represent the long and the punctum the *breve*. So it is in Fig. 7-3, which comes from the so-called "Bamberg codex" (known familiarly as **Ba**), a collection of exactly one hundred double motets that was put together at some point between about 1260 and 1290, to judge by its notational style.

Thanks to the explicit differentiation of longs and breves, it is now possible to indicate the trochaic rhythm of the familiar clausula without the use of ligatures. Because the individual notes now had intrinsic rhythmic values, and because there were no longer any indefinitely held-out notes like those in organum tenors, it was no longer necessary to align the parts in score. The layout first used in the motet manuscripts of the late thirteenth century, in which all the parts are entered on the same page but in their own separate locations, was a great space-saver and remained standard until the end of the sixteenth century. In the fifteenth and sixteenth centuries most of the music that was notated in this way was choral music, so this distributional layout came to be called "choirbook style." The Bamberg Codex is one of the earliest examples of it.

We do not know exactly when or where the virga and punctum were first used to represent the long and the breve. It happens in practical sources, like **Ba**, before any surviving theoretical source discusses it. (In fact, hints of such a distinction can be found in chant manuscripts as far back as the tenth century.) The earliest known theorist to prescribe the practice was Magister Lambertus, probably a University of

Paris instructor like Garlandia but of a later generation, in a treatise of ca. 1270. His description of mensural shapes and their relationship closely accords with the notation found in **Ba**, which probably means that **Ba**, though possibly copied in Germany, contains a Parisian repertoire. (The piece in Fig. 7-3 is obviously Parisian, of course, since it is just a texted version of a Notre Dame clausula.)

The fullest discussion of early mensural notation is found in a famous treatise called *Ars cantus mensurabilis* ("The art of measured song") by a German writer, Franco of Cologne, whose name has become attached to the notation he so definitively described. The principles of "Franconian" notation, first formulated by ca. 1280, though much supplemented and modified over the years, basically held good for the next two to three centuries.

Despite the mensural breakthrough, and not to take away from it, Franco's rhythmic notation did not absolutely transcend or replace the contextual aspects of "modal" notation. It represented a compromise of sorts between the intrinsic and the contextual (which is why there had to be all that supplementing and modifying over the years). A virga unambiguously represented a long rather than a breve, but that long could either be a perfect (three-tempora) long or an imperfect (two-tempora) long, depending on the context. In Fig. 7-3, the longs that alternate trochaically with breves in the motetus (texted duplum) and triplum parts are imperfect, while the longs that congregate spondaically in the tenor are perfect. A punctum unambiguously represented a breve and not a long, but that breve could be a normal one-tempus breve (*brevis recta*) or a two-tempora "altered" breve (*brevis altera*) as originally devised for the dactylic or "third mode" meter at Notre Dame, depending on the context. The contexts, which can be complicated, are spelled out to a degree in the accompanying table (Fig. 7-4), which outlines the basic principles of Franconian notation.

One of the cleverest Franconian innovations had to do with ligatures, where some apparently new graphemes were introduced. The new shapes, however, were based very systematically on the old. As observed in the previous chapter, the usual Gregorian binariae—the *pes* (ascending) and the *clivis* (descending)—happened to assume the rhythm BL in the first and second rhythmic modes as specified by Garlandia. Under the Franconian rules this rhythmic assignment was made intrinsic to the shapes irrespective of context. Then the fun began.

When written in their familiar *pes* ▗ and *clivis* ▀▘ forms, binariae were "proper" and "perfect." The former word applied to the appearance of the first note, the latter to the appearance of the second. If the first note in the ligature departed from its normal shape, whether by adding a tail to the pes ▗ or taking it away from the clivis ▀▖, then the first note received the opposite meaning and the ligature became LL. If the second note in the ligature departed from its normal shape, whether by reversing the termination of the pes ▗▘ or making the square termination of the clivis oblique ▚, then the second note received the opposite meaning and the ligature became BB. If both notes were affected—whether ▛ or ▚—then the whole ligature received its opposite meaning and became LB. That covered all possible two-note combinations. Additional notes were considered interpolations and were always read as breves.

E X. 7-2   Principles of Franconian notation

Three note values:

¶ (long), ■ (breve), ◆ (semibreve),

Longs are defined as "perfect" (i.e., containing three breves),

unless "imperfected' by a single intervening breve.

If two breves intervene between longs, the second is "altered,"

unless a "point of division" says otherwise:

Semibreves are to breves as breves are to longs.

When they come only in pairs they may be presumed equal:

Two note ligatures of traditional shape are said to
have "propriety and perfection" and are read BL:

(pes)   (clivis)

If the first note has an altered shape they are read LL
("without propriety but with perfection"):

If the second note has an altered shape they are read BB
("with propriety but without perfection"):

If both notes have an altered shape they are read LB
("without propriety or perfection"):

An upward stroke turns the ligature into a pair
of semibreves ("with the opposite propriety")

which may replace a breve at the biginning of a ligature:

All interpolated note are breves:

etc., etc.

And that is why the tenor in Fig. 7-3 is notated in *notae simplices* (longs and duplex longs, now called maximas) throughout. The three-note ligatures or *ternariae* that had represented spondaic or fifth-mode ordines in the Notre Dame style could no longer represent a group of three longs since middle notes were now breves by definition.

The remaining Franconian innovation was the division of the breve (or tempus) into semibreves, so that three note values were available. For the semibreve, too, an existing grapheme was co-opted. It was represented by the diamond shape that had originally been part of the *climacus*, the three-note descending neume in Gregorian chant notation. (For an example see the peak of the "omnes" melisma in the Gradual *Viderunt omnes* near the beginning of Fig. 6-2 in the previous chapter.) It had previously been adapted by the Notre Dame scribes to represent *currentes*, long descending "runs" of quick notes. (For the all-time champion run of *currentes* see the duplum voice in the organum on *Viderunt omnes*, right under the illuminated capital in Fig. 6-3.) Although the semibreve shape was derived, logically enough, from the quickest notes in the Notre Dame sign-system, the use of the semibreve in motets was not simply a way of speeding things up. Rather, the introduction of the semibreve made it possible to distinguish a third level of rhythmic activity. As we shall see, this was something that the development of the motet demanded.

Theoretically, the division of the breve into semibreves was similar to that of the long into breves: the longer value was assumed to be "perfect," meaning divisible by three. In practice, the division of the breve was duple from the first, and semibreves generally appeared in pairs. As the table shows, there was even a ligature shape to represent a pair of semibreves. Therefore most scholars assume that the notes in the pair were effectively equal in duration as performed, even though theorists called the first of them the *semibrevis recta* (one third of a breve) and the second the *semibrevis altera* (two thirds of a breve), implying a rather fussy lurching rhythm.

CONFLUENCE OF TRADITIONS

The motets examined thus far, all of them deriving from a specific clausula-protoype, demonstrate the descent of the motet from the liturgical repertory of Notre Dame. That is only half the story, though. A glance at another texting of the same *Ex semine* clausula will suggest the other half. Figure 7-4, allowing for the minor copying variants one must expect to find when comparing manuscripts, is musically identical to Fig. 7-3. The appearance of the notation, of course, is altogether different, but that difference should not mislead us. Since it comes from a Notre Dame source (our old friend W₂), the notation in Fig. 7-4 is pre-mensural. The motetus and triplum are laid out in score (although the tenor is now entered separately, to save space, as in Fig. 7-3), and the notes are graphically undifferentiated as to rhythm. But by now we know that the intended rhythm is the same one represented in modal notation in Fig. 7-2a and mensural notation in Fig. 7-3.

The real difference between Fig. 7-3 and Fig. 7-4, and it is a huge one, is a matter not of notes but of text. A different text to be sung to the same tune is called a *contrafactum* (or, in anglicized form, a "contrafact"). This particular contrafact involves a change not

FIG. 7-4 French motet, *Se j'ai ame/EX SEMINE* (W₂, fols. 136–136v). The triplum and motetus, sung to the same words, are vertically aligned. The tenor occupies the last two lines of music before the capital M that marks the beginning of the next motet.

only of words but of language. The *Ex semine* clausula has been effectively transformed into a French song for two voices over a vocalized or instrumental tenor. Its text, skillfully modeled to fit the irregular phrases of the original clausula, is as follows:

Se j'ai amé	If I have loved
N'en doi estre blasmé	I should not be blamed,
Quant sui assené	Since I am pledged
A la plus cortoise riens	To the fairest little
de Paris la cité.	creature in Paris town.
Onques en mon vivant	Never in my life, though,
N'en ai un biau semblant	Has she given me so much as a friendly glance,
Si est a touz fors (qu')à moi	Yet to all but me she is
franche et humiliant;	openhearted and meek.
Mes s'ele seust de voir	If only she could see
Cum je l'aim sanz decevoir,	How guilelessly I love her,
Ele m'ostast de doulor	She would take away my pain
Qu'ele me dounast s'amor.	By giving me her love.

Allowing for a bit of urbanization ("Paris town"), this is a trouvère poem in all but name. Indeed, at the point where we left it in chapter 4, we may recall, the trouvère *chanson* tradition was in the process of transplantation from its original abode in the aristocratic countryside to the towns of northern France. The new motet genre was its destination. It became the primary site for the production of French "literary song" in the late thirteenth century.

The motet in French was thus an interesting hybrid, crossbred from two exceedingly disparate strains. "We can imagine a schema," Richard Crocker deftly observes, "in which music from the monastery [that is, organum] converges on the cathedral, hence on the town, from one side; and music from the court [that is, the chanson] converges on the town, hence on the cathedral, from the other. They meet at the residences of the cathedral nobility."[6] If that seems a bit too schematic, since it casts the music, rather than the people who use it, in an active role, we can re-imagine the situation in more human terms. Let us imagine, then, that city-dwelling clerics (such as Johannes de Grocheio), who would have known and valued both the urbanized chanson and the prosulated discant, would have been the ones most apt to crossbreed the two and arrive at a new music that pleased them particularly. The great value of Crocker's formulation is that it emphasizes the co-responsibility of the courtly and the cathedral genres and their respective milieux for the birth and, especially, the rapid growth of the motet.

Again we need to be cautious when it comes to questions of priority and concordances. (A concordance is the reappearance of music or text in a new place.) Just as we cannot assume that a given clausula is older than a musically concordant motet just because historically the clausula came first, so we cannot assume that when a motet exists with texts both in Latin (sacred) and in French (secular), that the French must be the contrafact just because sacred music has the longer recorded history, or because measured rhythm was first notated in church. In the case of motets based on the *Ex semine* clausula, it is easy to make the false assumption, since all of them go back to a known Latin sacred prototype in modal rhythm. But as we have already seen, the French motet in Fig. 7-4 comes from an earlier source than the Latin one in Fig. 7-3 and uses an earlier method of notation.

Also of possible significance is the fact that the French motet is not a double motet. Its one text is evidently meant to be sung by the two upper voices in rhythmic unison. Take away the tenor and such a homorhythmic, syllabically texted piece would be called a conductus. So motets in which two voices sing a single text against a tenor have for that reason been christened "conductus motets," and are presumed to be early. It is modern scholars, however, who have done both the christening and the presuming. And a presumption, by definition, lacks supporting evidence.

The evidence does not allow us to state that the Latin motet was invented before the French. Only "common sense," our knowledge of early prosula technique, and our conjectures about the new genre's possible liturgical use support the Latin-first idea. On the other side of the scale there is the source evidence. The earliest sources for motets in French are actual trouvère manuscripts, such as the huge Manuscrit du Roi that was mentioned in chapter 4. It was put together between 1246 and 1254, which may actually be a bit earlier than the date of W_2, and no later than **Flo**, which seems to contain the earliest surviving Latin-texted motets.

There are even a few French pieces called "motet" in the Manuscrit du Roi that, being monophonic, are not related to the Notre Dame clausula at all. Like polyphonic motets they are written in mensural notation and are without sectional repeats. Like late trouvère chansons, on the other hand, some of them make use of "refrains"—the short, endlessly recycled verbal/musical tags or "hooks" we encountered in chapter 4. One of these monophonic motets quotes as a tag of this kind the refrain of Adam de la Halle's little rondeau *Bone amourete*, already familiar to us as Ex. 4-6. In the motet (Ex. 7-3), the refrain is split up, and the whole rest of the poem is inserted between its two halves:

Bone amourete m'a soupris	Good love has caught me off guard
D'amer bele dame de pris,	and made me love a prized beauty,
Le cors agent et cler le vis.	Comely of form and fair of face.
Et por s'amour trai grant esmai,	And for love of her I pay dearly,
Et ne por quant je l'amerai.	However much I love her.
Tant con vivrai de fin cuer vrai.	Nevertheless I will I live with fine true heart,
Car l'esperance que j'ai	for the hope I have
De chanter tous jours	of singing all the while
me tient gai.	keeps me gay.

EX. 7-3   Paris, BN 844 ("Manuscrit du Roi"), interpolation no. 8, transcribed by Judith Peraino

EX. 7-3 (continued)

car l'es - per - an - ce ke j'ai

de chan - ter tou - jours

me tient gai

Stanzas inserted within refrains like this were a distinct genre, called *motet enté* ("spliced" or "grafted motet"), and they were quickly assimilated to the polyphonic motet genre as it grew. The monophonic origins of the genre within the late trouvère repertory, however, should keep us from assuming that the motet is a polyphonic genre by definition. It is, rather, a hybrid genre, the product of multiple crossbreedings from various parent genres, both monophonic and polyphonic, both courtly and ecclesiastical.

A NEW *TROBAR CLUS?*

The undeniable fact is, however, that by the end of the century — that is, by Grocheio's time — the motet *was* a strictly polyphonic genre, and it reveled more than any other genre in its polyphonicness. To deny this fact about the motet on account of the genre's not-strictly-polyphonic origins or ancestry would be to commit what is called the "genetic fallacy" — the inadvertent or deliberate confusion of something as it is with what it may originally have been. (For a more obvious example, imagine claiming that our national anthem is not a patriotic song but just a drinking song.) And while we're on the subject of fallacies, it is also a fallacy (the so-called "pathetic fallacy") to say, as in this paragraph's first sentence, that the motet "reveled in its polyphonicness." Motets cannot revel. Only people revel. And it was people, notably Grocheio, who reveled in the complexity of the polyphonic, polytextual motet. For an example of the fully evolved, late thirteenth-century French motet that Grocheio reveled in, see Fig. 7-5, from the Bamberg Codex, and its transcription (Ex. 7-4).

The form of the piece is clearly discant- or clausula-derived, although there is no actual clausula counterpart to it. Two parts in trochaic meter ("first mode") are composed against a spondaic ("fifth-mode") cantus firmus borrowed from a Gregorian melisma. In this case the melisma comes from the Easter Gradual, *Haec dies*, already encountered in Ex. 1-7b. Compare the tenor in Ex. 7-4 with the notes sung to the italicized words in the final phrase of the Gradual: "quoniam *in seculum* misericordia ejus" (for His mercy endureth forever). The motet tenor consists of a double cursus of the chant melisma, its notes cut up into alternating groups of two and three longs or maximas.

FIG. 7-5 French double motet, *L'autre jour/Au tens pascour/IN SECULUM* (Ba, fols. 7–7v). The layout resembles that of Fig. 7-3. The tenor begins under the motetus part on fol. 7 and continues most of the way across the bottom of fol. 7v.

EX. 7-4 Transcription of Fig. 7-5

EX. 7-4 (continued)

mours chan-toit; et je dis, "Simple e coi - e, vo-len-tiers se roi - e,

dou ta-bour la dan-se de-me-ne - e; Ro-bin pas n'a-gre-e, quant

se il vous a - gre - e, vos a - mis." E - le res-pont cum _ se-ne - e:

il l'a es-gar-de - e; mais par a - a - ti - e fe-ra mieudre es - tam-pi - e.

"Si - re, lais-siés moi es-ter, ra - lés en _ vo con-tre - e, j'aim Ro-bin sans

Lors a sai - si son four-rel, prist son cha-pel, s'a sa cote es-cour-ci - e,

faus-se - té, m'a-mor li ai don-ne - e, plus l'aim _ que-riens ne - e; il s'en est a-

s'a fait _ l'es-tan-pi - e jo-li - e pour l'a-mour de s'a-mi - e. Ro-giers, Gui-os

EX. 7-4   (*continued*)

Triplum	Motetus
The other morning by a valley at daybreak,	At Eastertide all the shepherd folk
I found a shepherdess, and I watched her.	from one region
She was alone, singing of love, and I said:	gathered together at the bottom of a valley.
"Sweet and gentle one,	In the meadow Herbert led the dance
I would gladly be your lover,	with pipe and tabor.
If it pleases you."	Robin was not pleased when he saw it,
She replied most sensibly,	but out of defiance would do a better *estampie.*
"Leave me alone sir, return to your region.	Then he grabbed his drone, seized his bat,
I love Robin truly and I have given him my love,	tucked up his tunic,
I love him more than anyone.	and did the jolly *estampie* for the love
He has gone to play in the woods	of his sweetheart.
beneath the bower.	Rogier, Guiot, and Gautier
It would be vile of me not to love him,	are very envious indeed.
for he loves me faithfully.	Not one of them laughs, but they say defiantly
Never would I seek to leave him for you."	that before nightfall his pipe will be broken.

Tenor
Forever

That much is *à la* clausula, all right, but the motetus and triplum texts are both little pastourelles reminiscent of trouvère poetry, even down to the name of Robin the shepherd and the cliché beginning ("the other day . . .") that goes all the way back to the troubadours:

Triplum:	
L'autre jour par un matin	The other day at morn
dejouste une valée	down by a valley
A une ajournée	at break of day

Pastourelle ai trovée,	I spied a shepherdess
Je l'ai regardée;	and watched her a while.
Seule estoit,	She was all alone,
D'amours chantoit;	singing of love,
Et je dis:	and I said:
"Simple et coie,	"Guileless and bashful girl,"
Volentiers seroie,	gladly would I be,
Se il vous agrée,	If it would pleasure you,
Vos amis."	Your lover."
Ele respont cum senée:	She replied, thoughtfully:
"Sire, laissiés moi ester,	"Sir, let me be,
Ralés en vo contrée,	go back where you came from.
J'aim Robin sans faulsseté,	I love Robin without deceit;
m'amor li ai donnée,	I've pledged him my love.
Plus l'aim que riens née;	I love him more than any born thing.
Il s'en est alés juer	He's gone off to play
au bois, sous la ramée;	in the woods 'neath the trees;
Villenie feroie,	I'd do an awful thing
Se je ne l'amoie,	if I didn't love him back,
Car il m'aimme sans trechier,	For he has loved me faithfully,
Ja pour vous ne le quier laissier."	And I'd never leave him for the likes of you."

Motetus:	
Au tens pascour	At Eastertime
Tuit li pastour	All the shepherd folk
D'une contrée	from one locale
Ont fait assemblée	gathered together
Desous une valée.	at the bottom of a valley.
Hebers en la prée	Herbert, in the meadow,
A de la pipe et dou tabour	with pipe and tabor
la danse demenée;	led the dance.
Robin pas n'agrée,	Robin did not like it
Quant il l'a esgardée;	when he saw it,
Mais par aatie	but out of conceit
Fera mieudre estampie.	thought he'd do a better estampie.
Lors a saisi son fourrel,	So he grabbed his bagpipe,
Prist son chapel,	put on his hat,
S'a sa cote escourcie,	tucked in his coat,
S'a fait l'estanpie	and did an estampie,
Jolie	a jolly one,
Pour l'amour de s'amie.	to impress his girl.
Rogers, Guios et Gautiers	Roger, Guy and Gautier
en ont mont grant envie,	are right full of jealousy,
N'i a nul qui rie,	They none of them laugh,
Ains font aatie,	but say defiantly

K'ains ke soit l'avesprée,   that come nightfall
Iert sa pipe effondrée.   his pipe is going to be in pieces.

Naive and folksy as these texts seem, they are cast in a very urbane musical construction that belies their rustic nature. That jocular incongruity, which (along with polytextuality) intensified the essential heterogeneity of the motet genre, is already one delightful aspect of *ars combinatoria*, the art of combining things. And it is already a reason why Grocheio, the intellectual connoisseur, placed the motet at the summit of Parisian genres, for it was "a song composed of many voices, having many words or a variety of syllables, [but] everywhere sounding in harmony."[7] The harmonization of contrarieties (*discordia concors*) encompassed the texts as well as the tunes, even including the unsung, incongruously Latinate and liturgical text of the tenor. The duplum text, with its reference to "Eastertime" (*tens pascour*), alludes obliquely to the source of the chant melisma on which the whole polyphonic superstructure of the motet has been erected. Motets are full of in-jokes.

But that was not the only reason for Grocheio's devotion to the new genre. As usual, the theorist prescribes as well as describes, and this is his prescription for the motet:

> This kind of song ought not to be propagated among the vulgar, since they do not understand its subtlety nor do they delight in hearing it, but it should be performed for the learned and those who seek after the subtleties of the arts. And it is normally performed at their feasts for their edification, just as the song they call rondeau is performed at the feasts of the vulgar.

Very interesting, this: a song all about the shepherds and their faithful lassies, but not to be sung before Robin, Roger, and their gang, because they'd never understand it. In fact, the complicated polytextual song itself served to mark off the occasion at which it is sung—a university recreation or, as Grocheio charmingly puts it, a "feast of the learned"—as an elite occasion, at which and *through* which the members of Grocheio's new class could celebrate and demonstrate their superiority to the "vulgar." Now that seems to ring a bell. Where have we heard sentiments like these before? We heard them a few chapters back when we listened in on a mock debate (*joc parti*) between two troubadours, one of whom (Raimbaut d'Aurenga, alias Linhaure) espoused the values of *trobar clus*, the "difficult" poetry of the courtly elite. Do not prize "that which is common to all," he warned, "for then would all be equal." Grocheio's echo of these exclusionary values on behalf of the motet is a wonderful example of the way in which newly emerging elites—in this case an urban and literate elite, many of whose members had been drawn from the lower classes—ape or aspire to the status of an older, established aristocracy.

The self-congratulating "learned" class represented by Grocheio provided an audience that encouraged composers to experiment and vie with one another in the creation of *tours de force*, feats of ingenuity. The motet became a hotbed of technical innovation and "combinatorial" adventure. The one in Ex. 7-5 is an attempt to combine three disparate musico-poetic styles in one "harmony of clashes." The triplum is in the style of a *motet enté* like the one in Ex. 7-4: its non-repeating melody quotes an old refrain, *Celle m'a s'amour douné Qui mon cuer et m'amour a* ("She who has my heart and love did give her love to me"). The motetus is an actual rondeau, minus the opening refrain (also a famous one):

[A]	[*Li regart de ses vers euz*	The glance of her green eyes
[B]	*m'ocist*]	Just kills me.
a	Que ferai, biau sire Diex?	What can I do, good Lord?
A	*Li regart de ses verz euz*	The glance of her green eyes
A	*J'atendrai pour avoir mieix*	I will await in hopes of
B	merci	better treatment.
A	*Li regart de ses vers euz*	The glance of her green eyes
B	*m'ocist*	Just kills me.

And the tenor is the same tenor as in Ex. 7-4, only cast like the other parts in the trochaic first mode, with irregularities that only mensural notation could pinpoint with accuracy.

Though short and sweet, not to say trivial at first glance, this piece is very much a tour de force of *composing* in the most literal, etymological sense (from *componere*, to put things together). The task involved shoehorning into one harmonizing texture not one, not two, but three preexisting melodies, of which one contained, as an additional hazard, many musical repetitions of its own. The audience would have derived great

EX. 7-5 *J'ai les maus d'amours/que ferai/IN SECULUM* (Montpelier, Faculté de médicines H196 (**Mo**), f. 188ʳ)

EX. 7-5 (continued)

Triplum:
I have the pains of love without suffering when *she gave me her love who has
my heart and my love.* And since she has it, I well know that she will kill me.

Duplum:
What shall I do, good Lord God? *The glance of her green eyes* I shall await to
have better grace. *The glance of her green eyes kills me.*

pleasure out of penetrating beyond the first glance to recognize the three preexisting
tunes (all in different forms) and marvel at the skill with which they had been combined.

Such a piece was a triumph of literate contrivance, one whose craftsmanly intricacy
depended utterly on the written medium. Like the *trobar clus* of the troubadours, its
meaning was "shut up and obscure," so that "a man is afraid to do violence to it" by
casual oral delivery, as Peire d'Alvernhe (1158–80), one of the late Provençal poets, had
declared in defense of recherché, "difficult" art.[8]

TENOR "FAMILIES"

Of the three components that went into this brainy little song, the most frequently used
was the tenor. The "In seculum" melisma, like several others (including "DO-"[mino]
from the same parent gradual, *Haec dies*), was a great favorite with the university
crowd, used over and over again as a motet tenor. This, too, was an aspect of "tour de
force culture," in which emulation or outdoing—doing the same thing but doing it
better—was a cardinal aim.

But why the "In seculum" tenor in particular? It might have had something to
do with its eccentric tonal scheme. The Gregorian melismas, on which motets (like
clausulas before them) were constructed, are groups of notes excerpted more or less at
hazard out of larger tonal structures. They do not at all necessarily end on the final
of the parent chant's mode. Indeed, the "In seculum" melisma does not. The *Haec dies*
Gradual is in mode 2 transposed to cadence on A. The "In seculum" melisma ends on
F. And even within the melisma the final note is surprising, since it occurs only at the
end, after many repercussions (some of them quite convincingly cadential) on C.

When the melisma forms the tenor of a clausula that is then re-inserted into the
context of a full performance of the Gradual, the tonal disparity is minimized. When
it forms the tenor of a motet that is performed all by itself, the tonal disparity is

emphasized and becomes perhaps—or indeed almost certainly, in view of the tenor's popularity—a source of pleasure in its own right, for it is yet another aspect of *discordia concors*. (For modern listeners, who are trained to value tonal unity in a composition, it is perhaps a guiltier pleasure than it was for Grocheio and his contemporaries.) Wayward or unpredictable tonal characteristics, deemed a deviation or a defect in more recent music, are normal in medieval motets, and were probably even an allurement.

COLOR AND TALEA

An extraordinary witness to the popularity of the "In seculum" melisma is a little appendix of textless pieces, all based on it, found at the end of the Bamberg manuscript after the hundred motets that make up its main *corpus* or "body" of works. Although they are without text and written in score, these pieces are not really "clausulae," because they are written in mensural notation and have nothing to do with the actual Notre Dame repertory. (As far as the composers themselves were in all likelihood concerned, they were borrowing the "In seculum" tenor not from a Gradual but from other motets.) They were "abstract" pattern-pieces, intended for vocalizing or for instrumental performance, and as such count as the earliest written "chamber music." Fig. 7-6, an "opening" of two facing pages from the Bamberg manuscript, shows three of these pieces and the beginning of a fourth; Ex. 7-6 contains transcriptions of the two complete pieces.

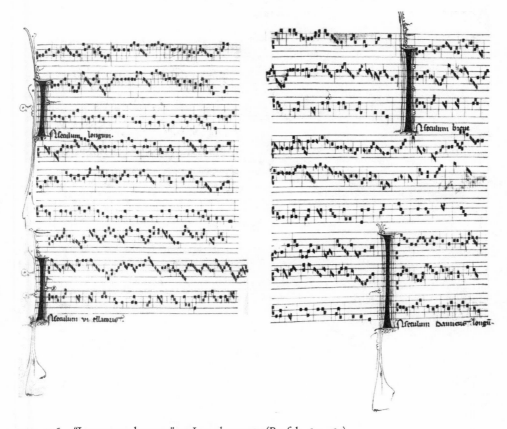

FIG. 7-6   "Instrumental motets" on *In seculum* tenor (Ba, fols. 63v–64).

EX. 7-6A   "Instrumental" (textless) motets, *In seculum longum*

EX. 7-6A   (*continued*)

EX. 7-6B   *In seculum breve*

EX. 7-6B   (*continued*)

Compare the tenors. They all cut up the "In seculum" melisma into three-note ordines. The first, called *In seculum longum* ("In seculum by longs") casts the tune in perfect longs throughout, as in the spondaic "fifth mode." The second, called *In seculum viellatoris* ("The fiddle-player's In seculum"), uses trochaic ("first mode") LBL patterns as fixed by the mensural ligatures. And the third, called *In seculum breve* ("In seculum by breves") reverses the patterns of the second piece into iambic ("second mode") BLB patterns, also fixed by the mensural ligatures.

All three tenors put the "In seculum" melisma through a double cursus. The melisma contains 34 notes, which when divided into three-note ordines leaves a remainder of one after the eleventh ordo. So in all three pieces, the twelfth ordo consists of the last note of the first cursus and the first two notes of the second cursus. As a result, the melody and the rhythmic "foot-unit" seem to go out of phase with one another in the second cursus, producing a new set of three-note ordines on which to base the polyphonic texture. In other words, the two aspects or dimensions of the tenor — the melody or pitch-succession, and the rhythmic ordo — have been conceptually separated.

This method of constructing tenors, in which a predetermined, repeated pitch-succession borrowed from a chant was coordinated with a predetermined, repeated succession of durations, opened up vast new possibilities for intellectual *tours de force* that were mined intensively during the fourteenth century, when the motet underwent a spectacular growth. The abstractly conceived pitch-succession was called the *color* by fourteenth-century theorists, and the abstractly conceived rhythmic pattern, especially when it went beyond the simple modal *ordines* found in these early examples, was called the *talea*. (This word, which literally means "measuring rod" in Latin, is obviously related etymologically to the Sanskrit word *tala*, by which Indian musicians refer to the fixed, cyclically repeated beat-pattern underlying the complex improvised surface rhythms in a musical performance.)

"The fiddle-player's In seculum" jibes well with the passage in Grocheio where the theorist praises fiddle players (*viellatores*) as the most versatile instrumentalists of the day. "A good performer on the *vielle*," he writes, "normally uses every kind of song and every musical form." It seems likely, then, that this piece was intended as an instrumental trio. The two pieces transcribed in Ex. 7-6 may also be instrumental trios, or at least performable that way, but there is no reason to rule out vocalized performance, especially since they are hockets, "cut-up songs," as Grocheio describes them, "composed in two or more voices." He lists hockets among the vocal genres, following organum and conductus, and comments that "this kind of song is pleasing to the hot-tempered and to young men because of its mobility and speed."

The pair of hockets in Ex. 7-6 certainly demonstrate that mobility and speed. They are in fact a single piece in two versions, *longum* and *breve*, of which the second goes exactly in "double time." Where the first is written in perfect longs, imperfect longs, and breves, the second has imperfect longs, breves, and (for the first time among the pieces selected for examination here) *semibreves*. Assuming that the "perfection" or beat-unit remains constant when the two pieces are performed in sequence, the second hocket goes at a really breakneck speed, especially considering the split-second timing that hocket-exchanges require. This is virtuoso music, demanding a *tour de force* from performers and composer alike. One or both of these pieces may be the famous *Hoquetus In seculum* attributed in Anonymus IV to "a certain Spaniard." They are found in a number of sources, and in one of them yet another voice—a texted quadruplum containing a trouvère-style love poem—is superimposed on the whole complex for a real combinatorial orgy.

THE ART OF MÉLANGE

Another motet with semibreves (in all parts this time, even the tenor) is given in Fig. 7-7 (facsimile) and Ex. 7-7 (transcription). Here the element of virtuoso composing ("fitting together") is most apparent in the motetus part, which is none other than *Robins m'aime*, the opening virelai from Adam de la Halle's *Jeu de Robin et Marion* (Ex. 4-9). The little tenor melisma, "Portare," clipped originally from an Alleluia verse, was used for many motets, but never, it seems, for a clausula. It goes through a triple cursus here.

Fig. 7-8 (transcribed in Ex. 7-8) displays one more virtuoso act of "combining" that uses material we have encountered before. This one is a real *quodlibet*—a grab-bag (literally "whatever you want") of found objects. At last we have an example of a macaronic motet,

FIG. 7-7   *Mout me fu grief/Robin m'aime/ PORTARE (Ba, fol. 52v).*

combining texts in Latin and the vernacular. Both the triplum (a French pastourelle) and the motetus (a Latin sermon) are stuffed with refrains, making the piece doubly a *motet enté*. The tenor, meanwhile, is drawn from a new source: it is a traditional "Gregorian" or Frankish chant melody, but one unrelated to the polyphonic repertory at Notre Dame. Despite some slight melodic embellishment it is familiar to us as the first acclamation from the Kyrie "Cum jubilo" (Ex. 3-5). It has been cast into a little talea consisting of a single long plus a first mode ordo, with a single cadential long inserted to complete the color after the fifth repetition of the talea. The whole tenor melody goes through a double cursus and starts up again a third time, but gets only as far as the third talea.

Thanks to the new resources of Franconian notation, the parts are neatly differentiated in rhythm — or, to be more exact, in *prosody*, the relationship of the text to the music. The triplum carries separate text syllables on semibreves; the motetus contains

EX. 7-7   Transcription of Fig. 7-7

EX. 7-7   (continued)

(3rd cursus [partial])

Triplum:
The departure of my dear sweetheart grieved me deeply, the pretty one with the bright face, as white and vermillion as rose set against lily, or so it seems to me; her ever so sweet laughter makes me tremble, and her gray-blue eyes, languish. O God, woe that I left her! Little, white lily flower, when will I see you? Worthy lady, red as a rose in May, on your account I suffer great grief.

Motetus:
Robin loves me, Robin has me; Robin asked for me, and he will have me. Robin bought me a chaplet and a little purse of silk; why then would I not love him? Robin loves me, Robin has me; Robin asked for me, and he will have me.

semibreves but places the text only on longs and breves, while the tenor, as noted, is confined to "modal" patterns of longs and breves.

This macaronic motet comes from the so-called Montpellier Codex (**Mo**), the most comprehensive and lavishly appointed motet book to survive from the thirteenth century. It contains more than three hundred motets of every description, ranging in date over the whole century, all gathered in eight fascicles, or separately sewn sections,

FIG. 7-8 *El mois de mai./De se debent bigami/ KYRIE* (Ba, fol. 14v).

of which the first six (including the one containing the macaronic motets) seem to have been compiled around 1280. It is best known for its "classic" Franconian motets, in which the voices are rhythmically even more strictly "stratified" according to pitch range (the higher the range the quicker the pace). This, too, is a refinement on the *discordia concors* idea, and the prosodic contrast is often mirrored at the semantic level. In one famous example from **Mo** (*Pucelete/Je langui/DOMINO*), the merry triplum describes the poet's enjoyment of his loving lassie in breves and semibreves; the droopy motetus complains of lovesickness in longs and breves; and the tenor keeps up an even tread of perfect longs.

The seventh and eighth fascicles of **Mo** date from the turn of the fourteenth century, Grocheio's time exactly. By now the fun and games aspect of *discordia concors* has so burgeoned as to invite free choice of found objects in all parts including the tenor, and the more extravagant the better. The motet in Fig. 7-9/Ex. 7-9 is one of those racy things Grocheio particularly recommends for his "feasts of the learned." Semibreves permeate all parts. The triplum and motetus texts are descriptions of just such medieval fraternity parties as Grocheio describes, at which young literati gathered to gorge on capons and guzzle wine and nuzzle girls and despise manual labor, and particularly to praise Paris, the fount of the good life for budding intellectuals. And the tenor? It consists of a fourfold repetition, prescribed by an early use of ditto or repeat marks in the notation, of a fruitseller's cry — "Fresh strawberries, ripe blackberries!" — possibly drawn directly "from life" as lived on the Parisian streets.

A motet like this one, in which both musical and subject matter are entirely urban and entirely secular, no longer has any direct relationship to the courtly and ecclesiastical traditions that historically nourished the genre. Its connection to the clausula or the trouvère chanson can be better demonstrated historically than stylistically. It has become independent of its traditions and ready to nurture the growth of new ones. As the American composer Aaron Copland once observed, when the audience changes, music changes.

THE "PETRONIAN" MOTET

To close our discussion of the thirteenth-century motet we can turn to the pair that opens the seventh fascicle of **Mo**. On the basis of citations by fourteenth-century writers they are attributed to a shadowy but evidently important composer and theorist named

EX. 7-8 Transcription of Fig. 7-8

Triplum: El mois de mai, que chan-te la mal-vis, que flou-rist la flour de glai,

Motetus: De se de-bent bi-ga-mi non de Pa-pa

Tenor: Kyrie

la rose et li lis: lor doit bien joi-e me-ner qui d'a-mours est es-pris;

que-ri, qui se pri-vi-le-gi-o spo-li-

si m'en-voi-se-rai, car je sui lo-iaus a-mis a la plus be-le qui soit en ces pa-

a-runt cle-ri: sed de fa-cto pro-pri-o

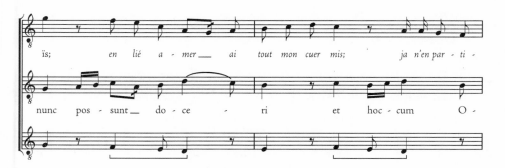

ïs; en lié a-mer ai tout mon cuer mis; ja n'en par-ti-

nunc pos-sunt do-ce-ri et hoc-cum O-

237

EX. 7-8 (continued)

Triplum:
In the month of May
when the thrush sings,
when the gladiolus, and the rose,
and lily bloom,
then those in love
should be joyful.
I will rejoice,
for I am the faithful lover
of the most beautiful one
in all these lands.
I have set my whole heart
on loving her,
I will never cease
as long as I live.
The great beauty
of her shining face,
her pretty body
made so wonderfully,
make me always
think about her.

Motetus:
Bigamists should complain about themselves,
not against the pope,
for they despoil themselves
of the privilege of clergy,
but now from their own deed
they can learn
and with Ovid
confess this to be the truth:
"Virtue is no less
to guard possessions than to seek them."

Petrus de Cruce (Pierre de la Croix?) in the treatises. These two motets, and another half dozen with similar characteristics (therefore also conjecturally ascribed to Petrus), are in a very special style that takes the device of rhythmic stratification to the very limit that contemporary notation allowed. Further, in fact, because Petrus modified Franconian notation and its attendant textures so as to exaggerate the layering effect.

Aucun/Lonc tans/ANNUN(TIANTES) gives us, in its motetus and triplum, a long and lingering last look at the loftiest class of trouvère chanson, and its tenor is also of a traditional type, borrowed from a Notre Dame organum. Fig. 7-10 shows its first

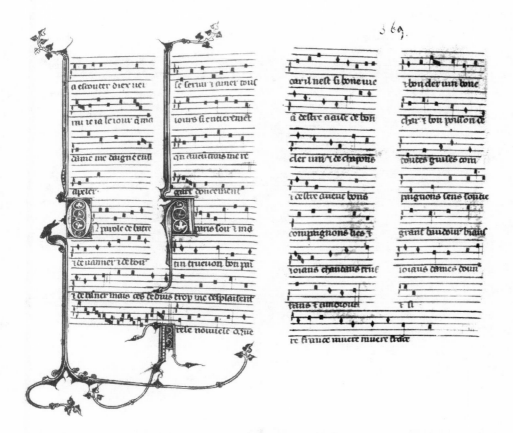

FIG. 7-9 *On a parole/A Paris/Frese nouvele* (Montpellier, Bibliothèque Inter-Universaire, Section Médecine, H196, fols. 368v–369). The beginning is again indicated by decorative capitals, halfway down the left-hand page.

page; Ex. 7-10 is a transcription of the same portion. The texture and prosody here are comparable to those in Ex. 7-8 (*El mois de mai/De se debent bigami/KYRIE*): the triplum has syllabically texted semibreves, the motetus has semibreves but carries syllables only on longs and breves or their equivalents, and the tenor moves in perfect longs throughout. And yet the sound and style of the piece are very novel indeed, owing to the flexibility with which the triplum part subdivides the basic beat (i.e., the *tempus* or breve unit).

Petrus marks off the triplum's breve units or *tempora* with little dots called *puncta divisionis* (division points) that function like modern bar lines, turning the tempora into measures. Between puncta there can be anywhere from two to seven semibreves (and according to several theorists, some composers around this time went as far as a ninefold subdivision of the tempus). In the setting of line 7, in which one measure is singled out to receive seven separate syllables, there is more than twice the usual number of semibreves in a tempus. Either they have to go by at more than twice the usual speed, turning a noble love song into a tongue twister, or the tempo of the whole has to be slowed down sufficiently to accommodate a "natural" delivery of the shortest note values.

The latter, it seems pretty clear, must have been the intention and the practice. The result is that the normal semibreve now becomes comparable in actual duration to

EX. 7-9   Transcription of Fig. 7-9

EX. 7-9 (continued)

a mes-tier, Pour so-la - cier Be-les da-mes a de-vis: Et tout ce truev' on a Pa-ris.

en - tre-deus De men-re feur pour ho-mes de - si-teus.

ve - le! Mue-re fran - ce! mue-re! mue-re fran - ce!]

Triplum:
The talk is of threshing and winnowing,
of digging and ploughing.
Such pastimes are not at all to my liking.
For there is nothing
like having one's fill
of good clear wine and capons,
and being with good friends,
hale and hearty,
singing,
joking,
and in love,
and having all one needs
to give pleasure
to beautiful women
to one's heart's content.
And all of this is to be had in Paris.

Duplum:
Morning and night in Paris
there is good bread to be found,
good, clear wine,
good meat and fish,
all manner of friends
of lively mind and high spirits,
fine jewels and noble ladies
and, in the meantime,
prices to suit a poor man's purse.

Tenor:
Fresh strawberries! Nice blackberries!
Blackberries,
nice blackberries!

FIG. 7-10 Petrus de Cruce, *Aucun/Lonc tans/ANNUN*, beginning (Mo, fol. 273), the first two pages of five.

EX. 7-10   Transcription of Fig. 7-10

Triplum: Au-cun ont trou-vé chant par u - sa - ge, Mes a moi en doune o-choi - son A-mours, qui res-bau-dist mon cou-ra - ge Si que m'es - tuet faire____ chan - çon. Car a - mer me fait da-me bele et sa-ge Et de bon__ re - non; Et je, qui li ai fait hou-ma-ge, Pour li ser-vir tout mon a - ge, De loi- al cuer sans pen-ser tra - hi - son, Chan-te-rai, car de li tieng un si douz he-ri-ta -

Motetus: Lonc tans____ me sui te - nu de chan - ter,____ Mes or ai__ rai - son de joi - e me - ner,____ Car bou - ne a - mour me fait de - si - rer La mieus

Tenor: ANNUN[TIANTES]

EX. 7-10 (*continued*)

EX. 7-10   (*continued*)

the normal breve in earlier motets, giving rise to a tempo at which the "perfect" division of the breve into three semibreves (or into an "altered" pair) is truly meaningful in transcription, like the one in Ex. 7-10. The spread between the longest and the shortest note values has reached a factor of 18 (3 × 3 × 2). As a result, the normal "modal" rhythms underlying the supple declamation of the triplum have now become so slow as virtually to fade from the surface of the music.

EX. 7-10 (*continued*)

Triplum:
There are men who live by writing songs
but I am inspired
by a love that so fills my heart with joy
that I can't stop myself writing a song.
For a fair and lovely lady
of high repute
has made me love her, and I
who am pledged to serve her
all my days without thought of betrayal,
shall sing, for from her do I
hold such a sweet bequest
that it alone can give me joy.
It is this thought that soothes my sweet sorrow
and gives me hope of curing it.
At the same time,
love may well complain of my
arrogance, and hold me prisoner;
I wouldn't think any the worse of her for that.
She knows how to lay siege so cleverly
that there is no defense from her;
Neither might nor rank
is of the slightest use.
And if it pleases her to return
my ransom at her whim, I shall
be her captive and give my heart
as collateral, by making it hers.
And I beg for mercy, since I have
no better plea on my behalf.

Motetus:
Long have I refrained from singing,
but now I have reason to flaunt joy
since true love has made me desire
the most accomplished lady
to be found in the whole world.
No other can be compared with her,
and when I so love such a precious lady
that I have great pleasure merely thinking about her,
well do I know
that a life of true love is
very pleasant, whatever people say.

Modal rhythm, in short, now loses the patterning and governing properties that were its original reason for being. Not only that, but the exaggerated rhythmic differentiation of the triplum from the supporting voices belies the origin of the motet style in the note-against-note texture of discant composition. Once again a connection that can be traced easily enough through time has been shed at the stylistic level. That is what is meant by stylistic evolution. One can trace it with interest, appreciate its vicissitudes, delight in the new possibilities it creates, and marvel at the ingenuity with which these possibilities are exploited, and yet remain skeptical of the notion that art makes progress.)

Business Math, Politics, and Paradise: The *Ars Nova*

NOTATIONAL AND STYLISTIC CHANGE IN FOURTEENTH-CENTURY FRANCE; ISORHYTHMIC MOTETS FROM MACHAUT TO DU FAY

A "NEW ART OF MUSIC"?

And yet (to pick up immediately on the closing thought of the previous chapter, and perhaps pick a fight with it) one can certainly point to times when changes in composing practice did take place for a definite composerly purpose, whether to enable specific technical solutions to specific technical problems, to enlarge a certain realm of technical possibility, or to secure specific improvements in technical efficiency. Why not call that progress?

No problem; but let us distinguish technical progress from stylistic evolution. The one affects the making only; the other is also the beholder's business. Technique is an aspect of production; style is an attribute of the product. Style, one might therefore say, is the result of technique. Hence stylistic evolution can be, among other things, a result of technical progress. But although all makers constantly try to improve their techniques, until quite recently no one ever thought deliberately to change his or her style as such. And whereas new techniques can replace or invalidate old ones, new styles do not do this, so far as the beholder is concerned. The fact that so many of us still listen to old music as much as (if not more than) to new music is sufficient proof of that.

To seek or abet style change in the name of progress means merging the concepts of technique and style. To do that required a sea change in the way artists (and not only artists) thought about means and ends. That change began to happen only near the end of the eighteenth century, and so we are a long way off from investigating it. But the question needs airing now, because the fourteenth century was indubitably a time of intensive and deliberate technical progress in the art of the musical *literati* — of those, that is, who made and used the music of the burgeoning literate tradition. Its result, inevitably, was an enormous change in musical style.

The best evidence we have that fourteenth-century technical progress in music was a highly self-conscious affair are the titles of two of the century's most important technical treatises, and the nature of the debate they sparked. The treatises were the *Ars novae musicae* ("The art of new music"), also known as *Notitia artis musicae* ("An introduction to the art of music") by Jehan des Murs (alias Johannes de Muris), first drafted between 1319 and 1321, and the somewhat later, even more bluntly titled *Ars nova* ("The new art [of music]"), a torso or composite of fragments and commentaries surviving from a treatise based on the teachings of Philippe de Vitry (1291–1361), known by the end of his life as the "flower of the whole musical world" (*flos totius mundi musicorum*), to quote a British contemporary.[1] The *Ars Nova* treatises began appearing around 1322–1323.

The authors, both trained at the University of Paris (where Jehan des Murs eventually became rector), were mathematicians as well as musicians—not that this should surprise us, in view of music's place alongside mathematics and astronomy in the traditional liberal arts curriculum. The new mensural notation that had been pioneered in the thirteenth century by Franco and company could not help but suggest new musical horizons to scholars who were accustomed to thinking of music as an art of measurement. And yet "Franconian" notation, geared toward an already existing rhythmic style and limited to supplying that style's immediate needs, only scratched the surface of the number relationships that might conceivably be translated into sound durations, whether for the sake of sheer intellectual or epicurean delight or as a way of bringing *musica practica*—or *musique sensible*, "the music of sense," as translated by Philippe de Vitry's younger contemporary Nicole d'Oresme[2]—into closer harmony with *musica speculativa* (the music of reason).

Though spurred originally by a speculative, mathematical impulse, the notational breakthroughs of Jehan and Philippe had enormous and immediate repercussions in the practice of "learned" music—repercussions, first displayed in the motet, that eventually reached every genre. So decisive were the contributions of these mathematicians for the musical practice of their century and beyond that the theoretical tradition of Philippe de Vitry has lent its name to an entire era and all its products; we often call the music of fourteenth-century France and its cultural colonies the music of the "Ars Nova." Neither before nor since has theory ever so clearly—or so fruitfully—outrun and conditioned practice.

MUSIC FROM MATHEMATICS

From a purely mathematical point of view, the Ars Nova innovations were a by-product of the theory of exponential powers and one of its subtopics, the theory of "harmonic numbers." It was in the fourteenth century that mathematicians began investigating powers beyond those that could be demonstrated by the simple geometry of squares and cubes. The leader in this field, and one of the century's leading mathematicians, was Nicole d'Oresme (d. 1382), the first French translator of Aristotle, whose writings (as we have already seen) encompassed music theory as well. His career as scholastic and churchman closely paralleled that of Philippe de Vitry: Philippe ended his ecclesiastical career as the Bishop of Meaux, northeast of Paris; Nicole ended his as Bishop of Lisieux, northwest of Paris. Nicole d'Oresme's *Algorismus proportionum* was the great theoretical exposition of fourteenth-century work in "power development" (recursive multiplication) with integral and fractional exponents; but it was precisely in Jehan des Murs's music treatise that the fourth power first found a practical application.

As for "harmonic numbers," this was a term coined by the mathematician Levi ben Gershom (alias Gersonides or Leo Hebraeus, 1288–1344), a Jewish scholar who lived under the protection of the papal court at Avignon. Gersonides's treatise *De numeris harmonicis* was actually written at the request of Philippe de Vitry and partly in collaboration with him. It consists of a theoretical account of all possible products of the squaring number (2) and the cubing number (3), and their powers in any combination.

All of this became music, first of all, in the process of rationalizing the "irrational" divisions of the breve into semibreves, with which, as we saw at the end of the previous chapter, composers like Petrus de Cruce had been experimenting at the end of the thirteenth century. And the other "problem" that motivated the Ars Nova innovations was that of reconciling the original twelfth-century "modal" concept of the longa as equaling twice a breve (that is, the two-tempora long of "Leonine" practice as later codified by Johannes de Garlandia) with the thirteenth-century "Franconian" concept of the longa as equaling a "perfection" of three tempora.

In turn-of-the-century "Petronian" motets, like Ex. 7-10, a breve could be divided into anywhere from two to nine semibreves. The obvious way of resolving this ambiguity was to extend the idea of perfection to the semibreve. The shortest Petronian semibreve (1/9 of a breve) could be thought of as an additional — minimal — level of time-division, for which the obvious term would be a *minima* (in English, a "minim"), denoted by a semibreve with a tail, thus:↑. Nine minimae or minims would thus equal three perfect semibreves, which in turn would equal a perfect breve. All of this merely carried out at higher levels of division the well-established concept of ternary "perfection," as first expressed in the relationship of the breve to the long. On a further analogy to the perfect division of the long (but in the other direction, so to speak), three perfect longs could be grouped within a perfect maxima or *longa triplex*.

We are thus working within a fourfold perfect system expressible by the mathematical term 3^4, "three to the fourth," or "the fourth power of three." The minim is the unit value. Multiplied by 3 (3^1) it produces the semibreve, which has three minims. Multiplied by 3×3 (3^2) it produces the breve, which has nine minims. Multiplied by $3 \times 3 \times 3$ (3^3) it produces the long, which has 27 minims; and multiplied by $3 \times 3 \times 3 \times 3$ (3^4) it produces the maxima, which has 81 minims. Each of these powers of three constitutes a level of musical time-division or rhythm. Taking the longest as primary, Jehan des Murs called the levels

1. *Maximodus* (major mode), describing the division of the maxima into longs;
2. *Modus* (mode), as in the "modal" rhythm of old, describing the division of longs into breves, or tempora;
3. *Tempus* (time), describing the division of breves into semibreves; and
4. *Prolatio* (Latin for "extension," usually designated in English by an ad hoc cognate, "prolation") describing the division of semibreves into minims.

And he represented it all in a chart (Fig. 8-1) which gives the minim-content of every perfect note value in "Ars Nova" notation.

First degree (Major mode)	◼ 81 Triplex long Longissima Maxima	◼ 54 Duplex long Longior Major	◼ 27 Simplex long Longa Magna
Second degree (Mode)	◼ 27 Perfect long Long Perfecta	◼ 18 Imperfect long Semilong Imperfecta	◼ 9 Breve Breve Brevis
Third degree (Time)	◼ 9 Perfect breve Breve Brevis	◼ 6 Imperfect breve Semibreve Brevior	◆ 3 Minor semibreve Minor Brevissima
Fourth degree (Prolation)	◆ 3 Perfect semibreve Minor Parva	◆ 2 Imperfect semibreve Semiminor Minor	↓ 1 Minim Minim Minima

FIG. 8-1   Harmonic proportions according to Jehan de Murs.

And now the stroke of genius: The whole array, involving the very same note values and written symbols or graphemes, could be predicated on Garlandia's "imperfect" long as well as Franco's perfect one, from which a fourfold imperfect system could be derived, expressible by the mathematical term 2^4, "two to the fourth," or "the fourth power of two." Again taking the minim as the unit value, multiplied by 2 (2^1) it produces a semibreve that has two minims. Multiplied by 2×2 (2^2) it produces a breve that has four minims. Multiplied by $2 \times 2 \times 2$ (2^3) it produces a long that has 8 minims; and multiplied by $2 \times 2 \times 2 \times 2$ (2^4) it produces a maxima with only 16 minims.

So at its perfect and imperfect extremes, the "Ars Nova" system posits a maximum notatable value that could contain as many as 81 minimum values or as few as 16. But between these extremes many other values were possible, because the levels of maximodus, modus, tempus, and prolatio were treated as independent variables. Each of them could be either perfect or imperfect, yielding on the theoretic level an exhaustive array of "harmonic numbers," and, on the practical level, introducing at a stroke as wide a range of conventional musical meters as musicians in the Western literate tradition would need until the nineteenth century.

To deal, briefly, with the speculative side (since it was that side that initially drove the engine of change), maximae could now contain the following numbers of minimae between the extremes we have already established:

[High end (all perfect) $3 \times 3 \times 3 \times 3$ (3^4) $=$ 81 minimae]
Any one level imperfect $3 \times 3 \times 3 \times 2$ ($3^3 \times 2^1$) $=$ 54 minimae
Any two levels imperfect $3 \times 3 \times 2 \times 2$ ($3^2 \times 2^2$) $=$ 36 minimae
Any three levels imperfect $3 \times 2 \times 2 \times 2$ ($3^1 \times 2^3$) $=$ 24 minimae
[Low end (all imperfect) $2 \times 2 \times 2 \times 2$ (2^4) $=$ 16 minimae]

By similar calculations one can demonstrate that the long can contain 27, 18, 12, or 8 minims; a breve can contain 9, 6, or 4 minims; and a semibreve can contain 3 or 2 minims. The array of all numbers generated in this way, beginning with the unit—1, 2, 3, 4, 6, 8, 9, 12, 16, 18, 27, 36, 54, 81—is the array of what Gersonides called harmonic numbers, since they are numbers that represent single measurable durations that can be fitted together ("harmonized") to create music.

PUTTING IT INTO PRACTICE

So much for the theory, which like all scholastic theory had to be exhaustive. The implications of all this tedious computation for *musique sensible*, by appealing contrast, were simple, eminently practical, and absolutely transforming. To begin with, maximodus was pretty much a theoretical level (except in the tenors of some motets) and can be ignored from here on. Moreover, in practical music it was the breve, rather than the minim, that functioned as regulator. Its position in the middle of things made calculations much more convenient. Lengths could be thought of as either multiples or divisions of breves. But then, as the "tempus" value, it had long been the basic unit of time-counting. Petrus de Cruce's use of "division points" (*puncta divisionis*) had already established it as the de facto equivalent of the modern "measure" (or bar, as the British say, and as we say when we aren't being too fastidious). It was this measure and its divisions, then, rather than the unit value and its multiples, that defined mensurations for practical musicians and those who instructed them.

So we can henceforth confine our discussion to the levels of tempus and prolation — that is, the number of semibreves in a breve and of minims in a semibreve. The former level defines the number of beats in a measure; the latter, the number of subdivisions in a beat. And that, by and large, is the way we still define musical meters. (One must include the qualifier "by and large" because our modern concept of meter includes an accentual component that is not part of Ars Nova theory.)

We end up with four basic combinations of tempus (T) and prolation (P):

1. Both perfect (*tempus perfectum, prolatio major*)
2. T perfect, P imperfect (*tempus perfectum, prolatio minor*)
3. T imperfect, P perfect (*tempus imperfectum, prolatio major*)
4. Both imperfect (*tempus imperfectum, prolatio minor*).

The first combination, with three beats in a bar and three subdivisions in a beat, is comparable to our modern compound triple meter ($\frac{9}{8}$). The second, with three beats in a bar and two subdivisions in a beat, is like "simple" (or just plain) triple meter ($\frac{3}{4}$). The third, with two beats in a bar and three subdivisions in a beat, resembles compound duple meter ($\frac{6}{8}$); and the fourth, with two beats in a bar and two subdivisions in a beat, is like our "simple" (or just plain) duple meter ($\frac{2}{4}$).

The resemblance between these Ars Nova mensuration schemes and modern meters is notoriously easy to overdraw. It is worth repeating that "meter," to us, implies a pattern of accentuation (strong and weak beats) whereas mensuration is only a time measurement. And it is also worth pointing out that when modern meters are compared, or when passing from one to another, it is usually the "beat" (the counterpart to the semibreve) that is assumed to be constant, whereas in *Ars Nova* mensuration the assumed constant was either the measure (the breve) or the unit value (the minim).

Because the beat (called the *tactus*, the "felt" pulse) was a variable quantity within the Ars Nova mensuration scheme, and because authorities differed as to whether the measure (*tempus*) was also a variable, an ineradicable ambiguity remained at the heart of the system that had to be remedied over the years by a plethora of *ad hoc* auxiliary rules and signs. Eventually the whole field became a jungle and a new notational "revolution" became necessary. (It happened around the beginning of the seventeenth century, and we are still living with its results.) Still, the extraordinary advance Ars Nova notation marked over its predecessors in rhythmic versatility and exactness is evident, and unquestionably amounted to technical progress. Everything that was formerly possible to notate was still possible under the new system, and a great deal more besides. As Jehan des Murs triumphantly observed, as a result of the Ars Nova breakthroughs "whatever can be sung can [now] be written down."

But do not confuse progress in notation with progress in music. In particular, do not think for a moment that duple meter was "invented" in the fourteenth century, as often claimed, just because the means of its notation and its "artful" development were provided then — as if two-legged creatures needed the elaborate rationalizations of the Ars Nova in order to make music to accompany marching or working or dancing. As Jehan's triumphant claim itself implies, "musique sensible" surely employed regular duple meter long before there was a way of notating it — and had, no doubt, since time immemorial. The unwritten repertory was then, and has always remained, many times larger than the literate repertories that form the main subject matter of this or any history text.

But even if the "imperfect mensuration" of the Ars Nova had had its origins in speculation about musical analogues to squares and cubes, and ultimately in speculation about how music might best represent God's cosmos, it nevertheless made possible the unambiguous graphic representation of plain old duple meter, and willy-nilly provided a precious link between what had formerly been an unwritable and historically unavailable practical background and the elite "artistic" or speculative facade. Lofty theory — the loftiest yet and perhaps the loftiest ever — had inadvertently provided the means by which musical art could more directly reflect the music of daily human life.

REPRESENTING IT

Like all previous notational reforms, the Ars Nova retained the familiar shapes of Gregorian "square" notation, modifying them where necessary (as in supplying the minim) but as slightly as possible. What mainly changed were the rules by which the signs were interpreted. The same notated maxima could contain 16 minims or 81 minims or any of several quantities in between. How was one to know which?

What was needed was a set of ancillary signs — time signatures, in short — to specify the mensural relationships that obtained between the notated shapes. Again, economy was the rule. These signs were adapted directly from "daily life" — that is, from existing measuring practices, particularly those involving time-measurement (*chronaca*) and "business math" (chiefly *minutiae* or fiscal fractions).[3]

In the fourteenth century, not only musical durations but weight, length, and the value of money were all measured according to the duodecimal (twelve-based) system inherited from the Romans, rather than the decimal (ten-based) system derived from counting on the fingers, only lately available in numerals borrowed from the Arabs.

Roman weights and measures survived longest in Britain and its cultural colonies. In America, despite long pressure to convert to the decimal metric system, introduced as an "enlightened" by-product of the French Revolution, we still divide feet into twelve inches and pounds into twelve ounces. (In Britain itself, the monetary system remained duodecimal until the 1970s, with twelve pence to the shilling, and 240 pence (12 × 20) to the pound.) Both "inch" and "ounce" are traceable to the Latin word *uncia*, which stood for the basic unit of duodecimal measurement, whether of weight, length, or money. The *uncia* was the equivalent, in those areas, of the basic unit of musical measurement, the *tempus*.

The standard Roman symbol for the *uncia*—on abacuses used for monetary transactions, for example—was the circle, and the symbol for one-half of an uncia (called the *semuncia*), logically enough, was the semicircle. It is hardly a coincidence, then, that the circle and semicircle were adopted as symbols for the division of the tempus (breves into semibreves) in Ars Nova notation, thus becoming the first standard time signatures used in Western music. The circle stood for *tempus perfectum*—i.e., the "whole" or "perfect" breve containing three semibreves—and the semicircle stood, correspondingly, for *tempus imperfectum*, with two semibreves to a breve.

The signs for major and minor prolation were adapted from the theory of *chronaca*, in which the shortest unit of time—sometimes called the *atomus*, sometimes the *momentum*, and sometimes, yes, the *minima*—was compared with the geometric point (*punctum*), defined by Euclid as that which cannot be subdivided. ("A point," Euclid wrote in his *Elements*, "is that which has no part.") The minimal time-unit was sometimes actually called the *punctum*, which is undoubtedly why the point, or dot, became the symbol for the musical minima and its mensuration. The major prolation, in which there were three minims to a semibreve, was at first indicated by placing three dots inside the circle or semicircle that represented the breve. The minor prolation was specified by a pair of dots.

Later on scribes figured out that they could save some ink by subtracting two dots from this scheme. Major prolation could just as well be indicated by a single dot, minor prolation by the absence of a dot. So by the end of the fourteenth century, the four tempus-cum-prolation combinations or meters listed above were represented by four standard time signatures: ⊙, O, ℂ, C. The last of them, the one that represented mensuration by two at all levels, still survives (as the sign for "common time"). In the light of the foregoing discussion, it should be obvious that explaining the "C" for $\frac{4}{4}$ meter as the initial of the expression "common time" is a folk-etymology. Its actual derivation was from medieval *minutiae* and *chronaca*, and its survival depended on its "imperfection." The main difference between modern notation and mensural notation, as we will observe in greater detail in a later chapter, is that although we certainly have our modern ways of indicating triple *meter*, the whole ancient idea of triple or "perfect" *mensuration* has been shed.

The table in Fig. 8-2 sums up the relationships specified by the mensural notation that was first employed by the Parisian musicians who promulgated the "Ars Nova"

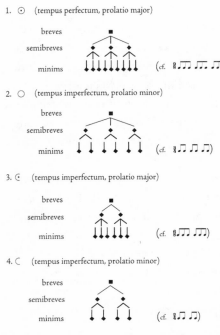

1. ⊙ (tempus perfectum, prolatio major)

breves

semibreves

minims   (cf. ⅜ ♫♫ ♫♫ ♫♫)

2. ○ (tempus imperfectum, prolatio minor)

breves

semibreves

minims   (cf. ⅜ ♫ ♫ ♫)

3. ℂ (tempus imperfectum, prolatio major)

breves

semibreves

minims   (cf. ⅜ ♫♫ ♫♫)

4. ℂ (tempus imperfectum, prolatio minor)

breves

semibreves

minims   (cf. ⅜ ♫ ♫)

FIG. 8-2   Ars Nova notation: the four signatures.

in the early fourteenth century, and these relationships remained the basis for musical notation in Europe almost to the end of the sixteenth century.

BACKLASH

Just as the technology-minded theorists of the "Ars Nova" represented the first self-conscious *avant garde* faction in European literate music, so they inspired the first conservative backlash. It is found in the seventh and last book of the mammoth *Speculum musicae* ("The mirror of music"), at 521 chapters the largest of all medieval music treatises, completed around 1330 by Jacobus (or Jacques) de Liège. The author was a retired University of Paris professor (thus Jehan des Murs's senior colleague) who had returned to his birthplace in Belgium to work on this grandiose project, which he intended as a *summa summarum*—a universal compendium—of musical knowledge. The young innovators of the "Ars Nova," by extending the boundaries of musical theory, threatened the completeness of Jacobus's account, so he tried to discredit their advance and thus neutralize the threat.

The basic ploy was to dismiss the Ars Nova innovations as so much superfluous complexity, and to show that their art, by admitting so much "imperfection," was thereby itself made imperfect when compared with what Jacobus called the "Ars Antiqua," represented at its unsurpassable zenith by Franco of Cologne. The term Ars Antiqua has also entered the conventional vocabulary of music history to denote Parisian music of the thirteenth century; it is a bad usage, though, since the term has meaning only in connection with its antithesis, and using it tends to ratify the notion that not just technique but art itself makes progress.

Citing a passage in Jehan des Murs's treatise in which the author explained the use of the term "perfection" in music by saying that "all perfection does in fact lie in the ternary number" (beginning with the perfection of God Himself, who is single in substance but a Trinity of persons), Jacobus maintained that "the art that uses perfect values more often is, therefore, more perfect," and that "the art that does that is the Ars Antiqua of Master Franco."[4] But of course basing an argument on what amounts to a pun is the very essence of sophistry. And besides, the innovations of the Ars Nova, while demonstrably a breakthrough, and controversial to boot, were in no sense "revolutionary." The granting of full rights to the imperfect was no challenge to the perfect. Rather, it was an attempt to encompass more fully the traditional "medieval" objective of translating number into sound, thus the more fully to realize the ideal significance of music as cosmic metaphor. By radically increasing the number of disparate elements that could go into its representation of harmony, moreover, the Ars Nova innovations only made the more potent the musical representation of *discordia concors*, the divine tuning of the world.

ESTABLISHING THE PROTOTYPE: THE *ROMAN DE FAUVEL*

That cosmological speculation was the aim, or at least the effect, of the Ars Nova project is apparent from the music that first issued from it. The earliest genre to be affected by the Ars Nova, and the most characteristic one, was — almost needless to say — the motet, already a hotbed of innovation and already the primary site of the *discordia concors*. The fourteenth-century transformation of the motet gives the clearest insight into the nature of the Ars Nova innovations and their purposes.

The earliest surviving pieces in which elements of Ars Nova notation are clearly discernable are a group of motets found in a lavish manuscript, compiled in or just after 1316, which contains an expanded and sumptuously illustrated version of a famous allegorical poem, the *Roman de Fauvel*. The poem, by Gervais du Bus, an official at the French royal court, is found in about a dozen sources, but this one, edited by another courtier, Raoul Chaillou, provided the poem with a veritable soundtrack consisting of 126 pieces of music ranging from little snippets of chant through monophonic rondeaux and ballades (the last of their kind) to "motetz à trebles et à tenures," meaning polyphonic motets, of which there are twenty-four. These musical items are meant as appendages or illustrations to the poem, on a par with the luxuriant manuscript illuminations. They were probably meant to adorn recitations of the *Roman* at "feasts of the learned," most likely at the home of some particularly rich and powerful "church aristocrat." What links all the musical numbers despite their motley variety of style, genre, text-language, and date is their pertinence to the poem's theme.

That theme is ferocious civil and political satire. The name of the title character, Fauvel, roughly meaning "little deerlike critter" who is *faus* and *de_vel* (false and furtive, "veiled") and of dull fallow hue (*fauve*), is actually an acrostic standing for a whole medley of political vices, apparently modeled on the list of seven deadly sins (the ones that are not cognates below are translated):

> F laterie
> A varice
> U ilanie (i.e., villainy, U and V being equivalent in Latin spelling)
> V ariété (duplicity, "two-facedness")
> E nvie
> L ascheté (laziness, indolence)

The manuscript illuminations represent Fauvel as something between a fawn and a horse or ass. Indeed, everyone "fawns" on him, from garden-variety nobles and clerics all the way to the pope and the French king. (Our expression "to curry favor" was originally "to curry favel," meaning to coddle Fauvel and win his base boons.) Fauvel is practically omnipotent; his feat of placing the moon above the sun symbolized the secularism and the corruption of court and clergy. Now he wants to pay back Dame Fortune for the favors she has granted him and proposes marriage—but this, too, is a trick; once married to Fortune Fauvel will become her master as well, and truly all-powerful. Fortune refuses but gives Fauvel the hand of her daughter Vaine Gloire, through whom he populates the earth with little Fauveaux.

The motet, whose first half is transcribed as Ex. 8-1, appears in the section of the *Roman de Fauvel* manuscript containing the description (accompanied by an

EX. 8-1   Philippe de Vitry, *Tribum/Quoniam/MERITO*, mm. 1–40

EX. 8-1 (*continued*)

Triplum
Furious Fortune did not fear
to turn quickly against the tribe
that did not recoil from a shameless rise [to power]
when she did not spare the governing leader of the tribe
from the pillory,
to be established as an eternal public example.
Therefore let future generations know . . .

Motetus
Since with the plots of thieves and
the den of shady dealers
the fox, which gnawed at the cocks
in the time when the blind lion reigned,
has suddenly been hurled down
to his reward in death . . .

Tenor
We suffered this deservedly.

illustration; see Fig. 8-3) of the Fountain of Youth, in which Fauvel, his wife, and his entourage—Carnality, Hatred, Gluttony, Drunkenness, Pride, Hypocrisy, Sodomy, and a host of others just as attractive—bathe on the day following the wedding. (In the illustration, the bathers enter from the right, clearly aged, and emerge rejuvenated from the bath, of which the topmost decorative spouts are miniature Fauvels.)

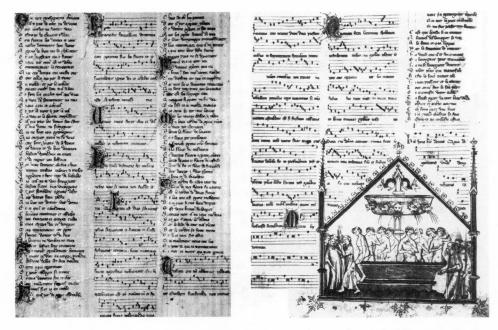

FIG. 8-3 Paris, Bibliothèque Nationale, Fonds Français 146 (*Roman de Fauvel*), fol. 41v–42, showing most of Philippe de Vitry's motet *Tribum/Quoniam/MERITO* and an allegory of the fountain of youth.

The triplum and motetus texts are laden with Fauvel-related allegories that have been associated by historians with the fate of Enguerrand de Marigny, the finance minister to King Philippe IV (Philip the Fair) of France, who was hanged following the death of the king, on 30 April 1315. His death is held up as an object lesson (*admonitio*) concerning the whims of Fortune and the dangers of concentrating political power. (The texts thus reflect the interests of the feudal nobility who opposed and sought to limit the power of the throne and forced concessions on Philip's successor Louis X.)

Because it corresponds so closely to the rhythmic and notational features soon to be set forth in the treatise *Ars Nova* (where a passage from it is actually quoted), the music of this little political tract in tones is thought to be an early work of Philippe de Vitry, who was the contemporary of Gervaise du Bus and Raoul Chaillou, and like Gervaise a court notary in his youth. With this work and the others that he composed in his twenties, Philippe established the fourteenth-century motet as a genre and provided the prototypes for a century of stylistic development. The differences between Philippe's motet and the one by Petrus de Cruce excerpted in Ex. 7-9 will virtually define the prototype.

To begin with, the text is in Latin, not French; its tone is hortatory, not confessional; and its subject is public life, not private emotion. Moralizing texts — allegories, sermons, injunctions — such as were formerly the province of conductus, would henceforth dominate the motet repertory. In keeping with the rhetorical seriousness of the texts, and to enhance it, the formal gestures of the fourteenth-century motet became more ample, more ceremonious, more dramatic than those of its progenitor.

Whereas thirteenth-century motets, like the discant clausulae on which they were generically based, began with all the voices together, the fourteenth-century motet tended to dramatize the tenor entrance. In *Tribum/Quoniam/MERITO* (Ex. 8-1), the voices enter one by one (*seriatim*), with the tenor last. The introductory section preceding the tenor entrance became so standardized that it was given a name, one with which we are familiar in another context: it was called the *introitus*, suggesting that the entering voices formed a procession. And just as in the case of the "introit" procession at the beginning of Mass, the most important participant (the celebrant, the tenor) enters last.

The tenor is the most important voice in the motet—the *dignior pars*, to quote one theorist, the "worthiest part"—because it is literally the "fundamental" voice.[5] In fourteenth-century motets it is chosen with care to reflect its liturgical dignity on the texted parts, although the fourteenth-century motet, even when in Latin, was by no means a liturgical genre. All of this is just the opposite of the situation that obtained in the early days of the motet, when such works were clausula-derived and performed in church. In the oldest motets—"prosulated clausulae," as we called them on their first appearance—the motetus and triplum texts were ancillary glosses on the tenor in the course of an ongoing liturgical performance of the item from which the tenor was drawn. Now it is the tenor that is chosen to support and gloss the orations up above. As the theorist Aegidius of Murino put it around 1400 in a famous motet recipe, "first take for your tenor any antiphon or responsory or any other chant from the book of Office chants, and its words should accord with the theme or occasion for which the motet is being made."[6] In Ex. 8-1, the tenor is drawn from the beginning of a matins responsory that is sung during Lent, the most penitential season. Its implied words—*Merito hec patimur* ("It is right that we suffered thus")—are plainly an extra comment on just desserts, and amplify the censorious allegories running above on the fate of corrupt politicians. The fact that the tenor is not a melisma from the chant but its incipit shows that it was probably meant to be recognized, at least (or at best) by the elite initiates for whose edification or solemn entertainment the motet was composed.

One final point of comparison: Whereas the tenor in Ex. 7-10, our "Petronian" motet, was allowed to "degenerate" into an undifferentiated sequence of longs during its second cursus, the tenor in the "Vitrian" motet maintains a strong, preplanned rhythmic profile from beginning to end. (As Aegidius instructs, "then take your tenor and arrange it and put it in rhythm" as a first composing step.) The tenor in Ex. 8-1 is cast in easily recognizable (even if slowed down) "second mode" or iambic *ordines*.

In the thirteenth century, its constituent note-values would have been breves and longs arranged *BLB(rest)*. Here, the note-values have been doubled in keeping with the increased rhythmic ambit of the Ars Nova style, so that the ordines are not "modal" but "maximodal," proceeding in longs and maximas. In the transcription, the tenor is barred according to the maximodus, with one measure equaling the perfect maxima. The upper parts are barred according to the modus, with one measure equaling the long. As one can see from the time signatures employed, the modus level here is imperfect, with the long (represented in transcription by the half note) divided equally into two breves (quarters). The mensuration of the breve (i.e., the tempus) is also imperfect, with the breve dividing equally into two semibreves (eighths).

TAKING A CLOSER LOOK

Comparing the notation of this motet as shown in Fig. 8-3, not only with later sources but with subsequent additions to the Fauvel manuscript itself, reveals the way in which Ars Nova notation emerged out of the Petronian style — a fascinating historical moment. The Fauvel manuscript is slightly earlier than the treatise of Jehan des Murs, in which the notation of the minim is introduced. In it, therefore, the level of prolation can be only indistinctly differentiated from that of tempus.

Looking closely at Fig. 8-3, in which the triplum part (*Tribum*, etc.) begins at the bottom of the third column of the left-hand page, one observes that the group of four notes over the syllable *que*, and the pair of notes immediately following, are both notated in semibreve-lozenges, even though both groups take the time of a breve. As in the Petronian motet, the breve units are marked off by "division dots" (*puncta divisionis*), there being no explicit way of showing by their shapes that the lozenges or diamonds in the first group are only half the length of those in the second. Nor can one distinguish the relative lengths of the notes in three-semibreve groups like the one on the triplum's second staff (over the syllable -*bun*-), in which (as the transcription reveals) each note has a different length.

In a hand too faint to be discerned in Fig. 8-3, an editor familiar with the new notational principles has gone over both the triplum and the motetus and added the minim-stems that not only distinguish levels of mensuration but distinguish the Ars Nova style from its predecessors. In the four-note groups, the second and fourth are given upward minim-stems, producing lilting trochaic triplet-patterns as shown in the transcription, thus defining the level of prolation as perfect or "major" (that is, triple). The implied time signature is $\mathbb{C}$. In the three-note groups, the first note is given a tiny downward stem, showing that it is a perfect (or major) semibreve, while the last is given an upward stem, turning it into a minim, leaving the time of an imperfect semibreve for the stemless note (see Ex. 8-2a). The perfectly practicable alternative, within the Ars Nova system, would have been to place stems on all the notes in the four-note group, and on the second and third in the three-note groups. This would have indicated imperfect or "minor" (that is, duple) prolation, implying the time-signature C (see Ex. 8-2b).

EX. 8-2 The two alternatives and their equivalents in modern notatation
a. Major prolation

EX. 8-2B   Minor prolation

The "French" preference shown here for the lilting "trochaic" subdivision of the semibreve (implying that the four-lozenge groups would have been lilted that way even before the stems were added) seems to resonate both with earlier "modal" practice and with the later French convention of performing pairs of eighth-notes or sixteenth-notes with a similar, and now definitely unwritten, lilt (the so-called *notes inégales* or "unequal notes"). As we shall see in a much later chapter, that practice is documented only for the seventeenth and eighteenth centuries, but it perhaps reflects a more widespread custom affecting unwritten repertories as well as written ones (compare the lilt in Viennese waltzes—or in jazz.)

MORE ELABORATE PATTERNING

In keeping with the idea of *discordia concors*, which emphasized belief in a hidden order and unity behind the world's apparent chaos, composers of Ars Nova motets placed particular emphasis on subtle patterning that unified and reconditely organized the heterogeneous surface of their work. One can bring this aspect of *Tribum/Quoniam/MERITO* to light by comparing mm. 10–13 in the transcription with mm. 34–37. The repetition thus uncovered initiates an interlocking series of periodicities that crosscut the more obvious periodicity of the tenor. The same melodic phrases in the triplum and duplum will turn up again in mm. 58–62, and the triplum-duplum combination in mm. 22–25 will recur in mm. 46–49 and again in mm. 70–73. Every one of these spots corresponds to a progression in the tenor from E to D, which crosscuts the tenor's more obviously repeating rhythmic ordo or *talea* (since in every case the E is the end of an ordo and the D is the beginning of another). And the thrice-recurring pair of alternating repetitions in the upper voices—mm. 10–13/22–25, 34–37/46–49 and 58–62/70–73 (**ABABAB**)—crosscut the tenor's double cursus, which begins right between the members of the middle pair (just after our example breaks off). This is an especially significant hidden periodicity, for it imposes on the structure of the motet at its most encompassing level a "perfect/imperfect" duality (three repeated pairs vs. two tenor *cursus*) that reflects the duality of note-value relationships at the heart of the Ars Nova system.

That duality is "thematized"—made the subject of demonstration—in a later motet by Vitry, *Tuba sacre/In Arboris/VIRGO SUM* (Fig. 8-4; Ex. 8-3), which displays with a special elegance the peculiar, highly persuasive combination of seriousness and playfulness that was so characteristic of the Ars Nova.

Here the tenor consists of a chant fragment (*color*) bearing the incipit *Virgo sum*, ("I am a virgin"), a verse that figures meekness and purity, supporting (and "coloring," in the sense of commenting on) a pair of solemn meditations in the triplum and motetus

FIG. 8-4 Phillippe de Vitry, *Tuba sacre/In arboris/VIRGO SUM* (Ivrea, Biblioteca Capitolare, MS 115, fols. 15v–16). The tenor notes that appear gray are notated in red ink to show a hemiola (3:2) proportion.

concerning the mysteries of Christian doctrine and the necessity of reconciling faith with reason. These earnest sermons, for all their gravity, are nevertheless cast in graceful melodies full of the characteristic "prolation lilt" that we encountered in the previous motet as well, and that must reflect the style of the contemporary song repertory. (Vitry is known to have composed French songs in addition to Latin motets, but neither they nor any other French songs survive from the period of his main activity.) Also songlike are the mode and the harmonic idiom. Up to the final cadence in each cursus — which comes as a harmonic surprise — the tunes in the upper parts depart from and cadence on the note C, so that they are in the functional equivalent of our major mode. As Giraldus Cambrensis (quoted in chapter 5) remarked at the end of the twelfth century, that mode was used in unwritten musics far more prevalently than in chant-influenced literate ones. There is no better example of Vitrian C-major "pop-lyricism" than the unaccompanied motetus melisma that launches the *introitus* to this very high-minded motet. And no less emphatically sweet are the harmonies at strategic moments. Note the long-sustained full triads (the first we've seen) at tenor entrances and cadences such as mm. 16, 25, 43, and 46. Also self-evidently playful are the hockets between the triplum and the motetus that regularly recur at the ends of taleae. A motet with such prominent hockets (to recall a comment by Johannes de Grocheio) is at once high-minded and hot-tempered. Entertainment values are unabashedly summoned to assist lofty contemplation.

As for the tenor, its rhythms are cast in no simple modal ordo, but in an arbitrary arrangement of values adding up to 24 breves, as follows (a number in italics indicates a rest): 4 2 2 2 2 3 2 1 2 4. Note the odd number in the middle. The composer might have indicated that one perfect long within a prevailing duple modus by simply dotting it — as we still do, even if we do not know that we are following the method introduced by the Ars Nova for converting imperfect values into perfect ones. Another way of indicating the perfect long would have been by applying to it an explicit mensuration sign. The way that Vitry actually did it was playfully ostentatious. He supplied the tenor with a supplementary performance direction — called a *rubric* (after the red ink in which such things were often entered) or a *canon*, meaning "rule" — that reads,

EX. 8-3   Philippe de Vitry, *Tuba sacre/In Arboris/VIRGO SUM*

EX. 8-3   (continued)

EX. 8-3 (*continued*)

Triplum

The trumpet of the sacred faith, God's own statement, herald of sacred mysteries cries out in the theater that Reason hesitates, in support of the sinners. More simply stated, one has to acknowledge and believe more firmly (or otherwise die) that God is necessarily in three equal persons, and that these three are one; that a virgin, not by the seed of man but by the spirit of the Word, has conceived while remaining ever a virgin; that both God and Man for the world have suffered.

But since all these transcendental things are the very life of the believer, unaware and neglecting, Reason, naturally acquired in steps, produces doubts and guesswork as it proceeds.

Faith, through which one can find a clearer road to the Beyond, one should always follow.

Motetus

On the top of the tree, flourishing, virginity presides, bearing a child. In the middle, Faith assists her in her labour while obscured by the trunk, Reason, followed by the seven sisters cherishing their *sophismata*, struggles to mount; the weakness of the branches causes her to crash. Therefore, one should either ask for the right hand of faith, or forever strive in vain.

Tenor

Free me, O Lord.

Nigre notule sunt imperfecte et rube sunt perfecte ("The little black notes are imperfect and the red ones are perfect"). Like so many of Philippe de Vitry's innovations, this one became standard practice. As a later theorist wrote, "red notes are placed in motets for three reasons, that is, when they are to be sung in some other mode, or other tempus, or other prolation than the black notes, as appears in many motets composed by Philippe."[7]

In every *talea*, then, six breves' worth of musical time is organized by perfect longs (that is, in "perfect minor modus"), requiring the use of red ink. It is here, of course, at the tenor's friskiest moment, that the hockets appear in the texted parts. Their rhythms, like the rhythm of the tenor, are the same each time. After three taleae, the note values are halved to coincide with the second cursus of the *color*, so that the tenor proceeds twice as "fast," and the red notes denote six semibreves' worth of time organized in perfect tempus. The frisky tempus shift becomes much friskier, since the perfect breve that now begins the red-ink patch crosscuts the basic tempus unit, producing a true syncopation—something that had never before been possible in notated music. Needless to say, the hockets in the upper parts get friskier, too; and again these puckish rhythms reappear each time the tenor syncopation returns. This passage introduces what was a permanent stylistic acquisition for fourteenth- and fifteenth-century music. "Coloration" (the use of a contrasting ink color, or, later, the filling in of notes ordinarily left "white") became a standard way of changing tempus in midstream to produce fascinating rhythms.

ISORHYTHM

The playful complexity of this tenor—an arbitrary (that is, "rational") talea that mixes mensurations and undergoes diminution by half—became a typical, even a defining feature of motets in the fourteenth century and beyond. Modern scholars use the term *isorhythm* ("same-rhythm") to denote the use of recurrent patterns or *taleae*, often quite long and cunningly constructed, that do not rely on traditional modal *ordines*. Motets that employ such recurrent patterns—often, as here, varied schematically on successive *colores*, or even within a *color*—are called isorhythmic motets. Despite the Greek derivation of the term, it is a modern coinage and a German one, first used by the great medievalist Friedrich Ludwig in 1904 in a pioneering study of the motets in the Montpellier Codex.

The first piece to which the term was applied, as it happens, was *On a parole/A Paris/ Frese nouvele*, familiar to us from the previous chapter (Fig. 7-9/Ex. 7-9). Yet according to current standard usage, that motet is not isorhythmic; the motetus, which Ludwig mainly had in mind, moves in phrases that are rhythmically similar but not identical, and in the tenor the color and the talea are coextensive, amounting to a simple melodic repetition. As currently used, the term isorhythm implies literal rhythmic repetition that, while often coordinated with melodic repetition (chiefly in tenors), is nevertheless independently organized.

A true isorhythmic tenor, like the one in Ex. 8-3, is built on two periodic cycles, the one governing pitch, the other duration. And this implies the separate, hence abstract, conception of melodic and rhythmic successions. The passages of tenor-coloration in this motet by Vitry are accompanied, as we have seen, by rhythmic recurrences in the upper parts as well, so that this particular isorhythmic motet has patches of "pan-isorhythm," in which all the voices are bound periodically (which of course means predictably) into recurrent patterns to which the ear cannot help looking forward.

Thus isorhythm and its attendant effects have at once an embellishing and a symbolic purpose. They enhance surface attractiveness, particularly when smaller note-values and hockets are called into play. At the same time the periodicities thus set in motion reflect the periodicities of nature (celestial orbits, tides, seasons), giving the senses—and, through the senses, the mind—an intimation of the ineffable *musica mundana*. The coordination of surface and deeper structure that this motet so well exemplifies, and their conjoint appeal to sense and reason, may all be subsumed under the heading of *rhetoric*—the art of (musical) persuasion. That was the all-encompassing aim to which every detail of the ceremonious late-medieval motet was geared, whether at the level of grandiose architecture or that of seductive detail. That rhetoric found its most eloquent expression in motets of doctrinal, civic, or political cast.

MUSIC ABOUT MUSIC

Before turning to the most exalted specimens, however, let us have another look at the playful side of Ars Nova composition, for it will cast light on the earliest emergence within musical practice of "art" as we know it. Art, as we know it, is a self-conscious thing, as concerned with manner as it is with matter. Its Latin cognate, *ars* (as in Ars Nova) simply means "method" or "way." The title of the treatise attributed to Vitry simply means "a new way [of doing things]." That is the sense of "art" that is implied by words like "artful" and "artificial." They mean "full of method," hence "full of skill," and ultimately "full of style." What makes an *artist*, in the familiar, current sense of the word, therefore, is high consciousness of style.

The earliest musical compositions that seem to exhibit this sort of awareness on the part of their makers emerge out of the Ars Nova milieu. In the previous chapter we observed deliberate compositional *tours de force*, to be sure, and we have been observing high artistry (in the sense of high technical prowess and rhetorical eloquence) since the very beginning. But nowhere yet have we observed the kind of self-regard exemplified in Ex. 8-4, which shows the end of an anonymous motet roughly contemporary with the works of Vitry that we have been examining.

It is found in a *rotulus*, a scroll-manuscript from about 1325. Little scrolls of this kind, of which very few survive, were the sort of manuscripts from which the proudly literate singers of motets actually performed, as opposed to the lavish codices, the illuminated presentation manuscripts, that preserve most of what we call our "practical" source material (to distinguish it from "theoretical" sources like treatises). In their day such codices were not practical sources at all, but items of wealth to be stored away—which is why we have them now. *Rotuli*, meant for use, were used up.

In terms of dimensions and complexity of structure, *Musicalis Sciencia/Sciencie Laudabili* is a fairly modest motet. It has no *introitus*. The tenor, which enters immediately, is the Christmas Alleluia, *Dies sanctificatus* ("A hallowed day has dawned for us"), one of the most famous of all Gregorian chants, which may be why the composer or the scribe did not bother, in this unassuming practical source,

FIG. 8-5 Lorenzo d'Alessandro, *Musical Angels*, a wall painting from the church of Santa Maria di Piazza, Sarnano, Italy. The angel at right is reading from a rotulus, or scroll manuscript of the kind used by singers in actual performance during the late Middle Ages.

EX. 8-4 *Musicalis Sciencia/Sciencie Laudabili*, mm. 121–67 (Paris, BN, Coll. de Picardie 67, f. 67′)

EX. 8-4 (*continued*)

to identify it. It is laid out in a single incomplete cursus, so that there is no *color* repetition. There is plenty of talea repetition, though: seven in all, of which Ex. 8-4 contains the last two. The syncopation at the end of each talea is produced, like the tenor syncopation in the previous example, by the use of red ink: the final maxima and long are counted in "imperfect mode." A second glance shows that the triplum and motetus voices are likewise governed by an eight-bar *talea*, so that the entire piece is "pan-isorhythmic" in seven rhythmically identical sections or strophes. Each of these strophes ends with a sort of *cauda* consisting of a melisma on the last syllable, which is held through an especially blithesome — and because of the melisma, an especially hiccupy — bunch of hockets, in which the singers have to emit single minims on open vowel sounds, without any consonants to assist in articulation. The line between virtuosity and clownishness can be a fine one.

Here are the triplum and motetus texts, abridged to eliminate a lengthy honor-roll of famous musicians:

> *Triplum:* The science of music sends greetings to her beloved disciples. I desire each one of you to observe the rules and not to offend against rhetoric or grammar by dividing indivisible syllables. Avoid all faults. Farewell in melody.

Motetus: Rhetoric sends greetings to learned Music, but complains that many singers make faults in her compositions by dividing simple vowels and making hockets; therefore I request that you remedy this.

Every one of the "faults" for which singers are berated by Music and by Rhetoric are flagrantly committed by the composer. The piece is a kind of satire. But such satire requires an attitude of ironic detachment, a consciousness of art as artifice, and a wish to make that artifice the principal focus of attention. These are traits we normally (and perhaps self-importantly) ascribe to the "modern" temperament, not the "medieval" one. Only we (we tend to think), with our modern notions of psychology and our modern sense of "self," are capable of self-reflection. Only we, in short, can be "artists" as opposed to "craftsmen." Not so.

MACHAUT: THE OCCULT AND THE SENSUOUS

Formal introduction to Guillaume de Machaut (d. 1377), the greatest poet-musician of mid-fourteenth-century France, can wait until the next chapter. Suffice it for now to say that he was the chief extender of the trouvère tradition, to which he gave a new lease on life by channeling it into new styles and genres that would thrive for almost two centuries. Machaut carried on the tradition of the French love-song motet into the fourteenth century and applied to it all the new technologies of the Ars Nova. But since the Latin devout genre that stood closest to the tradition of *fine amours* was the antiphon to the Blessed Virgin Mary, it is not surprising to find that Machaut's grandest, most rigorous essay in the most exalted genre available to him was an appeal to Mary in her role of divine "neck," or intercessor.

This lofty, ambitiously structured work—*Felix virgo/Inviolata/AD TE SUSPIRA-MUS*—is harmonically amplified by a the addition of a *contratenor*, a fourth voice composed "against the tenor" and in the same range. It also has a more formal *introitus* than any we have as yet encountered: it comes to a full cadence, supported by the contratenor and the tenor, the latter playing "free" notes (that is, not drawn from the cantus firmus or *color*) for no other purpose than sonorous enhancement.

The *color*, once it gets under way, turns out to be a tune we know, albeit in a somewhat different version (or "redaction"). It is a phrase from a variant of a melody already encountered in chapter 3 (see Ex. 3-12b): *Salve Regina*, the eleventh-century Marian antiphon that stood closest, formally and melodically, to the contemporary Provençal lyric. Machaut selected a 48-note passage from the version of this dirgelike Dorian melody that he knew by heart, encompassing the words ". . . to you we sigh, mourning and weeping in this vale of tears. O, therefore, [be] our advocate . . .," and applied to it a *talea* consisting of twenty rhythmic durations (sixteen notes and four rests) encompassing 36 tempora divided into two equal parts.

The first 18 tempora are organized into 6 longs under [O], the sign of perfection, and the second 18 are organized into nine longs under [C], the sign of imperfection, as shown in Ex. 8-5. It takes three such taleae to exhaust the color (3×16 notes $= 48$ notes), following which the whole color/talea complex is repeated in diminution, so that, relative to the motetus and triplum, the tenor now moves at the level of *tempus*, in breves and semibreves.

EX. 8-5   Guillaume de Machaut, *Felix virgo/Inviolata/AD TE SUSPIRAMUS*, tenor talea

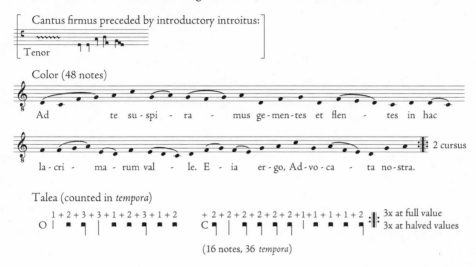

Everything we have observed about the tenor is true, in this motet, of the contratenor as well. Although a newly invented part rather than a cantus firmus (something that we can state with near certainty owing to its chromatic vagaries), the contratenor consists, like the tenor, of a color that is put through a double cursus, with each cursus encompassing a three-fold talea and with the second cursus in diminution. The contratenor's talea is in fact the same as the tenor's, except that it presents the two 18-tempora halves in the reverse or reciprocal order, with the imperfect longs under [C] preceding the perfect ones under [O]. Thus there is a constant interchange of time signatures between tenor and contratenor, and a perpetually maintained "polymeter" of perfect and imperfect mensurations. Because of their close relationship, we can be sure that the contratenor was composed at the same time as the tenor, and that both parts were conjointly laid out like a foundation to govern the proportions of the whole. In extremely formalized motets like this one, architectural analogies are virtually inescapable and in all likelihood envisaged aforethought.

Although the diminution of note values in the talea is quite salient to the ear (the more so because the texted parts choose that moment to break into hockets), the "polymetrical" superimposition and exchange of perfect and imperfect mensurations in the slow-moving lower parts is not. In this it resembles the harmonious orbits of heavenly bodies, which fit together according to the divinely ordained *musica mundana*, and which according to ancient tradition emit tones that the mind can infer, but that the senses cannot experience. Like the architectural analogy, this analogy too was surely present to the composer's imagination as he planned the trajectories of his supporting voices. It reflected the neo-Platonic worldview of every master of science or *magus* (the word, not coincidentally, from which "magician" is derived.) As a magus, Machaut believed that the world was hierarchically ordered, with intellectual elements occupying the highest realm; that superior elements in the hierarchy influenced inferior ones; and that the wise man might ascend through the levels of the world structure (or at least interact from below with higher levels) to gain special benefit from these influences.[8]

So writes Gary Tomlinson, a scholar who by means of musical parallels has sought to penetrate the arcane world of premodern occult philosophy. The fourteenth-century isorhythmic motet, possibly the most hierarchically conceived and rigorously ordered genre in the history of European music, was more concerned than any other to incorporate a representation of the higher "intellectual" elements and their controlling influence, which, being *hidden* from the senses, were in the most literal and etymological way *occult*. That is another way of interpreting the enormous value and emphasis that was placed on the "architecture" of the motet.

And yet the other special attribute of the motet was its heterogeneity, its power of harmonizing contradictions. So none of what has been said about its occultism should imply neglect of the sensuous surface, which in Machaut's hands was particularly and famously seductive, especially in the *introitus*, shown in Ex. 8-6. What made it so was an extraordinary harmonic idiom that, while emulated somewhat by the next generation

EX. 8-6   Guillaume de Machaut, *Felix virgo/Inviolata/AD TE SUSPIRAMUS*, mm. 1–33

EX. 8-6 (*continued*)

Motetus:
O happy Virgin, mother of Christ
Who brought joy to a sad world . . .

Triplum:
Virgin mother,
Beloved conqueress of pride
Without peer.
(Door-keeper of the) heavenly (palace.)

or two of French composers, nevertheless remained Machaut's unique and inimitable signature. It stemmed from the use of what we would call chromaticism, known in Machaut's day as *musica ficta* ("imaginary music") or *musica falsa* ("false music").

MUSICA FICTA

These terms should not be taken too literally. Indeed, Philippe de Vitry himself, as reported in *Ars Nova*, cautioned that "false music" is not false but real "and even necessary." All that the name implied was that the notes involved were not part of the gamut as defined long ago by Guido d'Arezzo, and that they had no predefined "vox," or position within a hexachord. So in order to solmize them—that is, find a place for them among the ut–re–mi's of traditional sight-singing—one had to imagine a hexachord that contained them, one that may have been "fictitious" with respect to the official theory of music, but whose sounding contents were fully presentable to the senses and in that respect altogether real.

And necessary, as Philippe de Vitry allowed, when their purpose was to make perfect a diminished fifth or an augmented fourth. As we know, a certain provision of this kind was made by the earliest theorists of harmony, when they incorporated B-flat into the modal system alongside B for use in conjunction with F. As a full-fledged member of the system, the B-flat was not musica ficta, and the F-based hexachord in which it was the "fa" was not considered "imaginary" but a real and integral part of the basic arrangement.

When, for example, an E was written against the B-flat, however, one had to go outside the system or beyond the basic arrangement to harmonize it. And that was musica ficta. The required E-flat was not conceptualized as we might conceptualize it, as an inflection of E. (There was no way of solmizing a direct progression E–E♭, and no practical use for such a progression.) Instead, it was conceptualized as the upper member of a melodic semitone, D–E♭, for which a solmization — *mi–fa* — could be inferred. So the E♭ a semitone above D was a *fa*, which placed it in an imaginary or "feigned" (*ficta*) hexachord with *ut* on B♭. Since the flat sign was itself a variant of the letter "B" to denote a B that was sung *fa* (in the "soft hexachord" on F) instead of *mi* (in the "hard hexachord" on G), so the flat sign in and of itself denoted *fa* to a musician trained to sing in hexachords. Thus a flat placed next to an E did not mean "sing E a half step lower," it meant "sing this note as *fa*." The result may have been the same so far as the listener was concerned, but understanding the different mental process by which the E♭ was deduced by the singer will make clear the reason why in most cases musica ficta did not have to be expressly indicated by the composer with accidentals. In many contexts the chromatic alteration was mandated by rule, and the rule was fully implied in the solmization, and so any singer who thought in terms of solmization would make the chromatic adjustment without being specifically told to do so, and, it follows, without even being aware of the adjustment as "chromaticism." It was not a deviation from a pure diatonic norm, it was a preservation of pure diatonic norms (in particular, perfect fourths and fifths) where they were compromised by a well-known kink in the diatonic system.

Musica ficta introduced to preserve perfect intervals was musica ficta *by reason of (harmonic) necessity* (in Latin, *causa necessitatis*), and was considered perfectly diatonic. Just as automatic, and diatonic, was musica ficta by long-established conventions — conventions that have left a trace on familiar harmonic practice in the form of the "harmonic minor." They mainly affected the Dorian mode, the one closest to our minor mode. For example, there was a rule that a single B between two A's had to be a B-flat (and, though it rarely required any adjustment, that an F between two E's had to be F natural).

Singers learned this rule as a Latin jingle: *una nota super la / semper est canendum fa* ("One note above la is always sung fa"). This adjustment had the effect of lowering the sixth degree of the Dorian scale, turning it into a sort of appoggiatura or upper leading tone to fifth degree, A, the note that formed the boundary between the principal segments of the scale. (And it turned the Dorian scale, for all practical purposes, into the minor scale.) It was a grammatical rule, not an expressive device; it was called into play automatically, and so it did not need to be written down.

There was a similar rule affecting lower neighbors to the final in Dorian cadences. Such notes were common enough in Dorian melodies to have a name: *subtonium modi*, as we may recall from chapter 3. The rule about neighbors raised the subtonium, a whole step below the final, to the *subsemitonium*, a half step below. The effect was similar to that of borrowing a leading tone in the minor mode and served the same purpose, strengthening the grammatical function, so to speak, of the cadence. By signaling a more definite close it made the final more "final." For this purpose the auxiliary pitch had to be raised, not lowered, thus forming the lower note in a *mi–fa* pair. To indicate it, a sign was needed that would instruct the singer to "sing *mi*." That sign, ♯, which we call a "sharp," was originally derived from the "square B" or *b quadratum* that functioned specifically as *mi* in the "hard hexachord." In places like Dorian cadences, where the *subsemitonium modi* or leading tone was called for by the routine application of a rule, it again could "go without saying." It did not need to be explicitly notated, though (like necessary flats) it could be notated and frequently, if haphazardly, was.

So often were musica ficta adjustments taken for granted—so often, in other words, were they left to oral tradition—that the term is often loosely (and, technically, wrongly) employed to refer only to "chromatics" that were unnotated. Scholars who transcribe early polyphony for nonspecialist singers cannot assume that the singers for whom they are preparing the edition will know the oral tradition governing these adjustments, and therefore indicate them in writing (usually with little accidentals placed above the staff). They often call this procedure "putting in the ficta," thereby implying that the word "ficta" applies only to what has to be "put in" in this way. They know better, of course. A C♯ is musica ficta whether it is explicitly notated or not, because there is no such note as C♯ on the Guidonian "hand." A B♭ is not musica ficta but musica *recta* (or *vera*), again whether explicitly notated or not, because there *is* such a note on the hand.

So the accidentals that are explicitly signed, often very abundant in fourteenth century music and particularly in Machaut's music, are just as much to be considered musica ficta (unless they are B♭s) as those mentally supplied by unwritten rule. Their purpose, however, was different. Instead of being musica ficta *causa necessitatis* (harmonically necessary adjustments), or even musica ficta arising out of conventions that all competent singers knew, they represented musica ficta *causa pulchritudinis*—chromatic adjustments made "for the sake of their beauty," that is, for the sensuous enhancement of the music.

Look now at the introitus to Machaut's motet (Ex. 8-6). The triplum has a signed C♯ at the moment when the motetus enters. It follows D. If it returned to D, then strictly speaking it would not need to be expressly "signed." But it does not return to D; instead, it skips to a wholly unexpected note, G♯. This note is not called for by any rule. Its only purpose is to create a "purple patch" in the harmony, especially in view of the weird interval it creates against the F-natural in the motetus.

An augmented second is, strictly speaking, a forbidden interval on the order of the tritone (and for the same reason: one of the voices sings *mi* while the other sings *fa*). It is clearly intentional, however, and cannot be removed by adjustment *causa necessitatis*. There can be no question of adjusting the expressly signed G-sharp, of course; why sign a note only to cancel it? The F cannot be adjusted to F-sharp for two reasons. First, it would only produce another dissonance (and a worse one)—a major second instead of an augmented second. And besides, the F can be construed as a *fa* between two *la*'s (since E is *la* in the hard hexachord on G) and therefore cannot be raised.

So the throb is there for its own sake. It is, literally, a heartthrob, expressing love for the Virgin the way so many similar harmonic throbs express love for the lady in Machaut's French songs. But it is also there for "tonal" reasons. All of the signed accidentals in the introitus are C♯s or G♯s. These tones at once depart from and emphasize the basic Dorian pitch set because they are "tendency tones," pitches altered chromatically in such a way as to imply — hence demand — cadential resolution to crucial scale tones. When the resolution is evaded or delayed — as it is in the case of the triplum's first C♯ (and even the G♯, whose resolution to A is interfered with by a rest where one is least expected) — a harmonic tension is engendered that will not be fully discharged until the introitus reaches its final cadence.

CADENCES

That cadence incorporates both the C♯ and the G♯, resolving in parallel to D and A, the notes that define the Dorian "pentachord." The defining or "structural" notes are each thus provided with a leading tone, the strongest possible preparation. For this reason such a cadence has been dubbed the "double leading-tone cadence." Thanks to its great stabilizing power it became the standard cadence in fourteenth- and early fifteenth-century music.

What gave it that stabilizing and articulating (form-defining) power had only partly to do with the doubled leading tone, however. More fundamentally, the structure of the cadence goes back to the earliest days of discant, when cadence was synonymous with *occursus*, the coming together of two parts in contrary motion. The earliest variation on the occursus (already endorsed by Guido in the eleventh century) was its inversion, in which the two parts moved out to the octave in contrary motion; and that basic cadential frame endured until the end of the sixteenth century. In the cadence we are now examining, at the end of the introitus to Machaut's motet, the essential two-part motion takes place between the motetus and the tenor, which move outward from the sixth e/c♯' to the octave d/d'.

No matter what else the other voices may be doing, no progression can be called cadential unless that "structural pair" is present in two voices (one of them, in keeping with the history of discant, almost invariably the tenor). The "double leading-tone" cadence, then, is only one of a number of possible ways of filling out the cadence-defining frame. It had its moment of popularity and was replaced in the mid-fifteenth century by another standard cadence type, and by the beginning of the sixteenth century by still another. We will take them up in due course, but it is worth pointing out up front that all of them incorporated — or, more strongly, were constructed around, or in various ways embellished — the old discant pair that went all the way back to Guido.

For a final technical point, it is worth observing that it was the structure of the cadence, defined by an imperfect consonance moving by step in contrary motion to a perfect one, that gave rise to the convention of *subsemitonium modi*, the use of cadential leading tones. The idea was to egg on the resolution of the imperfect consonance to the perfect one by making it larger — that is, closer in size to the perfect one. It was called, in fact, the "rule of closeness" (or, more fancily, "the rule of propinquity" after the Latin *propinque*, "near at hand").

The reason for raising C to C♯ before a cadence on D, then, was to make a major sixth with the tenor. The same effect could be achieved by lowering the tenor to E♭, making a major sixth with the unaltered triplum or motetus. There were times when that solution was preferable, but they were in the minority. The more striking alteration was the one that affected the higher part. As already noted, that type of alteration lasted into the era of "tonal" harmony in the form of the harmonic minor, which borrows its dominant function, replete with leading tone, from the major. Here we see the first step in that direction, and the reason for it.

CICONIA: THE MOTET AS POLITICAL SHOW

As seems altogether fitting, and in retrospect inevitable, by the late fourteenth century the motet had become preeminently "a vehicle for propaganda and political ceremony," to quote Peter Lefferts, a historian of the genre.[9] That crowning period in the history of the Ars Nova motet is best exemplified by works written not in France but in Italy, albeit by composers who had emigrated there from northern Europe.

Italy at the end of the fourteenth century was a checkerboard of city-states, many of them ruled by despots who had seized power violently, and who wished to establish legitimacy by an ostentatious display of power. Legitimacy was also a major issue for the church, since this was the time of the great papal schism (1378–1417), when two (and from 1409, three) rival claimants vied for the papacy, and when all subordinate clergy had to declare their allegiances to one, to another, or (as happened briefly in France) to none. This period of political and ecclesiastical chaos was a gold mine for the arts, and especially for music.

That is because one of the chief means of asserting political power has always been lavish patronage of the arts. Music received special attention at this time (writes Julie Cumming, another motet historian), because

> Nothing made as good a show or traveled as well as musicians ready to perform in public. Dignitaries of church and state traveled with their chapels, and put on the best show possible; they also listened to the music sung by the chapels of other dignitaries, and tried to hire the best possible musicians. Musicians met, exchanged repertoire, and looked for more lucrative and comfortable employment.[10]

Composers who had training in the techniques of monumental musical architecture, and who could produce works of grandiose (and somewhat archaic, therefore venerable) design, could put on the best of all such legitimizing shows for their patrons, and found a rich market for their skills. Such composers came from the north, the land of the Ars Nova, where such techniques had been chiefly developed. That is one of the reasons why the most sought after, the best paid — and therefore in retrospect the most typical — court and cathedral musicians of northern Italy in the fifteenth century were immigrants from France and Flanders.

The first of this distinguished quasi-official line was Johannes Ciconia. His surname, Latin for "stork," is probably a Latinized (that is, cosmopolitanized) version of a more prosaic French or Flemish family name. He was born in the Belgian town of Liège during the 1370s and received his basic training there, but by 1401 he was employed by the municipal cathedral in the north Italian city of Padua, where he died in 1412.

His chief Paduan patron was Francesco Zabarella (1360–1417), the cathedral archpriest or chief canon, and a famous university professor of canon law, who reached the height of his career as the chief negotiator of peace between Padua and Venice after the Venetian conquest of his native city. Thereafter he served both Venice and the Roman pope John XXIII as a diplomat. John made him bishop of Florence, and later a cardinal. Zabarella played a major role at the Council of Constance, where the end of the schism was brokered. It was he who finally persuaded his own patron, Pope John, to resign in the interests of church harmony. (John, the loser in the resolution of the schism, is not a pope but an "antipope" in the official history of the Catholic church, which is why his number could be reused by a much later pope, the illustrious John XXIII who convened the second Vatican council in 1962, at which the Latin liturgy, and with it the Gregorian chant, were decanonized.) At the time of his death, Zabarella was widely regarded as being next in line for the papacy.

In honor of this illustrious statesman and churchman, Ciconia composed two exceptionally grand isorhythmic motets. Their style is somewhat influenced by Italian secular genres to be described in a later chapter, but their culminating place in the development of the Ars Nova motet, and their consummate embodiment of the aesthetics of their genre, make this the appropriate place to analyze Ciconia's work.

It has been suggested that *Doctorum principem super ethera/Melodia suavissima cantemus* (excerpted in Ex. 8-7), the second and more ample of Ciconia's two Zabarella-inspired motets, was composed as a send off from Padua when Zabarella left to assume his bishopric at Florence. The triplum and motetus texts are of equal length, sung at equal rates, and they actually spell one another at times so that the two texts seem to interlock like a hocket in a single encomium to the honored patron. But the tenor layout and the mensural scheme are a virtual summation of Ars Nova practices, and in their combination of diversity and comprehensiveness they symbolize the harmonizing of competing interests — the *discordia concors* — that is the primary undertaking of any diplomat, as well as any motet. This motet, then, is emblematic both of its recipient and of the genre itself, especially in this phase of its history, when it had become primarily a political instrument.

EX. 8-7A   Johannes Ciconia, *Doctorum principem super ethera/Melodia suavissima cantemus*, mm. 1–14

EX. 8-7A (*continued*)

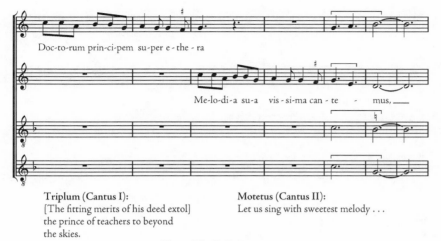

Doc-to-rum prin-ci-pem su-per e-the-ra

Me-lo-di-a su-a vis-si-ma can-te — mus, ___

Triplum (Cantus I):
[The fitting merits of his deed extol]
the prince of teachers to beyond
the skies.

Motetus (Cantus II):
Let us sing with sweetest melody . . .

Trans. Julie E. Cumming

EX. 8-7B *Doctorum principem super ethera/Melodia suavissima cantemus, mm. 45–58*

O Fran-ci-sce Za-ba-rel-le, glo-ri — a,   do — ctor, ___

O Fran-ci-sce Za-ba-rel — le, _ pro-te — ctor, ___

Triplum (Cantus I):
O Francesco Zabarella, glory,
teacher . . .

Motetus (Cantus II):
O Francesco Zabarella, protector . . .

Trans. Julie E. Cumming

EX. 8-7C *Doctorum principem super ethera/Melodia suavissima cantemus*, mm. 89–100

Triplum (Cantus I):
O Francesco Zabarella, [thou hast
provided] nourishment . . .

Motetus (Cantus II):
O Francesco Zabarella, [thou dost
watch over] the affairs . . .

Trans. Julie E. Cumming

The texts are laid out in three strophes, each of which is given the same highly ceremonious treatment: first a textless introitus in fanfare style, suggesting outdoor performance by wind instruments, perhaps in the Paduan cathedral square, followed by an almost homorhythmic tenor/contratenor complex in longer note-values (semibreves, breves, longs) that presents the same color and talea three times in notationally identical form.

In fact, the tenor/contratenor pair is written out only once, with a "canon" or special direction that specifies how it is to be altered on repetition. Although the tenor carries a Latin label (*Vir mitis*, "gentle man"), this seems to be nothing more than another encomium to Zabarella, not a text incipit. There is no known chant—and no conceivable chant—that bounces up and down by fifths, stutters through so many repeated whole-step oscillations, or descends by step through an entire octave the way this "melody" does. Clearly, the tenor and contratenor in this particular motet are not melodies at all, but harmonic supports.

The canon instructs the performers of the tenor and contratenor to read their parts each time under a different mensuration sign—C, O, and C, respectively. Thus despite their notational congruence, the actual rhythms of each presentation not only differ but undergo a progressive compression from perfect to imperfect time that resembles a traditional tenor diminution, but in three stages instead of two. The texted parts, meanwhile, are written chiefly in semibreves and minims, note values that are radically affected by the changing mensurations.

And yet the three stanzas are deliberately set so that they resemble each other melodically as much as possible in terms of contour, prosody (text distribution), and overall form, progressing each time from textless introitus through syllabically texted stanza to melismatic, hocket-ridden cauda. The result is a virtual set of strophic variations that in their fascinating interplay of sameness and difference symbolize the ideal of a harmoniously integrated society of free individuals — the ideal to which every northern Italian city state (or *res publica*, whence "republic") nominally aspired. Ex. 8-7 shows the fanfare-like introitus to each of the three strophes in turn.

DU FAY: THE MOTET AS MYSTICAL *SUMMA*

Guillaume Du Fay (ca. 1397–1474) lived almost exactly a century later than his namesake Guillaume de Machaut, and like Machaut he will be reintroduced in a later chapter. It is very important to consider at least one of his works right here, however, in order to appreciate the direct generic and stylistic continuity that linked Du Fay's creative output with that of his fourteenth-century precursors.

The reason for speaking in such urgent terms is that the beginning of "The Renaissance," for music, is often — though, as we will see, arbitrarily — placed around the beginning of the fifteenth century, and major historiographical divisions like that can act as barriers, sealing off from one another figures and works that happen to fall on opposite sides of that fancied line, no matter how significant their similarities. Not only that, but (as already observed in a somewhat different context) an appearance of stylistic backwardness or anachronism — inevitable when sweeping categories like "Medieval" and "Renaissance" are too literally believed in — can easily blind us to the value of supreme artistic achievements such as Du Fay's isorhythmic motets. They are not vestigial survivals or evidence of regressive tendencies, but a zenith.

The fact is, Du Fay's career was very much like Philippe de Vitry's a century earlier. He was a university-educated ordained cleric — in short, a *literatus* — whose musical horizons had been shaped by Boethius, by Guido . . . and by Philippe de Vitry. Like his predecessors, he thought in scholastic terms about his craft but in Platonic terms about the world. For him, no less than for the founders of the Ars Nova, the world was materialized number, and the highest purpose of music was to dematerialize it back to its essence.

Born in French-speaking Cambrai, near the border with the low countries, Du Fay followed in Ciconia's footsteps to early employment in Italy. He may have first gone down there as a choirboy in the entourage of the local bishop, who attended the Council of Constance, where Francesco Zabarella, Ciconia's patron, had shone. By 1420, when he was about 23, Du Fay was employed by the Pesaro branch of the notorious Malatesta family, the despots of the Adriatic coastal cities of west-central Italy. He joined the papal choir in 1428, and evidently formed a close relationship with Gabriele Cardinal Condulmer, who in 1431 became Eugene IV, the second pope to reign over the reunited postschismatic church.

Du Fay wrote three grandiose motets in honor of Pope Eugene. The first, *Ecclesie militantis Roma sedes* ("Rome, seat of the Church militant"), was composed shortly after the pope's election, at a very precarious moment for the papacy. That motet, expressive of the political conflicts that beset the new pope, is a riot of discord, with a complement of five polyphonic parts (three of them texted), and a sequence of no fewer than six mensuration changes. The second motet for Eugene, *Supremum est mortalibus bonum* ("For mortals the greatest good") is a celebration of a peace treaty between the pope and Sigismund, the Holy Roman Emperor. It is an epitome of concord, employing only one text and using a novel, sugar-sweet harmonic idiom of which (as we will see in chapter 11) Du Fay may have been the inventor. Near the end the names of the protagonists of the peace are declaimed in long-sustained consonant chords — concord concretized.

The third motet Du Fay composed for Eugene, *Nuper rosarum flores* ("Garlands of roses," of which the dazzling close is shown in Ex. 8-8), is the most famous one because of the way it manipulates symbolic numbers. In 1434, the pope, exiled from Rome by a rebellion, had set up court in Florence. In 1436, the Florence cathedral, under construction since 1294, was finally ready for dedication. A magnificent neoclassical edifice, crowned by a dome designed in 1420 by the great architect Filippo Brunelleschi, it was dedicated, under the denomination Santa Maria del Fiore, to the Virgin Mary. Pope Eugene IV, resident by force of circumstances in Florence, performed the dedication ceremony himself, and commissioned a commemorative motet for the occasion from Du Fay. This was to be the musical show of shows.

Nuper Rosarum Flores is cast in four large musical sections, plus an "Amen" in the form of a melismatic cauda. The layout is remarkable for its symmetry. The first and longest section begins with an introitus for the upper (texted) voices lasting twenty-eight *tempora*. The Gregorian cantus firmus, the fourteen-note incipit of the introit antiphon for the dedication of a church (*Terribilis est locus iste*, "Awesome is this place"), now enters, carried by a pair of tenors that present it in two seven-note groups, answering each to each as in biblical antiphonal psalmody.

Each of the succeeding sections presents the same 7 + 7 disposition of the tenor, and the same balanced alternation of duo and full complement (28 + 28 tempora, or 4 times 7 + 7). As in Ciconia's motet, the pair of tenors is written out only once, with directions to repeat. And again as in Ciconia's motet, each tenor statement is cast in a different mensuration: O, C, ₵ and (the part given in Ex. 8-8) ₵. These mensurations stand in a significant proportional relationship to one another. A breve or tempus of O contains six minims; a breve of C has four. The line through the signature halves the value of the tempus, so that a breve under ₵ contains three minims as sung by the texted parts running above, and a breve under ₵ contains two. Comparing these signatures in the order in which Du Fay presents them, they give the durational proportions 6:4:2:3. As anyone trained in the quadrivium would instantly recognize, these are Pythagorean

EX. 8-8 Guillaume Du Fay, *Nuper rosarum flores*, mm. 141–70

EX. 8-8 (*continued*)

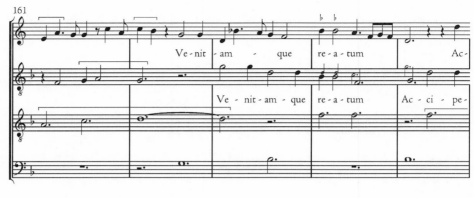

[... By ... the crucifixion of your son in the flesh,]
their Lord,
may they deserve
to receive kind favours
and pardon for their crimes. Amen.

proportions. In musical terms they can easily be translated from durations into pitch, for they describe the harmonic ratios of the most consonant intervals. Given a fundamental pitch X, Du Fay's numbers represent the octave (2X), the compound fifth, or twelfth (3X), the double octave (4X) and the twice-compound fifth (6X), as shown in Ex. 8-9.

EX. 8-9 Proportional numbers in *Nuper rosarum flores* represented as pitch intervals

Moreover, the complex of durational ratios also contains a symbolic perfect fifth (3:2) and a perfect fourth (4:3), all of it summed up in the final chord of the piece. Thus Du Fay's motet embodies a hidden Pythagorean *summa*, or comprehensive digest of the ways in which music represents the enduringly valid harmony of the cosmos. With its four different integers, it is the most complete symbolic summary of its kind in any isorhythmic motet. (By way of comparison, the proportional ground plan of Ciconia's motet, 3:2:2, incorporates only two integers, one of them repeated. The only harmonic intervals it can be said to express are the unison and the fifth.)

But that is by no means all. As Craig Wright has shown in detail (far more of it than we can pursue at the moment), the number symbolism in Du Fay's motet, reaching far beyond the specifically musical domain, makes contact with a venerable tradition of biblical exegesis that bears directly on the circumstances that inspired the work and the occasion that it adorned.[11] As we read in the second book of Kings, where the building of the great temple of Jerusalem is described, "the house which king Solomon built to the Lord, was three-score cubits in length, and twenty cubits in width, and thirty cubits in height" (2 Kings 6:2); that the inner sanctum, the "Holy of Holies," was forty cubits from the doors of the temple (2 Kings 6:18); and that the feast of dedication lasted "seven days and seven days, that is, fourteen days" (2 Kings 8:65). These, of course, are precisely the numbers that have figured in our structural analysis of Du Fay's motet. The durational proportions of the tenor *taleae* are precisely those governing the dimensions of Solomon's temple (60:40:20:30 cubits:: 6:4:2:3 minims to a breve); and the length and layout of the chant fragment chosen as *color* correspond to the days of the dedication feast ($7 + 7 = 14$). The relationship of all of this to the dedication feast for the Florence cathedral could hardly be more evident — or more propitious, in view of the Christian tradition that cast Rome as the new Jerusalem and the Catholic church as the new temple of God.

And yet there is more. The Florence cathedral was dedicated to the Virgin Mary, as the motet text affirms. That text is cast in a rare poetic meter with seven syllables per line. The introitus before the tenor entrance in each stanza lasts 28 (4×7) tempora, and the section following the tenor entrance likewise lasts 4×7. Seven is the number that mystically represented the Virgin in Christian symbolism, through her sevenfold attributes (her seven sorrows, seven joys, seven acts of mercy, seven virginal companions, and seven years of exile in Egypt). Four is the number that represented the temple, with its four cornerstones, four walls, four corners of the altar, and — when translated into Christian cruciform terms — four points on the cross, the shape of the cathedral floor plan. Four times seven mystically unites the temple with Mary, who through her womb that bore the son of God was also a symbol of Christian sanctuary.

All of this is mystically expressed in the occult substructure of Du Fay's motet, while on the sensuous surface, according to the testimony of the Florentine scholar Giannozzo Manetti, an earwitness,

> all the places of the Temple resounded with the sounds of harmonious symphonies as well as the concords of diverse instruments, so that it seemed not without reason that the angels and the sounds and singing of divine paradise had been sent from heaven to us on earth to insinuate in our ears a certain incredible divine sweetness; wherefore at that moment I was so possessed by ecstasy that I seemed to enjoy the life of the Blessed here on earth.[12]

What could better serve the church, better spiritually nourish its flock, or better assert its temporal authority?

A FINAL WORD FROM DANTE

That was the net effect, and the net aim, of the *discordia concors* that the motet so consummately symbolized. The ultimate verbal expression of the effect at which musicians aimed in the fourteenth century and its immediate aftermath was given by the greatest literary genius of the age, the poet Dante Alighieri, in his *Divine Comedy*. Significantly enough, it is in the third and last section — *Il Paradiso*, a description of heaven — that the motet is heard and described. The great poet's view of the peak musical genre of his day here coincides with that of the courtier Manetti, quoted above. Dante, who wrote around the time of Philippe de Vitry and the *Roman de Fauvel*, used a description of the motet as a metaphor for a world government of perfect justice, wholly attuned to the divine will, that perfectly harmonized multifarious humanity in bonds of social concord.

Dante portrays the sixth sphere of heaven as the abode of all the just rulers in the history of the world (Charlemagne among them, along with his biblical forebears Joshua and Judah Maccabee), who appear to him as singing stars. They assemble into a constellation in the form of an eagle, symbolizing the Roman Empire and its successor, Charlemagne's Holy Roman Empire, which had given the exiled Dante refuge after the Florentine wars of the Guelphs and Ghibellines.

In Canto XIX the eagle sings in the composite voice of "the congregated souls of rulers," and, says Dante, "I heard the beak talk and utter with its voice 'I' and 'mine' when its meaning was 'we' and 'ours.' . . . . Wheeling, then, it sang, then spoke: 'As are my notes to thee who canst not follow them, such is the Eternal Judgment to you mortals.'" In the next canto the Eagle falls silent and the starry lights that constitute it burst into a multitude of simultaneous songs. Dante is reminded of the sunset, when the brightness of the one great heavenly orb is replaced by the myriad tiny points of astral illumination: ". . . and this change in the sky came to my mind/when the standard of the world and of its chiefs/was silent in the blessed beak./For all those living lights,/shining still more brightly, began songs/that slip and fall from my memory." As Julie Cumming comments, for Dante,

> total comprehension of text or music is not necessary for appreciation. He describes in these passages the sublime musical experience of the inexpressible. This description of the musical experience is also a way of describing the apprehension of God: God's will is not comprehensible, but nevertheless it is possible to believe in it and appreciate it.[13]

This, at last, may be the answer to the riddle of polytextuality, to us perhaps the most salient feature of the French thirteenth- and fourteenth-century motet because it is the most uncanny. We need not assume that proper performance practice or greater familiarity rendered comprehensible to contemporary listeners that which is incomprehensible to us. The mind-boggling effect of the fourteenth-century ceremonial motet, confirmed by numerous witnesses, may have actually depended on the sensory overload delivered by its multiplicity of voices and texts. If so, it was not the first time that what we would call esthetic value and power would be extracted from the inscrutable. (A large part of the esthetic value, as well as the sacredness, of the earliest melismatic chant derived from what Dante might have called its slipperiness.) And it certainly will not be the last. Whenever the "sublime" is valued as an artistic quality, so is awe. And what produces awe must be unfathomable as well as thrilling.

Machaut and His Progeny

Machaut's Songs and Mass; Music at the Papal Court of Avignon; Ars Subtilior

MAINTAINING THE ART OF COURTLY SONG

Guillaume de Machaut may not have been the most prestigious French poet and musician of his time. In terms of contemporary renown, he may have been outshone by Philippe de Vitry. He is certainly the most important to us, however, and the most representative, owing to the extraordinary fullness of his legacy, a fullness that stands in stark contrast to the meagerness of Vitry's. Certain aspects of Machaut's legacy, moreover, lived on for a century and more in the work of later poets and musicians who definitely saw themselves as his creative heirs.

The first half of Machaut's long life was spent in service, chiefly as secretary to John of Luxembourg (1296–1346), a son of the Holy Roman Emperor Henry VII, who succeeded his father-in-law Wenceslaus as king of Bohemia in 1310. Machaut, who like his patron was born around the turn of the century, came from the environs of the ancient cathedral town of Reims in the north of France, not far from Luxembourg. There is actually a town called Machault about twenty-five miles from Reims, but there is no evidence to support the tempting assumption that it was the poet's birthplace.

He was in the peripatetic John's service by 1323 and traveled widely with him on campaigns across northern and eastern Europe, including Silesia, Poland, Prussia, and Lithuania, as well as the Alpine areas of Lombardy and Tyrol, which John briefly ruled. After his patron's spectacularly violent death, tied blind to his horse on the battlefield of Crécy, Machaut returned to Reims and lived out his last three decades as a tonsured cathedral canon, with few official duties

FIG. 9-1 Illumination from the largest of the "Machaut manuscripts" showing the poet composing *Les nouveaus dis amoureus* ("New Poems in Honor of Love").

beyond singing some minimum number of Masses and Offices each year. He was in effect a wealthy man of leisure, free to pursue his artistic callings. He died in 1377, remarkably aged for a man who lived during the century of the great plagues.

As his reputation as a poet grew, Machaut was commissioned by several kings and dukes to write *dits*, lengthy allegorical poems, in their honor. For these patrons and others, Machaut also supervised the copying of his complete poetical and musical works into rich manuscripts, several of which survive, making him the earliest musical *literatus* whose works come down to us in what amounts to an authorized collected edition.

Like the trouvères, his most kindred antecedents, Machaut belongs as much or more to literary as to musical history. He is universally regarded by today's literary historians as the greatest French poet of his age; his poetry is studied alongside that of Chaucer (whom he knew and influenced) and Dante, even if, unlike theirs, Machaut's literary output no longer enjoys a wide general readership. He is best known to today's connoisseurs for his music, not his poetry; since the revival of performing interest in "early music," he has come to enjoy a place in the concert hall and in recordings somewhat comparable to Chaucer's on the bookshelf.

His longest and most impressive works are nevertheless works of verbal art: extended narrative poems, much prized and cited in their day, in which the lyric compositions we now prize served as occasional interpolations. The earliest of these grand narratives, *Le Remède de Fortune* ("Fortune's remedy"), composed around 1349, has been compared to an *ars poetica*, a didactic treatise or compendium on lyric poetry, since it contains exemplary specimens of all the main genres, placed within a story that defines their expressive content and social use.

The very plot of the poem is motivated by poetry. The poet anonymously composes a *lai* in honor of his lady, who discovers it, bids him read it to her, and asks who wrote it. Embarrassed, he flees her presence and addresses a *complainte* to Love and Fortune. Hope, fortune's remedy, appears and comforts him with two ballade-type songs in praise of love: a *chanson royal* and a *baladelle* (the latter a poem in what much later was known as "binary form," with a stanza in two sections with complementary rhyme schemes, both repeated). The poet expresses his gratitude in a standard *ballade*. He seeks his lady out, finds her dancing, and accompanies her movements with a *virelai*. He confesses authorship of the lay, she receives him as her lover, and, after a day spent together at her chateau, they exchange rings and he expresses his joy in a *rondeau*.

This narrative followed and amplified the typical blueprint of a troubadour (or trouvère) *vida* of old. With it, Machaut deliberately gave the moribund art of the knightly poet-lover a new birth, distinguished in part—specifically, in the baladelle, the ballade, and the rondeau—by the use of polyphonic music in the latest style. The fact that these were the sections so favored points to an important difference between Machaut's courtly poetry and that of the trouvères. While operating on as lofty and aristocratic a plane as the knightliest trouvères, as a composer he preferred the "fixed forms"—that is, the dance songs with refrains. These, we may recall, had originally come into their own when the courtly art of the trouvères had moved from castle to city and became the property of the guilds. Machaut reinvested the urbanized, "popular" genres of *fine amours* with privileged (now we'd call it "chic") refinement.

REDEFINING (AND RE-REFINING) A GENRE

That reinvestment was accomplished not by a stylistic revival but a thorough stylistic renovation. Machaut was able to reelevate and recomplicate the style of courtly love poetry, even while retaining its more popular forms, because he possessed a polyphonic craft that went far beyond the attainments of any previous courtly *or* urban love-singer. Where Adam de la Halle's polyphonic rondeaux were cast in as simple and straightforward a polyphonic texture as could be—that of the syllabic *versus* or conductus setting—Machaut's were subtle, ornate, and full of a very recondite lyricism that made telling decorative use, as we have seen, of musica ficta "causa pulchritudinis."

We have already inspected one of Machaut's motets (*Felix virgo/Inviolata/AD TE SUSPIRAMUS*, Ex. 8-6) and seen how fully he had mastered the craftsmanly and constructive techniques of the Ars Nova. Ars Nova techniques, which had been developed specifically to serve the purposes of the motet genre, were "bottom-up" techniques. That is, they were techniques geared toward the erecting of highly stratified polyphonic superstructures over artfully contrived and elaborated foundations. And the foundations were wrought in turn from cantus firmus melodies appropriated, as a rule, from the high-authority repertoire of canonized church chant.

Machaut wrote some real masterpieces in this very formalized and architectonic idiom, the most extended being a giant *hoquetus* on the melisma DAVID that comes at the end of the Gregorian Alleluia *Nativitas* for the feast of the Virgin Mary's Nativity, already the basis (as Machaut surely knew) of a grandiose, "classic" setting in the Notre Dame style. (We know it, too: see Ex. 6-5.) Machaut's hoquetus was not meant as an appendage to that venerable composition, however. The DAVID melisma is sung not by the soloist(s) but by the choir, and so would not have been performed polyphonically in church. This was still music for "feasts of the learned," who delighted in high-spirited intellectual games.

As shown in Ex. 9-1, Machaut divides his 32-note *color* by a twelve-note talea lasting 30 tempora, and lets the two repetition-schemes run their course until they come out even (or in more evocatively "Boethian" terms, lets the two bodies orbit in musical space until they come into alignment). It takes three cursus of color and eight of talea, thus: $32 \times 3 = 12 \times 8 = 96$. Then, as a sort of cauda, he sets the color going once more to a shorter talea that divides its 32 notes evenly (8 notes in 27 tempora). Laying out the ground plan just described had to precede the composition of the hocketing upper parts, just as the foundation of an architectural edifice had to be laid before the rest could be erected. Instead of a full score, Ex. 9-1 gives just the foundational materials, the color, and the taleae. They can be followed, tracking each with one hand, while listening to a recorded performance. This will give a vivid idea of Ars Nova "isorhythmic" foundational architecture at its grandest.

By way of transition from the more speculative Ars Nova genres to the lyric genres more peculiar to Machaut, we may cast a sidelong glance at a whimsical hybrid: a motet

EX. 9-1 Guillaume de Machaut, hoquetus "DAVID," color and taleae

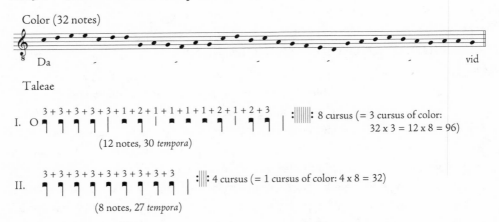

Color (32 notes)

Da - - - - - vid

Taleae

I. O 3+3+3+3+3+1+2+1+1+1+1+2+1+2+3

(12 notes, 30 *tempora*)

:||||||: 8 cursus (= 3 cursus of color: 32 x 3 = 12 x 8 = 96)

II. 3+3+3+3+3+3+3+3+3+3

(8 notes, 27 *tempora*)

:||||: 4 cursus (= 1 cursus of color: 4 x 8 = 32)

in three texted parts, all in French, in which the tenor is not a Gregorian chant but instead a traditional *chanson balladé* ("danced song") or *virelai* (Ex. 9-2: *Lasse/Se j'aime/ POURQUOY*). The song Machaut chose to do tenor duty was almost as "canonical" as a chant, however, having a textual pedigree going back to the thirteenth century. It satirizes courtly love as mere marital infidelity ("Oh God, why does my husband beat me? All I did was talk to my lover"). Ex. 9-2 shows Machaut's tenor in compressed note values (Machaut's are longs and breves, typical "tenor" values), with the constituent parts of the virelai—AbbaA, with "A" the refrain—labeled. The upper parts, meanwhile, behave in characteristic motet fashion. They are rhythmically stratified—the motetus moving in breves, semibreves, and occasional minims; the triplum in minims, semibreves, and occasional breves—and serve as glosses (here, ironic rhymed ones) on the tenor: "Alas, how can I forget/the handsome, the good, the sweet, the merry/[youth] to whom I've completely given/this heart of mine?" "If I love him truly, and he truly loves me, do

EX. 9-2 Guillaume de Machaut, *Pourquoy me bat mes maris*, tenor

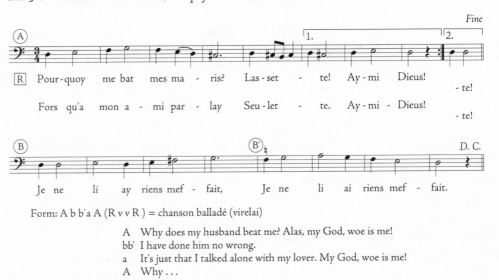

R Pour-quoy me bat mes ma - ris? Las - set - te! Ay - mi Dieus! - te!

Fors qu'a mon a - mi par - lay Seu - let - te. Ay - mi - Dieus! - te!

Je ne li ay riens mef - fait, Je ne li ai riens mef - fait.

Form: A b b'a A (R v v R) = chanson balladé (virelai)

A Why does my husband beat me? Alas, my God, woe is me!
bb' I have done him no wrong.
a It's just that I talked alone with my lover. My God, woe is me!
A Why...

I deserve to be treated so?" Ex. 9-3 shows the portion of the whole polyphonic texture corresponding to the tenor's first refrain.

There is good reason to suspect that even if the tenor's text is traditional, its tune is Machaut's, or else heavily edited by Machaut to accord with his own composing style (or, at very least, with contemporary performance practice; note, among other telltale signs, the musica ficta calling for the *subsemitonium modi*, the borrowed leading tone).

EX. 9-3   Guillaume de Machaut, *Lasse/Se j'aime/POURQUOY*, mm. 1–42

EX. 9-3 (continued)

Machaut's own virelais are very similar. Most of them are monophonic, presumably because of the three main fixed forms the virelai was the one that continued most often to serve a traditional social function — the *carole* or public (social) dance — and was most often performed by minstrels. Mensurally notated monophonic dances and dance-songs proliferated in written sources throughout the thirteenth and fourteenth centuries, beginning with the famous "Manuscrit du Roi," which contains eight *estampies royals*, long "stamping dances" in open-and-shut couplets, already mentioned in chapter 4 (and shown in Fig. 4-8). That being the case, *Lasse/Se j'aime/POURQUOY* might be looked upon through the other end of the telescope, so to speak: not so much as a motet built over a virelai, but rather as a polyphonically dressed-up virelai of an especially elaborate sort, in which the techniques of the motet serve to embellish a courtly dance.

THE TOP-DOWN STYLE

Mixing the attributes of the motet and chanson genres was a highly unusual effect. The genres were more typically thought of as distinct to the point of contrast — a contrast conditioned above all by their methods of composition. To appreciate the difference, and the new way of composing Machaut seems to have pioneered in his chansons, we will do best to begin with a monophonic composition — say, a typical virelai.

One of Machaut's best known pieces of this type, because it is so frequently performed by modern minstrels in "early music" ensembles, is the catchy *Douce dame jolie* ("Sweet, pretty lady"; Ex. 9-4). It is a very early instance of a literate, Ars Nova-style composition that is in duple time on all levels of mensuration. The purposely varied detail-work discloses the song's literate origins: the first three lines of the poem are set to what are in essence three repetitions of a single musical phrase, but each of them is subtly distinguished from the others. The music begins with rests, even though there are no accompanying parts, because without bars the only way in which an initial upbeat could be indicated was by showing the silent part of the hypothetical first measure. Like many duple-metered pieces of the time, it especially emphasizes syncopes.

EX. 9-4   Guillaume de Machaut, *Douce dame jolie* (monophonic virelai)

Fair sweet lady,
for God's sake do not think
that any woman has mastery
over me, save you alone.

For always without deceit
I have cherished you,
and humbly
served you
all the days of my life
without any base thought.

Alas! I am bereft
of hope and help;
and so my joy is ended,
unless you pity me.

Eight — only eight — of Machaut's thirty-nine virelais are polyphonic. Of these, six are in two voices only, a texted "cantus" ("song" or "singer") part and an untexted tenor. The nomenclature already suggests that a tenor has been added to a "song," or in other words, that the song existed as a monophonic composition before it was made polyphonic by a lower accompanying voice. This is just the opposite from the procedure we have observed in all the polyphonic genres of the twelfth and thirteenth centuries — organum, clausula, even the homorhythmic conductus, which had no preexisting tenor but created its own from scratch. Above all, adding a tenor to a preexisting cantus was the very antithesis of motet composition. Starting "at the top" was a whole new concept of composing — within the literate tradition, anyway (for we have always recognized the possibility, indeed the strong probability, that "accompanied song" was a minstrel specialty at least from the time of the troubadours.) Two kinds of additional evidence clinch the notion of "top-down" composition. One is the state of the musical sources. The virelai *En mon cuer* ("In my heart," Ex. 9-5), for example, is found as a two-voice composition in all the composer-supervised "collected editions" of Machaut's works — all, that is, except the one generally considered to be the earliest such manuscript, where its "cantus" is entered, like the other virelais in that manuscript, as a monophonic dance song. That was how it must have been originally composed. It is self-sufficient as a single voice. That is, it has a stable and satisfying cadence structure,

EX. 9-5   Guillaume de Machaut, *En mon cuer* (virelai a 2)

EX. 9-5 (continued)

and unlike its eventual accompanying tenor, it has enough notes to accommodate all the syllables of the text.

The remaining piece of evidence that Machaut wrote his songs from the top down, beginning with the self-sufficient cantus, comes from another of his famous narrative poems, *Le Voir Dit* ("The true tale"), composed in the early 1360s. This, too, is ostensibly an autobiographical poem, far less conventional in its scenario than *Le Remède de Fortune* and possibly, therefore, more reliable as autobiography. Its ten thousand lines embody, along with the narrative itself, some forty-six ultraliterary love letters exchanged between the sexagenarian poet and a precocious lass of nineteen, Péronne (or Péronnel) d'Armentières, whom he is pursuing as courtly lover. Along with the letters there are some lyric poems addressed by Machaut to his callow beloved, of which a few are set to music. In one of the letters accompanying a song Machaut tells Peronelle that he will send another as soon as he has put a tenor and a contratenor to it. Peronelle may not have been particularly interested in the implications of that statement, but to us they are profoundly revealing.

The upshot of all this scattered evidence is that *any* of Machaut's two-part virelais could have started out, and probably did start out, as monophonic songs, to which tenors were added later. A corollary implication is that monophonic performance was probably a standard option for all of Machaut's virelais. Another is that polyphonic performance was likewise a standard option: any monophonic virelai, that is, was eligible for accompaniment by a tenor, whether set down in writing or extemporized. And because Machaut's monophonic melodies had to be eligible for accompaniment in this way, they had to differ fundamentally in style from all previous monophonic melodies we have encountered.

Here is why: Whether set down or extemporized, any tenor had to make correct counterpoint with its "cantus." In addition to observing the rules of consonance, this meant making the proper kind of cadence—i.e., a discant cadence. A discant cadence, as we recall, either moved by contrary motion inward to a unison (i.e., made an *occursus*) or moved out by contrary motion to the octave. The latter type was by far the more common, owing to the fact that most discants were constructed over a Gregorian cantus firmus in the lower voice; and Gregorian melodies, as a result of their characteristic arch shape, almost always made their last approach to the final as a stepwise descent. For that reason, the usual *vox organalis* or *duplum*, just as characteristically, made its last approach to the final from below, via the *subsemitonium* or leading tone.

As we may remember from chapter 4, high "Latinate" troubadour and trouvère melodies were often all but indistinguishable, stylistically, from the late Frankish chants that were being composed at the same time. Accordingly, they too made their final approach to the final from above. That is the way unaccompanied melodies traditionally worked.

But now compare an unaccompanied (or a potentially unaccompanied) melody by Machaut. Both *Douce dame jolie* and *En mon cuer* make their cadential approaches not from above but via the *subsemitonium*. They are composed, in other words, on the model of a *duplum*, not a tenor, and they established a basic melodic type for courtly songs that would last for several centuries. They are, in short, monophonic melodies that were conceived in the context of polyphony, by a composer whose musical imagination had been definitively shaped by polyphony. Even the tenor melody in *Lasse/Se j'aime POURQUOY* (Ex. 9-3), that whimsical virelai-motet hybrid, makes its final cadences from below (see Ex. 9-2). In other words, it does not really behave like a tenor. Its eccentricity forces a peculiar cadence structure on the polyphonic texture that adds another level of irony to the piece.

CANTILENA

The new style of song-melody, composed with polyphonic accompaniment in mind, was called *cantilena*. By itself the melody was sufficient, making correct (*subsemitonium*) cadences and fitting the words. With the addition of a tenor, a self-sufficient two-part discant texture was achieved, in which cadences (to octaves or, more rarely, to unisons in contrary motion) were still correct according to the rules of discant. With the addition of a third voice, whether a texted triplum in the range of the cantus or an untexted contratenor in the range of the tenor, the two-part structure was sonorously enhanced and the harmonies made "sweet."

The most usual way of sweetening the harmony was to amplify the imperfect consonances into full triads; and the most characteristic place to observe this is, again, at cadences. A typical three-voice cadence in cantilena style has the cantus and the tenor describing their characteristic progression from sixth to octave, with a contratenor (or, less often, a triplum) doubling the cantus at the lower fourth (if a contratenor) or upper fifth (if a triplum), thus creating what we have already learned to identify as the "double leading-tone" cadence.

This full harmonic texture began to influence the composition of motets, as we saw in the previous chapter, when contratenors were added to the vocal complement. Although we now associate the contratenor-enriched texture primarily with Machaut, it may actually have been yet another innovation of Philippe de Vitry. Several of his extant motets do have contratenors; and, although they do not survive, Vitry is known to have written ballades, probably in the 1320s (when the polyphonic ballade is described as a popular novelty by Jacques de Liège), some twenty years before Machaut's earliest three-part cantilenas began appearing, at first in the *Remède de Fortune*.

One of the manuscripts containing the virelai *En mon cuer*, which we have considered in one part and in two, contains some extra ruled lines reserved for a triplum Machaut never got around to writing. That would have created three interchangeable versions of the song—or rather, three performance possibilities: cantus alone, cantus plus tenor, cantus plus triplum and tenor. Any of these possibilities is harmonically/contrapuntally correct; none of them can claim to be, in any exclusive sense, the "real thing." Again we are reminded that the line between creation and performance was still a blurry, permeable one. Machaut corroborates this in an odd way when he asks Péronelle, in one of the *Voir Dit* letters, to receive a special song from him and have it played by her minstrels "just as it is, without adding or taking away." For the sake of their special relationship, in other words, he was asking for something exceptional.

FUNCTIONALLY DIFFERENTIATED COUNTERPOINT

As an example of the standard cantilena texture "just as it is, without adding or taking away," we can look at yet another Machaut virelai, *Tres bonne et belle* (Ex. 9-6), the only one to come down in all its sources, exceptionally, as a three-voice composition. The final is C, putting the song in what we would call the major mode (and what Machaut, if he thought about it at all, would probably have called a transposition of the Lydian mode, normally pitched on F). The texted part or cantus has a plagal ambitus that puts the final smack in the middle of its range. The lower tenor and contratenor share a single authentic ambitus, from c to d'.

EX. 9-6   Guillaume de Machaut, *Tres bonne et belle* (virelai a 3)

EX. 9-6   *(continued)*

Although they occupy the exact same pitch space, however, the tenor and contratenor are not equivalent parts. Each of them behaves, so to speak, according to its station within the textural hierarchy. It is the tenor and only the tenor that makes the true discant cadence against the cantus, moving out from sixth to octave, whether on the final (mm. 3–4, 23–24, 34–35) or on some subsidiary degree (D in mm. 8–9 and 13–14, E in m. 32–33, the "open" cadence of the middle section). At such moments the behavior of the contratenor is also mandated: it invariably fills in the middle of the double leading-tone cadence. That is what defines it as a contratenor. A contratenor (or a tenor, or a cantus) is as a contratenor (or a tenor, or a cantus) does.

Thus, even if Machaut wrote all the parts in one sitting, and there is no reason to suppose that he did not, he nevertheless provided three grammatically viable or correct performance possibilities. Writing in this way—so that the cantus can be sung either alone, or in a duet with the tenor, or in a trio with tenor and contratenor—is often called "successive composition." We imagine the composer writing the cantus first, then adding the tenor, and finally the contratenor. We have already seen lots of evidence that this was often enough the actual procedure. But it does not follow that the composer had to write the parts separately, or that he could not conceive of a three part texture in a single act of composing.

Interpreting the idea of "successive composition" too literally can lead us into making unwarranted and probably fallacious assumptions about the way in which people "heard" music in those days—for example, that they did not "hear" harmony the way we "hear" it, but only an interplay of contrapuntal voices that just happens now and then to produce (as if by accident) what we call "chords." (The quotes around "hear," of course, are there to show that what is meant is not just hearing but conceptualizing on the basis of hearing.) What we call "successive composition," then, is merely the process of assigning strictly defined roles to the various parts in a contrapuntal texture. The reason for it does not seem to have much to do with how one "heard," but rather with the fluid and practical attitude that demanded not a single idealized text but a variety of performance possibilities for any song.

And that is why, even if he conceived all the parts in a song like *Tres bonne et belle* as a single harmonic unit, Machaut needed to differentiate the tenor and the contratenor in terms of function, if not style. For them to alternate roles on successive cadences, for example, would preclude a two-part performance of the piece, for in that case not all of the cadences would be properly enunciated no matter which of the two accompanying parts were used. And yet the fact that the tenor and contratenor had to be functionally distinct seems to have led to their being stylistically distinct as well. The contratenor, being in quasi-architectural terms the least "structural" voice (in that the other two voices could perform the piece without it), became willy-nilly the most "decorative" one—at once liveliest in rhythm (replete with hockets and syncopes) and most capricious in contour (leaping freely by sixths).

THE LUXURIANT STYLE

At their most luxuriant, Machaut's textures could accommodate four voices: the "structural" cantus/tenor pair, accompanied by both a triplum and a contratenor. This texture, which we have already observed in Ex. 8-5, was in effect a blending of the traditional motet complement (which included a triplum) with the newer cantilena complement (which included a contratenor). It was a rich all-purpose texture that could be adapted either to motet or to chanson designs.

The rondeau *Rose, liz* ("The rose, the lily") is found in all its composer-supervised manuscript sources with a full four-part complement. Ex. 9-7 shows the opening of the piece, up to the first cadence. Because the parts are still functionally differentiated within a structural hierarchy, there are four viable performance options: take away the triplum and the remaining voices will produce a texture like that of Ex. 9-6; take away the contratenor and the remaining texture will be like that of Ex. 9-5; take away the tenor and the cantus can stand alone, as in Ex. 9-4.

EX. 9-7   Guillaume de Machaut, Rondeau no. 10, *Rose, liz, printemps*, mm. 1–11

Note that the triplum and the contratenor behave similarly at the cadence. Both supply the "second leading tone," F♯, each in its respective register, producing parallel octaves. (The same was true of the cadences in the Machaut motet examined in the previous chapter.) The four-part texture is thus a sonorously amplified—and functionally redundant—version of the three-part texture. A functionally differentiated four-part harmony would not make its appearance for another century.

Of all the fixed forms, the ballade in three stanzas was for Machaut and his followers the noblest and most exalted—and musically, therefore, the most elaborate. In the manuscripts Machaut oversaw, the section containing ballades was headed, "Ci comencent les balades ou il ha chant," meaning, "Here begin the ballades or high song" (recall the *grand chant* of the trouvères). "Highness" (*hauteur*, whence "haughty") was expressed in the traditional way: by the use of an especially melismatic style. The ballade *De toutes flours* ("Of all the fruits and flowers in my garden"; Ex. 9-8), certainly exemplifies this. Otherwise it is very similar to *Rose, liz*, both in subject matter and (no surprise) in mode.

EX. 9-8   Guillaume de Machaut, Ballade no. 31, *De toutes flours*

EX. 9-8 (*continued*)

EX. 9-8   (*continued*)

(Additional strophes omitted. Underscoring denotes musical rhyme.)

a: De toutes flours n'avoit et de tous fruis
    En mon vergier fors une seule <u>rose:</u>
a: Gastés estoit li suerplus et destruis
    Par Fortune qui durement <u>s'oppose</u>
b: Contre ceste doulce flour
    Pour amatir sa coulour et s'odour.
    Mais se cueillir la voy ou trebuchier,
    Autre apres li famais <u>avoir ne quier.</u>

Of all flowers and fruits
there is in my garden a single rose.
All else has suffered the ravages
of Fortune, which is now setting its cruel heart
against this sweet flower,
to drain its color and its scent.
But if it droops or is plucked
I shall never want another one.

Mode, in this style, still means more than a scale and a final. It is still a formula family. The chief formula, of course, is the cadence: note the same doubled F♯s between the two "accompanying" voices (contratenor and triplum). And another important formula is the overall tonal progression. It is easiest to see this in a ballade, since the repeated opening section has the same sort of "open" (*ouvert*) and "closed" (*clos*) cadences we found in the monophonic songs of the trouvères, only now harmonically amplified. The first ending makes its open (or "half") cadence on what we would call the supertonic, and the second makes its closed (or "full") cadence on the final. The progression supertonic to final, of course, is also the way the tenor itself moves at the full cadence, and so the overall tonal progression is a kind of magnification of the full cadence.

Machaut reinforces the sense of cadential closure and rounds the whole piece off by means of a musical rhyme. Not only the final cadence but the whole final phrase of the first section returns at the end of the second (compare the first section from m. 22 with the second from m. 57); the repetition is made extra conspicuous by the use of an ear-catching syncopation in the tenor, preceded by a prolonged imperfect consonance (doubly prolonged in the second section!) that arrests the harmonic motion precisely when the doubled leading tone is sounding and demanding resolution (compare mm. 22, 56–57). In addition, the final line of poetry, which carries the musical rhyme, is a refrain uniting all three stanzas. Music and text thus work in harness to delineate the form and heighten its rhetoric.

WHAT INSTRUMENTALISTS DID

Proof of this ballade's distinction (or at least its popularity) is its inclusion, a generation or more after the composer's death, in a north Italian manuscript from about 1415 that is the earliest extant source of music composed or arranged for keyboard instruments. It is called the "Faenza Codex" after the Italian town to whose public library it now belongs. It may originally have been prepared by or for a church organist, because it contains a certain amount of service music, including an arrangement of the Kyrie *Cunctipotens genitor*, with which we are already familiar in both its original form (Ex. 2-14b) and as adapted for polyphonic performance (Ex. 5-8). The organ arrangement in the Faenza Codex is somewhat like the latter in concept. It is arranged in score, with the lower staff (left hand part) confined to the plainsong melody, held out as a tenor, while the right hand part carols away in a very florid counterpoint. Ex. 9-9 contains the first section.

EX. 9-9   *Cunctipotens genitor* from Faenza Codex

The arrangement of Machaut's *De toutes flours* follows the same idea. Ex. 9-10 gives the "A" section. It adapts Machaut's tenor as a cantus firmus, meanwhile transposing it up a fifth, lightly decorating it, and recasting its rhythms from simple-into-compound-duple patterns (or, in Ars Nova terms, changing the prolation from minor to major). Over it the right hand plays a version of Machaut's cantus that is so overgrown with embellishment as to be scarcely recognizable. (It is easiest to recognize at the musical rhyme: compare Ex. 9-10 at mm. 23 ff and 56 ff with the corresponding passages of Ex. 9-8.)

This arrangement (or *intabulation*, as arrangements for keyboard are often called) is extremely suggestive. It gives us grounds for surmising what instrumental virtuosos did at a time when practically no instrumental music was written down. Instrumental music, too, started out as an "oral" culture, if the term oral can be expanded to encompass the digital, based on listening, practicing, and emulating; and it left few traces before the sixteenth century for historian-sleuths to interpret. A book like the Faenza Codex, therefore, is a precious document. It reveals the way in which "standard"—or "classic"—vocal compositions may have provided highly skilled instrumentalists (like today's—well, yesterday's—jazz virtuosos) with a repertoire for specialist improvisation.

MACHAUT'S MASS AND ITS BACKGROUND

By a curious twist of fate, Guillaume de Machaut—best known in his day as a poet and, secondarily, as a composer of courtly songs—is best known today for what seems an entirely uncharacteristic work: a complete polyphonic setting of the Ordinary of the Mass. Machaut's *Messe de Nostre Dame* ("Mass of Our Lady") is in fact the earliest such setting to survive from the hand of a single known author. What might otherwise seem a liturgical anomaly in an otherwise basically secular career has instead loomed disproportionately large both within Machaut's output and in music historiography itself, because the "cyclic Mass Ordinary" (that is, a setting of the mostly nonconsecutive items of the Ordinary liturgy as a musical unit) became the dominant musical genre of the fifteenth and sixteenth centuries, and Machaut seems willy-nilly its prophetic harbinger.

The actual history of the polyphonic Mass Ordinary, while it might seem to diminish Machaut's legendary stature, is a much more interesting story than the myth of its single-handed invention by Machaut might suggest. The rise of polyphonic Ordinaries was a by-product of one of the most turbulent periods in the history of the Roman church—the phase during which, briefly, the church was not Roman.

AVIGNON

Until the fourteenth century polyphonic settings of the Mass Ordinary, or any part of it, were uncommon. In eleventh- and twelfth-century Aquitaine, as we know, one could find occasional polyphonic settings of the Kyrie. But these were fully "prosulated" Kyries, with syllabic verses that were "proper" to specific occasions or the places where

EX. 9-10 Guillaume de Machaut, *De toutes flours* as arranged in the Faenza Codex

EX. 9-10 (continued)

FIG. 9-2   An echo of the "Babylonian captivity," this altarpiece, executed ca. 1520 by the Venetian painter Antonio Ronzen for the church of Sainte Madeleine in Saint Maximin, France, shows Christ in chains before Herod against a background fancifully depicting the old papal palace at Avignon, the seat of the antipopes.

they were sung, not "ordinary" (in the sense of all-purpose). At Notre Dame de Paris, as we know, only the responsorial chants of the Mass Proper and the Office were set, and of these only the soloist's portion. The Ordinary was sung by the musically unlettered choir, and for that reason alone might well have been thought off-limits to polyphonic treatment. Therefore, before the fourteenth century one simply does not find settings of melismatic ("untroped") Kyries, to say nothing of the remaining motley assortment of Ordinary chants — the Gloria (an acclamation), the Credo (a contract), the Sanctus (an invocation of the heavenly choir), the Agnus Dei (a litany), or the "Deo Gratias" response to the Ite (dismissal formula).

The first center where Mass Ordinary settings began to proliferate was the papal court at Avignon. One of the larger cities in the southeastern corner of France, Avignon had become the papal see in 1309, when Pope Clement V, a Frenchman (born Bernard de Got), abandoned Rome at the behest of the French king, Philip the Fair. The next six popes after Clement were also French and also subservient to their kings. This virtual "capture" of the papacy by the French crown was dubbed the Babylonian Captivity by disapproving Italians like the poet Petrarch, who coined the phrase (but who nevertheless found profitable employment at Avignon in his youth). In 1378 Pope Gregory XI was prevailed upon to move the papacy back to Rome, touching off the Great Schism. It was more a national than a religious dispute. The French popes who, under royal protection, were elected to continue the line of Clement at Avignon, were later decanonized — ruled "antipopes" — at the Council of Constance that ended the Schism in 1417 and brought the papacy back within the Italian orbit where it remained almost without interruption until the election of Pope John Paul II, a Pole, in 1978.

Two surviving manuscripts, both of them full of Ordinary settings, comprise what music remains from the papal liturgical repertory at Avignon. These manuscripts are called the Apt and Ivrea codices after the towns where they may have originated, but where they are in any case kept today. Apt is close by Avignon to the east; Ivrea, a bit farther east, is now across the Italian border near Turin. Just why it should have been at Avignon that settings of the Ordinary began to flourish has never been fully explained. But it may have had something to do with the general Frenchification of the papacy during the Babylonian Captivity. The Apt and Ivrea settings employ textures associated with other genres popular in France and may have been deliberately modeled on them.

The most elaborate are in motet (or, when particularly melismatic, in hocket) style, built up from a cantus firmus that is often cast in isorhythmic taleae. The other characteristic "Ordinary" textures were far simpler and increasingly prevalent as the Avignon repertory developed. One was the homorhythmic (or "simultaneous") style previously associated with the conductus. It was often used for the wordier texts, such as the Gloria and Credo, where syllabic texting helped expedite their recitation. But most characteristic of all was the specifically French and originally secular three-voice "cantilena" (a.k.a. "ballade") style, composed in the top-down fashion we have associated with Machaut. Thus, even as the Latin-texted motet was becoming more brilliant and impressive than ever over the course of the fourteenth century (and more and more firmly associated with occasions of civic and ecclesiastical pomp), within the confines of the actual service liturgy there seems to have been a countervailing tendency toward modesty and simplification. This, too, may have been among the factors conducive to Ordinary settings, which were as liturgically bare as one could get.

It was one of the early Avignon popes who issued the most famous of all antimusical screeds. Pope John XXII, Clement's successor, was born Jacques Duèse in 1244, in the Provencal town of Cahors (a little to the north of Toulouse), and reigned from 1316 to his death in 1334. His bull, *Docta sanctorum*, promulgated in 1323, complained bitterly about hockets, "depraved" discants, and "wanton" polytextuality ("upper parts made of secular songs").[1] These motettish extravagances were to be condemned, but "consonances" that respected the integrity of the sacred texts were judged desirable, because music, in moderation, can "soothe the hearer and inspire his devotion, without destroying religious feeling in the minds of the singers." John might have been describing the Ordinary settings in the Apt and Ivrea codices.

Both manuscripts were fairly late artifacts of papal Avignon. Ivrea, the earlier of the two, was compiled around 1370. We have already encountered it as a source for one of Philippe de Vitry's motets (Ex. 8-3; Fig. 8-4). Apt was not put together until the time of the antipopes, about thirty years later. The music these sources contain could have been composed at any time up to the date of its inscription. That music consists not of complete or "cyclic" ordinary settings but of individual items ("Mass movements," as they are sometimes called, rather misleadingly) and occasional pairs. As a sample of Avignon service music, Ex. 9-11 contains the first section of a Kyrie from the Apt Manuscript. Motet-style hockets make an occasional appearance, and John XXII might not have entirely approved, but they are sung in the course of a melisma and no words are obscured. The piece is attributed to a local composer named Guymont.

When Ordinary settings were paired, it was primarily on the basis of shared textual characteristics, only secondarily on musical grounds. That is to say the Gloria and Credo, which contrast with the other Ordinary items by virtue of their lengthy prose texts, were a natural pair. Another natural pair were the Kyrie and the Agnus Dei, both of which are repetitive petitions or litanies. The Sanctus, though not a prayer, has a short repetitive text and could make an effective pair with either the Kyrie or the Agnus Dei. Finally, the Kyrie and the dismissal (*Ite, missa est*) were frequently set to the same chant melody and could thus easily be paired in polyphonic settings. Once selected for pairing, ordinary settings were furnished with shared musical characteristics like those of the Kyrie and Ite, ranging from the general (common mode, similar vocal complement, and ranges) to the more particular (common textural styles, mensuration schemes, or even, occasionally, a joint fund of melodic ideas).

A Gloria and a Credo from the Ivrea manuscript show many of these common features. They were in all likelihood conceived and executed as a pair by the anonymous composer, although they are not presented that way in the manuscript, where all the Kyries are grouped together for ease of reference, followed by a section of Glorias, one of Credos, and so on. Their beginnings, together with an incipit showing the original clefs and mensuration signs, are given in Ex. 9-12.

The clefs (which determine the vocal ranges) and the mensurations are among the factors linking them. They also share a final (D, making them Dorian or "minorish" pieces), which means that they will also share characteristic melodic turns and cadential patterns. Finally, they are both cast in the top-down cantilena texture. Only the top part is texted, which of course favors clarity of enunciation. The tenor and contratenor were probably meant to be vocalized, but the church organ could also have been used

EX. 9-11 Guymont, Kyrie

EX. 9-12   Original incipits and opening phrases in transcription

a. Ivrea 26 (Gloria)

EX. 9-12B   Ivrea 52 (Credo)

to accompany a soloist. Scholars are still debating this and many other points of "performance practice."

Of course the two pieces do not have everything in common. Each has its distinguishing characteristics, each makes its own expressive gestures. And yet the similarities between the settings far outweigh their differences, and quite deliberately so. Pairing like this served a purpose. The Gloria and the Credo sampled in Ex. 9-12 enclosed between them a significant portion of the service: the *synaxis*, given over to scriptural readings. The recurrence of familiar musical sounds to pace and punctuate the service added an extra level of inspiring ceremonial to it. There is a Sanctus in the Apt manuscript — see Ex. 9-13 for its incipit and opening phrase — that is even more similar in its melodic contents to certain portions of the Ivrea Credo than the Ivrea Gloria. It might well have been modeled on the Credo, to secure an additional return to familiar sounds that would thus inspiritingly organize even more of the service, encompassing the beginning of the Eucharist as well. Basing one polyphonic piece on

EX. 9-13   Incipit and beginning of A siglum. Apt 27 (Sanctus)

another like this was called *parody*, from the Greek for "alter the song." It did not at this point have any connotation of satire.

By the "middle third" of the century (ca. 1335–70), the Avignon styles had spread throughout France. The Agnus Dei sampled in Ex. 9-14 comes from a manuscript that originated in Cambrai, at the far northern end of the kingdom, near the border of what was then the Duchy of Burgundy. It is in the "simultaneous" or homorhythmic style reminiscent of the conductus, and like the conductus it carries a single liturgical text in all voices. That, plus the uniform rhythm producing chord progressions in which the individual lines are blended, suggests the possibility of choral performance. If that was indeed an option for this music, then we are dealing with the earliest choral polyphony in the European tradition. (Still, the earliest explicit call for *chorus* — as opposed to *unus*, "one" singer — in polyphonic church music is not found until nearly a century later, in Italian manuscripts of the 1430s.)

VOTIVE FORMULARIES

Another spur to the composition of Mass Ordinary settings was the growth of votive Masses — Masses celebrated not according to the church calendar but on special occasions. Such an occasion might be institutional, such as the dedication of a church or the installation of a bishop. Or it might be personal, marking the Christian sacraments or rites of passage (birth, christening, marriage, burial). Or — and this was the most frequent reason of all — it might be a posthumous memorial service. To have such a Mass celebrated in church on one's own behalf or on behalf of a loved one, one had to purchase it with a donation. Many votive Masses were "Lady Masses," Masses in honor of "Our Lady" (Notre Dame) the Virgin Mary, the intercessor supreme.

EX. 9-14 Agnus Dei from Cambrai, 1328 (Fascicle IV, no. 1), mm. 1–18

The earliest complete polyphonic Mass Ordinaries were votive formularies that were collected together and copied into special manuscripts for use in memorial chapels where votive Masses were offered on behalf of donors. Polyphonic votive Masses were the deluxe models, available to major donors who could afford the extra expense of skilled singers along with the best quality vestments, incense, altar cloths, and communion fare. The same manuscripts that contain them often contain monophonic formularies as well, for the less powerful or pecunious. The polyphonic Mass Ordinary, in short, was one of the finer fruits of a somewhat dubious practice—the practice of buying and selling the good offices of the church that, grown into an abuse, became one of the precipitating causes of the sixteenth-century Reformation.

Polyphonic Ordinaries for use at votive services come down to us in manuscripts from several ecclesiastical centers within the Avignon orbit. There is a "Mass of Toulouse" from the old capital of Languedoc, a hundred miles or so to the west of Avignon itself. There is a "Sorbonne Mass" from Paris. There is a "Barcelona Mass" from below the Pyrenees. They vary somewhat in their specific contents, but all of them contain a Kyrie, a Sanctus, and an Agnus Dei as a nucleus. The Barcelona Mass has a Gloria and a Credo as well, and the Toulouse Mass ends with a motet laid out over the Deo Gratias.

These were not cyclic compositions, however, but composites. They were not composed by a single author, or even composed for the specific purpose at hand. Their components were merely selected and assembled from the general fund of Avignon-style Mass Ordinary settings; individual items from these Masses turn up elsewhere, in other formularies or in miscellanies like the Apt and Ivrea codices.

The most complete and elaborate of these composite Mass-assemblages, one that Machaut must surely have known and possibly taken as a model, was the so-called "Mass of Tournai" from a Belgian (then Burgundian) cathedral town not at all far from Machaut's home city of Reims. A full set of six items, it was gathered together in 1349 for use at Lady Masses that were available to donors at a special altar that had been set aside for the purpose in the right transept or side-wing of the Tournai cathedral building.

The Mass is a stylistic hodgepodge of local favorites. The Kyrie is uncomplicated and somewhat archaic: its -note-against-note homorhythm is practically virgin-pure and its durational patterns are virtually modal (iambic, or "second mode"). Given a syllabic text it might have passed for a century-old conductus. Like the simplest chant Kyries it contains four brief musical sections to fill out a ninefold repetition scheme: a Kyrie for singing threefold; a Christe for singing threefold; a second Kyrie to be repeated once; and a final, somewhat more elaborate Kyrie to conclude. Its final is G.

The Gloria is cast in a texture that straddles the line between homorhythm and cantilena. What tips the balance in favor of the latter is the spread of vocal ranges, with the somewhat more active top voice occupying the octave above middle C, and the other two voices overlapping a somewhat lower tessitura, as a tenor/contratenor pair would do. There is a lengthy, melismatic Amen with motetlike features including a rhythmically stratified texture and some little bursts of hocket. The final of the Gloria is F.

The Credo is unambiguously homorhythmic, the three voices spitting out the lengthy text in lockstep, often in strings of uniform semibreves. The punctuation of the text is faithfully followed, each sentence being marked off from the surrounding ones by little textless bridge passages in the two lower voices. The final is D.

The Sanctus and Agnus Dei were pretty clearly composed as a pair. They collectively revert to the archaic style of the Kyrie, but their final is F, not G. And then, all of a sudden, the response to the Ite missa est is cast, as in the Toulouse Mass, as a full-fledged isorhythmic motet over a liturgical cantus firmus. It would have made Pope John XXII see red, for it sports an "upper part made of secular songs" in the form of a French-texted triplum about self-abasing service to the ladylove (here, of course, to be taken metaphorically as addressed not to the poet's lady but to Our Lady). The Latin motetus contains a more straightforward votive prayer on behalf of the donor, uttered, significantly, not to the Virgin but to her minions, the "lords" of the church, from whom indulgences and benefices flowed.

CI COMMENCE LA MESSE DE NOSTRE DAME

"Here beginneth the Mass of Our Lady," reads the heading following the motet section in one of Machaut's most sumptuous personally supervised manuscripts. It, too, was a votive Mass, one that the composer himself endowed with a bequest, to serve as a memorial to "Guillaume and Jean de Machaux [*sic*], both brothers and canons of the church of Our Lady (*l'eglise de Notre Dame*) of Reims." So reads the preface to an eighteenth-century copy of the composer's cathedral epitaph, which went on to quote a provision of his will stating that he had left three hundred florins to ensure "that the prayer for the dead, on every Saturday, for their souls and for those of their friends, may be said by a priest about to celebrate faithfully, at the side altar, a Mass *which is to be sung*" (italics added). In fact, the will was honored (though not with the music originally provided) until the middle of the eighteenth century.

So Machaut's Mass was intended to serve the same purpose as were the other Ordinary formularies of the period. (The familiar conjecture that it was composed for the Coronation of Charles V of France, which happened to take place at Reims in 1364, is still occasionally repeated but has long been discredited). And the detailed description of the Mass of Tournai given above is also, to an astonishing degree, a description of Machaut's Mass.

Although it is the work of a single author, it is no less a composite than the other Ordinaries of its time. Like the others, it is modally disparate: the final of the first three sections is D (minorish), while that of the last three is F (majorish). Like the Tournai Mass, it has a Gloria and Credo that contrast stylistically with the other components, and contrast in precisely the same way. The Gloria is a cantilena bordering on homorhythm, but with a grand motetlike Amen replete with hockets; the Credo is in a more rigorously homorhythmic style. Both movements have the same textless bridging passages as in the Tournai Credo. Again as in the Tournai Mass, the Sanctus and the Agnus Dei form an actual pair and are stylistically related to the Kyrie — but in a different mode. Yet again as in the Tournai Mass, the Kyrie is composed in four sections whose repetitions fill a ninefold scheme.

FIG. 9-3   Reims Cathedral, where Machaut lived and worked during the last thirty years of his life.

Yet however similar it may be to its predecessors and counterparts, Machaut's Mass is incomparably more ambitious. Although it lacks an actual motet (say, for the dismissal, where the singing of motets had apparently become customary), it has, throughout, a "specific gravity," so to speak, that bears comparison with contemporary motet composition, and in this it stood alone among the Ordinary settings of the fourteenth century. Partly that gravity is the result of the heightened emphasis given motetlike architectonics: the Kyrie, Sanctus, Agnus Dei, and Ite missa est are all based on isorhythmic tenors derived from canonical plainchant; within these large divisions, moreover, several subsections are pan-isorhythmic, with repeating taleas in all parts.

But architectural design and duration are not the only dimensions in which Machaut's Mass is remarkably big. The work is more sonorous than any of its counterparts as well, being cast throughout in the four-part texture identified in the previous chapter as the "luxuriant" style. It is a texture that crosscut traditional genres, adding both a high supplementary voice (endemic to the motet) and a low one (endemic to the cantilena) to round out the essential counterpoint of cantus (here called the triplum) and tenor.

With four elaborate movements in motet style, one quasi cantilena, and one quasi conductus, Machaut's Mass stands as a summa of contemporary compositional technique. Historically speaking, it is much more tellingly viewed as a culmination of a half-century of Avignon-oriented liturgical composition than as a dry run at the fifteenth century's cyclic Masses. Yet it is nevertheless something more than a summary of existing possibilities. The unprecedented four-part chordal textures of the Gloria and Credo explore novel sonorities and establish new possibilities. An attempt to account for a work of such heterogeneous complexity in all of its historical and technical dimensions is beyond the scope of a chapter like this, but sampling the strikingly contrasting Kyrie (Ex. 9-15) and Gloria (Ex. 9-16a), the only sections of the Ordinary that are performed in direct sequence, will in their very contrast at least register the

EX. 9-15   Guillaume de Machaut, *La messe de Nostre Dame*, Kyrie, mm. 1–27

EX. 9-15 (*continued*)

EX. 9-16A   Guillaume de Machaut, *La messe de Nostre Dame*, Gloria, mm. 1–29

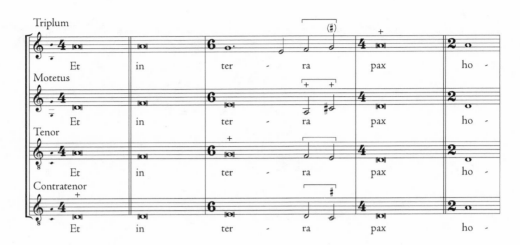

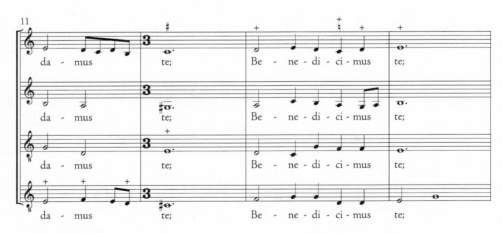

EX. 9-16A (*continued*)

Mass's stylistic extremes. The little dismissal response (Ex. 9-17) has been thrown in, too, as a reminder of the Mass's modal heterogeneity, and its consequent status as an irreducible sum of functional parts rather than the kind of unified whole we may be more in the habit of seeking (and therefore finding) in a work reputed to be a masterpiece.

KYRIE

The Kyrie is built around the same cantus firmus as the Kyrie from the Faenza Codex sampled in Ex. 9-9: the famous *Cunctipotens genitor* melody, which we have encountered by now in several guises. In the *Kyriale*, the official book of Ordinary chants, it is assigned to Mass IV, a lavish tenth-century formulary reserved for feasts of "double" rank. The fact that a setting of it is found in Faenza raises the possibility of *alternatim*

EX. 9-16B   Guillaume de Machaut, *La messe de Nostre Dame*, Gloria, final Amen

EX. 9-16B *(continued)*

EX. 9-17 Guillaume de Machaut, *La messe de Nostre Dame: Ite, missa est*

EX. 9-17 (continued)

performance with Machaut's Kyrie—a kind of responsorial performance in which sections sung in polyphony alternate with sections played on the organ or sung in plainchant. The Faenza setting is in fact the earliest presumed documentation of the practice, which became very widespread in the fifteenth century, especially in Italy and Germany.

This is not to imply that Machaut had any intention or premonition of such a thing. On the contrary, his unambiguous use of repetition signs shows clearly that his intention was to repeat his polyphonic settings rather than interpolate organ verses according to a practice he may or may not have known about. And yet the choice of the same cantus firmus for the Kyrie in Faenza, which contains other compositions by Machaut and his contemporaries, nevertheless suggests the possibility that the Faenza Kyrie may have been intended for insertion—or at least that it could have been inserted—into Machaut's very distinguished Mass. Despite its fame, in the early fifteenth century nobody regarded the work as an inviolable or canonical "classic" in our current sense of the word; such a concept did not yet exist. Machaut's Mass—any Mass—was functional music and as such was adaptable to circumstances and to local requirements.

In the first section of Machaut's setting (shown in Ex. 9-15) the *Cunctipotens genitor* melody, carried of course by the tenor, is cut up into bite-sized taleae of archaic cast: they actually correspond to "third mode" (LBBL) *ordines* as described a century earlier by Garlandia, with whose treatise a well-educated musician like Machaut had to be familiar. The contratenor, too, is composed of short recurring rhythmic "cells," although they are not strictly enough organized to be considered isorhythmic. Isorhythmic or no, there is a great deal of rhythmic repetition: the rhythmically active triplum at mm. 7–12, for example, a passage encompassing two measures of syncopation and one of hocket, is exactly mimicked by the rhythms in mm. 20–24; moreover, two measures in the same repeated passage—compare mm. 10–11 and mm. 22–23—are pan-isorhythmic (rhythmically identical in all parts).

The Christe section introduces a new level of rhythmic energy—syncopated, hockety minims—into the two uppermost parts. In the triplum it is the extremes of rhythmic activity—full-measure longs and rapid hockets—that recur most strictly. The most striking rhythmic effect—and a characteristic one—is that of wild activity regularly hitting the brick wall of utter stasis. Machaut was far from the only composer of his time to revel in this sort of radical rhythmic contrast. It displays the potentialities of the Ars Nova at maximum strength.

GLORIA

As a result of several recent discoveries, the Gloria of Machaut's Mass has emerged as perhaps the most fascinating "movement" of all. It was long thought to be a conductus-style setting like the Credo (perhaps modeled, like it, on the Credo of the Mass of Tournai). Recently, however, it has been demonstrated—by the American scholar Anne Walters Robertson, a historian of medieval musical liturgies—that it is a polyphonic setting of the Gloria that follows the Kyrie Cunctipotens in Mass IV, the same tenth-century "doubles" formulary.[2] The reason Machaut's use of this melody went undetected so long is that the version he used was the version he knew: that of the Reims service books of his time, not the reconstructed "original" version found in the printed chant books of the twentieth century.

Following on this initial discovery was an even more remarkable one, that Machaut did not use the preexisting tune in the traditional manner of a cantus firmus but instead paraphrased it—a technique that involved both embellishing and streamlining it, making it yet harder to detect—and, rather than confining it to the tenor, allowed it to migrate freely throughout the texture. A paraphrased chant is not only embellished but also cast in a rhythmic and melodic style approximating that of the contemporary "song" or (or *cantus*) style; that is one reason why Machaut's Gloria now tends to get classified as a cantilena rather than a conductus. Another is its pattern of open and closed cadences, which seems to fall into an AAB pattern repeated fourfold, reminding scholars of a strophic canso or ballade. Yet the work does not really conform to any ready-made category; it is a unique synthesis. The first of its main (AAB) sections is given in Ex. 9-16a.

Like all polyphonic settings of the Gloria, it begins with the words *Et in terra pax* ("And on earth, peace. . ."), because that is where the choir began to sing. (The opening phrase, "Glory to God in the highest," was traditionally an intonation sung by the priest or "celebrant," and so it had to remain in any properly liturgical setting.) In the score given in Ex. 9-16b, the polyphonic paraphrase is indicated by the use of little crosses ('+') above the chant-derived notes. Machaut was not in any real sense "quoting" the Gregorian chant, and it is altogether questionable whether he meant the paraphrase to be detected. It was, rather, a scaffolding device—there for the sake of (and of concern to) the builder, not the eventual users of the building.

The Amen (Ex. 9-16b) is a different story. From a fairly short chant melisma Machaut generated a very lengthy polyphonic one in "pseudomotet" style. "Pseudo" because the tenor is not really based on the plainsong but consists, rather, of a series of free variations on the plainsong's basic melodic shape, a leap up a fourth from the final and a stepwise return. And although the texture clearly reverts to the motet style of the Kyrie, with the tenor in lengthy note values that suggest bottom-up cantus firmus technique, there is no actual isorhythm, and no necessity therefore, of laying the tenor out as an actual foundation. The steady rhythmic diminution from a beginning in longs and breves to a concluding blaze of hocketing and syncopating minims (with an especially conspicuous flurry just where one least expects it, in the contratenor) is another playfully motettish touch: it mimics the behavior of a motet without actually being one.

DISMISSAL

The tiny dismissal response (Ex. 9-17), like the penultimate section of the Kyrie, is a sixteen-measure composition exactly bisected into two taleae (plus the unmeasured final note, conventionally written as a long but held like a fermata until cut off). The tenor and contratenor are once again the most rigorously isorhythmic voices, with the others most apt to repeat their rhythms when those rhythms are most distinctive. The second half of each talea (mm. 5–8 and 13–16), where most of the hockets and syncopes occur, is fully pan-isorhythmic. Balancing that, during the first three measures of each talea (mm. 1–3, 9–11) the tenor and contratenor are briefly identical in pitch as well as rhythm. Near symmetry, near congruence, near uniformity—that is the very interesting interactive space, between sameness and difference, that Machaut loved to explore.

SUBTILITAS

Machaut's art, like all "high" art in aristocratic France, was a connoisseur's art: an art of *literati* whose tastes were flattered by tours de force. Such a taste flattered the artist as well, and encouraged the fashioning, even in "secular" contexts, of complex artworks full of hidden meanings and arcane structural relationships. One might even look upon the musico-poetic legacy of the Ars Nova as another resurgence of the *trobar clus* favored by the noblest troubadours—"artistic art," as an early twentieth-century philosopher, José Ortega y Gasset, put it in trying to come to grips with the artistic avant-garde of his own day. The seeming redundancy of the expression is actually very apt. As Ortega explained, indulging his own elitism by using a fashionably obscure Greek term for "the common people," artistic art is "an art for artists and not for the masses, for 'quality' and not for *hoi polloi*." Its outstanding feature is *subtilitas*.

The easiest way of translating the word *subtilitas* into English would be to give its cognate, "subtlety." The word literally denotes fineness and delicacy, which are already aristocratic values (as anyone knows who knows the story of the princess and the pea). From the artistic point of view, even more pertinent are the word's connotations—the meanings it suggests by analogy or indirection. These include both allusiveness and elusiveness, qualities that point to something easily missed (as when we speak of "subtle wit" or "subtle irony"); or something faint and mysteriously suggestive (as when we speak of "a subtle smile"); or something requiring mental acuteness or agility to perceive (as when we speak of "a subtle point" in argument). In most general terms, the word suggests a focus on the small, on details.

Machaut created several works notable for intellectual cleverness and intricacy of detail. Of these the most famous was a "rondeau," the complete text of which reads as follows:

A	*Ma fin est mon commencement*	My end is my beginning
B	*et mon commencement ma fin*	and my beginning my end
a	*Et teneure vraiement.*	And this holds truly. (Or: And truly the tenor.)
A	*Ma fin est mon commencement*	My end is my beginning.
a	*Mes tiers chans trois fois seulement*	My third voice gets to reverse itself only
b	*se retrograde et einsi fin.*	three times before the end.
A	*Ma fin est mon commencement*	My end is my beginning
B	*et mon commencement ma fin.*	and my beginning my end.

But this is not really a rondeau at all, nor is the text really a text. The original notation of the piece, as entered in one of Machaut's personally supervised manuscripts, is shown in Fig. 9-4. The whole piece is transcribed as Ex. 9-18. For maximum amusement, compare the explanation that follows with the original notation before looking at the transcription.

The "text," although it makes reference to a famous religious proverb about eternity, is really a description of the piece, or a direction (rubric) for performance. The piece is notated as a rondeau among Machaut's other rondeaux as a sort of joke. The whole point of the piece is the strange way in which its first half ("my beginning") relates to its second half ("my end"), the rondeau being the one fixed form whose two halves, unlike those of the ballade, are played straight through, and whose final cadence, unlike the virelai's, comes at the end of the second half.

The piece is notated in two parts, but the text refers to the "third part," so we know that there is an unnotated part. That third part is labeled contratenor, so we know that the unnotated part is the tenor, of which we read that its end is its beginning. The contratenor is only half as long as the other notated part (the cantus), and we are told

FIG. 9-4   Guillaume de Machaut's rondeau *Ma fin est mon commencement*, as it appears on folio 136 of Paris, Bibliothèque Nationale, MS Fonds Français 9221, a manuscript containing the collected works of Machaut, copied for Jean Duc de Berry (d. 1416). The song begins on the fourth notated line. Only two of its three parts are written down: one without text (incorrectly labeled "Tenor" in this source; it should read "Contratenor," as it does in other manuscripts); the other with the text upside down and to be read backward (forming the tenor), while another performer reads it normally (forming the cantus). Only the first half of the (contra)tenor is given. At the point where it ends (the three-note ligature at the beginning of the fifth notated line), the musician reading it is to reverse direction and perform it again from back (*fin*) to front (*commencement*).

that it reverses itself. So we have a hint that it must double back on itself for "complete" statements of the two halves (AB) within the rondeau form, of which (the text reminds us) there are three. So this doubling-back or going backwards must also be the way the unnotated tenor is to be derived from the notated cantus. (Proceeding backward was known as *cancrizans* motion after the word for "crab," an animal evidently thought in those days to walk backward rather than sideways.) Thus the whole song can be "realized" from the rubric: Accompany the cantus with its own cancrizans (and note that when this is done, the tenor actually behaves like a tenor at the final cadence), and supplement the contratenor with *its* cancrizans to fill out the required length.

EX. 9-18   Guillaume de Machaut, *Ma fin est mon commencement* in transcription

EX. 9-18   (continued)

The result is what is given in the transcription. It is the sort of thing Machaut would have called a *resolutio*: an explicitly written-out (therefore "unsubtle") solution to a puzzle he expected adept musicians to solve directly from his incomplete notation and the textual hints. The joy of the piece consists not only in the enjoyment of its pretty sounds but in the triumph over unnecessary but delightful obstacles. One enjoys the puzzle-solving process as well as the result. Without the process the result would not be as enjoyable, just as without the hurdles an obstacle race would not be as exciting. And there we see the relationship between art and sport, something else that can be done (when not done "professionally") entirely for its own sake, and which, since it requires skill, is most thrilling to doer and spectator alike when it is most difficult. That principle of creative virtuosity is the root principle of *trobar clus*.

CANON

Another word for a rubric like the "text" in this eccentric "rondeau"—especially one that, as here, enables the reader to deduce a concealed (because unnotated) voice-part—is *canon*. It is a Latinized Greek word that originally meant a stiff straight rod, and by extension came to mean, in the first place, a measuring rod, then anything that sets a standard or imposes a rule.

We know the word "canon" best, of course, in a different connection: to us it means a composition in which at least two parts are related by strict melodic imitation. But that modern, familiar musical meaning is actually a direct extension of the earlier meaning, since when two parts are in strict imitation, only one of them need be written down. The other can be "deduced" with the aid of a rubric or some other sign that directs one performer to sing the same part as another but enter later; or enter later and a fifth higher; or enter later, a fifth higher, and twice as slowly; or enter later, a fifth higher and twice as slowly, beginning with the last note and proceeding to the first with all the intervals inverted. To realize the unnotated part you have to follow the directions given by the "canon." A piece with parts in strict imitation was thus "a piece with a canon," and eventually just "a canon."

There is of course a large unwritten repertory of simple imitative pieces sung for amusement. Anyone reading this book probably has known at least a few since childhood: "Row, row, row your boat," or "Frère Jacques," or "Hi ho, nobody home." They are the simplest of all polyphonic pieces for a group of children to learn, because you only have to learn one melody to sing all the parts. And while they have a definite beginning, they have no end—or rather, no composed ending. (They usually end in giggles or elbows-jabbed-in-ribs rather than in cadences.) Such songs just go round and round—whence their name, of course. (The Latin for a "round" is *rota*; we will encounter a famous example shortly.) What we call canons are usually far more complex and artful—often artful to the point of tour de force—and depend on writing both to get made and to get learned. They are fully finished works with composed endings as well as beginnings. And sure enough, such pieces came into their own, along with so many other tour-de-force genres, precisely in the fourteenth century. The original French name for them was *chace* (compare *chasse* in modern French), and it was a pun. The word is a cognate of the English "chase," which describes the behavior of the successively entering voices in a canon, each running after the last. The primary French meaning of *la chasse*, however, is "the hunt," and it is reflected in the novel subject matter of several *chaces* (and even more so, as we shall see, in the cognate Italian genre, the *caccia*).

There are four chaces in the Ivrea manuscript which, as we know, otherwise contains mainly Mass ordinary settings for the use of Avignon. One of them, *Se je chant mains*, begins with ironic reflections on its own departure from the customary topic of courtly song: "If I sing less of my lady than usual... it is for love of falcons." What follows is a three-part description of a falcon hunt, in which the middle section is truly a tour de force, but of a wholly new and off-beat type: a riot of hockets set to "words" mixing French, bird-language, and hound-language in an onomatopoetical mélange (Ex. 9-19). The interval of imitation in this *chace* is represented in the transcription as 21/2 measures; hence, the music sung by the top voice at the beginning of Ex. 9-19 turns up in the second voice in the middle of the third bar, and in the third voice at the beginning of the sixth bar. The use of onomatopoeia (imitation of natural sounds) in the hocket-ridden middle section of a *chace* became a standard feature: one of the other chaces in Ivrea has cuckoo calls in that place, and a third, *Tres dous compains, levez vous* ("Dearest companions, get up"), has an elaborate *carole* or circle dance for a middle section, replete with imitations of rustic instruments. (To a noble aesthete, one should realize, dancing peasants and the music they played were a part of "nature" — an attitude that persisted at least until the eighteenth century.)

The chace reached a pinnacle with Machaut, who incorporated it into two of his nineteen narrative and descriptive poems known as *lais*. The form of a lai, one may recall, was similar to that of the liturgical sequence, consisting of a series of paired versets or couplets, each pair set to a new melody or formula. In his *Lai de confort* ("Lay of Succor"), Machaut allowed the form of the poem to be entirely absorbed into a continuous three-part *chace* texture. In the *Lai de la fonteinne* ("Lay of the fountain"),

EX. 9-19   *Se je chant mains*, middle section

EX. 9-19 *(continued)*

only the even-numbered couplets are set as chaces, so that the use of the polyphonic genre actually serves to articulate and highlight the poetic form.

And not only the form but the sense as well, which it symbolizes on an allegorical plane transcending the "materialistic" onomatopoeia of the Ivrea chaces. Machaut's Lay of the Fountain is a meditation, by a lover whose lady has rejected him and who seeks solace in divine love, on the mysteries of the Virgin birth and the consubstantiality of the Holy Trinity — three Persons in one Godhead. The image of the fountain appears in the fourth pair of verses, the second to be set as a chace. It is a trinitarian metaphor: "Imagine a fountain, a stream, and a canal; they are three, but the three make one; a single water through all three must run." Just so, the chace serves as the metaphor's metaphor: a single melody running through all three voices in a musical representation of *trinus in unitate* ("three in one"), the verbal emblem of the Trinity (Ex. 9-20).

The manuscript source contains only the single melody, with signs near the beginning to indicate the second and third entrances, and another set of signs near the end to indicate the finishing notes for the second and third voices. Possibly another level of trinitarian symbolism, but certainly a source of aural delight, is the elegant use of hockets. A single line, of course, can no more sing hockets than a single hand can clap. The line is full of strategically placed rests, however; when it is sung by itself it seems full of holes that are plugged by the other voices when the hocket texture is complete. Thus, the single line attains fullness only when complemented by its two canonic counterparts, as the full concept of Godhead subsumes the three persons of Father, Son, and Holy Spirit. The theological message is entrancingly — yes, sensuously — delivered by the delicately wrought contrapuntal texture, the three statements of the tune fitting together like pieces in an aural jigsaw puzzle. That is *harmony* in the most literal, etymological sense. Like the Trinity itself, a well-wrought chace can be far more than the sum of its parts; and this particular chace is possibly Machaut's greatest feat of *subtilitas*.

EX. 9-20   Guillaume de Machaut, Chace 4 from *Lai de la fonteinne*

EX. 9-20 *(continued)*

EX. 9-20 (*continued*)

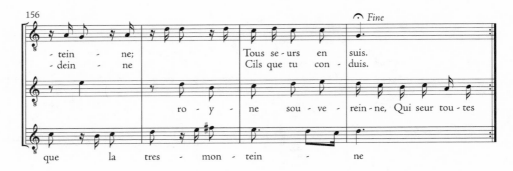

This three-in-one is not difficult to fathom;
I can explain it well enough:
Consider a fountain,
a brook, a canal.
They are three, yet these three
are deemed but one, whether large or small,
whether a vat or merely a bucket in size,
the container carries a single water
of a certain flavor.
Of this you may be sure.

O noble queen,
who illuminatest
all dark places
more brightly than the pole star,
you have given the water
and all the sweet fruits of life
human form in thy body.
Without pain
and beyond the reach of fate
are those who follow you.

ARS SUBTILIOR

The *subtilitas* with which Machaut expressed his implicitly aristocratic outlook on art and culture took an explicit and even somewhat technocratic turn in the work of the generations of poets and musicians who followed him, and who looked upon him as a creative father. One of the leading French poets at the end of the fourteenth century, Eustache Deschamps (ca. 1346–ca. 1407), the author of over a thousand ballades, actually labeled himself Machaut's apprentice, successor, and heir.[3] (According to at least one authority he was even more than that: he was reputed to be Machaut's nephew.) In his treatise *Art de Dictier et de Fere Chançons* ("The art of poetry and making songs") of 1392, Deschamps purported to transmit his master's teachings.

Most of the book concerns what Deschamps called *musique naturele* or "natural music," meaning poetic versification. (This was a time-honored use of the word "music"; recall St. Augustine's treatise *De Musica*, which concerned nothing but the meters of what we would call spoken poetry.) Nor is Deschamps known to have been what we would call a composer. But in one passage he juxtaposes *musique naturele* with *musique artificiele* or "artful music," that is, music as we would use the term. While either music can be practiced by itself, and while either is pleasant to hear, they achieve their fullest beauty, Deschamps maintains, in "marriage," through which "melodies are more ennobled and made more seemly with the words than they would be alone," and "poems are made more delightful and embellished by the melody and the tenors, trebles, and contratenors of music." This may seem an early enunciation of the idea that the various art media are mutually reinforcing and achieve their full potential in synthesis — an idea now typically associated with Romanticism and with Richard Wagner, an opera composer who wrote his own librettos. More likely Deschamps was merely invoking what he and his contemporaries took to be the normal state of affairs, in which poetry implied music and vice versa. The division of the two was an arbitrary rhetorical device that enabled Deschamps to specify what it was that each component — the verbal and the musical — contributed to the overall effect.

So it is noteworthy that the words are described as the bearers of gentility and seemliness — moral qualities — and the notes are the agency of artifice, embellishment, and delight. The period in which Deschamps lived was the period of the final (some say decadent) phase of the Ars Nova — an explosion of convoluted musical artifice and intricate embellishment that, it is often said, reached a height of sumptuous complexity unrivaled until the twentieth century.

To speak of rivalry in this case is quite appropriate, since the whole "explosion" was predicated on the idea of emulation — not just imitation, but the effort to surpass. And since contests of this sort can be objectively won or lost only on the basis of technique, technical virtuosity — in the handling of complex contrapuntal webs, in the contrivance of new rhythmic combinations, in the invention of new notational devices for representing them — became the primary focus. In the name of *subtilitas*, composers at the end of the fourteenth century became involved in a sort of technical arms race.

A treatise on advanced notation (*Tractatus de diversis figuris*) attributed to Philippus (or Philipoctus) de Caserta, an Italian-born composer who flourished around 1370–1390 at the papal court of Avignon, spelled it all out. Philippus wanted to go beyond the limits of Philippe de Vitry's practice, as set out in the *Ars Nova* treatises (and as exemplified by the motets in Ex. 8-1 and 8-3). Where Philippe had posited his four basic tempus/prolation combinations as alternatives, Philippus wanted to be able to combine them all "vertically," that is, as simultaneous polymeters.

To make these polymeters as explicit and unambiguous as possible, Philippus compiled or invented a great slew of bizarre note-forms to supplement the standard time signatures; they involved two (or even three) ink colors, filled and void note-heads, all kinds of tails and flags, sometimes employed in tandem (one extending upward from the note-head, the other down or to the side). He did all this, he said, to achieve a *subtiliorem modum*, a style or way of composing with greater *subtilitas*—with greater refinement, greater decorativeness, greater sophistication, and especially with ever more flamboyant technique. Since the 1960s this style has been called the "Ars subtilior" after Philippus's assertion, following a suggestion by the German musicologist Ursula Günther.[4] Previously it had been called the "mannered style," after the standard—that is, nineteenth-century—terminology of Germanic art history. That name obviously connoted a certain disapproval of excess; the idea of discarding it seemed remarkably timely in the 1960s, when many contemporary composers, especially in the academy, were enthusiastically advancing an *ars subtilior* of their own.

Philippus cast himself demonstratively as Machaut's heir by quoting the text incipit from one of Machaut's ballades, and the refrain of another, in a ballade of his own, *En remirant* ("While gazing at your darling portrait"), of which the first section is shown in Ex. 9-21. The choice of genre was significant: the grand strophic ballade had replaced the motet as the supreme genre for *ars subtilior* composers. The incipit of Philippus's ballad (both words and music) was later quoted in turn by Ciconia, the migrant Fleming whom we met in chapter 8, and who may have been Philippus's pupil. Thus did composers seek to establish and maintain dynasties of prestige. Ex. 9-22 shows the quotation from *En remirant* in Ciconia's virelai *Sus un fontayne* ("Beneath a spring. . ."). The quotations from Machaut come in the third strophe of Philippus's text, not shown in the example.

EX. 9-21 Philippus de Caserta, *En remirant* (ballade)

EX. 9-21 (*continued*)

The other way in which composers established prestige, of course, was through the sheer virtuosity of their composing, manifested at once in their contrapuntal control of very complex rhythmic textures and in their notational ingenuity. Fig. 9-5 shows the original notation of Philippus's ballade. It is not a particularly outlandish example of *ars subtilior* notation, but a representative one. Comparison with Ex. 9-21 will show the kinds of rhythmic stunts composers like Philippus enjoyed contriving and how they were achieved. As usual in this style, the tenor plays straight man to the cantus and

EX. 9-22   Philippus de Caserta, quotation from *En remirant* in Ciconia's ballade *Sus un fontayne*

contratenor, its relatively steady tread supplying an anchor to ground their rhythmic and notational subtleties.

The latter were of four main types. There are lengthy passages in syncopation initiated by innocent-looking little "dots of division," like the one that comes after the second note in the cantus. There is interplay of perfect and imperfect note values, represented by contrasting ink colors (red standing for the opposite of whatever the prevailing mensuration happens to be). The groups of three red semibreves near the beginning of the contratenor (fourth line from the bottom), and in the tenor (its single color shift), show this relationship of perfect and imperfect in most basic terms: the three red (imperfect) semibreves equal the same length of time as two black (perfect) ones. This very common and characteristic 3:2 proportion was called *hemiola* (from the Greek) or *sesquialtera* (from the Latin), both meaning "one-and-a-half."

There are superimposed and juxtaposed time signatures throughout. Most of them involve the two signatures that represented the extremes of mensural practice: ⊙, which denoted perfection at every specified level, and C, which denoted imperfect divisions at every specified level. The latter signature, moreover, is reversed to Ɔ, a diminution (reduced value) sign that could have various meanings depending on the context. Here it means that all values are halved, so that there are four minims rather than two in the time of a normal semibreve. There is a lovely little passage in which the three voices all go into diminished imperfect time, but not together: first the cantus (near the end of the first line in Fig. 9-5, on the words "en laquel"); then the contratenor, near the end of *its* first line (fourth up from the bottom of the page); and, finally, even the tenor, as if nudged by the other parts, bestirs itself for just four notes, its one and only signature change.

Finally, there are the *ad hoc* note shapes without which no self-respecting *ars subtilior* composition would be complete. There are two such shapes in *En remirant*, both borrowed, as it happens, from the Italian-style notation at which we will take a look in the next chapter. What seem like minims with stems down (near the end of the "A" section in the cantus, and again on its "rhyming" repeat near the end of the "B" section) are *sesquitertia* semibreves, meaning that four of them take the normal time of three. And the curious red notes with stems both up and down (called *dragmas*) near the end of the second line in the cantus are *sesquitertia* minims, reproducing the same 4:3 relationship at a higher level of rhythmic activity.

Perhaps you have noticed that the red dragmas mean the same thing as minims under Ɔ. Such redundancy is typical of *ars subtilior* notation and proves that notation as such was for composers like Philippus a focus of "research and development" in its own right.

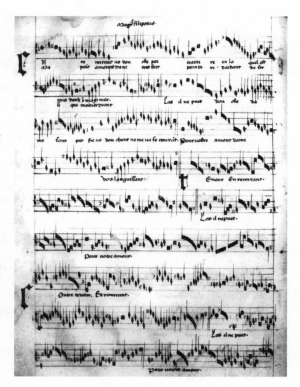

FIG. 9-5 *Ars subtilior*. Philippus de Caserta's ballade *En remirant*, as notated in Modena, Biblioteca Estense, MS α.M.5.24, copied in Bologna ca. 1410 (fol. 34v). The notes that look gray were entered in red ink.

That kind of showy overcomplexity is just the sort of excess—an excess of fantasy, perhaps, or maybe just an excess of one-upsmanship—that earned the *ars subtilior* its reputation as a "mannered" or "decadent" style. Many modern scholars seem to find it annoying as well as fascinating (perhaps because overcomplexity is a vice from which scholars have not invariably been immune). Contemporary audiences seem to have found it agreeable.

BERRY AND FOIX

But of course sobriquets like "decadent" imply judgment not only on the music, the musicians, and the notation they employed, but also on the audiences, which is to say the society that supported such a rarefied art. *Ars subtilior* composition flourished in two main centers. One was the south of France, the territory of old Aquitaine, whose traditions of *trobar clus* it was in a sense upholding. This territory included papal Avignon, as we know, as well as the duchy of Berry and the county of Foix at the foot of the Pyrenees, where Gaston III (known as Fébus, after Phoebus Apollo, the Olympian sun god), governor of Languedoc, maintained a court of legendary extravagance. The chronicler Jehan Froissart, one of Gaston's protégés, endorsed his patron's boast, made about 1380, that during the fifty years of his lifetime there had been more feats and marvels to relate than in the preceding 300 years of history. The *ars subtilior* is best understood, perhaps, as an expression of that culture of feats and marvels.

Like Froissart, many of the poet-composers of the *ars subtilior* worked under Gaston's protection and memorialized him in their work. One such court composer—Jehan Robert, who in the riddling spirit of the times signed his work "Trebor"—proclaimed in a grand ballade, suitably full of marvelous feats of syncopation and polymeter, that "if Julius Caesar, Roland, and King Arthur were famous for their conquests, and Lancelot and Tristan for their ardor, today all are surpassed in arms, renown and nobility by the one whose watchword is 'Phoebus, advance!'"

That ballade, like most of the grandiose dedicatory ballades that survive from its time and place, is found in a marvelous late fourteenth-century manuscript, a real feat of calligraphy that, having once belonged to Le Grand Condé, the great seventeenth-century general, is now kept at the Musée Condé in Chantilly, to the north of Paris. Its southern origins are well attested by its contents: besides the pieces in honor of Gaston Fébus, there are several dedicated to Jean, the Duke of Berry, whose court, located in the city of Bourges, rivaled Gaston's in magnificence. (Jean's fantastically sumptuous breviary or prayer book, known as the "Très riches heures" after the "hours" of the Office, is a well-known testimony to that magnificence; see Fig. 9-6.)

The poet-composer most closely associated with Jean's court, it appears, was a man named Solage, whose dates and even whose first name are unknown, but all ten of whose surviving works are found in the Chantilly codex. Seven of the ten are ballades (three of them making reference to the patron), but Solage's best known work is a bizarre rondeau called *Fumeux fume* ("Smoky smoke"; Ex. 9-23). It

stands out from the whole *ars subtilior* repertory for the way its composer makes a tour de
force out of chromatic harmony (or *musica ficta
causa pulchritudinis*) with the same exploratory
intensity that drove his contemporaries to
their recondite mensural caprices.

Such outlandish chromaticism (as observed in chapter 8) was another legacy of
Machaut, whose style Solage seems deliberately to have copied in several works. The
"smoke" connection was another link, albeit
an indirect one, with the earlier master. The
fumeux were a sort of waggish literary guild
or club, presided over by none other than
Eustache Deschamps, Machaut's self-desig-
nated poetic heir. According to Deschamps's
biographer Hoepffner, this society of whimsical eccentrics met at least from 1366 to 1381,
striving to outdo one another in "smoky"—
recondite or far-out—fancies and conceits.

FIG. 9-6 "The Adoration of the Magi,"
from the *Très riches heures du duc de Berry* (1416).

Solage, with his smoky harmonies and smokier tessitura, may have outdone them
all. Note, as one particular *subtilitas* that distinguishes this droll composition, that the

EX. 9-23 Solage, *Fumeux fume* (rondeau)

EX. 9-23 *(continued)*

A smoker smokes through smoke.
A smoky speculation.

Is, between puffs, his thought:
A smoker smokes through smoke.

For smoking suits him very well
As long as he keeps his intention.
A smoker smokes through smoke.
A smoky speculation.

accidentals drift flatward ("fa-ward") in the first section and sharpward ("mi-ward") in the second. The question of mode is altogether to laugh. The music begins on a concord of G, ends on F, with a middle stop on a ficta note, E-flat — "smoky speculation" indeed!

OUTPOSTS

As unpredictable as the final of *Fumeux fume* was the location of the other main center of *ars subtilior* composition. Cyprus, the most easterly of the major Mediterranean islands, off the southern coast of Turkey and the western coast of Syria, had been conquered during the Third Crusade in 1191 by an army under Richard Lion-Heart, who then bestowed it as a sort of consolation prize on Guy of Lusignan, the deposed ruler of the Latin kingdom of Jerusalem. The French-speaking Lusignan dynasty ruled Cyprus until 1489 when the island fell under the rule of the city-state of Venice. The highpoint of Cypriot French culture was reached at the end of the fourteenth century under King Janus (reigned 1398 – 1432), who in 1411 married the princess Charlotte de Bourbon whose entourage included a musical chapel.

The decade between their marriage and Charlotte's death in 1422 was a period of intense musical activity on the island, memorialized for us by a huge manuscript containing plainchant Masses and Offices and 216 polyphonic compositions in every contemporary French genre — Mass Ordinary settings, Latin and French motets, ballades, rondeaux, and virelais. (The manuscript is now kept at the National Library of Turin in northern Italy.) Although produced entirely by imported French musicians, it was a wholly indigenous repertory, and (with a single exception) a wholly anonymous one. Not one composition from the Cypriot manuscript turns up in any other source.

Ballades are predictably the most numerous genre. The 102 specimens in the Cypriot manuscript are the handiwork of supremely sophisticated craftsmen; one of them, *Sur toutes flours* ("Above all other flowers"), is well known to generations of struggling musicology trainees as the single most ferocious specimen of *ars subtilior* puzzle-notation in existence. The most distinguished body of French-Cypriot music, however, is the group of Mass Ordinary settings, consisting entirely of Glorias and Credos, most of them in musically linked pairs that (unlike such pairs in Western European sources) are entered consecutively, as actual pairs, in the manuscript.

One pair is unified by more than the usual common mode, meter, tessitura and texture. In addition to these, there is also a recurrent pan-isorhythmic passage that crops up twice in the Gloria and three times in the Credo. All the parts go into a threefold talea, jam-packed with syncopations, hemiolas, and hockets between the triplum and the tenor, that lasts an asymmetrical five tempora, followed by a cauda whose rhythms also recur on each appearance of the passage. The tenor, which moves more slowly than the other voices and has a very well-shaped melodic line, is not known to be a cantus firmus, but it may well be a paraphrase of an indigenous French-Cypriot plainchant. Example 9-24 contains the first occurrence of the common pan-isorhythmic passage in the Gloria.

Three Gloria-Credo pairs from a manuscript roughly contemporaneous with the Cypriot codex, by a composer who signed his name "Nicolaus de Radom," bear witness to the spread of Ars Nova styles and genres to the northeast as well as the southeast. Radom is a town midway between Kraków and Warsaw in central Poland, and the manuscripts that contain the works of this Nicolaus (or Mikolaj, as he would have

EX. 9-24   Pan-isorhythm in a French-Cypriot Gloria-Credo pair (MS. Torino, f. 32–33, 34–35)

EX. 9-24   (*continued*)

been christened) were associated with the royal chapel at Kraków, the seat of the joint Polish-Lithuanian Jagiellonian dynasty, one of the great ruling houses of Europe.

The reduced circumstances of present-day Poland — to say nothing of the periods of "partition" in the eighteenth and nineteenth centuries, when its more powerful neighbors divided its territory among themselves and the country simply disappeared from the map — make it all too easy to forget Poland's time in the sun, under the Jagiello kings. In the fifteenth and sixteenth centuries, the joint kingdom of Poland and Lithuania was a great European power, maintaining an empire that reached from the Baltic Sea in the north to the Black Sea in the south.

As a result of its status, and its diplomatic ties with western Europe, Poland had for centuries been an avid importer of polyphonic music from the West. There is even an indigenous Polish manuscript containing Notre Dame compositions of the "Leonin" and "Perotin" generations. Beginning around 1400, however, native Polish musicians began to produce advanced polyphonic music as well as consume it.

Foreign travel in the service of the church may have given them their earliest opportunity to master new styles. Ties between the Polish court and the papacy — and during the Schism, with Rome — were particularly strong. Nicolaus Geraldi de Radom, it so happens, is the name of a priest who was a member of the Roman *curia*, the administrative arm of the papal court, under Pope Boniface IX (reigned 1390–1404). If that is the same Nicolaus de Radom who wrote the Glorias and Credos that were entered into the Kraków manuscripts two decades later, it would explain not only his mastery of the burgeoning international style of his day but several musical details as well.

It has been pointed out, for example, that certain Glorias written in Italy at the height of the Great Schism seem to call attention to it, and to efforts toward its reconciliation, by ejaculating the word *pax* ("Peace!") as a hocket in three voices, each possibly standing for one of the rival claimants to the papal throne, or their negotiators. To the sue-for-peace Glorias in Italian sources — including one by Johannes Ciconia, whose connection with the conciliation of the schism we have already noted — we can add one by Nicolaus de Radom (Ex. 9-25).

EX. 9-25   Nicolaus de Radom, Gloria, mm. 1–20

Nor is this by any means the sort of provincial or primitive composition we might be inclined to expect from an "outlander." Such expectations, being prejudices, need to be faced and fought along with all our other preconceptions about the "main stream" of culture. As if expressly to disprove them, Mikolaj's Gloria is uniquely original among the Mass Ordinary settings we have encountered, for the clever — or should we say "subtle" — way it incorporates the characteristic opening gambit of the *chace*. But that very uniqueness is in its way typical — the typically playful Ars Nova attitude to genres and their potential cross-fertilization. Also typically playful is the rhythmic detail, especially the frequent hemiola shifts — three imperfect semibreves in the time of two perfect ones, indicated in the original with red ink and signaled in the transcription with brackets. Rhythms like these make implicit reference to the dance.

FAUX-NAÏVETÉ

Such references were made explicit in a special subgenre of chansons that stood at the opposite end of the rhetorical spectrum from the high-flown ballades associated with the *ars subtilior*. From the beginning the ballade was the loftiest of the fixed forms — the direct descendent of the noble *canso*, whose stanza structure it retained. The virelai was always the humblest, descending from the *pastorela*, later the *chanson baladé* — the literally danced songs with refrains that accompanied the carole. As we know, even in Machaut's time the virelai remained a largely monophonic genre. By the last quarter of the fourteenth century, even the lowly dance song had begun to put forth some *ars subtilior* plumage — but its "subtleties" were of a sort that accorded with its content. The virelai became the site of sophisticated, even virtuoso, parodies of rustic and "natural" music.

Just as it had been in troubadour times (and just as it would be, say, in the time of Marie Antoinette with her little "peasant village" for rustic play-acting on the palace grounds at Versailles), we are dealing here with the esthetic appropriation of a lifestyle. Adam de la Halle's "Play of Robin and Marion," we may recall, was played neither by nor for Robin and Marion. It was played by professional minstrels for a noble audience who enjoyed sentimentally contrasting the "simplicity" of the happy rustics on display with the artifice and duplicity of their own privileged lives. The anonymous virelai *Or sus, vous dormez trop* ("Get up, Sleepyhead"; Ex. 9-26), with characters suitably named Robin and Joliet, is another happy exercise in unrealistic "naturalism."

We have already noted some of its naturalistic (onomatopoetic) devices in the context of the *chace*, especially the ones in the Ivrea manuscript; and sure enough, Ivrea is among this popular virelai's numerous sources. Everything in it seems drawn from life: the mock-carole in the inner verses (the "B" section), where the text mentions drums (*nacquaires*) and bagpipes (*cornemuses*), and all three parts begin imitating them, even down to the bagpipe's drone in the contratenor; or the punning bird calls, in actual bird-French, in the "turnaround" (*volte*) and refrain (the "A" section), where the lark sings "what God is telling you" (*Que-te-dit-Dieu*), and the goldfinch is heard "making his song" (*fay-chil-ciant*).

Precisely where the birds take over, of course, we get a typical rhythmic "subtlety" — reiterated groups of four minims in the cantus part against a beat of perfect (three-minim) semibreves. This ornithological *sesquitertia* (4:3) proportion, a virtuoso turn for composer and singer alike, is a perfect paradigm of the *faux-naïf*, or patrician mock-simplicity: sophisticated artlessness, high-tech innocence — or, to quote Debussy joshing Stravinsky after seeing the latter's *Rite of Spring*, "primitive music with all modern conveniences."

This virelai, with its vivid, somewhat hedonistic portrayal of benign nature as something to enjoy rather than (as the contemporary motet would have it) to stand in awe of, makes a fitting close to this chapter — not just because it signals a new or a

EX. 9-26   Anon., *Or sus, vous dormez trop* (virelai), mm. 22–30

changed esthetic outlook that will find further expression in the music that will follow, but also because it reminds us that we need to take a closer look at the contemporaneous vernacular music of Italy, where throughout the fourteenth century composers had been celebrating "pleasant places" in song.

"A Pleasant Place": Music of the Trecento

ITALIAN MUSIC OF THE FOURTEENTH CENTURY

VULGAR ELOQUENCE

As we know, the rise of European vernacular literatures began in Aquitaine, toward the end of the eleventh century, with the troubadours. By the end of the twelfth century, there was a significant body of vernacular poetry in French. By the end of the thirteenth century, the current had reached Germany. In all cases, the rise of a vernacular literature was accompanied by the development of song genres as the medium for its performance and dissemination.

Why then, with the marginal (that is, marginally literate) exception of the *lauda*, did Italy wait until the fourteenth century before developing a vernacular literature with its attendant music? The answer seems to be that for a long time the Italian aristocracy preferred their courtly songs in the "original"—that is, Occitan (or, less precisely, Provençal), the language of southern France. Throughout the thirteenth century, Aquitainian troubadours, some of them refugees from the Albigensian Crusades, were officially attached to the feudal courts of northern Italy and to the royal court of Sicily down below, where their work was imitated by local poets who took over not only their models' subject matter and their forms but their language as well. Even Dante, in his unfinished treatise *De vulgari eloquentia* ("On high style in the vernacular") of 1304–1306, tells us that, before making up his mind that it would after all be possible to write poetry of profound intellectual substance in the Tuscan dialect of his native Florence, he, too, had at first planned to use the time-honored and internationally prestigious Occitan tongue.

And yet Dante was also among the earliest writers to attempt a separation of poetry and music, holding that for stylistically ornate, philosophically weighty "cantos" (*canzoni*) in high style, the decorative addition of music would only be a distraction. He advocated the creation of special "mediocre" (that is, "in-between") genres of pastoral *poesia per musica*—bucolic, descriptive poetry that would not be the main attraction, so to speak, but would furnish an elegant pretext for the creation of a secular music that, unimpeded by great verse, might itself aim higher than ever. Thus the Italian song genres, when they were at last established in the fourteenth century, gave rise from the beginning to a predominantly polyphonic and exceptionally decorative repertory.

That repertory had its own notation and its own generic forms, related by a common ancestry to those of contemporary France, but nevertheless distinctive and in some ways mysterious. It has been likened to a meteor or even a nova, "suddenly flaming into existence against an obscure background and, its fireworks spent, disappearing just as abruptly," in the words of its leading recent historian, Michael P. Long.[1] Thanks to Long's own research and that of several other scholars, that background is no longer quite as obscure as it once seemed.

The characteristic song-poem of *"trecento"* music — -so-called after the Italian word for the fourteenth century (the "[one-thousand-and-]three hundreds") to distinguish it from contemporary French "ars nova" developments — was called the *madrigale* (in English, madrigal). The name evidently descends from the Latin *matrix* (womb), the root of the Italian word for "mother-tongue" (*matricale*, whence *cantus matricalis*, "a song in the mother tongue"), and thus simply means a poem in the vernacular. It consisted of two or more three-line stanzas called *terzetti* (tercets), which are sung to the same music, and a single concluding one- or two-line "ritornello" in a contrasting rhyme scheme or meter. (The familiar sonnet form associated with Petrarch, and later of course with Shakespeare, is a related form that substitutes quatrains for tercets.)

The use of the word *ritornello*, seemingly a diminutive form of the word *ritorno* ("return"), to denote the one part of the song that does *not* repeat seems paradoxical on its face. The word is more likely derived not from *ritorno*, but from the Provençal *tornada* ("turnaround" or flourish), the "sendoff" verse that ended a stanzaic troubadour poem — for example, the *sestina*, a particularly dazzling *trobar clus* genre that had been invented by the twelfth-century troubadour Arnaut Daniel, for Dante the model of models (as he tells us in his *Purgatorio*.)

A striking confirmation of Dante's view of Arnaut Daniel as the supreme forerunner or progenitor of Italian mother-tongue literature is an illustration, discovered by the musicologist Kurt von Fischer, from a Bolognese legal treatise (Fig. 10-1).[2] It shows the three main practitioners of the early madrigal — Giovanni de Cascia, a certain "Maestro Piero," and in the middle, standing on a pedestal and with arm raised triumphantly, Jacopo of Bologna, the greatest musician of his generation. The three madrigalists are flanked, on the right, by a group of chanting monks, evidently representing music at its highest and best; on the left, they are flanked by Arnaut Daniel.

The three madrigalists, Piero, Giovanni, and Jacopo (to put them in order of apparent descending age), served side by side during the 1340s and early 1350s at the two richest north Italian courts, that of the Viscontis in Milan and that of the Scalas in Verona. Giovanni is shown holding a vielle or fiddle, which indicates that these poets may have performed their own songs as entertainers. The fact that they sometimes set the same texts suggests that they competed, as the troubadours had done, for

FIG. 10-1   The troubadour Arnaut Daniel and his madrigalist offspring, Giovanni da Cascia, Jacopo da Bologna, and Master Piero, depicted in a fourteenth-century Bolognese legal treatise now in the Hessian Provincial Library at Fulda, Germany.

prizes and favors. Their songs often address the same putative patrons—particularly a certain ANNA, whose name, though often concealed within other words like a troubadour *senhal* or code-name, is always written in the manuscripts in majuscules that proclaim her high birth and importance.

And sure enough, the Florentine chronicler Filippo Villani, in his *Liber de civitatis Florentiae famosis civibus* ("Book of famous citizens of the city of Florence"), tells us that Giovanni da Cascia, who came from the environs of Florence, "when visiting the halls of Mastino della Scala, lord of Verona, in search of a position, and competing in artistic excellence with Master Jacopo of Bologna, who was most expert in the art of music, intoned (while the lord spurred them on with gifts) many madrigals [and other songs] of remarkable sweetness

FIG. 10-2 Jacopo da Bologna's portrait page in the huge retrospective anthology of trecento polyphony known as the Squarcialupi Codex after one of its owners (Florence, Biblioteca Medicea Laurenziana, MS. Palatino 87).

and of most artistic melody." The sources of trecento polyphony often look like the big presentation chansonniers in which the music of the troubadours was retrospectively preserved. In particular this is true of the so-called Squarcialupi Codex (named after a famous organist who was one of its early owners), a magnificent compendium that was put together around 1415 as a memorial to the art of the trecento when that art was moribund or, possibly, already dead. Its expensive materials and lavish illuminations make it literally priceless; but it is priceless in another sense as well: it preserves dozens of compositions that would otherwise have been lost. Its contents are organized, like troubadour chansonniers, by authors, each section being introduced by a (no doubt fanciful) portrait of the composer. (Compare the "portrait" of Bernart de Ventadorn from the Paris 12473, Fig. 4-2.) Nowhere do we get a more vivid sense of how consciously the poet-musicians of the trecento thought of themselves as the inheritors and reanimators of the lost art of Aquitaine.

FIG. 10-3   Giovanni da Cascia, from the Squarcialupi Codex.

MADRIGAL CULTURE

But unlike the troubadours these Italian composers worked as polyphonists from the beginning: indeed, the earliest definition of madrigals, from a treatise on poetry dating from the early decades of the century, calls them "texts set to several melodies, of which one is primarily of longs and is called tenor, while the other or others is primarily of minims."[3] And unlike the troubadours, but like the Parisian composers of motets going back to the thirteenth century, the madrigalists seem to have practiced their art, at the beginning, largely as an aspect of university culture.

Jacopo of Bologna, universally recognized as the leading composer of his generation, came from the most venerable of all the Italian university towns. (The University of Bologna, founded in 1088, grew out of a school of Roman law that went all the way back to the fifth century CE.) The fact that Jacopo, in addition to his poems and songs, wrote a treatise on discant suggests that he may have actually been a university teacher. Bologna's only rival for academic eminence was Padua, site of Italy's second oldest university, founded in 1222 by refugees who had fled Bologna in the course of the long struggle between papal and imperial power known as the War of the Guelphs and Ghibellines. And thus it is probably no coincidence that the basic treatise on the theory and notation of trecento music was the work of a Paduan musician.

Marchetto of Padua (d. 1326) acknowledged the assistance of a Dominican monk, Syphans de Ferrara, in organizing his treatise, called *Pomerium*—"The Fruit Tree," containing the *flores et fructus*, the "flowers and fruits" of the art of mensural music—along scholastic lines. It is not clear whether Marchetto actually invented the notational system he expounded in this text completed in 1319 or just systematized it. Although he himself was a cathedral musician (his three surviving compositions are all motets, two of them Marian), his notational system was appropriated almost exclusively by the madrigalists and their thoroughly secular successors, which again implies dissemination through "liberal arts" rather than ecclesiastical channels.

The differences between the Italian and the French systems of notation, and they were considerable, may be explained by viewing the Ars Nova as a direct outgrowth of the "Franconian" notation of the thirteenth century, while the trecento system continued and refined the somewhat offbeat "Petronian" tradition—the tradition of Pierre de la Croix, the composer of those late thirteenth-century motets (like Ex. 7-9) that divided the breve into freely varying groups (or *gruppetti*, as we now call such things) of semibreves.

Marchetto classified all the possible meters of music into varying divisions of the breve. The short–long "Franconian" pairing of semibreves within a perfect breve Marchetto called "natural divisions" (*divisiones via naturae*, "dividing things nature's way"). Other divisions—long short, equal (imperfect), and the like—were classified as *divisiones via artis* ("dividing things up by way of art") or "artificial divisions,"

FIG. 10-4 Francesco Landini wearing a laurel crown, from the Squarcialupi Codex. Although the piece that the portrait illuminates, the three-voiced motetlike madrigal *Musica son* ("Music Am I"), is one of Landini's most complex, the great majority of his works were in the less venerable genre of the dance song (*ballata*).

and were represented by modifying the "natural" note shapes with tails. A descending tail doubled the length of a semibreve; an ascending tail halved it, producing the equivalent of a French minim. When it came to grouping the minim-shaped notes, the basic distinction was between what the French called major and minor prolation, what we call compound and simple meters, and what the users of Marchetto's system distinguished as *gallica* and *ytalica*—"French" and "Italian" styles.

When it came to varying the rhythms that occurred within a basic meter or *divisio*, the Italian system, with its wide variety of tailed note shapes, was exceedingly supple and precise. At least one of these special Italian note-shapes—the single eighth note with a "flag" (the unit value of the so-called *octonaria* meter that divided the breve by eight)—has survived into modern notation. The rarer Italian shapes were a major source for the novel signs used by *ars subtilior* composers—including, for example, the double-stemmed notes called *dragmas*, which we encountered in Fig. 9-2. But of course many of the *ars subtilior* composers (including Philippus de Caserta, their leading theorist) were Italians working in France. They were actually drawing to a large extent upon their native traditions. So what used to be called the "mannered" notation of the late fourteenth century was in fact a conflation of French and Italian practices that widened the possibilities of both.

A NEW DISCANT STYLE

Giovanni de Cascia's madrigal *Appress' un fiume* ("Hard by a stream") shows every distinctive feature of the budding trecento style (Ex. 10-1). The opening stanzas (tercets) enumerate a veritable shopping list of the ingredients that went into defining the bucolic scene — the "pleasant place" (in Latin, *locus amoenus*) inherited from the classical authors of "idylls" and "eclogues" like Virgil and Theocritus — within which all pastoral lyrics were set: a stream, a shade tree, flowers in bloom. It is the setting familiar from paintings and tapestries of noble outings, the same noble villas and their grounds where these agreeable songs were generally performed. The human ingredients are likewise idyllic: a beautiful lady, her graceful dance, her sweet song. In the ritornello the lady — Anna, of course — is secretly named within the word "fall in love" (an[n]amorar).

The setting is for two supple men's voices whose ranges lie about a fifth apart, with a common fifth in the middle that enables them to make cadences by *occursus* — that is, to the unison. Two-part discant counterpoint with *occursus* is something we have not seen in France since the twelfth century, and never in secular music. It is *the* characteristic madrigal texture. But it is no throwback. Everything else about the style is so new and fresh that the texture, too, is best seen in context as an Italian innovation — or, if you like, a reinvented wheel.

The way in which the music clothes the text is likewise characteristic. It is descriptive on several levels. Every line of the poem starts with a small melismatic flourish on the first accented syllable and ends with a large one on the last accented syllable, with most of the words occurring midway, in a clump. The words and music thus "alternate," so that the melismatic singing does not unduly interfere with verbal comprehension. We habitually call such singing "florid," perhaps without even realizing that the word derives from *flos* (plural *flores*), Latin for flower. The fourteenth-century Italians were in no doubt about this. Their word for "florid" singing was (and is) *fioritura*, "putting forth flowers," and Michael Long is surely (and illuminatingly) right to compare the obligatory melismas to "audible projections of the flowery landscapes of madrigal poetry," and to suggest that "the music of the madrigal was draped across its text like the floral garlands of which poets and theorists were so fond."[4]

It was to accommodate this kind of floral music that Italian musicians developed their lengthiest and most elaborate meters. *Appress' un fiume* is composed in what Marchetto and his followers called *duodenaria* — division by twelve. In transcription the breve is represented by the full measure (dotted half note) and the most characteristic melismatic motion is by sixteenths grouped in fours, making twelve to a bar in all.

EX. 10-1   Giovanni de Cascia, *Appress' un fiume* (madrigal)

EX. 10-1 (continued)

EX. 10-1 *(continued)*

> Close by a clear river
> Ladies and maidens danced around
> A tree adorned with lovely flowers.
>
> Among them, I saw one,
> Fair and courteous and tender,
> Who moved me with sweet song.
>
> ANNA, *to love your courteous*
> *countenance inspires me,*
> *The sweet glance and the elegant hand.*

(The occasional triplets were designated by special curlicues — they even look like floral fronds! — added to the note-stems.) But look what happens in m.17, when the text describes the lady's dance: the meter changes (from *.d.* to *.n.* in the original notation), duodenaria (3 × 4) giving way to *novenaria* (3 × 3) — motion by triplets (that is, *alla gallica*, "Frenchwise"). Even then "French" meant "fancy."

THE "WILD BIRD" SONGS

Jacopo da Bologna's madrigal *Oselleto salvagio* ("A wild bird"), of which the first tercet is shown in Ex. 10-2a, is one of those music-about-music pieces that cast such a fascinating sidelight on the esthetics of fourteenth-century art. One also gets from it a sense of what are sometimes called "the uses of convention."

Romantic esthetics (which we have inherited) tends to disparage conventions as being nothing but constraints on creative freedom. All that a convention is, however, is something agreed upon in advance by all parties. A contract — obviously a constraint — would be one sort of example, but so is language, especially in its semantic aspect. (Words mean what they do because we have tacitly agreed upon their definition — that is, by convention.) And so is an established artistic genre.

When artists work within well-established genres, they have made an unspoken contract with their audience, and, like the parties to a legal contract, have an awareness of what is expected from them. Yet there are many ways of honoring an expectation, in art if not in law. Not all of them are straightforward. Agreements can be honored "in the breach" as well as in the observance. Thus artists who work within established genres have the possibility of teasing their audience's expectations and producing irony. (There can be no irony, or even humor, in the absence of conventional expectations, as a moment's reflection will confirm.)

EX. 10-2A   Jacopo da Bologna, *Oselleto salvagio*, set as madrigal, mm. 1–30

EX. 10-2A (continued)

EX. 10-2B Jacopo da Bologna, *Oselleto salvagio*, set as caccia, mm. 1–12

EX. 10-2B *(continued)*

mo - do. Ta - le tal gri - da

Dol - ci ver - si - ti can - ta cum bel

for - te, ch'i' non lo - do.

mo - do. Ta - le tal gri - da

Per gri - dar for - te no se can - ta be - ne,

for - te, ch'i' non lo - do. Per

Tercets:
A wild bird during the season
sings sweet lines in a fine style.
I do not praise a singer who shouts loudly.

Loud shouting does not make good singing,
but with smooth and sweet melody
lovely singing is produced, and this requires skill.

Few people possess it, but all set up as masters
and compose ballate, madrigals and motets:
all try to outdo Philippe [de Vitry] and Marchetto [da Padua].

Ritornello:
Thus the country is so full of petty masters
that there is no room left for pupils.

Jacopo's poem begins as if setting the expected pastoral scene. The wild (or forest) songbird is a standard ingredient of "pleasant places." But having introduced the bird, the poet immediately turns it into a metaphor for song and proceeds to deliver a little sermon on the art of singing — an entirely nonconventional use of a conventional genre, but one that is tied intelligibly to the convention that is being "bent" or "sent up." By being the medium for a discourse on good singing, Jacopo's music thus becomes "exemplary." It must demonstrate the sweetness and moderation it proclaims.

Therefore it eschews the kind of "florid" virtuosity we saw in Giovanni's madrigal. It is cast in a meter — *senaria perfecta*, as Italian theorists would have called it — that characteristically moves exactly twice as slowly as Giovanni's *duodenaria*. In Jacopo's very lyrical setting, the fixed breve is divided into six semibreves grouped in pairs (rather than twelve grouped by four), hence eighth notes within $\frac{3}{4}$ time in transcription. One particular melodic feature that is especially characteristic of trecento music arises directly out of the *senaria perfecta* division. Note how frequently the paired notes take the form of descending seconds in the cantus part, cast in sequences (or, to revert to the familiar analogy, strung in garlands) with the first note in each pair repeating the second note of its predecessor in a sort of stutter. (The first instance is the delightfully syncopated initial "clump" of words in m. 5; compare it with the rhythmically more straightforward and typical clump in m. 23.)

This type of melodic motion may have been considered symbolically expressive; in later music it is called a "sigh-figure," which puts it in the category of "iconic" representation. That is, it symbolizes emotion by mimicking the behavior of a person responding to emotion. The idea that art expresses through imitation is an old Greek idea (hence the word *mimic* itself, one of several English words that come from the Greek *mimesis*, "imitation"; others are "mime," "mimetic," even "[m]imitation," which lost its initial *m* by being filtered through Latin). But it does not contradict the imitation theory in the slightest if we also notice that the sigh-figure falls very naturally under the hand of somebody playing on an *organetto*, a tiny "portative" (portable) organ held perpendicular to the body and played with one hand on the keyboard, the other on the bellows. To judge from the illuminations in the Squarcialupi Codex (including two given here as illustrations), rare was the trecento composer who did not play it. (To judge by the more detailed depictions of the portative in fifteenth-century paintings, it was fingered 2 – 3 – 2 – 3, etc., which would make a sequence of "sighs" virtually the easiest thing in the world to produce on it.)

But now a new irony, a new twist: Jacopo ostensibly eschewed virtuosity in his "wild bird" madrigal only to indulge it to the hilt in another setting of the same poem, in which the text is spat out so quickly that the first tercet (shown in Ex. 10-2b) takes only 12 measures in transcription. This version of *Oselleto salvagio* is a *caccia*. The word being so clearly cognate to the French *chace*, we may expect a canon. And a canon it is, albeit with a difference. For Italian poet-musicians the *caccia* was a type of madrigal (which is why Jacopo could recycle a madrigal poem in writing one). That meant a form in two sections (*terzetti* and *ritornello*), and it meant a texture consisting of a cantus (in this case running against itself in canon) over a tenor. So the Italian *caccia*, unlike the French *chace*, always had a "free" part.

But of course it was not literally free, since it had to concord harmonically with the canon that it accompanied. In fact it was more "bound," which is to say constrained harmonically and contrapuntally, than the canon itself. For obvious reasons, a voice accompanying a canon is generally written last. So the caccia was, of all fourteenth-century genres, the most necessarily and rigorously (and literally) "top-down" in compositional or generative method. Unlike the tenors of madrigals, those of caccias never carry the text. Does that mean that they were performed by instruments? The musicological jury is still out on that one, but it is clear enough that assumptions are risky. There are many proven instances in which the presence or absence of text is not a reliable indicator of performance medium. It is worth mentioning, therefore, that literary references to the performance of madrigals or caccias never use any verb but "sing."

Like the word *chace*, the word *caccia* had a built-in "extramusical" association, and so its subject matter frequently involved the hunt. (And like the chace, it frequently resorted to onomatopoeia, dog-language, and the like; compare Ex. 9-19 with Ex. 10-3). So again, the standard definition of the genre enabled a sophisticated composer like Jacopo to ring ironic changes on the genre's implications. A "wild bird" in the context of a caccia meant something different from what it meant in the context of a madrigal: not song but prey. But here, too, the topic was appropriate and relevant, and so its instant metaphorization is again suitably ironic.

Also ironic, of course, is the insistence on sweet, soft, and elegant singing, since the usual caccia text (like the one tendentiously excerpted in Ex. 10-3, replete with quail, dogs, and hunter's horn) contained so many invitations to "loud shouting." To sing the virtuosic music in Jacopo's caccia smoothly and in "lovely" fashion requires (as the poem warns) the ultimate in vocal control. Notice, too, that in the caccia setting of *Oselleto salvagio* the *octonaria* semibreve (that is, one-eighth of a breve, represented in transcription by a sixteenth note) gets to carry individual syllables of text. (In Giovanni de Cascia's madrigal, that level of duration was found only in melismas.) In its caccia guise, Jacopo's song could well have been a test for singers — or (as we have every reason to suspect) a contest piece.

BALLATA CULTURE

Besides motets and madrigals, Jacopo mentions a third musico-poetic genre in the *Oselleto salvagio* text — the *ballata*, which gradually stole pride of place from the madrigal over the course of the century. *Ballata* is the past participle of *ballare*, "to dance," identifying the genre as a dance(d)-song with refrain, thus associating it with the French *chanson balladé* or virelai. The French and Italian dance songs were counterparts in every way, and there is good evidence that as an "art" genre the ballata was directly influenced by the virelai.

Unlike the "learned" madrigal, cultivated in universities, the ballata began as a folk or popular genre, which is to say an oral and monophonic one. The beginnings of its literate tradition can be found in a favorite book of the period, the oft-translated

Decameron by the Florentine Giovanni Boccaccio (1313–75), the trecento's great prose classic. Like Chaucer's *Canterbury Tales* (for which it served as model), the *Decameron* is a collection of tales motivated by a situation that brings together a social microcosm, whose members regale one another with titillating, often ribald stories that vividly expose contemporary mores and social attitudes.

The setting is Florence in 1348, the year of the plague. A group of seven young ladies and three young gentlemen have fled the infested city to the suburbs, where they

EX. 10-3   Gherardello da Firenze, *Tosto che l'alba* (caccia)

From the mountain, he who was up there called out now to one,
now to another, and sounded his horn.

go from villa to villa, enjoying the sybaritic pleasures of the countryside as they wait out the epidemic. On each of ten days each member of the party tells a tale, and the day's entertainments are formally concluded with the performance of a ballata—either one known by heart or, in some cases, one improvised on the spot—by a member of the company, accompanied by others (again, extemporaneously) on various instruments. It was in ostensibly "transcribing" the fruits of the oral culture, as it were, that Boccaccio made literary genres out of the secular prose tale, on the one hand, and the ballata, on the other.

The ten *ballate* inset within Boccaccio's narrative consist of strophic stanzas with a refrain that either frames the lot or comes between each stanza and the next. (As usual, the oral tradition is not fully known to history.) One of them (*Io me son giovinetta*, "A girl am I [and gladly do rejoice at springtime]"), became a "classic," widely set by composers of a later age (beginning in the sixteenth century), when *ballate* were no longer used for actual dancing, and when (therefore) their form as such was no longer heeded by composers who set them to music.

Only one ballata by Boccaccio (not in the *Decameron*) was set by a contemporary: *Non so qual i' mi voglia* ("I know not which I would"; Ex. 10-4), with music by a Florentine composer who went by the name of Lorenzo Masini ("Lawrence, son of Thomas," d. 1372 or 1373). Like the virelai as practiced by Machaut, the ballata remained at first a largely monophonic genre even when written down by artistically trained composers.

Non so qual i' mi voglia resembles the ballate in the Decameron, and thus might be thought of as the "purebred" Italian ballata. But it was precisely Lorenzo's generation of trecento composers that began showing symptoms of musical Francophilia (as a credential, perhaps, of literacy and learnedness). Lorenzo wrote a famous caccia called *A poste messe* ("After Mass") in three parts, all of them canonic—in other words (but for the language of the text and the form of the poem) a *chace*. He also wrote a madrigal over an isorhythmic tenor in which each phrase is immediately followed by a syncopated rhythmic diminution—in other words, a madrigal-motet. And he even wrote a ballata to a French text—in other words a *virelai*.

LANDINI

Nevertheless, it is not until the next (last) generation of trecento composers that we begin to find *ballate* in a truly gallicized style—that is, ballate with their form adapted to the French manner by means of a "contained" refrain (or, to put it another way, with a "turnaround" or *volta* consisting of a new verse sung to the refrain melody), with open-and-shut cadences for the inner verses, and a three-part texture that included a contratenor. Such ballate could be called Italian virelais, and their great master—regarded by all his contemporaries as the greatest musician of the trecento—was a blind Florentine organist named Francesco Landini (1325–97).

Of all trecento composers Landini has by far the largest surviving body of works—though it is hard to say whether that fact reflects his greater productivity or the greater zeal with which his compositions were preserved. Out of more than 150 compositions by him that have come down to us, only fifteen (twelve madrigals, a caccia, and a couple of miscellaneous songs, one in French) are anything but polyphonic ballate. Of the ballate, about forty, or one-third, have the French three-part texture.

This enormous emphasis on what was originally the humblest and least literary of the trecento genres reflects a changed social setting. Where the early madrigalists had competed for laurels at the courts of the northern Italian nobility, Landini and his Florentine contemporaries made music for the Florentine ruling class, which was an urban mercantile and industrial elite. (As Dante noted sadly, there was no central court or noble residence in Florence; it was a republican city-state.) Landini's Frenchified ballata style may have reflected the tastes of that class, which maintained a lively commerce with their French counterparts. Florentine businessmen spent much of their time in French-speaking centers to the north and west, and learned the French language as a matter of business necessity. The later fourteenth century was a period during which the Tuscan vernacular language itself, to say nothing of the local art-music, suffered a great influx of gallicisms.

EX. 10-4   Lorenzo Masini, *Non so qual i' mi voglia* (ballata; text by Boccaccio)

Like many of the troubadours, Landini was born into the artisan class, which in Florence was no impediment to social prominence. His father had been a church painter, and he himself earned his living (and much of his local fame) as an organ technician. So it is not surprising that the works of an artisan musician within an urban industrial community should have differed greatly from those composed by *literati* (university-trained clerics) for dynastic courts. Landini's ballate do not so much evoke bountiful pastoral surroundings or extol voluptuary pleasures or narrate venereal conquests as communicate personal feeling — often the conventionalized love-longing of the troubadours (by the fourteenth century more a "bourgeois" affectation than a noble sentiment). Therein lay the difference between the "madrigal culture" of the noble north and the "ballata culture" of the Tuscan trading centers.

The three-voiced, thus presumably later *Non avrà ma' pietà* ("She'll never pity me," Ex. 10-5) was one of Landini's most popular ballate, and it is one of the most thoroughly gallicized as well. The texture, with a single texted cantus accompanied by an untexted tenor and contratenor, is indistinguishable from that of a virelai. The open and shut cadences of the middle verses or *piedi* (first on the "supertonic," then on the final) are reminiscent of Machaut. Besides the language of the text, only the "clumping" of the poem's syllables between melismas at the beginnings and ends of lines remains characteristically Italian.

And yet Landini's fingerprint is unmistakable, owing to the use of a cadential ornament originally so peculiar to him as to bear his name, though it eventually became a stylistic commonplace in the thoroughly internationalized music of the fifteenth century. Every one of the three standard "double leading-tone" cadences in the *ripresa* (refrain or "A" section) of *Non avrà ma' pietà* (mm. 10–11, 16–17, 28–29), and the final cadences (both open and shut) in the *piedi* show the same melodic progression to the final, in which the *subtonium* (or note-below-the-final) proceeds down an additional scale step (from the seventh degree above the final to the sixth) before leaping up to the ending note, its behavior resembling what we would now call an "escape tone." (Besides the structural cadences as noted, one can see the ornament in mm. 3–4 and 46–47 as well; all occurrences of it are bracketed in Ex. 10-5.)

This 7–6–1 cadence, sometimes called the "under-third" cadence, is more commonly called the "Landini cadence" or "Landini sixth." As the counterpoint in *Non avrà ma' pietà* shows, moreover, it is often allied with a hemiola pattern ($^6_8$ in the cantus against $^3_4$ in the tenor and contratenor) that produces a characteristic precadential syncopation. (The syncopation, too, would become a standard feature of fifteenth-century counterpoint, eventually emphasized by a characteristic dissonance that we now call a suspension.) For once the personalized term is not a misnomer. "Gregorian chant" may not have much to do with Gregory, nor the "Guidonian Hand" with Guido, but the Landini cadence is fairly associated with Landini, whose ballate were, as Michael Long has put it, "the first body of polyphonic works in which it appears with systematic regularity and structural weight"[5] — *structural* because the cadences it decorates are typically, though not exclusively, those that correspond to the ends of verse lines.

EX. 10-5   Francesco Landini, *Non avrà ma' pietà* (ballata)

EX. 10-5 (*continued*)

EX. 10-5 *(continued)*

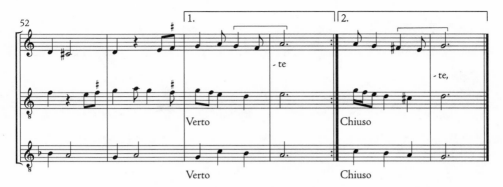

My lady will never have pity on me,
If you, Cupid, do not
Make her sure of my great passion.

If she but knew how much pain I bear
hidden, out of propriety, in my mind   aperto

On account of her beauty (for comfort
my sad soul can take only in this),   chiuso

Perhaps she herself would put out
The flames she kindles
And which increase my torment from day to day.

And yet the cadence can also be viewed as a typically trecento melodic pattern, found even in monophonic Florentine ballate, like *Donna l'altrui mirar* ("O Lady, who belongest to another") by Gherardello da Firenze (d. 1363), where it seems to recall the "sigh-figure" of expressively descending paired notes (Ex. 10-6). Gherardello, an older contemporary and countryman of Landini's, was also the author of the caccia *Tosto che l'alba*, sampled in Ex. 10-7. What Landini did was to give the "under-third" cadence a home within the newly Frenchified polyphonic texture, thus making it exportable.

One of the ways we know that Landini's ballata *Non avrà ma' pietà* was exceptionally popular is its inclusion in the Faenza keyboard manuscript, put together about two decades after Landini's death. We first met this manuscript in chapter 9 as a source for the Kyrie *Cunctipotens genitor* and for a ballade by Machaut. The mixed contents of the book is another indication that Italian and French styles were fast interpenetrating by the end of the fourteenth century. When we remember that Landini was the foremost organist in Italy, and that this had been his chief claim to contemporary fame, it is hard not to speculate on the extent to which the keyboard arrangements in Faenza may reflect his improvisatory skills.

Like the arrangement of Machaut's *De toutes flours* (Ex. 9-10), the arrangement of *Non avrà ma' pietà* (of which the first section is given in Ex. 10-7) consists of a virtuoso filigree over the original tenor. The filigree in this case conforms rather more to the

EX. 10-6 Gherardello da Firenze, *Donna l'altrui mirar* (monophonic ballata), cadences embellished with "Landini sixth"

A *O you who belong to another, look at the tears that flow from my eyes*
   until I wish a sweeter pain would kill me.

b Until now the sight of you brought me repose and peace,
b but now they are gone, Love.

a Mercy, woman, mercy, for I didn't think I would lose the peace which now is taken from me,
   or that I would have to serve honor above all else.

A *O you who belong to another, look at the tears that flow from my eyes*
   until I wish a sweeter pain would kill me.

EX. 10-7   Faenza version of *Non avrà ma' pietà*

2 da pars prima partis

outlines of the original cantus part than in the case of Machaut's piece; compare the notes marked "+" in Ex. 10-7 with the cantus of Ex. 10-5.

Certain features of the florid part in this setting have struck some commentators as unidiomatic for the keyboard. One is the tendency of the parts to cross, or to occupy the same note (= key). Another is the use of rapid repeated notes, as in the first cadence of the first part. These features would seem less problematical, the same writers have suggested, if the piece were re-imagined as a duet for two lutes, played (as was then the custom) with quills or plectrums. But if this is a notated lute duet, it is a completely isolated specimen. Nor are lutenists ever shown reading from sheet music in pictures before the sixteenth century.

At any rate, we may have here a kind of chance aural snapshot of the kind of music-making for which Landini was especially distinguished in his daily life as a musician, which was ineluctably "oral," not literate. (For one very obvious physical reason Landini could not have read any music, not even his own, from this or any book; it is worth mentioning, too, that he was only the first of many famous blind organists in the history of European music—the line extends right up to the twentieth century, with the organists Helmut Walcha and Jean Langlais, the latter also a noted composer.) But of course there is no reason to assume that this particular intabulation is a transcription of Landini's actual performances. On the contrary, the intabulator seems not even to have known that the work in question was a ballata: the sections after the first main cadence are marked "second part of the first part" and "second main part"; there is no indication that the "first part" is the one that actually ends the piece.

LATE-CENTURY FUSION

Landini's hilarious little madrigal *Sy dolce non sonò con lir' Orfeo* offers an especially rich and witty merger of French and Italian genres, all most inventively adapted to one another. Its distribution of voices, with the part labeled "contratenor" sharing the range of the cantus rather than the tenor, harks back to the texture of the motet rather than the virelai. And sure enough, a motet it is, albeit one with only a single text. What makes it conceptually a motet is the fact that it is built up from a tenor that has been laid out, foundation-wise, in advance. This we can tell even though the tenor quotes no cantus firmus, because it is fully isorhythmic in the Ars Nova manner.

Yet for all its "Frenchness," it is modeled exactly on, and illustrates, the structure of the Italian poem. A madrigal, we recall, consists of a number of three-line strophes called tercets—in this case three—followed by a contrasting ritornello. The tenor's thrice-repeated 21-measure *color* coincides with the tercet, and within each color the thrice-repeated 7-measure *talea* coincides with each of the tercet's constituent lines. The ritornello offers another surprise. It could also be viewed as isorhythmic in its tenor layout, with a twice-repeated color and a twice-repeated talea that happen to coincide. But since a coinciding color and talea amounts to plain repetition, we might also view the ritornello tenor as parodying a pair of *piedi* from a ballata, especially since the *colores* actually differ very slightly at their endings—one of them being "open" (cadence on G) and the other "shut" (cadence on F, the final). Ex. 10-8 shows the third tercet and the ritornello.

Landini even manages to work a few jesting references to the *chace* into the ritornello. The first little rash of texted minims in the tenor is mimicked in turn by the other two voices in successive measures. And on the rash's repetition, the other voices anticipate rather than follow the tenor, which now appears to have the last of three imitative entrances. The text is also a spoof, joshing the high-flown rhetoric of the early madrigalists, much given to classical and mythological allusions. Here no fewer than four mythological musicians—Orpheus, the prototype of lyric poetry (that is, poetry sung to the lyre); Philomel, the archetypal nightingale; Amphion, who could charm stones with his lyre; and the satyr Marsyas, master of the flute—are invoked,

EX. 10-8   Landini, *Sy dolce non sonò* (madrigal in motet style)

EX. 10-8 (*continued*)

EX. 10-8 (continued)

Tercets:

1. Not even Orpheus played his lyre as sweetly, when, singing of the love of the children of the gods, he attracted the beasts and birds of the wood

2. as did my rooster on the forest outskirts, with such sounds as were never heard by Philomel the nightingale herself in her woody bower.

3. Nor did Phoebus make better music when Marsyas scorned his reed pipe at the cost of his own life when bested in contest.

Ritornello:

He (my rooster) surpasses Amphion, the Theban wall-builder, and his effect is the very opposite of the Gorgon's.

only to be compared with the poet's little red rooster who can outsing them all. "Its effect," the poet deadpans, "is the opposite of the Gorgon's," whose ugliness turned men into stone. The concluding, rather Gorgonesque melisma, piling hockets atop snaking syncopations, adds a final touch of satire.

But who is this "rooster"? In Italian, the word is *gallo*. Might Landini's *gallo* not be a stand-in for a certain *gallico*—a certain Frenchman? If, as has been most plausibly proposed, we regard *Sy dolce non sonò* as a veiled tribute to Philippe de Vitry, the virtual (or, at least, the reputed) inventor of the isorhythmic motet, the whole concept of the piece and its affectionate parody of French genres takes on a new level of meaning.

The gallicization of the Italian style was matched, albeit a few decades later, by the Italianization of the French, both tendencies converging on an internationalized style that in fact became truly international. That was to be the great musical story of the fifteenth century. We can observe its beginnings from an angle opposite to Landini's—that is, from the French perspective—by analyzing the very different mix of generic ingredients in *Pontifici decora speculi*, a motet in honor of Saint Nicholas by "Johannes Carmen," a name we enclose in quotes because it is so obviously a Latin pseudonym ("John Song") for a Parisian composer active in the first decades of the fifteenth century. A likely patron for such a musician would have been Nicholas of Clémanges, the rector of the University of Paris from 1393 as well as secretary and chief legal defender of the notorious Benedict XIII, the unsinkable Avignon antipope; the prayer on behalf of St. Nicholas's "servants," then, might well have been a name-day tribute to the ancient saint's living namesake. Ex. 10-9 shows the first and second of its five quatrains.

But for the language of its text, this motet looks in its manuscript source for all the world like a chanson. Only the cantus part is texted, and there are an accompanying pair of voices (tenor and contratenor) that share the same pitch-space. The text, divided into five quatrains of iambic pentameters, all in the same rhyme scheme but with different actual rhyme-words (thus: abab/cdcd/efef/ghgh/ijij) resembles the conductus texts of old (or the new-fangled sonnet) far more than it does the typical motet text of its day. So why is the piece called a motet? Because it is isorhythmic: each texted stanza is sung by the cantus to the same talea. (There is no color—unless one is content to describe the nonrepetitive melody of the cantus as a single continuous color, which rather defeats the meaning of the word.) Thus, what usually characterizes the tenor in an isorhythmic motet here characterizes the cantus.

All of this is indeed unconventional for a French motet, but where is the Italian connection? It comes in the inconspicuous little "sign of congruence" (*signum congruentiae*) that directs a second singer to enter at the beginning when the first has reached the end of the first phrase. The work, in short, is a canon. But it is not just any sort of canon; it is a two-part canon for a cantus over a tenor. In other words, it is a *caccia*—but not an entirely conventional caccia, either, since it has a "French" contratenor in addition to the tenor.

Nor are conventional *caccie* isorhythmic. But like a motet, a caccia does have to be composed "successively." The canonic pair of voices have to be worked out in advance of the accompanying voices, just as an isorhythmic tenor, with or without a corresponding

EX. 10-9   Johannes Carmen, *Pontifici decora speculi* (motet in caccia style)

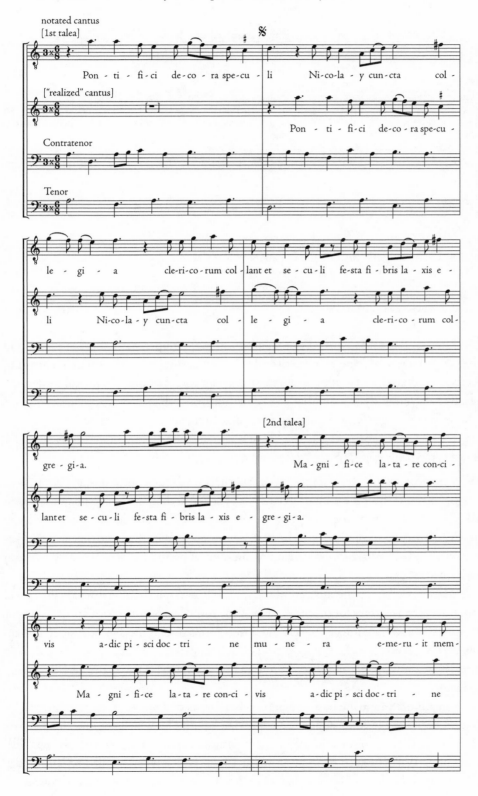

EX. 10-9 (*continued*)

bra-que la - sci-vis spre-vit o - dis de - de-re   te - ne-ra,

mu - ne - ra   e-me-ru - it mem- bra-que la - sci-vis spre-vit o - dis de - de-re

Let all the associations of clerics, the glories of the Papal mirror of
Nicholas, celebrate the festivals, even the festivals of this world,
with their tensions loosened. A citizen of great Patara has won the
rights to acquire the benefits of learning, and disdained to yield his
slender limbs to licentious hate; *etc.*

contratenor, has to be worked out in advance of the upper parts. So the motet and
the caccia have a genuine affinity; the addition of isorhythm to the canonic part(s) of
a caccia emphasizes that affinity. As in *Sy dolce non sonò*, Landini's madrigal motet, the
result is a genuine stylistic synthesis — something more than a stylistic juxtaposition or
a hodgepodge of genres — and a step toward genuine internationalization.

AN IMPORTANT SIDE ISSUE: PERIODIZATION

Was there a musical "Renaissance"? Was this it? To ask such questions, of course, is to
answer them. If there were no problems with the term, there would be no questions to
ask. The short answer to questions like these is always (because it can only be) yes and
no. A fair sorting of the issues is the best we can do or hope for, one that will address
not only the immediate case but also the question of periodization as broadly as it can
be framed.

The "yes" part of the answer addresses the broad question. Artificial conceptual
structures are necessary for the processing of any sort of empirical information. Without
them, we would have no way of relating observations to one another or assigning them
any sort of relative weight. All we would be able to perceive would be the daily dribble
of existence multiplied by weeks and years and centuries. That is the very antithesis
of history.

On a more mundane level, we need subdivisions of some kind in our conceptualization of history because subdivisions provide handles by which we can grip the part
of the story that interests us at the moment without having to contend at all times with
the whole. Without such conceptual subdivisions, which when applied to chronology
we call "periods," we would have no way of delimiting fields of research, or of cutting up

a book like this into chapters, or of organizing scholarly conferences, or (say it softly) of recruiting faculties of instruction at colleges and universities.

There is always the attendant risk that artificial conceptual subdivisions, hardened into mental habits, become conceptual walls or blinders. And there is also the related risk that traits originally grouped together for convenience will begin to look as though they are inherent (or *immanent*, "in-dwelling," to use the philosopher's term for it) in the material being sorted rather than the product of a creative act on the part of the sorter. When we allow ourselves to be convinced that traits we have adopted as aids in identifying and delimiting the "medieval" or "Renaissance" phases of history are in some sense inherent qualities of the Middle Ages or the Renaissance — or worse, that they express the "spirit" of the Middle Ages or the Renaissance — we have fallen victim to a fallacy.

That fallacy is called the fallacy of "essentialism." When an idea or a style trait has been unwittingly defined not just as a convenient classifying device but as something *essentially* "medieval" or *essentially* "Renaissance," we are then equipped (or rather, fated) to identify it outside as well as inside the boundaries of the period in question. They are then liable to take on the appearance of "progressive" traits (if they show up, as it were, in advance of their assigned period) or "regressive" ones (if they show up afterward). Not only does this confusion of assigned attribute with natural essence contribute to the teleological view of history as a directed march of styles (directed toward what, though, and by whom?); it also reflects back upon whatever it is that we are observing the values we associate with terms like progressive and regressive, which are borrowed from the language of politics and are never morally or emotionally innocent.

When periods are essentialized, moreover, we may then begin seeing objects classed within them in invidious comparative terms as more or less essentially medieval or Renaissance. We may become burdened with considerations of purity or fidelity to a *Zeitgeist* (a "spirit of the time") that never burdened contemporaries. And that is because unless we are very cautious indeed, we can forget that the Zeitgeist is a concept that we, not "the time," have constructed (or abstracted). We may then value some objects over others as being better, or even as being "the best" expressions of "the spirit of the Middle Ages" or "the spirit of the Renaissance." If this sort of essentialism seems innocuous enough, we might transpose the frame of reference from the chronological to the geographical, and reflect on what happens when people become concerned over the purity or genuineness of one's essential Americanism or Africanness or Croathood.

Subdivisions, in short, are necessary but also risky. Periodization, while purportedly a neutral — which is to say a "value-free" — conceptual aid, rarely manages to live up to that purpose. Values always seem somehow to get smuggled in. And this happens even when periodization is conducted on a smaller scale than the totality of history. Composers' careers are also commonly periodized. All composers, even the ones who die in their twenties or thirties, seem to go through the same three periods — early, middle, and late. No prizes for guessing which period always seems to contain the freshest works, the most vigorous, the most profound.

FIG. 10-5 Giotto di Bondone, *The Kiss of Judas*, a wall painting from the Scrovegni Chapel in Padua, Italy. Giotto's realism and his adoption of ancient Roman models have made him, for art historians, the first "Renaissance" painter.

The reason for raising these questions now is that the fourteenth century, and in particular the *trecento*, has been a period of contention with respect to musical periodization. In art history and the history of literature, scholars have agreed that the Florentine *trecento* marks the beginning of the Renaissance ever since there has been a concept of the Renaissance as a historiographical period. (That is not as long as one might think: the first historians to use the term as it is used today, for purposes of periodization, were Jules Michelet in 1855 and, with particular reference to art and literature, Jakob Burckhardt in 1860.) For art historians the first Renaissance painter, by long-established convention, is Giotto (Giotto di Bondone, ca. 1266–ca. 1337), a Florentine whose primary medium was the church *fresco*, or wall painting. In literature, it is Dante and Boccaccio, both Florentines, who for historians mark the great Renaissance divide.

The concept of the Renaissance in general historiography centers on three main considerations: secularism, humanism (sometimes conflated as "secular humanism"), and the rebirth—in French, *renaissance*—of interest in the art and philosophy of pre-Christian antiquity and its adoption as a "classical" model. All three concepts depend on the prior (and implicitly repudiated) notion of a medieval world that was sacred and inhuman in its outlook and shut off from the classical past. ("Essential" concepts can only originate as comparative ones: if we did not know "hot" we would not know "cold.") Applying them to the fourteenth-century Florentines, moreover, is done in hindsight, a hindsight that casts them as anticipators of trends that reached fruition later. ("Anticipations," being "progressive," are value-enhancers.)

Even though Giotto's output is almost entirely sacred in its subject matter and intent, he is regarded as an incipient secularizer because his figures, to the modern eye (and even to his contemporaries), have seemed more realistic—more "of this world"—than those of his predecessors. (Boccaccio: "he painted anything in Nature, and painted them so like that they seemed not so much likenesses as the things themselves."[6]) That greater realism, moreover, can be attributed to Giotto's adoption as a model for emulation of the artistic remains of ancient Roman culture in preference to the more immediate legacy of Christian (Byzantine) art. (Boccaccio:

"He brought back to light that art which for many centuries had lain buried under errors.") Dante's status as a proto-Renaissance figure depends above all on his being the first great Italian poet to use the vernacular, that is, a living language of this world, even as he adopted a pre-Christian classical poet, Virgil (who actually figures in Dante's *Divine Comedy* as the author's guide) as his model for emulation. And Dante is a protohumanist despite his divine (that is, inhuman) subject matter because of his passion for introspection, for analyzing and reporting his own physical and emotional reactions to the visions and events that he portrayed. Putting himself so conspicuously into the picture meant putting a man there, which ultimately meant putting Man there. Or so the periodizing narrative insists. Boccaccio's status as a proto-Renaissance figure is much easier to account for, given his realistic subject matter, his prose medium, and his irreverent style. Historians differ as to Dante's position with respect to the medieval/Renaissance divide. All agree on Boccaccio's place. But Dante and Boccaccio were contemporaries. Could they then belong to different periods?

It is not at all difficult to relate the proto-"Renaissance" indicators to the music of the trecento. Its secularism is self-evident; with the possible (and, for periodization, possibly troublesome) exception of the troubadours, on whose legacy the trecento poets and musicians so zealously built, no artists were ever so fully preoccupied with the inventory, and the pleasures, of this world. Its intimate connection with the rise of "the vulgar eloquence," to use Dante's term, is likewise a demonstrable fact. The special relevance of Landini, the foremost exponent of "ballata-culture," to Boccaccio's world could hardly be more conspicuous.

Landini's output can be related just as effectively as Dante's or Boccaccio's to what the literary historian Leo Spitzer called the shift from the poetic to the empirical "I"—from the poet as impersonal observer to (in Michael Long's words) "the poet as individual engaged in self-analysis."[7] This shift came about in response to the tastes of the Florentine public—an audience of self-made men—and can easily be viewed as a shift from the God-centered worldview of "The Middle Ages" to the Man-centered view of "The Renaissance."

Since the view of trecento music as a harbinger of the Renaissance turns it into a "progressive" repertory, hence extra-valuable for teleological history, the trecento-as-Renaissance view has won many advocates ever since the trecento repertory was rediscovered by musicologists around the beginning of the twentieth century. It has not caught on generally, however, partly because the rediscovery came after the conventional style-periodization of modern music history had been established, and partly because of the situation implicit in its very rediscovery.

That situation, simply put, is the extreme perishability of music compared with the other art media, and the consequent lack of classical models for it. There could be no revival of a pre-Christian classical past in music, since there was practically nothing left from that vanished musical culture to revive. As a result, the idea arose among musicians and their audience alike that music was an art virtually without a past—or at least without "a usable past." As one German writer, Othmar Luscinius, put it in

1536, at the very height of what we call "the Renaissance,"

> how strange it is that in matters of music we find a situation entirely different
> from that of the general state of the arts and letters: in the latter whatever comes
> closest to venerable antiquity receives most praise; in music, he who does not excel
> the past becomes the laughing stock of all.[8]

We have already observed a comparable attitude in Landini's madrigal *Sy dolce non sonò*, in which all the mythological (i.e., classical) masters of music were mocked by a comparison with (on the one hand) a "modern" musician (Philippe de Vitry), or (on the other hand) a barnyard fowl. Many modern historians prefer to view the beginning of the musical "Renaissance" somewhere between the beginning and the middle of the fifteenth century, a period from which we have many witnesses testifying to the general perception that music had been reborn—or rather, that a usable music had actually been born—in their own day. We will sample and evaluate their opinions on the new in later chapters; here it will suffice to quote the fifteenth-century theorist Johannes Tinctoris's opinion of pre-fifteenth-century music, including trecento music. Such songs, he wrote, were "so ineptly, so stupidly composed that they rather offended than pleased the ear."[9] Indeed Cosimo Bartoli, a Florentine scholar of the sixteenth century, observed (in a book about Dante!) that the composers of Tinctoris's time had "rediscovered music, which then was as good as dead."[10]

If we call that "rediscovery" the beginning of the "Renaissance" period for music, we are using the term in a very different way from the way it is used in general history. We are in effect endorsing and perpetuating an invidious comparison. The term, in such a usage, is not descriptive but honorific—a mark of favorable judgment—or even, as the music historian Reinhard Strohm has suggested, a mere "beauty" prize. The use of the term "Renaissance" to coincide with what fifteenth-century musicians saw as the birth of their art, or its rupture with its past, becomes downright paradoxical at the other end of the period. For at the end of the sixteenth century, musicians did in fact try to revive the art of pre-Christian antiquity—not in terms of its style (for they could not know what that was) but in terms of its effects as described by classical authors. Only then did music actually join "the Renaissance," as the term is understood by general historians. But this belated emulation of antiquity was precisely what led to the overthrow of what music historians now call the "Renaissance" period, and its replacement by the so-called Baroque!

Yet to try and avoid this terminological quagmire merely by pushing the beginning of the "Renaissance" back a hundred years to the trecento would scarcely help. As we will shortly see (and whether or not it makes sense to call it a "Renaissance"), there was indeed a stylistic watershed for music in the fifteenth century, as there was for painting and literature in the fourteenth. If there is to be a periodization, it should not contradict the actual history of styles. As already hinted, the fifteenth-century watershed came about as the result of the internationalization of musical practices—what might be called the musical unification of Europe. But it was not a "Renaissance," and there is no point in calling it that. We may as well admit that the term serves no purpose for music history except to keep music in an artificial lockstep with the other arts—a lockstep for which there is a need only insofar as one needs to construct a Zeitgeist, an "essential spirit of the age." So as far as this book is concerned, then, the answer is no: there was no musical Renaissance, and therefore no "Renaissance music." The latter term will only appear in this book surrounded by ironic quotation marks ("scare quotes") as if to say that although one may use it occasionally for convenience to designate music of a certain age, one should not take it as really descriptive of anything in particular.

Island and Mainland

MUSIC IN THE BRITISH ISLES THROUGH THE EARLY FIFTEENTH CENTURY AND ITS INFLUENCE ON THE CONTINENT

THE FIRST MASTERPIECE?

Ever since the late eighteenth century, when the first modern histories of music were written, the most famous piece of "ancient music" in the Western world (apart from chants in daily use) has been the little composition reproduced in its entirety in Fig. 11-1, a piece still known to many who have otherwise never run into any early music at all.

It is found in a manuscript that was probably compiled at the Benedictine abbey of Reading, a town in south central England some fifty miles west of London, around the middle of the thirteenth century. About three hundred years later the monastery was dissolved in the turbulent course of the English reformation. The manuscript eventually passed into the collection of Robert Harley (1661–1724), the first Earl of Oxford, sometime speaker of Parliament and Chancellor of the Exchequer, and a celebrated bibliophile. After Harley's death, his collection was acquired by the crown and joined the holdings of the British Museum, where the manuscript was catalogued (as "Harley 978") and became accessible to scholars and historians of music—a profession (or rather, at the time, an avocation) that was then just coming into being.

Harley 978 is actually a random assortment of old parchment and paper relating to the Reading Abbey, probably bound together by Harley himself. The musical portion consists of only fourteen leaves out of 180, containing thirteen miscellaneous pieces and a solmization tutor. Most of the pieces are monophonic conductus settings, but there is also a three-voice conductus, a version of the same piece entered *sine littera* in "modal ligatures" so as to fix the rhythm, and three two-voice textless pieces, probably dances (*estampies*).

And there is the piece shown in Fig. 11-1. From the beginning, scholars examining the manuscript knew that it was something special. For one thing, it had two texts in two different languages. Besides the expected Latin *versus* — *Perspice, christicola* ("Observe, O Christians!"), a poem celebrating the Resurrection — there is a text in English, in the local Wessex dialect, entered above the Latin, right below the notes, which celebrates the arrival of summer: *Sumer is icumen in / Lhude sing cuccu!* In modernized English, it goes like this:

> Summer has come! Loudly sing cuckoo! Seed is growing, the flowers are blowing in the field, the woods are newly green. The ewe bleats after her lamb, the cow lows after her calf. The bull starts, the buck runs into the brush. Merrily sing cuckoo! That's it, keep it up!

FIG. II-1 *Sumer is icumen in* (London, British Library, MS Harley 978).

And keep it up they do! But who are "they"? A long-winded rubric explains:

> This *rota* [round] can be sung by four companions, but not by less than three (or at least two), in addition to the ones on the part marked *pes* ["foot" or "pacer," or better yet, "ground"]. Sing it thus: While the rest remain silent, one begins together with the singers of the *pes*, and when he comes to the first note after the cross, another begins, and so on. Pause at the rests, but nowhere else, for the length of one long note.

So this piece is a round—a canon with a beginning but without a specified end—and it is to be sung over a repetitive phrase or ostinato (what *pes* means in this context) that is itself split like a round between two parts. (Or rather, since the two *pedes* are directed by their own rubrics to enter together rather than in sequence, they are sung in perpetual voice exchange: A against B, then B against A, and so on forever.) An accompanied round in as many as six separate parts! There is nothing comparable to such a conception in any other manuscript music of the period from any country, and no other six-part composition would be preserved in writing until the latter part of the fifteenth century, some two hundred years later.

The "Reading rota," as it came to be known, grew instantly famous in 1776, when it appeared, both in diplomatic transcription (that is, a reproduction of the original notation) and as written out (or "realized") in score, in *A General History of the Science and Practice of Music* by Sir John Hawkins. This was the first general survey of music in the Western literate tradition that (on the one hand) attempted to recount the whole chronological panoply and (on the other) was grounded rigorously in the empirical method—the inspection and analysis of documentary source material. Hawkins's history, in other words, was the first endeavor in the line of which the present book is the latest.

It had an instant competitor in the four-volume *General History of Music* by Dr. Charles Burney, the first volume of which appeared in the same year as did Hawkins's history. The second volume, published in 1782, contained a detailed discussion of the "Sumer canon" (as it is also commonly known) partly cribbed from Hawkins, which also included both a diplomatic transcription (only partial, Burney being a less laborious antiquarian than his rival) and a full realization in score (more accurate, Burney being also the better musician). Every subsequent history of music has done the same, and the present one, as you see, is no exception.

Having seen and discussed the original from a photographic facsimile (something for which Hawkins in particular would have given his eyeteeth), we will now proceed to the realization, in an ingenious space-saving version devised by the Irish musicologist Frank Llewellyn Harrison. The twelve phrases of the melody are all arranged over the double *pes* that accompanies the lot of them, with nine brackets showing the successive combinations of voices that occur when four "companions" sing the round as prescribed by the rubric (Ex. 11-1). Harrison, interestingly and uniquely, claimed that the Latin version of the canon was the original one, pointing out that the first five notes of the pes coincides with the incipit of *Regina coeli, laetare*, the Marian antiphon sung at Eastertide (compare Ex. 3-12a).[1] Whether to regard the undeniable resemblance as design or happenstance is anyone's guess.

Printed like this, as a twelve-part array, the Sumer canon looks very impressive indeed, and it is not difficult to see why it has been a celebrity of music history ever since there has been such a thing as music history. A certain nationalistic, promotional fervor has undoubtedly also played a part in the process of disseminating it. The canon has been a national monument in England since the days of Hawkins and Burney. It was printed as the frontispiece to the "S" volume in several editions of the big *Grove Dictionary of Music*, and even in the latest edition (the seventh, published in 2001) it has its own title entry, with a column and a half of text and a full-page photographic facsimile of the source. Every English school anthology (whether of songs or of poems) used to contain it, and every English child at school used to be able to sing it by heart. A book the present author was given as a child called it "the first masterpiece of music." Needless to add, it spawned legions of parodies, the most famous being Ezra Pound's "Winter is icumen in, lhude sing goddamn!" But just what has made it such a hit? Its "bigness," if we allow ourselves a moment to reflect, is somewhat illusory. A lot of parts get going at once, to be sure, but they are organized according to a very simple pattern, the repetitive pes with its implied harmonic oscillation between the final (F) and its "supertonic" (G)—the very oscillation that has governed the tonal design of many genres that we have already encountered, including all that have "open/shut" cadences or endings.

In fact, that oscillation has in a very significant way become more literally harmonic, as we understand the term today, than any music we have hitherto encountered. Once the second voice has entered, full F major and G minor triads sound on practically every beat. And that evocative alternation has meant "olde England," if not since the thirteenth century, at least since the time of Burney and Hawkins. Benjamin Britten (1913–76) was only the most conspicuous of many modern English composers when he appropriated it (tastefully embellished with a tonic pedal) to set the scene at the beginning of his

EX. II-I Sumer Canon, as realized by Frank Llewellyn Harrison

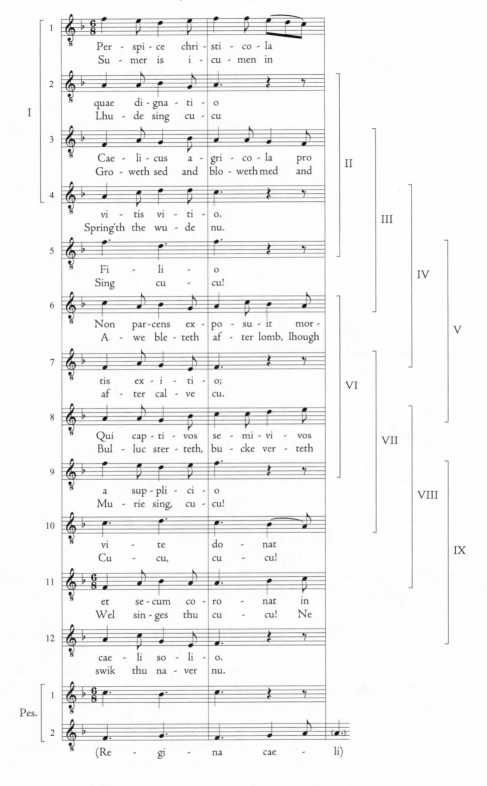

EX. 11-1 *(continued)*

The "Reading rota" (ca. 1250)

Perspice, christicola—	Pay heed, Christian—
que dignacio!	what an honor!
Celicus agricola,	The heavenly husbandman,
pro vitis vicio,	because of a blemish in the
filio	vine branch
non parcens exposuit	did not spare his son but exposed him
mortis exicio;	to the destruction of death!
qui captivos semivivos	and he (the Son) restores from torment
a supplicio	to life the half-living captives (of hell)
vite donat	and crowns them together
et secum coronat	with himself on the throne of heaven.
in celi solio.	

Sumer is icumen in—	Summer has come in—
lhude sing, cuccu!	loudly sing, cuckoo!
Groweth sed and bloweth med	The seed grows and the meadow blossoms
and springth the wude nu.	and the wood now puts forth shoots.
Sing cuccu!	Sing, cuckoo!
Awe bleteth after lomb,	The ewe bleats for the lamb,
lhouth after calve cu;	the cow lows for the calf;
bulluc sterteth, bucke verteth—	the bullock leaps, the buck breaks wind—
murie sing, cuccu!	merrily sing, cuckoo!
Cucce, cuccu—	Cuckoo, cuckoo!—
wel sings thu, cuccu!	Well do you sing, cuckoo!
Ne swik thu naver nu.	Do not ever cease now.

EX. 11-2 Benjamin Britten, *A Ceremony of Carols*, opening of *Wolcum yole!*

popular *Ceremony of Carols*, a Christmas school-piece for children's voices that he wrote in 1942. The "summer" progression, played on the harp, is actually the first harmony one hears, preceded only by a monophonic mock-Gregorian processional. (In Ex. 11-2 the music is transposed from A major to F major to aid comparison with Ex. 11-1.)

That basic harmonic—yes, chordal—to-and-fro so pervades the texture of the Sumer canon that anyone with half an "ear" (that is, the least bit acculturated into the idiom) could easily get into the swing of things and extend the piece "by ear" virtually *ad libitum* with additional simple counterpoints beyond the twelve written ones, the way kids at the piano do with "Chopsticks" or "Heart and Soul." And in bringing up the possibility of "ad-libbing," we are immediately reminded of Giraldus Cambrensis and his twelfth-century description of improvisational polyphony (and, just as in Britten's imaginative "transcription," harp playing as well) as practiced in his native Wales, quoted near the beginning of chapter 5.

Giraldus's account was set down in 1198, about half a century before the Reading Rota was set down. So is the Reading Rota a uniquely complex and innovative musical composition, the product of an anonymous English composer's prescient musical genius? Or was it a lucky (for us) written reflection of a widespread but otherwise unrecorded oral tradition—"acquired," as Giraldus informs us, "not by art but by long usage which has made it, as it were, natural," so that "children scarcely beyond infancy, when their wails have barely turned into songs could already take part"—possibly set down by a waggish monk who noticed the resemblance of a popular *pes* to the beginning of the *Regina coeli* chant, and fitted out a popular round with a Latin *contrafactum* that accorded with that chance resemblance?

If we assume the latter, then a great deal of what is otherwise strangely unique about early English music seems to fit into a historical pattern, and it turns out that that widespread oral tradition may not be quite so unrecorded as we might otherwise have thought. Once again the line between the oral and the literate—between "folk" and "artistic" practice, between "popular" and "aristocratic" culture, or define it as you will—turns out, fascinatingly and fruitfully, to be a blur.

VIKING HARMONY

Giraldus himself supplemented his observations of contemporary lore with a keen historical speculation. Noting that polyphonic folksinging in the British Isles was mainly endemic to two areas, Wales and the northern territory occupied by the old kingdom of Northumbria, he ventured that "it was from the Danes and the Norwegians, by whom these parts were more frequently invaded and held longer, that they contracted this peculiarity of singing."

There is a musical document, unknown to Giraldus, that seems to corroborate his theory. The Northumbrian style of "symphonious" singing, as Giraldus described it, consisted not of many parts in harmony, but only two, "one murmuring below and the other in a like manner softly and pleasantly above"—that is, "twinsong" (*tvísöngur*), to give it its old Scandinavian (or modern Icelandic) name. A late thirteenth-century manuscript, now at the University library in Uppsala, Sweden, but copied at a monastery on the Orkney Islands off the northern coast of Scotland, contains a strophic hymn setting that seems to fit Giraldus's description (Fig. 11-2; Ex. 11-3). From around 875 to 1231 the Orkneys were a Viking earldom under the Norwegian crown, and even afterward remained a part of the Scandinavian archbishopric of Nidaros—the most northerly of the Christian sees, with its seat at Trondheim, Norway—incorporating Iceland, Greenland, the Faeroe Islands, and the Western Isles of Scotland.

The hymn, *Nobilis, humilis*, sings the praises of St. Magnus (d. 1115, canonized 1135), the Norwegian patron saint of the Orkneys. By the time it was noted down the Orkneys were under Scottish temporal rule, but the music still undoubtedly represents a Nordic style of singing about which virtually nothing else is known. It cannot be connected with any other surviving Scandinavian music of the period (or even with the modern Icelandic

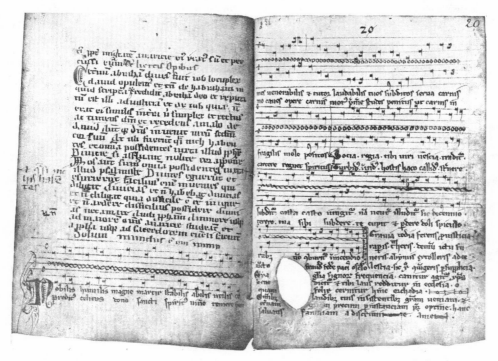

FIG. II-2 "Hymn to St. Magnus" (*Nobilis, humilis*) as it appears in its source, Uppsala (Sweden), Universitetsbiblioteket, MS C 233, fols. 19–20.

EX. II-3 *Nobilis, humilis* in transcription

O noble, humble Magnus, steadfast martyr, skilled useful, venerable guide and praiseworthy lord, protect thy subjects as they cope with the weaknesses of the flesh.

tvìsöngur, for that matter, which proceeds for the most part in parallel fifths). It seems to have been known elsewhere in the British Isles, however: the English theorist Robert de Handlo quoted the incipit of what appears to be its upper part in a treatise written early in the fourteenth century (with a text, *Rosula primula*, "Our dear first-among-roses," that substituted praise of the universally venerated Virgin Mary for the local Orkney saint).

The critical point is that the treatment of the third as primary normative consonance in *Nobilis, humilis* jibes with many early English musical remains. Besides the Sumer canon, with its normative triads, there is the roughly contemporaneous testimony of "Anonymus IV"—the Paris lecture notes, as we recall, of an English disciple of Garlandia—that English singers, especially those from "the area known as Westcuntre" (the West-country, bordering on Wales) called thirds, rather than octaves or fifths, "the best consonances."

And there is the tiny repertory of surviving English twinsongs, which maintains the emphasis on thirds, and also shares with the Sumer canon (and with Giraldus's account) the use of the F mode with B-flat, known to us as the major scale. These songs, among the earliest polyphonic vernacular settings to survive in any language, employ a more sophisticated sort of voice-leading, through contrary motion and voice-crossings, in addition to strictly parallel thirds; but they still seem, like the other pieces sampled in this chapter so far, to be the sort of "harmonizations" more often extemporized by ear than written down (Ex. II-4).

The most elaborate piece of this type is a translated sequence from the late thirteenth century, *Jesu Cristes milde moder* (from *Stabat juxta Christi crucem*, related to the famous *Stabat mater*). It is found in a manuscript that otherwise contains Latin-texted music, mainly plainchant (Ex. II-5). The two voices in this case are really twins. They occupy the same range and constantly cross, so that neither produces "the tune" or "the accompaniment." What is heard as "the tune" in a situation like this is actually a resultant of the constant voice-crossing. The voices are actually in a kind of "pivot" or "fulcrum" relationship, radiating outward from a central unison (to which cadences are ultimately made, *occursus*-fashion) through a third to a fifth; no larger interval is used. Although the F scale with B-flat is the medium through which the whole piece moves,

EX. II-4A   *Edi beo thu, hevene Quene*

EX. II-4A *(continued)*

> Blessed by thou, queen of heaven, comfort of men and joy of angels,
> spotless mother and pure maiden, there is none other such in the world.
> It is readily seen that of all women thou bearest the prize.
> My sweet lady, hear my prayer and have pity on me if it is thy will.

EX. II-4B *Foweles in the frith,* beginning

> Birds in the wood, and the fishes in the water, and I must grow mad,
> much sorrow am I troubled with for the best of bone and blood.

and although the third F–A is its most characteristic (and normative) harmony, it begins and ends on unison G, the fulcrum-pitch between F and A (a true tone "center," in a curiously literal sense).

Historians often call twinsong-type pieces like these "gymels," appropriating from the English musical vocabulary of the fifteenth century a handy word that actually derives from the Latin *gemellus,* "twin." A true fifteenth-century *gymel,* however, is something else: a temporarily split choral voice, like a modern orchestral "*divisi.*"

EX. II-5   *Jesu Cristes milde moder*, beginning

Jesu Cristes milde moder (British Library MS Arundel 248, late 13c)

Jesu Cristes milde moder
stud, biheld hire sone o rode (on the cross)
that he was ipined (pinned) on;
the sone heng, the moder stud
and biheld hire childes blud
wu (how) it of hise wundes ran.

Tho he starf (died) that king is of lif,
dreriere nas neuerre no wif (drearier was never woman)
than thu were, levedi (lady) tho (then);
the brithe (bright) day went into nith (night),
tho Jesu Crist thin herte lith
was inqueint (acquainted) with pine and wo.

INSULAR FAUNA?

The examples given so far are enough to show that English polyphonic music pursued a somewhat different line of development from the one we have traced on the European mainland. Indeed, it is tempting to look upon England as a sort of musical Australia, an island culture inhabited by, and sustaining, its own insular fauna — musical kangaroos, koalas, and platypuses. That, however, would be very much to exaggerate England's musical isolation or independence. It is also a considerable exaggeration to view the English preference for thirds as something altogether alien or opposed to continental practice, as if only in remote geographical corners (and behind closed doors, among consenting adults) could harmonies unsanctioned by Pythagoras or the *Musica enchiriadis* be furtively enjoyed.

We've seen plenty of thirds in music previously studied, and not even the English thought thirds so consonant that they could be used to end a (written) piece — assuming that a piece *has* an ending, as a rota does not. This very chapter, moreover, has already shown the British Isles to have been no isolated territory but a site of repeated invasion and colonization, with substantive musical effect — and we have not yet even mentioned the most momentous invasion of all, the Norman Conquest of 1066 that brought the English into an intense, long-lasting, and all-transforming intercourse with French language, society, and culture.

By the late thirteenth century, English and French culture were so thoroughly intermixed that their disentangling is no longer feasible. Nor was their intercourse a one-way street. England was politically subject to France, but culturally the shoe was often on the other foot. The English college at the University of Paris was a strong contingent, particularly around the turn of the thirteenth century — precisely, that is, when the "Notre Dame school" was consolidating. (Remembering that puts an interesting, possibly significant spin on all the voice-exchanging we observed in chapter 6 in the *organa quadrupla* attributed to Perotin.) And so it is not surprising to find occasional French pieces from the period exhibiting traits reminiscent of the Sumer canon.

Consider the conductus *Veris ad imperia* (Ex. 11-6), from the Florence manuscript. Though famous, it is an odd conductus. Yet no one would claim (or at least no one has claimed) that its peculiarities mark it as an actual English piece. And that is because its chief peculiarity is that its lowest voice (as written) is, most unusually for a conductus, a cantus firmus. More unusually yet, that lowest written voice is actually the highest sounding one, so that for the first fourteen measures this ostensible conductus is actually a sort of harmonized tune or cantilena — a tune that the reader may remember, because it has already appeared in this account as Ex. 4-2: the troubadour dance-song or *balada* entitled *A l'entrada del tens clar*, defined on its earlier appearance as "a sophisticated imitation folk song."

What marked *A l'entrada* as folklike was its repetition/refrain scheme: **aa'aa'B**, where the "prime" signs stand for "closed" endings, on the final. A peek at

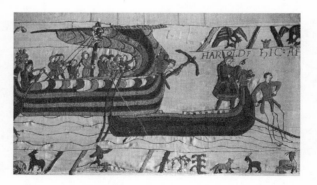

FIG. 11-3   William the Conqueror setting sail for England, from the Bayeux tapestry (eleventh century).

EX. II-6 *Veris ad imperia* (conductus)

At spring's command, Eya!
All things are renewed, Eya!
The first rustlings of love, Eya!
Weigh upon wounded hearts;
With plaintive melody,
With grace that guides,
(They weigh) upon wounded hearts.
In the midst of life,
The flower grows green among us.

the "tenor" of Ex. 11-5 shows that one of the closed endings has been replaced by an open one, so that the scheme is now the stuttering **aaaa'B**. Another way of accounting for the "stutter," of course, is to say that the "a" phrase has been turned into a *pes*. And now look what happens in the "upper" parts "over" that pes: what the triplum has the first time, the duplum has the second, and vice versa. Another way of putting this is to say that the two parts have made a voice-exchange. And they immediately repeat the exchange over the third and fourth repetitions of the pes, allowing for a different (closed) cadence the last time.

Voice-exchange over a pes—shades of the Sumer canon! And all the more so if we reflect that a round, shorn of its mock-imitative beginning, is just a perpetual voice-exchange disguised as a canon. (Gather three companions and sing "Row, row, row" or "Frère Jacques," beginning with the fourth entry!) But the use of an Occitan cantus-firmus tune (as well as the source situation) suggests that this is not an English piece, but a French one that uses similar devices. Is that an example of English "influence," then? Maybe, but why couldn't the English practice be an example of French "influence"?

That, too, is possible. There is no need to decide. This much can be agreed upon: what is only a sporadic and short-lived device, or set of devices, in French music became definitive in English music over the course of the thirteenth century. Again, there are at least two ways of interpreting this (or any) fact. One can assert, as some historians have done, that the musical predilections of the English contingent exerted an influence on French university musicians in proportion to their numbers; when their numbers declined, so did their musical influence. Or one can assert, as other historians have done, that certain French pieces especially appealed to the English imagination because their distinctive features recalled to the English their local oral practice—a practice previously inflected by the habits of their Viking overlords, but now reencountered within a literate context sanctioned by "mainstream" (read: French) cultural authority. And that is how the English were led to a national "school" of artistic, literate music making all their own. Guess which view is favored by English historians and which by French (as well as some influential Americans).

PES MOTETS AND *RONDELLUS*

Whatever their way to it, the English did develop their own "insular" ways of inflecting French genres of literate music. One of those genres was the motet. The English loved to use sequence melodies as tenors, as in the famous "Balaam" motet (Ex. 11-7a), which adopts for this purpose a versicle from the Epiphany sequence, *Epiphanium Domino*, that happily incorporates an internal repeat into each of its repeated strophes (Ex. 11-7b).

The text of the sequence verse is a paraphrase of Balaam's fourth prophecy from the Bible (Numbers 24:17) "A star shall advance from Jacob and a staff shall arise from Israel that shall smite the brows of Moab"—placed in a context that turns it into a forecast of the Star of Bethlehem that proclaimed the coming of Christ. And the motet text is a paraphrase of the sequence verse.

EX. II-7A *Balaam inquit, vaticinans*

EX. II-7A *(continued)*

Prophesying, Balaam said: "A star, the
new light of the world, will soon come forth
from Jacob, flickering in its new birth,
gleaming red."

EX. II-7B "Balaam" verse from sequence *Epiphanium Domino*

Ba - la - am de quo va - ti - ci - nans,   ex - i - bit de Ja - cob ru - ti - lans, in - quit, stel - la,
Et con - frin - get du - cum ag - mi - na   re - gi - o - nis Mo - ab ma - xi - ma po - ten - ti - a.

Balaam, prophesying of Him, said, "From Jacob there shall come forth a blazing star
and shall break the armies of the leaders of the kingdom of Moab by its mighty power."

Inserted into a performance of the sequence, the motet text would be the kind of
thing we might (very loosely) call a trope. And the likelihood that the piece was meant
to be inserted in this way seems good, since the text in question is the scantiest we have
ever seen in a motet. It consists of a mere four lines of Latin verse, enunciated twice: first
in the triplum and then in the motetus. While the triplum has the text, the motetus has
an untexted melody. When the motetus gets the text, it takes over the melody to which
the triplum had already sung it, and the triplum takes over the untexted countermelody:
voice-exchange! And that is why a sequence melody served so well: with its double

versicles it has a built-in pes to support the voice exchange. The particular manner of voice-exchange shown here, in which only one voice is texted at a time, is described by only one theorist, Walter Odington, a monk at the Benedictine abbey of Evesham, near the cathedral town of Worcester in the "West-country," who wrote around 1300. "If what one declaims, all others declaim in turn, this is called *rondellus*,"[2] he informs us, divulging a sure sign of English authorship, even when, as here, the music in question is found in a continental source (the famous Montpellier codex, alias **Mo**, familiar to us since chapter 7).

The texted exchange only comes at the repetition of the sequence's double versicle. But the first tenor statement also supports a textless exchange that counts, in Odington's definition, as a rondellus (for rondellus, he tells us, can be *cum littera* or *sine littera*). And then the whole double versicle is repeated in the tenor to support an extended cauda in hocket style, in which the voices exchange not only their tunes but their relative positions the second time around. The text and its liturgical tie-in have served as little more than a pretext, clearly, for the kind of elaborate musical game we have been reading about since the beginning of this chapter. Giraldus would have understood.

THE WORCESTER FRAGMENTS

There is an English source for the Balaam motet as well as the French one, but like almost all the English sources of the period, it is fragmentary—just a scrap containing the motetus voice. The wholesale destruction of "popish ditties"—manuscripts containing Latin church music—in the course of the Anglican reformation was a great disaster for music history. Between the eleventh century, the time of the staffless Winchester Tropers, and the beginning of the fifteenth, not a single source of English polyphonic music survives intact. All we have, for the most part, are individual leaves, or bits of leaves, that chanced to survive the holocaust for a seemingly paradoxical reason: having become liturgically or stylistically obsolete, the books that contained them had already been destroyed. The surviving leaves had been recycled, as we would now put it, for lowly utilitarian purposes. Some had been bound into newer manuscript books as flyleaves (the heavier protective leaves in the front and back of bound volumes), or as stiffeners for the covers or spine. Some had even been rolled up and inserted into organ pipes to stop little leaks that were causing the pipes to sound continuously (what organists call "ciphers").

As we can tell from the folio numbers on the surviving leaves and from tables of contents that have outlived their hosts, many of the manuscripts from which these shards remain were originally massive tomes, comparable to the Florence or Montpellier or Ivrea codices that so abundantly preserve the French repertory of the thirteenth and fourteenth centuries. And the surviving shards come from so many different parent sources that most historians take it as a fact that pre-Reformation Britain produced more manuscripts of polyphonic music than did any other country during those centuries. But all we have to go on now, if we want to reclaim memory of what appears to have been an exceptionally rich literate culture of music and sample its fruits, are these pitiful fragments from which no more than a few dozen whole pieces, or even self-contained sections, can be salvaged.

Many of the extant manuscript bits originated or at least were used at Worcester Cathedral, which confirms and supports Walter Odington's authority as a witness to the repertory he described, and the importance of "West-country" monastic centers as a hub for all that was most distinctive in English "popish" polyphony during these (to us) dark centuries. In the early part of the twentieth century, when systematic musicology was gathering steam in Britain, the loose leaves and strips from Worcester were collected and bound into three main codices — one kept in the Worcester Cathedral library itself, one at Oxford, and one at the British Library in London. These are now known as the "Worcester fragments." About three-quarters of this repertory can be dated to the last third of the thirteenth century, and confirms Odington's remarks about the prevalence in England of "pes" and "rondellus" techniques. We can be reasonably sure that the vast vanished body of music from the period reflected similar preoccupations.

Over and above the pes-motets like *Balaam* (or like *Alle psallite cum luya* — "Hey, come sing and play Alleluia" — its better-known companion in **Mo**), the Worcester fragments contain many rondellus-type compositions in conductus style. Odington's description of rondellus technique harks back unmistakably to Franco of Cologne's recipe for conductus, given in chapter 6. Where Franco wrote that the composer of a conductus must "invent as beautiful a melody as he can, and then use it as a tenor for writing the rest," Odington's instructions for composing a rondellus are these: "Think up the most beautiful melody you can, arrange it to be repeated by all the voices one by one, with or without text, and fit against it one or two others consonant with it; thus each sings the other's part." A circulation of parts in which all voices (usually three) participate is the quintessential "West-country" style, in which the age-old oral practices described by Giraldus Cambrensis are most fully absorbed into the developing literate tradition.

Flos regalis, a conductus in honor of the Virgin, is one of the largest and most characteristic pieces that can be salvaged from the dark centuries. It vividly reflects the way in which the English crossbred continental genres with indigenous performing traditions and harmonic idioms. It begins with a magnificent flourish of a cauda in the familiar trochaic ("first mode") rhythms of Notre Dame, grouped the French melismatic way into phrases of varying length. The first four lines of text are set in the "Franconian" conductus style, built from the ground up (tenor in "fifth mode") in regular four-bar phrases with occasional fast flourishes in the higher parts. The next two lines, however, in a slightly more lilting meter, are set as a three-part rondellus that runs through its entire *cursus* of voice-exchanges twice (once per line of text, as Odington implied). The remainder of the poem is cut up in the same way: four lines declaimed in longs *à la française* in a somewhat decorated homorhythmic texture, and the last two lines in purely English rondellus style. This last section is shown in Ex. 11-8.

NATIONALISM?

The harmonic idiom, too, is purely English (well, English-Scandinavian), even in the "French-textured" sections. No continental conductus sports strings of parallel or nearly

EX. II-8   *Flos regalis* (conductus/rondellus), mm. 87–117

EX. II-8 *(continued)*

parallel triads such as *Flos regalis* blazons forth from the very start. To this extent at least, the English idiom was indeed insular. And to an extent that continental composers may not have felt any need to match, the English seemed to flaunt their insular idiom within the "universal" (i.e., "catholic") ecclesiastical genres they had adopted.

This assertion of a local style within a universal genre may suggest the beginnings of something comparable to what we now call nationalism — a concept that, according to some historians, can be identified in England earlier than in other European nations. Those historians identify that emergence, it so happens, precisely around the 1270s and 1280s, the period of the pes motets and rondellus-style conductus settings so slenderly preserved in the Worcester fragments.

At this early date nationalism — or better, national consciousness — is identified with the crown, not with ethnicity, and is associated with propaganda aimed at conscripting a national army under the king's command. So far it may be viewed as merely a weaker, more abstract form of the personal loyalty one pledged to one's lord under feudalism. Nor is it easy to distinguish nationalism from imperialism: England's sense of itself as a nation had a lot to do with the efforts of the Anglo-Normans to conquer and rule their Celtic neighbors to the west and north. But an island country inevitably has a higher consciousness of its boundaries than a continental one, and this can promote a greater sense of civic "commonweal." As always, though, we should think twice before calling a tendency "progressive" simply because it "looks like us." There are reasons, after all, why the word "insular," denoting "island," tends also to connote the parochial, the provincial, and the narrow-minded. These too are often ingredients of nationalism.

"ENGLISH DESCANT"

In any case, the composers of the "Worcester school" rang many attractive changes on their parallel-triad (or, to put it in less anachronistic terms, their parallel-imperfect-consonance) style. Where *Flos regalis* featured parallel motion at the third and fifth, producing strings of chords in what we would call the $\frac{5}{3}$ (or "close-spaced") root position, a Marian conductus with a text that parodies the communion *Beata viscera* ("O blessed womb") shadows its tenor more rigorously with imperfect consonances. Doubling at the third and *sixth* produces what we would call strings of "six-three" (or "first-inversion") triads (Ex. 11-9). For reasons that will soon become apparent, *Beata viscera* has become the most famous individual item from the Worcester fragments. Its style exemplifies what is often called "English descant."

EX. 11-9   *Beata viscera* (conductus/motet), mm. 1–13

Blessed be the womb of the Virgin Mary, which, pregnant with the fruit of the eternal seed, . . .

When English descant was based on a plainsong, the cantus firmus was usually carried in the middle voice, following an English practice of "improvising" counterpoints above or below, and sometimes simultaneously, by the use of prescribed intervals. (Actually, this sort of "improvisation"—though it was known, oddly enough, as using "sights"—is exactly what we would call "harmonizing by ear.") When such settings were composed in writing, the cantus firmus often "migrated" between the middle and lower voices, so that the voices themselves did not have to cross. This seems to indicate an interest in chordal harmony as such: when the cantus firms is allowed to migrate to the lowest part instead of crossing it, the various parts are kept distinct in range. More significantly, the part written lowest in score can always maintain its function as "bass," making it easier for the composer to keep track of the harmony. In Ex. 11-10, a setting of a votive antiphon to the Virgin Mary that was often performed after Compline in Britain before the present selection of "Marian antiphons" became canonical, the voices cross once only and only for the duration of a single note (on "*genuisti*," near the end). The harmony is more mixed, between chords containing only perfect consonances and those admitting imperfect ones, than in the more popular "parallel" style, though there are local progressions that still bear traces of the English "oral" habit of extemporizing long sequences of full triads. But the general level of consonance is pervasive — far higher than in contemporary continental music.

EX. 11-10   *Sancta Maria virgo, intercede* (Marian antiphon)

Holy Virgin Mary, intercede for the entire world,
because thou hast given birth to the king of heaven and earth.

THE BEGINNINGS OF "FUNCTIONAL" HARMONY?

As a marvelous summation of everything we have learned to identify as English, consider the motet *Thomas gemma Cantuariae/Thomas caesus in Doveria* ("Thomas, jewel of Canterbury/Thomas, slain in Dover"). Ex. 11-11 shows its beginning. Discovered by fortunate accident in the flyleaves of an English (non-musical) manuscript from the fourteenth century that was acquired by the Princeton University Library around 1950, it is a dual martyrs' commemoration. The motetus celebrates Thomas de la Hale, a monk from the Benedictine priory at Dover, the chalk-cliffed English channel port, who was slain in a French raid that took place in August 1295, prefiguring the protracted conflict that became known as the Hundred Years War. The triplum celebrates another Thomas, the most eminent of all English martyrs: Thomas à Becket (1118–70), known since his canonization in 1173 as St. Thomas of Canterbury, who was murdered in the Canterbury Cathedral at the behest of King Henry II. The two texts in conjunction draw parallels between the two martyred Thomases, often sharing or paraphrasing each other's lines.

As might be guessed, the triplum and motetus, each representing a Thomas, are "twinned," sharing the same range and indulging in frequent voice exchanges and hockets. And they are accompanied by a tenor and a contratenor (the latter actually labeled "secundus tenor") that are twinned in the same ways, thus producing a double twinsong texture. That is already an English trademark, the first of many.

The whole piece is laid out, like the Sumer canon, as a set of variations over a *pes*. But that pes, even more explicitly than the one in the Sumer canon, is essentially a harmonic rather than a melodic idea. It is never literally restated even once, but its harmonic framework is restated some twenty-eight times. That framework consists of the same alternation or oscillation we have observed in every other English pes we have considered, between the final F (the "shut-cadence" note) and its upper neighbor G (the "open-cadence" note). They alternate in a regular four-bar pattern, as follows (where "I" means F and "ii" means G): I/I – ii/ii/ii – I.

The reason for using the roman I and ii (reminiscent of harmonic analysis) instead of the *claves* (note-names) F and G to represent the pes is that G is not invariably the lowest note in the "ii" portions. When G is the lowest note, the cadences are of the familiar "double leading tone" type. But sometimes, when one of the twinned tenors has G, the other one takes the C a fifth below, producing against the upper-voice

FIG. 11-4 The murder of St. Thomas of Canterbury in 1170, from a Latin psalter made in England ca. 1200.

leading tone not a "six-three" harmony but one of those characteristically English "ten-fives" we first encountered in "Kyrie Cuthbert." At such cadences the actual "bass progression" is not ii–I but V–I. No one reading this book will fail to take notice of the first occurrence in its narrative of a "V–I" cadential pattern, the most familiar and decisive of all harmonic closes to our modern ears. Just what the *historical* significance of that (to us) striking and significant progression may have been on its debut is a matter of considerable debate among historians — a debate that cuts very deep into the question of what the word "historical" really means. We will return to it.

For now, it will be enough merely to take note of the freedom with which the "ten-five" open-spaced triad is deployed in this motet, along with all the other full-triad sonorities we have been tracking in "English descant."

OLD HALL AND ROY HENRY

A caveat: Nothing that has been said about the distinctiveness and insularity of English music in the thirteenth and fourteenth centuries, or about its stylistic continuity, should be taken to imply that English composers were unaware of continental developments, or hostile to them. On the contrary, by the end of the fourteenth century, when evidence of English musical activity becomes much more abundant, it is clear that there were plenty of English composers who kept well abreast even of the most arcane *ars subtilior* techniques and paraded them proudly in their own work. Even they, however, were sure to put an English spin on whatever they appropriated.

A piquant case in point is a Gloria by a composer known to us only as Pycard. It comes from the earliest English source of decipherable polyphonic church music to come down to us relatively intact, a magnificent codex known as the Old Hall manuscript because at the time of its discovery by scholars it was owned by the College of St. Edmund in the village of Old Hall, near the town of Ware, to which it had been willed by a private owner in 1893. It had been previously owned by the composer John Stafford Smith, whose song "To Anacreon in Heaven," adapted to new words by Francis Scott Key, became "The Star-Spangled Banner"; in 1973 it was sold to the British Library. The fact that it had been in private ownership since the sixteenth century, and more or less out of sight, was probably what saved it from destruction.

The manuscript was compiled and copied during the second decade of the fifteenth century, but its repertory probably extends back at least a generation before that and represents the state of English music at or near the end of the fourteenth century. It is now thought to have been copied for the chapel of Thomas, Duke of Clarence, second son of Henry IV and younger brother of Henry V. Its contents consist predominantly of Mass Ordinary settings organized in sections according to category: first Kyries (a section now lost), then Glorias (followed by a few antiphons and sequences, the one major non-Ordinary portion, but appropriately placed), then Credos and so on. Within each section there are, first, some "English descant" settings notated in score, then some more modern (that is, motetlike) pieces notated in separate parts. Pycard's Gloria is of the latter type.

The piece is planned out in a very French sort of way. It apportions the text (the standard Mass Gloria "farced" with a Marian trope — *Spiritus et alme orphanorum* — that was very popular in England) into four sections, each consisting of a double pan-isorhythmic cursus. The lower parts have a recurrent color and talea that unite all eight cursus; the upper parts have four different taleae, one for each major section, each repeated once. As this description already begins to suggest, the four "real" voices in the texture are "twinned" just as they are in Ex. 11-11, the "Thomas" motet. The two upper parts, spitting out the text in rapid-fire bursts like fanfares, share a single range and a great deal of melodic material as well. Their very frequent if irregular imitations are clearly related to the old voice-exchange technique. The lower parts enunciate in tandem an old-fashioned English *pes* that oscillates between G and F as stable points. One of the parts is broken up "stereophonically" between two hocketing lines, so that the two-part pes actually requires the participation of three voices or instruments. (That is why there are four "real" parts even though the piece requires five players.) The combination of a popular English trope and the old English pes technique with isorhythm already justifies the remark about English "spin" on continental procedures. What justifies the reference to the *ars subtilior* is the changing rhythmic relationship between the upper voices and the pes. In the second pan-isorhythmic section (coinciding with the beginning of the trope) the upper parts continue singing as before, while the pes shifts over from longs equaling twelve minims (eighths) in the upper parts, to longs equaling nine minims. But the hocket-like splitting of notes in the pes means that in reality each note in the hocketing parts equals $4\frac{1}{2}$ of the minims running in the treble parts above. At the same time, by the use of red ink, those upper-voice minims are grouped by twos, hemiola-fashion, into semibreves, so that the actual ratio of lengths between the notes of the trebles and the notes of the pes is $1:2\frac{1}{4}(=4:9)$. Now that is *subtilitas!* This remarkable stretch is shown in Ex. 11-12.

Complications mount: during the next pan-isorhythmic section each pes note equals eight of the trebles' minims, but in the trebles those minims are grouped by threes. And so it goes, the pes steadily contracting in a series of "Pythagorean" proportions (12:9:8:6) until the voices at last come back into mensural alignment, but with the pes moving at twice its original speed. What makes the piece not only intelligible but palatable, even delightful, despite all cerebral complications is the mixture of all these artful linear subtleties with the typically English full triadic sonority and the use of jolly dancelike tunes to carry it through. Giraldus Cambrensis and his Welsh toddlers still lurk in the background.

So sophisticated is this music, so given was Pycard to mathematical and canonic wizardry in the other eight pieces preserved under his name in Old Hall, and so suspiciously Gallic is his name (cf. the ancient northern-French province of Picardie), that it has been suggested that he was actually a French composer whose works are preserved for some reason in an English manuscript (and in only one other, a fragment, also English). One scholar has even proposed identifying him with a chaplain named Jean Pycard (alias Vaux), not otherwise identified as a musician, who served John of Gaunt (d. 1399), Duke of Lancaster and Aquitaine, fourth son of Edward III, and progenitor of the English house of Lancaster, during his residence at Amiens, the Picard capital, in 1390.[3]

But a family named Picard or Pychard was prominent in England at this time, and it furnishes other possible candidates for identification with the composer. Nor is there any reason to suppose that a French composer would have been inclined to use a pes (or, before the fifteenth century, the *Spiritus et alme* trope). As to the Frenchness

EX. 11-11   *Thomas gemma Cantuariae/Thomas caesus in Doveria*, mm. 1–32

EX. II-II (*continued*)

I. Thomas, gem of Canterbury, killed for his faith, is now
   raised up to the heavenly host, *etc.*

II. Thomas, slain in Dover by a rival, is now forever with
    the Father on high, *etc.*

of Pycard's style, compare another Old Hall Gloria, in a purebred French cantilena style, by Leonel Power, indubitably an Englishman. It easily rivals Pycard's for sheer complexity and displays far fewer identifiable English traits (though the voice exchange followed by imitation at the very end of the excerpt in Ex. 11-13 is a giveaway, after all).

From the historian's point of view the Old Hall manuscript is truly a feast after a famine. About a hundred of its 147 pieces carry attributions, naming no fewer than twenty-four composers, so that we have more English musical names from this period to conjure with (even if many of them are nothing *but* names) than we have from any other country. And of all these names, it is fair to say that one has conjured up a fascination to equal all the rest combined: "Roy Henry," French for "King Henry," a royal composer!

EX. 11-12   Pycard, Gloria, mm. 25–48

EX. II-I2   (*continued*)

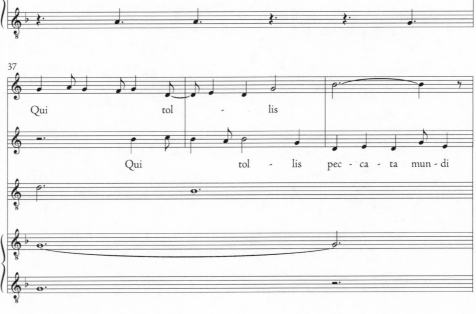

EX. II-12 (*continued*)

EX. II-13   Leonel Power, Gloria, mm. 1–14

But which Henry? The three kings of the house of Lancaster — the son, grandson, and great-grandson of John of Gaunt — were all named Henry. Henry VI, who acceded to the throne in 1421 at the age of nine months, can be ruled out, but Henry IV and Henry V, the father and the brother, respectively, of the manuscript's possible first owner, both reigned during the period of its compiling. Opinions still differ as to which of them may have composed the two pieces attributed to Roy Henry (and there is no guarantee that either attribution is anything but honorific), but as the two pieces differ radically in style it is not impossible that each of the two kings may have written one. An Alleluia setting in a different manuscript, attributed to "henrici quinti," might seem to clinch the case for the younger man; but as Margaret Bent, a specialist in the period, has dryly noted, the piece "is no more similar in style to the two Old Hall items than these are to each other."[4] The Old Hall Sanctus setting (Ex. 11-14) is the older of the two, to judge by its style and notation. Like the English descant settings of old (in particular, like Ex. 11-10), it is written in score, is basically homorhythmic, and freely mixes "perfect" and "imperfect" consonant chords. (The other "Roy Henry" piece is a Gloria in an advanced *ars nova* cantilena style, entered choirbook fashion in separate

EX. 11-14   Roy Henry, Sanctus, mm. 1–25

EX. II-14 *(continued)*

parts.) As befits its status as a royal composition — or at least as a composition carrying a royal attribution — it stands at the head of its section in the manuscript. Smoothly and skillfully written, maintaining the English predilection for full triadic sonority without resorting to actual parallelism, it can be taken as representative of "normal" English style (as opposed to the ostentatious complications of Francophiles like Pycard) just before that style became widely known and momentously influential on the continent.

FORTUNES OF WAR

Here is Roy Henry again (assuming he is Henry V) in Ex. II-15, this time doing what he did best and leaving the musical commentary to others:

EX. II-15 *Deo gratias Anglia* ("Agincourt Carol")

EX. II-15 (continued)

Ex. II-15 is a carol, the English version of the *carole*, the old French dance-song with refrain (here called the "burden"). Such songs had probably been sung in England since the Normans arrived in the eleventh century, if not before. But they left hardly a written trace until the fifteenth century, when they began to be composed by literate musicians using the latest polyphonic techniques. In the one shown here, the three-part writing in the "burden" (or refrain) has that distinctively English triadic sound first observed in the Sumer Canon, composed almost two centuries before.

By the time Ex. 11-15 was noted down, the genre to which it belonged had lost its necessary connection with the dance. It had become a "festival song," in the words of John Stevens, the carol's main historian.[5] The festival with which most written-down carols were associated was, yes, Christmas, although the songs we now call "Christmas carols" (especially those sung door-to-door or around the tree) are really hymns, and were largely the creation of the nineteenth-century sheet music industry.

For another illustration of the form, and a witty one, look at Ex. 11-16, a monophonic carol in popular style that is actually quite a bit younger than the earliest polyphonic examples. It comes from a Glasgow manuscript that contains a number of similar "unaccompanied" carol tunes. There is no chance of their being transcribed folk songs, though; their texts are urbane and literary through and through. This one, which describes the Annunciation (the event, so to speak, that made Christmas possible) is macaronic. It matches a burden in Latin, possibly meant for a chorus to sing, with verses in the vernacular (though the last verse ends with another, very familiar, line of Latin, quoting Mary's response to Gabriel's greeting in Luke 1:38 — "Behold the handmaiden of the Lord").

The burden, sung at the beginning and end and in between each verse, is an elegant pun. "Nova, nova" means something like "Extra! Extra!" "Ave" (Hail) is what the angel said to Mary when telling her she was to bear the Son of God, and it reverses the word "Eva" (Eve), the source of the original sin for which the coming of Christ brought redemption. So the redemption revokes and negates the sin for those who accept Christ: for them, "Ave (the virgin birth) remakes Eva" — a second chance.

EX. 11-16   *Nova, nova, ave fit ex Eva*

2. I met a maiden in a place;
   I kneeled down afore her face
   And said: Hail, Mary, full of grace;

3. When the maiden heard tell of this,
   She was full sore abashed y-wis;
   And weened that she had done amiss;

4. Then said the angel; Dread not thou,
   For ye be conceived with great virtue
   Whose name shall be called Jesu;

5. It is not yet six weeks agone
   Sin Elizabeth conceived John,
   As it was prophesied beforn;

6. Then said the maiden: Verily,
   I am your servant right truly;
   Ecce, ancilla Domini;

Deo gratias Anglia (Ex. 11-15), the carol in honor of Henry V, celebrates not a festival but a great event — one well known to fans of Shakespeare's history plays (or Laurence Olivier films). Found in a parchment roll copied some time during the first half of the fifteenth century, it commemorates the triumph of 25 October 1415, when King Henry and his small but well-equipped force of longbow men defeated a much larger French army on the field of Agincourt (now Azincourt) near Calais in the far north of France, near the point of shortest distance across the English Channel. It was the most important English victory in the Hundred Years War, a territorial conflict that actually lasted (off and on) for 116 years, from 1337 to 1453. In the battle's aftermath, England conquered and occupied much of northern France.

By 1420 Henry was able to march into Paris and (with the help of the Holy Roman Emperor and the Duke of Burgundy, his secret allies) claim—or, as he insisted, reclaim—the French throne. A treaty signed that year would have made him king of France after the death of the current ruler, Charles VI, whose daughter Catherine he agreed to marry. Henry died in 1422, before the terms of the treaty could be carried out (since Charles VI still lived). But the English armies continued to enjoy victories until by 1429 almost all of France north of the Loire River was in English hands. (It was at this point that the French rallied under Joan of Arc and eventually reclaimed most of their territory for the hereditary French heir, Charles VII.)

As the reader has surely guessed, there was an important musical repercussion from the political events just described. The English occupation of northern France in the 1420s and early 1430s brought a host of English "magnates" and administrators, both military and civil, to French soil. At their head was John of Lancaster, the Duke of Bedford, Henry's brother. Henry left behind a nine-month-old son and heir, Henry VI, who as the grandson of Charles VI was also heir by treaty to the French throne. (He was actually crowned in Paris in 1431, during the English occupation, but never reigned in France.)

Bedford and his brother Humphrey, the Duke of Gloucester, were named joint regents until the king came of age. Bedford had primary responsibility for prosecuting the war with France and administering the English occupation, duties that required his continued residence on French soil until his ally the Duke of Burgundy turned against him and made a separate peace with the French heir. From 1422 until his death in 1435, four years after he ordered the burning of Joan of Arc (who had been captured by the Burgundians, everybody's false friend, and sold to the English for a ransom), the Duke of Bedford was the effective ruler of France.

Bedford maintained a regal traveling household and retinue, including a chapel. Based largely in Paris, it was staffed by a substantial musical corps. The Duke also held many estates in Normandy, forfeited by French nobles who had been defeated and evacuated in the course of the English advance. One of these estates passed after Bedford's death to a man named John Dunstable, who is named in the deed as a servant and household familiar to Humphrey, Duke of Gloucester (*serviteur et familier domestique de Onfroy Duc de Gloucestre*), but who is named in another document (a bookplate in an astronomical treatise), and on his tombstone, as "a musician with the Duke of Bedford" (*cum duci Bedfordie musicus*).

The man thus rewarded in 1436 with a lordship in France was famous in his day as "an astrologian, a mathematician, a musitian, and what not" (to quote from one of his epitaphs). The striking thing about the musical works attributed to Dunstable is that, out of more than fifty surviving compositions (all but five on Latin religious texts), three-fifths are found only in continental manuscripts. This cannot be explained solely by the scarcity of English sources, since previously there had been nothing approaching such an English presence in continental ones. And the other striking thing about Dunstable's works is the enormous influence they had on continental composers — an influence readily, indeed enthusiastically, acknowledged by a number of witnesses. The only hypothesis that seems to unite all of these scattered facts and circumstances in a convincing pattern is one that places Dunstable in Paris at the head of the Duke of Bedford's musical establishment at the time when English prestige was at its height. That political prestige, plus the novelty and sheer allure of the English style (as we have already come to know it, but which was a revelation to continental musicians) conspired to produce a stylistic watershed in European music, after which for the first time there was truly a pan-European musical style — a literate musical *lingua franca* — of which the English, with Dunstable at their head, had served as catalysts.

DUNSTABLE AND THE "CONTENANCE ANGLOISE"

One of our best witnesses to Dunstable's prestige and his role as catalyst comes in the form of an aside in the course of an epic allegorical poem called *Le Champion des dames*, composed around 1440 by Martin le Franc, a Burgundian court poet. Le Franc, an enthusiastic partisan of the French in the Hundred Years War, wrote the poem to persuade Philip the Good, the Duke of Burgundy, to do what he eventually did: sunder his ties to the English and help the French drive them out. The presence of the English on French soil was baleful, Le Franc maintained; unchecked, it would lead ineluctably to an apocalypse, an end of historical time. Listing its portents, Le Franc pointed with a mixture of pride and dread at the perfection attained by the arts and sciences, beyond which no advance seemed possible. The fateful perfection of music, he alleged, was due especially directly to those accursed Englishmen.

At the beginning of the century, according to Le Franc, the great Parisian composers had been three: Johannes Carmen (whom we met in chapter 10), Johannes Césaris, and Jean de Noyers, called Tapissier ("the tapestry-weaver"). Their work had astonished all Paris, and impressed all visitors. But they had been totally eclipsed in recent years by a new generation of French and Burgundian musicians, who *ont prins de la contenance Angloise et ensuy Dunstable, Pour quoy merveilleuse plaisance Rend leur chant joyeux et notable*. ("have taken to the English guise and followed Dunstable, which has made their song marvelously pleasing, distinguished and delightful.")

Le Franc's vaguely eloquent phrase *la contenance angloise* — "the English something-or-other" (one dictionary gives "air, bearing, attitude" as well as "guise" as equivalents for the poetic *contenance*) — resists precise translation or paraphrase, and it is not clear whether Le Franc himself knew exactly what he was talking about. (The lines preceding the quoted ones are a merry hash of mangled technical terms.) But he was giving voice to the conventional wisdom of the day, and so it would remain for the rest of the century.

When the theorist Johannes Tinctoris, writing in 1477, made his famous announcement that there is not a single piece of music more than forty years old that is "regarded by the learned as worth hearing," he was dating the beginnings of viable music to precisely the time when Le Franc had been writing. Anything earlier, he contended, was "so ineptly, so stupidly composed that they rather offended than pleased the ear." And in a slightly earlier treatise Tinctoris had already identified "the English, of whom Dunstable stood forth as chief" as being the "fount and origin" of the "new art" that marked the boundaries of the viable.[6]

The "contenance angloise," whatever it was, had already made a sensation among the continental churchmen and musicians who heard the choirs of the bishops of Norwich and Lichfield, and the instrumentalists in the retinue of the Earl of Warwick, at the Council of Constance that negotiated the end of the Great Schism in 1417. English musical influence reached its peak in music composed on the continent, in the wake of this council, for the newly reunited Roman Catholic church.

The French musicians named by Martin Le Franc as having absorbed the new manner and brought it to perfection were Dunstable's contemporaries Gilles Binchois and Guillaume Du Fay. Tinctoris named them too, but as members along with Dunstable of the musical generation that had mentored Tinctoris's contemporaries, the truly perfect ones. It was just as much the fashion in "premodern" Europe to regard the present as a summit as later it became the fashion to regard the past as a "golden age."

Thus by the end of the sixteenth century Dunstable had grown sufficiently remote in time so as to lose his aura completely. Thomas Morley, a later composing countryman of Dunstable's, writing in 1597, produced a little scrap from a Dunstable motet just so he could show what "some dunces have not slacked to do, yea one whose name is John Dunstable (an ancient English author)," whose quoted passage "is one of the greatest absurdities which I have seen committed in the dittying of music." Or maybe Morley just couldn't resist a pun. In any case it was nothing personal, nor did it signal any substantive change of mind or heart among music theorists. Morley was merely doing what Tinctoris and Le Franc had done before him — namely, despising music that was older than he was.

If Martin Le Franc was right, it should be possible to show how Dunstable's music mediated between the music of Carmen, Cesaris, and Tapissier on the one hand, and that of Le Franc's Franco-Burgundian contemporaries Binchois and Du Fay on the other. It is indeed possible to do this, and very instructive. From such a comparison we learn that precisely those features that until the end of the fourteenth century most distinguished "English descant" from the music of the continent — features like "major-mode" tonality, full-triadic harmony (or at least a greater reliance on imperfect consonances), smooth handling of dissonance — had the most decisive impact on continental musicians in the early fifteenth century, and therefore must have constituted the so-called *contenance angloise*.

A pan-isorhythmic motet by Tapissier, *Eya dulcis/Vale placens*, is actually about matters the Council of Constance was convened to settle — "Rome, all Rome cries out, 'Away with the Schism,'" shrills the triplum at one point — though it probably was composed earlier, possibly in Avignon, where the composer, who died around 1410, had worked. Another possibility is that the motet was composed for the court of Duke Philip the Bold of Burgundy, who was then the chief rival to French power in northern Europe. In any case, one can easily see why Martin Le Franc said that music like this had stunned all Paris. It radiates power and authority.

Like the motet by Ciconia discussed in chapter 8 (also connected indirectly with the Council of Constance through its dedicatee, Francesco Zabarella), Tapissier's motet sports robust ceremonial fanfares preceding each talea, which suggest outdoor performance on loud winds. (Such wind bands did often accompany the choirs at the Council of Constance, we learn from literary descriptions, and the English trombones were particularly admired.) The text setting is hortatory, orotund, even a shade bombastic. It consists at times of longish strings of syllables on a reciting — or rather, a haranguing — tone. The rhythmic writing shows traces of the *ars subtilior*, the Avignon specialty, in its long chains of syncopes and its little rashes of polyrhythm.

The tonality of the whole is unabashedly disunified in the old French manner, recalling the *In seculum* motets encountered in chapter 7 whose wayward, unpredictable cadence structure was seen as a plus, as an aspect of variety (*discordia concors*). The three pan-isorhythmic taleae in Tapissier's motet all begin with fanfares on C, but make their respective cadences on F, C, and G. And then, just as in the *In seculum* motets, a single note evidently left over in the tenor's unidentified color comes out of the blue and forces a final chord on F that in no sense resolves the harmony but confuses it — pleasurably (or at least impressively) for its original listeners, one must assume, if not for us. Ex. 11-17 shows the last talea and its surprise ending.

The only fair comparison with Tapissier's motet would be another isorhythmic motet. Although he looms in traditional historiography (thanks to Le Franc and Tinctoris, among others) as a stylistic divider, Dunstable was at least as much a continuer and an adapter of traditional genres. He wrote a considerable number of isorhythmic motets, of which a dozen or so survive; indeed he was particularly expert in this loftiest of genres, as one might fairly expect "an astrologian, a mathematician, a musitian, and what not" to be. Like all his contemporaries, Dunstable was still brought up musically in the spirit of the quadrivium. But the content with which he invested the old forms — the new wine, as the old metaphor has it, that he poured into the old bottles — was indeed something different.

His motet *Salve scema/Salve salus*, in honor of St. Katharine (Ex. 11-18), is every bit as rigorous in its structural design as Tapissier's. The tenor and contratenor both have strictly maintained *colores* that sustain a triple cursus. Each color, moreover, supports a double cursus of a talea that is maintained strictly in the lower parts from beginning to end, for a total of six statements. With each repetition of the color, the talea undergoes a change in mensuration that increases its speed: the second color runs at $1\frac{1}{2}$ times the speed of the first, and the third is double the speed of the first. Moreover, the texted parts are pan-isorhythmic within a color statement of the lower parts: that is to say, whenever the lower parts repeat their talea at a given speed, the upper parts repeat their talea, too (compare mm. 1–18 with mm. 19–36, 37–54 with 55–72, 73–78 with

79-end). The difference is that the lower parts never change their *talea* while the upper parts do so twice, as indicated.

Yet if the structure of Dunstable's motet is traditional, its sound is worlds away (well, at least a channel away) from Tapissier's, thoroughly informed by sonorities we have learned to associate with English descant: uniform F-major tonality and euphonious triadic harmony, with thirds enjoying full rights (except in final chords) as consonances. When in each statement of their *color* the tenor and contratenor enter after the *introitus*, we even get a deliberate whiff of what old Giraldus Cambrensis had

EX. 11-17   Jean de Noyers (Tapissier), *Eya dulcis/Vale placens*, mm. 77–115

EX. II-17 (continued)

Triplum:
The lily of the lofty kingdom,
pressed with darts of great adversity,
beseeches thee, O fount of procreation,
to be the rose of consolation to the lily.
O thou our salvation,
now is a time of troubles;
their tears wet the faces of the people.
Distill peace upon our times.

Motetus:
It is holy to pray with the gifts
of the chosen; but it is yours
to command God, and give peace
and glory to men and angels.

called the "sweet softness of B-flat" (what we would call "plagal harmony"). Most of all, Dunstable's music displays an unprecedentedly smooth technique of part writing, its dissonances consistently subordinated to consonances in ways that begin to approximate the rules of dissonance treatment still taught in counterpoint class and analyzed in harmony class (passing tones, neighbors, and so on). Ex. 11-18 contains the last *color* statement. Note the double cursus of the pan-isorhythmic talea: after the eighteenth measure all the rhythms in all the parts repeat exactly.

EX. 11-18   John Dunstable, *Salve scema/Salve salus*, mm. 145–80

EX. II-18 (continued)

By contrast, Tapissier's texture bristles with "unprepared" and "unresolved" dissonance. The last six measures of the example abound in instances: triplum G making a seventh with the motetus (and tenor) A, and then skipping from it; triplum and motetus both skipping to a clashing E-F(♯) second, and so on. Such things had been perfectly normal in the French polyphonic style that grew out of continental discantus. They will not be found in Dunstable's piece. To ears trained to regard English descant as the norm, and to regard Dunstable as the "fount and origin" of viable music, Tapissier's dissonances can easily seem like blunders, and it is easy to see why Tinctoris would see fit to censure such music as "ineptly and stupidly composed." We have already seen the continental response to Dunstable's motet style in Du Fay's *Nuper rosarum flores*, analyzed for its numerical symbolism in chapter 8. There it was mentioned that the beginnings of "the Renaissance," for music, are often associated with the work of Du Fay (more often, in fact than with Landini). That is because modern music historiography has, perhaps somewhat uncritically, adapted the views of Martin Le Franc and Tinctoris—about the significance of the English style as marking a new beginning for the continent—to the conventional vocabulary of art history. What is "Renaissance" about Du Fay and his contemporary Binchois is exactly what Martin Le Franc said was "new" about them: that they "have taken to the English guise and followed Dunstable," particularly as regards harmony and part-writing. In fact the continental composers invented new ways—clever cookbook recipes, actually—for instantly transforming their style and donning that "English guise."

VOLUPTUOUSNESS AND HOW TO ACQUIRE IT

For a dose of English newness at its most radical, let us briefly consider Dunstable's most famous composition, then as now: *Quam pulchra es* ("How beautiful thou art"), a setting from the Song of Songs (Ex. 11-19). Verses from that book of the Bible had become exceedingly popular in England as a result of the burgeoning of votive services addressed to the Blessed Virgin Mary in her role as "neck," connecting (and mediating between) the Godhead and the body of the faithful. The love lyrics attributed to King Solomon, for which a long tradition of allegorical interpretation existed, now came into their own as votive antiphons.

Nevertheless, the Song of Songs remains an erotic poem, and its surface meaning no doubt conditioned the exceedingly sensuous settings its verses received from English composers, starting with the "Old Hall" generation and, through Dunstable and his contemporaries, eventually infiltrating the continent. A new style of discant setting emerged out of these Song of Songs antiphons; it is widely known in the scholarly literature as the "declamation motet," but a better name would be "cantilena motet" because of its similarity to the texture of the continental courtly chanson. Its seductive sweetness is the result of a control of dissonance so extreme as to remind Manfred Bukofzer, the historian who christened the new genre, of a "purge."[7] The homorhythmic texture of the old conductus is adapted in them to the actual rhythms of spoken language rather than to isochrony or to any preconceived metrical scheme. But the naturalistic declamation is not pervasive; rather it is used selectively to spotlight key affect-laden words and phrases, chiefly terms of endearment and symbols of feminine sexuality.

In *Quam pulchra es* there are from beginning to end only nine dissonant notes (circled in Ex. 11-19), and they all conform to the highly regulated dissonance treatment still codified in academic rules of counterpoint. (In other words, they can be named and classified.) There is an "incomplete neighbor" or "escape tone" on *pulchra*; there are unaccented passing tones on *ut* and *eburnea*; there is an accented passing tone on *videamus*, and there are three 7–6 suspensions at various cadences. Such a refining-out of dissonance requires effort. It is indeed conspicuous, and therefore expressive, reminding us that we normally take for granted a much higher level of dissonance as the norm.

No less expressive is the declamation. The words singled out for naturalistic setting in strict homorhythm include *carissima* ("dearest"), *collum tuum* ("your neck," perhaps symbolic as well as erotic), and *ubera* ("breasts"), the latter singled out twice, once by the male lover and another time, at the very end, by the female. Most dramatically set of all

EX. 11-19   John Dunstable, *Quam pulchra es*

EX. II-19 (continued)

EX. II-19 (continued)

How beautiful thou art, and how graceful,
my dearest in delights.
Your stature I would compare to the palm tree,
and your breasts to clusters of grapes.
Your head is like Mount Carmel,
your neck just like a tower of ivory.
Come my love, let us go out into the field,
and see whether the flowers have yielded fruit,
and whether the apples of Tyre are in bloom.

There will I give my breasts to you.

is the female lover's command — *Veni dilecte mi* ("Come, my beloved") — set off not only
by homorhythm and by long note values but also by time-stopping fermatas. Whatever
the allegorical significance of the Song of Songs verses within the Marian liturgy, the
music achieves its telling expressive potency by literally, if tacitly, "telling" — that is,
unmasking the allegory.

This, it is worth noting parenthetically, is only the first of many times that we will see music speaking the unspeakable and naming the unnameable, in many contexts of constraint. Its unique if largely unsung power to subvert the texts and occasions it adorns has already been given occasional notice in these pages, largely through the words of churchmen (Saint Augustine, Pope John XXII) who were sensitive to its potentially treacherous allure. In the case of the English declamation motet, the secret the music betrayed was as open a secret as could be.

One can well imagine the kind of impression music as voluptuous as this must have made on continental musicians when they finally had an opportunity to hear it. It opened up a whole new world of musical expressivity, and gaining access to it became item number one on the continental musical agenda. The first thing continental musicians must have noticed about the "English guise" was its luxuriant saturation with full triads, most conspicuous of all when they came in chains. Those chains, we recall, were a standard feature of English descant; now, in Dunstable's work they were absorbed into a more varied and subtly controlled compositional technique.

The only kind of parallelism Dunstable allowed was the kind that avoided perfect consonances in favor of the more mellifluous, more characteristically English imperfect ones. Thus, for example, the phrases *assimilata est palme* ("like the palm tree") and *ubera mea* ("my breasts") are made to stand out by the use of an exhaustive parallel motion of imperfect consonances, the contratenor shadowing the tenor at the third, the cantus at the sixth, as in the English descant setting of the *Beata viscera* Communion motet sampled in Ex. 11-9. And that is why *Beata viscera* has become the most famous piece of fourteenth-century English descant. It fortuitously foreshadowed the fifteenth-century pieces that marked an epoch in European music history, and has therefore been singled out in retrospect as "typical," which it was not.

The continental response to this exotic euphony came in surprisingly concrete form. Beginning in the 1420s — right on schedule, as it were, following the Council of Constance and coinciding with the Duke of Bedford's regency in France — pieces like the one in Ex. 11-12a turn up in profusion. Like *Beata viscera*, it is a Communion antiphon, based on a gregorian chant (Ex. 11-20a). It is notated as a "duo" (a piece "for two"), but a very curious one (Ex. 11-20b). The only intervals employed are octaves and sixths, with the octaves at the beginnings and ends of phrases and the sixths dominating in the middles, moving in parallel.

Now sixths are strange intervals for music in the "mainstream" theoretical tradition; while nominally consonances, they had always been described by theorists as an interval normally avoided. Here, bizarrely, they seem to be the prevalent interval. But the duo carries a "canon" or rubric that says, "If you desire a three-part piece, take the top notes and start with them, but down a fourth." When this is done, fifths are added to the framing octaves, and thirds are added to the sixths, so that the prevailing parallelism becomes exactly like the one in *Beata viscera*: an exhaustive parallelism of imperfect consonances amounting to a parallelism of triads, voiced for maximum smoothness with the "hard" and "hollow" perfect fifth avoided. In Example 11-20c, the beginning of the Communion is "realized" according to the given recipe; but any singer who can read the top part can deduce the unnotated middle voice from it by transposition, without any need for a special notation. Those handicapped by perfect pitch can substitute a different clef in their mind's eye (using what fifteenth-century musicians called "sights"), but most can make the transposition "by ear." Try it yourself with two companions: sing through Ex. 11-20b following the model indicated in Ex. 11-20c. When you do this,

EX. 11-20A   Guillaume Du Fay, *Vos qui secuti estis me* (Communion from *Missa Sancti Jacobi*), original chant

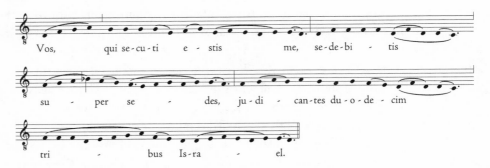

You who have followed me shall sit on seats judging the twelve tribes of Israel (Matthew 19:28).

EX. 11-20B   Guillaume Du Fay, *Vos qui secuti estis me* (Communion from *Missa Sancti Jacobi*), as notated (chant notes denoted by '+')

EX. 11-20C   Guillaume Du Fay, *Vos qui secuti estis me* (Communion from *Missa Sancti Jacobi*), first phrase as realized in performance

you will be simulating the "contenance angloise" just the way Martin Le Franc jokingly said Du Fay and Binchois did it: *En fainte, en pause, et en muance*, which roughly means "in faking, in relaxing, and in transposition [i.e., making hexachord mutations]."

FAUXBOURDON AND FABURDEN

Example 11-20 was actually composed by Du Fay himself. It is the concluding item in his *Missa Sancti Jacobi*, a "plenary" setting of the Mass for Saint James (that is, a setting that includes both the Proper and the Ordinary). Circumstantial evidence suggests that the Mass may have been written for the Church of San Giacomo Maggiore (Saint James the Greater) in Bologna, where Du Fay was sojourning in 1427 and 1428. If that date is correct, then Du Fay's Communion is the earliest surviving specimen of this technique for deriving three parts from two to achieve an instant-English effect. It would be rash, however, to call Du Fay the inventor of the technique or the year 1427 or 1428 the exact year of its invention on the basis of such scanty data. Still, Du Fay was one of the recognized specialists in the technique, with twenty-four surviving specimens to his name (four times as many as Binchois, the runner-up).

The other important distinguishing feature of the new style was that the cantus part, not the tenor, carried the original chant (transposed up an octave), as if reverting to the *vox principalis/vos organalis* texture of old. But that resemblance is fortuitous. By the fifteenth century, nobody remembered the *Musica enchiriadis* or any other treatise of its ilk. Their rediscovery had to await the zealous antiquarians of the modern age. Rather, the chant-bearing cantus was adapted by embellishment and rhythmic adjustment to the conventions of the contemporary "top-down" genre, the *cantilena* or *chanson*. The chant, in short, was disguised (or "paraphrased," as we now usually say) as a contemporary secular song.

Du Fay's ersatz-English Communion setting carries a label as well as a rubric. The setting is designated *fauxbourdon*, and the term became a standard one, sufficient in itself to take the place of the rubric. Singers seeing the word would know that the cantus part of the piece so labeled had to be doubled at the lower fourth, and that the tenor was so fashioned that a voluptuous array of parallel imperfect consonances *à l'anglaise* would emerge against the doubled line. The technique became understandably popular—faddish, in fact.

Just what the word *fauxbourdon* meant etymologically, or why it was coined (whether by Du Fay or some other French-speaking musician) to designate this particular manner of composing or arranging, remain enigmas. With only a handful of exceptions, the

FIG. II-5 Saint James with his pilgrim's staff, depicted in an illumination from the single extant complete source of Du Fay's *Missa Sancti Jacobi*, in which is the earliest fauxbourdon setting (Bologna, Civico Museo Bibliografico Musicale, MS Q 15, fol. 121, copied in Padua ca. 1420).

171 surviving pieces so labeled are all based on chants that have been transposed and embellished like the one in Du Fay's Communion. If *fauxbourdon* literally meant *faux bourdon* ("false bass," from the French *bourdonner*, to drone or sing in an undertone), then it might have referred to this transposition, leaving in the bottom voice what was usually found above (that is, a discant to a cantus firmus). If that seems a farfetched etymology, so are all the others that have been proposed from time to time. One explanation associates the *bourdon* in *fauxbourdon*, which can mean a pilgrim's staff, with St. James, who carried one, and who is depicted, staff in hand, in a miniature at the head of Du Fay's *Missa Sancti Jacobi* (Fig. II-5).

The enigma is compounded by the existence of a near-cognate English term, *faburden*, which denotes something comparable to fauxbourdon but not identical with it. How (or indeed whether) the two terms and practices are related has been a matter of considerable speculation and debate.

To begin with, the term faburden is not associated with individual written compositions but with an English technique of harmonizing chants at sight (*super librum*, roughly "off the book," or "off the page" in contemporary parlance). According to a treatise called *The Sight of Faburdon*, copied around 1450 and the sole surviving theoretical description of the method, two singers would accompany the singer of the chant with unwritten counterpoints, one (called the "deschaunte") above the written part and the other (called the "counter note") below. The "counterer" would sing thirds and fifths below the plainchant and the "discanter" would double it at the upper fourth. A didactic example of faburden that happened to be written in a Scottish treatise of the mid-sixteenth century shows the result (Ex. II-21). It is based on *Salvator mundi Domine* ("O Lord, Savior of the World"), a frequent English contrafact of the *Pentecost* hymn *Veni creator spiritus* (already encountered as Ex. 2-5c). The original chant is carried by the middle voice—the one voice, ironically enough, that was not notated at all in *fauxbourdon* settings.

The result, so far as the listener is concerned, differs from the *fauxbourdon* settings of Du Fay and his continental contemporaries only in pitch range, if it differs at all. In the case of *faburden* the chant is thought of as the "meane" or middle voice and the doubling part as the "tryble" above it. In the case of *fauxbourdon* the chant is thought of as the "cantus" and the doubling part as the contratenor below it. But it is a distinction that makes no audible difference, just as it makes no difference whether the lowest voice is thought of as making fifths and thirds against the middle or octaves and sixths against the top.

The reasonable and simple assumption would be that fauxbourdon was just the continental written-down imitation of the English oral practice. But the actual evidence does not fit that easy explanation. For one thing, *The Sight of Faburdon* (or at least its extant source) is a good deal later than the probable date of Du Fay's *Missa Sancti Jacobi*, in which the first use of the term *fauxbourdon* occurs. And for another, the word *faburden* is much more easily construed as a corruption of *fauxbourdon* than the other way around. (We can easily imagine etymologies for *fauxbourdon*, however flimsy; explaining *faburden* as "the bass that sings fa" (because it uses a lot of B-flats) is a rather desperate contrivance.) So what happened? Did the English borrow back a continental cookbook recipe for imitating the English? To believe that is neither simple nor particularly reasonable. What is likelier is that the term *faburden*, adapted from *fauxbourdon*, was applied retroactively by some English writers to one of many varieties of "sighting," or ad hoc chant harmonization, which had been practiced by the English all through the thirteenth and fourteenth centuries. This particular one happened to resemble, in a relatively crude and unembellished way, the very elegant written compositions from abroad that began to travel back to England, with their deft and graceful chant-paraphrases in the manner of the courtly chanson.

But *faburden* was and remained a "sight," an older English practice and an oral one. It can be documented in principle as far back as Anonymus IV, the first treatise that mentions sights. Thus it differed in kind, despite its belated similarity in nomenclature, from *fauxbourdon*, a later continental practice and an elegantly embellished, written one. Later, the technique became the property of organists, who used faburden "counters" or bass lines (like the bottom voice in Ex. 11-21) as grounds for improvisation, and, beginning in the early sixteenth century, kept little books of them handy. You can almost always tell a "faburden," as organists informally called the bottom line of a chant harmonization, by its initial rising fourth, the inevitable product of the "sight" technique. Since the "counter" had to begin at the fifth below the chant and proceed to the third below the chant, and since perhaps nine chants out of ten begin with a rising step progression, nine "faburdens" out of ten will begin with the rising fourth.

Lots of questions regarding the reciprocal early histories of fauxbourdon and faburden remain unanswered. For instance, did the inventors of fauxbourdon actually

EX. 11-21 *Salvator mundi Domine* in faburden

hear English choirs (at Constance, say, or in Paris) singing *super librum* — i.e., singing what eventually became known as faburden? Or did they hear something much more impressive, found a simple way of counterfeiting it, and gave the author of *The Sight of Faburdon* an idea for simplifying the technique of "sighting"? This last possibility, with its intriguing suggestion of a true cross-fertilization of cultures, is supported by a sentence in *The Sight of Faburdon* that calls the practice so designated only the lowliest and most commonplace of sight techniques.

Really skillful British extemporizers, going all the way back to the time of Giraldus Cambrensis, could come up with much more impressive harmonizations, not only in three parts but in four or even more. Desiderius Erasmus (Erasmus of Rotterdam), the great humanist scholar and a great Anglophile, reported in amazement, following one of his many visits to England toward the end of the fifteenth century, that in English churches "many sing together, but none of the singers produce those sounds which the notes on the page indicate." (This sounds a lot like Giraldus, in fact, except that the Welsh singers he described did not use books at all.)

We can share in Erasmus's amazement if we travel forward in time a bit for a quick look at the latest and most advanced treatise on *supra librum* singing from the British Isles. A manual copied in Scotland around 1580, but summing up two or three hundred years' worth of singers' lore, ends with a final chapter on "countering" in which twelve rules are given that, when mastered over considerable time, enabled a quartet of singers to take a simple line of plainchant (like Ex. 11-22a) and from it work up on the spot a polyphonic realization like the one shown in the treatise's final didactic example. The tenor sings a highly embellished version of the cantus firmus at the original pitch (each measure beginning and ending with the notated pitch, but with the middle filled

EX. 11-22A *Heir beginnis countering,* presumed cantus firmus

EX. 11-22B *Heir beginnis countering,* final example, mm. 1–6

EX. II-22B (*continued*)

most fancifully), and the other parts carol away even more ornately, albeit according to strict — and, no doubt, well-kept — secret formulas (Ex. 11-22b):

Compared to this, fauxbourdon (to say nothing of simple faburden) might seem like child's play. But the point of fauxbourdon, as practiced by the continental composers, was not so much the contrapuntal amplification of the chant as it was the transformation and elaboration of "plainsong" into "fancy song" (or, to use contemporary terminology, *cantus figuralis*, "figured" or patterned song). The raw material of plainchant was processed in this way into the highly refined style of the courtly "art song."

DU FAY AND BINCHOIS

It seems no accident, then, that Du Fay and Binchois (Fig. 11-6), the two most prolific masters of fauxbourdon were also the leading song composers of their generation. Nor is it a coincidence that the liturgical genre most characteristically treated in the fauxbourdon manner was the hymn, the most songlike of chant types.

Gilles de Bins, called Binchois (d. 1460) spent virtually his entire career as a court and chapel musician to Philip the Good, the long-reigning Duke of Burgundy, whose court was widely acknowledged to be the most magnificent in Western Europe at a time when art consumption was a prime measure of courtly magnificence. His fauxbourdon setting of *Veni Creator Spiritus* (Ex. 11-23) was written for Philip's chapel. Compare it with Ex. 11-21 to see how fauxbourdon and faburden relate to one another. It is not just that the settings are pitched differently because of the differing placement of the cantus firmus. Binchois's cantus part, while modest as such things go, is nevertheless an elegant paraphrase of the transposed chant melody. The embellishments occur mainly at cadences, where they invoke the typical formulas of the chanson style: the 7 – 6 suspension at the end

FIG. 11-6   Guillaume Du Fay and Gilles Binchois, French followers of Dunstable and the contenance angloise, as depicted in a manuscript of Martin le Franc's epic *Le champion des dames* copied in Arras in 1451.

EX. II-23   Gilles Binchois, *Veni Creator Spiritus*

of the first phrase (on *Creator*), the "Landini sixth" at the end of the second (on *spiritus*), and so on.

This is definitely an "art" setting, if a relatively unshowy one, and literate through and through, worlds away from the bald, nonfigural "sight" harmonization in Ex. 11-21. The artfulness is most apparent in the rhythmic design, which has been calculated with great subtlety both as to declamation and as to variety. The basic mensuration is that of *tempus perfectum*—semibreves grouped by threes into perfect breves. But Binchois applies hemiola at two levels, one above the basic mensuration (at the level of *modus*) and one below (at the level of *prolatio*). For an example of the latter, see the setting of the word *gratia*, where the cantus breaks momentarily into a trochaic pattern of semibreves and minims (quarters and eighths in transcription) that implies a grouping of three minims into perfect semibreves. And for the former, see what the tenor does immediately afterward (on *quae tu creasti*), where a series of imperfect breves (half notes in transcription) implies a grouping of three breves into perfect longs. That sort of supple, "natural" artfulness—artfulness within apparent simplicity—is the mark of a really successful assimilation of the "English sound" into the continental literate tradition.

We have already met Guillaume Du Fay (d. 1474) in chapter 8, and know from his extraordinary motet *Nuper rosarum flores* that he was an extremely ambitious composer. He had a brilliant international career, with phases in Italy (including a stint in the papal choir) and at the court of Savoy, a duchy in the Alpine region of what is now eastern France and western Switzerland, before returning to his native region as a canon at the cathedral of Cambrai, near the present-day border of France and Belgium. His setting of the Marian hymn *Ave maris stella* (previously encountered as Ex. 2-7a), while also fairly modest as befits the genre, is more ornate than Binchois's and assimilates the chant melody much more thoroughly to the style of the courtly chanson (Ex. 11-24). As befits Du Fay's glamorous career and his comprehensive stylistic range, even his hymn settings are unmistakably the work of the most enterprising composer of the age.

This greater assimilation is accomplished in two ways. First, Du Fay's chant paraphrase is far more decorative than Binchois's; there is nothing in the Binchois setting like the first measure of Du Fay's, in which the plainchant's opening leap of a fifth is filled in with what amounts to an original melody. The cadential structure of Du Fay's setting is also much freer from that of the plainchant than Binchois's—and quite purposefully so. The first cadence, for example, joins the finishing note of *maris* to the first note of *stella*, creating a stopping point on C, a note to which no cadence is made in the original chant. The alternation of cadences on C and D thus obtained in the first half of the setting is then replayed in the second half (C on *virgo*, D on *porta*), creating a bipartite structural symmetry not at all typical of plainchant melodies but very typical of courtly songs, whose "fixed forms" always comprised two main sections.

Even more boldly, Du Fay writes an alternate third part, labeled "*contratenor sine faulx bourdon*," that replaces the "derived" fauxbourdon voice with a full-fledged contrapuntal line that behaves exactly like the traditional chanson contratenor. It occupies the same register as the tenor, with which it frequently crosses. The first crossing is a marvelous joke, in fact. The first measure of the new contratenor coincides with — or rather, is disguised as — the beginning of the fauxbourdon realization, so that when the downbeat G replaces the expected F♯ in the second measure, it comes as an attention-grabbing surprise. That G forms a $^{10}_{5}$ chord with the other voices — a chord that simply cannot occur in a fauxbourdon. The contratenor stays under the tenor all the way to the end of the fourth bar, completely changing the harmonization of the chant-derived part and converting the setting for all practical purposes into a chanson. Then the contratenor reverts to its initial position above the tenor by leaping an octave, which (as we will see

EX. II-24A   Guillaume Du Fay, *Ave maris stella* in fauxbourdon

EX. 11-24B   *Ave maris stella* with "contratenor sine faulx bourdon"

in a moment) was a most typical sort of cadential behavior for a chanson contratenor at this time. All in all, Du Fay's setting shows him to be a singularly self-conscious artist and one especially aware of the distinguishing features and requirements of genres. As we have observed before, that sort of awareness enables an artist to play upon, and fully engage, the expectations of an informed audience.

As an example of the sort of contemporary courtly chanson Du Fay's hymn setting parodies, let us consider one of his own (Ex. 11-25). What to call it is already a problem, since it exists in different manuscript sources with two different texts, one in Italian and the other in French. The source containing the Italian text, *Quel fronte signorille* ("That noble brow"), also contains the note "Rome composuit" (composed in Rome),

EX. 11-25   Guillaume Du Fay, *Craindre vous vueil*

EX. II-25 *(continued)*

A	Craindre vous veuil, doulce dame de pris,	I wish to fear you, sweet and precis
	Amer, doubter, louer, en fais, en dis,	Love, honor, praise in acts and words
	Tous mon vivant, en quelque lieu que soye,	As long as I may live, wherever I may
B	Et vous donner, míamour, ma seule joye,	And give to you, my love and only joy,
	Le cuer de moy tant que je seray vis.	My heatr for as long as I may live.

a	Jamais ne suy anneuieux ne pensis	Never am I sorrowful or pensive
	Ne douleureux, quant je voy vo clair vis	Nor sad when I see your radiant face
	Et vo mainteing en alant par la voie.	And your bearing as you walk along.

| A | Craindre... (3 lines of refrain) |

a	De vous amer cel míest un paradis,	To love you that to me is paradise,
	Vëu les biens qui sont en vous compris;	Seeing all goodness with which you are endow
	Faire le doy quoy quíavenir un doye.	And i must love you whatever may come of it.
b	A vous me rens, lyes mieux que de soye,	To you I surrender, happy to live
	Joieusement, en bon espoir toudis.	Joyfully and always in good hope.

| A | Craindre... (5 lines of refrain) |
| B | |

which would date it to Du Fay's period of papal employment, between 1428 and 1434. There seems to be good reason, though, for believing that only the text was composed in Rome, and perhaps not even by Du Fay.

The French version, *Craindre vous vueil* ("To fear you is my wish"), is in the standard *rondeau cinquain* form, with a five-line stanza and corresponding refrain, and this fits the shape and cadential structure of the music very ingeniously. The poem has the rhyme scheme A A B/B A, with the slash showing the division between the refrain (first part of the music) and the remainder of the stanza. The music associates cadences on C with the "A" lines and cadences on G with the "B" lines. (By contrast, the Italian text has a four-line stanza, and the music ends with the cadence in m. 25 — off the final. That seems a sure sign of clumsy contrafactum.) In addition, the French text embodies an acrostic linking the names "Cateline" (whoever she may have been; some suggest the composer's sister) and "Dufai." The music was more likely fashioned to fit it than the other way around.

The octave leap noted earlier in Du Fay's "contratenor sine faulx bourdon" for *Ave maris stella* occurs in the very first cadence of *Craindre vous vueil*. It was standard contratenor behavior at cadences, alongside (and fast replacing) the "doubled leading tone" variety that had been customary in the fourteenth century (compare the second cadence a couple of measures later). Notice, though, that the "new" cadence is just another way of filling the same frame: the "structural pair" of cantus and tenor still make the cadence by moving from imperfect consonance to perfect consonance (here, from third to unison) in contrary motion. Yet another way of accompanying the same structural pair can be seen at the "medial cadence" of the rondeau. The superius and tenor again approach a unison; the contratenor, this time, does not leap up an octave, which would put it out of range, but drops a fifth to double the superius and tenor's pitch at the octave.

Thus there is now a choice of three possible contratenor moves (summed up in Ex. 11-26) to accompany the obligatory cadence-defining movement of superius and tenor. They will coexist throughout the century, with the second steadily gaining on the first, and (with the standardization of four-part textures, to be described in the next chapter) with the third finally displacing both of the others.

With more than sixty courtly chansons constituting more than half his surviving output, Binchois was his generation's great specialist in the genre, famous as a melodist both in his own day and in ours. Like Du Fay, he composed mainly *rondeaux cinquains*, but his greatest achievements were ballades. By the early fifteenth century, the ballade, the oldest and most distinguished of the courtly song genres, had become a genre of special grandeur, reserved for special occasions, chiefly commemorative and public. One of the grandest Franco-Burgundian ballades of all was *Deuil angoisseux* by Christine de Pisane

EX. 11-26 Cadential motion in superius/tenor pair accompanied by three different contratenors, doubled leading tone

EX. II-26B Octave leap

EX. II-26C "V –I"

(or Pizan, 1364 – ca. 1430) — one of the outstanding poets of the day, remembered now (in the words of the historian Natalie Zemon Davis) as "France's first professional literary woman"[8] — as set to music by Binchois for performance at the court of Burgundy.

By the time he set it, Christine's poem was already an old and famous one, composed on the death of her husband, Etienne Castel, a notary in service to the king of France, in 1390. Christine remained a quasi-official French court poet and a partisan commentator on the Hundred Years War. Her "Letter Concerning the Prison of Human Life" (*L'Espistre de la prison de vie humaine*) was intended in the first instance as a consolation to the widows left behind by the fallen heros of France on the battlefield of Agincourt, and at the end of her life Christine wrote "The Tale of Joan of Arc" (*Le Ditié de Jeanne d'Arc*), the earliest encomium to the intrepid Maid of Orléans, and one of the most authoritative, since it was the only one that dated from its subject's lifetime.

It is a bit ironic, then, to find in Binchois's setting of Christine's early ballade (Ex. II-27) a gorgeous epitome of the *contenance angloise*, the English-influenced style that testified so eloquently, if obliquely, to the ascendancy of France's enemy. It is a veritable orgy of F-major "euphony," opening with arpeggiations of the F-major triad in both cantus and tenor, sonorously supported by a pair of droning contratenors on the final and the fifth above. When the tenor reaches its high A at the end of the word *angoisseux*, the harmony sounding is the most brilliant possible spacing of an F-major triad: $^{10}_{8}$ over the final.

This ravishing four-voice texture is the "big band" sound of the day, achieved by replacing the contratenor in a three-part version of the song (itself achieved by providing a contratenor to add harmonious sonority to a self-sufficient structural pair) with a pair of complementary contratenors to amplify the sonority. The lowest voice in the transcription. could still function correctly as a contratenor by itself. It regularly makes its cadences by octave leap: see mm. 11–12, 21–22, 25–26, 28, 34–35, 44–45 (= 11–12), 53–54 (= 21–22), the final pair of cadences recapitulating the first pair since this is a "rhymed" or "rounded" ballade, in which the ending of the "B" section quotes the ending of the "A." The presence of the fourth voice makes it possible to complete the triad at each cadence by adding a third to the obligatory octave of cantus and tenor and the obligatory fifth of the contratenor.

FIG. 11-7 Christine de Pisane at her writing desk (London, British Library, MS Harley 4431, fol. 4).

Binchois's *Deuil angoisseux* can tell us an enormous amount about the esthetics of fifteenth-century courtly art. It is a marvelously effective, even hair-raising outpouring of emotion, and yet it scarcely conforms to our own conventional notions of what makes music sound "sad." Our present-day musical "instincts" demand that laments be set to extra slow, extra low music, harmonically dark ("minor") or dissonant. (We also expect such music to be sung and played with covered timbre and a greater than ordinary range of dynamic and tempo fluctuation.) Binchois's setting flatly contradicts these assumptions with its bright F-majorish (English) tonality, its high tessitura (especially in the tenor), and its very wide vocal ranges. Even the tempo contradicts our normal assumptions: the time signature carries a slash through it comparable to the slash in our familiar "cut time," which places the tactus on the breve, not the semibreve, causing all the note values to be shorter (hence, to go by quicker) than normal.

What is conveyed, in short, is not private anguish but a public proclamation of grief, as suggested in the poem itself with an *envoi* addressed to an assembled audience of "princes." The mood is one of elevation (*hauteur* in French): elevation in tone, in diction, in delivery, all reflecting the elevated social setting in which the performance took place. *Hauteur* had two specifically musical meanings as well, which relate metaphorically to

EX. 11-27   Gilles Binchois, *Deuil angoisseux*

EX. II-27 (continued)

EX. II-27 *(continued)*

Deuil angoisseux, rage desmesuree,
Grief desespoir, plein de forsennement,
Langour sanz fin et vie male ̗ree
Pleine de plour, díangoisse et de tourment,
Cuer douleureux qui vit obcurement,
Tenebreux corps sur le point de partir
Ay, sanz cesser, continuellement;
Et si ne puis ne garir ne morir.

Anguished grief, immoderate fury,
grievous despair, full of madness,
endless languor and a life of misfortune,
full of tears, anguish and torment,
doleful heart, living in darkness,
wraithlike body on the point of death,
are mine continually without surcease;
and thus I can neither be cured nor die.

the general concept: highness of pitch and loudness of sonority, both of which are exaggerated in Binchois's setting of Christine's lament. And rightly so, for fifteenth-century musicians still quoted Isidore of Seville, Pope Gregory's contemporary, on the qualities of a good singing voice: "high, sweet and loud."

Even "sweetness" comes in many varieties. To us it may connote a highly nuanced sort of tone production suitable for the subjectively expressive music of more recent centuries. The formal, conventionalized public rhetoric of the court called for a different sort of sweetness, the sort achieved by the "English" euphony of clear, uncomplicated, well-matched timbres, true tuning of harmonies, and sensitivity to the flexibly shifting rhythmic groupings we have already observed. Many scholars and performers have become convinced that the most desirable performing ensemble for a court ballade was one of voices unaccompanied by instruments, despite the absence of text in the tenor and the contratenors.[9] The singers of these parts may have vocalized or ad-libbed textual abridgments.

Again we are reminded that music in performance is something different from music on the page, and that even the most literately conceived music (and no music was ever more literary than the fifteenth-century court chanson) must be mediated through oral practices and traditions in order to become sound. That is why the study of "performance practice," which is precisely the collection and interpretation of evidence about the oral and unwritten, is and will always be one of the liveliest areas of "early music" research.

Emblems and Dynasties

The Cyclic Mass Ordinary Setting

THE INTERNATIONALISM OF THE UPPER CRUST

Johannes Tinctoris (ca. 1435–1511), a minor composer but a theorist of encyclopedic ambition, can be our very capable guide to the music of his time, the mid- to late fifteenth century. His twelve treatises, covering the properties and powers of music, the qualities of the modes, notation, counterpoint, form, mensural practice, terminology, and even (in his last work, called *De inventione et usu musicae*) what might be called musical sociology, attempt collectively to encompass all of contemporary music, its practices and its products alike. They are liberally illustrated with extracts not only from the works of ancient authorities but from the works of the leading composers of Tinctoris's own generation — the musical *literati* who staffed the principal courts and churches of Latin Christendom at the time of his writing.

Tinctoris, the theorist's Latin professional name, means "dyer." He was born near Nivelles (Nijvel in Flemish), a town in present-day Belgium, and attended the University of Orléans as a member of the "German nation" or non-French constituency there. No one knows today what his native language was or what his original surname may have been: in French it would have been Teinturier, in Dutch or Flemish de Vaerwere, in German Färbers. Around 1472, after a stint teaching the choirboys at Chartres Cathedral near Paris, and singing under Du Fay at the Cathedral of Cambrai, he entered the service of Ferdinand (Ferrante) I, the Aragonese (that is, Spanish) ruler of the kingdom of Naples in southern Italy, and seems to have remained in Naples until his retirement, if not his death.

Tinctoris's international, polyglot career, and in particular its southward trajectory from the Low Countries to Italy, were characteristic, even paradigmatic, for his time. The old Frankish territories were still the chief seats of musical learning, but the *nouveau riche* Italian courts, avidly competing with one another for the most brilliant artistic personnel, were becoming the great magnets for musical talent. Even after impregnation by the English, the basic technique of music remained French; but once the northerners began invading the south, it became impossible to tell by style where a piece of written continental music had been composed. Europe, musically, seemed one.

But this apparent musical unity should not be read as an indicator of cultural or social unity. Literate musicians, it is time once again to recall, served a tiny clientele of aristocrats and ecclesiastics. These elite classes did indeed identify with their

FIG. 12-1   Tinctoris at his writing desk, a portrait (possibly from life) by the Neapolitan artist Cristoforo Majorana from a late fifteenth-century manuscript of Tinctoris's treatises (Valencia, Biblioteca Universitaria).

counterparts throughout the length and breadth of Europe, but at less exalted social levels, Europe, musically and in every other way, was far from one. The minority culture of the literate cannot yet be taken as representative of society as a whole. It was just the surface cream — if a less complimentary analogy is desired, call it an oil slick — that only seems homogenized from our bleary historical distance. Owing to the nature of our sources of evidence, the surface slick tends to hide the rest from view; and unless we are careful to remind ourselves, we can easily forget that the vast majority of Europeans in the fifteenth century lived out their lives in complete ignorance of the music we are about to investigate.

THE "TINCTORIS GENERATION"

The musical literati from whom Tinctoris drew his didactic examples are the very ones whose works are found in practical sources throughout Europe irrespective of provenance. In the same preface to his book on mensural proportions in which he called Dunstable the fountainhead of contemporary music and consigned everything earlier to oblivion, Tinctoris cited an honor roll of his great coevals — a sort of musical peerage. Pride of place went to Johannes Ockeghem and Antoine Busnoys, who in their joint pre-eminence have, much like Du Fay and Binchois, haunted historical memory as a pair.

Ockeghem (d. 1497), the older of the two, came not from the East Flemish town of the same name, but from St. Ghislain, near the large town of Mons in the French-speaking Belgian province of Hainaut to the south. By 1443 he was a singer at the cathedral of Notre Dame in Antwerp, the leading church of Flanders. A *déploration* or chanson-lament Ockeghem composed on the death of Binchois in 1460 suggests a master-pupil relationship with the leading composer to the Burgundian court. It was at the court and chapel of the French king, however, that Ockeghem made his real mark, beginning in 1451. He became a great favorite of Charles VII, who elevated him to high

church rank as treasurer of the royal collegiate church of St. Martin of Tours in the
valley of the Loire, where the king had his
winter palace. Under Charles's successor,
Louis XI, Ockeghem became concurrently
a canon of Notre Dame de Paris. By the time
of his death he was surely the most socially
exalted musician in Europe, and the richest
as well: he was a major *rentier* or urban
property-owner, and rented out houses to
many persons of means and even eminence,
including Jean Fouquet, the great miniatur-
ist and portrait-painter, Ockeghem's court
counterpart among artists.

A famous manuscript illumination
from around 1523 (Fig. 12-2) perhaps
fancifully depicts Ockeghem (by then dead
a quarter century) and his chapel choir. The
great composer — famous for his deep voice
and so advanced in age when he died that his
official court eulogist, the poet Guillaume

FIG. 12-2   Ockeghem and his choir, depicted
ca. 1523 in a manuscript from Rouen (Paris,
Bibliothèque Nationale, Fonds Français 1537,
fol. 58v).

Crétin, lamented his not reaching a round hundred years — must surely be the burly,
bespectacled figure in the right foreground. The most valuable historical evidence in
this picture is the placement of the choristers' hands, visibly on the music rack and
palpably on one another's shoulders. The singers are not touching one another out of
camaraderie alone: as contemporary writers confirm, their hands were busily employed
in physically transmitting the tactus beat. As we will see, Ockeghem wrote some music
that kept his singers' hands quite full.

Busnoys (d. 1492), whose name suggests that he may have come from the town
of Busnes in northern France, was Ockeghem's counterpart (and Binchois's successor) at the court of Burgundy, where he served as "first singer" to Charles the
Bold (d. 1477), the last of the Burgundian dukes. As Ockeghem may have been
a pupil of Binchois, so Busnoys may have received instruction from Ockeghem at
Tours, where Busnoys served briefly during the 1460s, before joining the household
of the future Duke of Burgundy. (Charles the Bold and Louis XI, Ockeghem's
patron, were bitter enemies; between 1467 and 1477, one may say with confidence, the two composers had few opportunities to meet.) After Charles's death,
Busnoys remained in service to his patron's daughter Mary of Burgundy (who
was also the niece of the English King Edward IV). Her death in 1484 extin-
guished the Burgundian dynasty. There is evidence that Busnoys now retired to
the Belgian city of Bruges, becoming cantor at a parish church that was occasionally patronized by the Archduke (later Holy Roman Emperor) Maximilian, Mary's
widower.

Busnoys is perhaps the earliest major composer from whom autograph manuscripts survive, so that we know how he personally spelled his surname (often routinely modernized in the scholarly literature to Busnois). In a motet to his patron saint and namesake, the fourth-century Egyptian recluse St. Anthony Abbot, Busnoys worked his name into an elaborate multilingual pun that depends on the spelling with *y* to make (Greek) sense (see Fig. 12-3). Having received a master's degree (possibly at the University of Paris), Busnoys loved to show off his erudition—in particular, his familiarity with Greek—in little ways like this. And he was by no means exceptional in this quirk; the fifteenth century was one of those times when intellectual attainments and cerebral virtuosity were considered appropriate in an artist.

FIG. 12-3 Autograph copy of Busnoys's self-referential motet *Anthoni usque limina* (Brussels, Bibliothèque Royal Albert I, MS 5557, fol. 48v). The first pair of words in the first line of the text (*ANTHONI USque limina . . .*—"Anthony, you who to the furthest bounds . . .")—and the last pair of words in the last line (*Fiat in omniBUS NOYS*—"that understanding may come to all") contain a rebus of the composer's name.

Busnoys also put his formidable linguistic, musical, and architectonic skills to work in praise of his great contemporary and mentor. The motet *In hydraulis* ("On the Water organs"), written sometime between his stay at Tours and his patron's accession to the ducal throne in 1467, compares Ockeghem with Pythagoras and Orpheus, musicians of mythological stature. The motet is built over a *pes*, a repetitive tenor phrase in three notes (OC-KE-GHEM?) that is put through a series of transpositions that collectively sum up all the Pythagorean consonances (Ex. 12-1a). This whole complex of repetitions, moreover, which may be regarded as the *color* of the motet, is put through four complete repetitions, each of them under a different mensuration sign; the resulting speeds are calibrated to reproduce the same Pythagorean proportions—in another musical dimension, so to speak.

Ockeghem is actually named at the beginning of the second major section of the motet, and the phrase containing his name is turned into a musical emblem through

EX. 12-1A   Antoine Busnoys, *In hydraulis*, tenor layout

EX. 12-1B   Antoine Busnoys, *In hydraulis*, beginning of *secunda pars* (point of imitation on "haec Ockeghem")

Haec Ockeghem

a series of canonic entries (Ex. 12-1b). With its pes and its significant use of imitation and voice exchange, *In hydraulis* might be looked upon as a distant, university-educated descendant of the old Sumer Canon.

Ockeghem returned the compliment in the form of an even more elaborate motet called *Ut heremita solus* ("Lonely as a hermit"), of which the text has been lost, but whose incipit seems to combine a reference to Busnoys's hermit patron saint with an encomium, loneliness often being a trope for eminence (as in "it's lonely at the top"). The tenor of Ockeghem's motet is based on a six-note pes (AN-THO-NI-US BUS-NOYS?), to realize which requires solving an immensely difficult puzzle. (Compliments, at this rarefied, snooty level, are often hard to distinguish from challenges.) Most telling of all, its opening puts a variant of the same phrase that had carried Ockeghem's name in Busnoys's motet through another series of imitative voice exchanges (Ex. 12-1c).

EX. 12-1C   Johannes Ockeghem returns the compliment to Busnoys in *Ut heremita solus*

Besides Tinctoris's encomia to them, and their encomia to one another, there is further evidence in the surviving musical sources of the fantastic prestige that these composers achieved, and the veneration in which Ockeghem particularly was held. By all odds the most beautiful musical manuscript of the fifteenth century is a priceless presentation volume that contains Ockeghem's virtually complete collected sacred works and some of Busnoys's as well. It was commissioned in 1498 from the foremost scriptorium in Europe—the Flanders workshop of Pieter van den Hove, known as Petrus Alamire ("Peter A-above-or-below-middle-C")—as a memorial to the just-deceased Ockeghem by a courtier to the French king Charles VIII, the son and grandson of the composer's chief patrons. The intended recipient was possibly Philip I (the Handsome) of Spain, the son of the Holy Roman Emperor Maximilian by Mary of Burgundy, Busnoys's former employer. It was purchased by Agostino Chigi (KEE-jee), a great arts patron, for the collection of the rapacious Spanish pontiff, Pope Alexander VI (father of the notorious Cesare and Lucrezia Borgia). From there it went into the Vatican library, of which it is now one of the prize holdings. Fig. 12-4 shows a typically lavish opening from this manuscript, now called the Chigi Codex. The music shown is by Ockeghem, whose name appears at the upper left.

In addition to the superstars Ockeghem and Busnoys, Tinctoris's cast of characters included several other important contemporary Franco-Burgundian or Franco-Flemish composers. Johannes Regis (d. 1496) served as Du Fay's secretary at Cambrai during the last decade of the older man's life. Caron, whose first name is never given in the musical sources and is consequently uncertain (Tinctoris calls him Firminus, but there are archival references to a Philippe Caron as well), most likely trained at Cambrai under Du Fay and served the Burgundian court alongside Busnoys. Guillaume Faugues is known mainly by his works and by Tinctoris's references to him. Documents suggest that he received his early training at the cathedral of Bourges, France's second city under Charles VII and Louis XI, in the early 1460s.

The composers named thus far are not known to have visited Italy, but only Ockeghem's career is well enough documented to preclude the possibility of an Italian sojourn. Even in their physical absence, though, their music was widely circulated and performed in southern Europe, as Tinctoris's wide and deep knowledge of it already attests. Their works, and the works of many lesser French and Flemish masters, make up the bulk of the repertory preserved in the massive choirbooks that were copied during the reign of Pope Sixtus IV (1471–84) for use at his newly built and consecrated

FIG. 12-4 Opening of Ockeghem's *Missa caput* from the so-called Chigi Codex (Vatican City, Biblioteca Apostolica Vaticana, MS Chigi C.VIII.234, fols. 64v–65).

personal worship hall, the celebrated Sistine Chapel. These choirbooks survive to this day in the Vatican library. In 1472, Ockeghem received a personal communication from Duke Galeazzo Maria Sforza in Milan requesting help in recruiting French singers for his chapel. Several important composers of the early sixteenth century (among them Loyset Compère) who were too young to be noticed by Tinctoris, and who will therefore figure in a later chapter of this book, had their professional start in the Milanese court chapel choir around this time, possibly at Ockeghem's recommendation.

Beginning with the generation after that of Ockeghem and Busnoys — the generation Tinctoris called "younger composers," who were reaching maturity in the 1470s and lived into the next century — residence at the high-paying Italian courts became the rule. Their outstanding representative was Jacobus Hobrecht (better known as Obrecht, as habitually given in Italian sources), who after a distinguished career in Dutch and Belgian cities such as Antwerp, Utrecht, Bergen op Zoom, and Bruges was summoned to the magnificent court of Ercole I, the Duke of Ferrara, where he died of plague in 1505.

THE CYCLIC MASS

The major genre on which all these composers lavished their skills, and the chief vehicle for their fame, was a genre that did not exist before the fifteenth century. It may be fairly regarded as the emblem of the century's musical attainments, for it was a genre of unprecedented altitude.

The quality of "height" or *hauteur*, as we observed at the end of the previous chapter, was an important determinant of style within an aristocratic culture. It was the yardstick by which subject matter and rhetorical manner had been correlated since pre-Christian times. The classic formulation was given by Marcus Tullius Cicero (106–43 BCE), the Roman statesman and orator, who sought an ideal union of rhetoric and philosophy to guide human affairs. To make knowledge effective, it had to be cast in the proper expressive form.

Cicero distinguished three basic styles of oratory, which he called *gravis, mediocris,* and *attenuatus*: weighty, middling, and plain. The Carolingian rhetoricians and their scholastic descendants in the twelfth century had modified the Ciceronian doctrine to reflect literary rather than oratorical categories, substituting *humilis* ("low") for Cicero's plain-spoken style and associating it with the vernacular tongues that had replaced Latin for everyday speech, including the speech of the unlettered. In arguing for artistic literature in the vernacular, Dante had set himself the task of proving (on the basis of the troubadours' achievement) that vernacular languages could accommodate all three levels of discourse, identifying them in terms that had even more obvious social connotations: *illustre, mediocre, humile* (noble, middling, lowly).

It was Tinctoris who first applied a variation of this time-honored scheme to music. In his dictionary of terms, he designated three musical styles, calling them *magnus, mediocris,* and *parvus*: great (= high-ranking or lofty), middle, and small (= low-ranking).

He associated each of them with a genre. The small, predictably enough, was associated with the vernacular chanson. The middle was associated with the motet, especially as transformed by contact with English models, as we witnessed in the previous chapter.

The great or lofty style was the style of the Mass — a new type of standardized Mass composition in which five items from the Ordinary (no longer including the brief dismissal-plus-response formula) were set as a musical unit. A musical unit precisely, not a liturgical one, for there is nothing unified about the Kyrie, Gloria, Credo, Sanctus, and Agnus Dei as a set of texts. They had different histories, traced in the early chapters of this book; their structures were different, and they served different functions. Two are prayers, two are acclamations, one is a profession of faith. Only the Kyrie and the Gloria are consecutive in the liturgy.

Settings of the Ordinary in the fourteenth century, as we have seen, were of individual items, or occasionally of pairs. Such complete formularies as exist were ad hoc compilations of individual, musically heterogeneous items (even when, as in the case of Machaut, they were all the work of a single author), opportunistically assembled for "votive" — which from the church's point of view chiefly meant fund-raising — purposes.

And now, all of a sudden (or so it seems), the Mass Ordinary emerges as a unified musical genre — the most fully unified in history, covering a longer span, and shaped by more purely "musical," composerly (hence arbitrary) processes, than any we have yet encountered. The fact that its constituent sections were nonconsecutive in performance meant that its musical unity was "thematized" and made symbolic. The musically integrated Mass Ordinary setting now unified the whole service, symbolically integrating a process lasting as much as an hour or more by means of periodic inspiring returns to familiar, hence significant, sounds.

It was the most potent demonstration yet of the abstract shaping powers of music and their potential import in mediating between the human and the divine; and it was a kind of shaping for which the literate tradition and only the literate tradition could provide the necessary means. Consequently, the genre of the musically unified Mass Ordinary quickly acquired enormous prestige as a symbol of ecclesiastical power — the power, let us recall, of a church that was itself newly restored to unity, a church that frequently lent its support to temporal authorities, intervening in their affairs and disputes, and that just as frequently drew similar support from them.

Cyclic Mass Ordinaries were what chiefly filled those early Sistine chapel manuscripts, and thirteen of these mammoth cycles, posthumously collected together in one fantastically decorative presentation manuscript, were what attested to — or rather, what established — Ockeghem's claim to pre-eminence among the composers of his day. In short, the Mass Ordinary "cycle" became, in Manfred Bukofzer's words, "the focal point on which all the artistic aspirations and technical achievements of the composer converged," for it was the focal point of patronage and prestige.[1]

CANTUS FIRMUS AS TROPE OF GLORY

But first, its history: one that, like so much in the history of fifteenth-century music, begins with the English. And it begins at the moment when the device of paired movements based on a common cantus firmus tenor, already found in the Old Hall manuscript, was expanded to encompass all the major components of the Ordinary.

We cannot tell when that decisive moment occurred; all we can know are its first preserved fruits. One of the earliest is a Kyrie – Gloria – Credo – Sanctus set somewhat shakily attributed to Dunstable, based on a tenor derived from *Da gaudiorum praemia* ("O grant the prize that brings joy"), a responsory for Trinity Sunday (the Sunday after Pentecost). It is bound up with the family history of the Henrys of England and was very likely first performed at the wedding of Henry V and Catherine of Valois, his joyful prize and daughter of the French King Charles VI, which took place on Trinity Sunday, 2 June 1420. The same Mass seems to have been performed again at another royal occasion, the Paris coronation of Henry VI in 1431.

There, already, is a clue to the original purpose of the cyclic organization of the Ordinary: the use of a symbolic or emblematic tenor uniting its various sections renders the Ordinary "proper" to an occasion. The common cantus firmus acts like a trope, a symbolic commentary on the service. It was, or could be, a most potent device for insuring that there would be no separation of church and state.

More secure is the attribution to Leonel Power of a four-part Ordinary complex (a pair, so to speak, of traditional pairs: Gloria/Credo and Sanctus/Agnus Dei) all based on a tenor derived from the Marian antiphon *Alma Redemptoris Mater*. This composition, found only in northern Italian manuscripts copied around 1430 – 1435, is one of the best witnesses to the prestige of English music at the time and the leadership that English composers were exercising over musical developments on the continent.

Unlike Dunstable, his (probably) somewhat younger contemporary, Leonel Power does not seem to have made much of an international career. It was his music that traveled. Except for a brief French sojourn between 1419 and 1421 with his employer the Duke of Clarence (brother of Henry V, in whose campaign the Duke was participating), the composer spent his whole professional life in England, first as tutor to the choristers in the Duke's household chapel, and later as a member of the fraternity of Christ Church, Canterbury, where he died, probably aged around seventy, in 1445. One of his duties at the Canterbury church was to lead the choir that sang special votive services in the "Lady chapel," and it was presumably for this choir that he composed, on a suitable Marian hymn, the Mass that, because it was so widely circulated in manuscript copies, now looms so large in history.

Unifying the sections of Mass cycles on the basis of common tenors meant laying out a foundation in advance and building from the ground up. This architectonic conception had previously been the special distinguishing characteristic of the motet. And indeed, that genre was the source of the idea, even as the motet itself was undergoing change in the fifteenth century, a change that implied a "lowering" of its style. What happened, in effect, was that the rigidly conceived, highly structured style if the isorhythmic motet — the "high style" or *stylus gravis* of the fourteenth century — passed from the motet into the domain of the cyclic Mass, which was potentially a kind of isorhythmic motet writ large, with five or so discrete sections replacing the multiple color-talea *cursus* of old.

All the characteristics that mark a "high" style in the Ciceronian sense — weightiness, loftiness, nobility, vouchsafed by a highly rationalized, "artificial" idiom of "unnatural" intensity and complexity — became the property of the Mass, even as the motet loosened up under another strain of English influence to become more "naturally" declamatory, more personally expressive, more texturally flexible, thus assuming the position of a "middle" style. To appreciate this shift, keep Dunstable's *Quam pulchra es* (Ex. 11-19) in mind as a "middle style" foil to accompany and contrast with the brief account that follows of Leonel's Mass on *Alma Redemptoris Mater*.

The arbitrarily strict, the artificial, and the unnaturally formal — hallmarks of the high style — are very conspicuous in the fashioning and the treatment of Leonel's cantus firmus. Ex. 12-2a shows *Alma Redemptoris Mater* as it is found in the *Liber usualis*, the modern chant book, with the major divisions as extracted by Leonel for the purposes of his Mass setting, amounting to roughly half of the original melody, indicated with bars and Roman numerals. These divisions do not conform at all to the given (text-based) structural divisions of the chant. The break between Leonel's two major sections occurs in the middle of a ligature, and the end of the cantus firmus also comes in the middle of a word; nor is the last note of the cantus firmus even the final of the original melody's mode.

EX. 12-2A *Alma Redemptoris Mater* (eleventh-century Marian antiphon)

Thus there is no apparent rhyme or reason for Leonel's selection or apportionment of his cantus firmus material. That is not to say that there was no reason, only that it is not readily apparent. Possible reasons might have involved numerology or some other form of occult symbolism, or might have had some other connection with *musica speculativa*. Sometimes modern researchers stumble on these things, and sometimes they don't. In any case, the absence of an apparent rationale is not proof of the absence of a rationale. Nor is it proof of the presence of a rationale. Sherlock Holmes and his famous dog that failed to bark in the night notwithstanding, one can rarely make secure deductions from an absence. (It follows, then, that we can never know that a given piece of music has no preexisting cantus firmus; all we can know is that we have not yet discovered one.)

What is possible to say with certainty is that, whatever the reason for it, Leonel's selection and apportionment of raw material for his cantus firmus was entirely arbitrary (that is, "at will"), unrelated to the formal or semantic content of the antiphon from which it came. Similarly arbitrary is the processing of the raw material. Ex. 12-2b shows the actual tenor of Leonel's Mass in its entirety and in the original notation. The two sections marked I and II are cast in contrasting mensurations. (The first section, in accordance with an English custom for notating tenors that a few continental composers picked up, is meant to be performed "in augmentation," that is, in durations twice as long as those written.) The rhythms show an effort to include maximum variety. There is a profuse and unpredictable mixture of note values, including such standard options as hemiolas in the first (perfect) section and syncopations in the second (imperfect) one.

EX. 12-2B   Tenor of Leonel Power's Mass on *Alma Redemptoris Mater*

Once established, this arbitrary color/talea combo was cast in stone. It serves as the basis for all four extant sections of the Mass, without the slightest modification. This, of course, is the isorhythmic principle (though in somewhat simplified form, since the color and talea match up one to one), extended over a multipartite span that unifies the whole worship service. "Higher" than that one could hardly aim.

The beginnings of Leonel's Gloria and Sanctus are given for comparison in Ex. 12-3. The only difference between them, so far as the tenor is concerned, consists of the little "introitus" that precedes the first tenor entrance in the Sanctus. This, too, is arbitrary and counter-intuitive, since the Gloria has by far the longer text, and could benefit practically from the use of an introitus to take up some of the verbiage. Clearly, the introitus to the Sanctus serves an ornamental rather than a functional purpose, possibly in keeping with the fact, often exploited by composers of Masses, that the Sanctus is supposed to be an imitation of the heavenly choirs.

More important than the small difference is the overall uniformity. Two liturgical texts, with inherent shapes that have practically nothing in common, have been forced into a musical conformity. Owing to the uniform tenor, moreover, the two sections take the same amount of time. It means, of course, that the Sanctus text is stretched out in luxurious melismas and the Gloria text is crammed in as if with a shoehorn. But the fixed bipartite musical format prevails, and became standardized over time, both for Mass sections and for many motets.

EX. 12-3A   Leonel Power, *Missa Alma Redemptoris Mater*, Gloria, beginning

EX. 12-3B   Leonel Power, *Missa Alma Redemptoris Mater*, Sanctus, beginning

EX. 12-3B   *(continued)*

"CAPUT" AND THE BEGINNINGS OF FOUR-PART HARMONY

The direct adoption from the English of the cyclic Mass as the standard "high" genre, and the way the "Tinctoris generation" of continental musicians further developed all its compositional techniques, can be illustrated with a trio of Masses all based on the same cantus firmus melody: a grandiose *neuma* or supermelisma on *caput* ("head"), the concluding word of an antiphon, *Venit ad Petrum* ("He came to Peter"), that was sung at Salisbury Cathedral for the ceremony of "washing the feet" on Maundy Thursday during Holy Week preceding Easter. "Do not wash only my feet, but also my hands and my *head*," said Peter to Jesus in the Gospel according to John, in a line that became the antiphon that begat the Masses.

Sometime around 1440, an anonymous English composer (whose anonymity does not preclude his being a well-known personage) turned this magnificent melisma into a cantus firmus by following the procedures described above and produced a Mass similar in principle to Leonel's *Alma Redemptoris Mater* Mass, but much, much grander in scale. The vastness of the conception suggests no mere chapel votive service but a cathedral Mass attended by dignitaries and magnates in force (precisely the kind of stellar occasion, in short, for which isorhythmic motets used to serve).

As in Leonel's Mass, the cantus firmus of one "movement" is (with minor variables like rests between phrases) the cantus firmus of all. Each "movement" has the same overall bipartite structure articulated through the same contrast of perfect and imperfect mensurations. But each mensuration governs a full statement of the enormous cantus firmus, so that each "movement" embodies a double cursus of what is already a very lengthy melody. So this Mass would be twice as long as Leonel's even if the apparently missing (and probably heavily trooped) Kyrie from Leonel's Mass were restored.

In fact it is surely more than twice as long, because the "ideal" structure of this or any cyclic Mass (that is, the structure as composed) is not necessarily the same as its

FIG. 12-5 Salisbury Cathedral, home of the Sarum chant, the repertoire that included the *Caput* melisma.

practical structure (the structure as performed). The two sections of the Kyrie from the *Caput* Mass are composed — "Kyrie" in perfect time and "Christe" in imperfect — to satisfy the requirements of its structural plan. But they do not satisfy the requirements of the liturgy. In the actual liturgical performance of any Mass the words "Kyrie eleison" must be repeated following the words "Christe eleison"; and so we may assume that in the liturgical performance of this Mass, either the missing words were shoehorned into the "Christe," or the first section was performed *da capo* in order to complete the liturgical text.

But however impressive, length is not the most important dimension in which the *Missa Caput* has been magnified over and above its predecessors. More significant by far, historically speaking, is the amplification of the texture. The complement of voices has been increased to four — and that number of voices, in precisely the configuration found in this Mass, became the norm for a century or more of intense Mass Ordinary composition. Once something becomes normal it is quickly taken for granted; so let us seize this moment, while things we have long since taken for granted are still in the process of being formed, to witness the birth of "four-part harmony."

The *Caput* tenor is an unusually high-lying chant, making repeated ascents to the G that in the old eight-mode system was the highest theoretically recognized "scale note" of all. The original melisma is given in Ex. 12-4b for comparison with the tenor of the Kyrie, a portion of which is shown in Ex. 12-4a. The tenor's high tessitura puts it in a range far closer to, and apter to cross with, the contratenor above it than the "second

EX. 12-4A *Missa Caput*, Kyrie (sung with prosulas), mm. 11–25

EX. 12-4B   The *Caput* melisma

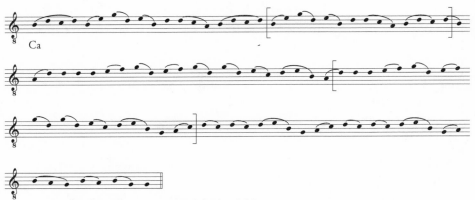

Ca

Bracketed repetitions omitted in Ockeghem's Mass.

tenor" below. Indeed, at its peaks it even crosses the cantus at times — sometimes quite dramatically, as when it makes its first ascent to the high G (m. 15) while the second tenor descends to its lowest note to put a maximum distance of a twelfth between the two parts that in earlier music used to cross so freely.

Although the sources that include the anonymous *Caput* Mass retain the nomenclature of voice-parts with which we are familiar, scribes in the mid-fifteenth century responded to the newly standardized, newly stratified four-part texture by adopting a new nomenclature, as shall we from now on. The now-obligatory voice that stays consistently below the tenor, like the more accustomed "nonessential" voice above it, was now thought of as a second *contratenor* — a voice written against the tenor and (functionally if not literally) "after" it — rather than a second tenor. To distinguish the two contratenors, one was called "high" (*altus*) and the other "low" (*bassus*).

No one reading this who has ever sung in a chorus will fail to appreciate the significance of this new nomenclature. The term *contratenor altus* metamorphosed into the Italian *contralto*, and *contratenor bassus* into *contrabasso* — terms that have long since been anglicized as "alto" and "bass." Moreover, once the word "high" became standard for a voice that was not in fact the highest one singing, the highest voice (till now the cantus or the triplum) became known as the "top voice" — *superius*, from which the word *soprano* is derived. And now we have our full familiar range of voice parts — soprano, alto, tenor, bass (SATB) — and can see how the word *tenor*, originally the "holding part" (which, in cantus firmus Masses, it still was), acquired the meaning that has since become standard: a high male range. (For that meaning to become primary, of course, a further major change was required — one that was still some centuries away: the substitution of mixed choirs for the all-male *schola* of the pre-Reformation Christian church.)

Now that both the range and the term for it have been established, let us take a close look at the *bassus* voice in Ex. 12-4a. It occupies a pitch space all its own and behaves in a new harmony-defining way. Like that of any contratenor, its movement tends to be disjunct — by skips — and it has a newly standardized role at cadences.

A cadence, we may recall, is defined theoretically as stepwise movement, by the "structural pair" (cantus and tenor), in contrary motion from an imperfect to a perfect consonance. That criterion is of course met here—and the original chant melisma is given in Ex. 12-4b just to show how the cantus firmus had to be modified at the ends of both its cursus in order to secure for the tenor a stepwise, properly "cadential" fall to the final. At the final cadences, both of the Kyrie and of the Christe, an A is interpolated in the tenor before the final to correspond with the *subtonium* F in the superius, preparing the cadence on G. The two voices make their resolutions in contrary motion, and that is the essential cadence (Ex. 12-4c).

EX. 12-4C   *Missa Caput*, Kyrie (sung with prosulas), mm. 50–52

Anyone who has studied counterpoint knows that the only way two additional voices can be added to the "imperfect" part of this cadence that will be both consonant with the structural pair and independent of it (in the sense that they will not be forced to double the "essential motion" of either cantus or tenor at the cadence) is to have them both sing D. At the resolution of the cadence the D above the tenor remains stationary, and the D below goes the only place it can—to G, doubling the tenor either at the same pitch or an octave below, depending on the available range. Because this cadence reinforces the effect of the tenor's descent to the final from above, it emphasizes the "authentic" modal ambitus and has a particularly forceful closing effect. It is conventionally called the "authentic cadence," probably because of its modal associations (but as with many terms in current, unambiguous and informal parlance, its etymology has not been researched, and its pedigree is uncertain).

At any rate, the progression in the bass, from the fifth scale degree (supporting the two "essential" pre-final tones) to the final, is congruent with what we are accustomed to calling a V–I or dominant–tonic progression. To call it that is to think of the motion of the lowest part as the essential cadential approach, and to associate the gesture toward closure with the "dominant" harmony. The question for historians is at what point such a way of conceptualizing cadences becomes justified (or to put it less prescriptively, at what point such a conceptualization matches that of contemporaneous musicians and listeners).

However they were conceptualized, such an approach and such a harmony were perceptually a part of virtually every final cadence from the mid-fifteenth century on. They admitted considerable variation from the beginning. For an idea of the possibilities, compare the lineup, in Ex. 12-5, of all the remaining sectional cadences in the *Caput* Mass (two per "movement"). In Ex.12-5a and b, from the Gloria, both the superius and the altus are decorated with "Landini sixths," producing pungent dissonances right before the resolution. A variation of the same configuration occurs at the end of the Credo (Ex. 12-5d), where the superius again has the Landini sixth but the altus has a simple lower neighbor, producing not a sixth but a seventh (the first "dominant seventh"?) above the bass.

Example 12-5g, from the Agnus Dei, is especially interesting since the bassus is modified so that the final chord is a richly sonorous full triad. Both the avoidance of the fifth progression in the bass and the presence of the third in the final chord, however, are justified by the fact that the chord in question is not actually a final chord. It is a sectional cadence only, immediately followed by the continuation of the Agnus Dei. The final cadence of the Agnus, Ex. 12-5h, returns to the concord of perfect consonances. The presence of an imperfect consonance in a final chord would not normally be countenanced in strictly composed polyphonic music (whatever may have gone on behind the closed doors of the oral tradition) until nearly the end of the next century.

EX. 12-5   *Missa Caput* a. middle of Gloria b. end of Gloria c. middle of Credo d. end of Credo e. middle of Sanctus f. end of Sanctus g. middle of Agnus Dei h. end of Agnus Dei

As long as the perfect concord was required at full cadences, the theorists, our only direct witnesses to contemporary concepts, went on calling the superius/tenor motion the essential cadential motion, with the V–I in the bassus beneath playing a no more than a contrapuntally mandated supporting role. Just as surely, however, by the middle of the seventeenth century the dominant – tonic cadence, articulated by the V – I bass, was fully conceptualized and had become for contemporary musicians the primary means of defining harmonic closure, as it remains for us today (that is, in our practiced habits of "hearing"). Over the two centuries between 1450 and 1650, in other words, a gradual conceptual change took place in the wake of a new perceptual reality. Roughly speaking, it was the change from "modal" to "tonal" thinking.

HOW CONTROVERSIES ARISE (AND WHAT THEY REVEAL)

The essential difference between these two concepts of pitch organization, the radical-ness of the change from the one form of cadential articulation to the other and the implications of that change, remain matters of debate among historians. They can be (and have been) tendentiously exaggerated, and also tendentiously minimized. Clearly, though, whatever the eventual implications of the V – I bass, its fifteenth-century intro-duction (like many other retrospectively momentous turning points in music history) was no conscious revolution. To call "tonality" a radical break with past thinking, an inspired invention, or (most telling of all) an unanticipated, world-transforming discovery is clearly to borrow without critical reflection from that all-embracing concept of the "Renaissance" that, unless vigilantly examined, can all too easily prejudice the study of fifteenth-century music.

Thus to look for a musical "Age of Discovery" to match the near-contemporary exploits of Columbus and Magellan is attractive but facile, just as it is facile to compare the "discovery" of "tonal" harmony based on the circle of fifths with the "discovery" of perspective by the painters of "Renaissance" Italy. In neither case was something discovered. Both discoveries were inventions. The invention of techniques for rendering a three-dimensional perspective by locating the viewer's eye in space is easily explained, moreover, as an attempt to imitate nature — that is, our natural way of seeing. That way of seeing existed before there was a technique for representing it on canvas. But what is the comparable preexisting natural model for tonal harmony? Natural acoustical resonance, some have argued, with reasonable but limited justification.

Yet it would be equally tendentious to minimize the difference between a harmonic syntax based on the concept of occursus — "closing in" on a unison or octave — and one based on fifth relations. On the basis of virtually all the music that we hear in daily life, we have learned to assign implied hierarchical functions to chords as well as to scale degrees. Composers have long since learned how to establish these harmonic (or, as we call them, "tonal") hierarchies, as well as dissolve them, and to move from one such ordering (through a process called modulation) to another.

These habits of the musical ear, and the techniques to which they gave rise, were a long time taking shape. A fully elaborated tonal system was not in place until the other end of the two-century time frame initiated by the change in cadential norms. By the late seventeenth century, the V – I close was only the most decisive member of a pervading system of fifth relations (the "circle of fifths") that governed harmonic relations at many levels. Equally important (and equally different from earlier practice), the tonal system was no longer dependent for its effects on strict voice leading.

For us, who live more than five hundred years later, what was for the fifteenth century the distant future has become the distant past. We are therefore much more fully aware than anyone could have been at the time of the range of implication the new cadential structure carried within it. And so we are justified in seeking the origins of modern harmonic practice at a period when that practice could not yet be predicted. The fact that some of the questions we now ask about fifteenth-century harmony would not have been meaningful to fifteenth-century musicians does not lessen their interest or their meaningfulness to us.

It should be clear, then, that to deny the perceptual reality of functional harmonic practice simply because it originated "unintentionally," as an incidental contrapuntal formula, is to commit the "genetic fallacy," as it is called, a rather hackneyed logical error that equates origins with essence. (According to the genetic fallacy no contrapuntal combination can ever become a harmonic norm, no drinking song can ever become a national anthem, no Russian composer can ever write an Italian opera, no African can ever become an American.) Committed innocently, an error is something from which one can learn; committed cynically, an error is something with which one can deceive.

This particular genetic fallacy — to reduce the "tonal system" to the chance product (or worse, the tenacious misinterpretation) of a contrapuntal accident — was a common academic strategy for undermining belief in the reality of the tonal system at a time around the middle of the twentieth century when the rights of "atonal" music — a music then practiced exclusively in the academy — were being defended against those who called it "unnatural." Instead of arguing that a basis in nature is only one of the criteria by which musical styles acquire perceptual viability (especially in academic or otherwise "high" or elite environments), an attempt was made to deny all natural basis to habits of musical "hearing." In this controversy, which we will have occasion to consider more fully in its own chronological circumstances, we can see especially clearly how fundamentally the writing of history can be influenced by current esthetic or political concerns.

So we will avoid taking sides in a misconceived argument and limit ourselves to the perceptual facts insofar as they are available, and with recognition that such facts are never entirely available. "Oral" practices that we know only imperfectly if at all — for example, the use of chord-strumming instruments in unwritten musical repertories and their effect in reconditioning musical "hearing" during the two centuries in question — unquestionably had an important bearing, but one that can never be fully documented, on the "transition" from modal discant counterpoint ("their" way of composing) to functional harmony ("our" way of hearing).

PATTERNS OF EMULATION

Leading composers of two "Tinctoris generations" of continental musicians — both that of the theorist's own contemporaries and the younger, up-and-coming generation — wrote *Caput* Masses in imitation (or rather, in emulation) of the one we have been examining, thereby casting themselves into a sort of three-generation dynasty. That these Masses were in fact responses to the older Mass and not two independently conceived Masses on the same cantus firmus tune is proved by the nature of the cantus firmus itself. It is a very little-used chant (neither from the Mass nor from the regular Office, but from a special service attended only by the clergy) that occurs only in English chant books. Ockeghem and Obrecht, the composers of the subsequent *Caput* Masses, would have been unlikely to encounter the tune anywhere else but in the tenor of the first *Caput* Mass, which circulated widely in continental manuscripts (in one of them under a spurious attribution to Du Fay that was long believed by scholars). Even more conclusively, the melody shows up in Ockeghem's and Obrecht's tenors in the precisely the same modified and rhythmicized form we have already observed in the first *Caput* Mass.

Ockeghem's Mass, because of its heavy dependence on a model, is presumed to be a relatively early work (possibly from the 1450s), but Ockeghem's works are not easy to date, since many of them are found only in manuscripts—like the magnificent Chigi Codex illustrated in Fig. 12-4—that postdate his death. That illustration, it so happens, shows the Kyrie from Ockeghem's *Caput* Mass, transcribed in Ex. 12-6, with which it may be compared. Of all the sections of Ockeghem's Mass the Kyrie is the freest in its relationship to the model, and therefore the most interesting and instructive one to describe.

EX. 12-6   Johannes Ockeghem, *Missa Caput*, first Kyrie, mm. 1–8

EX. 12-6 *(continued)*

The reasons for the freedom had to do with a necessary compression. The anonymous English *Caput* Kyrie, as English (but not continental) Kyries still tended to do in the fifteenth century, carried a full set of prosulas (included in Ex. 12-4a). To accommodate them, a very spacious musical treatment was necessary. Ockeghem, having only eighteen canonical words to set (3 × Kyrie eleison; 3 × Christe eleison; 3 × Kyrie eleison), streamlined his setting by pruning away the lengthy internal repetitions in the cantus firmus melody (bracketed in Ex. 12-4b), and then laying out the abridged cantus firmus to prop the whole Kyrie in a single cursus, divided into three parts in accordance with the liturgical form, observing both the mensuration contrast of the original *Caput* Mass (perfect time followed by imperfect) and the "da capo" resumption of perfect time that was implied in the older Mass but is now made explicit.

That single cursus can be easily viewed in Fig. 12-4, which shows an "opening," the visual unit formed by two facing pages in a choirbook — the back or *verso* of one leaf (*folio*) and the front or *recto* of the next — on which the four voice parts are entered for the group around the lectern to read from, as Ockeghem's own choir is shown doing in Fig. 12-1. The lower left area of the choirbook opening is the one normally occupied by the cantus-firmus-bearing voice: the tenor, by original definition. That placement puts the superius and tenor — the "structural pair" as they were regarded by composers and theorists — on one side of the opening, and the two compositionally "nonessential" contratenors, the altus and the bassus, on the other.

In Fig. 12-4 the positions of the bassus and the tenor seem to have been switched. In fact only their names have been transposed, in deference to the newer meaning of the term "tenor," then just coming into use, which designated a range rather than a function. And here we come to the nub of the distinction, drawn but not defined above, between an imitation and an emulation.

An imitation is simply a reproduction, a copy, a match — or, as often remarked, a compliment. An emulation is both an homage and an attempt to surpass. The dynasties of composers and of compositions that so distinguished the fifteenth and sixteenth centuries were dynasties of emulation. Works of "high" style became models for other works that aspired to highness in a spirit at once of submission to a tradition and mastery of it, and in a spirit at once of honoring and vying with one's elders. A composition regarded as especially masterly will come to possess *auctoritas* — authority. It sets a standard of excellence, but at the same time it becomes the thing to beat. A true emulation will honor the model by conforming to it, but it will also distinguish itself from the model in some conspicuously clever way.

The original *Caput* Mass set such a standard and inspired such emulation, and Ockeghem's way of distinguishing himself was to transpose the tenor down an octave so that it became the effective bass — no doubt originally sung by the composer himself, leading his choir not only with claps on the back but with his famously deep voice. That is what the little rubric says next to the "bass-playing-tenor" (in Latin, *bassus tenorizans*) in Fig. 12-4: *Alterum caput descendendo tenorem per diapason et sic per totam missam*, "Another head [appears] by lowering the tenor an octave, and thus for the entire Mass." It will not be missed that the "head" (*caput*) has now become the "foot" of the texture. That sort of playful cleverness was part of the emulation game; and yet (as is emphatically the case here) that playfulness, at its best, gave rise to music of high seriousness and eloquence.

Any practicing fifteenth-century musician would have been impressed with Ockeghem's sheer audacity in transposing this particular cantus firmus melody down an octave, to the foot of the texture. For it begins with the one note — B natural — that normally cannot function as a bass, since the diatonic pitch set can offer no perfect fifth above it with which it can resonate. To put it in more modern, avowedly somewhat anachronistic terms, it cannot function under normal conditions as a harmonic root. So Ockeghem creates abnormal conditions.

He goes ahead and writes an F above the cantus firmus B anyway, which forces alteration of the F to F♯ *causa necessitatis* ("by necessity"), producing what we would call a B-minor triad. But the F♯ is immediately contradicted by the superius's F-natural against the second cantus firmus note, D, producing what we would call a D-minor triad. This harmonic succession, by virtue of a root progression by thirds and a melodic cross relation, is still weird to the ear after half a millennium. Immediately reiterated and confirmed in the Gloria, it becomes a kind of signature for this Mass.

Nor is F/F♯ the only "cross relation" to be found in the work's harmonic texture. Within the first subsection of the Kyrie there is an equally teasing interplay of B-natural and B-flat (occasionally called for by specific notational sign). By harnessing the old devices of music ficta to new and especially pungent effect — an effect implicit in the cantus firmus that he has taken over from an earlier composer, but one that the earlier composer had not exploited — Ockeghem announces his emulatory designs on the *Caput* tradition and proclaims himself a worthy heir to his distinguished predecessor.

Who might this distinguished predecessor have been? Why should an anonymous English Mass have attracted such determined emulation? The likelihood, of course, is that in Ockeghem's day the Mass was not anonymous. Ockeghem probably knew for a fact something about which we now can only hazard guesses. The gargoylish manuscript illuminations in Fig. 12-6 give a fascinatingly oblique hint as to what he knew and we don't, namely the earlier author's identity.

They show dragons — dragons galore. In the bottom panel at left there is a huge dragon fighting with a centaur. At right there are two more dragons, one of which sports a grotesquely elongated neck that draws extra attention to its strangely maned head. A fourth dragon, in the lower right margin, is reduced to just a head emerging from a hellish cauldron.

Dragons' heads — what do they mean? Any fifteenth-century astrologer or navigator would have known. The Dragon's Head (*Caput Draconis*, now called *Alpha Draconis*), the topmost star of the constellation Draco, was the ancient polestar. The actual term "Caput Draconis" mysteriously appears at the head of the first appearance of the cantus firmus of the original *Caput* Mass in its most recently discovered source, a Dutch manuscript now in Italy, unknown to scholars until 1968. This manuscript, or one with a similar label on the cantus firmus, must have served the scribe who copied (or more to the point, the artist who decorated) the Vatican manuscript as his exemplar or copy-text. That scribe or artist seems to have interpreted the phrase "dragon's head" literally.

Or maybe not: the big dragon at bottom left is fighting with a centaur, and Centaurus, containing Alpha Centauri, the closest star to earth and one of the brightest in the sky, is another major constellation. For those in the know, what better way could there be than this — a visual pun linking the cantus firmus of this magnificent Mass with a bright heavenly orb — for evoking the great figure known to his contemporaries as "an astrologian, a mathematician, a musitian, and what not"? On the basis of the astrological reference, scholarly suspicion has begun to fall on none other than John

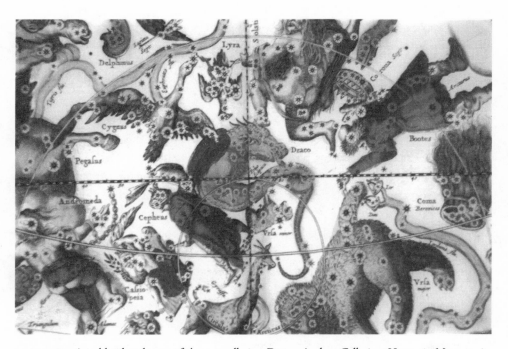

FIG. 12-6   An old sidereal map of the constellation Draco. Andrea Cellarius, *Harmonia Macrocosmica* (Amsterdam, 1708), plate 24: *Hemisphaerium stellatum boreale antiquum* (The Ancient Constellations of the Northern Hemisphere).

Dunstable (who, as it happens, did habitually use the term "Tenor secundus" for what later composers called "Contratenor bassus") as the author of the original *Caput* Mass.[2]

THE COMPOSER AS VIRTUOSO

Ockeghem's emulation of the original *Caput* Mass, whoever its author may have been, certainly shows him to have been inclined toward *tours de force*, for which the French, as we know, had a longstanding predilection. The most famous tours de force in all of fifteenth-century music, in fact, are a couple of Masses by Ockeghem — works with which his historical reputation, for better or worse, is indissolubly bound up.

One of them is called the *Missa Prolationum*, the "Mass of the Time Signatures." It is sung in four parts but written in two, both to be simultaneously realized as canons in an ascending cycle of intervals: the first section of the Kyrie is a double canon at the unison; the Christe at the second; the second Kyrie at the third; the Gloria at the fourth; the Credo at the fifth, and so on. The peculiar title advertises the fact that each of the two voices as written carries a double time signature: and when the Mass is actually sung, each of the four voices realizes its note-values according to a different mensuration scheme.

By writing canons in which the voices are in effect singing at different speeds, Ockeghem is able to start with all the voices singing together. When sufficient distance has been achieved between the canonic voices, Ockeghem employs additional notational devices that effectively neutralize the differing time signatures, and the canons proceed as normal ones. Only one little item in the *Missa Prolationum*, a duo, is truly a "mensuration canon," in which two parts derived from a single notated line move at different rates of speed throughout. In Ex. 12-7 that duo, the second Agnus Dei, is given in its original notation and in a two-voice realization. The lower voice reproduces the upper voice an octave below and at half the speed, and consequently ends halfway through the written part. This strict little duo, one of the simpler-textured items in the Mass, will give an idea both of its diabolically clever contrivance, and also of the smooth mellifluousness of the result (the truest art, to recall Horace's famous dictum once again, being the art of concealing art).

EX. 12-7A   *Missa Prolationum*, Agnus II, in the original notation as a single voice

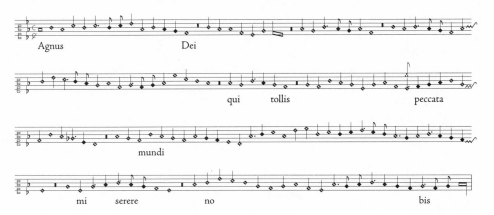

EX. 12-7B *Missa Prolationum, Agnus II, realized as a mensuration canon in two parts*

The other famous Ockeghem star turn is the *Missa cuiusvis toni*, the "Mass in any mode." It is notated without clefs. The singers can decide on one of four different clef combinations, each of which, when supplied mentally, fixes the notated music on one of the "four finals," (as described by the chant theorists) from D to G. When the final is D, the modal scale will be Dorian; when E, Phrygian; when F, Lydian; and when G, Mixolydian. In Ex. 12-8, the brief opening Kyrie is given all four ways. In order to make the harmony compatible with any mode, "authentic" cadences — impossible in Phrygian because "on the white keys" the "dominant" chord to E is diminished — had to be avoided throughout the Mass in favor of "plagal" ones.

EX. 12-8A   Johannes Ockeghem, *Missa cuiusvis toni*, Kyrie I, pitched on D (Dorian)

EX. 12-8B   Johannes Ockeghem, *Missa cuiusvis toni*, Kyrie I, pitched on E (Phrygian)

EX. 12-8C   Johannes Ockeghem, *Missa cuiusvis toni*, Kyrie I, pitched on F (Lydian)

EX. 12-8D   Johannes Ockeghem, *Missa cuiusvis toni*, Kyrie I, pitched on G (Mixolydian)

As noted above, Ockeghem's historical reputation rests disproportionately on these Masses "for better or worse," because not everyone is equally impressed with an elaborate technical apparatus that is seemingly constructed and exercised for its own sake. Charles Burney, the great eighteenth-century historian, captured well the appeal of the high style at its most hermetically "learnèd" when he wrote of the *Missa Prolationum* that "the performer was to solve canonical mysteries, and discover latent beauties of ingenuity and contrivance, about which the hearers were indifferent, provided the general harmony was pleasing."[3] For Ockeghem's clique of singers, as for all lovers of puzzles (or, more broadly, the members of any in-group), the notational complexities were not so much perceived to be a burden as their solution was experienced as a reward. To which it only need be added that like any *trobar clus*, the Masses of Ockeghem, chaplain to the French royal court under three successive kings of the Valois dynasty, were expected suitably to adorn, and in a sense to create, elite occasions. Intricacy of design and *facture* ("makery," as the French untranslatably put it) was one means of fulfilling this expectation.

Yet ever since the sixteenth century, when the Swiss music theorist Henricus Glareanus (Burney's chief source of knowledge about "Okenheim") illustrated the composer's work exclusively with these bizarre technical *tours de force*, Ockeghem has had a reputation for cold calculation that has rubbed off, until quite recently, on his whole era. "These compositions," Burney sniffed, "are given rather as specimens of a determined spirit of patient perseverance, than as models [worthy] of imitation. In music, different from all other arts, learning and labor seem to have preceded taste and invention, from both which the times under consideration are still very remote." As long as Ockeghem and his contemporaries were judged by an impressive but unrepresentative sample of their work, the verdict stood. Implicit in that condescending (mis)appraisal is a caution for anyone who would attempt to understand, let alone judge, the past on the basis of its fragmentary remains.

FARTHER ALONG THE EMULATION CHAIN

Obrecht's *Missa Caput* continues the emulatory line begun by Ockeghem and does so in a way that demonstrates with special clarity the composer's high consciousness of the tradition in which he was participating. He pays tribute to the founder of the dynasty by citing, at the beginning of his Gloria (Ex. 12-9a), the phrase that begins every movement of the original English *Caput* Mass (compare the beginnings of Ex. 12-9a and Ex. 12-9b). Such phrases, called "headmotives" or "mottos," were one of the most conspicuous devices through which composers spotlighted the formal unity of their music, a unity that was meant to rub off propitiously on the elite ritual occasions their music adorned.

EX. 12-9A   Jacobus Obrecht, *Missa Caput*, Gloria, mm. 1–5

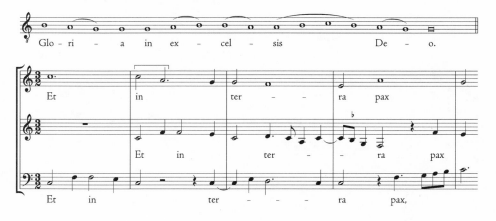

EX. 12-9B   Original *Missa Caput*, opening phrase

Obrecht also shows his awareness of Ockeghem's Mass by carrying farther the special technical maneuver that had distinguished it. That maneuver had been cantus-firmus transposition; but where Ockeghem had been content to make a single transposition of the cantus firmus, bringing it down an octave so that it became the de facto bassus of his Mass, Obrecht transposes it to five different pitch levels (one for each major section of the Mass) and has it migrate through the entire four-part texture. In the Kyrie it is located in the traditional tenor at its original pitch. In the Gloria, as can be seen in Ex. 12-9c, it is transposed up an octave to become the superius. In the Credo it is back in the tenor, but a fifth lower than before, so that it ends on C, the final of the Mass. In the Sanctus it is transposed an octave higher than the Credo pitch and is found in the altus. Finally, in the Agnus Dei, it is pitched an octave below its original pitch and placed in the bassus, so that Obrecht's Mass ends with a direct nod at Ockeghem's.

EX. 12-9C   Jacobus Obrecht, *Missa Caput*, Gloria, mm. 17–23

Within this highly conscious and deliberate continuity of tradition, however, there is a considerable transformation of style. Obrecht's preference is for a very active rhythmic texture, full of melodic sequences and syncopations, which contrasts markedly with the stateliness of the cantus firmus and emphasizes its emblematic status. A spectacular example are the bristly strettos that go off like sonic sparklers under the long-held final note of the cantus firmus at the end of the gloria (Ex. 12-9d).

EX. 12-9D   Jacobus Obrecht, *Missa Caput*, Gloria, mm. 213–end

There is nothing like this in any earlier polyphonic sacred music, although Ockeghem, too, enjoyed jacking up the level of rhythmic activity as the final close loomed (often dubbed his "drive to the cadence"). Without any real justification Obrecht's rhythmic athleticism is often cited as evidence of "secularization" and tied in with the overriding myth of the musical "Renaissance." It is perhaps more simply, and more plausibly, viewed as another instance of virtuosity both in the making and in the performing of an exceedingly elite musical repertory, the highest of the high.

THE MAN AT ARMS

The noblest and most copious dynasty of all was the long line of Masses based on a cantus firmus derived not from a church chant but from a secular (folk? popular?) song called *L'Homme Armé* ("The Man at Arms"). More than forty such Masses survive in whole or part, by authors of practically every Western European nationality (Flemish, French, Italian, Spanish, Scottish, German). The earliest was composed some time after 1454, and the latest, a colossal affair for three choirs plus organ, is somewhat doubtfully attributed to the Roman composer Giacomo Carissimi (1605–74). Practically every composer mentioned by Tinctoris, including Tinctoris himself, wrote at least one *Missa L'Homme Armé*, as did their pupils and their pupils' pupils. The principle of emulation, thus applied on such a massive scale, produced the very summit of fifteenth-century musical art and artifice.

The later composers in the line, Italians who were both temporally and geographically remote from the origins of the tradition, probably thought of it as a "purely musical" tradition, and a rather academic one at that, involving nothing more than a test-piece to establish professional credentials. The circumstances attending the earliest *L'Homme Armé* Masses — circumstances probably well known to the composers of the "Tinctoris" generations — suggest that there was originally a lot more to it. These circumstances point to the court of Burgundy, and in particular to a knightly order founded there, as the site and source of this most famous of all emulatory traditions in music.

In 1453, Constantinople (now Istanbul in Turkey), the largest and most splendid city in all of Europe, the capital of the latter-day Roman (Byzantine) Empire and the seat of Greek Christendom, fell after a two-month siege before the gigantic cannons of the Ottoman Sultan, Muhammad II ("The Conqueror"). Muhammad made it the capital of his empire, which it remained until 1918, and it has been a Turkish and a Muslim city ever since its conquest. The European response to this stunning event was one of horror and professed resolve, but little action. (Indeed, the armies of Constantine XI, the last Byzantine emperor, were defeated largely because no European power sent aid.) In immediate — if ultimately futile — reaction to the calamity of Constantinople, Duke Philip the Good of Burgundy vowed to go on a Crusade against the Turks. On 17 February 1454 he convened at Lille in northern France a great meeting of his own knightly retinue, known as the Order of the Golden Fleece. At this meeting, known as the Banquet of the Oath of the Pheasant, the Knights of the Order were sworn to the defense of Constantinople. Descriptions of the proceedings by court chroniclers recount the lavish musical performances that enlivened the banquet. At the climax, right before the oath itself was sworn, a giant led in an elephant on whose back was a miniature castle, from which a woman dressed in mourning sang a lament for the fallen city — perhaps one of four such Constantinopolitan laments that Guillaume Du Fay is known to have written, of which one survives.

This gives us some idea of the manner in which ceremonial music was "consumed" by the court of Burgundy, and the sorts of occasions that the great musicians of the day were expected to dignify. A great deal of sacred music has been circumstantially associated with the Order of the Golden Fleece, including many of the early *L'Homme Armé* Masses, which date from the period when the Order had become at least nominally a crusading order and when Philip the Good's famously belligerent son and eventual

successor Charles the Bold had become active in it. Charles is already known to us as the patron of Antoine Busnoys, who had entered his service shortly before Charles's accession to the ducal throne in 1467.

FIG. 12-7   Charles the Bold, duke of Burgundy, presiding over his Grand Council in 1474 (oil painting at the palace of Versailles, France).

The song *L'Homme Armé* was a special favorite of Charles, who identified himself with the titular "Man at Arms"[4] (probably Christ himself, if the connection with Crusades was there from the beginning). The song may even have been written for Charles. In any case, we know the song as a song, text and all, thanks to the chance survival of a manuscript containing a cycle of six anonymous *L'Homme Armé* Masses that bears a dedication to Charles and carries the original song up front like a blazon or motto (Fig. 12-8; Ex. 12-10). The song playfully incorporates a horn call — presented variously in three-note and four-note versions, dropping a fifth after an initial series of repeated notes or tattoo — that was possibly drawn from Burgundian town and castle life. A payment record from 1364 survives, detailing the purchase by Philip the Bold, the first Duke of Burgundy, of "a brass trumpet for the castle turret at Grignon, to be blown when the watchman sees men-at-arms."[5] A hundred years later that trumpet was still sounding in Burgundy, if the famous song is any indication.

The cycle of six Masses based on the tune as shown in Fig. 12-8 exactly fits the service requirements of the Sainte Chapelle at Dijon, the official chapel of the Order, where every week six polyphonic Masses and a Requiem were sung.[6] The Masses (and the song as well) have a durational structure that is built on the prime number 31: the song is 31 *tempora* (breve-long measures) in length and the subsections of the Mass are likely to be 31 or 62 (31 × 2) or 93 (31 × 3) measures long. Thirty-one was the prescribed number of men-at-arms in the Order and hence symbolized it. One of the Masses sounds the cantus firmus in canon between two tenors: its rubrics make elaborate veiled references to the titular "Man at Arms" and to

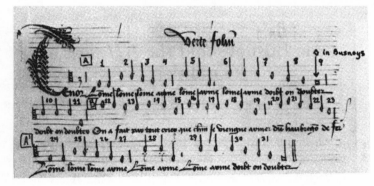

FIG. 12-8   *L'Homme Armé* tune as it is given in its single complete and texted source (Naples, Biblioteca Nazionale, MS VI E.40, fol. 58v).

485

EX. 12-10   Transcription of *L'Homme Armé*

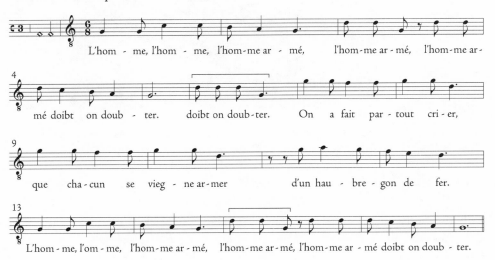

L'hom - me, l'hom - me, l'hom - me ar - mé, l'hom-me ar - mé, l'hom-me ar -

mé doibt on doub - ter. doibt on doub-ter. On a fait par - tout cri - er,

que cha - cun se vieg - ne ar-mer d'un hau - bre - gon de fer.

L'hom - me, l'om - me, l'hom-me ar - mé, l'hom-me ar - mé, l'hom-me ar - mé doibt on doub - ter.

another armed man "fashioned out of his very entrails" — as the second voice of a canon is fashioned out of the first, or as Charles the Bold had been fashioned out of the flesh of his father, the founder of the Order. Thus the circumstantial ("external") evidence associating the song *L'Homme Armé* and the Mass tradition based on it with the Order of the Golden Fleece in its late crusading (or at least blustering) phase under Charles the Bold seems to have ample "internal" corroboration.

So if Charles the Bold was the instigator of the *L'Homme Armé* tradition, special interest and authority attach to the *L'Homme Armé* Mass by Charles's own court composer. And indeed, Busnoys's *Missa L'Homme Armé* seems to have been regarded as a special "classic" — by contemporary composers (who emulated it with particular zeal and fidelity), by contemporary theorists (who cited it more often than any other then-current Mass composition), and by scribes for other potentates (including Pope Sixtus, one of whose Sistine Chapel choirbooks is its earliest surviving source). This account will follow suit, for the Mass's historical significance is matched by its exemplary style and form.

The word "exemplary" is used here in its strictest meaning (a meaning related to the strict meaning of the world "classic" as well): Busnoys's Mass exemplifies the style and form of the fifteenth-century cantus firmus Mass at its most characteristic, most regular, and most fully developed, and may be taken as a type-work for the "high" style as Tinctoris understood it. One of its most telling features is the technique — the multiple techniques, actually — by which the Mass is unified in many musical dimensions, for that musical unification, as we know, served as a metaphor for the unity of the service and the congregation and was fundamentally bound up with the concept of "highness" as devotional exaltation.

The most obvious way in which the Mass is unified, of course, is in the use of the cantus firmus. Each of its five constituent sections sends the *L'Homme Armé* melody through the tenor part, in augmented note values, in a cursus that joins the various subsections in an overarching continuity. The opening Kyrie (Ex. 12-11) may fairly represent all its fellows, the more so because all five sections begin identically, with a headmotive consisting of a duo for the superius and altus, three tempora in length, in which the lower part anticipates the cantus firmus tune, adding yet another level of unity. The first three measures of the Kyrie, as shown in Ex. 12-11, could (but for the words) as easily have been the first three measures of the Gloria, the Credo, the Sanctus, or the Agnus Dei.

It may appear odd, from the breakdown in Table 12-1, that Busnoys never divides the cantus firmus up among the Mass subsections according to its own very clearly articulated three-part (ABA) form, even though two sections of the Ordinary (the Kyrie and the Agnus Dei) are themselves tripartite in textual structure. But that is because the composer had his own musical plan in mind, one that overrode the structure of

EX. 12-11   Antoine Busnoys, *Missa L'Homme Armé*, first Kyrie, mm. 1–19

EX. 12-11   *(continued)*

the original tune and became standard for fifteenth- and early sixteenth-century Mass Ordinary settings. Table 12-1 sums up the apportionment of the cantus firmus in each section and subsection of the Mass. The treatment varies a bit according to the nature and the length of the various texts, but in all sections of the Mass, the cantus firmus is dramatically deployed in conjunction with the other voices to create a sense of climax, much in the tradition of the isorhythmic motet.

TABLE 12-1   Deployment of the Cantus Firmus in Busnoys, *Missa L'Homme Armé*

MASS SECTION	PORTION OF CANTUS FIRMUS USED
Kyrie	mm. 1–15
Christe	*tenor tacet*
Kyrie II	mm. 16–end
Et in terra	mm. 1–18
Qui tollis	mm. 18–end
Tu solus altissimus	complete
Patrem	mm. 1–15
Et incarnatus est	mm. 16–end
Confiteor	mm. 1–5, 12–27
Sanctus	mm. 1–19
Pleni sunt coeli	*tenor tacet*
Osanna	mm. 20–end
Benedictus	*tenor tacet*
(Osanna)	*ut supra*
Agnus I	mm. 1–15
Agnus II	*tenor tacet*
Agnus III	mm. 16–end

In the Kyrie and Agnus Dei, the single cursus of the cantus firmus is split right down the middle and alternates with a subsection in which "the tenor is silent" (*tenor tacet*) to quote the rubric in the choirbook from which such tenorless middle sections as the Christe eleison or the Agnus Dei II get their generic name. That alternation supplies the requisite "A–B–A-ness" to delineate the textual form. The sense of climax is achieved in every movement past the Kyrie by accompanying the cantus firmus, on its resumption, with voices notated in diminution. Speeding along against an unchanged tactus in the tenor, they reach a really dizzy pitch of virtuosity.

Following a custom already observed in the *Caput* Masses, Busnoys provides a cap to the entire Ordinary setting in the concluding Agnus Dei by manipulating the cantus firmus with a special "canon" or transformation rule. ("Gimmick" might actually be the best translation, flippant though it may seem.) The tenor appears to carry the tune in its usual form, but a jesting puzzle-rubric — *Ubi thesis assint ceptra, ibi arsis et e contra* ("Where [the armed man's] scepter is raised, there go lower and vice versa") — directs the singers to exchange roles with the basses, who sing the cantus firmus not only down an octave but also with all the intervals inverted. Ex. 12-12 shows the tenor entrance, following a lengthy *introitus*.

EX. 12-12   Antoine Busnoys, *Missa L'Homme Armé*, last Agnus Dei, mm. 14–22

489

In the lengthy Gloria and Credo, the cantus firmus gets a double cursus that in its accelerated repetition behaves more like the tenor of an isorhythmic motet than ever. The speed-up here is accomplished in two stages: first the accompanying voices go into diminution against the second half of the tenor tune, and then the tenor itself goes into diminution to join them. In the "Tu solus altissimus," the climactic subsection of the Gloria (Ex. 12-13), the whole cantus firmus is sung more or less exactly as shown in Ex. 12-11 (*ut jacet*, "as it stands," to use the contemporary jargon for "at the notated tempo"). All that differs is the amount of resting between phrases.

"PERVADING IMITATION"

With its vivaciously lilting, hemiola-infested rhythms and its fanciful little patches of voice-exchange on the "horn call" motif, Busnoys's "Tu solus" (Ex. 12-13) really crowns the Gloria. Not only its inherent qualities but also its placement testify to Busnoys's "art of shapeliness" and justify the high regard in which his work was held, as well as the dynastic influence it exerted on his contemporaries and juniors. And yet if we are to take a properly "historical" view of this Mass, it is on the relatively inconspicuous

EX. 12-13   Antoine Busnoys, *Missa L'Homme Armé*, Gloria, "Tu solus altissimus"

EX. 12-13 (*continued*)

tenor tacet sections that we must train our lens. They represent a new principle of composing — exceptional in Busnoys's time, but standard practice a hundred years later and for centuries thereafter.

In the absence of a prefabricated tenor to guide his fashioning hand, the composer proceeds instead in short spurts of *chace* or *caccia*-like writing. The superius, at the beginning of the Christe eleison (Ex. 12-14), guides the altus strictly for the duration of the first phrase. But the imitation remains strict only as far as the cadence, when it gives way to a conventional close. Then the bassus, entering, guides the superius strictly as far as the next cadence. Finally, all three voices come together for the third phrase: the altus, rejoining the texture, imitates the "headmotive" of the preceding duo, still functioning as a (would-be) guide. But the other voices pile in for a "free" discant, significantly the shortest of the sections because it is the one least guided. It culminates in another conventional close, this one borrowed from the chanson style: the altus plays the part of the tenor, and the bassus that of the "octave-leaping" contratenor. The Agnus Dei II follows the same format, but less strictly. Its duos begin with brief voice exchanges, then proceed in free discant. The final section begins with a duo for the outer pair that proceeds in a sequential fashion reminiscent of Obrecht as we have come to know him (but Busnoys was the earlier composer and provided the model for Obrecht, who was possibly his pupil).

EX. 12-14 Antoine Busnoys, *Missa L'Homme Armé*, Christe

EX. 12-14   *(continued)*

These modest three-part compositions, to which we may add the "Pleni sunt coeli" and the "Benedictus" subsections of the Sanctus, were epoch-makers. Out of earlier techniques of canon and voice-exchange the composer has worked out a manner of writing that replaces the cantus firmus (whether held out in the tenor or paraphrased in the superius) with a series of "points of imitation," as they have become known after centuries of standardization. Each point corresponds to a discrete portion of the text, the parsing of the words thus acquiring a far more direct role in the shaping of the music than in the sections of the Mass that are built over the cantus firmus — and each point comes to a full cadential close before proceeding to the next. Beginning with the generation of Obrecht, every composer of Masses and motets practiced the "pervading imitation" style when not using a cantus firmus. They all learned it, directly or indirectly, from Busnoys.

In the case of some composers, notably Obrecht, the learning-and-modeling process was exceptionally direct, testifying to the force of Busnoys's unsurpassed authority. Obrecht studied Busnoys's *Missa L'Homme Armé* with the same assiduousness he applied to the study of Ockeghem's *Caput* Mass and the anonymous English Mass before it. Obrecht's *Missa L'Homme Armé* appropriates Busnoys's tenor note for note; and there is another Mass, attributed by some specialists to Obrecht as well, that appropriates only the rhythms of Busnoys's tenor, not the familiar tune. (In this way the borrowing becomes not only more hidden but also more specifically an homage to Busnoys.) In such a case the lines of dynastic composerly fealty seem even stronger and more long-lasting than the lines of dynastic political fealty that spawned the original tradition of emulation.

There is a *Missa L'Homme Armé* by Faugues that quotes the headmotive of Busnoys's Mass in its Sanctus, just the way Obrecht had quoted the headmotive of the English *Caput* Mass in his Gloria. (At the same time, of course, Faugues made sure to surpass his model by casting the cantus firmus as a canon for two voices throughout his Mass.) Finally, there is a striking moment in Busnoys's Sanctus where the superius and altus suddenly drop out, leaving the tenor exposed over an energetic motive in the bassus (Ex. 12-15a). That motive was taken over by a whole slew of followers in their *L'Homme Armé* Masses, most impressively of all, in the true emulatory spirit, by Philippe Basiron, a pupil of Faugues, in his Agnus Dei (Ex. 12-15b).

EX. 12-15A   Antoine Busnoys, *Missa L'Homme Armé*, Sanctus, mm. 26–29

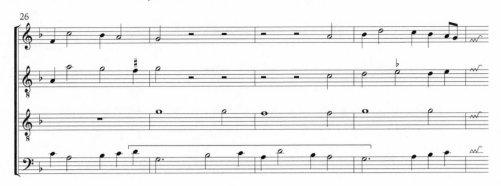

EX. 12-15B   Philippe Basiron, *Missa L'Homme Armé*, Agnus I, mm. 8–23

Not least among the reasons why Busnoys's *Missa L'Homme Armé* became the archetype of its genre was one that lay beneath the surface, in the realm of ideal, esoteric, even occult structure. The whole Mass is unified in a way that (like the ordering principles governing the isorhythmic motets of Machaut and Du Fay, surveyed in chapter 8) is unavailable to detection by the listening ear but can be easily grasped and relished by the rational mind. This aspect of the Mass, in other words, belonged to the level not of "music" as we understand the term, but of *Musica*, as understood in the enduring tradition of Boethius, first described in chapter 3.

When the durations of every subsection of the Mass are tabulated and measured against the initial *tempus* or counting unit established in the first Kyrie, a breathtaking array of "Pythagorean" proportions is revealed (Fig. 12-8). It resembles the one illustrated in Ex. 12-1a, from Busnoys's motet *In hydraulis*; but it is more hidden, farther-reaching, and far more complete. To pick one example: as shown in Fig. 12-8, the four written subsections of the Sanctus contain 36, 27, 18, and 24 tempora respectively. The ratio 36:27:18:24 reduces (when divided by three) to 12:9:6:8 — exactly the proportions of the anvil-weights in the old story of Pythagoras and the blacksmith's shop, an array that yields all the Pythagorean consonances as summarized all the way back in the first chapter of this book (see Ex. 1-9): the octave (12:6 = 2:1), the fifth (9:6 = 3:2), the fourth (8:6 = 4:3), and even the "tone" or major second, the difference between the fourth and the fifth (9:8).

The Agnus Dei, the concluding section of the Mass, has three subsections in the durational proportion 36:27:18, which when factored by nine reduces to 4:3:2, an array that precisely and economically sums up the perfect consonances, just as would the final octave/fifth/fourth harmony of any fifteenth-century Mass or motet (including this one). The subsections of the Kyrie have lengths can be represented as the ratio 18:16:18, reducing by a factor of two to 9:8:9, expressing the tone. Also striking is the fact that the opening sections of each of the five "movements" in the Mass collectively make an array of 18:54:54:36:36, which reduces to 1:3:3:2:2, expressing the most basic consonances, the octave and the fifth; while the concluding sections of each "movement" have identical durations (18 tempora), thus collectively expressing absolute unity.

Right smack in the middle of things — the middle subsection of the Credo, the middle "movement" of the Mass — a prime number occurs in the durational plan that seems to skew it. But that number is 31, symbolizing the Order of the Golden Fleece. So far from skewing the plan, the existence of 31 as a durational unit provides further evidence that Busnoys attached symbolic significance to durations and planned them out in advance, just as a composer of ceremonial motets might formerly have done.

It is worth reiterating that none of this impressive numerological edifice can be heard in performance, nor can it have been meant to be heard. Indeed, it is not even possible to sing the Mass with the ideal tempo proportions that would realize the ground plan accurately, for that would put the sections in diminution beyond the likely abilities of even the most agile singers. And that is precisely the point. *Musica* (as opposed to music) was not for the ear but for the mind. A shape that expressed unity on the level of Musica as well as on that of music was unified at something transcending the human level and approaching the divine, and hence served the mediating purposes of sacred music especially well—ideally, in fact, in every sense of the word.

AN ESTHETIC PARADOX (OR, THE PARADOX OF "ESTHETICS")

And this raises a final cluster of fascinating, somewhat troubling questions. When we perform music like this in concerts, what do we really hear, and how do we hear it? What is the relationship between the esthetics of modern music-listening and the esthetics of fifteenth- or sixteenth-century service music that is so often transplanted now from its natural habitat to the secular concert stage or to the even more casual venues where recordings are savored? What survives the translation process? What is lost in it? What, for that matter, may be gained?

These questions apply with particular urgency to cyclic Mass Ordinaries—large and impressively complex compositions in multiple parts, which from a certain point of view might seem to lend themselves especially well to modern concert performance. Their status as the paramount genre of their day—the highest in tone and the most prestigious for practitioners—prompts comparison with genres that enjoyed comparable standing in other historical periods. As Manfred Bukofzer, the most eminent historian of the genre, once put it, the cyclic Mass Ordinary in the fifteenth and sixteenth centuries "held as dominating and prominent a place in the hierarchy of musical values as the symphony did in the eighteenth and nineteenth centuries."[7]

The comparison between the cyclic Mass Ordinary and the symphony seems especially compelling because both genres are composites of smaller constituent units that are conceived and presented in a certain fixed, conventional order. The influence—inevitable, and inevitably anachronistic—of our knowledge of the symphony on our modern conceptualization of the cyclic Mass Ordinary is evident in the tendency to refer to the Kyrie, the Gloria, and so on, as the "movements" of the Mass. But a moment's reflection will confirm that the constituent sections of the cyclic Mass Ordinary actually have very little in common with symphonic movements, and that the nature of the two genres as wholes, however unified, is really just as dissimilar and incommensurable as is the nature of their component parts.

The manuscript choirbooks containing cyclic Mass Ordinaries, like those commissioned by Pope Sixtus for his chapel, can mislead us if we are not careful to remember certain aspects of the historical situation. They are not by any means the same kind of musical text as the scores that preserve and transmit classical symphonies or more recent compositions. They are service books that store music as economically as possible for active use. Each voice part, as we know, is separately inscribed for the individual singers' benefit, rather than space-wastingly aligned for a reader's perusal. The "movements," moreover, are entered in direct sequence, like those of a symphony, even though they were never performed in direct sequence. But that, of course, is how they are generally performed in concert and recordings today, as if Masses were in fact choral symphonies.

Modern transcriptions of cyclic Masses, like those on which we have been relying for most of our examples, "score" the works in accordance with modern practice and make them look more like symphonies than ever. So it is easy to forget (or ignore, or minimize) the fact that the "movements" of a cyclic Mass Ordinary, the first pair excepted, were spread out in performance over the whole length of the service, spaced as much as fifteen or twenty minutes apart, with a great deal of liturgical activity, including other music, intervening.

And that, over and above any urge to unify the works "esthetically," is why the "movements" of cyclic Masses were deliberately made to resemble each other as much as possible. As we have seen, they all begin exactly alike, with a "headmotive"; they all feature the same foundation melody, often presented in identical or near-identical form in the tenor; and—how completely unlike the movements of a symphony!—follow similar or identical standardized formal schemes.

All of this furthered the liturgical or spiritual purpose of the music in its original setting, adorning and integrating a festal rite. But take away all the intervening liturgical activity, and the uplifting symbolic recurrences of familiar music can seem merely redundant. When cyclic Masses are performed as choral symphonies, the music—"as music," as "esthetically" experienced—often palls. The ideal structure that makes such a strong appeal to our minds (our "organs of contemplation," as idealist philosophers have sometimes dubbed them) can actually tire the ear when presented without admixture in actual sound. Experiencing the music "as music," though we may think of it (or been instructed to think of it) as the "highest" way of appreciating music, is not inevitably or invariably the best way to experience it. And it can have little to do with what originally made it "high."

OLD AND YOUNG ALIKE PAY TRIBUTE

To return, in conclusion, to strictly historical and "dynastic" matters, it is absorbing to ponder the intricate relationships of homage that obtained among composers of cyclic Masses. Among the *L'Homme Armé* Masses that reproduce the moment from Busnoys's Sanctus depicted in Ex. 12-15a is one by Du Fay, the oldest and most distinguished composer to have joined the game. The corresponding passage in his Mass occurs near the end of the Credo (Ex. 12-16), and it is especially close to Busnoys's allowing for the speedy diminished note-values that one usually finds near the climaxes of large cyclic Mass sections.

EX. 12-16   Guillaume Du Fay, *Missa L'Homme Armé*, Credo, "Et exspecto"

The question, of course, is who was emulating whom? The discussion up to now would seem to favor Busnoys, and yet it might also seem commonsensical to assume that the younger composer imitated the older rather than the other way around—especially if the older composer were a composer of such unparalleled standing as the venerable Du Fay, by the 1460s definitely an aged man by contemporary standards. Common sense can seem especially persuasive in cases such as this, when there is little or no hard evidence against which to weigh it. (The earliest surviving source for both Masses is the same Sistine Chapel choirbook, which postdates the older composer's death.)

And yet in this particular case some other factors might also carry weight. One is the nature of the emulatory chain. As Ex. 12-16 already suggests with its very energetic syncopations (even including some interpolations into the cantus firmus), Du Fay's Mass is an especially—even an ostentatiously—elaborate composition. It is a true masterpiece, a demonstration of a great master's skills—and a great master's license, too; for Du Fay subjects the cantus-firmus tune to a great deal of embellishment almost amounting to paraphrase. The Mass also contains the single most complicated passage in all of fifteenth-century choral polyphony: a montage of four different mensurations, one for each voice, at the point in the Credo where the text, referring to God the Father, says "by [Him] all things are made" (*per quem omnia facta sunt*). The last three Latin words can also mean "all things are done," and that is what Du Fay has his chorus do, all at the same time. Once again we see that what may seem to us like nothing more than a pun ("the lowest form of wit") can be a serious symbol indeed, and the pretext for exalted creative play.

In any case, it contradicts the whole idea of emulation to imagine such a work as Du Fay's *Missa L'Homme Armé* at the beginning of the line; with such a starting point, where could it possibly go? Potential corroboration for the assumption that Du Fay came relatively late in the emulation chain is found in the inventory of the composer's property, drawn up after his death in 1474.[8] It lists six manuscripts of music, which the composer had willed to Charles the Bold, for transfer after his death. If the *Missa L'Homme Armé* were among the items contained therein (and Charles, after all, may have been the Armed Man himself), that would make it a late work indeed, as the style of the music already suggests.

In all likelihood, then, the *Missa L'Homme Armé* was the second-latest of Du Fay's cantus-firmus Masses. The cyclic Mass was a genre developed in the period of Du Fay's maturity, and one to which he, consequently, contributed little. Only four such Masses of his survive. Two of the others are based on plainsongs; one of them incorporates the music of a motet that Du Fay wrote for his own funeral, so it is probably the last of the four. The remaining Mass, the earliest, is the most famous. It embodies an intricate structure, very similar in its layout to a gigantic isorhythmic motet, based on a cantus firmus derived from the tenor of one of Du Fay's own chansons: *Se la face ay pale* ("If my face is pale, love's to blame . . .").

It has been suggested that this elegant love-song Mass was written for an aristocratic wedding, possibly during Du Fay's period in service at the court of Savoy in the 1450s.[9] That would put the Mass on *Se la face ay pale* in the same general category as the

L'Homme Armé Masses: sacred music in honor of secular authority. Alternatively, and more in keeping with motet practice, Du Fay's love-song Mass may have been intended, like Leonel's Mass on *Alma redemptoris mater*, for a Marian votive service, the cantus firmus now symbolizing the worshiper's love for the worshiped.

Either conjecture, if corroborated, would provide an explanation for the novel practice, of which Du Fay was a pioneer, of basing sacred music on secular tenors. Far from a blasphemy, it seems to have worked the other way, as a means of consecrating the secular. And thus, even if, as seems likely, Du Fay may have been a relatively late contributor to the *L'Homme Armé* tradition, he was among the founders of the larger tradition that made the *L'Homme Armé* cycles possible. Thus his dynastic authority lay behind that of Busnoys even as the authority of Busnoys's "classic" *L'Homme Armé* Mass may have called forth Du Fay's spectacular riposte in its turn. That is how artistic dynasties, as distinct from political ones, tend to work: they are elaborate cultural exchanges, not straightforward biological successions.

For one last, particularly revealing dynastic commentary, let us have a quick look at a later stage of the *L'Homme Armé* tradition. The composer who headed the next generation after Obrecht, and who was as commanding a presence among the musicians of his time as Obrecht had been — or Busnoys and Ockeghem before Obrecht, or Du Fay before Busnoys and Ockeghem, or Dunstable before Du Fay — was Josquin des Prez, to whom a whole chapter will shortly be devoted. It was Josquin's special good fortune to have been the protagonist of one of the great historical turning points for European music, when the printing revolution finally hit, and utterly transformed, its literate wing.

The very first printed volume of music devoted to the works of a single composer was a book of Masses by Josquin, issued by the Venetian printer Ottaviano Petrucci in 1502. Of the five Masses it contained, two of them — the first and the last, the alpha and omega — were based on *L'Homme Armé*. There could be no greater testimony to Josquin's stature than his laying claim in this way to the venerable tradition, and no greater testimony to the potency of that tradition than the way it was spotlighted by Petrucci in opening and closing this auspicious volume.

The opening work in the volume was called Josquin's *Missa L'Homme Armé super voces musicales*. The *voces musicales*, as we may remember from chapter 3, were the six solmization syllables of the Guidonian hexachord: *Ut−re−mi−fa−sol−la*. The special unifying *tour de force* of Josquin's Mass was to begin it with the cantus firmus pitched on C (the "natural" *ut*) for the Kyrie, and have it ascend step-by-step throughout the Mass so that in the final Agnus Dei (scored for a climactically enlarged five-part chorus) it was pitched on A (the natural *la*), the highest note of the hexachord, and transferred by way of zenith to the superius voice. No question, then, that Josquin was still engaging in the process of emulation — the process that continually asked, "Can you top this?"

Yet even as he attempted to top all his predecessors in his manipulation of the age-old cantus firmus, he paid them signal tribute in his headmotive (Ex. 12-17). If you do not immediately recognize this theme — the opening music, so to speak, in Petrucci's volume of the greatest Masses by the greatest composer of the day — go back to the beginning of this chapter and look again at its first musical example. Josquin's headmotive is modeled on the phrase with which Busnoys had set the name of Ockeghem in *In hydraulis* (Ex. 12-1b), and Ockeghem had returned the compliment in *Ut heremita solus* (Ex. 12-1c).

EX. 12-17   Josquin des Prez, *Missa L'Homme Armé super voces musicales*, Kyrie

Josquin, who wrote a lament on Ockeghem's death in which he referred to the older composer as his "bon père," his good (musical) father, was very possibly Ockeghem's pupil. Surely he knew Busnoys's *Missa L'Homme Armé* (for no musical *literatus* of his generation did not), and its special place in the *L'Homme Armé* tradition. How better to assert his place in the dynasty of "high style" composers than by making this most conspicuous reference to their most directly relevant work? And how better inaugurate and legitimate the "future" of music as a literate tradition — the phase of printed music, which has lasted until our own time and is only lately showing any sign of waning — than by making showy obeisance to the glories of the immediate past? Josquin's headmotive was thus a triple emblem: the emblematic unifier of his Mass, an emblem of heirship, and an emblem of the continuing vitality of the dynastic tradition.

Middle and Low

The Fifteenth-century Motet and Chanson; Early Instrumental Music; Music Printing

HAILING MARY

Over the course of the fifteenth century, the cyclic Mass Ordinary, a new genre, displaced the motet from its position at the high end of the musical style spectrum. That is one of the reasons why the motet, of all preexisting literate genres, underwent the most radical transformation during that time. From an isorhythmic, tenor-dominated, polytextual construction, it became a Latin "cantilena," a sacred song that primarily served devotional rather than ceremonial purposes. Connection with plainchant was retained but modified. Paraphrase — the technique pioneered in fauxbourdon settings, whereby an old chant was melodically refurbished and turned into a new "cantus" — began to dominate the motet just as the cantus-firmus technique was being appropriated by the Mass. Textual and expressive factors began to weigh more heavily than before both in the structure and in the detail-work of the newly renovated motet. The aim was lowered, so to speak, from the altogether transcendent to somewhere nearer the human plane. The result was the perfect embodiment of Tinctoris's *stylus mediocris*, the "middle style."

It became all the more fitting, then, that the middle style should continue to address the "middle being," the nexus and mediatrix between the transcendent and the human, especially as votive appeals to the Virgin Mary continued to burgeon in the liturgy. Accordingly, the latter fifteenth century witnessed the zenith of musical "Mariolatry." Its chief expressive outlet became the polyphonic arrangement of the Marian antiphons. For composers of the "Tinctoris generations," that was the basic motet category.

A wonderful introduction to the "classic" fifteenth-century Marian motet is a *Salve Regina* setting by Philippe Basiron (d. 1491), mentioned in chapter 12 as the composer of one of the numerous satellite Masses that surrounded Busnoys's enormously influential *Missa L'Homme Armé*. The original melody, signaled by the little crosses ("+") in Ex. 13-1a, has been familiar to us since the third chapter of this book (see Ex. 3-12b). As pointed out then, it resembles a troubadour canso — or, in terms more contemporary with the polyphonic setting, a ballade — in its repeated opening phrase. That repeated opening phrase is in fact identically paraphrased in Basiron's superius up to its cadence on both of its appearances in the motet, pointing up the composer's awareness of the melody's resemblance to a secular love song, and his wish to preserve that resonant resemblance in his cantilena setting.

EX. 13-1A   Philippe Basiron, *Salve Regina*, mm. 1–25

EX. I3-IA *(continued)*

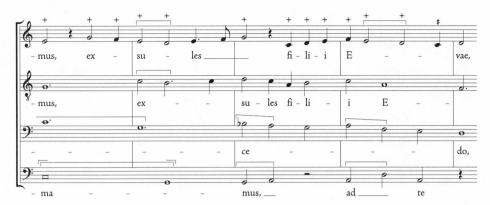

Basiron builds other generic resonances into his setting as well. The opening line of the chant paraphrase is accompanied by the altus only, creating the kind of duo one often finds in Mass Ordinary settings — or, more to the point, in the older isorhythmic motet — during the introit that preceded and heralded the entrance of the all-important tenor. The repetition of the opening superius phrase takes place over that entrance — and sure enough, the tenor behaves on entering just like a cantus firmus voice, in note-values outstanding for their slowness vis-à-vis the note-values of the introitus. The tenor seems to identify itself as — indeed, to impersonate — the bearer of the holy relic, the preexisting chant, when all the while the chant-bearing voice is the superius. The long-note tenor "melody" has never been identified, and in all likelihood will never be. It is a decoy.

What we have, in short, is a deliberate play on styles and genres by a supremely self-conscious composer-*literatus*: a paraphrase motet disguised as a cantus-firmus motet. The disguise is light and not seriously intended to deceive, of course: by the time the superius has descended its fifth between *sal-* and *-ve* in the first measure everyone in Basiron's envisaged audience would have surely recognized the most famous melody in all the liturgy. It is just a playful disguise, meant to amuse in an edifying sort of way. The deliberate playfulness — what we might call the "thematization" of genre — has a serious point. Incorporating elements of "low" (the superius in "pseudovernacular" style) and "high" (the tenor in "pseudoplainchant" style), the motet pitches itself, or balances itself, right in the middle, showing the composer's awareness of the rhetorical categories available to him, and his ability to exploit them meaningfully.

The *secunda pars* ("part two") of Basiron's *Salve Regina* shows a budding concern for choral "scoring." The cantus firmus migrates into the second and even the third voice from the top, and there is a great deal of interplay among various duos and trios drawn from the full four-part texture, with full four-part "tuttis," as we might call them, assuming in such a context a rhetorical, emphatic role. Particularly calculated for oratorical effect is the concluding triple acclamation to the Virgin — *O clemens, O pia, O dulcis* ("O thou gentle, O thou holy, O thou sweet") — in a progression from two to four voices, with the three-voice passage in the middle cast as a slightly modified fauxbourdon (note the altus and tenor in parallel motion at the fourth), the musical emblem of gentle sweetness (Ex. 13-1b).

For a remarkable contrast within a similar general approach, and certainly with no loss of expressivity, compare Ockeghem's grander setting of the same triple acclamation at the end of his *Salve Regina* (Ex. 13-2). The cantus firmus is now in the bassus (transposed down a fourth), paraphrased decoratively like Basiron's superius but nevertheless "held out" in tenor fashion. The rhetorical progression of intensity is achieved here not by augmenting the vocal complement, the way Basiron had done, but by an expanding melismatic luxuriance. The idea of "sweetness" is conveyed in harmonic terms, by means

EX. 13-1B   Philippe Basiron, *Salve Regina*, mm. 98–end

of melting cadences (or, to be grammatically precise, "half-cadences") to full triads with the third in the highest voice. Also noteworthy, for its bearing on the "prehistory" of tonally functional harmony, is the placement of the successive cadence chords—E minor, A-minor, D-minor—on a circle of fifths to the final. But notice that the sweet imperfect consonance over the final at the very end is treated as unstable; the piece cannot end until it has been "cleared" by the superius motion from F (third) to A (fifth).

EX. 13-2   Johannes Ockeghem, *Salve Regina*, "O clemens, O pia, O dulcis"

EX. 13-2 (continued)

PERSONAL PRAYER

These Marian antiphon settings sound a conspicuously personal note that we have
not previously encountered in liturgical music. That is another aspect of "middling"
tone; but it accords well with the votive aspects of Marian worship, the component

of the Christian liturgy that in those days was most intensely "personal." That, too, was something that could be thematized by a knowing composer, especially a knowing churchman-composer. The supreme case in point for a fifteenth-century motet is the third and most splendid setting Du Fay made of the Marian antiphon *Ave Regina coelorum*, copied into the choirbooks of Cambrai Cathedral in 1465. It is as impressive a motet as Du Fay or anyone ever composed, but it is impressive in an altogether different way from his earlier large-scale motet settings. Where the isorhythmic *Nuper rosarum flores* (Ex. 8-8) had impressed by its monumentality, *Ave Regina coelorum* impresses with an altogether unprecedented expressive intensity — unprecedented, that is, within the motet genre.

The personal and votive aspect of this motet are epitomized in a moving set of tropes that Du Fay interpolated into the canonical text of the antiphon, representing a prayer for his own salvation that he wanted sung at his deathbed, and that he wanted to go on being recited after his death in perpetuity, for which, a rich man, he provided an endowment in his will:

Ave regina coelorum,	Hail, O Queen of Heaven!
Ave Domina angelorum,	Hail, O Ruler of the Angels!
Miserere tui	*Have mercy on*
labentis Dufaÿ	*Thy failing Du Fay,*
Ne peccatorum	*throw him not into the*
in ignem fervorum.	*raging fire of sinners.*
Salve radix, salve porta	Hail, blessed root and gate,
Ex qua mundo lux est orta;	From whom came light upon the world!
Miserere genitrix Domini	*Have mercy, mother of God,*
ut pateat porta coeli debili.	*that the gate of heaven may be opened*
	to the weak.
Gaude, virgo gloriosa,	Rejoice, O glorious Virgin,
Super omnes speciosa;	That surpassest all in beauty!
Miserere supplicanti Dufaÿ	*Have mercy on thy suppliant Du Fay,*
sitque in conspectu tuo	*that his death may find*
mors ejus speciosa.	*favor in Thy sight.*
Vale, valde decora	Hail, O most lovely of beings,
Et pro nobis Christum exora	And pray to Christ for us.
In excelsis ne damnemur,	*Let us not be damned on high*
miserere nobis	*but have mercy on us,*
Et juva ut in mortis hora	*and help us that in our last hour*
Nostra sint corda decora.	*our hearts may be upright.*

The beginning of the motet, containing the opening canonical acclamation and the first of the votive interpolations, is shown in Ex. 13-3a. Again there is a teasing ambiguity between the old cantus-firmus style and the newer paraphrase technique. Both of the duos that together make up the introitus contain paraphrases of the Gregorian antiphon, first in the superius and then in the altus. When the tenor finally makes its dramatic entrance, it, too carries a chant paraphrase, albeit in longer note-values as befits a cantus firmus in the older tradition. But when the tenor intones the canonical chant, the other parts immediately switch over to the trope, so that a kind of old-fashioned polytextualism sets in.

The most dramatic touch of all, of course, is the sudden introduction of the E-flat in the superius on "Miserere," dramatizing in the most tangible way the shift from the impersonal diction of the liturgical chant to the personal voice of the composer. It is hard to ignore its affective significance in light of the text, which speaks of the composer's frailty and his fears. And so we have an early instance, and in this

EX. 13-3A   Guillaume Du Fay, *Ave Regina coelorum* III, mm. 1–29

EX. 13-3A (continued)

unexpected context a shattering one, of major – minor contrast in what would become
its traditional mood-defining role. The association of the Dorian interval-species with
woe and Lydian/Mixolydian with joy was as old as the Marian antiphons themselves
(as the contrast of *Salve Regina* and *Regina coeli laetare* in Ex. 3-12 sufficed to indicate). But
forcing the Dorian interval species into Lydian pitch space, as Du Fay does here, was
new and startling in a motet context (although, minus the "straightforward symbolism"

of affect, we encountered it two chapters back in Ex. 11-25, Du Fay's chanson *Craindre vous veuil*), and, in a newly "middling" way, expressive. Du Fay here speaks to Mary as human to human, seeking a human response (and getting it, at least, from his mortal listeners).

Was Du Fay aware, at such a poignant moment, of the inadvertent, irrelevant in-joke of having the added flat (which, to a fifteenth-century singer, meant "sing *fa*") occur on the text syllable "Mi-"? No doubt he was as aware of it as any singer would be, and found the irony irresistible — so irresistible that he strove to make it relevant to the affective content of the motet. Ex. 13-3b shows the way in which Du Fay set the one other text line that contained his name: *Miserere supplicanti Dufaÿ* ("Have mercy on thy suppliant, Du Fay"). This time the tenor, which never partakes of the tropes, is silent. Superius and altus engage in a little canon, both entering with E-flat on "Mi-" as the superius had done before. Even the bassus gets into the act, with a flatted "Miserere" at the fifth, that is on *A*-flat, which takes it even farther into flat space, and even closer to an adumbration of an actual major–minor "tonal" contrast.

EX. 13-3B   Guillaume Du Fay, *Ave Regina coelorum* III, "Miserere supplicanti Dufaÿ"

The flats persist until the cadence, where the superius evades occursus with the altus by means of a temporary escape to the third. That third, to remove any doubts caused by the previous infusion of flats, is designated major by specific sign — what we would call a "sharp" or "natural," which to a fifteenth-century singer meant "sing *mi*." And of course it comes on the "-fa-" of the name "Du Fay"! (And that is why the composer signaled his insistence on a three-syllable pronunciation of the name with the modified letter "ÿ.") It was an inescapable pun for a composer

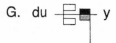

FIG. 13-1 Du Fay's rebus signature.

who enjoyed signing his name, both in letters and in musical documents, with the rebus shown in Fig. 13-1. The note on the staff, a C, is "fa" in the "hard" hexachord specified by the composer's first initial, G.

This solmization-inversion, paltry musicians' in-joke though it may be, nevertheless sparked the creation of one of the most affecting passages in the pre-Reformation sacred repertory. Nor is this the first time we have found the lowest form of wit producing, or helping to produce, the highest level of expression. Du Fay certainly recognized the pathos of what he had created and quoted it in the Mass he wrote to accompany his *Ave regina coelorum* motet at memorial services after his death (Ex. 13-4). Almost needless to say, the quotation comes in the second Agnus Dei, the only *tenor tacet* section of the

EX. 13-4 Guillaume Du Fay, *Missa Ave Regina coelorum*, Agnus II

Mass that includes the word "Miserere." There is no analogue to the second pun on "Du-fa-ÿ" here; the harmonic shift, though suggested by the pun, is no longer dependent on it for its effect.

The effect of anguished mortality is heightened in the Mass through additional chromaticism: a specifically signed F-sharp right before a specifically signed B-flat in each of the two voices in imitation. The resulting diminished fourth was something that might have been introduced into the motet by daring singers exercising their rights, so to speak, when it came to *musica ficta* — especially if those singers knew Du Fay's very late chanson *Hélas mon deuil, a ce coup sui je mort* ("Alas, my woe, at this blow I die"), where the same tortured interval is demanded for the very same expressive purpose (Ex. 13-5). No contrapuntal situation could demand such a rash of accidentals. It must answer to someone's specific expressive intent.

EX. 13-5   Guillaume Du Fay, *Hélas mon deuil*, mm. 1–8

Du Fay's Agnus Dei represents a new relationship between a Mass setting and its "raw material": it is not just a plainchant or a single line extracted from its polyphonic context that lies behind the Mass setting, but a preexistent polyphonic passage that is being cannibalized in its entirety. We are at the borderline between contrafactum — the fitting out of old songs with new texts for new purposes — and the kind of intricate polyphonic remodeling that in the next century would be called "parody."

THE ENGLISH KEEP THINGS HIGH

The musical cult of Mary reached its zenith in the place where the new-style motet began, in England. As usual, precious little pre-Reformation source material survived the sixteenth-century holy wars, but just as with the Old Hall manuscript at the front end of the century, a single enormous volume survives to tell us about British worship music at the back end. That book is the so-called Eton Choirbook, compiled for evensong (Vespers) services at Eton College during the reign of Henry VII (1485–1509), the first Tudor king of England, but containing a repertory that had been forming since Dunstable's time. (A motet by Dunstable himself is listed in the index to the manuscript, but about half of the original contents, including Dunstable's work, is lost.)

Eton College was founded by King Henry VI in 1440 to educate future government officials. It has long been famous as the largest of the so-called British "public schools," which are in fact private schools that charge tuition and to which entry is gained by competitive examination. Eton was founded jointly with King's College, Cambridge, and has ever since been a sort of preparatory school for King's, which still reserves a certain number of scholarships each year for Etonians. Both schools were (and King's still is) famous for their men-and-boys choirs.

Eton was officially franchised as "the College Roiall of our Ladie of Eton," and its charter, addressed to the Virgin Mary herself, proclaims its dedication "to thy praise, thy glory, and thy worship" (*ad laudem gloriam et cultum tuum*). The school's large choral endowment was specifically authorized by its statutes, as was the choir's daily obligation to serenade the Blessed Virgin, as it were, with a polyphonic votive antiphon. Every evening, the statutes directed, the choir was to enter the chapel in formal procession, two by two, sing the Lord's Prayer before the crucifix, and then proceed to the image of the Virgin, there to sing a Marian antiphon *meliori modo quo sciverint*, "as well as they know how."

The *Salve Regina* excerpted from the Eton Choirbook in Ex. 13-6 was specifically composed for this very purpose. Its author, William Cornysh (d. 1523), ended his life as the head of the Chapel Royal under Henry VIII. He was one of a brilliant generation of late fifteenth-century English chaplain-musicians; some of the others were John Browne, Richard Davy, Walter Lambe, and Robert Wylkynson, to name only those few who are more copiously represented in the Eton Choirbook than is Cornysh himself. Their works now barely survive, and so they do not command historical reputations comparable to those of either their continental counterparts or their English predecessors. Since 1961, however, when Frank Llewelyn Harrison published a modern edition of the complete manuscript, it has been apparent that, as Harrison put it, "the Eton music, like the chapel for which it was created, is a monument to the art and craftsmanship of many minds united in the object of carrying out the founder's vision of perpetual devotion."[1]

Shown in Ex. 13-6a and b are the beginning and end of this exceedingly lengthy motet. That length is the product of two characteristically English factors. One, which may easily be appreciated from the music as printed, is a veritable jungle growth of melismatic proliferation. The parts shown are not even the most florid sections of the antiphon, and yet they exceed in melodic extravagance any other music illustrated in this book except for the Notre Dame organa with which the Eton music is still clearly vying, at a time when continental motets have taken another expressive tack. Perhaps that is why Tinctoris, having praised the English for providing the stimulus that transformed continental style, immediately took it all back by complaining that "the English continue to use one and the same style of composition [he means the lofty style, of course], which shows a wretched poverty of invention."[2]

EX. 13-6A   William Cornysh, *Salve Regina*, beginning

EX. 13-6A   (continued)

A corollary to the melodic proliferation is the use of shorter note-values than anywhere (yet) on the continent. The boys in the famous Eton choir needed to be proper vocal athletes to negotiate their passagework in music like this, so that the official choral endowment of the college and the requirement that it be well staffed, amounted, then and now, to a kind of athletic scholarship for qualified students. And yet what the use of semiminims (sixteenth notes in transcription) accomplishes, in seeming paradox, is not the speeding up of the music, but just the opposite, its effective slowing down. That is because adding a new level of motion at the high end simply represents the limit of speed with a new symbol, increasing the spread of notated durations, while more of the change in actual note-lengths takes place at the opposite end, among the slow-moving "structural" voices.

EX. 13-6B   William Cornysh, *Salve Regina*, end

The main lengthener of English votive antiphons, however, was the exceptionally rich larding of the canonical texts with tropes. Any text that embodied prayer, and hence even potentially "votive" (like Kyries, for example), gave rise to another sort of jungle growth in the form of additional words. The concluding triple acclamation of the Salve Regina, shown in Ockeghem's already highly melismatic setting in Ex. 13-2, is an especially indicative case, since the tropes on "O clemens," and "O pia" so dwarf the canonical ejaculations. Cornysh set the text in this version:

O clemens:	O gentle one:
Virgo clemens, Virgo pia,	*Clement Virgin, holy Virgin,*
Virgo dulcis, O Maria,	*sweet Virgin, O Mary,*
Exaudi preces omnium	*Hear the prayers of all*
Ad te pie clamantium.	*who cry to thee devoutly.*
O pia:	O holy one:
Funde preces tuo nato	*Pour forth our prayers to thy*
Crucifixo, vulnerato,	*crucified son, wounded*
Et pro nobis flagellato,	*and scourged for us,*
Spinis puncto, felle potato.	*pierced with thorns, given gall to drink.*
O dulcis Maria, salve.	O sweet Mary, hail.

Imagine all of these words set with the same soaring melismatic abandon as the canonical ones, and it will be clear why the music of this motet could not be given here in its entirety. Even the concluding "Salve" is an interpolation, tacked on to give expressive meaning even to the final cadence, which now matches verbally the first grandly impressive "tutti" in the piece.

And that is yet another way in which the style of the Eton antiphons has been amplified: in terms of sheer sonority. The phenomenal upward extension of range in this music testifies to the Eton choirboys' astounding proficiency. Their ample numbers are suggested not only by the augmented complement of voices — five parts being the Eton norm, with several pieces going to six or even more — but also by the frequency with which the parts are split into "gymels" or twinsongs (in the original meaning of the terms), for final cadential chords like the one in m. 10, for even greater richness of sound.

All that magnificence comes at a price. The Eton music is thoroughly "official," collective, impersonal. It is institutional devotion *par excellence*. It makes no concession whatever to the "middling" tone that had long since begun to distinguish the continental votive motet and give it its compelling mien of personal urgency. That heightened expressivity came in part from a simplification of means. That simplification had originally come, as Tinctoris found it so ironical to recall, from England; but it was abandoned there as the English church became, under the Tudors, increasingly the partner and agent of royal authority.

And that especially necessitated the high style — a style that, as David Josephson, a historian of English music of the early Tudor period, describes it, "does not elicit the understanding, much less the participation, of the congregant. It is music of the

High Church. It awes, overwhelms, and perhaps oddly, comforts, as did the ritual to which it was attached, and the buildings in which it was sung."[3] The comfort was the comfort that comes from knowing and believing in something bigger, more powerful, more lasting, more important than ourselves — something with which our presence at worship puts us in touch, and something to which we pray, as embodied and personified in Mary. But note that the prayers addressed to her in the trope to the Salve Regina are collective, not personal: they use the first person plural, never singular; and they are generalized, never particular, rendered on behalf of the community for the salvation of all and for the common good.

The very peak of the High Church style came early in the next century, when English and continental music contrasted even more starkly than they are doing in this chapter, owing to continued continental drift, in the name of personalization, toward simplicity of texture and clarity of declamation. By the time of the English Reformation (or rather, just before it), when we will sample them again, the English and continental styles, particularly in the Mass, will appear downright antithetical despite their common ancestry. That musical divergence reflects a larger divergence in ecclesiastical mores. The one cannot be understood historically without taking due account of the other.

THE MILANESE GO LOWER STILL

A further step in the continental transformation — and stylistic "lowering" — of motet style was taken in Milan in the 1470s, when a custom was instituted within the Ambrosian rite of actually substituting votive motets addressed to Mary, more rarely to Christ or to local saints, for all of the Ordinary texts of the Mass (and in larger cycles, some of the Propers as well). Cycles of these *motetti missales,* or substitute motets for the Mass, were turned out in quantity. They are affectionately known by scholars as "*loco* Masses," from the word meaning "in place of," found in the rubrics that identify such pieces.

The most accomplished and widely disseminated cycles were those composed by the Flemish musicians employed at the court of the Sforzas (the brazenly self-styled "Usurpers" or "Governors-by-force"), a family of mercenary soldiers who in the middle of the century had suddenly risen from the peasantry to become by violent insurgency and advantageous marriage-making the ruling family of Milan. Among this clan of ruthless parvenus were some astute and enthusiastic patrons of the arts, notably the despotic Duke Galeazzo Maria Sforza, the temporal ruler of the city from 1466 until his assassination ten years later, and his brother, Cardinal Ascanio Maria Sforza (d. 1505), the city's ecclesiastical dictator.

Galeazzo's chief court-and-chapel composer was a very eminent and influential musician indeed, yet one whose current historical reputation does not adequately reflect his eminence and influence. Gaspar van Weerbeke, a Dutchman, was recruited, possibly from Busnoys's choir at the court of Charles the Bold, to lead the Milanese ducal chapel in 1471. From 1474 to around 1480 he was the Maestro di Cappella at the Milan Cathedral, and then went on to Rome, where he rose eventually to the leadership of the papal choir. His *motetti missales* seem so decisively to reject the lofty tone and the architectural genres of the Franco-Burgundian tradition that his style is often described as having been influenced by Italian popular (hence oral, undocumented) styles and genres. That may be one reason for his comparative neglect by historians and revivers of early music in performance, who have understandably tended to find most of interest in the loftiest and the lowest, and to take the stylistic middle for granted.

There is no real evidence to warrant the assumption that the music of the *motetti missales* is truly "popular" in style, but plenty of evidence that its style is, in the Tinctoris sense, "low." There is also evidence that the liturgical practice of substituting votive motets for Mass sections — and indirectly, then, the musical style of the result — was dictated by Duke Galeazzo himself, the grandson of an illiterate farmer, and may have reflected his plebeian personal tastes. The leading Italian member of the choir, later to make a great name for himself as a theorist, was Franchino Gafori (known from his treatises as Gaffurius), who inherited Weerbeke's position around 1490 and had three enormous choirbooks inscribed with the court chapel repertory for use at the cathedral (the so-called Milan *libroni*, the "big books"), thus insuring the survival of the *motetti missales* into our day. In a treatise written in the early 1480s, that is, shortly after the fact, Gafori refers to Weerbeke's motet cycles as the *motteti ducales*, the "ducal motets."[4]

What kind of motets are ducal motets? For one thing, their texts are mostly not canonical liturgical texts. Rather, they tend to be informal composites or pastiches of individual verses drawn from the Bible, from various liturgical items, or from rhymed

FIG. 13-2 Milan Cathedral (*Il duomo*).

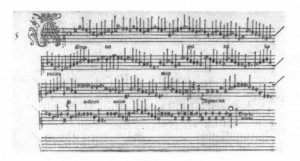

FIG. 13-3 The second Agnus Dei (starting in the middle of the third system) from Josquin des Prez's *Missa L'homme armé super voces musicales* as printed in *Missae Josquin* (Venice: Ottaviano Petrucci, 1502). The three parts are to be realized from the single notated line as a triple mensuration canon.

Latin *versus*, sometimes specially composed. For another, the music generally avoids all suggestion of the "tenor cantus firmus" style. Instead, it tends to resemble the style and some of the constructive methods of the *tenor tacet* sections that relieved and contrasted with the cantus-firmus bearing sections in cyclic Masses, especially those of Busnoys.

In such pieces, the absence of a foundational tenor had been compensated by the use of pervading points of imitation, in which the voices were treated as functionally equivalent, each providing the "authority" for the next. The beginning of Gaspar's airy-textured *Mater, Patris Filia* ("O Mother, daughter of the Father"), a motet *loco Agnus Dei* from one of his Mass substitution-cycles (Ex. 13-7), seems a clear application of this "tenorless" technique to a full four-part complement. The text, composed of three rhyming verses of votive supplication to the Virgin, reflects the threefold prayer of the Agnus Dei text. The inconsistent rhymes, scansion patterns, and syllable-counts in the verses meanwhile betray the origin of the text in an "extraliturgical" pastiche of stock Marian epithets.

Mater, Patris filia,	O Mother, daughter of the Father,
mulier laetitiae,	O woman of gladness,
stella maris eximia,	O peerless star of the sea,
audi nostra suspiria.	Hear our sighs.
Regina poli curiae,	O Queen of the remotest regions,
Mater misericordiae,	O Mother of mercy,
sis reis porta veniae.	Fling open, please, the gates of forgiveness.
Maria, propter filium	O Mary, for Thy son's sake
confer nobis remedium.	Grant us Thy aid.
Bone fili, prece matris	Good daughter, grant a mother's prayer
dona tuis regna Patris.	To us Thy people under Thy Father's rule.

Nowhere else have we seen a sacred composition in which the text is set as straightforwardly, line by line, as here. Every line begins with a fresh texture and comes to a full cadence. The first line, as already noted, begins with a full, four-part, regular, but very short-breathed point of imitation, succeeded by a cadential phrase after only ten measures (Ex. 13-7). The next couple of lines are set in what would have been fairly strict homorhythm but for the somewhat more active and decorative altus. Following that there are three short-breathed duos in a row, each of which comes to a full cadence, to bring the first verse to a close. A semblance of continuity is maintained by the retention of a common voice to link successive duos (the common presence of the

EX. 13-7   Gaspar van Weerbeke, *Mater, Patris Filia*, mm. 1–11

superius links the first and second; the common presence of the altus links the second and third).

Part of another, somewhat shorter and very lively motet *loco Agnus* from a different cycle of replacement motets (Ex. 13-8) shows a few more favorite textures and devices, from what might be called "paired imitation" at the beginning (the same little duo twice repeated, superius imitating altus, and tenor imitating bassus), rapid homorhythmic "pattersong" ("claustrum Mariae. . ."), and, finally, the sudden switch from duple to triple subdivisions of the beat, producing a high-energy, dancelike payoff (often called the "proportion" because of its strict common-pulse relationship to the previous tempo).

EX. 13-8   Gaspar van Weerbeke, *Quem terra pontus aethera*, mm. 1–23

EX. 13-8 (*continued*)

FUN IN CHURCH?

Gaspar van Weerbeke presided over a stellar group of young musicians in Milan, testifying to his employer's zeal in patronizing nothing but the best as an aspect of princely self-aggrandizement. That is to say: with great acuity, the Sforza dukes managed (in part through Gaspar's scouting "nose") to recruit at early phases of their

EX. 13-8   (*continued*)

careers a pleiad of future stars, including at least three whose future fame would eclipse Gaspar's own. They included Johannes Martini (d. 1498), who served briefly in Galeazzo's chapel choir in 1474, between stints at the rival court of Ercole (Hercules) I, Duke of Ferrara, where he eventually directed the chapel choir. In all likelihood, and in time-honored fashion, he used his invitation to sing at Milan as a stepping-stone toward the betterment of his rank at Ferrara.

Even more illustrious than Martini was the youngest northern star who trained under Gaspar van Weerbeke at Milan in the 1470s, a Frenchman named Loyset Compère (d. 1518) who eventually went back home to serve in the court chapel of King Charles VIII in Paris. It was on Compère that Gaspar van Weerbeke and his specially crafted Milanese music made the strongest immediate impression. An even greater number of *motetti missales* survives from Compère's pen than from Gaspar's, and Compère continued to develop this style and to apply it to new genres. His Marian pastiche, *Ave Maria*, is about as low in style as a motet can go, leading one to suspect a double purpose, hailing both Maria Virgo and Galeazzo Maria, both Virgin protectress and noble patron. In its patchwork of texts and tunes it is a virtual send-up of the ancient *ars combinatoria*, cast in very up-to-date patter declamation—syllables placed on minims!—that renders the texts with a dispatch bordering on flippancy.

In the motet's *prima pars* (first half), a cantus firmus is sneaked into the altus, the least "essential" (and therefore, so to speak, least conspicuous) voice, and paraphrased in such a way as virtually to disappear into the contrapuntal warp and weft. It was a familiar melody, however, and no doubt meant to be noticed (at second hearing, perhaps, with a furtive smile of recognition). The plainsong original, a sequence for the Feast of the Assumption (but often sung at other Marian services and appropriated, as it is here, for votive purposes), begins with the familiar words of the daily "Hail, Mary!" prayer, entered above the polyphony in Ex. 13-9.

Meanwhile, the tenor, the voice most likely to carry significant preexisting material, is confined to a monotone recitation of the prayer that the sequence quotes, as if mimicking the mumbling of a distracted communicant going through the rosary, the string of beads on which one counted off the "fifteen decades" ($15 \times 10 = 150$!) of Aves that a pious Christian was expected to recite each and every day. When the rosary recitation in Compère's tenor reaches the name of Jesus, the prayer shifts over to a patchwork of all-purpose litanies: "Kyrie eleison," "Hear us, O Christ," "Holy Mary, pray for us," and so on. The texture, meanwhile, gathers itself up from the opening fairly fragmented state through paired voices (beginning, of course, with the "structural vs. nonessential" opposition), proceeding through an opposition of high and low voices, and ending with an emphatic homorhythm.

The *secunda pars* expands the litany to include a wide variety of patron saints, mirroring the crowd of new names with a pervasively imitative texture in which the order and interval of entries, and the rhythmic values, are unpredictably varied. The motet explodes at the end into a long and exceptionally virtuosic triple "proportion." This is truly something new: funny church music — funny, but still pious. Piety of this

EX. 13-9 Loyset Compère, *Ave Maria*, mm. 1–18

EX. 13-9 (continued)

Hail, Mary, full of grace
The Lord is with thee, Virgin serene.
Blessed art thou among women,
and blessed is the fruit of thy womb, Jesus.

kind, though, is "humane"—pitched to the level of its hearers, rather than (like the English High-Church polyphony sampled earlier) way, way over their heads.

LOVE SONGS

These effects of whimsical, humanized religion seem to suggest the influence of the secular, vernacular genres of literate music—the official "low" style, according to Tinctoris. The vernacular genres, too, were undergoing significant change in the later fifteenth century, in stylistic terms aiming both higher and lower than before, and making many new points of contact across the generic and stylistic boundaries.

There was a new genre on the horizon, called the *bergerette*. Although its name ("shepherdess") suggests a pastoral style, it originated in French court circles, and so it is not surprising that Ockeghem was its first eminent practitioner. It was a sort of high-toned synthesis of two earlier "fixed forms," the rondeau and virelai. Its stanzaic structure was similar to the latter: a refrain enclosing a pair of shorter verses and a turnaround sung, when the poem was set to music, to the same music as the refrain, thus: A b b a A. Unlike the virelai, however, which could go on forever, the bergerette was a self-contained single strophe, in which the refrain and turnaround (the "A" sections) were ample five-line stanzas in their own right, comparable to *rondeaux cinquaines*.

An early classic of the genre was Ockeghem's *Ma bouche rit et ma pensée pleure* ("My mouth laughs but my thoughts weep," Ex. 13-10)—a classic by virtue of its wide dissemination (seventeen extant sources, a veritable record, indicating an original distribution in the hundreds) and its later emulation by younger composers, in one case as the tenor of a cantus-firmus Mass. The dates of its earliest sources suggest that Ockeghem's chanson was composed by the beginning of the 1460s.

EX. 13-10 Johannes Ockeghem, *Ma bouche rit*

EX. 13-10 (*continued*)

Qu'il eut____ le - bien   qui sa____ san - té____ des -

- chas - se   Et le plai - sir____ que la____

____ mort   me pour-chas - - se   Sans res - con -

-fort qui__ m'ai - de ne____ se - - queu - re.

2. Ha,   cuer per-vers, faul - saire et men - son - ger,   Dic -
3. Puis   qu'en ce point vous vous vou - lez ven - ger,   Pen -

Ha, cuer pervers
Puis qu'en ce point

Ha, cuer pervers
Puis qu'en ce point

EX. 13-10   (*continued*)

Vostre regueur veult doncques que je meure,
Mais Pitié veult que vivant je demeure;
Ainsi meurs vif et en vivant trespasse,
Mais pour celer le mal qui ne se passe
Et pour couvrir le dueil ou je labeure,
　Ma bouche rit . . .

My glance is gay, but my heart curses the hour
When it received the prize that now banishes its well-being.
And the pleasure that buys me death
Without hope of aid or consolation.

Ah, devious, lying, fickle heart,
How, pray, did you dare dream
of making such false promises to me?

Since you seek vengeance in this way,
think first of all of shortening my life;
I cannot live in the predicament you have put me in.

Your cruelty, then, wills me to die,
but Pity wishes that I go on living;
Thus alive I die and dead I live,
Only to hide the incessant pain
and mask the sorrow I endure.

My mouth laughs . . .

The outstanding textural novelty here is the use of almost systematic imitation entirely confined to the superius and the tenor, the voices that make up the structural pair. The incipits of both musical sections are imitations at the octave at a time interval of two tempora. They could hardly be more conspicuous. Thereafter, the alerted ear will pick up the imitation at the fourth on the final melisma of the second line of the refrain, at the last line of the refrain ("Sans reconfort. . .") , and (more subtly) at the last line of the second musical section, the very end of the music as notated. This final one is less pronounced not only because it is shorter but also because it is covered up by the movement of the other voices. Elsewhere, Ockeghem is careful to lay bare the points of imitation by having the second entering voice rest while the first enunciates the motif that will be imitated.

This kind of superius – tenor imitation, in which the nonessential voice or voices do not participate, could be called "structural" (as opposed to "pervading") imitation. We have already observed it in Gaspar's substitution motet, *Mater, Patris filia* (Ex. 13-7). It became a standard practice in motets (especially Milanese motets) as well as chansons, and typifies the convergence of the middle and low genres — a convergence that, depending on the context, can be construed as the lowering of the middle or the raising of the low.

In the case of the bergerette, it is clearly a case of raising the low, for raising can be observed in other ways as well. We have already noted the textual enlargement. No less significant is the casting of the music in two absolutely self-contained sections, with the second (here, the *residuum*, "the rest") actually labeled as such. That amounts to mimicry of the musical structure of the motet, or even of the two-part motet's model, the individual cyclic Mass "movement." In later bergerettes, including those of Busnoys, the *residuum* is often set off from the refrain by the use of a contrasting mensuration, again mimicking the motet or Mass section.

From the "tonal" point of view, too, Ockeghem's *Ma bouche rit* is novel and exceptionally "high." It is one of the earliest polyphonic compositions to incorporate a final "Phrygian" cadence, by way of a sighing tenor half step down to E, as an emblem of special melancholy or seriousness. At least as reflected in the surviving sources, on which alone we can base our knowledge of the past, Phrygian polyphony seems to have been a special predilection of Ockeghem, who bequeathed it as a standard resource to succeeding generations (and even Du Fay, possibly, who wrote a handful of Phrygian pieces at the very end of his career, probably after Ockeghem had already set the standard.) The earliest Phrygian Masses and motets, as well as the earliest Phrygian chansons (all bergerettes), were Ockeghem's.

Josquin des Prez, who was reputed to be (or, at least, who cast himself as being) Ockeghem's star pupil, made a great production of emulating Ockeghem's Phrygian music, among many other emblematic things, in his *Missa L'Homme Armé super voces musicales*, already familiar to us as an Ockeghem tribute (see Ex. 12-17). The ground plan of that Mass required pitching the final of the cantus-firmus melody on each of the six notes of the natural hexachord in turn. E's turn came in the Credo, and Josquin announces the arrival of the Phrygian mode by positively screaming out the Phrygian half-step progression at the outset (Ex. 13-11).

To acquire the versatility required to compose polyphony in any mode, one must study models. Josquin slyly tells us what model he studied for the Phrygian in the Agnus Dei II, a famous tour de force that, owing to the fascination it exerted on theorists in Josquin's day and on textbook writers since, has become the most famous part of the Mass. Outwardly an emulation of the *Missa Prolationum*, this mind-boggling little piece exponentially outstrips Ockeghem's example by "answering" the older master's two-part mensuration canon (Ex. 12-7b) with one in three parts, immeasurably more difficult to devise. And the tempo relationship of the three simultaneous parts — 1:2:3 — has been a famous challenge to performers since the sixteenth century. Josquin's single notated line is reproduced in Fig. 13-3 directly from Petrucci's volume of Josquin Masses, while Ex. 13-12 gives a transcription.

Where have we seen the beginning of Fig. 13-3 before? Look again at *Ma bouche rit* (Ex. 13-10), this time paying attention to the part to which no attention was paid the first time around. The contratenor, the "nonessential" voice that keeps out of the "structural imitation" that monopolized our gaze, is the source (the cantus firmus, if you will) for Josquin's amazing melodic line that reproduces itself in counterpoint at three different speeds and at two different pitch levels. It was probably a special joke to appropriate a lowly contratenor, a joke underscored for those who got it by the "laugh" embodied in the name of the parent song, springing unexpectedly to mind in the midst of Mass.

Josquin, trickster supreme, had a special fondness for contratenors, where one is least likely to look for anything special. The altus voice in his motet *Christe, Fili Dei* ("Christ, O Son of God"), a *loco Agnus Dei* substitute that comes at the end of a cycle of Milanese-styled *motetti missales*, carries a hidden message very much like the one in the

EX. 13-11   Josquin des Prez, *Missa L'Homme Armé super voces musicales*, Credo, mm. 1–13

F I G . 13-4 Lorenzo de'Medici, "the Magnificent" (1449–1492), depicted among the artists whom he patronized by the Florentine painter Ottavio Vannini ca. a century after Lorenzo's death.

E X . 13-12 Josquin des Prez, *Missa L'Homme Armé super voces musicales*, Agnus II, realized in three parts

Ockeghem-based Agnus Dei just considered. The motet is laid out in three well-defined sections corresponding to those of the Agnus Dei chant. The first two sections end with the Agnus Dei prayer itself (*miserere nobis*), and the motet is thus ostensibly addressed to Christ (the Lamb of God) himself. Section 1 is given in Ex. 13-13a.

The threefold invocation "Christe fili Dei" is set each time to the same music. It consists of what by now we might fairly expect, namely an imitative duo for superius and tenor, the "structural pair." That is what arrests the immediate attention and occupies the mind's foreground. Yet the very end of the text gives away the votive game: if Christ is to hear our prayers, they must be mediated by his *sanctissima mater*, his "most holy Mother, Mary," ever our intercessor.

And now we notice the subliminal message that the altus has been insinuating all along; for it carries, throughout, a borrowed melody, and a very famous one—the superius of the rondeau *J'ay pris amours* ("I've taken love as my motto"), probably the most popular French chanson of the late fifteenth century (Ex. 13-14). The altus, then, crooning this love song in the midst of prayer, is in effect sending a secret love letter to the Virgin while the text ostensibly addresses her Son. In a much less formal way, Josquin is doing what Du Fay had done in his *Missa Se la face ay pale*. Where Du Fay's Mass had displayed the borrowed secular tune as an emblem, Josquin allows it to infiltrate his texture as an inconspicuous "nonessential" voice.

The borrowed melody's big moment comes at the end, where Mary is finally alluded to in the text, and the altus and bassus treat the final phrase of *J'ay pris amours* to a fully exposed point of imitation (Ex. 13-13b). This reference, one must assume, was meant to be heard and recognized, and to color retrospectively the whole motet. Josquin's ostensibly secular song-paraphrase within the ostensibly sacred genre of the motet,

E X. 13-13A Josquin des Prez, *Christe, Fili Dei* (loco Agnus Dei in cycle *Vultum Tuum deprecabuntur*), mm. 1–11

though novel in method and effect, was not really a new idea. It was only the latest manifestation of what by the fifteenth century was already a fairly ancient practice — the fusing of the popularized sacred and the sacralized secular — whose tradition reaches back some four hundred years, all the way to the original *Salve Regina* chant, cast in the form of a *canso*, a courtly love song to the Virgin.

Thus it would be a mistake to regard this fusion of sacred and secular as an "essential" (meaning an *exclusive*) trait of the burgeoning "Renaissance." Its significance is far more inclusive than that, suggesting that categories and oppositions we may be inclined to regard as hard and fast — sacred *vs.* secular, spiritual *vs.* temporal, high *vs.* low, literate *vs.* oral — were never quite as firm or constant as we might like to pretend.

EX. 13-13B Josquin des Prez, *Christe, Fili Dei* (loco *Agnus Dei* in cycle *Vultum Tuum deprecabuntur*), mm. 28–end

Unless policed (by churchmen, by schoolmen, by snobs, and by "theorists" of all kinds) they tend to merge and fecundate one another.

INSTRUMENTAL MUSIC BECOMES LITERATE AT LAST

The elegantly crafted *J'ay pris amours* seems the perfect late fifteenth-century chanson, and so it was evidently regarded at the time. Its popularity was something phenomenal,

EX. 13-14   *J'ay pris amours* (anonymous rondeau)

Soprano

1. 4. 7. J'ay pris a - mours _____ à ma de - vi - - - - -
3. S'il est au - cun _____ qui m'en des - pri -
5. Il ___ me sem - ble que c'est la gui -

Tenor

Bass

[A] [B]

— se Pour ___ con - qué - rir _____ joi -
— se Il ___ me doit _____ e -
— se Qui _____ n'a rien, _____ il ___

[C]

- - - eu - - se - té, 2. 8. Eu - - -
— stre _____ par - - don - né.
_____ est _____ de - - bou - té. 6. Et _____

[D]

— reux _____ se - ray en cest _____ e - sté, ___
___ n'est _____ de per - son - ne _____ ho - no - ré. ___

EX. 13-14   *(continued)*

se puis ve - nir___ a mon em-pri – – – se.___

N'est-ce point droit que je y vi – – – se?___

I have chosen love willingly
to win joy.
I shall be happy this summer
If I arrive at my goal.

If any man thinks badly of me for that,
he has my pardon.
    I have chosen love . . .

It seems that love is the fashion;
the man who has none is spurned everywhere,
and no one honors him.

Am I not right, then, to aim at it?
    I have chosen love . . .

Trans. Lawrence Rosenwald

to judge by the usual standards of wide dissemination and emblematic or emulatory recycling in later music—so phenomenal, in fact, that its present-day status as an anonymous composition is something of a phenomenon in itself. Its nearest rival for favor was *De tous biens plaine* ("Full of all good things"), by the Burgundian court composer Hayne van Ghizeghem, whose surviving output consists entirely of rondeaux. Like *J'ay pris amours*, Hayne's song was appropriated as a Marian emblem for cantus-firmus Masses and motets, including a famous motet by Compère that translated the opening words into Latin (*omnium bonorum plena*), addressed them directly to the Virgin, and called down her blessings on a whole honor roll of French and Flemish musicians.

J'ay pris amours is conceivably another song by Hayne, or one by his Burgundian colleague Busnoys, but any of the leading French-speaking composers of their generation would be a plausible candidate. Despite the song's anonymous status, its quality leaves little doubt that its composer was a major figure. The opening phrase, in a manner that became increasingly popular (possibly as a result of this very song's success), starts with a motto or *devise*, just as the text says: a five-note phrase, very strongly profiled in rhythm and contour, that is set off from what follows by a short rest.

It is set off in another way as well, since it is held immune from the systematic "structural imitation" that unifies the rest of the song. Starting with the second phrase, the superius and tenor move in pretty strict imitation at the octave, with occasional freer imitation at the fifth (as in mm. 8–10—the kind of thing one calls a "tonal answer" in a fugue), and with one ingenious spot where the tenor recalls a prior motif from the superius (compare mm. 20–23 with mm. 3–4). Structural imitation briefly becomes pervasive in the final "point": the phrase initiated by the superius in m. 23 is matched not only by the tenor, as expected, but also by the contratenor (end of m. 25).

The paramount historical significance of favorite songs like *J'ay pris amours* and *De tous biens plaine* lay in the later work they inspired, which led to a new genre, born in the late fifteenth century without precedent in the literate tradition, but probably reflecting the longstanding practice of virtuoso improvisers. In his treatise called "On the invention and use of music" (*De inventione et usu musicae*), Tinctoris described the work of "two blind Flemings," obviously barred by their handicap from involvement in literate repertories, who nevertheless put their learned colleagues to shame with their flamboyant improvisations on standard tunes, reminiscent in Tinctoris's description of jazz solos: "At Bruges I heard Charles take the treble and Jean the tenor in many songs, playing the fiddle (*vielle*) so expertly and with such charm that the fiddle has never pleased me so well."[5]

That would have been in the writer's youth, before he went south to serve the king of Naples. Could these blind brothers have been the same blind fiddlers that, according to Martin le Franc in *Le champion des dames*, astonished and abashed the court musicians of Burgundy, including Binchois and Du Fay, with their amazing virtuosity? Probably not; the one description relates to the 1430s, the other to the 1460s; but that only strengthens our impression that virtuoso fiddling on the trebles and tenors of familiar chansons had a long history before its earliest reflections in the written sources.

Three such early reflections are found in a manuscript now kept at the municipal library of Perugia in northern Italy. It is a compendium of music treatises, including one, called *Regule de proportionibus* ("Rules of proportions"), that contains dozens of little problem pieces, mainly in two parts, of which so many are known to be by Tinctoris himself that the assumption is inescapable that so are the rest. Each one introduces some new difficulty of notation, preparing the way for a three-part monster called *Difficiles alios* (translatable in this context as "The hardest ones of all") that Bonnie J. Blackburn, its discoverer, wittily describes as "the musical equivalent of a bar examination," having passed which one could claim the title of *musicus* — a fully trained musician.[6]

Three of the study-pieces on the way to the exam are textless duos in which one part consists of the superius of *J'ay pris amours* — a well-known tune whose familiarity makes it an effective "control" — and the other consists of a virtuosic counterpoint to it, after the fashion of those blind fiddlers' teams described above. The difference, of course, is that Tinctoris's duo is a proving ground for literate, rather than "oral" virtuosity — virtuosity not just in singing and playing *per se* but also in reading and using complicated notation. The easiest and most straightforward of the three duos is given in Ex. 13-15.

From duos that test and display virtuoso reading skills it is but a step to untexted chanson arrangements that test and display virtuoso compositional skills — and a familiar step indeed, given the tradition of competitive compositional *tours de force* with which we have been acquainted since the thirteenth century. The one by Henricus Isaac whose beginning is given in Ex. 13-16a is found in a late fifteenth-century Florentine manuscript, and must therefore date from the composer's period of service to the

EX. 13-15   Instrumental duo on *J'ay pris amours*

great Florentine Duke Lorenzo de' Medici ("il Magnifico"). The original treble is preserved against a new and very florid tenor that may represent the type of brisk and airy counterpoint with which the itinerant Flemish fiddlers used to wow their audiences. The compositional tour de force, however, is in the contratenor, which Isaac has fashioned entirely out of repetitions and transpositions of the opening *devise*, the memorable five-note motto that distinguished the original tune.

An even more ambitious tour de force is the one whose beginning is shown in Ex. 13-16b, by Martini, found in the same Florentine manuscript. It consists of the original structural pair, the treble and tenor together, with their many intricate imitations and motivic interrelationships, accompanied by a new contratenor that runs against itself in strict canon at the unison, at a mere minim's time lag. Needless to say, the original notation is in only three parts with a rubric denoting the canon, so that the piece turns into a tour de force for the reading musicians as well as the composer. There is another bizarre canonic arrangement of precisely this kind by Josquin, based on the superius and tenor of that other great hit, *De tous biens plaine*. Obviously, the two pieces represent a sort of informal competition ("If you can do it on *De tous*, I'll do it on *J'ay pris!*") between friendly rivals.

EX. 13-16A Henricus Isaac, *J'ay pris amours*, mm. 1–13

EX. 13-16B   Johannes Martini, *J'ay pris amours*, mm. 1–4

Besides these, there is a *J'ay pris amours* setting by a minor contemporary of Martini and Josquin named Jean Japart in which the original superius is actually performed as the bassus, transposed down a twelfth and sung back to front (the rubric simply says *Vade retro, Sathanas*: "Get thee back[wards], O Satan"). There is one by Busnoys, titled *J'ay pris amours tout au rebours* ("I have taken love the wrong way round"), in which the original tenor is inverted, so that all its intervals are turned *au rebours*. There is one by Obrecht, clearly meant to be the chanson arrangement to end all chanson arrangements, in which the superius and tenor are each used as the cantus firmus twice, migrating systematically throughout a four-part texture. There is even an anonymous arrangement in which the treble of *J'ay pris amours* is shoehorned into counterpoint with the tenor of *De tous biens plaine*.

What was the purpose of all this beguiling ingenuity? Amusement for the composer? Yes, of course, but not only for the composer. There was an audience to sustain it, a public audience that was soon to become, in the classic economic sense, a "market." The existence of that audience is attested by a new kind of musical text-source called a partbook: a volume, or rather a set of volumes, each of which contains a single part — superius, tenor, contratenor, etc. — from a polyphonic texture. The earliest set of partbooks is the so-called *Glogauer Liederbuch* ("Songbook from Glogau"), a set of three books compiled and copied in the late 1470s in or near the town of Glogau in Silesia, a border district between Germany and Poland, which has often changed hands between the two countries. (Glogau is now Glogów, Poland, and the partbooks now belong to the old Royal Library in Kraków.)

The *Glogauer Liederbuch* contains a huge miscellany of Latin-texted, German-texted, and textless compositions, with which, evidently, the retired canons and brothers at the local Augustinian monastery amused themselves in convivial singing and playing. That has been the chief use of partbooks ever since. Nowadays we associate them with what we call chamber music — string quartets and the like — a genre that, while by now thoroughly professionalized, began as a convivial one. The music in the *Glogauer Liederbuch*, whether texted or not, can be regarded as the earliest extant chamber music — for chamber music can be vocal as well as instrumental, if it involves an ensemble and if its primary or original purpose was convivial. The genre of vocal chamber music has more or less died out, but there was an enormous literature of it, attesting to an enormous market for it, in the sixteenth century. We will take a close look at it shortly.

For now, though, let us concentrate on the textless and (presumably) chiefly instrumental repertory. Significantly, the *Glogauer Liederbuch* contains no fewer than three textless arrangements of *J'ay pris amours*. They are not found elsewhere and are thus probably the work of local composers, which testifies all the more strongly to the widespreadness of the genre and its attendant practices. These arrangements are identified not by the original French words but by a German tag, *Gross senen* ("Great longing").

Their beginnings are lined up for comparison in Ex. 13-17. The first consists of the original superius and tenor plus a new contratenor, placed, very unusually, in the topmost position. The other two are based on the original tenor only, accompanied by two new voices. In Ex. 13-17b, the tenor is in the traditional tenor position, in the middle. Ex. 13-17c replaces the contratenor bassus of Ex. 13-17b with a contratenor altus, retaining both the tenor and the superius of the previous arrangement. There is even a fourth *Gross senen* piece in the *Glogauer Liederbuch*, as shown in Ex. 13-17d. It is based on the superius of the preceding pair of arrangements and thus contains no original *J'ay pris amours* material at all, but is still demonstrably a part of the famous song's tradition. It is not the musical child of *J'ay pris amours*, but its grandchild. The family resemblance can be discerned only by those who are familiar with the middle generation.

EX. 13-17 *Gross senen (J'ay pris amours)* settings from the Glogauer Liederbuch
a. Original superius and tenor beneath a new cantus part

EX. 13-17B Original tenor with two new voices

EX. 13-17C   Superius and tenor of the preceding with a new contratenor

c.f. (original tenor)

EX. 13-17D   Superius of the preceding with two new voices

So the chanson arrangement (or *Liedbearbeitung*, as the composer(s) of the *Gross senen* pieces would have called it) was a very important genre historically. A few scattered predecessors aside (like the "vielle players' *In seculum*" given in the Bamberg motet manuscript discussed in chapter 7), it was the earliest form of instrumental chamber music, in effect the earliest form of "functionless" or "autonomous" instrumental music.

The word "functionless" should not be misunderstood: obviously, everything that is used has its use. If the Glogauer chanson arrangements were played for recreation and enjoyed, then recreation and enjoyment were their function. But providing the occasion for active (players') or passive (listeners') enjoyment of sound patterns is a very different, far less utilitarian sort of function from marching or dancing or worship. It emphasizes leisure, contemplation, pleasure in sensuous diversion and abstract design — in a word, "esthetics."

We are witnessing, in short, the earliest manifestation of the condition of "absolute" art or art-for-art's-sake as defined a good three centuries later by the German thinkers who invented and named the philosophical category known formally as esthetics, or inquiry into the nature of the beautiful — particularly Immanuel Kant, who coined the phrase "purposeless purposiveness" (*Zweckmässigkeit ohne Zweck*) to capture its paradoxical fascination. Anybody who attends concerts and sits still, intently watching and listening while people on stage zealously hit skins with sticks, blow into brass tubes or cane reeds, and scrape horsehair over sheep gut, will know what purposeless purposiveness is all about without elaborate explanations, and the skin-hitters, tube-blowers, and gut-scrapers know best of all.

Of course the modern concept of "absolute music" is not completely or even accurately defined if we do not emphasize the supreme value placed on it as an art-experience since the nineteenth century. By contrast, the fifteenth-century forerunner, compared with a cyclic Mass or a motet or even with a texted courtly song, was of all genres the lowest and the lightest, mere fluff. And yet the leisured clerical senior citizens who sat around amusing themselves with the *Glogauer Liederbuch* in the last decades of the fifteenth century could nevertheless be described as the earliest literate "music lovers" in the modern, esthetic sense.

MUSIC BECOMES A BUSINESS

It was the spread of that kind of music-loving that supported the earliest music business—written music as a commodity possessing monetary exchange value. It is no accident that the very earliest printed publication containing polyphonic music was a set of partbooks largely given over to textless chanson arrangements, including some of those on *J'ay pris amours* with which we are now familiar. It was brought out in 1501 by Ottaviano Petrucci, the same enterprising Venetian printer who the next year brought out the volume of Josquin Masses mentioned at the end of the chapter 12. Its highfalutin pseudo-Greeky title was *Harmonice musices odhecaton A*, which means, roughly, "A Hundred Pieces of Polyphonic Music, Vol. I." Petrucci knew his market. The next year he issued his second volume of chamber music, called *Canti B numero cinquanta* ("Songs, vol. II, numbering fifty"), and in 1504 came *Canti C numero cento cinquanta* ("Songs, vol. III, numbering one hundred and fifty"), equal in size to the other two collections combined—proof positive of successful marketing.

The production of printed music books, and the new music-economy thus ushered in, was a crucial stage in the conceptualizing of a "piece" or "work" of music as an objectively existing thing—a tangible, concrete entity that can be placed in one's hands in exchange for money; that can be handled and transported; that can be seen as well as heard; that can be, as it were, gazed upon by the ear. This "thingifying" of music (or reification, to use the professional philosopher's word for it), leading to its commodification and the creation of commercial middlemen for its dissemination—this was the long-range result of literacy, and the vehicle of its triumph.

From this point on, music would be defined, at least for the urban and the educated, as something that was *primarily* written: a text. So fluff though it was, the instrumental chanson arrangement—the commercialized, middle-class by-product of the high-purpose, high-class genres of the day, amounting to the bastard offspring of Mass, motet, and chanson—was indirectly of decisive importance to the future of literate music and music-making in the West.

"SONGS" WITHOUT WORDS

The word *canto* ("song"), as used by Petrucci in his titles, refers specifically, if paradoxically, to something that was not sung—namely, textless, instrumental items of chamber music. The usage was in fact common at the time; in the *Glogauer Liederbuch* and other German sources, the Latin equivalent of Petrucci's Italian word—*carmen* (plural *carmina*)—was used in the same meaning: an instrumental piece based on, or in the style of, a song: a "song without words."

The actual chanson arrangement was, by Petrucci's time, only one kind of carmen (to adopt, as less confusing, the Latin term for our descriptive purposes). Another, equally popular kind consisted of *tenor tacet* subsections extracted from Masses and motets, sometimes identified as such, more often not. The *tenor tacet* piece, we may recall, was the hotbed of pervading imitation—a "purely musical" sort of patterning if ever there was one, which could sustain a "purely musical" listener's interest. One famous example, published in Petrucci's *Odhecaton* and found in many manuscripts as well, was a Benedictus by Isaac (Ex. 13-18). It came from a Mass based on the tenor of Busnoys's chanson *Quant j'ay au cuer* ("Since I hold in my heart. . .") that was probably meant for Marian feasts and votive observances. The tenorless Benedictus contains no hint of the cantus firmus, however. Its emphasis on pure patterning pleasure, as well as its floridity, conspired to make it appear a very paradigm of "instrumental style" in the opinion of modern scholars—until, that is, the Mass from which it was extracted was discovered and notions of "instrumental" vs. "vocal" style had to be radically revised.

EX. 13-18   Henricus Isaac, Benedictus from *Missa Quant j'ay au cuer*, as it appears (without text) in Petrucci's *Odhecaton*

EX. 13-18 (*continued*)

The final stage, of course, consisted of specially composed songs-without-words in a style adapted from those of chanson arrangements and *tenor tacet* sections, but without preexisting material. Such pieces amounted to the earliest repertoire of "abstractly" conceived chamber music, intended for an audience of playing and listening connoisseurs. The earliest important contributors to this genre were the same composers already encountered in connection with the chanson arrangement. The most prolific was Henricus Isaac (d. 1517), a Fleming who worked in Florence, later at the Austrian court of the Holy Roman Emperor Maximilian I. The runners-up were Martini, Josquin des Prez, and Alexander Agricola (d. 1506), who wrote his share of Masses, motets, and songs for the courts and churches of France and Italy, but whose chief claim to fame was a whole raft of *carmina* that eventually found their way to the commercial presses of Petrucci, including (to give an idea of his fertility) no fewer than six instrumental arrangements of *De tous biens plaine*. Agricola also wrote carmina in the more modern imitative style, free (as far as anyone knows) of borrowed material.

Ex. 13-19 shows the beginnings of two late fifteenth-century carmina of the latter type—original *carmina* without known prototype. Both have significant titles. *La Alfonsina* (13-19a), from Petrucci's *Odhecaton*, was the work of Johannes Ghiselin (alias Verbonnet), a Picard or northern French composer who worked in Italy alongside Obrecht and Josquin at the court of Ferrara. The title translates as "Alfonso's little piece," after the composer's patron, Alfonso I d'Este, Duke of Ferrara (and husband of the notorious Lucrezia Borgia).

A similar piece by Josquin in Petrucci's *Canti C* is called *La Bernardina* ("Bernardo's little piece"). Giving carmina the names of people was a handy way of getting around the problem of what to call a piece in this "purposeless" genre, and could be applied to producers as well as consumers. One of Martini's best-disseminated pieces of this kind (found in a dozen manuscripts, including the *Glogauer Liederbuch*) was called *La*

Martinella ("Martini's little piece"). Somewhat later, Ludwig Sennfl (ca. 1486 – ca. 1543), a Swiss-German pupil of Isaac, identified a few of his carmina by naming their finals: *Carmen in la* ("Song in A"), *Carmen in re* ("Song in D"), and the like., anticipating the practice of identifying abstract or "functionless" instrumental music by naming its key ("Sonata in A major," "Symphony in D minor").

La Alfonsina and other pieces of its type were in essence a kind of souped-up version of (or "answer" to) Isaac's Benedictus. The opening point of imitation in *La Alfonsina* is a veritable rewrite of Isaac's, disguised (or rather, displayed) by reversing the order of its constituent phrases. The brisk minim motion that came in the middle of Isaac's opening "theme" now comes at the beginning, and it is carried through the entire rising octave for additional virtuoso verve. The attractive passage near the end of the Benedictus in which the tenor sings florid sequences against the sustained parallel tenths of the outer voices is mirrored in Ghiselin's piece near the middle: two parts cast in imitative sequences against one part, the superius, cast in descending dotted longs that crosscut the prevailing meter. Ghiselin adroitly tightens things up into a pair of strettos (points of imitation at a reduced time lag and with overlapping entries) in conclusion. It is a brilliant little piece.

Ile fantazies de Joskin (Ex. 13-19b) is found in a manuscript thought to contain the repertoire of the ducal wind band (or *alta*, "loud ensemble") at Ferrara. Like most

EX. 13-19A   Johannes Ghiselin, *La Alfonsina*, mm. 1–19

pieces of its type (or of its parent types) it fluctuates between pervasive and structural imitation, with fanfare-like strettos reflecting the probable medium of performance (sackbuts or trombones and double-reed instruments called shawms or bombards, depending on range).

EX. 13-19B   Josquin des Prez, *Ile fantazies de Joskin*, mm. 1–12

The significance of the title is in the use of the word *fantazie* (fantasia). The word has had several musical meanings. The earliest one was a textless musical theme or idea, something produced out of imagination rather than on the basis of an earlier authority like a cantus firmus. Later the word came to denote an instrumental composition in a systematically imitative style. (Still later it came to denote a demonstratively "free-form" composition, ruled by imagination rather than strict formal procedure.) Josquin's little piece, probably composed around 1480, links the first meaning with the second. The transfer of imitative texture to the instrumental medium was the real signal of its ascendancy. It was now polyphony's basic *modus operandi*, and so it would remain throughout the sixteenth century, which might appropriately be called the century of imitative polyphony. In any case, as we are about to see, the perfection of imitative polyphony in the sixteenth century meant for contemporary musicians the perfection of the art of music itself.

Josquin and the Humanists

JOSQUIN DES PREZ IN FACT AND LEGEND; PARODY MASSES

WHAT LEGENDS DO

As with Machaut in chapter 9, we are going to take time out, so to speak, and devote a whole chapter to a single composer. This time the close-up will be on Josquin des Prez (d. 1521), whose work has already figured, alongside that of Busnoys, Ockeghem, Obrecht, Isaac, Martini, and others, in chapters 12 and 13. It is appropriate to single him out at this point, not only because of the intrinsic quality of his music (although that is axiomatic) but also—and mainly—because Josquin became a legend in his own time, remained a legend throughout the sixteenth century, and became one again when he was discovered by modern historians. Burney, in the late eighteenth century, called him "the type of all Musical excellence at the time in which he lived," and so he has remained in the eye of history.[1] His supreme legendary status has caused Josquin to be studied more intensively, and in greater detail, than any contemporary. Yet in seeming (but only seeming) paradox, that same legendary status has also worked to hide him from view.

To the student of history, the Josquin legend is if anything even more important than the composer himself, because in describing it and accounting for its formation we may gain some critical insight into certain momentous changes that took place in the sixteenth century affecting attitudes toward music and its creators. These changes, in their relationship to the body of contemporary thought known as humanism, provide whatever justification there is for the use of the word "Renaissance" as applied to music.

In his unprecedented stature and his undisputed preeminence in the eyes of his contemporaries and posterity, Josquin has never failed to remind recent historians of Ludwig van Beethoven (1770–1827), who was similarly regarded three centuries later, and who retains a similar quasi-legendary aura. Drawing parallels between them is easy; doing so has become traditional in music historiography. Unease with this tradition has occasionally been expressed by those who see in it a danger to an unprejudiced view of Josquin and his time. Certainly we learn little if we merely assimilate what is less familiar to what is more familiar. To think of Josquin merely as a fifteenth- or sixteenth-century Beethoven would be like placing him behind the nearer figure and thereby obscuring him from view.

Worse, drawing parallels between historically remote figures simply on the basis of their perceived greatness may lead to the perpetuation of what many regard as an insidious art-idolatry that discourages critical thinking about artists and their work. Unease is certainly justified if unwarranted parallels are drawn between the two

FIG. 14-1 Jean Perréal, *The Liberal Arts: Music*, a fresco from the cathedral of Le Puy in Auvergne, France. The shorter figure, possibly because of his characteristic hat, has been speculatively identified as Josquin des Prez. The one extant representation of Josquin that was possibly rendered from life — a woodcut published in 1611 copied from a panel portrait in oil that once adorned the walls of the church of Sainte Gudule in Brussels — is often reproduced; it shows a somewhat similar headdress and features that are not imcompatible with those in the Le Puy painting.

composers as persons, or if such parallels lead to (or even result from) an ahistorical, contingent but mistakenly universalized concept of "essential" musical greatness. Yet at the same time drawing parallels between Josquin and Beethoven as cultural figures can also shed light on the ways in which "cultural figures" are constructed.

The kind of legendary or symbolic status that both Josquin and Beethoven achieved in their times can tell us a lot about those times. Both composers broke through to plateaus of prestige and cultural influence beyond the reach of their predecessors. It can seem that by the sheer force of their example they caused the world to look not only upon their music but upon music itself, with new eyes, and to listen with new ears. A more accurate way of putting it, perhaps, would be to say that they each provided an apt focal point for the crystallization of new attitudes about music and about artistic creation.

Josquin was the first composer to interest his contemporaries and (especially) his posterity as a personality. He was the subject of gossip and anecdote, and the picture that emerges again resembles the popular conception of Beethoven: a cantankerous, arrogant, distracted sort of man, difficult in social intercourse but excused by grace of his transcendent gift. Josquin, like Beethoven, was looked upon with awe as one marked off from others by divine inspiration — a status formerly reserved for prophets and saints. Among "musicians," it had formerly been reserved for Pope Gregory alone (at least when his dove was present).

This, indeed, is the kernel of our popular conception of artistic genius to this day. But saying "to this day" implies a false continuity. Josquin was so regarded, and Beethoven was so regarded, but between Josquin's time and Beethoven's there were other times (and, of course, places) in which artists were not so regarded or valued. The "humanistic" sensibility that elevated Josquin and the "romantic" one that elevated Beethoven had an important component in common, though: namely a high awareness and appreciation of individualism. In both cases, moreover, that high awareness and appreciation stemmed on the one hand from cultural and social conditions, and on the other from economic and commercial ones.

Here the parallels must end, because the applicable conditions were not the same in Josquin's and Beethoven's times. We will deal with Beethoven when the time comes. For now the task will be to understand Josquin against the background of his time — a time that formed him, to be sure, but one that he helped form as well. Powerful individuals and historical conditions are never in a fixed or static relationship. Their formation is inevitably reciprocal, and for that reason all the more inexhaustibly fascinating.

A POET BORN NOT MADE

On the most worldly level (as forecast in chapter 12), Josquin was able to achieve an unprecedented reputation thanks to newly available means of dissemination, through which his works achieved an unprecedented circulation. He was the chief protagonist and beneficiary of the nascent "music biz," the dawn of commercial music printing. He was, in short, the first composer who made his reputation — and especially his posthumous reputation — on the basis of publication. And as his reputation grew to legendary proportions Josquin became the first musical object of commercial exploitation. One of the chief tasks of modern Josquin scholarship has been to weed out the many spurious attributions made to him by sixteenth-century music publishers in an endeavor to capitalize on what we would now call his name-recognition. "Josquin" became a commercial brand name, music's first. The section given over to "Doubtful and Misattributed Works" in the catalogue that follows the article on the composer in the latest edition of *The New Grove Dictionary of Music and Musicians*, the standard English-language music encyclopedia, lists 14 Masses (as against 18 authenticated ones), 7 separate Mass sections (as against 7), a whopping 117 motets (as against 59), and 36 secular songs or instrumental pieces (as against 72). Most of the spurious items come from posthumous prints.

Yet that commercial exploitation was linked inextricably with the loftier aspects of the Josquin legend. The lion's share of the sixteenth-century Josquin trade took place in the German-speaking countries, where the music business especially flourished, and where most of the doubtful attributions were made. Sixteenth-century Germany was both a hotbed of humanistic thought and the cradle of the Protestant reformation. Both were individualistic movements, and Protestantism placed a high value on the achievement and expression of subjective religious faith.

Certain qualities of Josquin's music — none of them qualities he invented but ones at which he particularly excelled — were interpreted as personally expressive and communicative. Turning that around, they were also interpreted as the inspired expression of a forceful personality. Martin Luther, the founder of German Protestantism, famously declared that Josquin alone was "master of the notes: they must do as he wills; as for other composers, they have to do as the notes will."[2] The qualities humanist thinkers valued so highly in Josquin were mainly qualities we have so far associated with Italy and with the "lowering" of style — lucidity of texture, text-based form, clarity of declamation. As these qualities were reinterpreted in the sixteenth century, Josquin became willy-nilly the protagonist of a new ordering of esthetic values. Through the writings of German humanist theorists like Henricus Glareanus (Heinrich Loris, 1488–1563), his most enthusiastic exponent, his works became the classics on which the new esthetic rested. Glareanus went so far as to declare Josquin the creator of an *ars perfecta*: a "perfected art" that could never be improved. That is exactly the definition of a classic.

When Josquin began his long career, sometime during the third quarter of the fifteenth century, music was still traditionally ranked alongside arithmetic, geometry, and astronomy as part of the quadrivium, the arts of measurement. By the time of his death in 1521, music was already more apt to be classed with the arts of rhetoric. Glareanus, in 1547, asserted the new classification outright. He placed music among the "arts dedicated to Minerva," the Roman goddess of handicrafts and the creative arts. These included what we now would call the fine arts, such as painting and sculpture, but also the arts of poetry and eloquence. Music was now to be regarded as a branch of poetic eloquence, an art of persuasion and disclosure. Although his works could be (and often were) cited as exemplifying it, Josquin was hardly responsible for this change; it was a by-product of classical humanism, the rediscovery of old texts (particularly those by Roman orators like Cicero and Quintilian) that stressed the correspondence between music and heightened speech and defined its purpose as that of swaying the emotions of listeners. Josquin was, however, immediately cast by the promulgators of musical rhetoric as the chief model for emulation.

The first unequivocal musical rhetorician, predictably enough, was a German humanist with Lutheran leanings: Nikolaus Listenius, who in 1537 published a musical primer for use in German Latin schools. The little book, straightforwardly called *Musica*, was very popular and influential. In less than fifty years it went through more than forty editions. Basically a method for training choirboys, it contained dozens of short musical illustrations, mostly cast in the form of little duets called *bicinia*, either specially composed or extracted from the works of famous masters. (Though a Latin word, the term *bicinium*, along with its three-voice counterpart, *tricinium*, was coined by German pedagogues like Listenius in the sixteenth century to specify a piece devised or culled for use at singing schools.)

Listenius's bicinia were mostly of his own composition, but the same year as his *Musica* appeared, another German singing master, Seybald Heyden, published a competing text called *Artis canendi* ("On the art of singing"), in which the illustrations were duos "sought out with especial care," as the author put it, "from the best musicians," with Josquin in pride of place.[3] Beginning in 1545, the early German music publisher Georg Rhau issued several books of bicinia for the Lutheran Latin schools, and he was followed by many competitors, whose books kept coming out in quantity until the second decade of the seventeenth century. Thanks to all these publications, the music of Josquin remained on the lips of choristers and in the minds of composers (who trained as choristers) throughout the sixteenth century and beyond. They circulated well beyond the borders of Germany, moreover, crossing back into the countries where Josquin had actually lived and helping to assure his immortality there as well. The age of printing made such cross-fertilizations easy and normal.

As a pedagogical aid, Listenius's primer was one among many, albeit one of the first and perhaps the foremost. Its unique distinction, and its enduring importance in music history, lay in its humanistic revision of musical values. This was a side issue for Listenius, who was mainly concerned simply with teaching boys how to sing. He could not possibly have attached anything like as much significance to it as we are about to do. But then, authors are not always the best predictors where the import of their works is concerned.

In his prefatory chapter, Listenius divided the realm of music not into the traditional two branches — *musica theoretica* (rules and generalizations) and *musica practica* (performance) — but into three. The third item, the humanistic novelty, he called *musica poetica*, a term borrowed from Aristotle, for whom *poetics* was the art of constructing or making things. *Musica poetica* could be translated simply as musical composition (or, more literally, as "making music"), but that would not capture its special import. Composition, after all, had been going on for centuries without any special name. It had been regarded as the application of *musica theoretica* and the arbiter of *musica practica*. In a sense it was the nexus between the two, at least within the literate practice of music. Within that practice it could be taken for granted.

But once music was taken to be a form of rhetorical expression — of a text, of emotion, or of a composer's unique spirit or "genius" (which originally meant exactly that: spirit, whence "inspiration") — it could no longer be regarded simply as the application or the result of rules and regulations. There had to be something more in a composition that moved its hearers — something put there by a faculty that (as experience certainly attested) went beyond what could be learned by anyone. And that, of course, is our familiar definition of talent or genius — something essentially unteachable yet developable through education. It is a notion that we owe to the humanists.

Josquin was the main protagonist of this new idea from the moment of its earliest formulation, albeit posthumously. One of the earliest musicians to put the thought in writing was Giovanni Spataro (c. 1460–1541), the choirmaster of the Cathedral of San Petronio in Bologna. Like Tinctoris, whom we met in chapter 12, he was a minor composer but an encyclopedic theorist, described by one writer as "the epitome of the experienced and informed Renaissance musician."[4] And indeed, his work does sum up the musical attitudes to which the idea of "The Renaissance" can be most fruitfully applied, if only retrospectively.

The bulk of Spataro's theoretical works dates from the period immediately following Josquin's death. They constantly celebrate Josquin as the master of all masters. Spataro is best known, however, for his letters, which are voluminous (his recently published collected correspondence running more than a thousand pages), just as encyclopedic as his treatises, and very lively. In one letter, sent on 5 April 1529 to a Venetian musician named Giovanni del Lago, Spataro vividly summed up the quality or faculty to which Listenius would shortly give a name: "The written rules," Spataro wrote,

> can well teach the first rudiments of counterpoint, but they will not make the good composer, inasmuch as the good composers are born just as are the poets. Therefore, one needs divine help almost more than one needs the written rule; and this is apparent every day, because the good composers (through natural instinct and a certain manner of grace which can hardly be taught) bring at times such

turns and figures in counterpoint and harmony as are not demonstrated in any rule or precept of counterpoint.[5]

Utterly new as a philosophical thought, if not as a musical reality, was the idea of a music that cannot be defined by rules (that is, by *musica theoretica*) yet is not therefore inferior (as Boethius, for example, would have assumed) but actually superior to rule-determined craft. The gap between the rules and the art, the part that requires "natural instinct," "divine help," even *grace*—that is, the free, unmerited favor or love of God—that is what the term *musica poetica* was invented to cover. The idea of grace, of course, is a Christian idea (and one to which Protestantism would give a whole new definition). But the idea of genius is pre-Christian; it was genuinely an idea recovered from the ancients, and thereby qualifies as a "Renaissance" idea. It is related to the Platonic notion that artists create not by virtue of rational decision but because they are gifted with "poetic frenzy." The ancient idea most precisely embodied in Spataro's letter is the idea that one is born to art. It is a knowing paraphrase of an aphorism attributed by tradition to the Roman poet Horace: *poeta nascitur non fit*, "a poet is born not made."[6] Josquin was the first "born" composer in this new sense, the first composer "by grace of God." He did not know that he was that, of course. The terms, as well as the humanistic discourse or belief-system that undergirded them, arose in his wake and were applied to him retrospectively, which is to say anachronistically. But that is just the point. Because he was made retroactively, anachronistically, the emblem of the new discourse, Josquin was able to have the posthumous historical influence that so conditioned the development of sixteenth-century music. It was (as far as Josquin the man was concerned) a distinction entirely unasked-for and unmerited. In that sense it was indeed a state of grace.

JOSQUIN AS THE SPIRIT OF A (LATER) AGE

With few exceptions, the many literary encomiums that form our idea of Josquin's personality all date, like Luther's, from after the composer's death and more likely reflect the ideas and values of the writers than they do Josquin's own. One exception is a jovial sonnet, "To Josquin, his Companion, Ascanio's musician," by Serafino dall'Acquila, a poet who served alongside him in the entourage of Cardinal Ascanio Sforza toward the end of the fifteenth century. It consists of some friendly advice to the composer not to envy finely dressed courtiers, because he has something more valuable than they: namely his *si soblime ingegno*, his "talent so sublime."[7] That may give a hint of what later became more seriously known as the "aristocracy of talent"—something, again, that we are apt to associate with the Beethoven legend—but if so, it is a hint as slight as the mood is light.

The posthumous Josquin anecdotes embody a fully formed humanist ideology, and are therefore as biographically suspect as they are culturally illuminating. One of them was retailed by a minor Flemish composer and theorist named Adrian Petit Coclico, who claimed in the preface to his *Compendium musices* of 1552 that he had studied composition with the master himself. The claim is generally written off as braggadocio, not only because of its self-congratulatory implications but also (and mainly) because it is a classic application of the new, three-pronged, conceptualization of music as an art that was first propounded by Listenius in 1537. According to Coclico, Josquin taught *musica theoretica* along with *musica practica* to one and all; but only the elect were worthy of instruction in *musica poetica*. "Josquin," he wrote," did not judge everyone capable of the demands of composition. He felt that it should be taught only to those who were driven by an unusual force of their nature to this most beautiful art."

From an even later source, a "commonplace book" (a collection for writers of miscellaneous items for quotation) issued in 1562 by a Swiss humanist who wrote under the Roman patrician name of Manlius, we get another revealing glimpse of "Josquin"—revealing, that is, of humanists rather than of Josquin. In this story he supposedly takes a singer roughly to task for having had the temerity to add ornaments to one of his compositions in performance: "Tu asine!" Manlius has him shout, "You ass! Why do you decorate my music? Had I wanted embellishments, I'd have written them myself. If you wish to improve upon well-made compositions, compose a piece yourself and leave mine alone!"[8]

This, no doubt, was the kind of thing sixteenth-century choirmasters and composers did shout at their singers, under the influence of humanist ideals of eloquence as implying "divine simplicity." Putting the thought in Josquin's mouth lent it authority, and publishing it in a commonplace book made that authority available to all who wished to invoke it. But one may doubt whether Josquin ever said it, especially since the attitude it embodies toward the sanctity of the literal text is obviously beholden both to "print culture" and to Protestant fundamentalism—both of them cultural phenomena that rose to prominence and eventual dominance only after Josquin's time.

RECYCLING THE LEGEND BACK INTO MUSIC

The greatest popularizer of the Josquin legend, however, was someone who was also concerned to popularize (or repopularize) Josquin's music. This was Glareanus, the author of a great treatise that circulated piecemeal in manuscript for decades and was finally published in 1547 under the title *Dodekachordon*. Glareanus was a different sort of theorist from most of those whom we have encountered. He was neither a composer nor a practical musician but rather an all-round scholar of the purest humanistic type, a disciple of Desiderius Erasmus and a professor at the University of Freiburg im Briesgau in what is now the southwest corner of Germany, where he held chairs not in music but in poetry and theology. As a music theorist he consciously modeled himself on Boethius, the classical prototype of the encyclopedic humanist. But his actual musical views differed radically from everything Boethius had stood for.

Glareanus's main theoretical innovation, reflected in the pseudo-Greeky title of his book ("The Twelve-Stringed Lyre"), lay in the recognition of four additional modes beyond the eight modes established by the Frankish theorists of Gregorian chant. These modes, which Glareanus christened Ionian and Aeolian (together with their plagal or "hypo-" forms), had their respective finals on C and A, and hence corresponded to what we now know as the major and minor scales. Neither was a necessary invention.

FIG. 14-2 Heinrich Loris, who wrote as Henricus Glareanus, in a sketch by Hans Holbein found in the margin of a copy of Desiderius Erasmus's *Praise of Folly* (1515) at the Kunstmuseum, Basel, Switzerland.

Through the use of B-flat, a fully accredited tone in the gamut since at least the eleventh century, the Lydian had long since provided the theoretical model for the major and the Dorian for the minor. But Glareanus's terminology made it unnecessary to account for the use of C and A as finals by calling them transpositions of other finals. Very typically for a humanist, Glareanus sought to represent his innovation as a return to authentic Greek practice. It was anything but that.

Glareanus illustrated all twelve modes by citing the works of Josquin, and he was among the first theorists to use mode theory (as adapted by himself) to analyze polyphonic music. As Glareanus conceived of modal polyphony, the various strands of a polyphonic texture were (usually) cast alternately in the authentic and plagal variants of the modal scale represented by the composition's final. Typically, the structural pair of superius and tenor represented the authentic and the contratenors (altus and bassus) the plagal.

Again, it is questionable whether Glareanus's novel terms and methods contributed materially to the understanding of contemporary music. But he certainly did succeed in grounding contemporary music in a discourse of classical authority, turning Josquin into the musical equivalent of a classical master like Horace or Cicero. That being the essential humanist task, Glareanus, musically insignificant though he may appear, was culturally very significant indeed. It was he, if anyone, who brought "the Renaissance" to music, and made Josquin des Prez the first "Renaissance" composer.

Glareanus's anecdotes are mainly of the "aristocracy of genius" variety, centering on Josquin's reputed service at the court of King Louis XII of France, and on the audacity, tempered with wit, with which the composer supposedly comported himself in the presence of his royal patron. To remind the king of a forgotten promise, for example, Josquin is said to have composed a motet on the words *Memor esto verbi tui servo tuo* ("Remember these thy words unto thy servant") from the very lengthy Psalm 118. And when the king, thus reminded, made his promise good, "then Josquin, having experienced the liberality of a ruler, immediately began, as an act of gratitude, another Psalm"[9] — a motet on the words *Bonitatem fecisti servo tuo, Domine* ("Thou hast dealt well with Thy servant, O Lord, according to Thy word"), which actually come from the same Psalm.

By now, this second motet is definitely known not to be a work of Josquin's. *Bonitatem fecisti* is securely attributed to a younger, minor contemporary of Josquin named Elzéar Genet, alias Carpentras, under whose name it was published in 1514 by the very authoritative Petrucci, in a volume called *Motetti della corona* ("Crown motets") that supposedly contained the repertory of the French court chapel, including *Memor esto*. There is, however, a manuscript that attributes both motets to Josquin: a songbook compiled in the 1540s by another Swiss humanist named Aegidius Tschudi, where the two motets mentioned in Glareanus's story are entered side by side. And who was Tschudi? A pupil and disciple of Glareanus.

The whole story begins to look fishy. Having noticed the textual relationship between a motet of Josquin's and a motet of Carpentras, Glareanus (or some member of his immediate circle) probably invented the tale that linked them so symmetrically around Josquin and the King, in the process fabricating the second attribution to Josquin as well. It is another case, and a very telling one, of *se non è vero, è ben trovato* ("not true, perhaps, but well made up"), and what it reveals, precisely, is how the Josquin legend was constructed: when, and why, and by whom.

WHAT JOSQUIN WAS REALLY LIKE

But is the story wholly false? Even if the attribution to Josquin of *Bonitatem fecisti* is obviously an embellishment, the authenticity of *Memor esto* (Ex. 14-1) is well attested. It is a prime example of Josquin's characteristic "paired imitation" style, in which an opening imitative duo (here the tenor and bassus) is answered, when it reaches its cadence, by a complementary duo (here the superius and altus), and is entirely typical of his psalm motets, just as its high degree of "motivicity" (to use an ugly but handy word coined by Joshua Rifkin to denote the building up of long melodies and dense textures out of repetitions and transpositions of a tiny—here, a four-note—phrase) is generally typical of Josquin's mature style. Can the motet's connection with Louis XII and his forgotten promise be confirmed or, more decisively, disproved?

Not really. There is no documentary corroboration that Josquin wrote the motet during his period of presumed service at the French court, somewhere between 1494 and April 1503. The only guide we have to dating the work is the age of its sources, always a rough and potentially treacherous criterion. The oldest manuscript containing *Memor esto* is a Sistine Chapel choirbook of uncertain but (for our present purpose) uselessly late date. It was copied during the reign of the Medici pope, Leo X, who ascended the papal throne in 1513 and who died in 1521, which is also the year of Josquin's death. The manuscript contains the work of several members of a distinctly younger generation—Jean Mouton, Antoine de Févin, Adrian Willaert—whose relationship to Josquin was confessedly discipular. And it contains Josquin's last Mass, the famous *Missa Pange lingua* on the venerable Phrygian hymn melody we have known since chapter 2 (see Ex. 2-7b), which was presumably written too late for inclusion in Petrucci's third and last volume of Josquin Masses, which came out in 1514.

That classic work is worth a parenthetical quote at this point (Ex. 14-2), since it is so securely associated with Josquin's latest period, and therefore exemplifies his latest technique: that of subjecting a chant paraphrase to the same paired imitation technique we have just observed in *Memor esto*. The *Missa Pange lingua* takes the paraphrase technique a step further than the point where we left it: the chant paraphrase is no longer confined to the "cantus" voice alone, but through imitation suffuses the entire texture.

EX. 14-1 Josquin des Prez, *Memor esto*, mm. 1–14

As we have already seen, the year 1514, in which the third volume of Josquin's Masses appeared, was also the year in which Petrucci issued both Josquin's *Memor esto* and Carpentras's *Bonitatem fecisti* in his *Motetti della corona*, and there is no demonstrably earlier source for either motet. The probable earliest source for *Memor esto* turns out to be not a manuscript but a print. And since even that print long postdates the events

EX. 14-2 Josquin des Prez, *Missa Pange lingua*, Kyrie I

recounted by Glareanus, it can neither corroborate nor refute them. Indeed, a modern biographer of Josquin has found another version of the story about Josquin and the king, only this version involved a different king, Francis I (reigned 1515–47), Louis's successor, whom Josquin could never have served.[10]

That sort of confusion is the usual situation with Josquin, alas. Determined research has produced an intermittently detailed but stubbornly gapped picture of his career. The details, moreover, have fluctuated greatly over the years, as more recent findings have not only supplemented earlier ones but at times invalidated them. The facts, then, have always, and necessarily, been complemented by an ever-changing web of speculation and inference.

According to the most recent scholarly consensus (summarized by Richard Sherr, the editor of *The Josquin Companion*, published by the Oxford University Press in 2000), Josquin was born in or near the town of St-Quentin in Picardy, a northeasterly region of France, about 20 miles south of the cathedral city of Cambrai where Du Fay had worked. The first document to mention him is a bequest of land from his uncle and aunt, dated December 1466 and executed in the town where they lived, Condé-sur-l'Escaut, a fortified town in northernmost France, right across the river from Belgium. This deed, first reported by the Canadian archivists Lora Matthews and Paul Merkley in 1998, gives the future composer's name as Jossequin Lebloitte dit Desprez.[11] Only since then has even so basic a fact as his original family name, Lebloitte, been known to modern scholarship.

The first documents to mention Josquin as a musician place him, from 1475, at the opposite end of France: in Aix-en-Provence near the Mediterranean coast, where he served in the chapel choir of René, King of Sicily and Duke of Anjou, who was then living in semi-retirement and devoting himself to artistic pursuits. "Good King René" died in 1480. The last document placing Josquin in Aix is dated 4 August 1481. In February 1483 he reappears in Condé to claim the land bequeathed to him in 1466. The next year, as noted above, he entered the service of Cardinal Ascanio Sforza, a Milanese aristocrat and churchman who made many trips to Rome accompanied by his full entourage.

For a period of about 40 years it was thought by modern scholars that Josquin had been at Milan much earlier than 1484. In 1956, the Italian musical bibliographer Claudio Sartori published an article in which he reported a document that attested to the arrival of "Iudochus de Picardia" as a *biscantor*, or singer of polyphony, at the Cathedral of Milan in 1459.[12] This Iudochus (sometimes called Ioschinus in the documents) went from the cathedral to the personal chapel of Galeazzo Maria Sforza, the duke of Milan (and Ascanio's brother) in 1474. Inasmuch as there was an already established connection between Josquin des Prez and Ascanio, the assumption that Galeazzo's Iudochus — who hailed, like the famous composer, from Picardy — was in fact the same man was irresistibly attractive, for it managed to fill in a decade and a half of the composer's early biography.

To make it possible for Josquin to have been a biscantor in 1459, Sartori postulated a birth date for him around 1440. There was no document to preclude the new birth date and it became an accepted fact, even though it introduced an unexplained anomaly into his biography: namely, that the works of the most famous composer of his time only began to appear in the extant sources when he was in his forties, normally the point at which a composer's "late" period, in those days, began. It was not until 1998 that Mathews and Merkley were able to produce documents showing conclusively that Jossequin Lebloitte dit Desprez and Sartori's Iudochus de Picardia (known to be active in Milan until 1479) had different fathers, and therefore had to be different men. (They also discovered documents attesting to the death of Iudochus in 1498.) Josquin's birth date was duly re-emended to ca. 1450–55, just where the Belgian musicologist Edmund vander Straeten, the first modern scholar to attempt a reconstruction of the composer's biography, had located it in 1882.[13]

That would put Josquin in his mid- to-late thirties when, as a document dated June 1489 attests, he joined the papal chapel choir in Rome. It was here, as a member of the most prestigious musical establishment in western Christendom, that he began to make his mark as a composer and his music began to circulate, most conspicuously in the output of Ottaviano Petrucci, the pioneering Venetian music printer. Petrucci's initial offering, the *Odhecaton*, was issued in May 1501 and contained six carmina attributed to Josquin. In February 1502, the first printed music book devoted to a single composer (*Liber primus missarum Josquini*, "The first book of masses by josquin") came off Petrucci's presses, followed in May by *Motetti A numero cinquanta* ("First book of motets, numbering fifty"), in which a motet by Josquin was given pride of place.

At this point Josquin seems to have left the papal service. In April, 1503, a document lists "Jusquino/Joschino cantore" as a member of the choirs attending Louis XII of France and Philip the Fair, Duke of Burgundy (and later King of Spain), at Lyons. That is the only literary evidence (besides Glareanus's anecdotes) of Josquin's possible service to the French royal court. Meanwhile, in September 1502, an agent from the court of Ercole (Hercules) d'Este, the Duke of Ferrara, advised his employer, in a letter that has become famous, to hire Isaac as *Maistro della cappella* rather than Josquin, since Isaac is "more sociable" and "composes new things more quickly," while Josquin, though he "composes better," does so "only when he pleases not when he is requested to, and has demanded 200 ducats in salary, while Isaac is content with 120."[14]

Court payment records from June 1503 to April 1504 show that the Duke ignored his scout's advice and hired Josquin. Duke Ercole has received much praise from historians for showing such keen artistic judgment, but he was probably acting on less lofty impulses. For one, there was the lure of conspicuous consumption—the same impulse that motivates the purchase of expensive designer jeans or luxury cars. Indeed, a rival scout had recommended Josquin to the Duke a month earlier, advising him that "there is neither lord nor king who will now have a better chapel than yours if Your Lordship sends for Josquin," and that "by having Josquin in our chapel I want to place a crown upon this chapel of ours."[15] Lewis Lockwood, a scholar who did extensive research on the rich musical establishment at Ferrara, comments that Josquin was being touted to the Duke as "a crowning figure, and the implication is that, by hiring him, Ercole can aspire to higher status than most dukes can claim." Very shrewdly,

Lockwood noted a further implication: "the musician of great reputation can confer upon a patron the same measure of reflected glory that had traditionally been attributed to poets and painters."[16] This represented a new level of prestige for music itself, and Josquin was its protagonist. The Josquin legend had been born, and was already doing its historical work.

The most immediate evidence of that work was a Mass in which Josquin kept the implied promise to memorialize his patron the same way poets and painters had traditionally done it. One of his most famous and widely disseminated works, both in his own day and in ours, it bore the title *Missa Hercules Dux Ferrariae* ("The Mass of Hercules, Duke of Ferrara") and was published by Petrucci in his second volume of Josquin Masses (1505), when — assuming dangerously for the moment that it was actually composed at Ferrara — the work was almost brand new. The Mass continued to circulate, in whole or in part, in manuscripts and prints until the 1590s. Since Josquin's rediscovery by music historians, it has had several modern editions and many recordings. More than anything else, perhaps, this Mass has served to keep alive the name of Hercules, the Duke of Ferrara.

One of the reasons for the Mass's popularity is the clever way in which Josquin fashioned its cantus firmus out of his patron's name and title. It is an abstract series of pitches, usually presented in the tenor in long notes of equal value, arrived at by matching *voces musicales* (that is, solmization syllables) to the vowels (or *vocali*) in the phrase *Hercules, Dux Ferrari(a)e*, thus:

HER-CU-LES DUX FER-RA-RI-E = rE-Ut-rE-Ut-rE-fA-mI-rE

or

EX. 14-3   "Hercules, Dux Ferrari(a)e" in musical notation

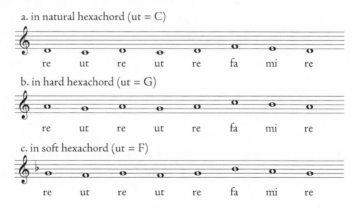

Ex. 14-4 is the Hosanna from the Missa Hercules, in which the *soggetto cavato dalle vocali* ("the theme carved out of the vowels,"[17] as the Italian theorist Zarlino would later call it) is put through some basic exercises like transposition (from the natural hexachord up a fifth to the hard hexachord) and diminution. Fig. 14-3 shows a page from Petrucci's third *carmina* collection (Canti C, 1504), containing another piece based

EX. 14-4 Josquin des Prez, *Missa Hercules Dux Ferrariae*, Hosanna

EX. 14-4 *(continued)*

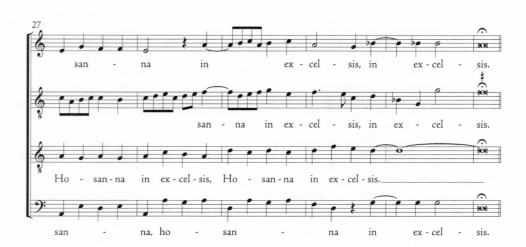

FIG. 14-3 Josquin, *Vive le roy*, from *Canti C numero cento cinquanta* (Venice: Petrucci, 1504), fols. 131v–132.

on a *soggetto cavato*, a little fanfare, almost certainly meant for a wind band, based on the vowels of the phrase *Vive le roy* ("Long live the King!"), treating the *V*, as per Latin usage, as a *U* (and the *y* as an *i*), thus:

UIUE (L)E (R)OI = Ut-mI-Ut-rE rE sOl-mI = C E C D D G E
(or G B G A A D B depending
on the hexachord)

This bit of fluff is actually the only evidence we have, beyond the single document and Glareanus's gossip, to place Josquin at the court of Louis XII, the only patron he is supposed to have served whom one would have greeted with the words of this *soggetto*. But of course there is no reason why the king so greeted had to be the composer's patron. The evidence is no "harder" than the stories.

By May 1504, Josquin is listed as provost, or head canon, of the collegiate church of Notre Dame in his ancestral home town of Condé-sur-l'Escaut. There he died on August 27, 1521, probably aged about seventy. Josquin had done as many aging musicians of eminence, like Machaut and Du Fay, had done before him: he retired to a clerical sinecure, where he continued to compose on commission up to the end of his life.

At the very end, again like Du Fay, he also composed for himself. His will, discovered by the musicologist Herbert Kellman in the French government archives at Lille and first described in 1976, contains a provision that after his death the Notre Dame choir was to stop before his house during all festival processions and sing his polyphonic setting of the Lord's Prayer in his memory.[18] The beginning of that eloquent piece, composed in six tightly woven parts and found only in sources that were copied or printed after the composer's death, is shown in Ex. 14-5. It may be fairly taken as his swan song and dated around 1520.

Thus Josquin's professional career spanned some 45 busily creative years and yielded a preserved output that dwarfed that of any earlier composer (plus an attributed output, as we have seen, that dwarfed the preserved one). The hugely, exasperatingly ironical fact is that, with only a tiny number of exceptions or possible exceptions like the ones discussed above, we cannot correlate Josquin's enormous musical legacy with the sketchy biographical framework just outlined, and so we have no reliable chronology of his work.

Lacking the evidence on which to base a strictly documentary chronology, historians have had to construct a stylistic chronology — that is, a chronology based on our ideas about the evolution of Josquin's style. And here we have to contend not only with the absence of facts but with the presence of myth. It is no wonder that many mistakes have been made and many agonizing reappraisals necessitated. We are still nowhere near a wholly reliable chronology and unlikely ever to reach it.

EX. 14-5   Josquin des Prez, *Pater noster*, mm. 1–17

But the ultimately encouraging thing about mistakes is that one learns from them. The history of Josquin chronology has not yet produced a good Josquin chronology, but it has yielded a number of excellent cautionary tales. They tell us more about ourselves, and the way in which we come to know what we know, than they do about Josquin. One of them is particularly rich in implications about the relationship between perception and prejudice.

A MODEL MASTERPIECE

Ever since the sixteenth century, the motet *Ave Maria . . . Virgo serena* has been not only Josquin's most famous work but also, in at least two senses, his exemplary opus. One meaning of "exemplary" is *representative*. On this work, above all, generations of musicians, music students, and music lovers have formed their idea of Josquin's methods, his characteristics, and his excellence. Another meaning of "exemplary" is *example-setting*. The whole "perfected art" of sixteenth century sacred music, it sometimes seems, was formed on the example of this one supreme masterpiece. Its stylistic influence was enormous and acknowledged. To a degree previously unapproached by any one composition, it was regarded as a timeless standard of perfection, a classic.

This is the motet that Petrucci chose in 1502 to open his first motet collection, the earliest such printed collection in history. In 1921 the Dutch Jesuit musicologist Albert Smijers chose *Ave Maria . . . Virgo serena* to open the inaugural volume in his pioneering edition of Josquin's complete works. It is found in almost two dozen manuscript sources from half a dozen different countries, including the present-day Czech Republic and Poland. It was the basis for many later compositions. It was arranged for keyboard instruments and for the lute. In our time, it has been recorded more times than any other work of Josquin, to say nothing of his contemporaries. Except for *Sumer is icumen in*, perhaps, it is the piece of "early music" today's music-lovers or concertgoers are most likely to know.

The text is a pastiche of three different liturgical items: a votive antiphon to the Blessed Virgin Mary, framed by a prefacing quatrain that quotes both the words and the music of the sequence for the Feast of the Annunciation (commemorating the occasion at which the archangel Gabriel uttered the original "Hail, Mary!"), and a closing couplet that voices a very common prayer formula of the day:

Ave Maria,	Hail, Mary,
gratia plena,	full of grace,
Dominus tecum,	the Lord is with thee,
Virgo serena.	virgin serene.

(1) *Ave*, cujus CONCEPTIO,	Hail, thou whose conception,
solemni plena gaudio,	full of solemn joy
coelestia, terrestria,	fills all things in heaven and earth
nova replet laetitia.	with renewed gladness.

(2) *Ave*, cujus NATIVITAS	Hail, thou whose birth
nostra fuit solemnitas,	became our solemn rite,

ut lucifer lux oriens   a light arising like the morning star
verum solem praeveniens.   going before the true sun.

(3) *Ave*, pia humilitas,   Hail true humility,
sine viro fecunditas,   fruitfulness without man,
cujus ANNUNTIATIO   whose annunciation
nostra fuit salvatio.   has become our salvation.

(4) *Ave*, vera virginitas,   Hail, true virginity,
immaculata castitas,   immaculate chastity,
cujus PURIFICATIO   whose purification
nostra fuit purgatio.   has become our cleansing.

(5) *Ave*, praeclara omnibus   Hail, most glorious one
angelicis virtutibus,   in all angelic virtues,
cujus ASSUMPTIO   whose assumption
nostra fuit glorificatio.   has become our glorification.
O mater Dei,   O mother of God,
memento mei. Amen.   remember me. Amen.

The central antiphon is a metrical hymn that echoes Gabriel's "Ave"—one of the prime emblems in Christian theology and art—through five stanzas that recall in turn the five major events of Mary's life, each of them commemorated by a major feast in the church calendar: The Immaculate Conception (December 8), Nativity (September 8), Annunciation (March 25), Purification (February 2), and Assumption (August 15). There was even a latter-day Marian votive office called La Recollection des Fêtes de Notre Dame, which originated in the dioceses of the Burgundian Netherlands, near Josquin's native turf, wherein each of these feasts was recalled, and where this antiphon would have been especially appropriate.

Entirely in keeping with the humanist rhetoricians' ideals of clarity and force of expression, Josquin's music is shaped closely around the words of the antiphon. The shaping process may be observed and described at three distinct levels. The most concrete is that of *declamation*, the fit between notes and syllables. Then there is the level of overall structure or *syntax*, the ways in which the various parts of the text and those of the music relate to each other and to the whole. Finally, there is the level of textual illustration, ways in which the shape of the music or the manner of its unfolding can be made to parallel or underscore the *semantic* content of the words.

All three aspects of the new text-music relationship are vividly exemplified by the setting of the opening prefatory quatrain. It is based not only on the text of the Gregorian sequence for the Annunciation, but on its melody, too, as set forth over the polyphony in Ex. 14-6a. The preexisting tune is not treated as a traditional cantus firmus, borne by the tenor. Neither is it paraphrased by the superius in cantilena style. Instead, just as in Josquin's very late *Missa Pange lingua*, the four phrases of the paraphrased chant melody are each made in turn the basis for a lucid, airy point of imitation, so that the texture is fully penetrated and integrated by shared melodic material, and the voices are made

EX. 14-6A Josquin des Prez, *Ave Maria . . . Virgo serena*, mm. 1–8

functionally equal. Relatively little fifteenth-century music unfolds in this way, but in the sixteenth century it became the absolute norm.

The first phrase of the melody is quoted quite literally from the chant, even in terms of its rhythm. The declamation is nearly syllabic. Thereafter the chant is more or less decoratively paraphrased: but melismas tend to come at or near the ends of phrases, and accented syllables are placed on longer note-values, both procedures being calculated to maintain the intelligibility of the text.

The final entry, in the bassus, is in each case the least adorned and the most straightforwardly declaimed. It is the "crown" of the point. The fact that the crown comes at the bottom of the pitch range, and that the first three points proceed as identical straightforward descents from top to bottom, can be interpreted as a "semantic" illustration of Gabriel's descent, as divine messenger, from God's abode in heaven to Mary's abode on earth.

As a final point about shaping, and about Josquin's exemplary craftsmanship, note the difference between the final point, on "virgo serena," and the three previous ones. The order of entries is varied at last; but more importantly, so is the time interval between the entries, which is subtly tightened, stretto-fashion — the tenor following the superius after only one beat instead of two, and the four voices all gathering in to

EX. 14-6B   Josquin des Prez, *Ave Maria . . . Virgo serena*, mm. 9–14

sound together for the first time at the cadence. All of these effects, so carefully and subtly planned, serve to mark off the prefatory quatrain from what follows. It is an ideal instance of the way in which the shape of the text "humanistically" governs, and is reflected by, the shape and syntax of the music.

Every succeeding textual unit is marked off cadentially in similar, but never identical, fashion. And each one is purposefully shaped around its words, often by artful "scoring" devices. The first stanza of the votive antiphon ("Ave, cujus conceptio," Ex. 14-6b) begins with a homorhythmic superius/altus duo that is immediately imitated by the complementary tenor/bassus pair in what we have already seen to be typical Josquin fashion. After the first two notes, however, the altus slyly joins them in a mock-fauxbourdon texture, so that there is not only a "paired" repetition of the opening phrase but also an increment from two voices to three, preparing for the emphatically homorhythmic four-voice tutti on "solemni plena gaudio," which just happens to coincide with the first "affective" or emotion-laden word in the text. All three levels of textual shaping have been cunningly made to work in harness to produce a simple, "natural" rhetorical effect. The tutti having been achieved, it is maintained through the full-textured syncopated sequences that dramatize the word "filled" and achieve cadential release at a melodic high point coinciding with the next affective word, "laetitia." The stanza beginning "Ave, cujus nativitas" opens with another pair of duos that introduce close imitation at the fifth rather than the octave or unison, and the new, harmonically richer contrapuntal combination persists through the next tutti ("Ut lucifer"), the superius/tenor and altus/bassus pairs here operating internally at the octave and reciprocally at the fifth. The third stanza of the votive antiphon ("Ave pia humilitas," Ex. 14-6c) is foreshortened by splitting the text between rigorously maintained high and low voice-pairs, setting off the total integration of the lilting fourth stanza, which moves in dancelike trochees and chordal homorhythm throughout.

But not quite. Closer examination by eye reveals what the ear perceives with delicious immediacy: within the seeming rhythmic unanimity, the superius and tenor are actually engaged in a canon at the fifth, at a mere semibreve's interval, and a "triplet" semibreve at that. Where all the other voices have trochees, the tenor has iambs (or

E X. 14-6C   Josquin des Prez, *Ave Maria . . . Virgo serena*, mm. 20–28

EX. 14-6c *(continued)*

perhaps better, considering the words, displaced trochees). This fourth stanza, poised as it is between the chordal and the canonic, is a little miracle of textural balance and a *locus classicus* of the artful simplicity (or "natural" artistry) humanists prized as evidence of genius—the "poet born not made." It exemplifies to perfection another ubiquitous Latin maxim popularly ascribed by the humanists to Horace: "art lies in concealing art" (*ars est celare artem*).

The fifth, climactic stanza ("Ave praeclara," Ex. 14-6d) is set in the most traditional texture to be found in Josquin's motet, one that we observed first in the chansons of the previous generation: the "structural pair," superius and tenor, are in strict imitation throughout, phrase by phrase and at a fixed time interval, while the "nonessential" voices, altus and bassus, supply fanciful nonimitative counterpoints. It is also the most heterogeneous texture to be found in the motet, and gives rise, in the nonessential voices, to the most ornate (albeit still relatively modest) melismatic tracery to be found anywhere in the motet. The suitability of the melodic ascent in the structural pair to the meaning of the word "assumptio" is self-evident, just as the floridity of the nonessential pair matches the word "glorificatio."

But meaning is never entirely inherent. It is also relational. The textural intricacy of the climactic stanza offsets the really stark homorhythm of the concluding prayer (Ex. 14-6e). The starkness comes about by virtue of the entrance of all four parts together on a "hollow" or "open" perfect consonance on "O." Everywhere else, four-part

EX. 14-6D   Josquin des Prez, *Ave Maria . . . Virgo serena*, mm. 28–35

EX. 14-6E   Josquin des Prez, *Ave Maria . . . Virgo serena*, mm. 36–end

homophony implied triadic harmony. Here the four voices are absorbed into the perfect consonance so as to sound like an amplification of a single voice. And once again, the motivation is textual: for the one and only time in this composite text, the first person singular pronoun (*mei*, "of me") replaces the plural (*nostra*, "our"). There can be no question that the composer of this motet saw himself as the "performer" of the words, a musical rhetorician par excellence.

PARODIES

And for that he was supremely valued by the humanist musicians of the sixteenth century, who were inspired by Josquin's example and propagated it zealously. Glareanus reproduced the whole motet in his treatise, ostensibly as an illustration of the Ionian mode with its final on C, but in fact as an example to his readers of "genius" at work. Its impact on Glareanus's contemporaries was profound. Where Glareanus verbally proclaimed the work an emblem of perfected style, his friend and colleague the Swiss composer Ludwig Sennfl proclaimed it so by musical deed.

Sennfl (ca. 1486–1543) had been a pupil of Henricus Isaac, and succeeded his teacher as the court chapel composer to the Holy Roman Emperor Maximilian I. His *Ave Maria . . . Virgo serena* was published at Nuremberg in 1537, by which time Sennfl had joined the court and chapel establishment of Duke Wilhelm of Bavaria at Munich. In his *Ave Maria* motet, Sennfl did on a vast scale what we have already observed in miniature on the level of carmina and chanson arrangements. It is a gigantic "parody" or reworking of Josquin's motet, in which the younger composer did everything in his considerable power to monumentalize the work of the older composer, and with it, posthumously monumentalize its creator.

The texture is expanded from four voices to six; the length of the work is trebled by means of overlapping imitative repetitions and transpositions of Josquin's melodic motives; and most impressive of all, the opening six-note chant-derived motto that carries Gabriel's words "Ave Maria" is turned into a motto that recurs like a clarion in the tenor part throughout the length of the piece. Josquin's "Ave" had been to Mary, but Sennfl's, clearly, was to Josquin. The younger composer's resourcefulness in exhausting the contrapuntal potential of the motivic material bequeathed him by Josqin, and the finely wrought textures that balance imitative polyphony with rich harmony, are clearly meant to display both Josquin's genius and his own. Sennfl not only admires Josquin's legacy but claims it.

FIG. 14-4 Ludwig Sennfl, drawn by Hans Schwarz in 1519.

A single excerpt, the final prayer (Ex. 14-7; compare Ex. 14-6e), will give an idea of the way sennfl replaces Josquin's spareness with opulence: note particularly her Josquin's ascetic open fifths at the concluding "Amen" have been enlarged into a gorgeous plagal cadence.

Even before Sennfl paid his tribute to Josquin's emblematic motet, it had been reworked into an entire Mass by Sennfl's somewhat older, unhappily short-lived contemporary Antoine de Févin (ca. 1470–1512). Most unusually, Févin was of

EX. 14-7   Ludwig Sennfl, *Ave Maria...Virgo serena*, mm. 76–80

aristocratic birth but nevertheless pursued a professional career as a musician — which is to say, a career in service. He was a member of Louis XII's musical establishment at the time when Josquin is popularly supposed to have worked there, and it was on the basis of their presumed relationship that Glareanus called Févin "Josquin's happy follower" (*felix Jodoci aemulator*).

Whether or not Févin and Josquin enjoyed a personal relationship, Glareanus accurately described their musical relationship. And yet Févin, while basing his technique and his stylistic preferences squarely on Josquin's, was nevertheless an innovator. His Mass on *Ave Maria . . . Virgo serena*, published by Petrucci in 1515, bears a novel relationship to its musical model, in a manner dictated by the very nature of the model (which is to say dictated, albeit indirectly, by Josquin).

In the new style exemplified by Josquin's motet the texture is so mobile and protean — now imitative, now homorhythmic, now proceeding by one sort of pairing, now by another — that no single voice-part has enough self-sufficiency to bear appropriation either as a tenor for cantus-firmus treatment, or as a melody for paraphrase. Instead, the polyphonic reworking of such a piece has to adopt the whole polyphonic texture as its model. The adaptation consists of a thorough reweaving of the texture, producing a new polyphonic fabric from the same fund of melodic motives.

Févin and his contemporaries called this new technique *imitatio*, and called a Mass in such a style a *Missa ad imitationem* ("Mass in imitation of") or simply a *Missa super* ("Mass on") followed by the name of the model. A fairly obscure late-sixteenth century German composer in the humanist tradition, Jakob Paix, published a mass in this style in 1587 under an affected pseudo-Greeky equivalent, *Missa parodia*, which means exactly the same thing as *Missa ad imitationem*. Since "imitation" already meant something else in modern musical parlance, modern scholars have adopted Paix's term for the polyphonic reweaving technique. We now call such Masses "parody Masses," and try to forget that the term now ordinarily suggests some sort of caricature or lampoon.

The Kyrie from Févin's *Missa super Ave Maria* (Ex. 14-8), one of the earliest true parody Masses, gives a good idea of the new genre and its possibilities. ("True" parody Masses are distinguished here not from false ones, but from earlier works — like Du Fay's *Missa Ave Regina Coelorum*, quoted in chapter 13 — which are basically tenor cantus-firmus Masses but which might occasionally draw informally on additional voices from a polyphonic prototype; such Masses were also composed by Ockeghem, Martini, Faugues, Obrecht, and Josquin himself.[19]) It is set in three parts, following the structure of the text. The "Christe section," like the outer "Kyries," uses the whole four-voice complement. (There is no need for a "tenor tacet" reduction where there is no tenor cantus firmus to withhold for effect.) The first section (Ex. 14-8) opens with a superius/altus duo on the opening motto-phrase of Josquin's motet, with a melismatic extension that takes it one scale degree higher for its climax. The tenor enters with what sounds like a repetition of the same point, but in fact the tenor sings an elision of the first two phrases from the motet, imitated by the altus and then by the superius, while the bassus enters at the lower fifth, providing a harmonization that reemphasizes the F reached by the superius in the first phrase. The closing phrase reiterates the opening,

EX. 14-8   Antoine de Févin, *Missa super Ave Maria*, Kyrie, first section

EX. 14-8   (*continued*)

but only in the superius. The other voices sing nonimitative counterpoints, the tenor making a brief recollection of "gratia plena" just before the final cadence.

The "Christe" appears to begin with a new point woven out of the "gratia plena" motive, but it is actually the altus counterpoint, derived from "cujus assumptio" near the end of Josquin's motet, from which most of the fabric is actually woven. The final "Kyrie" is especially ingenious. The motivic material for its first point of imitation is provided by the tenor's version of the third phrase ("Dominus tecum") in Josquin's motet. What had been an accompanying melisma — part of the background, as it were — in the original motet is moved on reweaving into the foreground. Févin's final point is woven more straightforwardly out of Josquin's "Virgo serena" phrase. In its general effect, the Mass Kyrie is a reworking of the opening quatrain from the motet, but with subtle variants and digressions at the reworker's discretion.

FACTS AND MYTHS

Févin was "Josquin's happy follower" chiefly in matters of texture — the texture exemplified in *Ave Maria*, with its rhetorically supple alternation of pervading imitation and emphatic chordal declamation. The full integration of musical space — rather than the hierarchical stratification of parts found in older music, with each part carrying out its own particular functional assignment — implied not only a new technique but a whole new philosophy of composition.

The technique as such was given an early general description in 1523, two years after Josquin's death, when the Florentine theorist Pietro Aaron published his compendium *Thoscanello de la musica*. Aaron, a Jew, was the first major writer on music to use the Italian vernacular rather than Latin, for which reason he is often looked upon as the first "Renaissance" music theorist. His book went through several editions, the last of which was published in 1539, when the new style Aaron was the first to recognize theoretically was fully established in practice.

The description in the *Thoscanello* was actually foreshadowed by Aaron himself in an earlier treatise published in 1516, a year after Févin's Mass was published; it is a less detailed and distinctive formulation than the one now classic, but it mentions Josquin explicitly as one of the composers whose methods it describes. No wonder, then, that Aaron is looked upon as the literary harbinger of "high Renaissance" music, and Josquin as its master architect.

Both aspects or poles of the "*Ave Maria* style" are represented in Aaron's discussion. The functionally integrated, imitative style of the opening quatrain is reported as a recent innovation, replacing the older discant practice in which the voices were laid out one at a time. "The moderns," Aaron somewhat gloatingly observed, "have considered better in this matter," his complacent tone recalling Tinctoris, whose works Aaron had studied well. "Modern composers," he continued, "consider all the parts together rather than by the method described above." And when all the parts are considered together, each is free to play whatever role composer may wish to assign it.

As to the homorhythmic, declamatory style, Aaron is the first theorist to consider what we would call chords as autonomous harmonic units that may be described and crafted individually. The theorist devotes much attention to matters of spacing and doubling in four parts, and to making cadences — in short, to what is still taught today in "harmony class." The ideal of integrated musical texture or "space," and the ideal of compositional freedom and mastery in tandem, have seemed to many influential modern scholars to be closely allied to notions we now associate with the "Renaissance" mentality, especially as contrasted with that of the "Middle Ages." In an ingenious and seminal article of 1941, Edward Lowinsky radically opposed the "medieval view of space" (as solidly layered and bounded) to the "Renaissance concept of space" (as free, wide open, yet "organically" integrated and harmoniously proportioned) and claimed that the transition from the one to the other had taken place around the time of the Copernican revolution in astronomy, suggesting a time-frame of 1480 to 1520. At the beginning of this period, Lowinsky maintained, the medieval view of space and the world was unquestioned; by the end, it had been decisively overthrown.

The "exact parallel" to the Copernican revolution, on this view, was the modification in compositional method that Aaron described near the end of the period of cosmological transformation. "Of all the changes in the manner of composition since the emergence of polyphony," Lowinsky concluded, this was "the most vital and the most fateful one."[20] Josquin, in Aaron's account as interpreted by Lowinsky, assumed truly colossal stature as a culture hero, becoming a veritable musical Copernicus. And *Ave Maria . . . Virgo serena* acquired a renewed — indeed, a magnified — emblematic status as the prime musical embodiment of its *Zeitgeist*, to use a word common in discussions of the "history of ideas" to denote the essential spirit of a time.

It became customary to link up Josquin's motet with Aaron's description of "simultaneous conception" and to assume their chronological proximity. And that automatically made Josquin's motet a relatively late work, one that demonstrated the composer's "perfect technical mastery, stylistic maturity, and profundity of expression," in Lowinsky's eloquent words. So obviously did it exemplify Josquin's "mature motet style," as Lowinsky put it in another study, that the historian allowed himself a categorical assertion.[21] The work had to be written, he contended, after the change Aaron had described was essentially completed, and when composers had begun relying on what the German humanist Lampadius of Lüneburg, writing (like Listenius and

Heyden) in the vintage year of 1537, called the *tabula compositoria* — a preliminary draft in full score that preceded the copying of the individual parts in choirbooks.

"A glance at this music," Lowinsky wrote of the *Ave Maria*, "will be enough to suggest how greatly the conception of such a piece must have been facilitated by the introduction of the score." Even more strongly, he claimed that "a polyphonic texture of this density can scarcely be manipulated without the aid of a score." Since Lampadius implied that the use of scores had begun around 1500, and since an archival search yielded no full scores that could be dated much earlier than that, the turn of the century became by extension the presumed date of Josquin's motet.

A highly erudite and resourceful scholar, Lowinsky refined the date still further, and even managed to infer the exact occasion for which *Ave Maria . . . Virgo serena* had been composed. He suggested that it was written for a votive service held on 23 September 1497 at the Church of the Blessed Virgin in Loreto (a shrine near Rome much favored by pilgrims), at the behest of Cardinal Ascanio Sforza, then Josquin's patron, who had just recovered from a prolonged and serious illness, in fulfillment of a sickbed vow (*voto*, whence "votive").

This was an admirably crafted hypothesis. The proposed date fell within the time frame stipulated by the "Copernican revolution" the motet was held to typify; it came close to the origins of the *tabula compositoria* as described by Lampadius; it was just early enough to account for the motet's earliest sources, yet late enough to qualify as the work of Josquin's full maturity. (According to his then extrapolated birth date, the composer would have been nearing sixty.) The proposal fit the facts insofar as facts were known (or at least believed), and also fit in with, and supported, an inventive and intellectually fertile assessment of the culture that produced it.

Imagine both the excitement and the consternation, then, when a young American scholar named Thomas Noblitt asserted — in an article written in German and published in 1974, mainly consisting of a detailed physical

FIG. 14-5 The tomb of Cardinal Ascanio Maria Sforza, Josquin's employer (1509; in Santa Maria del Popolo, Rome).

description of a German manuscript that was one of the motet's remoter sources — that *Ave Maria . . . Virgo serena* had reached Germany and was copied there no later than 1476.[22] All at once the work went from being the very paradigm of Josquin's ripest and most "humanistic" style to being his very earliest datable work. It now predated, in some cases by decades, all the developments it had formerly exemplified: musical humanism, "simultaneous conception," the *tabula compositoria*, the "northern Renaissance" itself. The innocent redating of a source turned into a threat — to some, an intolerable threat — to the Josquin legend.

One reaction to the shattering news was denial. The article on Josquin des Prez in the 1980 edition of the *New Grove Dictionary*, the one that followed Noblitt's report, dismissed his claim out of hand (as resting on unspecified "questionable assumptions") and proceeded to argue on purely stylistic grounds that the famous motet "can hardly have been composed much more than 15 years earlier" than its publication by Petrucci, who had accorded it the place of honor.[23] "In fact," the venerable dictionary declared, Josquin's *Ave Maria* self-evidently typified "the motet style of Josquin's middle years," namely "the mid-1480s." The conclusion, and the evident premise on which the dating relied, was that "the musical form precisely mirrors that of the text, yet without any sense of constraint." Of course, to base conclusions on premises is the very definition of circular reasoning. And the introduction into the argument of the inescapably value-laden concept of "constraint" and its overcoming gives considerable insight into the way myths arise and how they function. It begins to suggest what may have really been at stake, and what sort of a culture hero Josquin had really become.

Lowinsky, too, had charged his discussion of musical space and its changing conceptualization with matters of high cultural and ethical (not to say political) import. "Simultaneous conception," as preached by Aaron and practiced by Josquin, meant "the emancipation of the composer from the *cantus firmus* technique."[24] Not only that, but "the principle of imitation," as it "gradually penetrated all the voices," was also an emancipating force, for "imitation was based on motives freely invented by the composer, who could now obey fully the impulses and inspiration he received from the text." Josquin's late works, of which *Ave Maria . . . Virgo serena* was one, were "great musical structures freed from all the shackles of the medieval tenor."

We have, it seems, come back to the view of Josquin as a surrogate Beethoven: Beethoven as the voice of the French revolution, who proclaimed liberty and equality and in so doing became "The Man Who Freed Music," to quote the subtitle of what was for a long time the standard popular biography of the great composer (by Robert Schauffler, first published in 1929). But we return to the Josquin/Beethoven nexus from a new perspective that allows us to see that the correspondence so often drawn between the two legendary figures is not drawn so "simply on the basis of their greatness," but reaches much farther down into the stuff of the culture that does the drawing.

That culture — our culture — is one wedded to the ideal of personal liberation. That is a value that arose alongside modern historiography itself in the nineteenth century. It expresses above all the aspirations of a socially mobile, economically empowered, highly educated but nonpatrician segment of the population: in short, the expanding and optimistic nineteenth- and twentieth-century middle class. That is the class that has mainly supplied the world with its professional historians, and so it is not surprising that the stories professional historians have told express the values of that class, a class undreamed of in Josquin's day.

If, having been brought up in a middle-class culture that professes social justice and equality of opportunity, we have learned to place a high value on political and personal freedom and on emancipation from shackles and constraints of every kind, then we are liable to see manifestations of these values in all areas of life, including art, as progressive, and will try to abet them. The converse of this tendency is the tendency to see all sequent narratives, including the narrative of musical style-evolution, as metaphors for the master narrative of progress and liberation.

If we are now becoming more acutely aware of this tendency and are taking steps (and alerting our students and readers) to spot it and possibly avoid it, it is neither because we are suddenly wiser than Lowinsky (as great a music historian as ever lived) and his contemporaries, or because our class-bred values have necessarily changed, or because we are no longer wedded to high ideals, but because the exponential increase in the amount of available (and often apparently contradictory) information, and the occasionally dramatic consequences of that growth (such as the controversy surrounding the re-dating of *Ave Maria ... Virgo serena*) have forced a confrontation with basic questions of epistemology — questions of how we know what we know, and whether we really know it.

It is because commitment to high ideals, and the tendency to universalize them, can themselves shackle empirical perception and impede rational inference that we try to bring them to full consciousness and surmount them in our professional work. It betokens not the abandonment of emancipation as a goal but rather its application at a higher conceptual level, the one that conditions our own beliefs and actions. It is much easier to see how values become prejudices on the lower levels of scholarly work than at the higher ones. If, therefore, we raise our conceptual sights higher than before, it is in hopes of being freed to engage more directly with the perceptual materials of our trade (like manuscripts), and derive concepts from them (like the dates of their contents) with more confidence.

That is why it has been thought valuable to devote so much space in a book like this to so relatively dry and inconsequential a matter as the date of Josquin's *Ave Maria*. Its ramifications are anything but inconsequential. They can alert us to the dangers of looking for "good vibes" in history. When Lowinsky's excellent hypothesis was shown no longer "to fit the facts insofar as facts were known," continued commitment to it is exposed as prejudice, no longer fitting facts but only a predefined notion of a Zeitgeist.

Thus, to believe that pervading imitation "emancipated" music or its composers from the "tyranny" of the cantus firmus, however thrilling or gratifying it may be to us personally, only makes problems for us as historians. For one thing, it renders us unable to understand how it is that imitation and cantus firmus techniques can coexist so happily — and especially in Josquin's work, as we may see in Ex. 14-9, the beginning of *Benedicta es, coelorum regina* ("Blessed art thou, O Queen of the Heavens"), a sequence motet that circulated mainly during Josquin's "posthumous" period (that is the period of his widespread dissemination in German prints). *Benedicta es* was a particular favorite of Glareanus himself, and popular, thanks to him, with all the German humanists.

In fact, like so many ancient musical techniques, cantus firmus writing has never died out at all. Imitation no more replaced cantus firmus than (to recall an analogous

EX. 14-9   Josquin des Prez, *Benedicta es, coelorum regina*, mm. 1–10

EX. 14-9 *(continued)*

EX. 14-9   (*continued*)

Blessed art thou, O queen of heaven,
and governess of the whole world,
and healer of the sick.

discussion in the first chapter of this book) literacy replaced oral practices. The one joined the other, affecting it, to be sure, but never altogether supplanting it. Cantus firmus technique is still an available option, and one universally studied by aspiring composers even now. So neither literacy nor pervading imitation can be simply understood as liberations. Their histories are far more complex—and far more interesting—than that. And that is one more reason why the narrative in this book is making such strenuous and self-advertising efforts to avoid concepts like "The Middle Ages" and "The Renaissance." When turned into dueling Zeitgeists they are obstacles, not aids, to seeing things, let alone understanding them.

What happens now if we accept the date that Thomas Noblitt's physical evidence (specifically, the watermark in the paper on which it was copied) assigned to Josquin's *Ave Maria . . . Virgo serena?* Nothing very terrible. Quite the contrary: all at once it takes its place in a new and telling context, that of the Milanese *motetti missales*. Compare it with the works of Gaspar van Weerbeke sampled in the previous chapter (Ex. 13-7, Ex. 13-8), or especially with Compère's *Ave Maria* (Ex. 13-11), and its membership in their family becomes obvious. The reader may already have noticed, in fact, that Josquin's opening quatrain is based on the very same sequence melody that Compère appropriated in the altus of his litany motet: a local favorite, no doubt.

Ave Maria ... Virgo serena thus stands revealed as belonging to the tradition of the Milanese "ducal motets" identified in chapter 13 with Galeazzo Maria Sforza, the brother of Ascanio Sforza, Josquin's sometime patron. Far from the revolutionary work that Lowinsky sought and found in it, it now appears to be fully representative of its fifteenth-century parent repertory, even if, as we are all likely to agree, its artistic quality far outstrips that of its companions. Though exceptionally realized and full of idiosyncratic detail, its style nevertheless reflects its time and place. Both in its avoidance of a cantus-firmus-bearing tenor and in its close-fitting text-music relationship it resonates less with lofty humanism than with its near-opposite, the stylistic "lowering" associated in chapter 13 with the influence of local, nonliterate popular genres.

When Noblitt's article was published, Josquin des Prez was still erroneously identified with the Iudochus de Picardia who had sung in the Milanese cathedral choir as early as 1459. For a while, it was argued that the famous *Ave Maria* was actually intended for use in a "loco Mass" as described in the previous chapter. Now that Josquin's early presence in Milan has been disproved, the relationship between his motet and the Milanese tradition is no longer quite so obvious. But Josquin certainly was in Milan during his time of service to Ascanio Sforza, most securely documented for the period 1484–85. Some scholars have tried to reconcile Noblitt's source evidence with this later date, reasonably arguing that music copied on paper with a 1476 watermark need not have been entered immediately after the paper was procured, and that the year 1476 should not be regarded as anything more than a "terminus post quem"—the earliest possible date rather than necessarily the actual one.[25]

Even 1485, however, is too early a date to support the claims that Lowinsky made for the motet, or for its composer's intentions. To acknowledge this, however, is by no means to deny the status of *Ave Maria ... Virgo serena* as an exemplary (or even "prophetic") sixteenth-century composition. It survived in print, in memory, and in use, and achieved renewed currency thanks to the work of the humanists who appropriated it. It did indeed play an important part in establishing a genuine tradition of musical humanism. Works of art certainly can and often do transcend their time and place of origin (as anyone attending concerts today can attest), and works that have so survived can exert influence at the farthest, most improbable temporal and geographic remove.

In the nineteenth century, for example, the first century to have a "modern" historical sense, the century-old vocal works of J. S. Bach were revived and had a far more direct impact on contemporary composition, as we shall see, than they ever had during the composer's lifetime. In the twentieth century, an even more history-obsessed age, much older repertories exhumed by musicology (including "medieval" and "Renaissance" ones) have often influenced the newest music.

The survival and posthumous influence of Josquin des Prez, and certain of his works, was an early example of this process of "remote reception"—perhaps the earliest. But if *Ave Maria ... Virgo serena* was an exemplary sixteenth-century composition, it was not Josquin who made it so, but the sixteenth century.

A Perfected Art

SIXTEENTH-CENTURY CHURCH MUSIC; NEW INSTRUMENTAL GENRES

In this splendid, noble art
So many have been famous in our age
They make any other time seem poor.[1]

ALL IS KNOWN

The lines quoted as epigraph were penned in 1490 by Giovanni Santi, court painter to the Duke of Urbino, when his son Raffaello Santi, known to us as Raphael, was seven years old. That boy, of course, whose gifts were recognized early and stimulated with papal patronage, would soon make his father's time seem poor. The art of Raphael is now a standard of perfection in painting, "the clearest expression," according to one modern authority, "of the exquisite harmony and balance of High Renaissance composition."[2] That standard of perfection has remained in force, so to speak, whenever and wherever "perfection," as a standard, has been valued (see Fig. 15-1)

Something similar may be observed in the music of the sixteenth century, particularly as practiced in Italian centers of patronage. Fifteenth-century writers — Tinctoris, for one — were often as complacently sure as Giovanni Santi was of the unprecedented richness of their age. But in the sixteenth century there was an enormous striving after an objective standard of perfection — of surpassing "harmony and balance" — that, once achieved, would remain good for all time.

This happy status quo, many musicians of the latter half of the sixteenth century believed, had been reached in their time. Music, they argued, was now an *ars perfecta,* a

FIG. 15-1   Raphael (Raffaelo Santi or Sanzio, 1483–1520), *Alba Madonna,* ca. 1510.

"perfected art." After floundering in the "lowest depths" of decay during an age of barbarism (what those who believe in the Renaissance call the Middle Ages), it had rescaled the "heights of perfection" it had known in ancient times.[3] Its technique now admitted of no further development. What was needed was codification: the casting of the perfected style in permanent rules so that it might never be lost again, so that its harmony and balance might be preserved and passed along even to those who had not the genius to discover it for themselves. For no one needed to rediscover what had already been discovered. The age of discovery was past. All was known. An age of "classicism" — of conformity with established excellence — had dawned. It was a great age for theorists.

The outstanding codifier of the *ars perfecta* was Gioseffo Zarlino (1517–90), from whose great treatise *Le Istitutioni harmoniche*, first published in 1558 and reissued twice thereafter, the historical judgments in the preceding paragraph were taken. The title of Zarlino's four-volume manual was itself a sign of the times. Often translated as "Elements" or "Principles of Harmony," or something equally neutral, it really means "The Established Rules of Harmony." And harmony, both in the narrow musical sense and in the wider esthetic sense, was what it purported to impart by methods tried and true. "If we follow the rules given up to now," Zarlino promised at the conclusion of his third volume, on counterpoint, "our compositions will be free of reprehensible elements, purged of every error and polished, and our harmonies will be good and pleasant."[4] Harmony and balance are matters of proportion, and proportion is a matter of quantities. Therefore it will not surprise us to find Zarlino writing that "music is a science subordinate to arithmetic."[5] He even appended one final chapter to the last volume that carried the cautionary heading, "The Senses are Fallible, and Judgments Should Not Be Made Solely by Their Means, but Should Be Accompanied by Reason."[6] That begins to smack of Boethius. If we are hasty to invoke the dueling Zeitgeists, we may be tempted to slap the label "medieval" on the quintessential "Renaissance" theorist.

FIG. 15-2 Gioseffo Zarlino, anonymous portrait at the Civico Museo Bibliografico Musicale, Bologna.

But like most paradoxes, this one is only seeming. Zarlino was merely trying to lend authority to his rules and discourage whimsical experimentation on the part of his students. New ideas, to say nothing of thrill-seeking, could degrade a perfected art. Elsewhere he invokes something that would never have occurred to Boethius to invoke, namely "natural philosophy." That is what we would call *science*, in the modern empirical (or "Galilean") sense that is thought to have arisen during the "Renaissance" as a by-product of its secularism. Those who think of the sixteenth century as the cradle of modern science tend to call it the "early modern" period. Zarlino was the first "early modern" theorist.

The really valuable fruit of Zarlino's rationalized empiricism was his recognition of harmony, as it actually functioned in "early modern" music, as being worthy of theoretical attention, and his ingenuity in devising a rationale for it. For a long time now—at least since the beginning of the fifteenth century, and most likely before that in unwritten repertories—the triad, first imported into continental music from England, had been the de facto normative consonance for all European polyphonic music. Before Zarlino, however, no theorist had recognized it as an entity, given it a name, or legitimized its use.

THE TRIAD COMES OF AGE

All theory we have studied up to now has been discant theory, in which two voices (the "structural pair") define harmonic norms and in which only perfect consonances enjoy full freedom of use. If nowhere else, composers of written music still honored this ranking of consonances at final cadences, where as we have seen, triads had to be purged of their thirds for full cadential finality. Zarlino was the first theorist to accept the triad as a full-fledged consonance. Not only did he accept it, he dubbed it the *harmonia perfetta*—the "perfect harmony." He rationalized giving the triad this suggestive name not only on the basis of the sensory pleasure that triadic harmony evoked, nor on the basis of the affective qualities that he ascribed to it, although he was in fact the first to come right out and say that "when [in a triad] the major third is below [the minor] the harmony is gay, and when it is above, the harmony is sad."[7] Along with these factors Zarlino cited mathematical theory, so that he could maintain, like a good Aristotelian, that according to his rules reason held sway over sense. The "perfect harmony," he asserted, was the product of the "perfect number," which was six.

Just as Glareanus had come to terms with modern practice by adding two more finals to the Frankish four to account for contemporary melodic styles, Zarlino added two more integers to the Pythagorean four in order to generate the harmonies of contemporary music that he now wished to rationalize. The perfect Pythagorean harmonies could all be expressed as "superparticular" ratios of the integers from 1 to 4. That is, they could be expressed as fractions in which the numerator was one more than the denominator, thus: $2/1 =$ octave; $3/2 =$ fifth; $4/3 =$ fourth. But, said Zarlino, there is nothing special about the number four, and no reason why it should be taken as a limit.

Ah, but six! It is the perfect number because it is the first integer that is the sum of all the numbers of which it is a multiple. That is, one plus two plus three equal six, and one times two times three also equal six. So a harmony that would embody all the superparticular ratios between 1 and 6 would be a perfect harmony, and a music that employed such harmony would be a perfect music. In effect, that meant adding a major third (harmonic ratio 5:4) above the fourth and a minor third (ratio 6:5) above the major third, producing a very sonorous spacing of tones, a kind of ideal doubling of the triad in six voices (three roots, two fifths, one third), as shown in Ex. 15-1.

EX. 15-1 Gioseffo Zarlino's *senaria* (chord of six), based on C

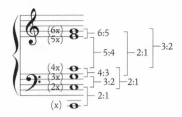

Nowadays this configuration is recognizable as the beginning of the natural harmonic series (or "overtone" series), which since the eighteenth century has been the standard method of explaining the triad and asserting its "naturalness." Zarlino, needless to say, would have jumped for joy to see this confirmation of his rational speculation in the realm of "natural philosophy." But nobody knew about overtones as yet in the sixteenth century.

What people certainly did know is that when pitches were stacked up in this way they sounded good. In rich textures of five and six voices, which were increasingly common by the late sixteenth century, this ideal spacing and doubling was widely practiced, and compositions ended more and more frequently with full triads sonorously spaced. (See the end of Sennfl's luxuriant parody of Josquin's *Ave Maria* in Ex. 14-7 for an illustration of the practice in advance of the justification for it.) Now both of these harmonically enriching practices—larger vocal complements, triadic endings—had a properly "theoretical" support. They were among the finishing touches, so to speak, that defined the *ars perfecta* as the last word in harmony.

"IL ECCELENTISSIMO ADRIANO" AND HIS CONTEMPORARIES

The other main finishing or perfecting touch that distinguished the "classic" polyphony of the mid-sixteenth century higher genres (Mass and motet) was the full rationalization and codification of dissonance-treatment, a polishing or smoothing-out process if ever there was one. Here again, Zarlino was the authoritative theorist, but in matters of

FIG. 15-3 Adrian Willaert, in a woodcut that served as frontispiece to *Musica nova* (Venice, 1540), a collection of ricercars for organ or instrumental ensemble by Willaert and several of his Italian disciples.

high gloss he confessed his particular indebtedness to his revered teacher and mentor, to whom he never referred except as *il eccelentissimo Adriano*, "the most excellent Adriano." We know him as Adrian Willaert. Thanks in part to Zarlino, Willaert looms in history as the great mid-century stylist.

Born around 1490 in West Flanders (now Belgium), either at Bruges or in a smaller town to the south, Willaert was the last in the line of Flemings and Frenchmen who dominated Italian court and chapel music since the early fifteenth century. In a way he was Josquin's creative grandchild, for his primary teacher was Jean Mouton (ca. 1459–1522), a member of the French royal chapel under Louis XII and Francis I and an important composer of motets. The poet Ronsard, writing in 1560, called Mouton Josquin's best pupil.[8] Other writers, too, called attention to their special affinity.

It is unlikely, though, that Mouton could actually have studied with Josquin. He could have known the older man only in the period of his own relative maturity—and even at that, only if Josquin really was in residence at the French court, for which there is no clear evidence. It is certain, however, that association with Josquin, the greatest luminary of the day, was as good for Mouton's reputation as it would be for anyone else's, and that Mouton consciously emulated Josquin's motets in his own. The style characteristics he educed from Josquin—paired imitation, clear declamation, a rhetorical approach to form—he passed on to Willaert in turn.

He also passed on what Glareanus, who admired Mouton the most of all the composers of the immediate post-Josquin generation, called his *facili fluentem filo cantum*: his "leisurely flow of melody,"[9] the result of a studied regularity of rhythmic motion and a sophisticated technique for evading or eliding cadences, an important development about which there will be more to say in connection with Willaert and Zarlino. Willaert was by no means its only inheritor, or (by that token) Josquin's only creative grandchild. Before looking closely at his work, we can create a context for it by briefly inspecting that of his two most important contemporaries, both slightly younger than Willaert but shorter-lived. Between them, they succeeded in developing Mouton's leisurely flow into a majestic sound-river, in which the various component voices, no longer functionally distinguished in any obvious way, constantly enter and leave, contributing their individual, elegantly shaped lines to a generous yet impervious texture that leads a seemingly inexhaustible life of its own.

GOMBERT

The "post-Josquin" style at its most seamless and luxuriant can be sampled in the work of the Fleming Nicolas Gombert (ca. 1495–ca. 1560). Gombert, too, was reputed to have been Josquin's pupil, but the information comes from a late, remote observer—a German theorist named Hermann Finck, writing in 1556—and is very likely just another use of "Josquin" as a brand name.[10] Finck probably drew an erroneous conclusion from Gombert's humanistic elegy for Josquin (*Musae Jovis*, "O Muses of Jove!") that had been commissioned in 1545 by the Antwerp publisher Tylman Susato to adorn a book of Josquin's chansons.

In fact, Gombert was a member of the élite chapel choir of Charles V, the greatest of the latter-day Holy Roman Emperors, and from 1529 the master of the choirboys. In 1540 he was dismissed from his post for sexually abusing one of the boys in his charge and spent some time thereafter in penal servitude as a galley slave on the high seas. He seems to have retired afterward to the Belgian cathedral town of Tournai as a canon of the same church of Notre Dame where the famous composite Mass Ordinary now known as the "Mass of Tournai" had been sung a couple of centuries earlier (see chapter 9). During this final period of relative calm and modest material security he was something like a freelance composer specializing in motets. More than 160 survive from his pen, of which more than half evidently date from after 1540.

One such is *In illo tempore loquente Jesu ad turbas* ("While Jesus was speaking to the crowd"), a six-voice gospel motet that was first published in Antwerp in 1556. Example 15-2 contains its opening point of imitation, and the beginning of the next. To speak of pervading imitation here would be an understatement. The texture is woven out of motives (*fantazies*) of the composer's invention, but there is no longer any correspondence (as there had been in Busnoys or Josquin) between the number of voices and the number of imitative entries. The music proceeds deliberately, in great wavelike sections. Each is woven out of countless entries large and small, and all entries begin recognizably (though not literally) alike. Zarlino's term for this kind of highly redundant approximate imitation with free continuation was *fuga sciolta*, which might be translated as "free imitation," as opposed to what he called *fuga legata* (what we would call canon).

The musical phrase associated with "in illo tempore" enters sixteen times, as shown. The next phrase, on "loquente Jesu ad turbas," will have fourteen entries in all, more

EX. 15-2   Nicolas Gombert, *In illo tempore*, mm. 1–23

EX. 15-2 (continued)

EX. 15-2 (continued)

closely spaced in time. The number of statements of a given motif and their rate of entry are Gombert's primary means of both formal articulation and rhetorical emphasis. Varying them, often quite markedly and asymmetrically, allows the composer to monitor and control the shape of the composition without resorting to stark contrasts of texture. Rhetoric remains as a shaping force, but within new limits defined by a proud emphasis on craftsmanship. Expression is sublimated into "finish."

The texture might be compared with a finely wrought tapestry: a weave of melodic strands that are given a high profile at their beginnings, receding from there into the harmonic warp and woof. What brings the river metaphor to mind, with its suggestion of placid, time-forgetful flow, are the harmonic and rhythmic dimensions. The harmonic or tonal plan is extremely stable. Its stability is achieved by a strong emphasis on what might be called the "structural pitches," so defined on the basis of their function within the built-in structure of the mode, in this case what Glareanus had dubbed "Ionian," with C as final.

Every entry of the first phrase ("in illo tempore") is either on the final or on the *tuba* or reciting tone (to recall some Frankish terminology from long ago), namely G. Entries on the final proceed by a rising fifth to the tuba, describing the modal pentachord. Entries on the tuba proceed not in literal but in reciprocal fashion, by a rising fourth to the final, describing the modal tetrachord. The second phrase (beginning "loquente") seems to vary the scheme a bit: entries are on G or its fifth, D; but the finishing or cadential notes are again in every case either G (the tuba) or C (the final).

This modal regularity is reinforced by range-deployment (*tessitura*): the old structural pair, cantus and tenor (plus the "quintus" or fifth voice, which coincides with the tenor's range) are the first to enter, moving from tuba up to final. That suggests a plagal ambitus (to recall the old chant-theorists' term), and the suggestion is confirmed by the overall range of those parts, with the initial G functioning as a lower limit and the final located in midrange. The remaining parts — the old nonessential pair of high and low contratenors, plus the "sextus," or sixth voice that doubles the range of the bass — are pretty strictly confined to the "authentic" octave. For them the final is the lower limit.

The other factor suggesting an endless stream is uniformity of texture and, above all, of rhythm. Once all six voices have entered, they remain constantly in play until the end. The nearly three-tempus rest in the bass between its last "in illo tempore" and its first "loquente" is about the longest rest in the entire motet; there are no radical contrasts in texture, whether for structural delineation or for rhetorical effect. Even more tellingly, once the six voices are in play, there is steady motion on every minim (quarter notes in transcription) until the very end.

That is to say, some voice moves on every minim pulse, so that the "resultant," were the moving parts to be summarized on a separate staff for analytical purposes, would be a steady stream of quarter notes, occasionally decorated by eighths. As the motet proceeds, moreover, the regularity of the minim pulse is progressively emphasized by the increasingly syllabic text-setting. Harmonic smoothness is assured by the pervading use of consonance on every minim, cadential suspensions alone excepted. Otherwise, once the six voices are all in play, the only dissonances are on the "weak" eighths, and are all of them fully classifiable according to our modern harmonic terminology: mainly passing notes and incomplete neighbors (*échappées*).

One can readily see the sort of stylistic perfection at which Gombert was aiming. We have little information about the way in which such music struck listeners, but we do know that it enjoyed great prestige among composers, who found Gombert's technical control impressive enough to go on vying with it for several generations. Indeed, as late as 1610, more than fifty years after Gombert's motet first saw the light of day, Claudio Monteverdi (1567–1643), who will get lots of attention later in this book but who was not yet born at the time of Gombert's death, published a parody Mass that rewove and recast *In illo tempore* on a truly heroic scale. Gombert was first and last a composer's composer.

CLEMENS

Willaert's other important contemporary was the fantastically prolific Jacobus Clemens (or Jacob Clement, ca. 1510–56), jestingly dubbed "Clemens non papa" by his Antwerp publisher, Tylman Susato, as if anyone would confuse a Dutch composer with the Roman pope. The silly nickname, however, has stuck. His sacred music falls into two very different groups. The larger portion consists of the traditional Latin Masses, of which he wrote 15, and motets, of which he wrote a staggering 233 — a proportion that gives an extreme but not inaccurate idea of the relative weight of the two genres in the output of most "post-Josquin" church composers: the opposite of what it had been pre-Josquin. It is a fair measure of their "rhetorical," which is to say humanist, orientation. In these works Clemens uses the same integrative techniques that we have observed in Gombert, if with a somewhat less determined rigor and a bit more caprice.

One of Clemens's best known motets is *Qui consolabatur me recessit a me* ("He who once consoled me has abandoned me"), first published in 1554, of which the beginning and end are given in Ex. 15-3. The text is what is known as a Biblical cento, a patchwork of Bible quotations put together for votive, possibly even nonliturgical, expressive purposes. Such centos, very common at the time, are enigmatic to us since we do not really know their purpose. They may have served for votive services in church, or they may signal the advent of a new genre, made available by music-printing, of "pious chamber music" (as Joseph Kerman has christened a somewhat later English repertory) meant for performance at home.[11]

EX. 15-3A   Jacobus Clemens, *Qui consolabatur me recessit a me*, mm. 1–24

EX. 15-3A (continued)

Many if not most motet texts in this great age of motet writing were nonstandard and nonliturgical. Even Gombert's *In illo tempore* is an example: described above as a gospel motet, it is really just a "gospel-style" motet, in which a narrative formula much used in the gospels (*In illo tempore*, literally "At the time when") is appropriated to introduce a fairly torrid paean to the Virgin Mary disguised as praise of her son: "Blessed is the womb that bore Thee, and the breasts that gave Thee suck." We might hazard a guess, therefore, that Gombert's motet was intended for use at a typical pre-Reformation "Lady Mass." But it is no more than a guess.

By the same token, the *Qui consolabatur me* patchwork was presumably designed to beautify or symbolize a mournful occasion; the textual fragments assembled in it speak of tears, bitterness, and loss. So spectacularly affect-laden are its words that the

EX. 15-3B   Jacobus Clemens, *Qui consolabatur me recessit a me*, mm. 78–end

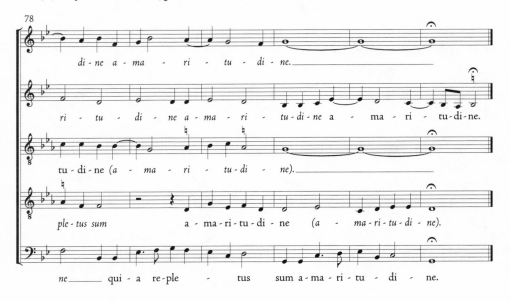

motet was once a mainstay in an elaborate hypothesis according to which the mid-century composers of Catholic Holland and Flanders often expressed a covert leaning toward Lutheranism, with its emphasis on personal religious feeling, by engineering secret chromatic modulations to color their music through the wholesale infusion of unwritten *musica ficta* accidentals.[12] That theory has been, if not disproved, at least shelved for lack of supporting evidence. But even without secret chromaticism Clemens's motet is a strikingly affective work, in which expressivity is heightened and buttressed by what we may — at least in direct contrast with Gombertian rigor — fairly term poetic license.

On the face of it, Clemens's procedures seem just as rigorous as Gombert's, even more so. There is the same redundancy of overlapping interwoven entries in the opening point of imitation. Clemens, in fact, brings each voice in exactly twice, producing a precisely calculated, symmetrical "double point," the second part in rhetorically effective stretto. But the rhythm does not settle when expected into Gombert's regular minim pulse. Indeed, that second statement in stretto is a moment of unexpectedly arrested rhythmic motion: a rhetorical pause, so to speak, that serves (as pauses do) to focus attention. On what?

On some unusual pitch relationships, to begin with. The reader may already have noticed that the piece carries an unusually flat-full key signature. That in itself is no indication of chromaticism: quite the contrary, in fact. What key signatures do is transpose diatonic modes intact. That is what they do nowadays with modern major and minor scales, and that is what they did in the sixteenth century, too, when major and minor scales, under the rubrics Ionian and Aeolian, were incipient. Looking at Clemens's first point of imitation in terms of its cadence, it is evident that the two flats in the superius, contratenor, and bassus have simply transposed the Ionian mode down a whole step — most likely to "darken" it in keeping with the prevailing affect. That first point, just like Gombert's in Ex. 15-2, establishes the regularity of the mode by alternating entries on the tuba and the final. (Where Gombert had paired his entries at the octave, Clemens pairs the first two at the descending fifth, making a direct, rhythmically regular and highly affirmative progression from full-tempus tuba to full-tempus final.)

But in the second point, the one in stretto, the entries are highly irregular. The tenor, exactly repeating its first phrase with another entry on the final, is the only voice to reiterate one of the structural pitches, as we have been calling them. The contratenor does not imitate it but actually enriches it harmonically by doubling it at the third, beginning on D, so that its intervallic structure departs from precedent. The next voice to enter is the "quinta vox" or "fifth voice," imitating not the tenor but the contratenor at the fifth below. It is forced by the curious extra flat in its signature to imitate the nonstandard intervallic configuration as well.

And that, of course, is why that extra flat is there: the normal rules of *musica ficta* would not have demanded it. It has to be explicitly signed because it is a departure from modal regularity. Thus it is a true "chromaticism," if a mild one. Finally, the outer voices both enter on E-flat, in their respective octaves. Here the normal rules of *musica ficta* do demand the A-flat that had to be specifically supplied by signature in the quinta (and, as we now notice, in the tenor as well). The A-flat is no part of the Ionian scale. It is a "Mixolydian" infusion. The mode of the motet has been "mixed" and rendered unstable.

That instability is confirmed (to put things a bit paradoxically) at the other end of the motet. The final cadence is made, unexpectedly, on G, retrospectively coloring the motet Dorian, possibly because the last word of the text—*amaritudine*, "bitterness"—called for a dark harmonization, or possibly because the composer, for all his harmonic daring, remained a bit squeamish about ending the motet somewhere other than on one of the four traditional finals. He was not squeamish, however, about ending on a full triad. By the middle of the century, as Zarlino would report, such endings were standard; indeed, the presence of the third in the final chord was routinely dramatized, as it is here, by suspensions and lower neighbors.

The other branch of Clemens's sacred output is at the opposite stylistic extreme from the loftily expressive motet just sampled. His four volumes of *Souterliedekens* ("Little psalter songs"), published in 1556–1557, contain three-voice polyphonic settings of all 150 Psalms in what was then a recent translation (or rather, a paraphrase) into Dutch verse. The translation and publication of "metrical psalms," as they are generally called, in vernacular languages became a virtual craze in the wake of the Reformation, even in countries that did not immediately participate in the rise of Protestantism. They were meant both for public worship in the form of congregational singing and for home use, and were a bonanza for publishers.

The psalm translations Clemens set (on commission from his publisher, the enterprising Susato) had first been issued in 1540 by an Antwerp printer named Simon Cock. It was the first complete set of metrical psalms to appear anywhere in Europe. To make it even more useful and marketable, Cock's book provided popular or folk tunes—love songs, ballads, drinking songs, and familiar hymns—to which each of the metrical paraphrases could be sung. One of these tunes was printed above each psalm. They were in fact the first music ever printed in the Low Countries from movable type. But the whole purpose of their inclusion was that they were widely known by heart.

This kind of appropriation from oral tradition is known in the scholarly literature as "contrafactum" (literally, a "makeover" or counterfeit). Latin terminology makes anything sound arcane, but this is one practice everybody knows. It is what we informally call "parody," and it is familiar to anyone who has attended a revival meeting, learned a school or camp song (which rarely have their own tunes), or participated in a convivial "roast." The practice obliquely acknowledges the fact that verbal literacy is far more widespread than musical literacy in most societies, including our own. The idea is to get everyone singing together as quickly as possible, without wasting any time on frills. Familiar tunes, whatever their origin, can be sung by everyone immediately, without any special instructions.

Accordingly, Clemens did not just set the texts published by Cock. Presumably on orders from Susato, he incorporated the familiar tunes as well, either in the tenor, following tradition, or in the superius where it would be all the more conspicuous. As published by Susato, then, the psalms became musically semiliterate, so to speak: still available for unison singing as contrafacta but also available in an elegant harmonization for the literate. The one selected for inclusion here (Ex. 15-4) is a setting of Psalm 71, "In Thee, O Lord, have I placed my hope" (or *In te, Domine, speravi*, as it was traditionally sung in church). Clemens's superius voice incorporates an old Dutch love song, *O Venus bant*, which begins "O shackles of Venus, O burning fire! How that lovely gracious girl has overwhelmed my heart!" Again, there was no question of incongruity between the nature of the original text and the utilitarian purpose to which its tune was being adapted. Togetherness in prayer was the objective — indeed it was the vision that motivated the whole religious reform — and anything that facilitated togetherness in prayer was meet and righteous.

EX. 15-4   Jacobus Clemens, *Souterliedekens*, Psalm 71 (*In te, Domine, speravi*)

EX. 15-4   (*continued*)

In thee, O Lord, do I put my trust:
let me never be put to confusion.
Deliver me in thy righteousness, and cause me to escape:
incline thine ear unto me, and save me.
Be thou my strong habitation, whereunto I may continually
resort . . . (Psalm 71, King James version)

Needless to say, this homely domestic psalm is not an example of *ars perfecta* but a contrast or alternative to it. It can serve here as a preliminary reminder that the *ars perfecta*, despite Zarlino's claims and the undeniable quality of the music he espoused, was never truly a universal style. And more, it shows that even as the *ars perfecta* was being perfected, there were forces at work that would compromise and eventually supplant it. The popularization of religious art in the name of reform was only one of these forces.

WILLAERT AND THE ART OF TRANSITION

And yet the perfection of the *ars perfecta* shows up all the more clearly against its rough-hewn rival. Of course the rough-hewn metrical psalm was just as deliberately rough-hewn as the perfected style was deliberately perfected. We have just seen examples of both from a single composer, who chose his styles according to his purposes. The difference shows up particularly well at the "joints"—the line ends and cadences: pronounced and emphatic in the metrical psalm, artfully smoothed over in the Latin motet. Indeed, there is no place where Ex. 15-3a, the opening of *Qui consolabatur me*, could have broken off without interrupting something in progress.

The place chosen to break it off, the spot where the setting of the line "recessit a me" ends, is a particularly vivid case in point. A cadence on B-flat is elaborately foreshadowed and contrapuntally prepared to take place between the superius and the "quinta vox" in m. 23 and thus bring the first section of the motet to a graceful conclusion. But the quinta fails to follow through with the expected B-flat, leaping instead to E-flat. The superius, as if surprised, veers off into a little melisma to mark time till the next available B-flat harmony. But the next point of imitation (its words — *quaero quod volui*, "I seek what I desire" — almost seeming to mock the poor superius) has already got ten underway, introduced right under the surprising tenor E-flat by the bass, and the superius finally trails off without full cadential support.

This sort of thing was where the true art of "perfected" composition lay. As Richard Wagner would put it many years later, the art of composition was the art of transition. Here is where Willaert was the supreme technician, and that is why, for Zarlino and all who read his treatise, Willaert was the perfector of music and the preceptor supreme.

In part, of course, Willaert owed his supremacy to the fact that in Zarlino he had what Josquin had in Glareanus, namely an ardent propagandist. Partly, too, it was a matter of favorable location and business acumen. Willaert lived and worked in Italy, at once the focal point of patronage and the center of the burgeoning music business. He was lucky enough to find an admirer in Andrea Gritti, the doge (chief magistrate) of republican Venice, who chose him, over several candidates with more seniority, for one of the most prestigious and lucrative cathedral posts a musician could aspire to — *maestro di cappella* at the splendid eleventh-century church of St. Mark's, one of Europe's architectural glories. He was installed in 1527, when he was in his middle thirties, and served until his death in 1562.

He also struck up a profitable relationship with the local music printers, Antonio Gardane and the brothers Scotto, the undisputed captains of the sixteenth-century Italian music trade. Beginning in 1539, Gardane and the Scottos brought out about two dozen volumes devoted to Willaert's works, comprising Masses, motets, and

FIG. 15-4   St. Mark's Cathedral, Venice.

several genres of secular vocal and instrumental music. The man became a one-man music industry.

And yet Willaert's preeminence did depend at least in equal part on the specific qualities of his music. His secret, the thing that made him, rather than Gombert or Clemens, the true "classic" of his time, and the arbiter supreme of established excellence, was his stylistic moderation and lack of idiosyncrasy. Moderation, and a certain impersonalism, are traits commonly correlated with classicism. Willaert possessed them, one might almost say, to an extravagant and individualizing degree.

He achieved the extraordinary balance, clarity, and refinement identified with perfection by avoiding Gombert's density and Clemens's conceits. In effect, he leapfrogged backwards over the achievements of his "post-Josquin" contemporaries and deliberately restored some basic elements of Josquin's own style, as idealized and propagated by the humanists. The result was a leaner, cleaner idiom that Zarlino could more easily codify and that could then become a true lingua franca, a medium of international commerce. Thus it was Willaert, above all, who made Josquin (or rather, "Josquin") a truly representative sixteenth-century composer.

The process can be most keenly illustrated by a motet of Willaert's that parallels a motet of Josquin's with which we are familiar. His *Benedicta es, coelorum regina*, published by Gardane in 1545 (Ex. 15-5), draws its melodic material from the same Gregorian sequence that had previously served as motet source both for Josquin (see Ex. 14-9) and

EX. 15-5A   Adrian Willaert, *Benedicta es, coelorum regina*, mm. 1–15

EX. 15-5B   Adrian Willaert, *Benedicta es, coelorum regina,* mm. 24–31

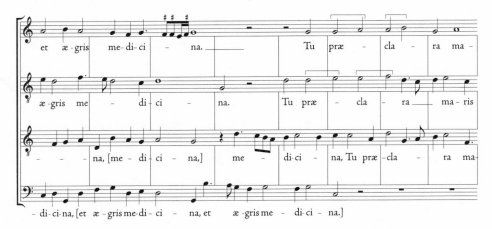

EX. 15-5C   Adrian Willaert, *Benedicta es, coelorum regina,* mm. 144–50

for Mouton, Willaert's teacher. The two settings, Josquin's and Willaert's, would thus seem related in a direct line of succession. And yet they are actually quite dissimilar. Josquin's setting observes a radical functional distinction between the cantus firmus voices and the "free" ones, each group treated separately, if equally, in imitation. In Willaert's motet the chant material is thoroughly absorbed into the imitative texture, and there are no essential functional distinctions among the voices.

But this observation, even as it puts distance between the two settings of *Benedicta es,* links Willaert's with the opening of Josquin's *Ave Maria,* the model of models. That is the work with which Willaert's *Benedicta es* (like most of his other motets) has most in common. There is the same varied pairing of voices, the same canny deployment of the texture so that tuttis are rare and climactic. That texture, in consequence, is airier and simpler than Gombert's or Clemens's, and for that reason all the closer to Josquin's.

Texting is more often on the semibreve than on the minim, and it is more nearly syllabic (hence more intelligibly declaimed) than in the work of Willaert's immediate predecessors. There are even suggestions, at times, of Josquin's rhetorical use of homorhythm for emphasis. Willaert was famed for his attention to declamation. Zarlino included a famous, nearly unprecedented set of declamation rules in his treatise that is widely presumed to reflect Willaert's explicit teaching.

Where Willaert is nevertheless recognizably a "post-Josquin" composer is in his use of harmony. The obvious giveaway is the final chord of the piece, a full triad approached plagally—even now the most typical sort of "Amen" cadence (see Ex. 15-5c). Note that Willaert's spacing of the final chord, with the intervals progressively smaller as the pitch ascends—octave, major third, minor third reading up—corresponds to the theory of the *senaria* (six-as-perfect-number) as set forth by Zarlino. Were there a fifth part, it would certainly take the D between the Gs, so that the intervals of the senaria would line up even more completely: fifth, fourth, major third, minor third. (A sixth voice, theoretically, would go an octave below the low G, but in practice it is freed by the limitations of human vocal range to double one of the existing Gs.)

There is also the more disciplined and regular handling of dissonance—more regular not only than Gombert's or Clemens's, but even more regular than Josquin's. As one example of a dissonance that might occur in any of the others but not in Willaert, see m. 21 in Gombert's *In illo tempore*, near the end of Ex. 15-2. The dissonance is in the superius: before moving to B, its C is held against the Gs in the tenor and sextus, producing a 4–3 suspension, and against the D in the quintus, producing a 7–6 suspension—but also against the B in the bassus, which produces a 9–8 suspension against what we would call the leading tone. Today's students learn to avoid that one by applying the rule that one does not sound the resolution tone (in this case B) against the suspended tone (in this case C). Zarlino's readers were the first students to be so instructed in writing, and Zarlino must have learned the rule from Willaert.

The most important way in which Willaert's style differs from Josquin's, however, is that Willaert (like Gombert and Clemens) was at all times concerned to maintain a seamless, "leisurely flow of melody," as he had learned to do from his teacher Mouton. And so he was at all times concerned with mitigating, eliding, or actually evading cadences. Even without benefit of Zarlino, Willaert's motet is already a veritable textbook on smooth cadence-avoidance.

Sometimes the avoidance is achieved by what we still call the "deceptive cadence." The first example of this comes at the very first cadence in Ex. 15-5: the end of the opening superius/altus duo (m. 8). The altus drops out instead of sounding its octave G against the one in the superius, and at the same time the bassus sounds an unexpected E a third below the final. That E, however, while unexpected harmonically, is very much expected melodically: the deceptive cadence arises right out of the bassus/tenor imitation of the opening point. Nothing could be smoother. Sometimes the avoidance is more subtle. The phrase "Et mundi" (first heard in the superius in mm. 13–14) is calculated to enter against, and draw attention away from, cadences that have been prepared in the other parts.

An especially ingenious cover-up is the one that hides the literal repeat of the opening superius/altus duo in m. 28 (Ex. 15-5b) behind continuing, harmonically diversionary action in the lower parts. Where earlier composers, including Josquin, had often inclined toward overtly modeling the shape of their chant-derived motets on that of the chant itself (in this case the "double versicles" of the sequence), Willaert, while actually honoring the melodic repeat, tries to obscure the fact. The aim seems always to be the avoidance of anything that will sectionalize the music, except where the composer expressly wishes to sectionalize it. The abstractly conceived, "purely musical" or composerly form of the polyphonic motet, in two cadentially articulated halves expressly labeled "first part" and "second part," takes precedence over the form of the liturgical model. The result is a music that is carefully and expertly controlled in every dimension, yet one without a hint of flashy tour de force. That is as good a description as any of a "classic" style.

THE PROGRESS OF A METHOD

Classicism, by definition, is teachable. We can be sure that every one of the technical observations just made about Willaert's music corresponds to the composer's conscious practical intentions because the techniques involved were abstracted and explicitly transmitted as methods by Zarlino. A fairly hilarious instance of this abstraction and transmission is a *bicinium* that Zarlino devised to demonstrate "how to avoid cadences" (*Il modo di fugir le cadenze*). Its object is to give as many examples as possible of Willaert's technique of making the voices "give the impression of leading to a perfect cadence, but turn instead in a different direction"[13] (Ex. 15-6).

EX. 15-6   Gioseffe Zarlino, *Il modo di fugir le cadenze* (*Istitutione harmoniche*, Book III)

EX. 15-6 *(continued))*

Because he was so obviously and enthusiastically a perfecter of method, and because like many methodical types he seems to have had both a flair and a taste for pedagogy, Willaert enjoyed an enormous celebrity as a teacher. No previous composer left behind so distinguished a list of pupils or so explicit a technical legacy. The pupils included two famous Flemings. One of them, Cipriano de Rore (ca. 1515–65), was appointed to succeed Willaert as St. Mark's choirmaster, no doubt owing to the lingering preference given northerners, like the lingering preference for Europeans as orchestra conductors that can still be observed in America today. In both cases, the foreign artist is presumed to be closer to the origins or the "essence" of the art he professes; and that is because the art in question is in both cases perceived as an imported luxury, a perception that contributes markedly to its prestige. (The irony, as we will see in a later chapter, was that Rore, despite his foreign birth, was a crucial participant in the Italianization of music, albeit in the secular sphere.)

Partly owing to ill health, Rore was unsuccessful in the St. Mark's post and withdrew after a couple of years. He died in 1565 and was replaced by Zarlino, a fellow pupil of Willaert but an Italian, who held it until his death in 1590. Afterward the musical leadership at St. Mark's remained in native hands, reflecting a lessened sense that high art music was an imported product. Largely thanks to Willaert, Venice was full of outstandingly learned Italian musicians: Nicola Vicentino, Girolamo Parabosco, Costanzo Porta, and above all Andrea Gabrieli, to name only his most famous Italian pupils. It was Willaert's very supremacy in Venetian music and his very success as a teacher that finally overcame the Franco-Flemish hegemony. Indeed, by the end of the century Italy would become the great training center for musicians in the literate tradition, and some of Willaert's Italian pupils would become distinguished teachers in their turn.

The other important Fleming whom Willaert trained, or at least decisively affected, was the Ghent-born Jacques (or Jachet, or Jakob) Buus (ca. 1500–65), who in the 1540s worked under Willaert as second organist at St. Mark's and published three books of music for his instrument. The fact that Buus was the first distinguished musician in the literate tradition to be chiefly concerned with instrumental music gives him considerable historical significance, and a place in this narrative a little out of proportion, perhaps, to his actual musical achievement. But he, too, played a role of some consequence in the perfecting of the *ars perfecta* and its further cleansing, so to speak, by dint of transference to a wordless medium.

That medium was the *ricercare*. The word, etymologically related to our word "research," connotes seeking and finding. That is an old metaphor for what we now think of as artistic "creation," familiar to us at least since the days of the troubadours, the "finders" of courtly love songs. Terminology based on the seeking rather than the finding end of the process may go all the way back to the Vulgate, the standard (fourth century) Latin translation of the Bible, where the term "composer" is rendered in one place (Ecclesiasticus 44:5) as *requirentes modos musicos*, "seekers of tunes."

As a musical term, the word *ricercare* goes back to the beginning of the sixteenth century and is first encountered in early printed lute tablatures. A tablature or intabulation is a form of notation, still used to indicate guitar or ukulele chords in popular sheet music, that prescribes not the sounds to be produced but the hand placements or other actions that go into producing them. The *Intabolatura de lauto* by Francesco Spinacino, published in Venice by Petrucci in 1507, contains the very first known use of the term (in a variant spelling, *recercare*) and also illustrates the use of tablature. What looks like a staff in this source is actually a stylized picture of the neck and fingerboard of the lute, each line representing a string. The numbers superimposed on the lines represent the frets behind which the player's fingers are to be placed, and the headless stems above show the rhythm.

Early lute tablatures like this one are only marginally a part of the literate tradition. What they really contain are recordings, as it were, of the kind of performances virtuoso instrumentalists gave of vocal music. Practically all the pieces in Spinacino's collection are arrangements of currently fashionable motets and chansons. The book opens, in a manner that will hardly surprise us, with an *Ave Maria* by Josquin (not the famous piece discussed in the previous chapter but a short setting of the traditional prayer), and goes on to provide intabulations of the most popular songs of the day, including both *J'ay pris amours* and *De tous biens playne*.

The only original compositions in the collection are the ricercari, and they are minimal, consisting mainly of finger-flexing scale segments and flourishes. The first one, shown here, suggests by its title, *Recercare de tous biens*, that it was intended as a prelude before playing the intabulation of the song itself. It, too, was probably a transcription of an unwritten virtuoso practice, and the whole book probably served as a primer — a book of notated examples for emulation as a part of one's training in that unwritten practice — rather than a collection of finished texts.

Some of Spinacino's ricercari have minuscule points of imitation, to show another kind of thing that virtuoso improvisers were expected to toss off. Whether these impulsive little passages underlie the development of the kind of ricercare that

Buus practiced, which was composed "strictly" (that is, in pervading imitation) throughout, is hard to say. It is worth remembering, though, that a great deal of what a church organist does to this day is also improvised — such as grinding out music by the yard to accompany liturgical actions of indeterminate or unpredictable length: communions, for example, where the length of the ceremony depends on the number of mouths to fill. That is where church organists probably played their ricercari. The first organ ricercari were published in Venice in 1523 by Marco Antonio Cavazzoni, then the organist at St. Stephen's Church in that city. They still resemble the fairly raw written-out improvisations of the lutenists. But eventually the Venetian organ ricercari began to take on a suitably dignified, recognizably ecclesiastical style.

That style, of course, was the style of the *ars perfecta* motet. And just as the first published lute ricercari appeared in Venice, the strict church motet-ricercare seems also to have been a Venetian innovation and one perhaps attributable to Willaert and his immediate circle. The earliest strictly composed ricercari appeared in Venice in 1540, in a set of four partbooks called *Musica Nova*. Eighteen of the 21 textless pieces in the collection are called ricercari. Although the title page calls them "suitable for singing or playing on organs or other instruments," and the partbook format made possible home performance by ensembles, there can be little doubt that they were primarily composed for the organ and for church, and that performance by ensembles was a secondary option offered by the publisher to stimulate sales.

All of the composers represented in the collection were church men. Pride of place, naturally, went to Willaert. One of his ricercari is printed first, but only two of the remaining twenty were his. As the *maestro di cappella*, he would have had little need to compose or perform ricercari himself. The lion's share, thirteen in all, were by a composer called "Julio da Modena" in the edition, but identifiable by comparison with other sources as the organist Julio Segni, who did indeed hail from Modena, but who from 1530 to 1533 served as Willaert's first organist at St. Mark's and probably composed his ricercari at that time. (The remaining composers represented in *Musica Nova*, Girolamo Parabosco, and Girolamo Cavazzoni, Marco Antonio's son and a future luminary of the instrument, were then teenagers receiving instruction from Willaert.)

So Buus, Willaert's second organist at St. Mark's, was following in a tradition perhaps established by Segni, Willaert's former first organist, in composing ricercari for the keyboard in the clean "perfected" style of a Willaert motet — ricercari so nicely crafted and precisely voiced that they could be published in partbooks and marketed as actual ensemble music. It was a complete about-face from all previously known keyboard practice, and its justification cannot be sought within the domain of the keyboard. There is no reason why keyboard music should ape the contrapuntal consistency of contemporary vocal music save an ideological reason: that the perfection of style achieved by the high art music of the literate tradition was held to be a universally valid achievement. The hegemony of the literate tradition had begun. Academic music had been born.

ACADEMIC ART

An academic style is one in which the process of making is considered to be of paramount value, and therefore one in which the maker's technical apparatus is at all times on display. It is a species of tour de force in that its "art" is demonstratively advertised, never concealed, but it has a different character from other tours de force that we have encountered because the primary addressee of the compositional display is not the casual beholder (or ordinary "consumer"), but rather the initiated connoisseur of craft, which in practical terms means the composer's fellow practitioners or producers. It is an art of guild secrets, of tricks of the trade, of a self-selected and exclusive professional class. It is a new, inner-directed manifestation of the aristocracy of talent. Its remuneration comes not in the form of public acclaim but in professional prestige.

The all but interminable fourth item from the 1547 collection *Ricercari di M. Jacques Buus, Organista in Santo Marco di Venetia da cantare, & sonare d'Organo & altri Stromenti . . . , Libro Primo, a quatro voci* (Ex. 15-7) has long been a famous piece because of the way it takes things to extremes. A motetlike ricercare will generally proceed like a motet through several points of imitation, each based on a new *soggetto* or "subject" (to use Zarlino's word) as if crafted to fit a new line of text. Buus's fourth ricercare proceeds similarly and at unusual length, but with every one of its points based obsessively on the same five-to seven-note motivic "head." Ex. 15-7a shows the beginning of the ricercare with the motivic heads set off by brackets. Ex. 15-7b tunes in again at the very end, some 83 measures (and a good ten or a dozen minutes) later, to find the same motive still chugging away. While applying a technique that had its origins in text-setting, Buus's ricercare has thus clearly and deliberately transcended those origins and has entered the utopian realm of abstracted technique. The aim now is not to match a *soggetto* to a phrase of text but to show everything that can be done with a given *soggetto* within the technique normally applied to texts. It is, in effect, the great motet in the sky. The irony, of course, is that a technique devised to particularize the musical potential of a specific text — that is, in the humanistic sense, to enhance its content through rhetoric — has left rhetoric behind in its pursuit of an ideal, exhaustive (which means, ultimately, a generalized) consummation. From text-realization the technique has turned toward self-realization. Depending on one's point of view, that turn can be seen as an ascent or a descent — or, perhaps, just a deviation. At any rate, the name of the genre seems eminently justified: the composer's aim has indeed been deflected from expression or communication to pure "research." It will not be the last time.

In pursuit of its own exhaustion, Buus's *soggetto* appears in myriad variants. Most entries are rhythmically unique, all have independent continuations, and a few have independent preparations (for example the bassus in m. 7 and m. 10). The whole piece has a rudimentary "macrostructure" or overall form, shaped around a section in the middle that features rhythmic augmentation of the *soggetto* and counterpoint in syncopes. Enlargement in another dimension is achieved by varying the pitch of entries far beyond what can be found in any texted piece. The vast majority of entries are made exactly where one would expect to find them in a motet: on G, the final, and at the higher fifth or tuba (D). A large number also take place at the reciprocal — that is, lower — fifth (C). Yet in the course of the piece the *soggetto* is transposed to every note of the scale, even B. At times the secondary pitches stake out little contrasting tonal regions. Thus the tonal contrast, too, announces a sectional division and contributes to the perception of an overall shape. Rhythmic and tonal contrasts, in short, function in this ricercare the way the words of the text do in a motet, as formal articulators.

EX. 15-7A   Jacques Buus, Ricercare no. 4, mm. 1–15

EX. 15-7B   Jacques Buus, Ricercare no. 4, mm. 98–110

Yet the overall impression is one not of sections succeeding sections but rather the ultimate "leisurely flow of melody" — so leisurely as to attract a great deal of censure over the years from modern writers who have found it dull. Listened to the way modern listeners are encouraged to listen to "classical" music — that is, as object of one's full attention, with no other purpose than to repay that attention — Buus's ricercare can indeed seem dull. Given its technical rigor and its uneventfulness, it is easy to write it off as music that only a composer could love; and that is actually not too bad a characterization of much academic composition.

But while academic, Buus's ricercare is not "absolute music" in the our modern sense of the term; such a thing did not yet exist, even if a certain amount of sixteenth-century music is now listened to in that way. Rather, Buus's ricercare, like virtually all the music of its time, had a definite role to play within a social occasion. Its primary purpose was to fill time otherwise empty of sound in church. Viewed as accompaniment to action — yes, as background music — the piece seems quite apt to its purpose. That purpose, in fact, explains the curious fermatas that appear about two-thirds of the way through the piece. They denote not a "hold till ready," but an alternative ending — to be used, we may assume, on days when there was a light turnout for Mass and the communion ritual could be correspondingly curtailed.

SPATIALIZED FORM

Julio Segni has been identified as someone who held the position of "first organist" under Willaert and Buus as one who, somewhat later, served under him as "second organist." The terms were not solely indications of rank. Since the late fifteenth century, St. Mark's Cathedral actually had two organ lofts, each with its designated player. It was inevitable that antiphonal music-making would be cultivated there, with the cathedral cappella split into two groups, one standing in a hexagonal enclosure called the *pergolo* (when it wasn't occupied by the Doge and his retinue), the other across the nave in the Gospel pulpit.

It was also inevitable that such performances took place primarily at Vespers, because that is where the singing of full psalms was prevalent. Psalms were antiphonal by biblical tradition, after all, and were even characteristically structured (in "hemistichs") according to that implied performance style. Willaert was not the first *maestro di cappella* to set Vespers psalms for "split choirs" (*cori spezzati*); he had an important predecessor, for one, in Francesco Santacroce, the choirmaster at the nearby city of Treviso. But, typically, it was Willaert who "classicalized" the practice and gave it an orderly procedure. In his settings, the two four-part choirs alternate verse by verse, then come together in eight parts for the concluding doxology, turning a formulaic termination into an impressive musical climax. Published by Gardane

FIG. 15-5 St. Mark's Cathedral, interior view showing the *pergola* (hexagonal enclosure) and the Gospel pulpit, where two choirs sang antiphonal psalms.

in 1550 and reprinted in 1557, Willaert's Vespers Psalms were exemplary not only from the sonorous and formal point of view but also from the standpoint of declamation, increasingly an "issue" for sixteenth-century church musicians, as we shall see. Here, too, "il eccelentissimo Adriano" established a standard of perfection.

ALTERNATIVES TO PERFECTION

But let us conclude this chapter with some reminders that perfection, as a standard, is a matter of attitude and values. The ideals implicit in the *ars perfecta* were not universally shared at any time or in any place, as we have only to glance across the English Channel to discover. When last we looked, English church music had already diverged significantly in style from the continental variety, and the stylistic differences, it was already evident, indicated a difference in attitude. But if Josquin's style and Cornysh's already made for a striking contrast, just compare two excerpts from the Sanctus of a Mass by John Taverner (1490–1545), Willaert's exact contemporary (Ex. 15-8).

The luxuriant melismatic cantus-firmus polyphony that characterized the Eton Choirbook antiphons has continued its jungle growth. Neither textual declamation nor structural imitation play anything like the role they had long since come to play in the humanistically influenced church music of continental Europe from the Low Countries to Italy. None of the music examined up to now in this chapter sported anything

EX. 15-8A   John Taverner, *Missa Gloria Tibi Trinitas*, Benedictus, mm. 7–21

EX. 15-8A (continued)

so old-fashioned as a traditional plain-chant cantus firmus in long notes. Taverner occasionally unifies the texture with repetitions among the voices, but such imitations are still close to their conceptual origins in such "medieval" devices as voice-exchange and hocket (see in particular the higher moving parts at "Domini" in Ex. 15-8a).

The impression is of a music — and a religious attitude — supremely untouched by "Renaissance" humanism. Such music is still a loftily decorative art rather than one expressive of its occasion. And it is still one that insists upon the difference — or rather the distance — between the human and the divine.

That was explicitly the reaction of a Venetian diplomat who was privileged to attend High Mass at one of Henry VIII's royal chapels, sung by choristers "whose voices," he marveled, "were more divine than human." His other comment is best left in his own Italian words: *Non contavano ma giubilavano,* "they did not so much sing as jubilate," the last being a word that has carried a charge of religious emotion for us since the days of St. Augustine, who described jubilus-singing as "a mind pouring itself forth in a joy beyond words."

At the most basic level, it came down to a difference in how music and words were supposed to connect. Where continental musicians strove to make their music reflect both the shape and the meaning of the texts to which it was set, and none more successfully than Willaert, the insular musician remained true to an older attitude, according to which the music contributed something essentially other than what human language could encompass. The English melismas continued to hide the text, so to speak, from aural view, and thus preempt it. Next to the work of Taverner, the *ars perfecta* is revealed as a fundamentally rationalized art, an art whose tone had been lowered in the name of reason, brought down to earth.

The English still sought the opposite. Their music, aspiring to raise the listener's mind up above the terrestrial, provided a sensory overload: higher treble parts than anywhere else, lower bass parts, richer harmonies — including that special English tingle, the suspended sixth (given a spotlight at the very end of Taverner's Sanctus; see Ex. 15-8b). Motivic imitation — an orderly, rational procedure if ever there was one — is only a sporadic decoration here, never a structural frame.

EX. 15-8B   John Taverner, *Missa Gloria Tibi Trinitas*, Benedictus, mm. 26 – end

The heaviest overload of all came in the guise of length, a heavenly expanse in which the listener is lost by design. An early Tudor setting like Taverner's of the Mass Ordinary — a text that can be recited in a couple of minutes — will typically last about three-quarters of an hour, and that is minus the Kyrie, which in Tudor England was always full of tropes, left in plainchant, and considered a part of the Proper. A Tudor polyphonic Mass setting begins with the Gloria. And even so, it is half again as long as a full five-section continental Ordinary from the sixteenth century, which will usually clock in at under thirty minutes if sung straight through at a comparable tempo.

It is often said (and even echoed, somewhat ironically, here) that the English music of the early sixteenth century represented a survival of medieval attitudes that had, owing to the so-called Renaissance, become outmoded on the continent. Dueling Zeitgeists again: they simplify the story but do not clarify it. For the "Renaissance"

Zeitgeist is represented in this dichotomy in a very selective and tendentious guise. As students of humanism have long agreed, humanism as a mode of thought is by no means to be equated, in its totality, with rationalism or "modern" empirical attitudes. It retained a great deal of magical thinking about nature and about human nature, and about the influence of the cosmos on the human constitution, all of it fully sanctioned by a different strain of classical thought from the one on which the *ars perfecta* theorists relied. The god of the perfectionists was orderly Aristotle, the great observer and classifier and logician. The god of magical thinkers was Plato, who believed in a realer reality than that which either our senses *or* our empirical logic can grasp.

The transrational and transsensible powers of music that the ancients described — its *ethos*, to use their word for it — lay altogether outside the Aristotelian ken of those highly professionalized musicians of the *ars perfecta* like Zarlino or Willaert. But they attracted the keen attention of neo-Platonist humanists (mainly literary men), many of whom practiced astrology and tried to harness the occult power of music to aid them in calling upon cosmic forces. Chief among them was the Florentine physician, classical scholar, and musical amateur Marsilio Ficino, the founder of the Platonic Academy of Florence, a bastion of humanism and an emblem of "The Renaissance" if ever there was one. He thought that music was the best avenue available to humans for "capturing celestial benefits," and even tried to codify the practice of "channelling astral influxes" in a treatise called *De vita libri tres* ("Three books on life"). Needless to say, Ficino's treatise has little in common with Zarlino's. It prescribes no actual method of composition, but instead gives three rules by which to judge the products of composition, drawing on the magical powers of correspondence or analogy — that is, of shared attributes. A three-sided relationship is set up between the active force, the stars, and the passive receiver, the human organism, with the song, which imitates the attributes of the stars in a form assimilable by the human organism, as the effective mediator of the influx. As translated by Gary Tomlinson, the leading modern investigator of the occult branches of musical humanism, Ficino's rules are these:

(1) To examine what powers in itself and effects from itself a given star, constellation, or aspect has, what these remove and what they provide; and to insert these into the meanings of our words so as to detest what they remove and approve what they provide.

(2) To consider what star chiefly rules what place or person, and then to observe what sorts of tones and songs these regions and persons generally use, so that you may supply similar ones, together with the meanings just mentioned, to the words which you are trying to expose to the same stars.

(3) To observe the daily positions and aspects of the stars and investigate to what speeches, songs, motions, dances, moral behavior, and actions most people are principally incited under these, so that you may imitate such things as far as possible in your songs, which aim to agree with similar parts of the heavens and to catch a similar influx from them.[14]

Thus, to channel the benefits of Venus, one makes a song that is "voluptuous with wantonness and softness"; to channel the sun's influence one makes a song that has "grace and smoothness" and is "reverential, simple, and earnest"; and so on. Not technical perfection but uncanny efficacy is the goal. What did these songs sound like? Who sang them? Did they work? Wouldn't we like to know! But Ficino never wrote down any of his astrological songs, and (as Tomlinson has emphasized) they are irrevocably lost behind the oral curtain to those, like us, who depend on our literacy (and on empirical reasoning rather than analogy) for knowledge.

Not only Ficino's explicitly astrological songs, but a great deal of more ordinary music-making, too, was credited with irrational magical force during what we now call the Renaissance. There is a famous memoir by a French diplomat, published in 1555, of the playing of the Italian lutenist Francesco da Milano (1497–1543), that resonates with what Ficino called *raptus* or trance, what modern anthropologists call "soul loss," and what the more recent language of spiritualism calls "out-of-body experience." Francesco had been hired to entertain the company at a noble banquet:

> The tables being cleared, he chose one, and as if tuning his strings, sat on the end of the table seeking out a fantasia. He had barely disturbed the air with three strummed chords when he interrupted the conversation that had started among the guests. Having constrained them to face him, he continued with such ravishing skill that little by little, making the strings languish under his fingers in his sublime way, he transported all those who were listening into so pleasurable a melancholy that — one leaning his head on his hand supported by his elbow, and another sprawling with his limbs in careless deportment, with gaping mouth and more than half-closed eyes, glued (one would judge) to the strings of the lute, and his chin fallen on his breast, concealing his countenance with the saddest taciturnity ever seen — they remained deprived of all senses save that of hearing, as if the spirit, having abandoned all the seats of the senses, had retired to the ears in order to enjoy the more at its ease so ravishing a harmony; and I believe that we would be there still, had he not himself — I know not how — changing his style of playing with a gentle force, returned the spirit and the senses to the place from which he had stolen them, not without leaving as much astonishment in each of us as if we had been elevated by an ecstatic transport of some divine frenzy.[15]

The last phrase in this description of musical shamanism or sorcery, about "ecstatic transport" and "divine frenzy," is rife with neo-Platonist buzzwords. At the other end of the passage we get a valuable clue to the music through which the sorcerer wielded his magic. To "seek out" (*chercher* in French, *cercar* in Italian) is the root word behind *ricercare*, and a *fantasia*, as we already know, is an early way of describing "made up" (as opposed to quoted) music. We get a glimpse of a ricercare-in-action, the kind of thing that only occasionally got written down, and the kind of effects it could produce, not on the permanent page but in ephemeral performance. The passage celebrates the power of the artist-improviser, the diametrical opposite from the artist-creator of the literate *ars perfecta* ideal. It celebrates the power of music in performance, something lost when music becomes text, and therefore lost to the historian's direct experience.

Lest we think for that reason that the account must be wholly fictional, and lest we therefore despise it, we might reflect on other manifestations of musical soul-loss as experienced by the audiences of charismatic performers throughout history and into our own time. Later we will read about the uncanny mesmeric effects achieved by

Romantic virtuosi like Paganini on the violin and Liszt on the piano. Those effects, in the twentieth century, have largely been ceded to what are now known as popular entertainers: Frank Sinatra, Elvis Presley, the Beatles, Michael Jackson. These are the names of Francesco da Milano's most recent heirs.

Like him, and like Paganini and Liszt when performing, they work primarily in an oral medium. While there is certainly some contact between their art and preserved musical texts of various kinds, it is a secondary contact of a sort already available to Francesco da Milano. But it did not constitute his art, the way the music text of a Willaert or a Buus constituted the *ars perfecta* in Francesco's time, or a symphony by Beethoven in Paganini's time, or a string quartet by Arnold Schoenberg in Frank Sinatra's time.

The *ars perfecta*, the Beethoven symphony and the Schoenberg quartet, being primarily textual, are more adequately recorded in history than the performances of Ficino, Francesco, Paganini, or Sinatra. The historical record is partial (in more than one sense). It leaves out a lot — not necessarily because it wants to but because it has to. The danger is that we will forget that anything has been forgotten, or value only what is not left out, or think that that is all there ever was. As the fox who couldn't reach the grapes reminds us, there is a tendency to despise what one can no longer have. What we no longer have (until the twentieth century) are recoverable performances. It is a bad mistake to think that texts can fully compensate their loss, or that they tell the whole story, or that the story that texts tell is the only story worth telling.

PEEKING BEHIND THE CURTAIN

In its penetration (through publications like *Musica Nova* or Buus's ricercari) of the instrumental domain, long the bastion of the unwritten and the spontaneous, the *ars perfecta* can seem to embody a crowning triumph for literacy. All that was captured, though, was the elite protruding tip of a huge iceberg. The vast majority of instrumentalists continued as before to perform by a combination of ear, hand, and memory. Even church organists more often improvised their accompaniments to liturgical action than read them off their music rack. (And they still do; organists are perhaps the only literate musicians who still receive training in the art of improvisation.) Even those who did read their music (or rather, Buus's or Willaert's music) off the rack did not read it literally, the way we might imagine them doing on the basis of our own education and experience. Again a reminder is due that literacy has never totally eclipsed orality, even in those repertoires and fields of practice where it can seem most firmly ensconced. And there is no reason to expect that it ever will.

Which is by no means to disparage the degree of ready literacy that existed among sixteenth-century church musicians. Choral sight-singing, practiced since Guido's time, will hardly amaze us nowadays. We can do that. But the idea of an organist putting four separate partbooks on his music rack to play a ricercare at sight is somewhat stunning. Yet any sixteenth-century organist could do it, even a mediocre one. For anyone aspiring to a professional post it was considered a requisite, not an exceptional, skill.

Nevertheless, we should not suppose that what came out of the organ under those circumstances were the notes in the partbooks and nothing but the notes. No performer treated musical texts in those days with the scrupulous reverence our contemporary practice sanctions and enforces; and this, too, is evidence that despite the burgeoning availability of music books and the academization of certain composerly techniques in the sixteenth century, oral performance practices remained alive and well.

We have very specific evidence of what we would call freedom even in the performance of Buus's ricercari. Less skilled organists, or lazy ones, liked to copy the music they played into keyboard tablatures rather than go through the brainy effort of mentally "scoring" a set of partbooks. Music publishers catered to this set with publications containing transcriptions of favorite organ pieces into the kind of notation that simply tells you at a glance, like a modern keyboard score, where all your fingers have to go. One of Buus's ricercari was published both ways (Ex. 15-9, Fig. 15-6).

EX. 15-9A   Jacques Buus, Ricercare no. 1 from *Il secondo libro di recercari* (Venice: Gardane, 1549), opening point, scored from partbooks

EX. 15-9B   Jacques Buus, Ricercare no. 1, opening point, as it appears in *Intabolatura d'organo di recercari* (Venice: Gardane, 1549)

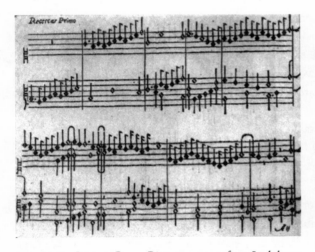

FIG. 15-6   Jacques Buus, Ricercare no. 1 *from Intabolatura d'organo di recercari, Libro primo* (Venice: Gardane, 1549).

The differences between the two versions are the differences between, on the one hand, an idealized conception or premise in writing from which all performances will derive (the piece set down for all time), and on the other, an actual performance — that is, a once-only "oralized" and ephemeral realization (the piece as we are hearing it right now). Our age tends to minimize the distinction and try to realize all pieces in performance just the way they have been set down, thinking in this way to capture their timeless essence. Such a performance is often called an "authentic" one. A better term for it might be a "literalistic" one, were that term not burdened with a negative connotation in ordinary usage; for what such a performance really represents is a fully "literacized," text-dominated concept of music.

That was certainly not the sixteenth-century way, and we have to keep it constantly in mind that the music we know from its written traces — the music we know by sight, so to speak — was not the music that anybody in the sixteenth century actually heard. That great submerged iceberg of sound is gone forever from today's ear, hand and memory. All we have to go on if we wish to hear it again are a few didactic guides, some scattered practical examples like the one in Ex. 15-9b, and our imaginations.

The didactic guides, especially, give a tantalizing glimpse of a lost world of music-making. The two earliest authors of printed method books for instrumentalists were Sylvestrodi Ganassi dal Fontego (1492-ca. 1550), who actually worked alongside Willaert in St. Mark's, and Diego Ortiz (ca. 1510–ca. 1570), a Spaniard who worked at the court of Naples. Ganassi published two books. The first, a method for wind players called *Fontegara* (Venice, 1535), deals mainly with the vertical whistle-flute or recorder. The second, a double volume for string players called *Regola rubertina* (Venice, 1542–43), mainly deals with the "leg-viol" or viola da gamba. (Its title, "Ruberto's rules," is a tribute to Ruberto Strozzi, a member of a celebrated Italian family of noble musical amateurs.)

After some rudimentary instruction on playing technique, both manuals shift over to the more creative aspects of instrumental performance, which grew directly out of the kind of music-making Tinctoris had described a hundred years earlier, when he wrote about the two blind brothers who converted famous songs into dazzling instrumental displays (see chapter 13, Ex. 13-15). In the sixteenth century, the virtuoso instrumentalist's repertoire was still largely parasitic on vocal music. The art of instrumental virtuosity was the art of *passaggii* or passage work, in which the plain "classical" lines of sacred or secular songs in the *ars perfecta* style were converted into flamboyantly ornamental sonic cascades and necklaces. One learned the technique by systematically breaking down a song into its component intervallic progressions — up a third, down a fourth, and so on — and memorizing dozens of note patterns to decorate each interval, which one could later apply in actual performance to any song, and on the basis of which one could eventually evolve one's own personal style of playing "diminutions" (or "divisions"), as this process of substituting many short notes for each long one was called.

The *Regola rubertina* also contains a number of "preludizing" pieces called "recercars" like Spinacino's (or Francesco's) for the lute. Such pieces were evidently better suited to string technique, whether plucked or bowed, then wind. Ortiz's *Trattado de glosas* or "Treatise on embellishments" (Rome, 1553), which like Ganassi's *Regola rubertina* is addressed to viol players, also contains "recercadas" galore, in addition to even more systematic instruction in diminution. Ortiz's methods are more sophisticated and detailed, and give us an even more embarrassing sense of how little we know of old music when all we know is what was written down — and, even more important, what is lost from music as well as what is gained in the process of its becoming literate.

The first half of Ortiz's text is devoted to diminution technique in the abstract. The second half consists of model recercadas for every occasion, showing how diminution technique, once internalized, was applied in practice. First come the "free" improvisations — actually strings of little cadence formulas subjected to transposition, sequential treatment and diminution. Then there are recercadas based on individual voice parts extracted from polyphonic classics. This is just a more thoroughgoing application of the embellishment practices shown in Ex. 15-9b.

Then come the really creative exercises, the ones that really give a glimpse of a vanished musical culture. They begin with recercadas in the cantus firmus style (or as Ortiz has it in his native language, recercadas over a *canto llano*, a "plainsong"). Here the player had to be able at one and the same time to imagine a discant against a familiar tenor and to embellish it with diminutions. What is particularly interesting and instructive about Ortiz's examples is the source of his cantus firmus. Although he says that the technique he is imparting may be applied to any church chant (and might well have provided music to accompany the same moments in the service as Segni's or Buus's organ ricercari), the actual tenor Ortiz selected on which to compose his illustrative examples was one that had been used for over a century by dance bands.

DANCES OLD AND NEW

We have seen written traces of instrumental dance music going back to the thirteenth century (Fig. 4-8). But of course dance music, being an eminently functional genre, was one of the slowest to "go literate" in any major or transforming way; and when it did, it did so piecemeal. The earliest extensive manuscript collections of instrumental dances come from the fifteenth century and were devoted to the noblest and courtliest ballroom dance genre or the time, a processional dance for couples known in Italian as *bassadanza* and in French as *basse danse*. The English equivalent would be "low dance," the adjective referring to the dignified gliding steps — low and close to the floor — that the noble ballroom dancers employed. The lower the steps, one might say, the higher the social rank of the dance. Peasant dances — oftentimes mimicked by the nobility for their fun and games — were the ones for leaping and prancing.

The appearance of the music in the early *bassadanza* collections was strange, and for a long time it succeeded in misleading historians. It consisted of long strings of unaccompanied square notes that looked for all the world like Gregorian chant, arranged over weird strings of letters (Fig. 15-7). Comparison with a few scattered polyphonic *bassadanza* settings finally cracked the code: what the collection contained were bass lines (or rather, in contemporary parlance, tenors) over which musicians trained in the specialized art of dance accompaniment improvised discant by ear. (The letters under the notes in some sources represented the dance steps.)

Although an unwritten practice, this sort of ensemble improvisation by reed and brass instruments was a high art indeed. The standard ensemble, as depicted in Fig. 15-8, was a trio consisting of a pair of shawms (early oboes) and a slide trumpet or trombone. This little band was called the *alta capella*, a term that (confusingly enough)

FIG. 15-7   *Il re d'Espagna*, from Michel de Toulouze, *L'art et instruction de bien dancer* (Paris, 1496); here it is titled "Casule la novele" ("New Castile").

means "high ensemble," even though it was used exclusively for accompanying "low" dancing. (As usual, there is less paradox here than meets the eye: when applied to instruments, the terms "high" and "low" — *alta/bassa* in Italian, *haut/basse* in French — distinguished loud from soft; the alta capella was thus a "loud" ensemble.) "Alta" musicians formed something of a guild and treasured their techniques as guild secrets; no wonder there is no written source of instruction in their craft. It was passed along for generations by "word of mouth" — by example and emulation. As far as we are concerned, it is irrecoverably submerged in that unheard and unhearable "iceberg." We don't have any theoretical guide to it; all we have are a few written specimens (or imitations) of the practice, few of them actual dances.

If not dances, then what? Carmina, bicinia, lute intabulations — even Masses! From these chance survivors we know that the most popular *bassadanza* tenor of all (the one shown in Fig. 15-7) was traditionally called *Il re d'Espagna* ("The King of Spain") or simply *La Spagna*. That may even be why Ortiz, a Spaniard working abroad, selected it for his specimen improvisations. But long before Ortiz, Henricus Isaac had taken it into his head to flatter and amuse his *bassadanza*-loving patron, the magnificent Lorenzo de' Medici of Florence, with a Mass built over the Spagna tenor as cantus firmus.

For the most part Isaac hid the dance tune behind a thicket of paraphrase and polyphony. But all at once the second Agnus Dei gives away the game. Convention decreed that this middle section of the last part of the Mass Ordinary be cast as a "tenor

FIG. 15-8   Loyset Liedet, *Ball at the Court of King Yon of Gascony* (Paris, Bibliothèque de l'Arsenal, Manuscripts Français 5073, fol. 117v).

tacet" setting, in three voices, and so it is. But very whimsically and unconventionally, Isaac transferred the tenor tune to the bassus voice, where it is laid out in a series of even breves just as it would be in a *bassadanza* collection. And it is accompanied by the superius and the altus in a polyphony so rough and ready—glorified antiphony, hocket-like exchanges, sequences that track the tenor down the scale—that it simply has to be a sly send-up of an actual alta capella, caught in the act of improvising, perhaps even drawn "from life" (Ex. 15-10).

Ortiz provides six different recercadas over the Spagna tenor, the idea being that after having mastered them the pupil can then go on to make up his own. Ex. 15-11 shows the beginnings of all six. This is another way in which the written can suggest to us the unwritten, although Ortiz was not training anyone in the art of dance accompaniment. Like virtuosos both before and after him, in a tradition that continues to this day, he appropriated a sublimated dance style—dance music, not for active dance use but for receptive listening—as his vehicle for a display of dexterity.

EX. 15-10   Henricus Isaac, *Missa super La Spagna*, Agnus II

EX. 15-10   (*continued*)

EX. 15-10   (*continued*)

EX. 15-11   Diego Ortiz, *Tratado de glosas* (1553), six recercadas on *La Spagna*

The same principle operates in the final portion of Ortiz's book, which gives another sort of peek into the world of the unwritten, and a truly momentous one. "The better to complete this work," he writes, "I thought I'd include the following recercadas on these bass lines (*cantos llanos*) that are usually called tenors in Italy, but that are mainly played as written here, in four parts, with the recercada over them."[16] What follows is a series of recercadas in which the model solo improvisation is accompanied not by a single cantus firmus line playing itself out in abstract long notes from beginning to end, but rather by short, very rhythmic ostinato chord progressions: harmonic templates or frameworks that are repeated as often as necessary to fill out the time required for the improvisation (as in "real life" they were repeated as often as necessary to fill out the time required for dancing).

Ortiz's instruction method for viol players is the earliest written source to contain these "tenors," for which the standard historian's term is *ground bass* (or simply *ground*).

Five grounds, all quite similar in their harmonic structures, were in especially widespread use; they are given, together with their traditional names, in Ex. 15-12. The duple-metered pair called *passamezzo* — old (*antico*) and new (*moderno*) — were the ones most closely associated in Ortiz's time with actual ballroom dancing: the *passamezzo* (from *passo e mezzo*, "a step and a half") was the somewhat livelier couples dance that replaced the *bassadanza* at sixteenth-century Italian courts. "Composed" passamezzos first appeared in lute tablatures in the 1530s. But the Spanish violist's frozen improvisations were the first written compositions to suggest the traditional use of these repetitive cadential formulas, which were employed in Italy not only to accompany dancing but also to guide the extemporaneous singing of popular poetry since at least the beginning of the fifteenth century (as we may learn from any literary account of court life, such as Castiglione's *Book of the Courtier*).

EX. 15-12   Traditional ground-bass tenors

a. *Passamezzo antico*

EX. 15-12B   *Romanesca*

EX. 15-12C   *Folia*

EX. 15-12D   *Passamezzo moderno*

EX. 15-12E   *Ruggiero*

Until Ortiz published his handbook in 1553, all of this activity had gone on behind the curtain of the unwritten. Ortiz brought it comprehensively into the visible world of notation for the first time, whence it proliferated hugely in ways that would in time utterly transform literate practice. We have only to observe that the Italian word for poetry sung over a ground bass like the Romanesca (Ex. 15-12b) or the Ruggiero

(Ex. 15-12e) was *aria*, or that the harmonic scheme itself was then called an *aria per cantare* (literally a "space for singing"), to realize the extent of that transformation, since from the seventeenth century onward the aria has been one of the ubiquitous genres of "art" music in the West. Needless to say we will return to it.

But the creation of new genres is only a part, and not even the most important part, of the revolution in Western music-making wrought by the use of grounds. For grounds are the first indisputably harmony-driven force in the history of Western music-making. They are the first musical frameworks, in other words, to be defined *a priori* in harmonic and cadential terms, hence the first musical structures to which the modern term "tonal" can be fairly applied. Their tonality in the mid-sixteenth century was not yet precisely congruent with modern major-minor tonality. The *passamezzo moderno* progression employed by Ortiz in his *Recercada segunda* (Ex. 15-13) is still unmistakably "Mixolydian" in its use of a triad built up over F, a note that is not even part of the modern G-major scale. And yet it makes its cadence through a modern G-major dominant chord (even preceded by the subdominant), for which purpose a leading tone (F♯) had to be imported from outside the "pure" modal scale. Ex. 15-13 shows the first two of six run-throughs of the ground.

EX. 15-13   Diego Ortiz, *Recercada segunda* (on the *passamezzo moderno*)

That F♯, by the way, is no longer to be explained by the old rules of *musica ficta*, which were based on rules of discant voice leading. There are no longer any "voices" to speak of in that sense; harmonies are now functioning as independent perceptual units produced by strumming strings or striking keys, quite unconfined by counterpoint. It seems virtually certain that harmonic progressions as such were developed on—indeed, right "out of"—strumming and striking instruments for which no notation existed at the time. A leading tone strummed or struck within a chord belongs to no particular voice. It is a harmonic free agent, a necessary component in a closing formula that by recurring regularly articulates a structurally significant span of time.

But what makes the cadence recognizable as a closing formula, hence grammatically effective, is not just its regular recurrence but the way it "telegraphs" its ending—that is, the way it signals its ending in advance. It does this not only by the use of the leading tone but also by means of an increased rate of chord change—what modern theorists call an accelerated "harmonic rhythm." Harmonic rhythm as a structural articulator is an eminently "tonal" concept, not a modal one. We seem poised right on the cusp, as it were, between the older modal system, with a different scale species on each final, and the modern tonal (or "key") system, with only two scales, each of which can be transposed to any pitch (the transposition itself defining the pitch as a final or "tonic").

Yet it should not be thought that the "tonal revolution" was a sudden thing, just because it has swung so suddenly into our historical purview. That is an illusion created by our source material, which is of necessity confined to the literate sphere. What is suddenly made literate and visible can be cooking behind the curtain for centuries, and in this case certainly was. For all that time, literate music-making had been proceeding on a discant basis and a modal one, while much unwritten music had surely been operating on a strophically cadential basis and a tonal one. The watershed that now looks to us like a "tonal revolution" was in fact the meeting place of two long coexisting traditions.

The meeting could only take place because the traditions were now both at least partly literate ones. It was because his "Treatise on Embellishments" was the first overt act of "tonal insurgency" that Ortiz (otherwise hardly known as a composer) looms so large in the present discussion. It was a giant step in the direction that now seems favored by history. It was a step, however, that neither the author nor any of his contemporaries could have known he was taking. That, of course, is not because he or they were in any way obtuse. Nor is it because we see things more clearly than they could. It is merely because the "step" can only be perceived as such in hindsight. The step as such is something created by our perspective.

The End of Perfection

PALESTRINA, BYRD, AND THE FINAL FLOWERING OF IMITATIVE POLYPHONY

UTOPIA

B efore turning our attention to the many other ingredients in the seething cauldron that was sixteenth-century music, it will make sense to pursue the *ars perfecta* to the end. For indeed, the perfected art had an end, and it was near at hand. It had to be, for anything perfect, in this world, is doomed. Perfection cannot change, yet nothing in human history stands still. The only way to preserve the perfected art was to seal it off from history. This was done, but the price was high. The *ars perfecta*, as we shall see, still exists, but not in a way that matters anymore. In the sixteenth century it claimed all the greatest musical minds in Catholic Christendom. Later, it harbored nonentities, and the church that maintained its artificial life-support system gradually lost its significance as a creative site for music. The sixteenth century was the last in which the music of the Catholic church made history. From then on it was history.

The *ars perfecta* came about because musicians had something timeless, universal, and consummate to express: God's perfection as embodied and represented by God's own true church, the institution that employed them. Although nowhere stated by Zarlino, still less by Willaert (who wrote a quantity of secular music in genres we will soon be taking up), the values of musical perfection, however mediated by humanism, implied and reflected belief, as the Credo of the Mass puts it, *in unam sanctam catholicam et apostolicam ecclesiam*: "one holy universal church, sent by God." The standards to which musicians serving such an institution aspired transcended the relativity of taste, just as the doctrines of religion are held by believers to represent an absolute truth, mandating in turn an absolute standard of behavior — one that does not aim to gratify the individual and that cannot be altered to suit the wishes or purposes of individuals, or the changing values and fashions of secular society.

Therein lay both the beauty and the despair of the *ars perfecta*. It was the music of Utopia — a term coined by Thomas More, not at all incidentally, during the sixteenth century. The world was its enemy. Perfection had to be enforced in order to exist at all. And yet music, a human product, did inevitably change. Many deplored the changes; the word used to sum them up — "Baroque" — though now regarded as a neutral identifying tag like "Renaissance," was originally a term of opprobrium, used by jewelers to describe a misshapen pearl or by critics to describe a bombastic utterance. It meant "distorted."

That is what music surely became from the perspective of the *ars perfecta*, as would anything that deviated from a standard of perfection. By the second half of the sixteenth century the forces of "distortion" were rife, and some of them had arisen within the church itself. Others were the result of literary movements. Still others were the outcome of a radical turn within musical humanism, which had always been an uneasy ally of religious transcendentalism. There were also pressures brought by the burgeoning music trade, pressures that reflected the overall rise of mercantilism and that militated further against the prestige of religious art. As we shall see, moreover, in every one of these responses that led away from perfection and toward the "Baroque," it was Italy that took the lead. What is usually called the "Baroque" period might more truly be called the period of Italian dominance in music.

By century's end the *ars perfecta* was only one style among many—no longer privileged, no longer where the action was. In a way its fate mirrored the larger fate of the Roman Catholic Church, which was left at the end of the sixteenth century a transformed institution—no longer truly "catholic," but much more truly "Roman." It was no longer truly "catholic" because it was no longer the undisputedly universal Western church; now it had to compete for adherents with a whole variety of Reformed churches that had sprung up to the north for a variety of reasons, doctrinal (Germany, Switzerland) and political (England). It was more truly Roman because its power, having become more localized, was more and more strongly concentrated among the Italian bishops and cardinals. The last non-Italian pope before the election of John Paul II in 1978 was Adrian VI, a Netherlander who was elected in 1522 and reigned, rather ineffectually, for only twenty months. For more than 450 years, from Clement VII to John Paul I, the nationality of the Roman pope was a more or less foregone conclusion. The same sixteenth-century transfer from Netherlandish to Italian leadership took place in Roman Catholic music.

The two composers to be chiefly treated in this chapter—Giovanni Pierluigi da Palestrina (ca. 1525–94) and William Byrd (1543–1623)—were the outstanding members of the last generation of musicians who kept the *ars perfecta* faith unquestioningly. Theirs was the last generation of musicians who unanimously saw the highest calling of their art in divine service, and whose primary social relation as artists was to institutions of the Catholic religion. They brought the *ars perfecta* to its greatest stylistic heights even in the period of its cultural decline. Their actual relationship to religious authority differed diametrically. Palestrina was the quasi-official musical spokesman of Catholic power, Byrd its clandestine servant in adversity. The difference is reflected in their music, to be sure, and with intensity; but that difference found expression within a fundamental stylistic agreement, which after all is what the *ars perfecta* was all about.

PALESTRINA AND THE ECUMENICAL TRADITION

The first native Italian to be a major creative player in this narrative (as opposed to theorists like Aaron or Zarlino), Giovanni Pierluigi da Palestrina—the name means "Giovanni Pierluigi, from Palestrina"—was born either in Rome or in the nearby ancient town whose name he bore, called Praeneste by the Romans. He died in Rome, by tradition in his 69th year, on 2 February 1594. By then he had been either directly in the papal service or at the musical helm of one of the major Roman churches for more than forty years, beginning in 1550 with the election of Pope Julius III (formerly the bishop of Palestrina), and ending ten popes later, with Clement VIII. That is the central fact of Palestrina's career. He was the pope's composer, a veritable papal institution in his own right.

That status made him the recipient of an amazing and paradoxical commission: in 1577, at the height of his fame, Palestrina (then choirmaster of the Cappella Giulia at the Vatican, named after Julius III, his original patron) was enjoined by Pope Gregory XIII to revise the plainchant that bore the sainted name of the pope's predecessor and namesake, Gregory I. That chant was supposed, by long tradition going back to the Franks, to be divinely revealed (as we have known since the first chapter of this book). Yet it was now subjected to a "modern" stylistic and esthetic critique, and purged of its "Gothic" impurities completely in the spirit of the *ars perfecta*. Palestrina did not complete the project, which reached publication only in 1614; indeed it is not known how much of the revision he (or his appointed assistant, Annibale Zoilo) actually accomplished. The result, however, was exactly what one might expect: a simpler, less tortuous, more "directed"—in short, a more "classic"—melodic line.

In Ex. 16-1, a matins responsory for Easter is given in two versions. The one printed below is the "perfected" version published in 1614 by the Medici Press in Rome (and therefore called the Editio Medicaea), which remained standard until the end of the nineteenth century. The one above is the "restored" text prepared in the nineteenth century by the Benedictines of Solesmes expressly to supplant the Editio Medicaea and put back the "barbarisms, obscurities, inconsistencies, and superfluities" Gregory XIII had ordered pruned away.[1] By then, of course (and under the influence of Romanticism), the "Gothic impurities" had taken on the aura of authenticity.

EX. 16-1   Responsory *Angelus Domini*, in Medicean and Solesmes (Roman) versions

631

Both the Medici and the Solesmes editions carried the papal imprimatur, and so each in its respective time carried the only authority that mattered so far as the church was concerned. What was different was the source of authority the editors themselves relied upon to guide their work. In the nineteenth century it was "scientific" philological method: historical evaluation and comparison of sources. In the sixteenth century the authority came from within: from the religiously informed musical sensibility of the editors, especially the one originally appointed to execute the task, who had become something like the gatekeeper of the church's musical utopia.

That same status as a virtual musical pope—the musical head of what Catholic reformers pointedly referred to in those days of religious unrest as the Hierarchical Church—made Palestrina the most prolific composer of Masses that ever lived. Complete settings of the Ordinary securely attributed to Palestrina number 104 (exactly the same number, by bizarre coincidence, as that of symphonies traditionally attributed to Haydn) and another dozen or so survive with disputed attributions to the composer, whose fame, like Josquin's before him, had made him a brand name. Forty-three were published during his lifetime, in six volumes beginning in 1554. Another forty were posthumously issued, in another six volumes, the last appearing in 1601. The resurgence of the Mass as dominant genre is striking after such a long period—beginning with Josquin and Mouton and encompassing all the mid-century composers whose works we examined in the previous chapter—when motet composition had decisively overshadowed the Mass. It testifies to the quasi-official, "papal" and hierarchical character of Palestrina's activity.

Not that he neglected the motet by any means, with upwards of four hundred to his credit, including a celebrated book of fairly lively works based on the Song of Songs and another fifty with Italian rather than Latin texts, called "madrigali spirituali." Palestrina also composed two ambitious books of service music that sought to outfit the whole church calendar with items of a particular type: the first of these was a book of Vespers hymns that appeared in 1589; the other, considered by many to be his masterpiece, was a complete cycle of Mass Offertories that appeared in the last full year of his life, 1593. Finally, and definitely least, come two books of secular part-songs (madrigals)—but even in this genre, which Palestrina devalued in his devout maturity and even went so far as to recant, he wrote one indisputable "classic" (*Vestiva i colli*, "The hills are bedecked").

The man couldn't help setting an example, it seemed. His staggering output is not only in itself exemplary (of industry, the opposite of one of the deadly sins) but implies commitment to what has already been identified as the "classical" ideal, that of conformity with established excellence—or, better yet, the refinement of existing standards. To do best what everybody does is the aim of a classicist. One does not question aims, one strives to improve one's performance. Practice makes perfect. Continual striving after the same goal is the kind of practice that results, at the very least, in facility. That is how one becomes prolific, and why certain historical periods (the "classical" ones) are so full of prolific composers. The sixteenth century was the first of them.

Palestrina exemplified that aim and that facility, perfected his style to a legendary degree, and in so doing brought the *ars perfecta* to its final pitch. But no matter how you explain it, that output of Masses remains a fairly mind-boggling—and a very telling—achievement. The idea of setting the same text to music a hundred times is on one level the ultimate stylistic exercise, the supreme expression not only of the *ars perfecta* but of the religious and cultural attitudes that undergirded it. It bespeaks a ritualized and impersonal attitude toward composing—a "catholic" attitude. The aim is not to express or illuminate the text, as one might seek to illustrate the unique text of a votive motet, but rather to provide an ideal medium for it. A body of work produced under such ritualized conditions and with such transcendent aims will constitute a *summa*—an encyclopedic summation of the state of the perfected art.

And that seems only just, because no composer ever harbored a more demanding sense of heritage than Palestrina. He practiced the branch of Western musical art that had the longest written tradition, and that had just begun to monumentalize its great figures. Hence Palestrina was easily the most historically minded composer we have as yet encountered. He was the first to do what so many have later done in his name (in counterpoint class, if no longer in church schools)—that is, deliberately master archaic styles as a basis for contemporary composition.

BESTING THE FLEMINGS; OR, THE LAST OF THE TENORISTAS

All but six of Palestrina's hundred-odd Masses are based on preexisting music. That in itself is not remarkable; the polyphonic Mass Ordinary cycle was from the very beginning a cannibalistic genre. But Palestrina was the only late sixteenth-century composer who retained an active interest in the techniques of the early fifteenth-century composers whose work he discovered in the manuscripts of the Sistine Chapel, where he worked in the years immediately preceding the publication of his first volume of Masses in 1554. (He was pensioned out of the Sistine Chapel choir in 1555 owing to Pope Paul IV's decision to enforce the long-dormant rule of celibacy there; Palestrina was one of the three married members who had to be let go.)

That first volume (Fig. 16-1) was dedicated to Palestrina's protector, the recently elected Pope Julius III, and opened with a Mass based on the Gregorian antiphon *Ecce sacerdos magnus*—"Behold the great priest"—presumably composed in celebration of Julius's investiture. It was an old-fashioned tenor cantus-firmus Mass, written in imitation of the oldest music preserved in the Vatican manuscripts and possibly still performed there on occasion in Palestrina's day. The final Agnus Dei even has some old "poly-mensural" tricks such as we have not seen since Josquin's early days.

Palestrina demonstrated his intimate familiarity with the work of Josquin (dead before Palestrina was born) and also his lively, somewhat jealous admiration for it, in the most explicit and traditional way: by basing a Mass on Josquin's celebrated sequence motet *Benedicta es*. He was the latest composer to pay this sort of direct homage to Josquin. But he often reached back further yet for his models, rooting himself as deeply as he knew how in the Franco-Flemish legacy, even taking part, enthusiastically if

(a)   (b)

FIG. 16-1   (a) Title page of Palestrina, *Missarum liber primus* (Rome: Dorico, 1554), showing the composer kneeling before Pope Julius III. (b) Title page of Cristobal de Morales, *Missarum liber secundus* (Rome: Dorico, 1544), showing the composer kneeling before Pope Paul III. It is obvious that the printer recycled and retouched the earlier plate to produce the second.

belatedly, in its ancient emulatory games as if staking a claim to the tradition on behalf of Italy.

This retrospective strain comes particularly to the fore in Palestrina's third book of Masses, published in 1570. Of its eight Masses, two were as old-fashioned as could be. One of them, called *Missa super Ut re mi fa sol la*, was based on the old solmization hexachord, the *voces musicales* on which Josquin had playfully based a *L'Homme Armé* Mass almost a hundred years before. And sure enough, the other tenor Mass in the volume is a *Missa super L'Homme Armé*, one of the very latest contributions to the noblest emulatory line of all. (Palestrina's most recent predecessor had been the Spanish composer Cristóbal de Morales, who had worked before him at the Sistine Chapel and published a pair of *L'Homme Armé* Masses in the 1540s.) In so demonstratively bringing up the rear, so expressly establishing a connection between his work and the half-forgotten wellsprings of the Franco-Flemish art, Palestrina could not have staked his claim on tradition more plainly.

That he regarded himself not as an antiquarian—a mere caretaker of the tradition—but as an active emulant within it is clear from the nature of the compositions themselves. They are cast on a grand scale, combining feats of ancient contrapuntal craft with the sonorous, mellifluent style that had come into vogue only during the

Willaert period. The *Missa L'Homme Armé* is scored for a five-part chorus and the *Missa super Ut re mi fa sol la* for one in six parts. In both cases the final Agnus Dei adds a part, as was by then customary, for an extra-grand finale. In the hexachord Mass the extra (seventh) voice is cast as a canonic part against the cantus firmus, shadowing it at the lower fifth. Ex. 16-2 gives the beginnings of both of these final Agnus settings. In them, we may see the blazing sunset of the Franco-Flemish tradition in its Italianate "perfected" phase.

EX. 16-2   Giovanni Pierluigi da Palestrina, *Missarum liber tertius* (1570)
a. Missa L'Homme Armé, final Agnus Dei

EX. 16-2A *(continued)*

The most spectacular Mass in Palestrina's third book, though, and the most telling instance of emulation, is his *Missa Repleatur os meum laude* (Mass on "May my mouth be filled with praise"), ostensibly based on a motet by Jacques Colebault (1483–1559), a French composer who worked in Italy and was known there as Jacquet (or Jachet) of

EX. 16-2B   *Missa super Ut re mi fa sol la,* final Agnus Dei

EX. 16-2B   (continued)

Mantua. Jacquet's motet was itself a contrapuntal tour-de-force, embodying throughout a chant-derived canon at the fifth between the "structural" voices. Palestrina, using the same basic material, constructed a vast canonic cycle in which both the pitch interval and the time interval progressively contract toward unison. In the Kyrie, sampled in Ex. 16-3, the opening section has a canon at the octave at a time lag of eight semibreves.

EX. 16-3A   Jacquet of Mantua, *Repleatur os meum laude*, opening point

EX. 16-3A *(continued)*

EX. 16-3B Giovanni Pierluigi da Palestrina, *Missa Repleatur os meum laude*, Kyrie I

EX. 16-3B (*continued*)

EX. 16-3C Giovanni Pierluigi da Palestrina, *Missa Repleatur os meum laude,* Christe

EX. 16-3C (continued)

EX. 16-3D Giovanni Pierluigi da Palestrina, *Missa Repleatur os meum laude*, Kyrie II

EX. 16-3D (*continued*)

(In characteristic art-conceals-art fashion, the canon is hidden behind a general point of imitation for the five voices in the texture, in which the two canonic parts are the third and fifth entries, the latter further obscured by being placed in an inner voice.) In the middle section (Christe eleison), the canon is at the seventh at a time lag of seven semibreves, and in the closing section, the canon is at the sixth, at a time lag of six semibreves.

Palestrina is not vying here merely with Jacquet. He is after much bigger game: none other than Ockeghem, whose *Missa Prolationum*, another progressive canonic cycle (but with expanding pitch intervals) had set the Netherlandish benchmark for artifice, and whose preeminence had lately been decreed anew in Italy, in a specifically humanistic context. The famous Florentine polymath or "Renaissance man" Cosimo Bartoli, in a commentary to Dante called *Raggionamenti accademici*, wrote that "in his day Ockeghem was, as it were, the first to rediscover music, then as good as dead, just as Donatello discovered sculpture."[2] Bartoli's observations, published in 1567 (three years before Palestrina's Mass), echo all too clearly the famous theses of Giorgio Vasari, whose "Lives of the Painters" (1550) virtually created the popular notion of the Renaissance in the visual arts. Now there was such a notion for music, too, and Palestrina was getting in on its ground floor.

PARODY PAIRS

More than thirty of Palestrina's Masses are of the paraphrase type — pioneered by Josquin in his late *Missa Pange lingua* and standard practice (as we have seen) for *ars perfecta* motets — in which a Gregorian chant is absorbed into a pervadingly imitative texture. But the lion's share, accounting for almost exactly half of Palestrina's output in the genre (fifty-three to be exact), are parody Masses, in which the motives of a polyphonic model are exhaustively rewoven into new textures. The sources of these Masses were most often motets by composers whose works were popular in local liturgical use during Palestrina's youth. More than twenty times, though, Palestrina based a Mass on one of his own motets (or even madrigals, including *Vestiva i colli*).

When this is the case, it suggests that both the motet and the derivative Mass may have been meant for performance in tandem on the same major feast. Palestrina provided three such motet-plus-Mass sets for Christmas. The one on *O magnum mysterium* ("O great mystery!" — motet published 1569, Mass in 1582) has become particularly famous, and with good reason. The motet begins with a marvelously effective rhetorical stroke: a series of colorful (i.e., chromatic) chords and a reiteration of "O!" that conspire vividly to portray a state of wonder. The chords are connected for the most part along an ordinary circle of fifths (the C being elided) — ordinary, that is, to us; in Palestrina's time it was a striking novelty, and the speed with which the implied bass progression traverses the tritone from E to B-flat is still a little disorienting and "uncanny." The string of successive leading tones (G♯–C♯–F♯–B), each contradicting the last, does the very opposite of what a leading tone is supposed to do in "common practice" (known as such to us but not, of course, to Palestrina). Far from tightening the focus on any particular harmonic goal, it keeps the tonality of the music blurred until the cadential suspension, coinciding with the "uncanny" B-flat, concentrates expectations on A (Ex. 16-4).

That is the sort of thing one fairly expects in a "humanistically" conceived motet, especially one with a text as charged as this one is with emotion. The composer "recites" the text like an orator, highlighting its meaning by modulating his harmonies as an orator modulates his tone of voice. When colorful harmonies or effects imitative of speech patterns occur in tandem with affective words, they seem to "point to" or refer to those words, ultimately to symbolize them. Such symbolism, in which signs

EX. 16-4   Giovanni Pierluigi da Palestrina, *O magnum mysterium*, opening phrase

EX. 16-4   (*continued*)

point to something "outside" the system of sounds themselves (in this case to words and their embodied concepts) is called "extroversive" symbolism (or, more formally, *semiosis* — "signing"). Humanistic, rhetorical text setting encourages such effects, which became increasingly prevalent during the sixteenth century.

When the motet is transformed through parody technique into a Mass, what had been affective and rhetorical becomes syntactical and structural. The "uncanny" progression that launches the motet on a note of awe serves the Mass as a suitably ear-catching "head motive." Each of its five constituent liturgical units opens by invoking the phrase before proceeding to other business, stirring memories of its predecessors and thus integrating the service by structuring its duration around a series of strategic returns to symbolic, hence inspiring, sounds (Ex. 16-5). Within the Mass, the symbolism or semiosis is entirely "introversive" (inward-pointing). What is emblematized or signaled is precisely the integration of the service — already an emotionally intensifying, uplifting, effect, but one that carries no external concepts with it.

(This remains true even if, as suggested, the motet is also performed as part of the same Mass service. Places where motets might be sung, so far as we know, are the same sorts of places as those where a ricercare might be played: during the elevation of the host or during Communion, when there is an activity that takes up time that is otherwise unfilled by sounds. Thus the motet *O magnum mysterium*, if performed at Christmas Mass, would be performed only after three or four Ordinary items had already been sung. Once it has been performed, of course, the referents for its harmonic and declamatory effects will be both introversive and extroversive at the same time. That kind of mixture or complexity of reference is the normal state of affairs for music, which is why musical symbolism or "expression" has always been such a complicated, contentious, and even mysterious issue.)

PALESTRINA AND THE BISHOPS

Palestrina placed the ancient elite and ecumenical art to which he claimed the key at the service of "the one holy, catholic and apostolic church" at the very moment when the church, under pressure from the northern Reformation, was renewing its age-old mission as the "Church Militant" (*ecclesia militans*). As we will see in a later chapter, that rekindled militancy was ultimately subversive of the ars perfecta. But in its early stages it created the demand for a new clarity in texture that could be seen as the

EX. 16-5A   Giovanni Pierluigi da Palestrina, *Missa O magnum mysterium*, Kyrie, beginning

ultimate refinement—the ultimate perfecting—of the traditional style. Clearly that was how Palestrina saw it. By seizing the opportunity to satisfy that demand, he created a prestigious masterwork, an influential style he could call his own, and a durable personal legend.

At least as early as the 1540s, and particularly in Roman circles, some churchmen had taken a negative attitude toward the music of the post-Josquin generation, which for all its technical excellence ran counter, they thought, to the proper role and function of church music. To put their concerns in a nutshell, they thought that the elegantly wrought imitative texture that had gained universal currency was far too artistic, and therefore not sufficiently functional. Such music, in its preoccupation with its own beauty of form, exemplified the sin of pride, and interfered with the intelligibility of the sacred texts to which it was meant to be subordinate.

EX. 16-5B   Giovanni Pierluigi da Palestrina, *Missa O magnum mysterium*, Gloria ("Et in terra. . . "), beginning

The complaint, as such, was nothing new. We have heard it before from John of Salisbury, who railed at the vainglory of the singers at Notre Dame, and even from Saint Augustine, who had nothing more than the seductive beauty of Gregorian chant to contend with. Made against the music of the incipient *ars perfecta*, however, it carried considerable conviction, because imitative texture was an artistic value first and last, and was hardly reconcilable with the demands of textual intelligibility no matter how much attention a composer like Willaert paid to correct declamation. As one indignant bishop, Bernardino Cirillo Franco, put it of contemporary composers (and with the text of the Mass Sanctus in mind), "in our times they have put all their industry and effort into the compositions of fugues, so that while one voice says 'Sanctus,' another

EX. 16-5C   Giovanni Pierluigi da Palestrina, *Missa O magnum mysterium*, Credo ("Patrem omni potentem. . . "), beginning

says 'Sabaoth,' still another 'Gloria tua,' with howling, bellowing, and stammering, so that they more nearly resemble cats in January than flowers in May."[3]

The part about howling, bellowing, and stammering was just all-purpose invective, but the point about imitation was a fair one, and it proceeded, moreover, from a genuine, specifically Italian humanist impulse—"specifically Italian," because as we have seen, English musicians, for one example, could be every bit as devout and yet quite indifferent to the matter of textual intelligibility, seeing music as serving another sort of religious purpose that had little to do with humanism. In Italy, though, what had been a crotchety minority opinion in the 1540s had become a concern of powerful "mainstream" Catholics by the middle of the next decade, when Palestrina was beginning to establish himself as a papal musician.

According to Bishop Cirillo Franco himself, writing a quarter of a century later around 1575, one of these mainstream figures was Cardinal Marcello Cervini, who in 1555 was elected pope, and who promised his friend the bishop that he would do

EX. 16-5D   Giovanni Pierluigi da Palestrina, *Missa O magnum mysterium*, Sanctus, beginning

EX. 16-5D (continued)

EX. 16-5E   Giovanni Pierluigi da Palestrina, *Missa O magnum mysterium*, Agnus Dei, beginning

something about the problem. Cirillo Franco claimed that in due course he received from Rome "a Mass that conformed very closely to what I was seeking."[4] Cardinal Cervini reigned, as Pope Marcellus II, for only twenty days before his sudden death; but there is nevertheless evidence that corroborates Cirillo Franco's testimony about the pope's concern for "intelligible" church music. The diary of Angelo Massarelli, Pope Marcellus's private secretary, contains an entry dated Good Friday (12 April) 1555, the third day of the pontiff's brief reign. Marcellus came down to the Sistine Chapel to hear the choir, of which Palestrina was then a member, sing the gravest liturgy of the church year. "Yet the music performed," Massarelli noted,

> did not suit the solemnity of the occasion. Rather, their many-voiced singing exuded a joyful mood. . . . Accordingly, the pope himself, having beckoned to his singers, directed them to sing with proper restraint, and in such a way that everything was audible and intelligible, as it should be.[5]

Palestrina was one of the singers who heard this fatherly lecture from the pontiff. His second book of Masses, published in 1567, is prefaced by a letter of dedication to King Philip II of Spain (best remembered in English-speaking countries as Queen Elizabeth's rejected suitor and later her military adversary), in which Palestrina testified to his resolve, "in accordance with the views of most serious and most religious-minded men, to bend all my knowledge, effort, and industry toward that which is the holiest and most divine of all things in the Christian religion — that is, to adorn the holy sacrifice of the Mass in a new manner."[6] The seventh and last item — the valedictory, as it were — in the book that had opened thus, with the composer's statement of pious or chastened resolve, was a Mass entitled *Missa Papae Marcelli*, "The Mass of Pope Marcelli," or even "Pope Marcellus's Mass." And indeed, it was a Mass that conformed very closely to what Bishop Cirillo Franco had been seeking, for it set the sacred words "in such a way that everything was audible and intelligible, as it should be."

Was this the Mass that Bishop Cirillo Franco received from Pope Marcellus, as promised? To believe that one would have to imagine Palestrina writing the Mass, and Pope Marcellus dispatching it, within seventeen days, which was all the earthly time the pope had left. That is certainly not impossible. But by 1567 the "intelligibility movement" had gathered a powerful impetus, and the dedication to Pope Marcellus may have been commemorational, honoring the unlucky and lamented pontiff whose reign had been so abruptly terminated, but who was now looked back upon as the spur that had set an important musical reform in motion.

That reform had reached a critical point in the year 1562, when the Nineteenth Ecumenical Council of the Western Church (popularly known as the Council of Trent, after the north Italian city where it met), finally got around to music. The Council of Trent was an emergency legislative body that had been convened in 1545 by Pope Paul III to stem the tide of the Protestant Reformation. Music, clearly, was not terribly high on the Council's agenda, but it, too, could play a part in the general effort to revitalize the church through modesty and piety, to some extent to personalize its religious message, and by so doing to steal some of the Protestants' thunder. Appropriate music could be of assistance in the project of adjusting the traditionally unworldly, impersonal (and indeed rather haughty) tone of Catholic worship to the point where it might meet the comprehension of the ordinary worshiper halfway.

That, ideally, was the purpose that motivated the "intelligibility" crusade, and it was explicitly formulated by the Council in its "Canon on Music to be Used in the Mass," promulgated in September 1562. The singing of the Mass, this document decreed, should not be an obstacle to the worshipers' involvement but should allow the Mass and its sacred symbolism "to reach tranquilly into the ears and hearts of those who hear them."[7] Music was not provided in church for the benefit of music lovers: "The whole plan of singing in musical modes should be constituted not to give empty pleasure to the ear, but in such a way that the words be clearly understood by all, and thus the hearts of the listeners be drawn to desire of heavenly harmonies, in the contemplation of the joys of the blessed." It was left to musicians to find the means for implementing these general guidelines, but it was up to the bishops and cardinals to make sure that those means were found. In the years immediately following the Council's Canon, several important princes of the church took an active part in overseeing the work of composers. One of them was the redoubtable Cardinal Carlo Borromeo, the Archbishop of Milan and the chief enforcer, as papal secretary of state, of the Council's decrees. Borromeo directly charged Vincenzo Ruffo, the *maestro di cappella* at Milan, "to compose a Mass that should be as clear as possible and to send it to me here," that is to Rome, where it might be tested.[8]

This commission was issued on 10 March 1565. Several weeks later, on 28 April, according to the official diary of the Papal Chapel Choir, "we assembled at the request of the Most Reverend Cardinal Vitellozzi at his residence to sing some Masses and to test whether the words could be understood, as their Eminences desire."[9] That Ruffo's Mass was among these seems virtually certain; the effort of this composer, famed earlier for his contrapuntal skill, to conform to the dictates of the Cardinals is touchingly evident (see Ex. 16-6).

Whether Palestrina's *Missa Papae Marcelli* was among the Masses tested that day is a matter of conjecture, but the notion is made plausible by the date of the Mass's publication two years later, and it has formed the basis of one of the most durable myths in the history of European church music. The legend exaggerated the test at Cardinal Vitellozzi's into a public trial, thence into a virtual musical Inquisition, with music coming "very near to being banished from the Holy Church by a sovereign pontiff [Pius IV], had not Giovanni Palestrina found the remedy, showing that the error lay, not with music, but with the composers, and composing in confirmation of this the Mass entitled *Missa Papae Marcelli*."[10]

The words just quoted are from an aside by Agostino Agazzari, the *maestro di capella* of the Jesuit Seminary in Rome, in the course of a treatise on instrumental music that he published in 1607, a dozen years and more after Palestrina's death. It is the first report of the post-Council intervention by the hierarchy of the Church Militant in the affairs of music to cast it in such radical and confrontational terms, and the first explicitly to associate the *Missa Papae Marcelli* with those events. It is hard to know

EX. 16-6   Vincenzo Ruffo, *Missae Quatuor concinate ad ritum Concilii Mediolani*

whether Agazzari was drawing on "oral history" here, or on unsubstantiated rumor, or on his imagination.

But if he was the first to cast Palestrina as music's heroic savior, he was certainly not the last. The legend passed from pen to pen throughout the seventeenth and eighteenth centuries, until it reached a seemingly unsurpassable peak in 1828 in the first full-length biography of Palestrina, by the priest Giuseppe Baini, a papal musician and composer in his own right and a follower in Palestrina's footsteps as a Sistine Chapel chorister. *"Povero Pierluigi!,"* Baini wrote: "Poor Pierluigi! He was placed in the hardest straits of his career. The fate of church music hung from his pen, and so did his own career, at the height of his fame. . . ."[11]

But Baini's account was only seemingly unsurpassable. It has been surpassed many times over in popular history — "Church music was saved forever. Italian music was founded at the same time. What if Palestrina had not succeeded? The mind staggers"[12] — and was even worked up into an opera. The latter, a "musical legend" in three acts called *Palestrina*, by the German composer Hans Pfitzner (to his own libretto), was composed in 1915, and first performed in Munich two years later, while World War I was raging. Not only Palestrina (tenor) but Cardinal Borromeo (baritone), Pope Pius IV (bass), Angelo Massarelli (transmuted into the general secretary to the Council of Trent) and even Josquin des Prez are cast as characters (the last as an apparition). Women's roles are entirely incidental: Palestrina's daughter, his deceased first wife (another apparition), and three angels.

In act I, Cardinal Borromeo issues the commission to a reluctant Palestrina, whom he has to cajole with actual imprisonment and threatened torture. The spirits of the dead masters (including Josquin) exhort the composer to add "the last stone" to the jeweled necklace of musical perfection, and an angel intones the first motive from the Kyrie of the *Missa Papae Marcelli*, followed by the whole angelic host who dictate to Palestrina the music that saved music (see Fig. 16-2). Act II shows the assembled Council of Trent engaged in luridly acrimonious debate over music, with a sizable faction calling for its outright abolition. Act III shows the outcome of the musical show trial: Palestrina, released from prison but tormented by self-doubt, receives the plaudits of the singers and compliments from the pope himself, for having emerged victorious as the savior of music.

Pfitzner's *Palestrina* is an important work — or rather, at the least, a work that raises

FIG. 16-2   Angelic dictation scene from Pfitzner, *Palestrina* (Munich, Prinzregententheater, 12 June 1917).

important issues. They are issues, admittedly, that were probably more consciously pondered in Pfitzner's time than in Palestrina's, but they are issues that are still hotly contested today. They are spelled out in a quotation from the nineteenth-century German philosopher Artur Schopenhauer that the composer placed at the head of the score as an epigraph: "Alongside world history there goes, guiltless and unstained by blood, the history of philosophy, science and the arts."[13] The question thus raised — whether the history of art is an idyllic parallel history, a transcendent history that is separate from that of the (rest of the) world, or whether world history and art history are mutually implicated — has been the urgent subtext of this book from the very first page.

The Palestrina legend was a good symbolic medium for broaching this enormous question because the bishops' call for "intelligible" church music, backed up by the legislated decrees of the Council of Trent and the implied power of the Inquisition and of the "Holy Roman Empire" under whose auspices the Council was convened, was a clear instance of public political intervention in the affairs of art and its makers, as opposed to the accustomed pressures of private patronage. It brings to mind — to our contemporary mind, at least — many other such interventions, some of which have had serious and even tragic implications.

FREEDOM AND CONSTRAINT

Such parallels are only too easy to overdraw, and we may take comfort on behalf of poor Pierluigi that he never suffered the imprisonment or mortal duress that the operatic Palestrina had to endure. Not only that, but Palestrina's third book of Masses, published in 1570, contained the extremely complicated and "artificial" works in Netherlandish style already discussed and sampled in Ex. 16-2 and 16-3. Clearly there was never any actual inquisitorial ban on any form of Catholic worship music, at least in territories subject to the strictures of the Council of Trent.

Still and all, the style of the *Missa Papae Marcelli* remains arguably a coerced, official style — not a style, in other words, that Palestrina or Ruffo or any other composer would have adopted spontaneously (to judge by their prior output and the values implied therein) but one imposed by an external force to suit purposes that arguably ran counter to the interests of composers, but that were not negotiable. And yet the style was (or could be made) a very beautiful and moving one, and one that later artists found sufficiently inspiring to emulate willingly. As Pfitzner implied in his melodramatic way, it was a tribute to Palestrina's artistic imagination to have found so successful a means of reconciling artistic and ecclesiastical criteria — a manner, moreover, that was very much in the spirit of the Church Militant.

As the Credo and the Agnus Dei from the *Missa Papae Marcelli* especially confirm, Palestrina's post–Council-of-Trent style was not a chastened, ascetic, quasi-penitent affair like Ruffo's but a style of special opulence, grace, and expressivity. *Missa Papae Marcelli* is a "freely composed" Mass, one of the few by Palestrina that incorporates no preexisting material — or, at least, none that has been acknowledged by the composer or subsequently detected. The composer's shaping hand is all the more crucial, then, and the Mass is given a musical shape more elegant than ever, in demonstrative compensation for the loss of the usual external scaffold.

The opening idea of the Kyrie, the one intoned by the angel in Pfitzner's opera, is both the subject of the Mass's first point of imitation (Ex. 16-7) and the Mass's main melodic building block; and it embodies the quintessence of his style, as identified by the many who have studied it with an eye toward extracting from it a compositional method.

EX. 16-7 Giovanni Pierluigi da Palestrina, *Missa Papae Marcelli*, opening Kyrie

That quintessence is the "recovered leap." This model motif (we'll call it the "Ur-motif," German-style) begins with an ascending leap of a fourth, which is immediately filled in, or "recovered," by descending stepwise motion. (Fascinating never-to-be-answered questions: Was the similarity of this phrase to the opening phrase of the old *L'Homme Armé* tenor (Ex. 12-10) fortuitous or emblematic; and if emblematic, of what?) It is the double reciprocity—immediate reversal of contour after a leap, the exchange of leaps and steps—that creates the "balanced" design with which the name Palestrina has become synonymous. The wealth of passing tones (many of them accented), vouchsafed by the stepwise recovery of skips, is what gives Palestrina's texture its much-esteemed patina. Otherwise the style of Palestrina's Kyrie does not differ especially from the *ars perfecta* idiom with which we are familiar, because the Kyrie is a sparsely texted, traditionally melismatic item where textual clarity was not of paramount concern.

It is in the "talky" movements of the Mass—the Gloria and Credo—that the special post-Tridentine qualities emerge. The setting of the very first phrase of polyphony in the Credo (Ex. 16-8) can serve as paradigm. The bass has the Ur-motif, its first note twice reiterated (or, to put it more in sixteenth-century terms, its first note broken into three) to accommodate two unaccented syllables. Four of the six voices sing the phrase in choral homorhythm, with melodic decorations taking place only where syllables are held long, so as not to obscure the text. The top voice uses its chance for decoration to mirror the Ur-motif, substituting a reciprocal fifth from C to G (embellished with passing tones) for the bass's fourth from G to C. That fifth having been achieved, the contour is reversed and the melody descends to its starting point, just like the Ur-motive in the bass.

EX. 16-8   Giovanni Pierluigi da Palestrina, *Missa Papae Marcelli*, Credo, mm. 1–8

The second phrase of text ("factorem coeli. . .") employs another sort of reciprocity: it is scored for a different four-voice sample from the six available parts, chosen for maximum contrast. The two voices that had played the most conspicuous melodic role in the first phrase are silenced and replaced by the two voices that had been silent before. The result is a kind of ersatz antiphony within the single choir, and it is a device that will in effect replace imitation as the prime structural principle for the Credo. The replacement bass, meanwhile, sounds the Ur-motive a second time, its notes broken up into a new rhythmic configuration to accommodate another set of words, and it is again doubled homorhythmically by remaining voices.

The close on the final (C) at "terrae" is emphasized by a gorgeous, and very characteristic, double suspension (7–6 in the alto over the bass A, 4–3 in the first tenor over the bass G). This ornamental approach to functional articulation is one of the secrets of the post-Tridentine style: to create opulence out of sheer grammatical necessity is a high rhetorical skill. It reaches a peak in the Sanctus, characteristically the most luxuriant movement of all, since it is identified by its liturgical Preface as a portrayal of the heavenly choirs (the source, evidently, of Pfitzner's sentimental representation).

The music at the beginning of Palestrina's Sanctus (Ex. 16-9), so magnificently evocative of infinite space, is in essence just a rockingly reiterated cadence with a decorated suspension (passed from Cantus to Bassus II to Bassus I). Again, reiteration and varied choral distribution take the place of imitation. Ever increasing spaces are then suggested by extending the span between suspension-cadences from two bars to three (mm. 7–9) and then moving the cadential target around from C to F to D to G (mm. 10–16) so that when C finally comes back (not until m. 32, not shown) it carries enormous articulative force and effectively finishes off a section.

EX. 16-9   Giovanni Pierluigi da Palestrina, *Missa Papae Marcelli*, Sanctus, mm. 1–16

EX. 16-9 *(continued)*

This sort of tonal planning, necessitated by the absence of a cantus firmus and the need to keep the music "in motion" without the propulsion that pervasive imitation can afford, amounted to something quite new. The harnessing of tonal tension by delaying cadences (or, more subtly, delaying points of necessary arrival) undoubtedly depended on aural memories — on the composer's part and that of his audience as well — of the sort of improvisatory music over ground basses that we observed briefly at the end of the previous chapter.

Returning to the Credo, we can summarize its structure as a strategically planned series of cadential "cells," or "modules," each expressed through a fragment of text declaimed homorhythmically by a portion of the choir in an iridescently shifting succession and rounded off by a beautifully crafted cadence. In the middle section ("Crucifixus") Palestrina apes the tenor-tacet sections of old by scaling down the performing forces to a four-voice "semichoir," but the nature of the writing does not differ; it still consists of a kaleidoscopic interplay of homorhythmically declaimed, cadenced phrases.

The third and last part ("Et in spiritum") returns to the full six-part complement, which is deployed more frequently than before at full strength, reaching a massive tutti at the final "Amen" (Ex. 16-10) that develops the arching "recovery" idea — upward leaps followed by downward scales — into a thrilling peroration. (The first tenor attempts for a while to swim against the tide with downward leaps and upward scales, but is finally caught up in the cadential undertow; the plagal cadence at the very end is an embellishment of the long-sustained final C in the second tenor — an archly deliberate whiff of the old, decisively superseded cantus-firmus texture.)

The expressivity of this music arises out of the cadence patterns, not to say the "tonal" progressions. It is with Palestrina that we first begin to notice — and, more, to feel the effects of — strategic harmonic delays. It is an expressivity that is based almost entirely on "introversive" (inward-pointing) signification and the emotion that delayed fulfillment of expectations produces in the listener. There is little or no extroversive symbolism in this — or any other — Mass setting by this time. As one can readily imagine, relying on extroversive symbolism when setting the same text repeatedly would drastically restrict rather than enhance one's creative choices.

EX. 16-10   Giovanni Pierluigi da Palestrina, *Missa Papae Marcelli*, Credo, mm. 186–97

EX. 16-10 *(continued)*

The only text-derived symbolism one can point to in the Credo are the virtually inescapable contrasting melodic contours on the phrases *"descendit de coelis"* and *"et ascendit in coelum."* To contradict the implied "directions" in the text at these points would be bizarre. The reason why this particular pair of images has become such a compulsory trope or "figure" for translation into sound seems to be precisely that it is a pair—or rather, an antithesis. (By way of contrast, look back at Ex. 16-1, the Easter responsory chant, and note how the single word "descendit," in the absence of its

EX. 16-11   Giovanni Pierluigi da Palestrina, *Missa Papae Marcelli*, Agnus Dei, mm. 1–15

EX. 16-11   (continued)

opposite, is allowed to ascend melodically.) As we shall see in the next chapter, figural symbolism in music thrives on antithetical relations, and antithetical figures in texts seem to demand musical illustration.

The opening point in the Agnus Dei (Ex. 16-11) recapitulates the beginning of the Kyrie (compare Ex. 16-8), an effect calculated to give this "freely" composed Mass an especially rounded and finished shape. The technique of composition, not only here but in all the melismatic sections of the Mass, reverts to the freely imitative style Zarlino called *fuga sciolta*. Only phrase-beginnings are imitated; continuations are "freely" adapted to the harmonic design. The concluding Agnus (designated "II" but meant for the third section, with its separate textual ending "Dona nobis pacem") expands, following custom, into seven parts. It is very unlikely that anyone listening to this triumph of art-concealing art (Ex. 16-12a) could tell without following the score that its luxuriant contrapuntal unfolding was scaffolded around a three-part canon (bassus I, altus II, cantus II) based, initially, on the Ur-motive. It is a very spaciously laid out canon in which the parts hardly overlap, again putting a kind of antiphony in place of imitation. The interval of the canon is a rising fifth that proceeds in two

EX. 16-12A   Giovanni Pierluigi da Palestrina, *Missa Papae Marcelli*, Agnus II, mm. 1–10

stages, from bassus to altus and from altus to cantus, so that the first and third voices are in fact a ninth apart. That layout, strange from the purely intervallic point of view, is harmonically a very strategic move, giving further evidence of Palestrina's inclination to plan his works out "tonally," in terms of fifth-related harmonic regions.

The payoff comes at the end. The last phrase of the canon begins with the Bassus's "Dona nobis pacem" in m. 40. Its progression from the final (I) to the subsemitonium or leading tone (vii) by way of an initial descent to the subdominant or lower fifth (IV) elegantly prepares the final cadence in the second Cantus a ninth above: supertonium (ii) to the long-held final (I) by way of an initial descent to the

EX. 16-12B Giovanni Pierluigi da Palestrina, *Missa Papae Marcelli*, Agnus II, mm. 40–53

EX. 16-12B *(continued)*

tuba (V). These sequences of degree functions, modeled on those of the ground basses and reinforced by constant use, were eventually stereotyped into the familiar tonal cadences of what we, looking back on it, call the "common practice." Palestrina's I–IV–vii//ii–V–I, arising out of his strange canon-by-two-fifths, is none other than the essential frame of the common-practice circle of fifths, lacking only the middle pair (iii–vi) for completion.

CRYOGENICS

The final stage in Palestrina's texturally clarified, harmonically saturated, motivically economical—in a word, "classical"—*ars perfecta* polyphony is reached in the book of Offertories that he published in the last year of his life. *Tui sunt coeli* (Ex. 16-13) is the one for Christmas. Compared with the *Missa Papae Marcelli* this pervasively imitative composition might seem a relapse into some bad old pre-Tridentine habits. But this is pervasive imitation with a difference. The points are tightly woven out of laconic motives that are precisely modeled on the pronunciation of the words.

Many motives ("et tua est terra," "orbem terrarum," etc.) are well-nigh syllabically texted in all parts. Elsewhere, Palestrina deploys the *fuga sciolta* technique in a way that maximizes intelligibility. The words are concentrated at the heads of the motives, the parts that all the voices have in common. In the first point, for example, the syllabically texted head exactly coincides with the verbal phrase; everything that follows is freely molded melisma. Thus every entrance stands out in note-lengths, in texting style, and

EX. 16-13   Giovanni Pierluigi da Palestrina, *Tui sunt coeli* (Offertory), mm. 1–22

EX. 16-13 *(continued)*

Thine are the heavens, and thine is the earth: the world and
the fulness thereof thou hast founded: justice and judgment
are the preparation of thy throne.
(Psalm 88, verses 12 and 15)

by virtue of its wide skips, from the placid melismatic note-river that murmurs in what
is definitely the aural background.

At the same time that this sense of perspective has been introduced into the
polyphonic texture, a similarly hierarchical sense of perspective orders the harmony as
well. It is virtually taken for granted by now that imitation will be "tonal" rather than
literal. The setting of the text incipit ("Tui sunt coeli"), for example, contains entries
on the final (D) and on the tuba (A). In every case, the downward contour is adjusted
so that the two notes in question will define its limits: either A proceeds downward
to D by way of G (producing the intervallic succession step+fourth) or D proceeds
downward to A by way of C (producing the intervallic succession step+third).

In a way that is almost shocking for Palestrina, the next interval, while reversing
direction as expected, does so by means of a spectacular leap that emphatically requires
a full "recovery." The ensuing stepwise melismatic "tail" (*cauda*) supplies precisely that.
And it does not come to rest until full recovery—return to the starting note—is
achieved, which is how Palestrina is able to maintain melodic tension over a considerable
melismatic span, and why the tunes in his late compositions, however decorative, always
have a pressing sense of direction.

To pick one example: the altus, entering first, has to recover the whole sixth from
B-flat to D in its descending melisma; it proceeds immediately as far as E, but then
reverses direction; it then overshoots its top and skips down from C so as to require
another recovery before it can go farther; that recovery having been made, it teasingly
moves down again to the E; finally it gives the ear what it craves, through a circle of
fifths; the D having at last been regained, the voice now—and only now—can rest.
The line is complex and tortuous, but as it keeps making and (eventually) keeping
promises, it sounds at all times purposeful, never meandering.

The high tonal definition and tonal stability established at the outset is maintained throughout the motet, and the projecting and achieving of tonal goals are among the factors contributing fundamentally to the impression of the music's overall "shape," the coherence of its unfolding. We are, in other words, just about at the point where it makes sense to start replacing the old "modal" terms like "final" and "tuba" (first employed some seven centuries earlier to assist in a purely melodic classification) with modern terms like "tonic" and "dominant," which refer to harmonic functions. The age of functional tonal harmony, it can be argued, begins with pieces like this, although the full panoply of tonal functions will not come into play until complete diatonic circles of fifths become standard — in about a century's time, and also in Italy.

The extraordinary lucidity and rational control that Palestrina achieved in his late work corresponds quite closely with the ideals of the Society of Jesus, popularly known as the Jesuits, a religious order founded by Palestrina's older contemporary Saint Ignatius of Loyola (1491–1556, canonized 1622), devoted equally to learning and to the propagation of the faith. The use to which Palestrina's music has been put in educational institutions both sacred and secular substantiates the affinity. The incipient tonal functionalism one finds in his music does seem to have something to do with his being an Italian composer — the first to achieve parity with the northern masters of the literate tradition, and for that reason an inspiring historical figure for Italian musical nationalists in years to come, especially after the period of Italian musical hegemony that began quite soon after his death had ended. (To Giuseppe Verdi, for example, Palestrina was not only the pure spring of Italian melody but the best shield against the "German curse.")

The relevance of Palestrina's nationality to his tonal practice, and the way the latter inflected his style, had to do above all with the nonliterate musical culture that surrounded him in his formative years, as it did every Italian — the art of *improvvisatori*, whether poets declaiming their stanzas (*strambotti*) to stock melodic-harmonic formulas (*arie*) or instrumentalists making their brilliant divisions and *passaggii* over ground basses, all defined by regularly recurring, cadential chord progressions. The earliest written "part music" to emulate these improvisations were settings of Italian poetry that began appearing near the end of the fifteenth century, and were published in great quantities in the early 1500s by Petrucci and the other early printers. These simple part songs called *frottole* have long been viewed as a major hotbed of functional or "tonal" harmony, and we will see some specimens in the next chapter. Palestrina, being (after Ruffo) the first important native-born Italian composer of church music, was among the first to transfer something of their tonal regularity to the loftiest literate genres. And it was the technical regularity of his music, along with its towering prestige, that made Palestrina the basis of the most enduring academic style in the history of European music. At first this was a matter of turning the Sistine Chapel — the pope's own parish church — into a musical time capsule, sealing it off from history by decree and freezing the perfected polyphonic art of Palestrina into a timeless dogma, as it were, to join the timeless dogmas of theology. Long after the "concerted" style that mixed separate vocal and instrumental parts (the topic of a coming chapter) had become standard for Catholic church music, especially in Italy, the Sistine Chapel maintained an *a cappella* rule that forbade the use of instruments and mandated the retention of *ars perfecta* polyphony as its standard repertory.

Palestrina remained the papal staple: he is thus the longest-running composer in Western musical history, the earliest composer whose works have an unbroken tradition in performance from his time to ours. What is even more remarkable, composers continued to be trained to compose in the *a cappella*, *ars perfecta* style (or what was taken as the "Palestrina" style) for Roman church use long after Palestrina's time. By the early seventeenth century, two styles were officially recognized by church composers: the *stile moderno*, or "modern style," which kept up with the taste of the times, and the *stile antico*, or "old style," sometimes called the *stile da cappella*, which meant the "chapel" style, which is to say the timelessly embalmed Palestrina style, a style that had in effect stepped out of history and into eternity.

Ex. 16-14 is the opening of *O magnum mysterium*, a setting of the same text Palestrina himself had set (Ex. 16-4) and then made the basis of a Mass (Ex. 16-5). It was composed for the Sistine Chapel by a member of the choir named Balthasar Sartori, and it is preserved in a Sistine Chapel manuscript alongside the works of Du Fay, Ockeghem, Busnoys, Josquin, and of course Palestrina. The manuscript's date, however, is 1715 — a century and a quarter after Palestrina's mortal expiration. When it was put together, the streets and theaters of Rome were filled with the sounds of Vivaldi concertos and Scarlatti operas. Inside the Sistine Chapel, though, it was as if Palestrina had never died. In the most literal sense he had been canonized.

Of course a connoisseur can easily tell an eighteenth-century imitation like this one from a Palestrina original; but that it is a studied attempt to write in "the Palestrina style" is nevertheless patent. Interestingly enough, it is not the style of Palestrina's own *O magnum mysterium* that Sartori's motet imitates, but the much more rarefied, cerebral, and impersonal — one might even say "Jesuitical" — style of the late Offertories like *Tui sunt coeli* (Ex. 16-13). Only such a style, rather than an "expressive" one, could aspire convincingly to "timelessness." But the *stile antico* lived on longer still and has assumed another role entirely in Western musical culture. In 1725, ten years after the manuscript containing Sartori's motet was compiled, an Austrian church composer named Johann Joseph Fux (1660–1741), who as it happened was trained in Jesuit schools and colleges, published a treatise called *Gradus ad Parnassum* ("Stairway to Parnassus," that is, to the abode of the Muses). Like many Catholic musicians of his time, Fux composed "bilingually," turning out operas and oratorios in the *stile moderno* of the day, and Masses and motets in the immutable *stile antico*. His treatise was a brilliantly successful attempt to reduce the *stile antico* to a concise set of rules, which Fux accomplished by dividing the realm of old-style polyphony into five "species" (as he called them) of rhythmic relationships, as follows

1. Note against note (or *punctum contra punctum*, whence "counterpoint")
2. Two notes against one in cantus firmus style
3. Three or four notes against one in cantus firmus style
4. Syncopation against a cantus firmus
5. Mixed values ("florid style")

EX. 16-14   Balthasar Sartori, *O magnum mysterium*, mm. 1–10

EX. 16-14   (continued)

— and prescribing the "dissonance treatment" for each. Fux's rationalization of the *stile antico* gave it a new lease on life, not only as an artificially preserved style of Roman Catholic church music but also as basic training for composers. As the bible of the "strict style," Fux's *Gradus ad Parnassum* became the first "counterpoint text" in the modern sense and the greatest schoolbook in the history of European music. Starting with the generation of Haydn, musicians — at first in Austria, gradually everywhere — used it to gain facility in "the first principles of harmony and composition," which were regarded by teachers as an eternal dogma in its own right, a bedrock of imperishable lore that "remains unaltered, let taste change as it will."[14] Thus the *stile antico*, in the form of Fux's rules, became the gateway to the *stile moderno*.

Its derivation from Palestrina, far from being forgotten in the course of its transformation, was emphasized for its prestige value. Indeed, Fux cast the whole treatise in the form of a dialogue between the master "Aloysius" (= Palestrina, "Petroaloysius" being the Latinized form of Pierluigi) and the pupil "Josephus" (= Fux). Either in itself or as absorbed or cribbed by later writers, Fux's treatise remained current into the twentieth century, when several other major counterpoint texts educed from Palestrina were written, further updating the *stile antico* as a purely pedagogical style, no longer in active use even in church.

FIG. 16-3   Johann Joseph Fux, author of *Gradus ad Parnassum*.

The most influential of these books was *Kontrapunkt*, by Knud Jeppesen (1892–1974), a Danish musicologist and composer, who based his method on his doctoral dissertation, a fresh description of Palestrina's style that was published in English in 1927 as *The Style of Palestrina and the Dissonance*. Either in the original or in its English language edition, published in 1939, Jeppesen's *Counterpoint* was standard pabulum in European and American conservatories and universities at least until the early 1960s, when the author of this book worked his somewhat lugubrious but finally profitable way through it. Many have questioned its relevance to modern composition by now, and its hold on the curriculum has loosened. But for historians traditional counterpoint training is invaluable. His territory has been shrinking, but Palestrina lives.

BYRD

The fate of William Byrd, Palestrina's somewhat younger, longer-lived English contemporary, was rather different. He was a far more versatile composer, adept in every contemporary genre both sacred and secular, who made an important contribution to the early development of instrumental chamber and keyboard music, realms about as far removed from Palestrina's sphere of interest and influence as can be imagined. In this chapter, however, we will concentrate on the side of Byrd's output that overlapped with Palestrina's, and on his position as a late — arguably, the very latest — great master of polyphonic service music in the Catholic tradition, of all European musical traditions the most venerable.

With Byrd we truly reach the end of the line. His work was never canonized the way Palestrina's was but had to await revival by musical antiquarians in the nineteenth and twentieth centuries. The reason was simple and cruel: the church he served had also reached the end of the line in England. Far from the official musical spokesman of established religious power, Byrd became the musical spokesman of the losing side in a religious war: that of the so-called recusants or refusers, loyal Catholics in an England that had anathematized the pope and persecuted his followers. Byrd's latest, greatest music, on which we shall focus, was the music of a church gone underground.

CHURCH AND STATE

The English reformation was totally unlike the German and Swiss ones whose musical effects we have yet to consider. It was led from above by the monarch; it was as much a political as a religious commotion, and it carried a portentous tinge of nationalism. Its origin was a quarrel between King Henry VIII and Pope Clement VII, who had refused Henry's request for annulment of his marriage to his first wife, Katharine of Aragon, for failing to produce a male heir to the throne. (Behind the pope's ostensibly ecclesiastical judgment there lurked another political power: Charles V, the Holy Roman Emperor, Katharine's nephew, whose troops had already sacked Rome once, taking Clement prisoner, and threatened to do it again.) When Henry divorced Katharine in defiance

(a)

(b)

FIG. 16-4   (a) Henry VIII, portrait by Hans Holbein the Younger (1540). (b) Elizabeth I bestriding the map of England, portrait by Marcus Gheerhaerts (1592).

of the church, the pope excommunicated him, and the king retaliated in 1534 with the Act of Supremacy, which made the king the head of the Church of England.

This act of treason against the church hierarchy polarized English opinion (to put it as mildly as possible) and had to be enforced by violence. The author of *Utopia*, Sir Thomas More, who had served Henry as Lord Chancellor of the realm, was the most notorious victim: he was imprisoned and beheaded in 1535 for his principled refusal to recognize Henry's religious authority and was canonized by the Roman Catholic Church as a martyr on the four hundredth anniversary of his execution. The English monasteries, loyal to the traditional church, were forcibly dissolved beginning in 1540.

Musical repercussions were inevitable — and decisive. They were not quite immediate, however. Henry himself was an enthusiastic music lover. He played the organ, lute, and virginals (a small harpsichord-like instrument), and even composed in a modest way; thirty-four small compositions attributed to him survive, all but one in a single manuscript. The inventory of his property at his death in 1547 listed a fabulous instrumentarium for the use of his "waits" (household musicians): 56 keyboard instruments, nineteen bowed strings, 31 plucked strings, and upwards of 240 wind instruments of all descriptions.[15] He took great pride in the virtuosity of his chapel choir (as we know from the amazed reaction of an Italian diplomat, quoted in the previous chapter). We have already had occasion to admire the music that choir performed (see the works of Cornysh, Henry's own court composer, and Taverner, quoted in Exx. 13-6 and 15-8). The activities of this choir did not cease when the Church of Rome gave way to the Church of England, nor did the performance of the Latin liturgy. Except for its repudiation of the pope's authority, the newly established national church did not at first differ much, doctrinally or liturgically, from the "universal" one.

It was during the reign of Henry's son, Edward VI, who became king at the age of nine and died six years later, that the Church of England began to show real signs of doctrinal Protestantism. Henry's loyal Archbishop of Canterbury, Thomas Cranmer, now asserted his own half-Lutheran, half-Calvinist objections to the Catholic liturgy, chief among them being his widely shared antagonism toward the idolatrous worship of the Virgin Mary, the very aspect of Catholic worship that, as we know, had produced some of the greatest glories of fifteenth- and sixteenth-century polyphony, and especially in England. It was at Cranmer's instigation, in conjunction with Henry's suppression of the monasteries, that the notorious search-and-destroy missions against books of "Popish ditties" — particularly Marian votive antiphons — took place, thanks to which so little early English polyphony survives. Under Edward, organs were destroyed as well; English organ-building did not resume until the seventeenth century.

Cranmer also shared the hostility of many Catholic churchmen toward the impious overelaboration of polyphonic music at the expense of the holy word, no doubt sharing Erasmus's sarcastic view that the attention of English monks was entirely taken up with music. He collaborated with a zealously anti-Catholic composer named John Merbecke (d. ca. 1585) on a new English liturgy, with texts translated into the vernacular and with strict limits placed on the style of the music. The Anglican ideal was an ascetic polyphonic style more radically stripped down than anything ever imagined by the Council of Trent. "Anglican chant" consists of chordal harmonizations of traditional chant, but a traditional chant that had itself been rigorously purged of all melismas.

Cranmer and Merbecke's first strike against the so-called Sarum (or Salisbury Cathedral) rite, the gorgeous Catholic repertoire of the English church that Henry took such delight in showing off, came in 1544, with a book of stripped-down litanies in English. This was truly drab stuff, and Henry wouldn't buy it. Under Henry's weak successor, the real development and stabilization of the Anglican liturgy got under way.

The first collection of metrical psalms in English appeared in 1548, but no music attended it. The need for new music became urgent that same year, though, when Edward VI, or rather Cranmer acting in the boy-king's name, issued an injunction finally abolishing the Sarum rite. English choirs, the statute read, "shall from henceforth sing or say no Anthems of our lady or other saints but only of our lord, and them not in Latin but choosing out the best and most sounding to Christian religion they shall turn the same into English setting thereunto a plain and distinct note, for every syllable one."[16]

In 1549, Cranmer published the first *Book of Common Prayer*, a comprehensive translation of the liturgy. It was accompanied by the Act of Uniformity, making its use mandatory, and consequently making the celebration of the traditional Latin Mass a

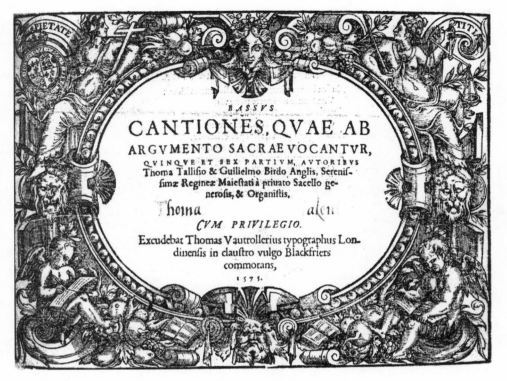

FIG. 16-5   Title page of *Cantiones*, published by Thomas Tallis and William Byrd in 1575.

criminal act, grounds for persecution. Merbecke finally followed up in 1550 with *The Booke of Common Praier Noted*, providing the only legal liturgical music for the Church of England. These publications, while quickly superseded, set the tone for the Anglican musical reform.

Not that a style founded on "plain and distinct note, for every syllable one" necessarily precluded good music, or even masterworks. Consider the hymn *O nata lux de lumine* as set by Thomas Tallis (1505–85), the greatest composer in England after the death of Taverner, who was organist at the chapel royal all through the period of reform (Ex. 16-15). Though fantastically adept at the most grandiose and intricate polyphonic designs — he celebrated the fortieth birthday of Queen Elizabeth I with a truly elephantine motet, *Spem in alium*, for forty independent voice parts deployed in eight five-part choirs! — Tallis also developed a sideline in Reformation austerity that he continued to cultivate even after the height of stringency had passed.

O nata lux, published in 1575 but (to judge by its archaic original notation) composed a good deal earlier, fulfills every condition set forth in the Edwardian statute of 1548 save that of language (no longer insisted upon by the 1570s). Yet it remains one of Tallis's most impressive works for the subtlety of rhythm and (particularly) harmony with which he was able to compensate the absence of contrapuntal interest. Let this hymn, rather than one by Merbecke or another equally gifted, represent the officially approved music of the Anglican reformation. It shows as clearly as the *Missa Papae Marcelli* that coercion can be met with creative imaginativeness, and that artists can find opportunity in constraint.

EX. 16-15 Thomas Tallis, *O nata lux de lumine*, mm. 1–9

O Light of light, by love inclined,
Jesu, redeemer of mankind,
With loving-kindness deign to hear
From suppliant voices praise and prayer.

The music of the Anglican church did not develop in any more smooth or orderly a fashion than did the church itself. After Edward things took a dialectical turn, to put it a little euphemistically. The boy-king was succeeded by his half-sister, Mary I ("Bloody Mary"), Henry VIII's daughter by Katharine of Aragon. She was a loyal Catholic and undid the whole reform except for the confiscation of monastic property. What was

FIG. 16-6 "Persecutions Carried Out against Catholics by Protestant Calvinists in England," sixteenth century.

instituted through violence had to be suppressed through violence. Cranmer was burned at the stake. Protestantism again became an illegal heresy. Mary died in 1558 after a reign even shorter than Edward's, but one that brought the country to the brink of a religious civil war.

It was in this atmosphere that Mary's half-sister Elizabeth I ascended the throne. She achieved a compromise—a synthesis, so to speak, known as the Elizabethan Settlement—between the antithetical religious factions, that by letting English politics simmer down allowed the nation's economy to surge, its international prestige to bloom, and the arts to flourish. One of her first decisions was to reinstitute the Acts of Supremacy and Uniformity, but with far less anti-Catholic doctrinal and liturgical zealotry. "Mariolatry" and "popish ditties" were no longer actively persecuted, and the Book of Common Prayer was actually translated, for the use of colleges, into Latin (as *Liber Precum publicarum*). While the Catholic Church remained legally abolished, recusants were not to be subject to legal reprisal, at least for a while.

Gradually, however, tolerance of recusants was withdrawn, and penal measures against them reinstituted, following numerous rebellious plots and attempts on the childless Elizabeth's life that would have placed Mary Stuart (Mary Queen of Scots), a loyal Catholic, on the throne. Pope Pius V and his successor Gregory XIII (both of them major patrons of Palestrina) also did their best to destabilize Elizabeth, the former by formally (and superfluously) excommunicating her in 1570; and the latter by authorizing a clandestine army of English Jesuit missionaries, who began to infiltrate the British isles from their base, the English college at Douai in the north of France, beginning in 1580. This gave rise to new reprisals, including grisly public executions. Matters reached a head (so to speak) with the decapitation of Mary Stuart herself in 1587, after which life could be easily as dangerous for Catholics in England as it had been under Edward.

THE FIRST ENGLISH COSMOPOLITE

The religious predicaments of the Elizabethan period and its steadily eroding religious "settlement" were epitomized in the recusant William Byrd's long career as the country's foremost musician, a career that spanned virtually the whole of Elizabeth's reign. At the beginning, Elizabeth's tolerance of ritualism within the Church of England made it possible for a high art of Latin polyphony to flourish again. Yet it was a changed art nevertheless. It had been affected—one might even say contaminated—by continental styles, and proudly so. Byrd was the great protagonist of this change, which in the face of English withdrawal from the universal church might seem a bit paradoxical. Yet it reflected in its particular domain the same heightened cultural commerce with continental Europe that distinguished the Elizabethan age generally.

Henry VIII had begun importing continental musicians for his personal entourage as early as 1520. One of them, Philip van Wilder, a Fleming brought over as a "lewter" (lutenist), was a particularly gifted composer. His lovely *Pater noster* for high voices (Ex. 16-16), though published in Antwerp in 1554 (a year after the composer's death), was probably composed for the "young mynstrells" at Henry's court, a boys' ensemble in Philip's charge. It counts as one of the earliest *ars perfecta* compositions to be written on English soil.

EX. 16-16   Philip van Wilder, *Pater noster*, beginning

EX. 16-16 (*continued*)

Another famous émigré was Alfonso Ferrabosco (1543–88), a Bolognese composer whom Elizabeth hired in 1562. According to a Venetian intelligence report a dozen years later, Alfonso had become "one of the grooms of the Queen's privy chamber, [who] enjoys extreme favour with her Majesty on account of his being an excellent musician."[17] Royal favor meant royal protection, which could be a critical matter for Catholics like Alfonso—and like Byrd, who was able to hold high official positions, at least for a while, without converting to the new faith (although he did furnish it with some excellent music, including a Great Service for "Evensong," the Anglican Vespers-plus-Compline).

Even later, though cited for recusancy, and perhaps fined (and although at least one recusant was actually arrested for owning one of Byrd's late books), he was never greatly troubled by the law—although, as we shall see, he gave good cause for trouble—because Elizabeth did not think it impossible for her favorites (such as the Earl of Worcester, one of Byrd's patrons) to be "a stiff papist and a good subject."[18] Despotisms have arbitrary beneficiaries as well as victims.

Alfonso's impact on the new English church music was particularly pronounced, as Byrd's first important publication makes clear. This was a volume of motets called

Cantiones ab fual argumento sacras vocantur, which Byrd published jointly with his mentor (and possible teacher) Tallis in 1575, five years after his appointment as organist to the royal chapel. (Tallis's "O nata lux," quoted in Ex. 16-15, comes from this book.) Amazingly enough, it was the first book of Latin-texted music ever printed in England, and Tallis and Byrd were themselves literally the publishers, having been granted a patent from the queen giving them a monopoly on English music-printing and staved manuscript paper.

Dedicated (naturally) to Elizabeth (and, it follows, probably used in her chapel), the volume opens with a series of prefatory and dedicatory poems that positively trumpet rapprochement between the musicians of England—formerly insular and print-shy but now aggressively modern and entrepreneurial—and the great names of ecumenical Europe: Gombert, Clemens, even the relative newcomer Orlando (de Lassus; see the next chapter), and their ambassador, as it were, to the English, "Alfonso, our Phoenix."[19] What the poem proclaims the music confirms. Joseph Kerman, who took the trouble to go through the work of Alfonso Ferrabosco for the first time since the sixteenth century, was able to establish that William Byrd owed his virtuosity in the techniques of the *ars perfecta*—a virtuosity the older Tallis never quite achieved—directly to the example of Alfonso, his Bolognese contemporary and companion in the royal service. The works of Byrd that show Ferrabosco's impress most faithfully, moreover, were precisely the ones he chose for his debut appearance in print.[20] The Italianate motets in the 1575 *Cantiones*, most of which have liturgical texts (though of course not Marian ones) and were clearly meant for official service use, assert Byrd's claim as a contender on the ecumenical stage.

As his career went on, however, he had less and less opportunity to play the role of official church composer in the *ars perfecta* style. There was obviously no room for a Palestrina in England. There was no chance to make one's reputation composing Masses, and the range of suitable texts for motets was stringently circumscribed by the narrow limits of Catholic-Anglican overlap (mainly psalms). A composer like Byrd was thus confronted with a choice. One could shift one's career focus over to the Anglican sphere altogether, which (given Byrd's connections) would by no means have required personal conversion, but would have entailed renunciation of the calling for which one had trained—and renunciation, too, perhaps, of a sense of personal authenticity. Or one could renounce the official arena and withdraw into the closet world of recusancy.

As life became more difficult for Catholics in England, Byrd took the latter course. He and Palestrina were comparably devoted to the universal church, but where Palestrina's devotion brought him worldly fame and fortune, Byrd's meant the virtual relinquishment of his career. In contrast to Palestrina, Byrd's pursuit of the *ars perfecta*, while it arguably brought the style to its climax of perfection, ran entirely counter to the composer's worldly self-interest. There is not another case like it in the history of Western church music, which, through Byrd, reached a stylistic climax on an agonizing note of personal sacrifice and risk.

Withdrawal took place in stages. In 1589 and 1591, Byrd published two volumes of *Cantiones sacrae*, the first dedicated to the Earl of Worcester. These were motets of a very different sort from the ones in the book of 1575. Their texts, no longer liturgical, were biblical pastiches, mostly of intensely plaintive or penitential character:

O Domine, adjuva me ("Deliver me, O Lord"), *Tristitia et anxietas* ("Sorrow and distress"), *Infelix ego* ("Unhappy am I"). Others, with texts lamenting the destruction of Jerusalem and the Babylonian captivity, easily support allegorical readings that may covertly have expressed and solaced the sentiments of the oppressed Catholic minority. One in particular — *Circumspice, Jerusalem* — has been linked persuasively with the arrival from France of a party of Jesuit missionaries with whom Byrd is known to have consorted: "Look around toward the East, O Jerusalem," the text proclaims, "and see the joy that is coming to you from God! Behold, your sons are coming, whom you sent away and dispersed!" These pastiche motets, it is now widely believed, were never meant for service use, but rather provided (under cover of the irreproachable source of their individual verses) a body of "pious chamber music," as Kerman has called it, for the use of recusants at home.

THE MUSIC OF DEFIANCE

The final stage was devoted to the setting of forbidden liturgical texts, coinciding with Byrd's effective retirement, at the age of fifty, from the royal chapel and his removal to a country home, where he joined a recusant community headed by a noble family named Petre. It was for this community and others like it, evidently, that his late work was intended. From 1593 to 1595, Byrd issued three settings of the Mass Ordinary, one a year, respectively for four, for three, and for five voice parts. This, finally, was music that could only be sung behind closed doors. The first Mass Ordinary settings ever printed in England, they were issued without title pages (but as Kerman observes, "Byrd's name was coolly entered as author at the top of every page").[21]

In 1605 and 1607, Byrd followed up with two ambitious volumes of Propers, called *Gradualia*. In them, he supplied England's clandestine Catholics with a comprehensive body of gorgeously wrought but modestly scaled polyphonic music for their whole liturgical year — a veritable Magnus Liber, to recall the first such attempt, at Notre Dame de Paris, as long before Byrd's time as he is before ours. More immediately, Byrd was following in the footsteps of Henricus Isaac who about a hundred years earlier had received a commission from the Swiss diocese of Constance to set the whole Graduale to polyphonic music, and responded with three big books called *Choralis Constantinus*; they were finally published between 1550 and 1555, long after Isaac's death in 1517, in an edition by his pupil Ludwig Senfl, who put the finishing touches on the last items.

Isaac's settings, based on Gregorian chants as advertised by the title of his book, used the cantus-firmus and paraphrase techniques of his time. Byrd's settings, employing no traditional melodies, were (like his Ordinaries) the concise and tightly woven epitome of a half-century's striving after imitative perfection. (Between 1586 and 1591, another Proper omnibus, the *Opus musicum* by the flamboyant Austrian Catholic composer Jakob Handl, containing a record-breaking 445 motets in an ostentatious variety of styles, many of them avant-garde for the time, was published in Prague.)

Byrd's preface to the Gradualia contains one of the most eloquent humanistic descriptions of musical rhetoric ever penned. Sacred words, he wrote, have an *abstrusa et recondita vix* (translatable as "a cryptic and mysterious power"). Yet what Byrd affected to attribute to the words, however, was really the power of his own musical inspiration. "As I have learned by trial," he continued, "the most suitable of all musical ideas occur as of themselves (I know not how) to one thinking upon things divine and earnestly and diligently pondering them, and suggest themselves spontaneously to the mind that is not indolent and inert."²² One pictures the composer walking about, pen in hand, mulling and muttering the words he is to set, deriving his musical ideas from their sound as uttered in his own earnest voice, and weaving the polyphonic texture out of motives so acquired. It is the consummate balance of distinctive personal enunciation and lucid formal design that is so affecting in Byrd's last works. His way of shaping musical motives — so closely modeled on the precious, threatened Latin words — into contrapuntal structures of such dazzling technical finish at once sums up the whole notion of the *ars perfecta* and raises it one final, matchless and unprecedented notch.

In the case of the Masses, the works are literally without precedent. The tradition of Mass composition in England was decisively broken by the Reformation. Nor were the grandiose festal Masses of Taverner and his generation — implying a secure institutional backing and leisurely confidence in execution — suitable models for Masses that would be sung by undercover congregations in rural lofts and barns, using whatever vocal forces the congregation itself could muster up. Nor is there any indication that much continental Mass music — unprintable stuff in England — could have come Byrd's way. This was a wheel that he would have to reinvent.

He did it on the basis of his own motet-writing experience, in which he had worked out a very personal synthesis of *ars perfecta* imitation and rhetorical homophony. Byrd's Masses are in effect extended, multipartite "freestyle" motets of this kind, affording a whole new way of approaching the text, a manner unprecedented on the continent where composers wrote their Masses by the dozen. Byrd was one composer — the one Catholic composer, as Kerman has remarked — who did not take that text for granted, but who set it with unexampled and unparalleled awareness of its semantic content: a very idiosyncratic awareness, in fact, as befitted his plight and that of his community.²³

The only continental Mass, as it happens, that is in any significant way comparable to Byrd's settings is the *Missa Papae Marcelli*, where Palestrina had also, if for very different reasons, adopted a cell- or module-oriented technique of composing, playing imitation off against homorhythm. Since the most revealing comparisons are those that discover difference in a context defined by similarity, it will repay us to concentrate on the same two sections from Byrd as we did from Palestrina: the Credo and the Agnus Dei (Ex. 16-17). And the first difference we discover is that where Palestrina had segregated the two techniques (systematic imitation, declamatory homorhythm), Byrd integrates them with singular terseness and word-responsiveness.

The contrast shows up particularly in the Agnus Dei, where the one by the official Catholic was contrapuntally rich and calmly imposing, the ones by the closeted Catholic (besides being leaner, not necessarily by choice) are rhetorically complex and restlessly significative. "Restlessly," because the rhetoric and the signification of the setting changes radically, as Kerman has keenly observed, from Mass to Mass. To make the comparison finer yet, then, let us contrast Byrd with Byrd as well as Byrd with Palestrina.

MUSICAL HERMENEUTICS

The Mass in Four Parts, the earliest of the settings, was composed almost immediately after Byrd's second volume of protest-motets was issued, and retains something of their tortured mood. The mode—transposed Dorian, but with a specified E-flat that "Aeolianizes" it into something more nearly resembling plain G minor—contributes to the mood, of course; but more potent by far is the astonishing degree of dissonance, which grates most where it is least expected, in the Agnus Dei, a text outwardly concerned with gentleness, deliverance from sin, and peace.

Byrd's setting, unlike practically any continental setting, is one continuous piece, not a triptych. The three invocations of the Lamb, all strictly if concisely imitative in texture, are nevertheless distinguished from one another by the progressive enrichment of their "scoring": the first for a duo, the second for a trio, and the last, with its new words (*dona nobis pacem*, "grant us peace") for the full complement. It is when those very words are reached, amazingly, that the voices begin rotating in a stretto based on a syncope, and the dissonance level—a suspension on every beat, emphasizing the sharpest discords (major seventh, minor second, minor ninth)—begins to approach the threshold of pain. The music (Ex. 16-17) is unprecedented both in its sheer sensuous effect and in its exceptional rhetorical complexity.

EX. 16-17   William Byrd, Mass in Four Parts, Agnus Dei, mm. 40–56

EX. 16-17 (*continued*)

There is irony in it, to be sure. One is surely meant to sense a contradiction between the meaning of the word "peace" and the extreme tension of Byrd's discords. But move up from the level of literal meaning to that of implication, and the apparent irony is trumped by a naked truth: they only beg for peace who have no peace. Once one has thought of this, one can hardly view this Agnus Dei as anything other than a portrait of the artist as recusant—or, more appropriately perhaps, a portrait of the general mood that reigned where such a Mass as this was sung.

The Mass in Five Parts, the last of the settings, displays a very different "reading" of the same text, yet one just as complex and profound. Again there is a rhetorical progression of harmonic density that gives shape to the threefold petition, from three parts to four to the full five. The first acclamation uses harmonic color to distinguish Christ's metaphorical name ("Lamb of God") from the actual prayer. By first withholding, then reintroducing the B-flat, Byrd reminds us that the flat has, ever since Guido of Arezzo, been a "softening" device. The harmonic softening on *miserere* can only refer to the act of mercy itself, rather than the petition. The emphasis, therefore, is not on what is lacking (as in the Mass in Four Parts) but on what is given. That emphasis is maintained to the end.

In the second acclamation, like a magician, Byrd makes the conflict of *B-durus* and *B-molle* express the same idea by reversing roles. By transposing the cadence from F to G, where the B-flat darkens the tonic harmony and the B-natural brightens it, Byrd again makes the point that the Lamb of God will not fail its pious petitioners. The third acclamation (Ex. 16-18) is again something different. The whole choir gathers itself up for a pair of sudden homorhythmic outbursts—literal "calls" to the Lamb of a kind no other composer had thought to make. Again we are reminded of the plight of the persecuted. But this time the leisurely *dona nobis pacem* comes as a relief, and expression of confidence, of faith.

EX. 16-18   William Byrd, Mass in Five Parts, Agnus Dei, mm. 33–42

The kind of detailed interpretive analysis these descriptions of Byrd's Agnus Dei settings have attempted is what literary scholars call hermeneutics. Byrd's is the earliest music—certainly the earliest Mass Ordinary music—to have called forth such interpretations from modern critics, because his Masses and his alone seem to offer true interpretive readings of their texts. These are the kinds of readings "official" settings like Palestrina's do not encourage, precisely because they are official. That is, precisely because they are official they take meaning as something vested and given rather than as something that arises out of a human situation. Byrd's Masses, precisely because they are written out of a very extreme human situation, open up new levels of musical meaningfulness. It goes without saying (but better, perhaps, with saying) that the only meaningfulness we can speak of meaningfully is the meaningfulness the music has for us now. But that meaning includes our impressions (impressions conditioned by specific historical awareness) of what meaningfulness the music may have had for Byrd and his co-congregants.

The Credo from the Mass in Five Parts also invites hermeneutic reading, and such reading is of course to be recommended as an exercise in "historical imagination." Here let it suffice to call attention to one particular phrase, since it resonates so strongly with the premises on which this chapter is based. At the beginning of the chapter, when justifying the pursuit of the *ars perfecta* to its end, it was pointed out that the "perfect art" would have had no reason for being were it not for the artist's belief in the perfection of God's church as an institution: belief *in unam sanctam catholicam et apostolicam ecclesiam.*

Compare Palestrina's setting of these works in the Credo of the *Missa Papae Marcelli* (Ex. 16-19a) with Byrd's (Ex. 16-19b). Palestrina sets them gracefully but somewhat perfunctorily as a double module — a parallel period in five parts, the basses exchanging at the repeat. The line is both preceded and (especially) followed by more dramatic music. The "confiteor," the personal acknowledgment of one's baptism, that comes after the lines about the church is set off by longer note values and a higher high note. The *et unam sanctam* passage, one feels, was something on the way to something bigger. At any rate, Palestrina's very evenly paced recitation is clearly the work of a man for whom this text is a comforting ritual formula, not a risky personal declaration.

EX. 16-19A Giovanni Pierluigi da Palestrina, *Missa Papae Marcelli*, Credo, mm. 145 – 53

EX. 16-19A *(continued)*

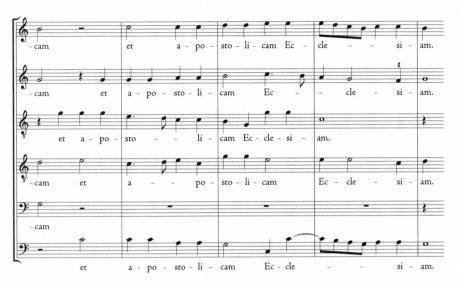

EX. 16-19B William Byrd, Mass in Five Parts, Credo, mm. 157–68

Byrd's setting of the line begins with a violent chordal tutti that disrupts a pair of elegant polyphonic trios, and continues in agitated homorhythmic declamation replete with a near-bombastic repetition of the words *apostolicam ecclesiam*—"a church *sent by God*" (not instituted by a king!)—that sends the passage to its melodic peak. After this shriek of Catholic defiance, the concluding Amen, entirely set apart from the rest by a cadence and a fermata, comes across as no mere ending formula but as a genuine intensifier, the very essence of affirmation. The whole history of the English Reformation and the plight of the recusants seems to be contained in this Credo as in a musical microcosm. At the very least, for Byrd these words were just what they were not (because they did not need to be) for Palestrina: a personal, rather than an institutional, Credo; a profession of dangerous personal faith.

THE PEAK (AND LIMIT) OF STYLISTIC REFINEMENT

Passages from two pithy motets in Byrd's *Gradualia*, one from each book, show the ultimate degree of refinement not just of Byrd's art but of the whole art of Catholic church polyphony. *Ave verum corpus*, the sacramentary hymn for the feast of Corpus Christi, is probably the best known piece from these late books, possibly Byrd's best known sacred work outside of the Masses. Partly because its text is a hymn, and partly because of the way (reminiscent of the ending of Josquin's *Ave Maria*) it addresses Christ using the first person singular, it is one of Byrd's most unwaveringly chordal settings. Not only that, the motet is virtually without conventional dissonance; even cadential suspensions are often avoided. At the same time the harmony is famously wayward and, by implication, discordant. Why the seeming contradiction between the stark simplicity of the texture and the fractious harmonic ambience? As usual, the answer is to be sought in the domain of rhetoric.

The subject of the motet is one of the great marvels of Christian dogma: the transubstantiation of the Communion Host into the body of Christ. We have already seen Palestrina using unusual harmonies to delineate a *magnum mysterium*; but where Palestrina uses a chromaticism that arises out of a speeded-up sequence of ordinary fifth-relations, Byrd exploits with special expressive intensity a harmonic usage that, while not unknown in continental music, was cultivated with special gusto by English composers and is for all practical purposes an English trait.

That special feature is called the "false (or cross) relation"; it consists in the immediate juxtaposition or brief simultaneous occurrence in two voices of a diatonic scale degree and its chromatic inflection (often pitting the major vs. the minor third in a triad). Successive cross relations pervade the motet; simultaneous cross relation occurs at the moment of prayer, *miserere mei* (Ex. 16-20), in which the bass's F rubs directly against F♯, the sustained chord third in the tenor, creating a dissonance to add urgency to the words addressed to God.

For a last look at Byrd, and at the *ars perfecta*, we can focus on *Non vos relinquam*, the Vespers antiphon to the Magnificat for the feast of Pentecost, known in England as Whitsunday. The Pentecost liturgy, being the climax of the jubilant post-Easter season known as Paschal Time, resounds throughout with the word "Alleluia," the emblem of

EX. 16-20   William Byrd, *Ave verum corpus*, mm. 36–43

exaltation. That was another word Byrd never took for granted, but clothed in countless specially expressive guises. Here he throws in an extra "Alleluia" of his own to rebound against the first word of the liturgical text in what was known as a "double point": a complex of two motives that unfold in perpetual (and perpetually varied) counterpoint (Ex. 16-21). It was something he had inherited from Ferrabosco (who had inherited it from the Continent), but which Byrd took to a new level of suppleness and concision.

The remaining ejaculations on "Alleluia," for each of which Byrd invented a new motive and wove a new point, are liturgical. In his setting they punctuate a texture that has become so interpenetrated with imitative cells and little homorhythmic blasts as to make the task of unraveling them a wholly pointless and thankless exercise. This is the ultimate—the farthest point the *ars perfecta* reached before it gave way to new *stili moderni* or froze into the mummified state known as the *stile antico*. Byrd, who lived until 1623, was the very last composer for whom the *ars perfecta* was not a *stile antico* but a living style to sustain the best imaginings of the greatest musical minds.

Our comparative survey of Palestrina and Byrd at the latest extremity of the *ars perfecta* has shown nothing if not the extraordinary versatility that pliant medium had achieved over the century of its growth since the humanist embrace of Josquin. Why was it abandoned? It is not enough simply to invoke progress (at best) or change (at least) as the general, inevitable condition of human history. One must try to account for

EX. 16-21 William Byrd, *Non vos relinquam* (*Gradualia*, Book II)

I will not leave you orphans,
alleluia:

changes, especially changes as fundamental as this one, in specific terms, as responses to specific pressures.

In the three chapters that follow, three such pressures will be identified and described in turn. There was the joint pressure of the new markets opened up by printing for secular music, and of the literary movements that influenced the ways in which secular poetry was set. There was the pressure, already a haunting presence in the last two chapters, of religious unrest. And there was the pressure of what might be called "radical humanism," the true Renaissance idea, which (paradoxically in the light of conventional style-periodization and its attendant labels) actually brought about the loss of faith in "Renaissance" styles and ideas, leading to their disintegration and the birth of the "Baroque."

None of these pressures accomplished their evolutionary work suddenly. To account for each of them it will be necessary once again to step back in time and renarrate the story of sixteenth-century music from a new perspective. Breaking down a complex story of change into several perspectives is admittedly an artificial analytical technique, and one not normally available to those who actually live through the change in question.

Therein lies both the advantage and the disadvantage of retrospect. We can perform our dissection, if we are lucky, to our satisfaction, and persuade ourselves that we understand the change better than those who experienced it. But they are the ones who felt (or resisted) its necessity, suffered the losses, and rejoiced in the gains. Our understanding is rationalized, articulate, and imaginary; theirs was immediate, real, but inarticulate. The reconciliation of the two, as well as the resynthesis of all the different stories our analytical perspectives entail, must take place in the reader's mind.

Commercial and Literary Music

Vernacular Song Genres in Italy, Germany, and France; Lasso's Cosmopolitan Career

MUSIC PRINTERS AND THEIR AUDIENCE

Alongside the Masses, motets and instrumentalized chansons for which Ottaviano Petrucci is best remembered, the enterprising Venetian printer also
issued Italian songbooks for the local trade. That trade was exceedingly brisk.
The first such book, *Frottole libro primo*, came out in 1504, the fourth year of Petrucci's
business activity. It was his seventh publication. A scant decade later, in 1514, Petrucci
issued his eleventh Italian songbook, in addition to two volumes of *laude*, Italian
part-songs of a similar style but with sacred texts, and two volumes of previously
published songs arranged for a single voice with lute accompaniment.

The fifteen volumes described thus far, each containing about fifty or sixty songs,
accounted for more than half of the printer's total output as of 1514. Four books were
issued in the year 1505 alone, and by 1508 three of the four had sold out and been
reissued. When Petrucci's first competitor, the Roman printer Andrea Antico, set up
operations in 1510, his cautious maiden outing was yet another book of Italian songs.
Canzoni nove, it was called: "New songs." But most of them were not new. They were
pirated from Petrucci, whose copyright was good only in Venice. Clearly we are dealing
with a craze that was created by the music printing business and that in turn sustained it.
It was the first great instance in the history of European music of commodification: the
turning of artworks, through mass reproduction, into tangible articles of trade — items
that could be bought, stockpiled, and sold for profit.

Although books of Latin church music and Franco-Flemish court music were
Petrucci's and Antico's prestige items, the humble vernacular songs were their moneymakers. The same held true in every other country to which music printing, and
with it the music business, spread. The first music book printed in Germany, by the
Augsburg printer Erhard Öglin, was a prestige item: Latin odes by Horace set by a
humanist schoolmaster, Peter Treybenreif (alias Petrus Tritonius), to illustrate the
classical meters. The moneymakers began appearing a little later with part books issued
by Öglin (1512), Peter Schöffer in Mainz (1513), and Arnt von Aich (Arnt of Aachen)
in Cologne (1519), all with flowery sales puffs in place of titles.

Arnt von Aich's title page, for example, says *In dissem Buechlyn fynt man LXXV.*
hubscher Lieder myt Discant. Alt. Bas. und Tenor. lustick zu syngen ("In this little book you

will find seventy-five pretty songs with superius, altus, bass and tenor [parts] to sing for fun"). The first musical incunabulum to appear in England (London, 1530) was similar. A gorgeously appointed effort in the Petrucci style, its title page read, "In this boke ar conteynd. XX. songes. ix. of iiii. partes, and xi. of thre partes" (twenty partsongs, nine for four voices, and eleven for three). It contained vernacular settings by many of the famous composers of Henry VIII's chapel royal (Cornysh, Taverner, etc.) but it survives, alas, only in fragments.

In France, music printing got under way when Pierre Attaingnant set up shop in Paris in the mid-1520s and secured for himself a royal patent or monopoly (a necessary protection for such a risky undertaking). His first book was a breviary, a book of Mass texts, issued in 1526. His first music publication followed two years later: *Chansons nouvelles en musique*, "New Songs with Music," imprinted 1527 but actually issued in 1528. That same year he issued five more sets of part books, averaging thirty songs apiece, and one set of dance music, plus one volume of motets. That would remain Attaingnant's effective ratio between the universal sacred and the local secular repertory for the duration of his career as printer, which lasted until 1557.

Attaingnant was more than a printer, and had an impact on the music trade that far exceeded his activities as publisher. For he was the inventor of a new laborsaving and cost-cutting method for music typography that swept Europe in the 1530s and completely transformed the business, making real mass production and high-volume distribution possible. The method employed by Petrucci and the other early Italians had required a triple impression. A page was fed to the presses once for the staves, again for the notes, and yet again for the titles and texts. The result was stunning, and Petrucci's early books were never surpassed as models of printerly art, but the process wasted time and was overly exacting: a great deal of spoilage took place due to "misregistration" (failure of the impressions to line up exactly with one another).

FIG. 17-1   Above: Specimens of Pierre Attaingnant's movable music type (Plantin-Moretus Museum, Antwerp). Opposite: Superius part from Claudin de Sermisy's *Tant que vivray*, in *Chansons musicales, esleus de plusieurs livres par ci-divant imprimés, les tous dans un seul livre . . . réimprimées par P. Attaignant* [sic], *imprimeur et libraire de musicque* (Paris, 1536). The typically wordy title translates as "Songs with Music, Chosen from Several Books Printed by the Above-Named, All in One Book Reprinted by P. Attaingnant, Printer and Seller of Musical Books."

Attaingnant's method was much more like alphabetic typography. Every possible note- and rest-shape was cast along with a short vertical fragment of the staff on a single piece of type. When these were placed in a row by the compositor like bits of letter type and printed, the staff-lines joined together, or nearly so. The result was far less elegant than Petrucci's, but so much more practical and economical that the older typographical method could not stand a chance against the new. Attaingnant's method remained standard as long as typography was the print medium of choice for music — until the eighteenth century, that is, when copperplate engraving came into widespread use.

Who bought the early printers's wares? Petrucci's early volumes, with their cumbersome production methods and handsome appearance, were luxury items. We know some-

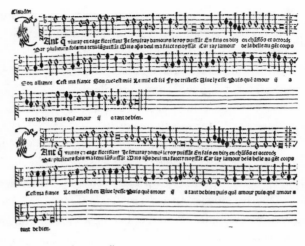

FIG. 17-1 (continued)

thing about their prices because of the meticulous purchase records kept by Ferdinand Columbus, the explorer's son and one of the great early bibliophiles. (His collection, more or less intact, became the basis of the famous Biblioteca Colombina in Seville, Spain.) No musician, Columbus nevertheless acquired several Petrucci items on a buying expedition to Rome in 1512; and in the words of Daniel Heartz, whose study of Attaingnant remains virtually the only investigation of early music printing from the consumption as well as the production standpoint, "for the price of any one of them he might have acquired several literary works of equivalent size."[1]

Thus the practical utility of the early Petrucci volumes was at least matched, and probably exceeded, by their value as "collectibles," items of conspicuous consumption — and in this they did not differ appreciably from the twelfth- to fifteenth-century presentation manuscripts of polyphonic music with which we are familiar. The very fact that Petrucci's volumes, particularly of court and church music, survive today in greater quantities than those of his eventual competitors shows that their primary destination was not the music stand but the library shelf.

The trend, however, was toward economy and utility, which is why Attaingnant was so successful. Even before the Paris printer revolutionized the trade, Antico experimented in Rome with smaller, less decorative formats, single woodblock impressions, and (consequently) lower prices, to meet the needs "especially of students of music," as he stated in his application for a permit. He managed to undersell Petrucci by more than fifty percent, forced down the price level of the whole industry, and eventually squeezed Petrucci, the immortal founder, out of the music trade altogether.

Few surviving music books testify to their household use, partly because such use itself led to deterioration: Heartz, lamenting the large number of lost Attaingnant prints, has rather pessimistically suggested that, as a rule, "an inverse ratio exists between the popularity of music prints and their chance of survival." Nevertheless, we know from literary accounts that household entertainment — both aristocratic and bourgeois, both as provided by professional entertainers and by convivial amateurs — was the chief use to which vernacular songbooks were put, increasingly so as the sixteenth century wore on and printed music became less a bibliophile's novelty or prestige purchase and more a normal household item.

Diaries, prefaces, and treatises make reference to the ritual of passing out part books at social functions or around the table after meals. The ability to sing at sight and play an instrument increasingly became a vital social grace on a par with dancing. Self-tutors, like the *Plaine and Easie Introduction to Practicall Musicke* (London, 1597) by Thomas Morley, the musician-entrepreneur who inherited William Byrd's monopoly on the British music trade, were a favorite sales item in and of themselves — the sixteenth century's popular and commercial answer, so to speak, to the learned theoretical treatise of old.

Morley's book opens with a preface in the form of a dialogue in which one gentleman confides to another his social embarrassment when "supper being ended and the music books (according to the custom) being brought to the table, the mistress of the house presented me with a part earnestly requesting me to sing; but when, after many excuses, I protested unfeignedly that I could not, every one began to wonder; yea, some whispered to others demanding how I was brought up."[2] Conversation manuals, etiquette books in which upwardly mobile burghers were trained in the manners of genteel society, often contained model dialogues to teach their readers how to take part in such a musical party: how in polite company, each member with a part book in hand, one inquires who is taking which part, who begins the song, on what pitch, and so on (for an example from a Flemish etiquette book of around 1540, see Weiss and Taruskin, *Music in the Western World*, pp. 151–153).

Finally, one of the main consequences of the music trade and its commodifying practices was that music traveled faster, farther, and in greater volume than before. Particularly was this true of Attaingnant's aggressively marketed editions and those of his competitors in Paris and Lyons, the other main French publishing center, who did a booming international business, particularly in northern Italy. As we shall see, this ease of travel led to some surprising hybrid styles and genres.

VERNACULAR SONG GENRES: ITALY

And what were the songs like that the early printers printed, the early collectors collected, and the early consumers consumed? They differed markedly, like their languages, from country to country, in contrast to the sacred lingua franca of the ars perfecta. At first they all reflected the earlier courtly fixed forms in their poetry, but their novel musical textures reflected the new conditions of trade.

The Italian part-song or *frottola* as published by Petrucci in the early years of the century was a lightweight affair; the name was derived from the Latin *frocta*, meaning a motley group of trifling objects. A whiff of that slightly pejorative nuance clung to the genre. The best translation of frottola might be "a trifling song." Formally speaking, it was very much like the last Italian vernacular genre we encountered, several chapters back, in the late years of the fourteenth century. That was the *ballata*, the "dance song," which (like the French virelai) consisted of a number of strophic ballade-like stanzas (aab) and a *ripresa* or refrain with music corresponding to the "b" of the stanza. As noted in chapter 4, a representation of the form that truly reflected its structure would be B aab B, but since convention requires that the first letter in any representation of a formal scheme be an A, the scheme usually given is A bba A.

With the *frottola* — or, to be a little more precise, the *barzelletta* (possibly named after the French *bergerette*), the most popular refrain form of several — the scheme is actually a little simpler, since the refrain now takes in all the music of the stanza. Thus the *barzelletta* can be straightforwardly represented as AB aab AB, which begins to look a little like the old French rondeau. If it helps, then, one could think of the barzelletta as a modified ballata or a hybrid virelai/rondeau. As that old-fashioned pedigree attests, of all sixteenth-century vernacular genres the frottola was the most aristocratic. As a sample, Ex. 17-1 contains a barzelletta from Petrucci's seventh book of frottole (1507).

EX. 17-1   Marco Cara, *Mal un muta per effecto*

EX. 17-1 *(continued)*

The suave but simple music of this song was the work of Marco Cara (d. ca. 1525), one of the two leading frottolists employed at the smallish court of Mantua in the north-central Italian area known as Lombardy. The mistress of that court was the duchess Isabella d'Este, the daughter of Ercole I of Ferrara, famous in music history as the patron whose name Josquin des Prez turned into a Mass tenor (see Ex. 14-3). Isabella, who probably would have hired famous Flemings if she could have afforded them, instead became the patroness who oversaw—through Cara and his colleague Bartolomeo Tromboncino ("the little guy with the trombone")—the rebirth of Italian song as a literate tradition.

Everything about Cara's song, however, bespeaks its origin in oral practice. And that is the answer to the famous question posed by the apparent gap between the late fourteenth-century ballata, obsolete by 1430, and the early sixteenth-century frottola. What happened to the fifteenth century, the *quattrocento*, when Italian music seemed to disappear? The answer is that the frottola *was* a quattrocento genre that for want of prestige and noble patronage had not managed to establish itself as a literate one. The sudden explosion of frottola writing was just that: an explosion of *writing* (or writing down), stimulated by the printing trade, not a sudden or unprecedented explosion of creativity.

Oral genres, as we have long since learned, are formulaic genres. The attractively lilting or dancelike rhythms in Cara's frottola are all stock formulas, common to dozens of barzellette, that were originally devised for the musical recitation of poetry in the so-called *ottonario*, a popular eight-syllable trochaic pattern favored by Italian court poets and musicians. The original rhyme scheme of the ottonario verse (somewhat modified in Cara's song) is abab/bcca; the music supplies three phrases—a, b, and c (plus a decorative flourish for the end of the refrain)—keyed to the specific requirements of the rhyme scheme. Each line or pair of lines takes the musical formula corresponding to its place in the rhyme scheme; and each formula ends with a cadence, made emphatic by a pitch-repetition on the last trochee. The cadences thus create a pattern of open and closed phrases that works tonally to define and project the poem's formal scheme.

Such formulas were "popular" both in the sense that they were widely used and enjoyed and in the sense that, compared with the lofty poetry of the *trecento*, they represented in their obvious and jingly rhythms a debased poetic tone — even an "antiliterary" one, as their leading American historian, James Haar, has put it.[3]

A musical composition like the one in Ex. 17-1, then, was not so much a song as a kind of matrix for song-making; a melodic/harmonic mold into which countless poems could be poured. The song as it appears in print is a sort of transcription from life: a snapshot of an improvisation, or of a pattern abstracted from countless improvisations. The "improvisatory hypothesis" is strengthened by the inclusion in several Petrucci frottola prints of textless *aere* or *modi* — "arias" or "ways," recitation formulas for declaiming poems in various meters (see Ex. 17-2 for the "way of singing sonnets" as given textlessly in Petrucci's fourth book) — and by the inclusion of what the publisher called *giustiniane*: lavishly ornamented "Giustinian songs," named after Leonardo Giustiniani or Giustinian (1383–1446), a Venetian courtier who was famous for extemporizing florid impromptu arias to his own accompaniment on the *lira da braccio* or "arm-held lyre," a sort of bowed lute much favored by humanists for its pseudoclassical associations. Again the impression is that of a model for decorative singing, a style of improvisation that could be learned from such examples and applied to other songs — indeed, to any song.

The appearance of Cara's songs in Petrucci's book as four-part polyphonic settings in correct if rudimentary counterpoint might seem to contradict the improvisatory hypothesis. Anything is possible with practice, of course, but improvisation is generally a soloist's domain. Closer inspection of Ex. 17-1 lessens the apparent contradiction. Only the cantus part is texted. The other parts do not always have enough notes to accommodate the words, particularly at cadences. Now there is no reason to think that singers could not easily have adapted the lower parts to the words for a fully texted vocal rendition; but that does not seem to have been the primary medium for these songs. Rather, putting them in part books was just the most versatile or adaptable or presentable (or — perhaps more to the point — saleable) way of marketing them.

FIG. 17-2   Poetry recitation to the accompaniment of a lira da braccio: woodcut from Luigi Pulci's epic *Morgante maggiore* (Florence, ca. 1500).

As to the primary medium, connect these facts. Petrucci issued three books of frottole arranged by a lutenist named Franciscus Bossinensis ("Francis from Bosnia") *con tenori et bassi tabulati et con soprani in canto figurato*, "with the tenors and basses written in lute tablature and the sopranos in staff notation." One of the primary tasks for which the *Regola rubertina*, Silvestrodi Ganassi's mid-century viol treatise, trained its readers was that of reducing notated part-songs to solo songs with instrumental accompaniment. Especially pertinent: in several contemporary writings, including Baldesar Castiglione's famous *Book of the Courtier*, Marchetto Cara is described as a renowned "singer to the lute"[4] — that is, a self-accompanied vocal soloist, if not an improviser.

The conclusion is virtually inescapable that frottole were originally and primarily solo songs for virtuoso singers to lute or other instrumental accompaniment; that

EX. 17-2   "Modo di cantar sonetti" from Ottaviano Petrucci, *Strambotti, ode, frottole, sonetti. Et modo de cantar versi latini e capituli. Libro quarto* (1505)

Bossinensis, far from arranging Cara's and Tromboncino's part-songs for a secondary medium, was in fact returning them from a printer's all-purpose adaptation to their original medium for the benefit of amateurs—parvenus who could not "intabulate" by ear or at sight like professionals (or true aristocrats); and that this soloistic mode of performance was a standard option throughout the century. (From which it will follow that the "monodic revolution" of the early seventeenth century that, as we shall soon see, ushered in the "Baroque era" was no revolution at all, and that "Baroque" singing styles—"improvised" ornaments and all—were perfectly familiar and available to "Renaissance" musicians.)

The frottola was the first literate musical genre since the fourteenth century to be produced by Italians for Italians. Its style was so different from that of the *oltremontani*, the northerners (from "over the mountains") in Italy who furnished the wealthier Italian courts and churches with polyphonic music, that one senses a deliberate opposition of taste, one that was maintained all through the *quattrocento* when, as Haar has observed, "one expected the polyphonists to be *oltremontani*, the improvisatory music makers to be Italian."[5] Only in the sixteenth century did crossovers begin to occur. The Italian pupils of Willaert and others of their generation eventually took over the *ars perfecta* genres, as we have seen. Crossover in the opposite direction was much rarer. The very act of converting the frottola repertory into a written repertory like that of the *oltremontani* could of course be viewed as a crossover phenomenon; but frottole actually composed by *oltremontani* were veritable hen's teeth.

It is quite revealing of some stubborn biases of music historiography that these hen's teeth—especially the two items out of the six hundred or so in Petrucci's collections that bear the name of "Josquin Dascanio"—are now the most famous representatives of the genre. And very unrepresentative representatives they are! This is especially true of the one frottola that every "early music" enthusiast is likely to know: *El Grillo* ("The cricket"), from Petrucci's third book (1504), of which the refrain is given in Ex. 17-3.

Josquin Dascanio, if re-spelled with an apostrophe after the "D," translates as "Ascanio's Josquin"—in other words, Josquin des Prez during his period of service to Ascanio Sforza, the bishop of Milan. It would be too much to say that *El Grillo* would never have become famous were it not for the brand name it bore; it is a delightfully amusing composition and deserves its popularity. And yet the fact remains that it was not singled out for popularity in its own day. It is found only in the one source from which it is quoted here, whereas many other frottole and related items (including the other Josquin Dascanio number printed by Petrucci, a Latin-refrained but otherwise Italian lauda called *In te Domine speravi*) were copied and recopied dozens of times.

And the fact also remains that the piece shows Josquin Dascanio to have been very much of an outsider where the frottola was concerned, perhaps even a little "unclear on the concept." Cara's song (Ex. 17-1), a typical frottola, is basically an elegant medium for the poem. It does not compete with the words, so to speak, in rendering their meaning. It is not, to recall Haar's useful distinction, a "literary" song. Josquin's setting is literary through and through. It was probably meant as a carnival song, to be sung in costume, and with appropriate (not overly decorous) gestures.

The music corresponds in clear (and clearly intentional) ways with the semantics of the text: *chi tiene longo verso* ("he holds out his verses long") is illustrated by literally holding out the verse long; the hockets and the patter on *dale, beve grillo, canta* ("go on, cricket, drink and sing") is so clearly meant as a literal imitation of the cricket's actual "chirping" (or leg-rubbing) that we get the point even though the imitation is far from literal or even in any way accurate. Such "imitations of nature" are delightfully

EX. 17-3 "Josquin Dascanio," *El Grillo*, mm. 1–21

amusing. It will be well to keep in mind, though, when we come shortly to a later Italian repertory that relied heavily on "musico-literary" imitations and illustrations, that no matter how seriously they may be intended, such things operate, as they do in Josquin's clever nonsense song, on mechanisms of wit — the drawing of unexpected or unlikely correspondences — and are basically a form of humor.

GERMANY: THE *TENORLIED*

The German counterpart to the frottola, as purveyed in the printed songbooks that appeared in Germany from 1507 (making that country chronologically the second to take up the music trade), is now known as the *Tenorlied*. That is the modern scholarly term for what contemporary musicians called a *Kernweise* (roughly, "core tune"): a polyphonic setting of a *Liedweise*, a familiar song-melody, placed usually in the tenor — or else a song that resembled a *Liedweise* setting in texture. In other words, it was a cantus-firmus setting of a lyrical melody, either traditional or newly composed, in what by the early sixteenth century would have been considered in other countries a fairly dated style.

That is no surprise. We know that Germany took up the monophonic courtly song a bit later than its western and southern neighbors. The earliest German composer of polyphonic courtly songs, the latter-day Minnesinger Oswald von Wolkenstein (see chapter 4), had been dead for little more than half a century when the print revolution transformed German music; the earliest German printed songs merely continued the process he had fairly recently initiated of adopting courtly love lyrics to the polyphonic literate tradition. Again we may observe that there is no uniform march of styles, and that styles arise and decline in particular historical and social contexts.

The Tenorlied makes its earliest appearance in the form of folksong settings in manuscripts from the second half of the fifteenth century, beginning around 1460. The earliest such manuscript, the source of the three earliest identifiable Tenorlieder, was called the Lochamer Liederbuch and came from Nuremberg in the south of Germany. The biggest source of early *Liedweisen* settings is the vast miscellany called the Glogauer Liederbuch from around 1480, familiar to us as the earliest surviving set of part books, which came from the German far east.

By the print period Tenorlieder were more often newly composed songs than settings of traditional *Liedweisen*. The one printed in Ex. 17-4 comes from Peter Schöffer's first *Liederbuch* ("Mainz," 1513), the third set of printed part books to see the light in Germany. Its very curious history recommends it for inclusion in a history book like this, rather than one, say, on a more famous tune or by a more famous composer. The shapely, stately tune is evidently a *Hofweise*, a newly composed melody in a courtly, vaguely Minnesingerish style. About the composer, Jörg Schönfelder, all that is known is that he *may* have been a member of the court chapel choir in Stuttgart (since other songs in the same book are by known members of that choir).

Peter Schöffer did not include any attributions in his original print. (The authorship of its contents, where known, was determined by comparison with other sources.) Therefore, when the young Johannes Brahms came upon the book in the early 1860s (when on the lookout, as a struggling choir director in Vienna, for "a

EX. 17-4   Jörg Schönfelder, *Von edler Art* (1513)

cappella" material that would not require the hiring of any extra musicians) he mistook its contents for folk songs, then the object of a craze in romantic-nationalist Europe. Struck by the stately beauty of Schönfelder's melody, he made it the first item in a collection of *Deutsche Volkslieder*, German folk songs for mixed chorus dedicated to his Vienna choir and published in 1864 (Ex. 17-5). Brahms placed the tune where tunes

EX. 17-5 Johannes Brahms, *Von edler Art* (1864), mm. 1–10

went in the nineteenth century (that is, on top), and considerably enriched the harmony and the contrapuntal texture, but the melody is Schönfelder's exactly, precluding the possibility that the tune was in fact a folk song in oral circulation rather than an old *Hofweise* that Brahms found in its actual printed source.

Brahms was a canny arranger and a very knowing one; as we will see later, he was a true connoisseur of old music and a virtuoso contrapuntist, perhaps the most history-obsessed composer of the whole history-obsessed century in which he lived. The technique he employed at the beginning of his arrangement of Schönfelder's tune — that of prefiguring the tune's first entry with preliminary imitations (*Vorimitationen* in German scholarly jargon) at the octave and the fifth — was one he picked up from the actual practice of sixteenth-century composers, especially Ludwig Sennfl.

Sennfl, whom we already know as the author of a magnificent tribute to Josquin des Prez, was the great master of the Tenorlied. He kept the German music presses rolling, publishing more than 250 such songs by the time of his death in 1543. In keeping with the side of him that we have already observed, Sennfl strove to bring this peculiarly German genre into the international mainstream of music as he knew it, which really meant reconciling it with the style and technique of Josquin, the "universal" paragon. He wrote Tenorlieder that subjected familiar tunes to bizarrely inventive manipulation, the way Flemish composers treated Mass tenors: by canon, by inversion, in quodlibets ("whatnots," name-that-tune medleys or contrapuntal combinations), in contrasting modes, whatever. Even when not showing off, Sennfl fashioned his Tenorlieder with a "Netherlandish" finesse, and that ultimately meant integrating the texture.

Nowhere is this more the case than in *Lust hab ich ghabt zuer Musica* (Ex. 17-6), Sennfl's clever autobiography in song. It is all about his apprenticeship at the court of the Holy Roman Emperor with Henricus (by then known as Heinrich) Isaac, second only to Josquin as international Flemish star; and the music actively demonstrates the fruits of Sennfl's learning as described in the text. The text is a tour de force in its own right. The initials of its twelve stanzas are an acrostic of the composer's name. (It is from this acrostic that we know he spelled his name "Sennfl," rather than "Senfl," as given in most sources of his work and in most modern reference books.) The tune, plainly a newly invented *Hofweise*, is cast in the retrospective ballad or "Bar" form of the Minnesingers, with its repeated opening phrase (all that our limited space allows Ex. 17-6 to display). But the opening of the song obviously apes the *ars perfecta* motet with an elaborate point of "Vorimitation," in which the actual entrance of the tune sounds at first like just one voice out of four.

The tune itself is a little odd, a little contrived. It literally turns the Palestrina ideal of recovered motion on its head, what with its funny downward skip of a fifth after a step, outlining a major sixth that must then be laboriously recovered by stepwise ascent. A systematic stepwise ascent of a sixth, of course, is the old Guidonian hexachord. And sure enough, Sennfl pitches his entries so that they alternately count off the notes of the "soft" hexachord on F and the natural one on C. And then, when the *Stollen* or opening phrase is repeated, we see the reason for the odd contrivance: the poem spells out the actual *voces* of the hexachord — ut, re, mi, fa, sol, la — each syllable assigned to the proper note. A "literary" device if ever there was one, it nevertheless could only have occurred (or appealed) to a practical musician. But it's just a little joke, and Sennfl apparently did not mind that on all the subsequent stanzas of his song, the rising scale is detached from its textual referent and no longer has any illustrative role to play. The fast descending scales in the accompanying parts, some of which are in the

EX. 17-6   Ludwig Sennfl, *Lust hab ich ghabt zuer Musica*, mm. 1–15

Long have I loved music: from the time I was a boy till now. Starting with the simplest do-re-mi, going on to further study,

Trans. Lawrence Rosenwald

same hexachord positions as the thematic ascending scales, also stop being illustrative after the first stanza, becoming instead one of many superb craftsmanly touches in the consummately worked-out texture.

THE "PARISIAN" CHANSON

During the fifteenth century, the word "chanson" connoted an international courtly style, an aristocratic lingua franca. A French song in a fixed form might be written anywhere in Europe, by a composer of any nationality whether at home or abroad. The French chanson was thus nearly as ecumenical or "travelable" a style within its rarefied social domain as the Latin motet. In addition to the examples given in previous chapters (Du Fay in Italy, Binchois in Burgundy, Isaac in Austria, Josquin everywhere), one could add the names of two English composers, Robert Morton and Walter Frye, both of whom wrote French rondeaux in the purest "Burgundian" style (although only Morton is known to have actually worked on the continent).

The age of printing brought a change: a new style of French chanson that was actually and distinctively French the way the frottola was Italian and the *Hofweise* setting German. Its centers were the printing capitals: Paris to the north and Lyons to the south, with Paris (through Attaingnant) sufficiently out in front that the genre is generally known as the "Parisian" chanson. Its great master was Claudin de Sermisy (ca. 1490–1562), who served King Francis (François) I as music director of the Chapel Royal and furnished the voracious presses of Attaingnant with dozens of chansons for publication as household music.

Attaingnant's very first songbook, the *Chansons nouvelles en musique* of 1528, opens with a run of eight songs by Claudin (as his pieces were signed), plus another nine scattered later in the volume for a total of seventeen, more than half the total contents. The second item in the collection, Claudin's *Tant que vivray* (Ex. 17-7) to a text by Francis I's court poet Clément Marot, has always been *the* textbook example of the new chanson for the sake of its memorable, very strongly harmonized tune.

EX. 17-7   Claudin de Sermisy, *Tant que vivray*, mm. 1–16

EX. 17-7 (continued)

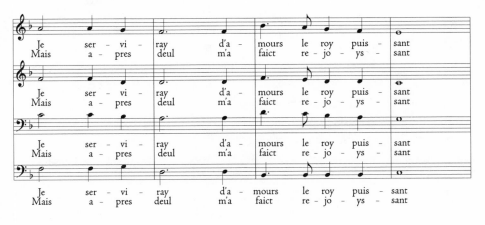

As long as I am able bodied,
I shall serve the potent king of love
through deeds, words, songs, and harmonies.
Many times he made me languish,
but after mourning, he let me rejoice,
because I have the love of the fair lady with the lovely body.

Her alliance
is my betrothal.
Her heart is mine,
mine is hers.

The interesting historical question is where this sudden new style could have come from. It did not rise up like the frottola from subterranean improvisatory depths; it wasn't there all along in oral tradition, so far as we can tell. It really was a new invention. Hypotheses about its origins include the impact of Italian musicians who were welcomed at the French court following King Francis's conquest of Milan in 1515 (this would reinstate the frottola as a stimulus on the chanson). Another guess is that court musicians, possibly spurred by the King's taste, began to copy the style of urban popular music (this would give the chanson an oral ancestry after all). A third conjecture is that the print market and the chance to make a quick profit caused musicians to lower their sights: this could be called the sell-out theory.

These theories, while they all allude to factors that may have had a bearing on the situation and are hence all plausible in some degree, are nevertheless completely speculative and somewhat circular. That is, they are inferences drawn not from any evidence of the processes they describe, but from the nature of the perceived result, the Parisian chanson itself. And they are all subject to refutation in some degree. For one thing, the later history of sixteenth-century secular music (as we shall see) suggests that by the 1530s Italian musicians were learning as much from the French as the other way around. For another, no composer seems to have gotten rich during the sixteenth century on the basis of publication, printers generally paying authors in kind, in printed copies rather than in cash.

The main generative influence on the new chanson style may not have been musical at all; it may well have been the newly humanistic poetic idiom of Marot and his contemporaries that spurred the musicians. Claudin's chanson clothes the syllabification of its poem in a musical scansion that seems as strict and formulaic as those we observed in the frottola. As Howard Mayer Brown, an important historian of the genre, has noted, "some chanson melodies are virtually isorhythmic, so closely do they fit the patterned repetitive rhythms of the poetry."[6] This sharp observation tends not so much to confirm the direct influence of the frottola on the chanson as it confirms the more general notion that national musical styles arose out of vernacular poetic idioms, in this case the *chanson rustique*.

The opening long–short–short rhythm seems to suggest a dactylic meter, and its ubiquitous presence at the beginnings of chansons has even misled some commentators into assuming that chanson verse was largely made up of dactyls. But it is not a dactyl, and the reason why it became so conventional is worth a small digression. For one thing, the initial "pseudodactyl" became an identifying tag, a sort of trademark that identified the Parisian chanson and (more to the point) some later derivations from it. And for another, it offers a stunning illustration of how from the very beginning of the "music business," the business side of music affected the artistic side.

Instead of a dactyl, the tag in question is just a three-syllable pickup that has been distended so that the piece need not begin with a rest. In a scoreless notation without bars, upbeats could not be indicated in relation to what followed; they could only be indentified as "off the beat" by preceding them with a rest. Example 17-8a shows an alternative, "undistended" version of the pickup, notated the only way it could have been at the time. The reason why such a rhythm was considered undesirable at the beginning of a piece had nothing to do with any "purely musical" consideration. It was a purely practical matter having to do with the way in which music was packaged for sale.

People singing a chanson together sang from printed part books, each of which contained only a single line. The social consequences of that drab little fact are illustrated in the Flemish etiquette manual mentioned above, which gives a model polite conversation for domestic music-making:

> Rombout: Give me the bass part.
> Antoni: I'll do the tenor.
> Dierick: Who'll sing alto?
> Ysaias: I, I'll sing it!
> Dierick: Who begins?
> Ysaias: No, not I. I've a four-beat rest.
> Antoni: And I one of six.
> Ysaias: Well then, you come in after me?
> Antoni: So it seems. It's up to you then, Rombout![7]

If a piece began with a rest in all parts, the answer to the preliminary question, "Who begins?" would be a chorus similar to that elicited by the Little Red Hen (not I... not I... not I). To avoid confusion and wasted time, then, all the parts began at the beginning. Everyone could "be first." Even pieces that began with points of imitation had to be similarly adjusted if published in part books. In Ex. 17-8b, the opening point from a motet by Clemens non Papa (published in part books by Susato of Antwerp in 1553) is laid out in score. The motif on which the point is based is a syncopated idea. The first voice in, however, begins at the beginning, the first note being extended back, as it were, to remove the rest (and with it, the syncopation) just so that there would be someone to answer the question, "Who begins?"

EX. 17-8A   Hypothetical beginning for *Tant que vivray*

MUSIC AS DESCRIPTION

A new sort of "literary music" — or rather a possibly unwitting revival of an old sort — came into being when Attaingnant, still in his first year of publishing activity, brought out a slim volume devoted to the works of a single composer. The title page read *Chansons de maistre Clement Janequin*, and it contained only five items. Those five, however, took up as much space as fifteen had occupied in Attaingnant's first collection. Four of them became famous and vastly influential all over Europe, and (most amazingly of all) remained in print for almost a century.

The composer, Clément Janequin (ca. 1485–1558), was a provincial priest from Bordeaux in the south of France, who never held a major appointment either at a large cathedral or at court. Despite his clerical calling, he was almost exclusively a chanson specialist: he wrote two Masses (both of them based parody-fashion on chansons of his that had become popular) and a single book of motets, but more than 250 chansons, many of them broadly humorous or racy or downright

EX. 17-8B   Clemens non Papa, beginning of motet *Musica dei donum*

Music, gift of the most benevolent God . . .

lewd. When thinking of Janequin it is hard not to recall his near-exact contemporary, François Rabelais, the novel-writing monk whose name became synonymous with gross drollery. It was Janequin who gave the "Rabelaisian" mood its musical embodiment.

The four big chansons of 1528 define the Rabelaisian genre. Broad they certainly are, in more ways than one. Where the average length of a "Parisian," semi-courtly chanson like *Tant que vivray* is thirty to forty measures (counting the breve or "tempus" as a measure), the longest item in the 1528 book, divided into two "partes" as if it were a motet, totals a whopping 234 measures, six times the normal length. What could be the text of such a monster chanson? Here is where things get even curiouser, because if "text" is taken to mean something meaningful written in French words, then these colossal pieces have hardly any text at all.

In the original publication of 1528 the contents are listed the normal way, by incipits (first lines). Nine years later, the volume was reissued in a deluxe "quarto" edition with double-sized pages, and with each item most unusually given a title, so popular had they become. The first (excerpted in Ex. 17-9), called *La guerre* ("The war") is the 234-measure monster. It commemorates the battle of Marignano, the Milanese conquest of 1515, and its text, once past the opening salute ("Hear ye, gentlemen of France, of our noble King François") consists almost entirely of battle sounds: guns and cannon-fire, bugles, war whoops, laments for the fallen. (It must have been written a good deal earlier than its publication date, since by 1528 Francis had been defeated, captured, ransomed, and forced to give up all his Italian territorial claims.)

The second item, *La chasse*, is a hunting piece full of horn calls and barking dogs. We know (as Janequin possibly did not) that such pieces, written in the form of canons both in France (where they were called *chace*) and Italy (where they were called *caccia*) were a popular genre close to two centuries before. The fourth item in the Janequin chanson book, called *L'alouette* ("The lark"), begins with the line "Or sus, vous dormez trop" ("Get up, you sleepyhead"), which we encountered in another fourteenth-century genre, the "birdsong virelai." But there is nothing in the fourteenth century to compare for sheer ornithological frenzy with Janequin's third item, *Le chant des oyseux* ("The song of the birds"), a huge composition in which another refrain about lovers awakening alternates with five different birdsong collages.

These orgies of onomatopoeia, sheer imaginative play on a par with Rabelais's hilarious lists, amount at times to long stretches of what might best be described as pure texture. The beginning of the second part of *La guerre* (quaintly listed in 1528 by its incipit, "Fan Frere le le lan fan"), which depicts the height of battle, holds a single chord for a veritable eternity (Ex. 17-9). The singers have nothing resembling a tune to sing, and nothing resembling words to say, just a concatenation of lingual sound effects—a virtuoso turn for performer and composer alike. As befits such a stunning tour de force, it inspired emulation on a grand scale, beginning with Philippe Verdelot, a Flemish composer active in Italy, who at the request of the publisher

Susato skillfully added a fifth voice to the piece to augment its already loaded textures and, no doubt, promote sales. Janequin liked Verdelot's added voice well enough to include it in his own revised edition of the work, and that is how it is presented in Ex. 17-9.

EX. 17-9 Clément Janequin, *La guerre*, a 5, with Verdelot's extra voice (secunda pars, mm. 1–6)

To call a piece like Janequin's *La guerre* "literary" is to interpret the word a little loosely. It would make no sense to say that such a work "expresses" its text. (How do you express "fan frere le le lan fan"?) Rather, the text and the music work together to evoke the sounds (and not only the sounds) of the world at large, and in so doing point outside the work in a way that the music of *Tant que vivray* had no business or interest in doing. But construing the word more strictly, in terms of the relationship between the music and the text, Janequin's onomatopoetic chansons are not literary. The music is still basically a medium for the recitation of the text; the two components still touch mainly on the phonological (or declamational) level, not the semantic one. Onomatopoeia is presentation, not representation. It has no semantics.

LASSO: THE COSMOPOLITE SUPREME

Real literary music—indeed a virtual literary revolution in music—is looming up on our horizon, but before immersing ourselves in it and becoming absorbed in its consequences, there is a loose end to tie up. "Loose end" hardly does justice to a composer thought by many of his contemporaries to be the most brilliant musician alive, but Orlando di Lasso is a blessedly unclassifiable figure who sits uncomfortably in any slot. It was his unparalleled versatility, the very quality that makes him retrospectively a loose end, that made him such a paragon in his day.

One of the last of the great peripatetic Netherlanders, Lasso was born in Mons, now an industrial town in southern (French-speaking) Belgium, in 1532. His baptismal name was Roland de Lassus, but by the age of twelve he was already a professional chorister in the service of the Duke of Mantua, where he adopted the Italian name by which he was and remains best known. By the 1570s he was the most famous com-

FIG. 17-3   Orlando di Lasso at age sixty-seven, an engraving published in 1599.

poser in Europe, hailed by the French poet Pierre de Ronsard as "the more than divine Orlando, who like a bee has sipped all the most beautiful flowers of the ancients and moreover seems alone to have stolen the harmony of the heavens to delight us with it on earth, surpassing the ancients and making himself the unique wonder of our time."[8] From a humanist there could scarcely be any higher praise.

From 1556 until his death in 1594 (the same year as Palestrina's), Lasso served faithfully as court and chapel musician to the Dukes of Bavaria in Munich. Thus he was born a French speaker, was educated in Italy, and reached his creative maturity in Germany, making him the very model of the cosmopolitan musician of his age. But whereas the earlier cosmopolitan ideal — the ideal of the *ars perfecta*, brought to its peak by Palestrina — had been ecumenical (that is, reflective of religious universalism and hence nation-transcending), Lassus was brought up in the age of music-printing and was an eager and ambitious child of the burgeoning age of worldly music-commerce. Thus his brand of cosmopolitanism was not ecumenical but polyglot. He and Palestrina were complementary figures, and in many respects incommensurable ones; between them they summed up the contradictory ideals and leanings of a musical world in transition.

Lasso's appointments were secular, though they did entail the writing of huge quantities of service music, and his allegiance was always a dual one: to his patrons (with whom he was on terms of unprecedented familiarity and from whom he actually received a patent of nobility in his own right), and to his many publishers. During his lifetime a staggering seventy-nine printed volumes of his music (and only his music) were issued, a total that leaves his nearest competitors in a cloud of dust; and his work was included in forty miscellaneous publications as well. Lasso volumes continued to

FIG. 17-4 Concert at the Bavarian court chapel directed by Orlando di Lasso from the keyboard (frontispiece by the Bavarian court painter Hans Mielich to a manuscript now in the Bavarian State Library, Munich).

be issued posthumously all over Europe — Graz, Munich, Paris, Antwerp — until 1619. His output covered every viable sacred and secular genre of continental Europe: Masses (almost all of them parody settings), motets (including many full calendrical cycles in various genres), and vernacular settings in all the languages he spoke. His work has never been published in its entirety; his sons tried to issue his entire backlog after his death but gave up in despair. Nobody knows exactly how much music Lasso wrote, but his published works, including those published only in modern times, number more than two thousand items.

From this vast assortment any selection at all would be invidious and unrepresentative. So without undue hand-wringing we will limit ourselves to what was most representative of the age rather than the man. We will get our most vivid quick impression of Lasso's special character if we forgo his magnificent legacy of Catholic church music (where, after all, he had competitors and counterparts) and sample the full range of his secular work, which was unique, choosing a single piece in each of four languages. Each of them, moreover, illustrates this cagey chameleon-composer's bent for witty mixtures and juxtapositions of styles.

Je l'ayme bien (Ex. 17-10) is from Lasso's very first publication, a miscellany called *D'Orlando di Lassus il primo libro dovesi contengono madrigali, vilanesche, canzoni francesi e motetti a quattro voci* ("The First Book by Orlando di Lasso, containing madrigals, vilanescas, French chansons, and motets for four voices") published in Antwerp by Susato in 1555, when the composer was 23 years old. The Parisian chanson style, by then a quarter century old, has been elegantly reconciled to the *ars perfecta* in Lasso's setting, in which a striking melody that might have prompted an exquisite harmonization from Claudin is given an elaborate imitative exposition, which supplies the exquisite harmonies all the same.

Matona (i.e., "Madonna") *mia cara* (Ex. 17-11), informally known as "the lansquenet's serenade," was printed rather late in Lasso's career, in a 1581 volume of "low style"

Italian songs (*Libro de villanelle, moresche, et altre canzoni*) published in Paris. It is thought, however, to date from an earlier period, perhaps Lasso's earliest, when he accompanied his first employer, Ferrante Gonzaga of Mantua, on expeditions throughout Italy. *Lansquenets* were Swiss or German lance-bearing mercenaries (soldiers of fortune) who enlisted as infantrymen in foreign parts. The word itself is a jocular French corruption of *Landsknecht*, German for "trooper" or "foot soldier". There was also an Italian variant, *lanzichenecco*, and Italian armies such as Ferrante's were full of them.

EX. 17-10   Orlando di Lasso, *Je l'ayme bien*

I love him very much and will love him always.

There could be no better emblem of Lasso's inveterate cosmopolitanism than this silly Italian song, written by a Fleming in imitation of a clumsy German suitor who barely speaks his lady's language. The genre to which it belongs, called *villanella* or town song (or to be excruciatingly precise, a *todesca*, meaning a villanella with a ridiculous German accent), was a strophic song with refrains and hence the direct (and deliberately debased) descendant of the frottola or "trifling song" of old. The refrains are usually nonsensical or onomatopoetic; here, it takes the form of the lovesick lansquenet's feeble attempts to serenade his lady on the lute.

EX. 17-11 Orlando di Lasso, *Matona mia cara*

EX. 17-11 (continued)

don, di-ri-di-ri, don, don, don, don, Don, don, don, di-ri-di-ri, don, don, don, don.

don, di-ri-di-ri, don, don, don, don, Don, don, don, di-ri-di-ri, don, don, don, don.

don, di-ri-di-ri, don, don, don, don, don, Don, don, don, di-ri-di-ri, don, don, don, don, don.

don, di-ri-di-ri, don, Don, don, Don, don, don, di-ri-di-ri, don, don, don.

My luffly lady, pleass recivv my zong.
I zing beneat' dye vindow, to vinn you ofer.
Plink, plink, plink . . .

Another jokey piece is the one shown in Ex. 17-12 that begins "Audite nova" ("Hear the news!") in the solemn manner of a Latin motet, but that quickly shifts over to a preposterous tale about a dimwitted farmer ("Der Bawr von Eselskirchen," literally "The farmer from Ass-Church") and his honking goose, the latter rendered musically in the manner we have come by now to expect. The song comes from a volume of miscellaneous items in various languages that Lasso published in Munich in 1573. German songs suffered the most precipitous decline in tone between the heyday of the Tenorlied, about a half- or quarter-century earlier, and the rustic, mock-homespun *Lieder* of Lasso's time, which were really villanelle set to German words. The nobler Tenorlied, as we will see in the next chapter, had gone out of the secular tradition into a new sacred domain.

Finally, as if to atone for representing so imposing and varied an output as Lasso's with fluff (albeit the kind of fluff no one else could have composed), it is time to consider a serious Latin setting. But here, too, there were genres in which Lasso stood virtually alone by virtue of his wit and intellectual elan. One of them was the setting of classical or classicistic texts, the latter being the work of humanist writers in imitation of the classics. His most notorious work in this category was the *Prophetiae Sibyllarum* ("The sibylline

EX. 17-12   Orlando di Lasso, *Audite nova*

Au - di - te _____ no - - - va! _____

Au - di - te no-va, au-di-te, au - di - te no - va!

Au - di - de, au - di - te no - - va!

Au - di - te no - - va!

EX. 17-12 *(continued)*

Audite nova! [Hear the news!]
The farmer from Eselskirchen (Jackass-church),
he has a big fat g-g-goose,
and it has a long, thick, sturdy neck.
Bring the goose here!

prophecies"), published posthumously in 1600 but perhaps written as early as 1560. (They were performed before King Charles IX of France, whom they astonished, in 1571.)

The sibyls, according to one authority, were in antiquity "women who in a state of ecstasy proclaimed coming events, generally unpleasant, spontaneously and without being asked or being connected with any particular oracle site."[9] Over the formative years of Christian religion, the tradition of the sibyls was assimilated to that of biblical prophecy. The sybilline prophecies — originally collected in a book supposedly sold in the sixth century BCE by the Cumaean sibyl, who lived in a cave near Naples, to Tarquin, the last of the legendary kings of Rome — came to be read increasingly as foretelling not natural disasters or the like but the coming of Christ and the Last Judgment. (Hence the reference to the sibyl in the Dies Irae sequence, known to us since chapter 3.)

In the fifteenth century, the number of sibyls was stabilized at twelve, a number full of Christian resonances (the minor prophets, the apostles). The twelve sibyls are best known today from Michelangelo's renderings on the ceiling of the Sistine Chapel. The twelve anonymous prophetic poems Lasso set to music appeared for the first time as a supplement to a 1481 Venetian edition of a treatise on the sibyls as prophets of Christ by Filippo Barbieri, the Inquisitor of Sicily. They were reprinted in Basel, Switzerland, in 1545, and that, presumably, is how they found their way to the composer.

FIG. 17-5   The Cumean sibyl, as rendered by Michelangelo on the ceiling of the Sistine Chapel in Rome.

These venerable quasi-pagan mystical texts as summarized by a Christian classicistic poet obviously demanded some form of unusual musical treatment to render their uncanny enigmatic contents. Drawing on a kind of humanistic musical speculation that was just then rife in Italy (and to which we will return in a couple of chapters), Lasso adopted a style of extreme, tonally disorienting chromaticism (as he proudly proclaims in a three-line poetic prologue of his own contriving), coupled with a starkly homorhythmic, vehemently declamatory manner that brought the weird words and the weirder harmonies very much to the fore. The result is hair-raising, not only as an expression of religious mysticism, but as the revelation (so to speak) of an alternative path for music

EX. 17-13A   Orlando di Lasso, *Prophetiae Sibyllarum*, Prologue

These songs proceed by chromatic progressions.
They tell of how the twelve Sybils,
one after the other, once sang the
hidden mysteries of our salvation.

that challenged the absolute validity of the *ars perfecta*. The two extracts included in Ex. 17-13 are the prologue, with its brash expository sweep by fifth- and third-relations from triadic harmonies on the extreme sharp side (as far as B major) as far flatward as E-flat major; and the end of the Cymmerian sibyl's prophecy, which contains the most radical single progression in the cycle, entailing the direct motion in the altus, on the last line of text, through a diminished third (now how are you supposed to solmize *that*?).

THE LITERARY REVOLUTION AND THE RETURN OF THE MADRIGAL

The extremity of style represented by Lasso's sibyls, while eerily astonishing as befits the subject, is not unintelligible in musical terms, relying as it does on harmonies and progressions that, taken singly, were part of ordinary musical language. (The progressions are not even "chromatic" to any huge extent, as the sixteenth century defined the term, since even where accidentals are involved, the voices usually move by half step from one scale degree to another — the definition of diatonic motion — rather than by inflecting single scale degrees.) It is in the aggregate that they overwhelm. Still, although musically intelligible, such a style is not easily explained on purely musical grounds: that is, it would be hard to account for Lasso's musical decisions or their motivation without taking the text into consideration. Are the motivations then

EX. 17-13B   Orlando di Lasso, *Prophetiae Sibyllarum, Sibylla cimmeria*, mm. 35 – 46

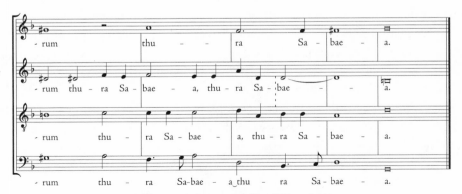

Magi shall bring to the boy myrrh, gold, and Sabean frankincense.

"extra-musical"? Is the result "literary"? Do such motivations or such results make the product artistically impure? And is artistic impurity an artistic vice?

These questions have been debated for centuries, and no matter what we may resolve or agree upon among ourselves, they will go on being debated for centuries, for the question behind all the other questions is a fundamental question of values. The best we can do is to try to understand the various positions that have been taken (including our own, whatever they may be) in their historical context.

In the sixteenth century the contention was between the proponents of the *ars perfecta*, a wholly or autonomously musical style founded on a specific musical history and valued for its universality (which meant its relative indifference to words), and the proponents of stylistic mixture in the name of expression, which implicitly denied universal or autonomous musical values. Many composers, Lasso emphatically included, saw no need to choose between the two principles, but adapted their style according to functional and textual requirements. Partisan positions were more apt to be espoused by theorists and patrons.

Still, even within the relativist camp distinctions and nuances can be observed. Even Lasso's sibylline style was addressed more to the overall character of the text — its supernatural origin, its quality as mysterious utterance — than to the specifics of its semantic content. Indeed, when it came to the mechanics of the word–music relationship, Lasso came down in this case on the side of phonology and rhetorical declamation, just like the chanson composers. If "literary" music means music that embodies or is responsive to semantic meaning, Lasso's sibylline motets do not qualify.

But a great deal of sixteenth-century music did qualify, and it is to that style, and to the movement that supported it, that we now turn. It was a revolutionary movement, and it transformed music fundamentally and irrevocably.

Its first fruits did not look very revolutionary, and the origins of the movement remain unclear. The trend toward literary music, which first involved settings of Italian verse, was long viewed as a slow evolutionary outgrowth of the frottola. More recently, however, it has been proposed that the trend was the product of two other currents — or rather, that it was the product of their confluence, which took place not in the main centers of frottola activity (Mantua for composition, Venice for publication), but in Florence, during the 1520s, when the frottola craze had already begun to subside.[10]

These two currents were (1) the "Petrarchan movement," a literary revival of archaic (fourteenth-century) poetic genres, and (2) the application to settings of Italian texts of styles and techniques previously associated with "northern" polyphony, both sacred (Latin motets) and secular ("Franco-Flemish" chansons).

The influence of the Petrarchan revival is already suggested by the revival of the word *madrigal* to identify the new style of Italian verse setting. There is no musical connection at all between the sixteenth-century madrigal and its *trecento* forebear. The latter had quite died out and been forgotten. It was initially brought back to sixteenth-century consciousness not as a musical genre but as a literary one, a species of pastoral verse discussed with examples in a fourteenth-century manuscript treatise on poetry, the *Summa artis rithimici vulgaris dictaminis* ("Survey of the art of vernacular poetry") by Antonio da Tempo, published as a printed book in 1507.

The influence of "northern" musical idioms on the new genre is betokened by the simple fact that the first sixteenth-century "madrigalists" of note were not Italians but *oltremontani* who like so many of their musical contemporaries had found gainful employment in Italy. It is to the confluence of high old literary ideals with sophisticated imported musical techniques that we owe, in the words of James Haar, the madrigal's leading "revisionist" historian, "the beginnings of a musical vocabulary adequate to meeting the intellectual and emotional demands of the verse."[11]

The protagonists of the literary revolution in its earliest phases were the humanist scholar (and later cardinal) Pietro Bembo (1470–1547), the chief instigator of the Petrarchan revival, and the composers Philippe Verdelot (ca. 1480–ca. 1530), a Frenchman, and Jacques Arcadelt (d. 1568), a Walloon or French-speaking Fleming. Verdelot's first book of madrigals was published in 1533, though he was mainly active in the 1520s and wrote five times as many madrigals as he published. Between 1539 and 1544, Arcadelt published five books of madrigals for four voices and one for three. By the mid-1540s, the madrigal had been established as the dominant musical genre for Italian poetry and retained its supremacy for over a century, albeit with many modifications along the way to accommodate changing styles and social functions. By the end of the sixteenth century, moreover, madrigals were an international craze, both in the sense that Italian madrigals were eagerly imported and performed abroad, and in the sense that they inspired emulations in other countries and other languages, particularly English.

"MADRIGALISM" IN PRACTICE

Bembo's revival of Petrarch was a watershed for Italian poetry and for the reestablishment of the Florentine or Tuscan dialect as a standard literary language. Precociously erudite, the future cardinal published an edition of Petrarch's complete works in 1501, when he was thirty. Four years later, he published a dialogue on courtly love that included a selection of illustrative verses of his own composition in the style of Petrarch, demonstrating what Bembo took to be the great poet's essential devices and themes. The most famous part of the book was the chapter devoted to lovers in conflict, in which the device of antithesis—the immediate confrontation of words, feelings, and ideas with their opposites—was exploited in spectacular fashion. In a later work, *Prose della volgar lingua*, Bembo drew out of Petrarch the idea of an antithesis of styles ("heavy" *vs.* "light") as well. His polar categories—*gravità* (gravity or dignity) and *piacevolezza* (pleasingness or "charm")—were to be realized technically by the mechanics of the verse: phonology or sound-content, rhyme-scheme, meter.

These theories were enormously stimulating to musicians; Bembo's poems, and eventually those of Petrarch himself, became a *locus classicus*—an endlessly returned-to source—for composers of madrigals, who began to specialize in the expression of violent emotional contrasts that could be effectively linked with musical

contrasts—high/low, fast/slow, up/down, consonant/dissonant, major/minor, dia-
tonic/chromatic, homorhythmic/imitative—as bearers (or at least suggesters) of
semantic meaning. Musical tones all by themselves may not possess much in the way
of semantic reference; in other words, they may not *denote* objects or ideas with much
precision. But antithetical relationships between tones and tone-constructs can *connote*
plenty. (We have already seen this, of course, in the predictable "ascendit/descendit"
contrasts in sixteenth-century Mass settings like Palestrina's: this convention may
already have been a "madrigalism," an extension of the "Petrarchian antithesis," first
exploited in madrigals, to another textual realm.)

An ideal starting point for observing the growth of "literary music" through the
madrigal, and its growing antagonism to the impersonal universalism of the *ars perfecta*,
would be *Il bianco e dolce cigno* ("The white delightful swan," Ex. 17-14), the first item
in Arcadelt's first book of madrigals (1539), the most frequently reprinted music book
of the whole sixteenth century (some 53 times, the last in 1642!). It was possibly the
sixteenth century's most famous single piece of art music, surely the one that most
people knew by heart (as they did not and could not know a legendary but rarely heard
work like the *Missa Papae Marcelli*).

Like most madrigal poems, the text of Arcadelt's swan song is *inordinato*, to
use the contemporary word: it consists of a single stanza in lines of varying length,
without refrain or any other obvious formal scheme, and the music does not impose
one either. This is the most dramatic way in which the madrigal differs from the
other vernacular genres of the sixteenth century. Most of the others were in some
sort of fixed form, descended mainly from the ballata: to those already mentioned
one could add the Spanish *villancico*, a dance-descended song that enjoyed a big
burst of polyphonic creativity under Ferdinand and Isabella (whose main court
composer, Juan del Encina, composed upwards of sixty). Even where the poems
were devoid of refrains or strophic repetitions, like many "new style" chansons,
composers were more observant of their forms, and certainly of their meters, than of
their contents.

A madrigalist, by contrast, went after content and its maximal musical representation, and, as time went on, was more and more willing to commit what offended
humanists like Vincenzo Galilei called a "laceramento della poesia"—mangling or
trampling on the form of the poem—in order to get at that content. Composers of
Arcadelt's generation, and especially *oltremontani* like Willaert and (later) Lasso, tended
to recite the poem fairly straightforwardly, aiming at a general mood of gravity or
charm. Their settings are mild compared to what came later. But even Arcadelt's swan
poem is built à la Petrarch around an antithesis (the swan's sad death, the poet's
happy "death" in love), and the composer gives two vivid hints of the particularizing
impulse that would later become such a fetish among madrigalists. Both of them involve
(implicit) antitheses.

The first high-powered affective word, *piangendo* (weeping), receives the first
chromatic harmony (Ex. 17-14a). There is nothing intrinsically weepy about the chord
itself: it is just another major triad. But in context it contrasts with the diatonic norm

and is therefore, like the word with which it coincides, a "marked" feature (to use a modern linguists' term). As to the second hint, there could be nothing more ordinary, or less particularly "expressive," in music of the sixteenth century than a point of imitation (although we should note that points of imitation were not common in Italian secular music before the motet-writing *oltremontani* began putting them in.) Yet Arcadelt's imitative setting of the thrice-repeated last line (Ex. 17-14b), by standing out from the homorhythmic norm, becomes "marked," and therefore illustrative of the sense of the line, which refers to a multiple, repetitive act — and underscores the "charming" double entendre: *lo piccolo morte* ("the little death") was the standard Italian euphemism for the climax of the sexual act.

Because it so privileged the humanistic axiom that music should be the servant of the *oratione*, the sense of the poetry, and therefore "imitate" it, the madrigal became a hotbed of musical radicalism and experimentation. Because of its "literary" premises, it was tolerant of audacities that in any other genre would have been thought blunders or (at the very least) lapses of style. Any effect, however bizarre or however it transgressed the rules demanded by the universal standard of the *ars perfecta*, could be justified on a "literary" basis.

Real crimes against perfection begin to show up in the 1560s, beginning with the madrigals of Cipriano de Rore (1516–1565), the Flemish associate (and pupil?) of

EX. 17-14A Jacques Arcadelt, *Il bianco e dolce cigno*, mm. 1–10

The white and gentle swan
dies singing, and I,
weeping, approach the end of my life.

Willaert. He was unusual among the *oltremontani* for the enthusiasm with which he followed the literary premises of the madrigal into uncharted musical terrain. *Dalle belle contrade d'oriente* ("From the fair regions of the East") comes from Rore's fifth and last book, published posthumously in 1566.

The whole poem consists of one sustained, multileveled antithesis: narrated recollection of physical pleasures at the beginning and the end as against the sudden outpouring of emotional anguish in the middle, expressed in "direct discourse" or actual quoted speech. The multiple contrast is expressed with unprecedented violence in the music. The narrative portions at the two ends are full of delightful descriptive effects:

EX. 17-14B   Jacques Arcadelt, *Il bianco e dolce cigno*, mm. 34–46

I would be content to die a thousand times a day.

the rocking rhythms where the poet speaks of enjoying bliss in his lover's arms ("fruiva in braccio. . . "), the tortuous imitative polyphony where the intertwining of the lovers' limbs is compared with the snaky growth of vines.

Musical descriptions like these, as observed in the previous chapter, usually depend on the uncovering of unsuspected correspondences and are basically humorous no matter what is actually described. That is why the middle section (Ex. 17-15), with its serious content and agonized mood, adopts a wholly different approach to the task of "imitating nature." Here the imitation is no easy matter of analogy or metaphor: what is imitated is the actual speech of

FIG. 17-6   Cipriano de Rore, anonymous portrait in the Kunsthistorisches Museum, Vienna.

the disconsolate lady, replete with sniffles and sobs, especially poignant when, after an unexpected rest representing a sigh, she blurts out her harmonically wayward, syncopated curse upon Eros ("Ahi, crudo Amor"). In keeping with the agonized mood, the soprano part (corresponding in range to the lady's voice) makes a direct "forbidden" progression through a "minor semitone" from C-sharp (as third of an A major triad) to C-natural (as root of a C minor triad). It is a supremely calculated effect, needless to say, but it is fashioned to resemble a spontaneous ejaculation, following an old theory of Aristotle's that, speech being the outward expression of emotion, imitation of speech is tantamount to the direct imitation of emotion.

The direct imitation of tortured speech, evoking a single subject's extreme personal feeling by the use of extreme musical relationships, is as far from the aims of the *ars perfecta* as can be imagined. The musical means employed, judged from the standpoint of the *ars perfecta*, are full of bombastic exaggeration and distortion — in a word, they are "baroque." But Rore's exaggerations and distortions only begin to suggest the violence that the last generations of madrigalists, working around the turn of the century, would wreak on the consummate musical idiom their fathers had perfected.

PARADOX AND CONTRADICTION

Just as it was in the realm of Catholic sacred music, when the generation of Willaert gave way to that of Palestrina, so it was in the realm of the madrigal: native Italian talent gradually took possession of the elite genres. The first of the great Italian-born madrigalists was Luca Marenzio (1553–99), who spent most of his career in Rome, with short forays in other Italian centers and, at the end of his rather short life, at the royal court of Poland. He published nine books of madrigals over a period of nineteen years beginning in 1580; his reputation was so far-reaching by the time of his death that all nine books were reissued together in a collected memorial edition, published in Nuremberg in 1601.

Solo e pensoso ("Alone and distracted," Ex. 17-16), from Marenzio's ninth and last book (1599), has for its text a famous verse by Petrarch himself, one that was frequently set by the madrigalists. Marenzio's setting of the opening couplet, a stroke of "nature-imitating" genius, illustrates another possibility for "painting" a text musically, one to which the late generation of madrigalists had increasing recourse. Music "moves," and in its movements it can analogize physical movement, even physical space. The opening image of the poem is that of numbly wandering "with slow and halting steps." The

EX. 17-15   Cipriano de Rore, *Dalle belle contrade d'oriente*, mm. 26–48

EX. 17-15   *(continued)*

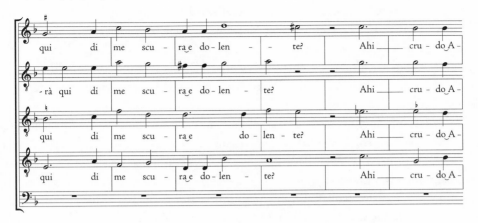

Hope of my heart, sweet desire,
You go, alas! You leave me alone! Farewell!
What will become of me here, gloomy and sad?
Alas, cruel love, how false and brief
are your pleasures

steady tread of semibreves in the accompanying voices suggests the steps pretty clearly. But what are they accompanying?

They are accompanying a soprano voice moving in semibreves (whole notes) through perhaps the first complete chromatic scale in the history of European art music. (The part ascends through fifteen semitonal progressions, covering more than an octave, and descends through eight.) What better way to indicate unpremeditated movement through deserted fields, parts unknown? The soprano's half steps are unpredictably treated as diatonic or chromatic, as sixteenth-century terminology would have it. In modern terms, and perhaps somewhat oversimply, the diatonic semitone is the one that progresses from one scale degree to another (every diatonic scale has two), and the chromatic semitone is the one that inflects a single degree and (by definition) cannot be found in any diatonic scale.

Using chromatic semitones is obviously incompatible with modal integrity, though it would be a gross overstatement to call madrigalistic chromaticism "atonal," as some have done. Marenzio takes care to bring things into tonal focus at the end of the couplet (making use, in fact, of techniques of tonal focusing that were as new as his chromaticism) and by extending the last note long enough to sustain a normal authentic cadence. But the new freedom of movement did play hob with modal theory—and even more so with tuning systems: it was precisely this kind of harmony that made tempered tuning, which finally eliminated the actual difference in size between the two kinds of semitone, a necessary invention.

The free intermixture of major and minor semitones was something the madrigalists pioneered, because they were the first musicians to have need of such a device for their pictorializing purpose. They had some predecessors in a certain crackpot brand of musical humanism that sought to recover the nondiatonic modes of Greek music (the "chromatic genus," which used minor semitones, and even the "enharmonic genus," which used quarter tones). A radical humanist named Nicola Vicentino built himself around 1560 a monster keyboard instrument called the *arcigravicembalo*, with fifty-three

EX. 17-16   Luca Marenzio, *Solo e pensoso*, mm. 1–24

EX. 17-16 (continued)

EX. 17-16   (*continued*)

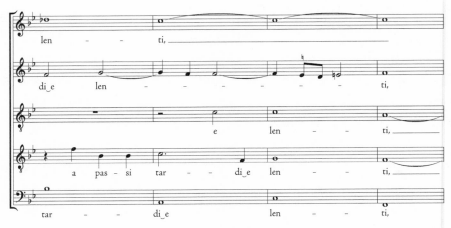

len - - ti, _____

di_e len - - - - ti,

e len - - ti, _____

a pas - si tar - - di_e len - - ti, _____

tar - - di_e len - ti,

Alone and thoughtful I pace the most deserted fields
with slow and heavy steps,

different pitches within the octave, on which he could experiment in search of the miracles of *ethos* (emotional contagion and moral influence) that the ancient Greek musicians were reputed to have achieved with their music. But it came to nothing.

There was also a negligible tendency on the part of some sixteenth-century musicians to experiment with complete circles of fifths as another way of encompassing the totality of chromatic pitch space. This tendency, too, demanded a radical revision of tuning systems if it was to work. It produced some curious little pieces, in particular a motetlike composition by the German composer Matthias Greiter (ca. 1495–1550) that transposed the beginning of a song called *Fortuna desperata* ("Hopeless fortune") twelve times by fifths in order to symbolize the rotation of Dame Fortune's wheel. But it, too, came to nothing. The chromaticism of the madrigalists came to something because its purpose was communication (or representation) of feeling, not pure (or mere) research. It was at first something that only unaccompanied voices, able to adjust their tuning by ear, could effectively perform.

Yet in its very realism, the expressivity of the madrigal contained the seeds of its own undoing. The opening couplet of Marenzio's setting of *Solo e pensoso* is miraculously precise in depicting the poet's pensive distraction, but can an ensemble of five voices represent his solitude? One makes allowances for convention, one can easily answer, but in that case why the chromatic experimentation? Its purpose, clearly, was to surmount convention in the interests of expressive exactness. It was a literary, not a musical

FIG. 17-7   Enharmonic keyboard comparable to Vicentino's, by Vito Trasuntino (Venice, 1606), now at the Museo Civico Medievale in Bologna.

exactness that was sought, and it exposed a contradiction between literature and music, the two media that madrigal composers were trying to fuse. The motivating "literary" idea brought literalism in its train; and once literalism was admitted, absurdity had to be confronted. There was no way out of the bind.

Another composer who set *Solo e pensoso* to music was Giaches (originally Jacques) de Wert (1535–96), an Antwerp-born composer who was taken to Italy as a child, became a naturalized citizen of Mantua, and grew up to all intents and purposes an Italian composer. A very prolific madrigalist, he published eleven books by the time of his death, and a twelfth was issued posthumously in 1608. *Solo e pensoso*, from his seventh book, was published in 1581, when Marenzio was only beginning his career. It, too, is full of the sort of expressive distortion music historians sometimes designate as "mannerism," borrowing a term from art history (think of El Greco's blue-skinned elongated saints).

Wert portrays the poet's distraction by the use of crazy intervallic leaps that utterly mock the smooth recuperative gestures of "perfected art." The madrigal's opening motive (Ex. 17-17) proceeds through two successive descending fifths, a rising major sixth (an interval for which you'll search all of Palestrina in vain), a falling fifth, a falling third, and two rising sixths. And by beginning with a point of imitation, Wert contrives to have the word *solo* actually sung "solo." But when the other parts enter, the illusion of solitude is broken even more decisively than in Marenzio's setting, because the five voices move so much more independently of one another. No way out.

EXTERIOR "NATURE" AND INTERIOR "AFFECT"

A particularly vivid example of antithesis, and of the audacities the use of musical metaphors could sanction, is *A un giro sol* ("At a single glance"), first published in 1603 in the fourth madrigal book by Claudio Monteverdi (1567–1643). The long-lived Monteverdi had a multifaceted career that included pioneering work in genres that properly belong to the seventeenth century; we will review his biography and survey his output in a later chapter. Here we will consider him as a late madrigalist exclusively, who attracted particular hostile attention from proponents of the *ars perfecta* who saw him as a particular threat precisely because his work was so persuasive.

The poem on which Monteverdi based his madrigal is cast in an unusual form that mirrors its rhetorical content. Its eight lines divide into two quatrains in differing rhyme schemes (abab *vs.* aabb) — but that is the least of their differences. The first quatrain is an "objective" nature description, and a cheerful one; the second is a subjective internal portrait, and miserable. The two quatrains are linked by a play on the word *occhi* (eyes). In the first, the eyes are the sun's, a metaphor for rays of light. In the second, the eyes are those of the poet, shedding tears.

This particular outer/inner antithesis — all the world is happy; only I am miserable — was a veritable madrigalian cliché because it was so perfectly suited to musical imagery of every kind. The "objective" description in the first part employs devices of the simpler sort. There is straightforward onomatopoeia in the "laughing" melismas. There are metaphors of motion and direction: the wavelike undulation of the sea — a

EX. 17-17   Giaches de Wert, *Solo e pensoso,* opening point

spatial metaphor that would have a long musical life indeed — is portrayed at first at a leisurely pace, then more lively in response to the wind (Ex. 17-18a). And there is a slightly more complex analogy to qualities of light (the brightening day) by means of shared attributes: as the sun rises, so does the vocal tessitura.

The big turnaround on *"sol io"* (I alone) is signaled by a brusque chromaticism, signaling a new tonal and emotional terrain. Really intense dissonance will follow when the bitter complaint against the lady's cruelty is enunciated. Monteverdi well understood the paradox of "persona" in the madrigal — a group of singers impersonating a single poetic sensibility — and exploited it. The line beginning "Certo!" is set on every occurrence for two singers in unison, so that it sounds like a single voice that "breaks" into a grating minor second when *cosi crudeleria* ("such a heartless one") is recalled (Ex. 17-18b). Thereafter, the two voices move in a suspension chain to a cadence, but a cadence that is trumped and frustrated every time by the next semitone clash. The dissonance is kept gnashingly high at all times and can seem excessive even now; this lover's pain remains palpable after four centuries.

Monteverdi's "baroque" dissonances were notorious. His madrigal *Cruda Amarilli*, published in 1605 in his fifth book, had already been a cause célèbre for five years because it had been angrily attacked by Giovanni Maria Artusi (1540–1613), a pupil of Zarlino and a latter-day proponent of the *ars perfecta*, in a treatise published in 1600 and pointedly titled *L'Artusi, overo Delle imperfettioni della moderna musica* ("Artusi's book concerning the imperfections of modern music"). Like most treatises it is in dialogue form. Artusi puts his criticisms in the mouth of a wise old monk, Signor Vario, to whom the other character, Signor Luca, has brought the unnamed Monteverdi's latest. "It pleases me, at my age," says Signor Vario, "to see a new method of composing, though it should please me much more if I saw that these passages were founded upon some reason which could satisfy the intellect. But as castles in the air, chimeras founded upon sand, these novelties do not please me; they deserve blame, not praise. Let us see the passages,

E X. 17-18A   Claudio Monteverdi, *A un giro sol*, mm. 16–27

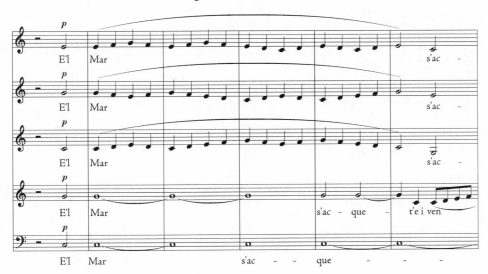

The sea quiets down, and the winds

however."[12] Then follow seven little extracts from *Cruda Amarilli*, each containing some offense against the rules of counterpoint as laid down by Zarlino. The most famous infraction is the first, a skip in the most exposed voice, the soprano, from an A that enters as a dissonance against the bass G to an F that is also a dissonance: two sins at a single stroke. What Artusi left out of his discussion, however, is the very thing that motivated the trespasses, and that alone can explain them — namely the text. This testifies either to a devious strategy on the author's part or, more likely, to his inability to comprehend the literary basis of the new style or admit that musical procedures could legitimately rest on textual, rather than musical grounds. In this position he has had successors in every subsequent century, right up to the present.

The all-determining text of *Cruda Amarilli* ("Cruel Amaryllis"), like those of countless other madrigals, is an excerpt from *Il Pastor Fido* ("The faithful shepherd"), a play by the contemporary courtly poet Giovanni Battista Guarini (1538–1612). A classic of the

EX. 17-18B Claudio Monteverdi, *A un giro sol*, mm. 43–55

Forsooth! When there was born
such a cruel one as you,
born also was my death!

"pastoral" mode, in which the purity and simplicity of shepherd life is implicitly contrasted with the corruption and the artificiality of court and city, Guarini's "tragicomic" play (i.e., a play about the sufferings of "low" characters) was one of the most famous Italian poems of the sixteenth century. In a fashion that may recall the competitive or emulative practices of the early generations of Mass composers, Guarini's play attracted more than one hundred composers great and small. That spirit of competition — to achieve the most accurate depiction of the poem's emotional content or (to give the same idea a more ordinary human twist) simply to come up with the most far-out setting of a given text — should certainly not be discounted as a force driving radical experimentation.

What proved so stimulating to the musical imagination was the new "affective" style in which the poet cast his "pathetic" monologues, that is, the monologues depicting the *affetti* or sentiments of suffering lovers, expressed not only in words but in sighs and tearful ejaculations like *ohimè!* ("oh me oh my") or *ahi lasso!* ("ah, weary me," whence "alas") — the very phrase to which Monteverdi's main "transgression" (Ex. 17-19) was

EX. 17-19 Claudio Monteverdi, *Cruda Amarilli*, mm. 1–14, encompassing the first of Artusi's "spots"

set. Thus composers were encouraged to develop an "affective" style of their own, analogizing the one that was being developed (also to the consternation of classicists) in literature. The remarkable thing is the way the new musical style came into its own just as — or even because — the poetry was becoming less "articulate" in its eloquence, more given over to elemental plaintive sounds, rhetorical "music." The two arts seemed to be converging, meeting in the middle; each giving something up (stylistic "perfection," exalted diction), each gaining something else (heightened expressivity). Out of that nexus a momentous style transformation was bound to occur.

The ultimate madrigalian stage was reached by Carlo Gesualdo (1560–1613), the Prince of Venosa near Naples in southern Italy. A colorful figure, himself a nobleman in no need of patronage (and with a biography rich in lurid anecdote as only a nobleman's could be), Gesualdo's name derives equal notoreity from his having ordered the murder of his unfaithful first wife and from his astonishing musical compositions. It would be the wiser course, perhaps, to resist the temptation to link the two sides of his fame, but there is no gainsaying his music's lurid aspect, reported in his day (by a diplomat slightly annoyed by Gesualdo's "open profession" of an art better practiced by his employees) as being an art "full of attitudes."[13]

Gesualdo brought to its peak the tradition of "uncanny" chromatic artifice initiated fifty years earlier by Lasso, and applied it to the new, supercharged vein of erotic love poetry. *Moro, lasso* ("I shall die, O miserable me") comes from his sixth and last book, published in 1611, about the latest date at which continental music in the "a cappella" polyphonic style could claim to represent a current idiom rather than a *stile antico*. Before we even touch upon the music, it would be well to take a look at the poem, just to satisfy ourselves that it is indeed a poem with meter and rhyme:

Moro, lasso, al mio duolo	I shall die, O miserable me, in my suffering,
E chi me puo dar vita,	and the one who could give me life,
Ahi, che m'ancide	alas, kills me and is unwilling
e non vuol dar mi aita!	to give me aid.
O dolorosa sorte,	O painful fate!
Chi dar vita me puo,	The one who could give me life,
ahi, mi da morte!	alas, gives me death.

Gesualdo's harmonic progressions, more fully saturated than any predecessor's with true chromatic voice leading (often in two, sometimes even in three voices at once), is often compared with much later music (most often, perhaps, with Wagner's). Those inclined to make such comparisons — such as Igor Stravinsky, the famous Russian composer then living in Hollywood, who became fascinated with Gesualdo in the 1950s and even orchestrated three of his madrigals — are also inclined to look upon Gesualdo as a "prophetic" composer, so far ahead of his time that it took two and a half centuries for the rest of the world to catch up with him.

As ought to be clear long before we reach Wagner's work, however, such ideas are based on dubious historical assumptions. The most groundless one is that all of music is moving in one direction (say, toward Wagner and beyond), and therefore some music is farther along the path of destiny than other music. But by the time we reach Wagner, we will see that his chromaticism depends for its effect (and even its sheer intelligibility) on a great deal of aural conditioning that Wagner's contemporaries had all been subjected to (as have we), but that Gesualdo's contemporaries had not. Gesualdo's harmony, however radical, was in no sense ahead of its time. As in the case of Lasso, its ingredients were familiar and its progressions not unprecedented. What was unique in his music was not its sound or its syntax, but its concentrated intensity.

Within the terms of sixteenth century style, moreover, Gesualdo's greatest audacities are not harmonic *per se*, but consist rather in the frequent pauses that disrupt the continuity of his lines, often followed by harmonically disconnected resumptions that coincide (as in *Moro, lasso*) with the *ahi*'s, the affective or downright suggestive exclamations of desire or (given their proximity to words invoking death) of satiation (Ex. 17-20). This linguistic realism, betokening emotional realism and even physiological realism, can still make us uncomfortable when listening to Gesualdo in public. That discomfort has led many writers, even modern ones, to write the Prince of Venosa's extravagances off as being inartistic, even (as befits a prince) "amateurish."[14] Poetry lovers also resist Gesualdo, for his fragmented, discombobulated music completely devours the poem in the course of realizing its *affetti*, turning it into what often sounds like fairly inarticulate prose.

Gesualdo's modern reputation (or modernist reception) poses interesting historical questions. On the one hand, as suggested above (and as the Italian scholar Lorenzo Bianconi has eloquently complained), by drawing factitious connections between Gesualdo and other daring harmonists, the modern revival of interest in him has fueled the invention of "an imaginary, heroic history of visionary prophets"[15] (Lasso → Gesualdo → Wagner → Stravinsky, or something of the sort) and has obscured rather than illuminated the actual historical and cultural conditions that nourished their various activities. On the other hand, without benefit of some of these false historical notions, interest in Gesualdo would never have quickened in the twentieth century the way it did; his works would have been studied and performed far less than they have been, and probably with far less understanding.

Which is not to say that modern understanding of Gesualdo (or any cultural figure from the past) is or can ever be the same as contemporary understanding. It is motivated by new interests and a different intellectual climate, and the passage of years or centuries irrevocably alters the context in which any artifact of the past is perceived. Modern understanding, then, cannot be anything other than new understanding and—if difference is automatically equated with loss (which of course it need not be)—it can only be "misunderstanding."

But it is an inevitable misunderstanding, even a necessary one. There is little to be gained in complaining that the disproportionate interest we now take in Gesualdo's chromatic madrigals, at the expense of his sacred music or his instrumental dances or any other less spectacular side of his output, is "a mistaken overemphasis," as Bianconi so challengingly puts it.[16] Our modern (mis)understandings of the past are not mistakes but the products of changed historical conditions. We value in Gesualdo

EX. 17-20   Carlo Gesualdo, *Moro, lasso*, mm. 1–12

I shall die, miserable, in my suffering,
and the one who could give me life,
alas, kills me

something his contemporaries could not have valued, because we know what they (and he) did not—namely, their future, which is now our past. That knowledge can hardly be erased from our consciousness.

So what interests us now bespeaks our condition and no one else's. No amount of historical learning can replace new understanding with old understanding. All one can hope to do is add depth and detail to our misunderstanding. (That is where the sacred music and the instrumental music can usefully fit into even the most biased modern appreciation of Gesualdo.) If that seems a paradoxical thing to say, that has been precisely the intention.

POSTSCRIPT: THE ENGLISH MADRIGAL

Both the music printing business and the cultivation of vernacular art music had a relatively slow start in England. The beginning, splendidly signaled by the publication of *XX. Songes* in 1530, did not take hold. William Byrd, who with Thomas Tallis sought and received monopoly rights on music printing, turned out to be an ineffectual or indifferent businessman. He did not publish even his own settings of English poetry until

he had turned his patent over to a printer-musician named Thomas East, who finally made a go of it. Apart from compositions for the Anglican liturgy, Byrd's vernacular settings can be found in two volumes printed by East in 1588 and 1589: *Psalmes, sonets and Songs of sadness and pietie*, and *Songs of sundrie natures, some of gravitie, and others of myrth, fit for all companies and voyces*. Most of the songs are grave and semireligious; they are mainly set for solo voice with instruments and show no interest in the new directions being taken on the continent toward "literary" experiment.

Byrd's songs were representative. Little of the English song literature that circulated in manuscript during the sixteenth century was set for vocal ensembles, but consisted rather of instrumentally accompanied solo "ayres," either with "consorts" of viols or with lute as backup. Whether for viols or for

FIG. 17-8 Detail from the huge painting *The Wedding at Cana* (1562) by Veronese, which now faces Leonardo da Vinci's *Mona Lisa* in the Louvre, Paris. The players of the viols were secret portraits of the painter and his colleagues, the size of the instruments they play corresponding to their ages: Tintoretto (Jacopo Robusti) is at left, bowing a tenor viol held lute-style. Opposite him, the aged Titian (Tiziano Vecellio) is sawing away at a gigantic bass viol. Between them, holding a little viol on his shoulder, is Veronese himself (real name Paolo Caliari).

lute, the accompaniments were often contrapuntally intricate, the texts melancholy, the style basically motetlike, but respectful of the structure of the poem in a way that the madrigal was not.

The most important sixteenth-century composer of English verse settings untouched by madrigalian influence was not Byrd but the lutenist John Dowland (1563–1626), like Byrd a recusant Catholic who, upon being refused the post of lutenist to the court of Elizabeth I in 1594 (because of religious discrimination, he claimed) went abroad and spent the early years of the seventeenth century at various German and Danish courts, returning to England in 1609 and finally securing appointment as one of the King's Lutes at the court of James I in 1612.

Dowland was a supreme virtuoso of his instrument, who could write for it in a very strict contrapuntal style. For this reason he found it easy to arrange his lute ayres, most effectively, for publication as vocal ensembles after the madrigal had caught on in England. But his work belongs to the earlier tradition, a tradition that goes back (like most pre-madrigalian continental vernacular genres as well) to the strophic dance song. Most of Dowland's ayres are cast in the form of one of the two main ballroom dances of Elizabeth's time: the stately duple-metered *pavan* and the lively triple-metered *galliard* with which the pavan was often paired in the ballroom, characteristically full of lilting "hemiola" syncopations. Both pavan and galliard consisted formally of three repeated "strains" or cadenced phrases, the middle cadence (or half-cadence) being on a contrasting harmony.

The pavan was originally an Italian dance called *paduana* after Padua, its putative city of origin. (There is also a theory, no longer much believed, that it was originally a Spanish dance named after the *pavón* or peacock because of its proud movements.) The most famous of all pavans is Dowland's song "Flow My Tears" (see Ex. 17-21 for its first strain), which he not only arranged as a part-song but also transcribed for five-part consort of viols without voice under the title "The Lachrymae Pavan" (*lachrimae* being Latin for tears), in which form he published it in 1604 together with six more pavans all based on the same head motive: a falling tetrachord, traditionally emblematic of lamenting (Ex. 17-22).

The *galliard* was also originally a north Italian court dance; its name derives from *gagliardo*, Italian for "robust." Dowland's galliard songs are wonderful examples of expert English text-setting. They are based on poems in iambic pentameter, the Shakespearean meter, with hemiolas — the breaking of a normal triple bar (say, $\frac{3}{4}$) bar into two smaller ones ($2 \times \frac{3}{8}$) or grouping two of them into one larger bar ($2 \times \frac{3}{4} = \frac{3}{2}$) — allowing for interesting inversions and cross-accents that adapt the regular meter to the normal enunciation pattern of English speech. The witty lover's complaint, *Can shé excúse my wróngs with vírtue's clóak?* (i.e., can she claim virtue as her excuse for thwarting me) is a particularly complex — and therefore a particularly delightful — example (Ex. 17-23a). The title as just given is marked to show the normal iambic-pentameter scansion. Example 17-23b shows how Dowland's hemiolas actually stress the words in performance. This is English musical prosody at its most original and authentic.

EX. 17-21   John Dowland, "Flow My Tears," first strain

The situation changed, very abruptly, in 1588, the year of the great sea battle with the Spanish Armada, hence a year usually associated in English history with victory and conquest. In music it went the other way. It was the English who were conquered by the Italians, to the point where a decade later Thomas Morley could complain, in his *Plaine and Easie Introduction to Practicall Musicke*, that "such be the newfangled opinions of our countrymen, who will highly esteem whatsoever cometh from beyond the seas, and specially from Italy, be it never so simple, contemning that which is done at home though it be never so excellent."[17]

Morley (1557–1602) had scant right to grumble so. As translator, as arranger, as monopolistic publisher and as literary propagandist he deserves most of the credit or the blame for the English craze for Italian music that flared up after the 1588 publication of *Musica Transalpina* ("Music from across the Alps"). This was a large anthology of fifty-seven Italian madrigals (grouped in sections for four voices, for five, and for six) with their texts translated into English by a London music lover named Nicholas Yonge, who had long made it a hobby to sing Italian madrigals at home and to translate their texts for his friends, knowing that so literary a genre as the madrigal will only be sung "with little delight" by those ignorant of the language.

EX. 17-22 John Dowland, "The Lachrymae Pavan," opening

EX. 17-22 (*continued*)

g. Lachrimae verae

EX. 17-23A John Dowland, *Can shee excuse my wrongs*, first strain

Voice

Can shee ex - cuse my wrongs with ver - tues cloake:
Are those cleere fiers which van - nish in - to smoake:

Lute

mf poco marcato

Shall I call her good when she proves un - kind.
Must I praise the leaves where no fruit I find.

EX. 17-23B John Dowland, *Can shee excuse my wrongs*, voice part rebarred to show hemiola scansions

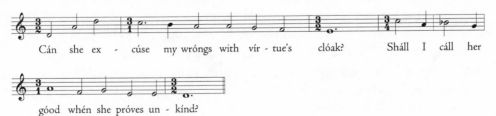

Cán she ex - cúse my wróngs with vír - tue's clóak? Sháll I cáll her

góod whén she próves un - kínd?

(One of the madrigals Yonge Englished was Palestrina's ubiquitous *Vestiva i colli*.) Yonge's bestseller was followed two years later by *Italian Madrigals Englished*, mainly containing Marenzio, freely paraphrased by a well-known poet, Thomas Watson. And then it was Morley's turn to make a killing. Aiming for the widest possible appeal, he concentrated at first on the lighter submadrigalian Italian genres that had descended from dance songs, becoming ever more frivolous as the madrigal became ever more serious: *canzonetti* (little homorhythmic songs), *balletti* (little dances), and the like. These are the genres that have the *falala* nonsense refrains (parodying solmization) that are so firmly associated with English "madrigals" as commonly defined (and as sung by glee clubs). Their continued currency goes all the way back to Morley's popularizing efforts.

Morley's first book of Italian translations, *Canzonets, or Little Short Songs to Four Voices: Selected out of the best and approved Italian authors*, came out in 1597. His *Madrigals to Five Voices: Selected out of the best approved Italian authors* appeared the next year, and also consisted, for the most part, of canzonets. But his Italianate composing activity actually preceded his editorial work. In 1593, Morley had published a book of two-voiced canzonets of his own; in 1594 he put out a book of four-part madrigals under his own imprint as publisher; and in 1595 he issued a shady little book that bestrode the borderline between composing and arranging: *The first book of ballets to five voyces*, issued in both English and Italian versions, in which no name is given as author except Morley's, but in which almost every item is so closely based on an Italian model as to amount to plagiarism, except that Morley very skillfully amplified the "falas" far beyond anything in his models.

Morley's dance-song "Now is the month of Maying," for example, now a glee club evergreen, was really a balletto, *So ben mi c'ha bon tempo*, that Morley found in a goldmine of a book published five years earlier in Venice, called *Selva di varia ricreatione* ("Forest [i.e., a big bunch] of various recreations") by Orazio Vecchi, the great Italian master of submadrigalian frivolity (including "madrigal comedies" — farces with texts made up entirely of madrigal spoofs). Ex. 17-24 shows the first strophe, complete with falas, from both pieces.

Morley's publications are a fitting conclusion to a chapter all about early musical entrepreneurship. Once he got the commercial ball rolling, there was no stopping it, or so it seemed. Between the mid-1590s, when Morley began, and the early 1620s, when Thomas Tomkins (1572–1656) published his last madrigal book, about fifty prints containing madrigals or "madrigals" (that is, songs the English called madrigals but which the Italians would have called something else) were issued, by almost as many composers, some of whom were remarkable musicians indeed, fully worthy of their transalpine forebears. Emblematic of the whole movement was a collection published by Morley in 1601: *The Triumphes of Oriana*, consisting of madrigals by 21 composers, all in praise of Queen Elizabeth and ending with a common refrain, "Long live fair Oriana." Thus nationalism, public relations, and entrepreneurship conjoined to turn the century's most quintessentially Italian musical genre, or at least a lightened variant of it, into a genre the English accepted as their own.

The most eminent English madrigalists, or at least the most serious, were the three W's: John Ward (1571–1638), John Wilbye (1574–1638), and Thomas Weelkes

(1576–1623). They combined the kind of musico-literary imagination that marked the best of the Italian madrigalists with outstanding contrapuntal techniques, making them absolutely the last composers whose work exemplified the sixteenth-century polyphonic style as a living, rather than an embalmed, tradition. To illustrate their work, Ward's *Upon a Bank* (Ex. 17-25), published in 1613, makes an apt counterpart to Monteverdi's *A un giro sol* (Ex. 17-18). It is based on the very same kind of overall "Petrarchian" antithesis — a jolly description of nature followed by a lament — and features a wealth of delightfully subtle imagery in the opening pictorial part. Here is the text of that part, with the words most ingeniously "painted" set in italics:

> Upon a bank with roses set about,
> Where pretty turtles [i.e., turtle doves] *joining bill to bill*,
> And gentle springs *steal softly murmuring* out,
> Washing *the foot* of pleasure's sacred hill. . . . . . .

EX. 17-24A   Thomas Morley, "Now is the month of Maying"

747

EX. 17-24A (continued)

EX. 17-24B Orazio Vecchi, *So ben mi c'ha bon tempo*

The most impressive thing about Ward's descriptive technique is its strategy. In order to paint "joining" with a sudden homorhythm, he precedes it with a passage of hocketing text repetition. In order to paint "the foot" with a bass entrance, he withholds the voice from the whole preceding line. The strategy, of course, is based on a particularly fine awareness that relationships are what impart musical meaning, and that the simplest sort of relationship to contrive is an antithesis. Pictorialisms that seem more "direct" or "essential" are in fact the opposite, resting on specifically musical conventions that must be learned before their effects can be perceived. Thus Ward's brook "murmurs" by way of a melisma whose down-and-up contour may seem self-evidently (like Monteverdi's) to describes a wave. But that is because we have all internalized a spatial (up/down) analogy that is by no means given in the sounds themselves. Even more convention-bound is Ward's depiction of "stealing softly": it is ingeniously matched to a suspension, the lowest voice stealing softly to a dissonance beneath the higher ones. But to get this particular joke one needs concepts that come only with technical musical training.

EX. 17-25   John Ward, *Upon a Bank*, mm. 12–27

EX. 17-25   (*continued*)

The pictorialism in Ward's first quatrain show an enormous affinity for those in Monteverdi's. It is the second quatrain, the affective one depicting the wounded cupid, that suggests the difference between the English madrigalists as a school and their Italian counterparts. Or rather, it reinforces our sense of that difference, amounting, it could almost be said, to a deficiency or a blind spot on the part of the English. Compared to the Italian, the English madrigalists deliberately curbed emotional intensity (here, for example, by deflecting love, as suffered subjectively, to "Love" as objectified in the adorable, unthreatening form of Cupid), and avoided any but jocular references to sex. In other words, what had fueled the most powerful moments in the most serious Italian madrigals, and in particular provided the impetus for the most extreme chromatic experiments, was anxiously relegated by the English madrigalists to the lighter vein.

A typical example is the coy double entendre in *Fair Phyllis*, a mock-pastoral by the minor madrigalist John Farmer (and yet another glee-club perennial), in which the shepherd "wanders up and down" in search of the shepherdess, finds her, kisses her, and then, because of a repeat sign, "wanders up and down" and "finds her" again. No need for chromaticism here, thank you; and there is generally far less interest in chromaticism among the English than among the Italians, which more than anything else hints at what all that Italian chromaticism really meant.

Was this reticence a national characteristic? It certainly did not arise out of religious scruples alone (for all that Weelkes and Ward were churchmen by profession). The church to which the Italian composers confessed was assuredly no less officially censorious of illicit sex than the Church of England. Was it "purely musical" conservatism? Or was it (as Joseph Kerman suggests) "a fundamental dislike of stopping the composition abruptly for the purpose of momentary word-painting"?[18] But if so, why? Kerman, ostensibly restating the same proposition more succinctly, may in fact suggest the reason: the English, he writes, "saw chromaticism as a disruptive force and tended to reject it accordingly."[19] But of course Gesualdo, too, saw chromaticism as a disruptive force—and embraced it enthusiastically. Was it only musical continuity that the English saw as threatened? Now that chromaticism has been established as both a musical and an expressive resource, it will be something to watch—indeed to monitor—as time goes on.

Reformations and Counter Reformations

Music of the Lutheran Church; Venetian Cathedral Music

THE CHALLENGE

What we now call the Protestant Reformation was in fact a series of revolts against Roman Catholic orthodoxy and the authority of the hierarchical church with roots going back to the fourteenth century (John Wyclif in England, Jan Hus in Bohemia, both successfully suppressed). They took radically different forms in different places. (The one sixteenth-century Reformation movement with which we are already familiar, the English, was the most "radically different" of all, since it was, uniquely, led by the Crown.) They did, however, reach a joint peak in the first half of the sixteenth century and achieved a lasting rupture in the history of European Christendom, for which reason they now appear in retrospect to have been a concerted movement, which they were not.

What the continental reform movements had in common was an antifeudal, antihierarchical individualism; a zeal to return to the original revealed word of scripture (a by-product of humanism, which encouraged the learning of Greek and Hebrew, the original scriptural languages); and confidence that every believer could find a personal path to truth based on scripture. They shared a disdain for formulaic liturgical ritual or the "caking up" of scripture with scholastic commentary; they reviled the worldliness of the professionalized Catholic clergy and its collusion with temporal authority, especially that of the supranational Holy Roman Empire, the very existence of which testified to that collusion.

What is now thought of as the first overt act of the sixteenth-century religious revolution took place in Germany in 1517, when an Augustinian monk named Martin Luther (1483–1546) nailed 95 "theses" or points of difference with Roman Catholic authority to the door of the castle church in the town of Wittenberg, as a challenge for debate. The precipitating cause of this bold act was Luther's horror at what he considered the venal abuse by the local church authorities of what were known as indulgences: the buying of "time off" from purgatory for one's ancestors or oneself by making contributions to the church coffers.

Among underlying factors that brought things to a head in the sixteenth century was the steady growth of mercantilism — that is, of economic enterprise and money-based

FIG. 18-1   The beginning of the Reformation: Martin Luther posts his ninety-five theses on the church door at Wittenberg.

trade. Protestantism, capitalism, and nationalism went hand in hand, it has often been observed, and renewed Europe in ways that ultimately went far beyond religion. Their mutual interactions were extremely various. One manifestation of mercantilism, as we know from the previous chapter, was the growth of the printing industry. This not only facilitated the dissemination of humanistic learning and secular music; it also allowed the rapid spread of Protestant ideas. In return, the Reformation provided a big new market for printers (and, as we shall see, for music printers).

It cannot be said that music ranked very high on the Reformation agenda, but the effects of the Reformation were felt very keenly in the musical sphere. For it was a revolt within the very stronghold of cultivated music, the source of much or most of its richest patronage. Just think how much of the music we have considered up to now has been bound up with the liturgy that was now coming under attack, and how much the now-suspect opulence of the Roman church hierarchy had meant to the material support of musicians, especially those whose work, committed to writing, forms the basis of music-with-a-history. Under particularly ascetic "reform" conditions, one could imagine music leaving history again. And in some of the reformed churches, it did just that.

For nowhere do the differences among the reformed churches show up more clearly than in their attitudes toward music. What they shared was a hostility to the pope's music: rich, professionalized, out of touch with ordinary life—just like the hierarchical clergy itself. What they hated, in other words, was the *ars perfecta*, whose very perfection now came under moral suspicion. But musical agreement among the reformers ended there. They had no united positive vision of music's place in religion.

Most negative of all was John Calvin (1504–64), the Geneva reformer, whose emphasis on austerity and complete rejection of the sacraments left very little room for music in his services, and none at all for professional music. The only musical artifact of the Calvinist or Huguenot Church was the Geneva Psalter, a book of psalms put into metrical verse (partly by the famous poet Clément Marot) for singing to the tunes (or *timbres*) of popular songs. It was first published in 1543 and reissued three times thereafter with various harmonizations by the one-time chanson composer (and eventual Huguenot martyr) Claude Goudimel (ca. 1514–72).

These psalm settings were similar in concept to Jacobus Clemen's *Souterliedekens*, briefly discussed and sampled in chapter 15, but far simpler. Goudimel's preface to the last edition, published in 1565, strongly implies that even the simplest polyphonic psalm harmonizations were rejected as frills in Calvinist services, to be allowed only in home devotions. For all practical purposes, then, the Calvinist Church turned its back on music as an art. To the extent that music was cultivated as an art, it had no place in church; to the extent it had a place in church, it was to be "uncultivated" and unlettered. The same could be said for the Swiss German reformed church of Ulrich Zwingli (1484–1531), which was of all the Protestant churches the most hostile to liturgy, and which sponsored public burnings of organs and liturgical music-books.

The great exception to this pervasive music-hatred was the largest and most successful of the Reformed churches, the Lutheran; and as Luther was quick to point out, there was a lesson in that. Although he was by far the most spectacular and histrionic of the reformers, Luther was in some ways the most conservative, retaining a far more regular and organized liturgy than his counterparts, and in particular keeping the sacrament of the Mass (renamed the Lord's Supper in its modified Lutheran form). Unlike his counterparts, moreover, Luther was personally a fervent music lover, who played several instruments, loved to sing and even composed a bit, and who did not fear the seductiveness of melody the way Calvin or Zwingli (following St. Augustine) did, but instead wished to harness and exploit it for his own purposes. His most widely quoted remark on music — "Why should the Devil have all the good tunes?" — speaks directly to this wish.[1] Even more unlike the Swiss reformers, Luther urged the cultivation of polyphonic or "figural" music in churches and schools as well as homes.

But the polyphonic church music he favored was still of a different order from anything we have seen up to now. It was not totally divorced from the music of the *ars perfecta*, since Luther wanted the music of his church modeled after that of Josquin des Prez, which (like many Germans) he treasured; and Josquin had been a great figure for the *ars perfecta*, too. But still, Luther opposed professionalization and hierarchy, seeing his church (in accord with his conception of the original Christian church) as a universal priesthood of all believers.

The music he wanted for it was not the music of a professional choir, but a music of a *Gemeinschaft* — a congregational community. He described his musical ideals in the preface to a schoolbook called *Symphoniae jucundae* ("Pleasant polyphonic pieces"), issued in 1538. All men are naturally musical, he begins by observing, which means that the Creator wished them to make music. "But," he continued, "what is natural should still be developed into what is artful." With the addition of learning and artifice,

> which corrects, develops, and refines the natural music, then at last it is possible to taste with wonder (yet still not comprehend) God's absolute and perfect wisdom in his wondrous work of music. Here it is most remarkable that one single voice continues to sing the tenor, while at the same time many other voices trip lustily around it, exulting and adorning it in exuberant strains and, as it were, leading it forth in a divine dance, so that those who are the least bit moved know nothing more amazing in the world. But any who remain unaffected are clodhoppers indeed and are fit to hear only the words of dung-poets and the music of pigs.[2]

From the previous chapter we recognize the kind of music that Luther is praising here with characteristic delicacy. It is the Tenorlied, or as Luther would have called it, the *Kernweise*, the peculiarly German song genre in which traditional cantus-firmus writing, increasingly outmoded in other European centers, was given a new lease on life by the growth of the printing trade. Luther was a great devotee of the genre, and of its foremost practitioner. Next to the divine Josquin he worshiped Ludwig Sennfl, just the sort of composer the other continental reformers despised. "I could never compose a motet like Sennfl's, even were I to tear myself to pieces in the attempt," wrote Luther in admiration; "but on the other hand," he could not resist adding, "Sennfl could never preach as well as I."[3]

He wrote this after receiving an actual musical tribute from Sennfl, with whom he corresponded, and who, while never declaring himself a "Lutheran" or breaking with the religion of the Holy Roman Empire, his employer, sympathized sufficiently with Luther the man to egg him on at a low point in his career (his confinement under arms at Coburg in 1530) with a motet based on Psalm 118, verse 17 — "I shall not die, but live, and I shall declare the works of the Lord" — based on the traditional Mode 7 psalm tone as sung in Germany. Luther took the verse forever afterward as his motto, and even tried to make a setting of it himself, as if vying with Sennfl (though never seriously) in the *ars perfecta*.

In Ex. 18-1a Luther's tiny setting, in traditional tenor cantus-firmus style, is set alongside the portion of Sennfl's motet in which the tenor gets the tune. They make a touching contrast. Luther's is a musically amateurish but eloquent shout of faith

EX. 18-1A Claudio Monteverdi, *A un giro sol*, as set by Martin Luther

EX. 18-1B   Claudio Monteverdi, *A un giro sol,* as set by Ludwig Sennfl

and endurance: there are no actual errors, but the outer voices move uninterestingly in parallel tenths (a technique much used in "supra librum" or improvised polyphony, and taught to composition students as a quick fix) and the altus is all too clearly a filler, with little melodic profile. Sennfl's setting is the suave work of a professional, full of subtle stylistic felicities: "Vorimitation" in the soprano, the lilting metric displacement in the outer voices (on "sed vivam") to bridge the gap between tenor phrases, and so on and on.

THE LUTHERAN CHORALE

The Tenorlied texture was not only distinctively German—although that was important enough in its own right to emphasize at a time when a German national church was asserting itself against the supranational authority of "Holy Rome" both as ecclesiastical and as temporal power. It was also ideally adaptable to the musical needs of the emerging Lutheran Church. In keeping with the communitarian ideals of the reform, the Lutheran Church at first advocated the use of full congregational singing in place of the traditional service music—or any music, whether plainchant or "figural," that required the use of a professional choir and thus created a musical "hierarchy." The lay congregation could thus become its own choir even as the whole congregation of the faithful, not the minister's ordained authority, now constituted the priesthood. A service in which the minister's preaching was answered by congregational singing would be more than a mere sacramental ritual; it would become "evangelical"—an occasion for actively and joyously proclaiming the Gospel anew, and affirming the bonds of Christian fellowship.

The unit of congregational singing, hence the distinctive musical genre of the Lutheran Church, was the strophic unison German hymn known as *Choral* ("chorale" in English), a term that originally meant "chant," as in "*gregorianischer Choral.*" Chorales were meant to take the place of the Gregorian chant, especially the Gradual (in conjunction with the Gospel) and the Sanctus/Agnus Dei pair in conjunction with the Eucharist. Many of the earliest ones were actually adapted from favorite chants, particularly (but not only) hymns. Some were direct translations. The Latin Advent hymn *Veni redemptor gentium* ("Come, redeemer of the Heathen") became *Nun komm, der Heiden Heiland*; the Pentecost favorite, *Veni creator spiritus* (Ex. 2-7c) became *Komm, Gott Schöpfer, Heiliger Geist.*

Others were freer adaptations. One of the most famous of all Lutheran chorales, the Easter hymn *Christ lag in Todesbanden* ("Christ lay in Death's bondage"), descended from *Victimae paschali laudes*, the Latin Easter sequence, as mediated through an earlier German adaptation—a popular twelfth-century *Leise*, sung mainly in street processions not in church—called *Christ ist erstanden* ("Christ is risen"). Only the first line—the incipit or "tag," as it were—of the Latin sequence is retained; it is immediately balanced by an answering phrase in the complementary modal pentachord; and the melody thus created is immediately repeated in conformity with the popular "Hofweise" or court-song model, the traditional bar form (*aab*) that now survived only in Germany (Ex. 18-2).

In keeping with the "why should the Devil..." theory, many Lutheran chorales were adapted from secular songs. One with a particular resonance, and a particular irony, was *Innsbruck, ich muss dich lassen* ("Innsbruck, I now must leave thee"), a song composed by Heinrich Isaac (ca. 1450–1517) during his period of service to the "Kaiser" (Caesar), Maximilian I, the Holy Roman Emperor, one of whose capitals was the Austrian city of Innsbruck. Ex. 18-3 contains Isaac's original setting, underlaid both with the original text and with the clever Lutheran *contrafactum*, in which the sentiments of the very worldly original words are, with only a few adjustments, "universalized" and assimilated to a typical expression of Lutheran contempt for the (or rather "this") world.

Finally, there were newly composed chorales, but composed as far as possible to resemble traditional melodies. Many of the most famous tunes are attributed to Luther himself, probably as an honorific. The most famous one of all, with an attribution to Luther that dates from within his lifetime and is therefore possibly trustworthy,

EX. 18-2   *Christ lag in Todesbanden compared with Victimae paschali and Christ ist erstanden*

Christ lay in death's bondage, imprisoned for our sins.
He rose again and brought us life.
Wherefore we should be glad and grateful to God, and sing Hallelujah.

EX. 18-3   Heinrich Isaac, *Innsbruck, ich muss dich lassen*, underlaid both with original text and with Lutheran *contrafactum*, mm. 1–9

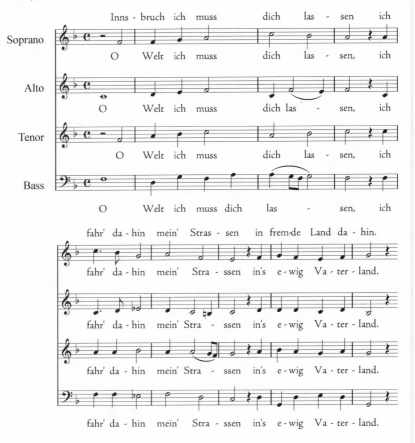

is *Ein' feste Burg ist unser Gott* (famous in English as "A Mighty Fortress"), a hearty *Verkündigungslied* ("faith-proclaiming song") as Luther termed it, for which he adapted a text from his own translation of Psalm 46 ("God is our refuge and strength" in the King James version). The melody, it has been plausibly suggested, was adapted from the formula-stock of the Meistersingers — the contemporaneous German guild-musicians (see chapter 4). Fig. 18-2 shows the famous hymn as it appeared in its first published source, a book of "new, improved sacred songs" (*Geistliche Lieder auffs new gebessert*) issued in 1533 by the printer Joseph Klug in Wittenberg, Luther's own town. Like almost all the newly composed chorales, it follows the "bar" form of the *Hofweise*.

Nine years earlier, also in Wittenberg, the first book of polyphonically arranged chorales had already appeared, the work of Johann Walther (1496–1570), formerly a Saxon (East German) court singer, who had become Luther's main musical consultant and assistant. Essentially a collection of Protestant Tenorlieder (though they were called motets) based on chorale melodies, Walther's *Geystliches gesangk Buchleyn* ("Little sacred songbook"), which boasted a preface by Luther himself, was chiefly intended for use at religious boarding schools, so that "young people," as Luther put it in the preface, "who should and must be trained in music and other proper arts, would free themselves from

FIG. 18-2 Luther's *Ein' feste Burg* (A Mighty Fortress) as printed by Joseph Klug (*Geistliche Lieder*, 1533).

love songs and other carnal music and learn something wholesome instead."[4] The book remained standard curricular fare for many years and went through many editions.

The level of musical training at such schools was high, to judge by the sophistication of Walther's settings. His setting of *Christ lag in Todesbanden* (Ex. 18-4), for example, treats the tune to a point of *Vorimitation* before the tenor enters; and the tenor, when it does come in, comes in as twins: up to the double bar the setting is canonic, and remains pretty strictly imitative thereafter. But even at its most elaborate, the Lutheran *Liedsatz* (polyphonic chorale setting) was clearly organized around the cantus firmus

EX. 18-4 Johann Walther, *Christ lag in Todesbanden*

EX. 18-4   *(continued)*

Here is the true Easter lamb of sacrifice,
as God of old ordained.
It is he who hung upon the cross in
ardent love for us.

and dominated by it. The accompanying parts, though provided with text, were often played on the organ or by ensemble instruments; this set the precedent for the important instrumental genre called "Chorale prelude" (*Choralvorspiel*) that kept the traditional art of cantus-firmus writing (and improvising) alive among Lutheran composers into the eighteenth century.

The two settings of *Ein' feste Burg* in Ex. 18-5 are at two textural extremes. The first is by Martin Agricola (1486–1556), the choirmaster at the Protestant "Lateinschule" or humanist academy for boys at Magdeburg in Eastern Germany (hence his Latinized pen name). In its homespun simplicity it is almost a discant setting. The other, which sports as much motetlike pseudo-imitation as the composer could work into it without altogether compromising the tenor's ascendancy, is the work of Stephan Mahu, a composer in the service of the Austrian Archduke Ferdinand I (a Hapsburg and therefore a member of the ruling family of the Holy Roman Empire), who like Sennfl was probably a sympathetic or nationalistic Catholic, not a Lutheran. The settings are representative of their composers' positions: Mahu's is internationalist, ars-perfectified; Agricola's is provincial, wholly indigenous, Lutheran-specific.

That both styles were welcomed and deemed useful within the big tent of Lutheranism is clear from the fact that they appeared together in the most comprehensive musical publication of the early Lutheran church, the *Newe deudsche geistliche Gesenge* ("New German sacred songs"), a collection of 123 four- and five-part settings for school use, published at Wittenberg in 1544 by Georg Rhau, a church musician who became the more or less official printer to the Reformation church, and for whom the Lutheran revolt was a commercial bonanza. Rhau met Luther in 1519, while occupying the position of cantor at the St. Thomas Church in Leipzig (the same position J. S. Bach would hold a couple of centuries later). He wrote the Mass that consecrated the opening of the great theological debate between Luther and Johann von Eck, his main orthodox opponent, which led to Luther's excommunication.

Rhau's close association with Luther cost him his job at Leipzig, but vouchsafed him a second career that made his fortune. Rhau's printing and publishing activity was not confined to music; he also issued books on theology, catechisms, Luther's sermons, even mathematics texts for use in the Lutheran schools. The voluminous music publications, though, are historically the most significant, because they give a complete picture of the early Protestant musical repertory and its surprising wide stylistic reach. Rhau's

EX. 18-5A   *Ein' feste Burg ist unser Gott*, as set by Martin Agricola

EX. 18-5B *Ein' feste Burg ist unser Gott,* as set by Stephan Mahu

energetic activities, at once religiously dedicated, nation-centered, "populist," and highly profitable, epitomize the overriding reform doctrine—the so-called "Protestant work ethic"—that initiative and ambition fired by personal faith are the best road to the accomplishment of good works, and that the best insurance of the common welfare is freedom to pursue one's enlightened self-interest.

In the later sixteenth century, Lutheran *Liedsätze* (chorale-settings) developed both in Agricola's direction, so to speak, and in Mahu's and Walter's. Utilitarianism reached an extreme with the publication (Nuremberg, 1586) of a little book with a monster title: *Funfftzig geistliche Lieder und Psalmen mit vier Stimmen auff contrapunctsweise (für die Schulen und Kirchen in löblichen Fürstenthumb Würtenberg) also gesetzt, das eine gantze Christliche Gemein durchaus mit singen kann* ("Fifty sacred songs and psalms in four-part counterpoint for the

FIG. 18-3   Front and back of the title page to *Newe duedsche geistliche Gesenge* (New German Spiritual Songs, Wittenberg: Rhaw, 1544). The portrait is that of the printer, Georg Rhaw.

schools and churches of the honorable principality of Württemberg, set in such a way that an entire Christian congregation can sing along throughout"), arranged by Lucas Osiander, the town pastor of Stuttgart and tutor to the Prince of Württemberg in south-central Germany.

Osiander was not a professional musician, and his primitive harmonizations of psalm tones and chorale melodies may seem to have little artistic value, but they were the first recognizable "four-part chorales" (or *Cantionalsätze*, "hymn-settings," as they were officially called) of the kind that remained standard for congregational singing (and not only for congregational singing but for basic harmony instruction) for centuries—indeed, into our own time. Within two or three decades there would be dozens more published *Cantionalsatz* collections, reaching an early culmination in the one—or rather, the three—by an indefatigable Lutheran musician named Michael Praetorius, whose work ethic is reflected in his magnum opus, called *Musae Sioniae*, an encyclopedic compendium of Lutheran music in nine volumes, of which the last three (published in 1609–1610) contained 742 choral harmonizations, based on 458 hymn texts. Ex. 18-6 contains *Cantionalsätze* of *Christ lag in Todesbanden* by Osiander and Praetorius for comparison.

The basic texture of these settings seems to have been adapted from the Calvinist psalters, but the melody is placed consistently in the soprano part rather than the tenor, so that a listening congregation could the more easily sing along by ear, as the title recommends. The idea of transposing the cantus firmus to the soprano may have merely been an obvious solution to a practical problem, but it may also reflect the influence of the villanella or other Italian song styles that were making their way in Germany thanks to the book trade. In any case, Osiander's were the first "Bach chorales." They not only show the antecedents of the practice that J. S. Bach would bring to its stylistic peak a century and a half later, but they also give some idea of the extreme utilitarianism and stylistic conservatism of the atmosphere in which Bach would work his compositional miracles.

That basic conservatism can also be seen in the more elaborate kind of "chorale motet" that ostensibly sought reconciliation with the international style. In these pieces,

EX. 18-6A *Christ lag in Todesbanden,* from Lucas Osiander, *Funfftzig geistliche Lieder* (1586)

EX. 18-6A (*continued*)

sein und sin - gen Al - le - lu - ja, Al - le - lu - ja.

2. Den Tod niemand zwingen könnt
   bei allen Menschenkindern,
   das macht' alles unsre Sünd,
   kein Unschuld war zu finden.
   Davon kam der Tod so bald
   und nahm über uns Gewalt,
   hielt uns in seim Reich gefangen.
   Alleluja.

3. Jesus Christus, Gottes Sohn,
   an unser Statt ist kommen
   und hat die Sünd abgetan,
   damit dem Tod genommen
   all sein Recht und sein Gewalt,
   da bleibt nichts denn Tods Gestalt,
   den Stachel hat er verloren.
   Alleluja.

EX. 18-6B *Christ lag in Todesbanden*, from Michael Praetorius, *Musae sioniae* (1609-10)

Christ lag in To - des - ban - den für un - ser Sünd ge - ge - ben
Er ist wie - der er - stan - den und hat uns bracht das Le - ben

des wir sol - len fröh - lich sein Gott lo - ben und ___ dank - bar sein

EX. 18-6B   *(continued)*

each successive line of the chorale was treated as a point of imitation, so that no one voice could be identified unequivocally as cantus firmus. A three-part school setting (*tricinium*) of *Ein' feste Burg* (Ex. 18-7) by Sethus Calvisius, the cantor of Leipzig's St. Thomas Church at the end of the century, is a good example of the new technique whereby the polyphonic texture more or less evenly absorbed the chorale tune ("more or less," because the middle voice, like an old-fashioned *altus*, has less tune and more filler than the others). But the setting, however artful, remains essentially utilitarian, and it hews closely enough to the traditional tune so that no one could possibly miss it. The art of concealment, so dear to the Netherlanders and even to Josquin, was

EX. 18-7   Sethus Calvisius, *Ein' feste Burg* (1603)

EX. 18-7 (*continued*)

essentially foreign to the Lutheran ideal. And so were all "literary" pretensions, radical experiments, or efforts at rhetorical persuasion. Rarely do the *Choralsätze* of the first Lutheran century indulge in any semantic or illustrative play or aspire to any startling or stirring compositional effect.

A Lutheran musician was an honest tradesmen. His aim was not to bowl you over or attempt sublime disclosure but to furnish an attractive, craftsmanly, not overly polished setting for a cherished article of common faith. Even at its fanciest, Lutheran church music was a town music, not a court music, enhancing and solacing the day-to-day life of students, churchgoers, and families at home. Its esthetic ignored the rare and the recondite, seeking beauty in the commonplace. It did not reject the *ars perfecta* but placed limits on its exercise.

Within those limits—within any limits—masterpieces could be created. *Ein Lämmlein geht und trägt die Schuld* ("A little lamb goes forth and bears the world's guilt"), a chorale tricinium composed by Benedictus Ducis (born Benedikt Herzog), a provincial pastor from the East, for use as a substitute for the Agnus Dei at the Lutheran "Lord's Supper," is a tiny masterpiece (Ex. 18-8). Its modest perfection can serve as a foil against which the Catholic response to the Lutheran challenge can be musically assessed.

THE RESPONSE

That response took a turn that could never have been predicted at mid-century, when all that the leading Catholic bishops seemed to want was an intelligible liturgy. That

EX. 18-8   Benedictus Ducis *Ein Lämmlein geht*

EX. 18-8 *(continued)*

A little lamb burdened by the guilt of the world's children, patiently bearing the sins of all sinners, growing sick and faint, gives itself to the slaughterhouse bench. Forsaking all joy, accepting insult, scorn, mockery, fear, wounds and scars, Cross and Death, saying: "I will suffer gladly."

trend, the one associated with Palestrina, could be interpreted as an attempt to meet the Lutheran reform musically on its own ground — grounds of modesty. It did not threaten the *ars perfecta*; on the contrary, it sought to amend and thus preserve it.

But the Catholic reaction to the Reformation, now called the Counter Reformation, eventually took on a mystical, enthusiastic, and antirationalist character that spelled fundamental theological change — and with that, of course, came musical change. This did fundamentally threaten the *ars perfecta*, which was if nothing else a rational style. As the "church militant" turned toward pomp and spectacle, and as Catholic preaching turned toward emotional oratory, church music began to turn toward sensuous opulence and inspirational "sublimity," the instilling of awe. For the late Counter Reformation, church music became a kind of aural incense, an overwhelming, mind-expanding drug.

"To attain the truth in all things," wrote St. Ignatius of Loyola in his *Spiritual Exercises*, "we ought always to be ready to believe that what seems to us white is black, if the Hierarchical Church so defines it."[5] God-given though it was, human reason had its limits. To place excessive trust in it was a hubris on which the Devil could play, if it led proud thinkers away from faith. This much of Counter Reformation teaching was in harmony with the spirit of the Reformation that spurred it. To that extent Reformation and Counter Reformation were united in reform. The huge difference was the source of the faith the two churches espoused. The one placed it in the hands of an infallible Hierarchy, the other in the spirituality of the individual believer. It became the job of the Counter Reformation to win souls back from Luther by fostering emotional dependency on the Hierarchy, which (like the feudal hierarchy it supported) viewed itself as God's own institution among men.

The highest spiritual premium was placed on what was called the ecstasy, or, more loosely, the "religious experience"—a direct and permanently transforming emotional apprehension of the divine presence. The most famous literary description of religious ecstasy, visually immortalized by the seventeenth-century sculptor Giovanni Bernini, is from the *Vida* (1565), or autobiography, of a Spanish nun, Saint Teresa of Avila, an epileptic, whose seizures were accompanied by visions. In one of them (the one portrayed by Bernini), she was visited by a beautiful angel, who, she wrote,

> thrust a long dart of gold, tipped with fire, through my heart several times, so that it reached my very entrails. So real was the pain that I was forced to moan aloud, yet it was so surpassingly sweet that I would not wish to be delivered from it. No delight of life can give more content. As the angel withdrew the dart, he left me all burning with a great love of God.[6]

There can be little doubt that—paradoxically though it may appear—it was the extravagant sensuality of Saint Teresa's description that made it a spiritual classic. (At first her visions, so tinged with the erotic, aroused suspicion: the *Vida* was originally composed as an apologia, at the behest of the Inquisition.) And it is that spiritualized sensuality or sensualized spirituality that Counter Reformation art reflects at its most potent.

In music, that sensuality had two main avenues of expression. One was transfer to the religious domain of the techniques of quasi-pictorial illustration and affective (often highly erotic) connotation that had been developed by the madrigalists. The other was the augmentation of the sheer sound medium and its spectacular deployment, so that sound itself became virtually palpable. Both of these strains can be found at a high level of early development in the *Opus musicum*, the mammoth, calendrically organized collection of Latin liturgical music published in Prague between 1586 and 1591 by Jacobus Gallus (or Jakob Handl, or Jacov Petelin—in all cases the surname means "rooster"), a composer from Slovenia who worked in Bohemia, both Slavic areas within the Austrian dominion of the Holy Roman Empire.

FIG. 18-4 Gian Lorenzo Bernini, *The Ecstasy of Saint Teresa of Avila* (1652) at the church of Santa Maria della Vittoria in Rome. Compare Bernini's hectic sensuality with the "perfect" art of Raphael in Fig. 15-1.

Mirabile mysterium (Ex. 18-9), a Christmas motet, is literally mystical. That is, it seeks to portray—give direct apprehension of—a mystery that lay at the very foundation of church dogma: the fleshly incarnation of the Holy Spirit in Jesus Christ, God become Man. In it, for the first time, we may observe the chromatic techniques of Lasso, Marenzio, and Gesualdo—techniques involving the direct "irrational" inflection of scale degrees—applied to a liturgical text (that is, a text meant, unlike Lasso's Sibylline Prophecies, for actual performance in church) as a way of rendering uncanny secrets and imparting uncanny sensation. It is music that seeks to provide a religious experience.

The opening point of imitation, announcing the "marvelous mystery," already includes a chromatic inflection that gives rise to marvelously mysterious harmonic progressions (Ex. 18-9a). A suggestion of commixture of opposites is already given at the words *innovantur naturae*, where sharped notes and flatted notes are combined "vertically" in harmonies that had no theoretical explanation—in terms of the *ars perfecta* theory books this was indeed an "innovation of nature." The thesis is stated in terms of a bald opposition: the distance from God to man is dramatized by a precipitous octave descent in all voices, from which, in emphatic violation of the Palestrina ideal, a further descent is made into a region where the singers' voices will sound weak and

EX. 18-9A Jacobus Gallus, *Mirabile mysterium*, mm. 1–11

helpless, like man before God (Ex. 18-9b). Where the text says that what God was, God remains, the word *permansit* is stretched out for an "eternity." And where the text says that what man was not a man shall assume, the word *assumpsit* is "painted" according to its etymological meaning, by strange *rising* intervals — an octave in the soprano, a minor sixth in the tenor, and a weird augmented second (normally forbidden by "nature") in the bass.

But the most esoteric musical effect is reserved for the moment of mystery: the preternatural passing of the one substance into the other "without mixture" calls forth a possibly unprecedented triple chromatic inflection, disguised by false relations (Ex. 18-9c). On *passus* the bass's B is inflected to B♭ both by direct progression and by transfer to the soprano; The alto's D♯ is inflected to D-natural by transfer to the tenor; and the soprano's F♯ is inflected to F-natural by transfer to the alto. In the process both

EX. 18-9B   Jacobus Gallus, *Mirabile mysterium*, mm. 16–28

soprano and alto sing intervals (diminished fourth and diminished third respectively) that do not exist at all within the rules of the *ars perfecta*. More "innovations of nature." Simply "side-slipping" from a B major to a B♭ major triad would not have conveyed the "marvelous mystery." What makes it marvelous and uncanny is the way in which the voices all exchange their positions in passing between those two mutually exclusive harmonies. That exchange, to quote another mystical Christmas antiphon, is truly an *admirabile commercium*: a dazzling interchange. To account for the musical effect takes a musician; to discuss the mystery takes a theologian; but the uncanny experience is available to all through sheer sensory perception.

The other mode of Counter Reformation sensuality is well conveyed by Gallus's setting of the Passion narrative from the Gospel of John, a grandiose Easter motet in three long sections. Music for multiple choirs, pioneered rather tamely by Willaert and some of his Venetian contemporaries for antiphonal Vespers psalms, became a craze (in churches that could afford it) by the end of the century. Both the spatialized effect and the multiplication of voice parts contributed to the "overbowling" or awe-inspiring result, bypassing reason and boosting faith.

The Passion, the Gospel account of Christ's suffering and death, is recited at Mass during the Holy Week that precedes Easter: on Palm Sunday it is read from the Book of Matthew, on Wednesday from Luke, on Thursday from Mark, and finally, on Good Friday, it is read from the Book of John. The Passion reading was always specially marked by music: originally by the use of special recitation or "lesson" tones, from the fifteenth century on by the use of polyphony. The earliest polyphonic settings were

EX. 18-9C   Jacobus Gallus, *Mirabile mysterium*, mm. 43–47

Today the awesome mystery is revealed,
and our natures are renewed:
God is made man.
That which he was he remained;
that which he was not, he assumed,
suffering neither contaminatioon
nor division.

responsorial. The narrative was chanted; only the lines given to the "crowd" (*turba*) were multiplied polyphonically for chorus, usually in a simple style like fauxbourdon. Later the words of other characters who speak directly within the narrative were set polyphonically, and finally the words of Christ were also so set, leaving only the voice of the Gospel narrator or evangelist in chant.

The earliest complete polyphonic setting of the Passion text—including the evangelist narration, the *exordium* or sung title ("The Passion of Our Lord Jesus Christ According to. . ."), and a *conclusio* or final prayer—dates from the first decade of the sixteenth century. Each of its sources names a different composer; Rhau picked it up in 1538 and issued it in print for the first time, attributing it (surely wrongly) to Obrecht. Its Italian origin (or at least its Italianate orientation; some sources attribute it to a French-born composer named Antoine de Longueval) is evident from its use of *falsobordone*, a way of setting psalm tones in four-part harmony (triads in what we now call root position) that was developed "by ear" in imitation of fauxbourdon (see Ex. 18-10). This setting already shows a tendency to treat parts of the choir antiphonally for dramatic effect.

In Gallus's St. John Passion, two four-part choirs, differentiated in range, are treated in antiphony. The low choir is reserved for the *vox Christi*, the voice of Christ, whose gravity it betokens. The high choir takes the parts of all other characters, such as the thief who speaks to Jesus from the adjoining cross, and also the Evangelist during the narration of the Seven Last Words, when the narrator and the voice of Christ are the only two "characters" in play. The combined choirs represent the *turba*: at these moments the setting takes on the traditional, impressively thundering, harmonically static but rhythmically active quality of the *falsobordone*.

EX. 18-10   From the "Longueval" Passion, mm. 10–21

EX. 18-10 *(continued)*

(Pilatus then turned to the Jews, saying: "Behold your king!")
At which the priests cried out, saying: "We have no King but Caesar."

The full eight-part chorus takes over the Evangelist's role for the conclusion, encompassing the announcement of Christ's death and the general prayer (Ex. 18-11), where antiphony seems to strengthen the idea of generality (the lower choir "seconding" and joining in with the pleas of the higher). The triple Amen, mandated by the length of the piece it concludes and the need for an appropriate peroration, shows the composer's high awareness of himself as orator and rhetorician—that is, a persuader. If such a music proclaims it, we may very well believe that what seems to us white is black.

AUGENMUSIK

Compared with the sheer sonic magnitude of this Passion setting, the inherent drama of the choral characterizations, and the composer's self-dramatization at the end, the use of "madrigalisms" like those in *Mirabile mysterium* is secondary and sporadic. There is a spectacular one at the very beginning of the third and last part of this grandiose work, however, and it is of an especially "literary" kind. At the first mention of the word "crucify" (Ex. 18-12), a really jarring harmony (a C♯-minor triad, we would call it) is introduced—simply for its shock-value, it might appear—as a way of underscoring the horror of the event.

But there is another dimension to it as well. The harmony is produced by the abrupt and "unprepared" apparition of sharps in all parts. The word for "sharp" in German is *Kreuz*—"cross." Thus the strange harmony is not only an audible effect; it is a visual effect as well—or rather, a literary pun based on the visual appearance of

EX. 18-11   Jacobus Gallus, St. John Passion, tertia pars, end

the notated music. (Another instance of such a visually inspired pun, and a popular one among madrigalists, was setting the word *occhi*—"eyes"—as two semibreves on the same pitch side by side, each representing an eye; yet another was coloring all the notes in a lament or funeral piece black.) The Germans have a word for this sort of thing: *Augenmusik*, "eye-music." It may seem a particularly trivial or frivolous variety of "madrigalism," but it carries an important cultural message. Composers who indulge in Augenmusik tacitly equate notation with music, or at least give evidence of regarding the notation as being as much a part of the music as the performance. The music, in short, has become indelibly associated with its written embodiment (not to say "text," which for music can merely mean the words to be sung). Musicians who think this way have come to regard music as being a primarily literate, secondarily oral medium rather than the other way around. So it has been regarded, by composers in the so-called "classical" or "art music" tradition, ever since. This is, in fact, the most accurate definition possible of that notoriously hard-to-define yet definitely recognizable tradition, the tradition of which this book is a history.

EX. 18-12   Jacobus Gallus, St. John Passion, tertia pars, mm. 1–7, high voices only

"CONCERTED" MUSIC

The polychoral style and the Counter Reformation attitudes associated with it reached their pinnacle in Venice, the city of its birth, at the hands of two musicians from the same family, both of whom served as organists at St. Mark's under Zarlino. Andrea Gabrieli (ca. 1532–85) competed successfully, after several failures, for the first organist's position in 1566 and held the post until his death. During that period there were several major quasi-secular celebrations held at the cathedral—the outstanding one being the *trionfi* following the naval victory over the Turks at Lepanto in 1571—and Gabrieli's music for these occasions revealed an enormous aptitude for ceremonial splendor, a talent he continued to develop as the cathedral's musical resources were expanded. He also furnished music for theatrical presentations, including a set of choruses for up to six voices performed in March 1585 at a gala performance of Sophocles's tragedy *Oedipus tyrannis*. It is the earliest surviving music specifically composed for a humanist revival of Greek drama, which puts Gabrieli in the line that led, eventually, to opera.

Andrea's collected sacred works, published the year after his death, contain several spectacular Masses and motets that employ larger and more varied forces than any previous written music. Especially indicative of the trend is a Mass for sixteen voices organized into four antiphonally deployed four-part choirs, performed in 1585 to welcome (and impress) a party of visiting Japanese princes. One of the choirs was marked *a cappella*, designating it and it alone as intended for performance by voices (and voices alone) on all four parts. The intended performing medium for the other choirs can be deduced from the title page of the collection: CONCERTI/*continenti Musica DI CHIESA*/*per voci, & stromenti Musicali; à 6.7.8.10.12.&16.*

Concerti! A momentous word. From Andrea's title page one can learn what it originally meant: works expressly combining voices and instruments—written, that is, in what is still sometimes called the "concerted" style—in which the contrast and interplay of timbres are an integral part of the musical conception. From the employment lists at St. Mark's it is possible to infer that these works by Gabrieli mixed and alternated voices with wind instruments such as cornetti—not modern cornets but instruments held and fingered like oboes but played with a brass cup mouthpiece—on the upper parts (or choirs) and trombones on the lower, with the organ playing along with everything and providing the sonic glue that held the whole timbrally and spatially variegated surface together.

Gabrieli's "concerted" Masses and motets were quickly imitated—so quickly as to suggest that the practice was an established one, at least in the great churches of northern Italy, long before it was specified in print. The very next year, in 1589, the Bolognese musician Ascanio Trombetti, associated with the church of San Petronio, a great center for instrumental music, published *Il primo libro de motetti accomodati per cantare e far concerti* ("The first book of motets arranged for singing in conjunction with instruments").

The terms *concerto* and *concertato* became standard in titles. Beginning with the double-choir *Concerti ecclesiastici a otto voci* ("Church concertos [= concerted motets] for eight voices") by the Bolognese organist Adriano Banchieri (Venice, 1595), publishers supplied a new standard feature: a separate part for the organist to assist the player in his new role as omnibus accompanist. Banchieri supplied a primitive score (*spartitura* = "parts extracted") for this purpose that summarized the basic harmonies of his first choir.

A few years later, in a more modest publication called *Cento concerti ecclesiastici, a una, a due, a tre & a quattro voci* ("One hundred church concertos for 1, 2, 3, and 4 voices," Venice, 1602) by a peripatetic north Italian friar named Lodovico Viadana, a more streamlined organ part was devised. Since some of Viadana's "concerti" were actually accompanied solo songs (in keeping with yet another sort of radical anti-*ars-perfecta* practice that we will investigate in the next chapter), there was nothing to "score." Instead, as the title page advertised, there was a *basso continuo per sonar nell'organo, nova inventione commoda per ogni sorte de cantori, & per gli organisti:* "a continuous bass line to play on the organ, a new invention for the convenience of all kinds [i.e., any number] of singers and for the organists." The *basso continuo,* a term that caught on and has been standard ever since, was an independent organ part written as one line, but realized in full harmonies (with radical implications: for the first time in "composed" or literate music chordal harmony functioned as a sonorous filler or background, independent of controlled part writing). In effect, the notated line was to be played by the left hand, and the unnotated chords by the right. It was called "continuous" because it played straight through the composition, no matter what went on above it.

In view of the radical harmonic implications of the new style, it should be reemphasized that neither Banchieri nor Viadana suddenly invented any new technique of accompaniment. All they did was publish written aids to help organists do what they did anyway by longstanding "oral" tradition. Organists had been accompanying ensembles since whenever, but previously they had to do it from the same choirbook or part books as the other musicians. As we have already seen, organists had to be able to open a whole set of part books in front of them on the music rack and follow them all at once (unless they went to the trouble of writing out a *spartitura* for themselves, as many did). From around the turn of the century, though, no music print was complete (or competitive) without the new laborsaving device of a separate organ bass-book.

Eventually, the most common kind of organ part for church "concerti"—for example, the pioneering *Prima parte dei salmi concertati* ("First installment of Psalms in concerted style," 1609) by Girolamo Giacobbi, another musician from San Petronio in Bologna—was something in between Banchieri's *spartitura* and Viadana's *basso continuo.* What Giacobbi—or rather his powerful publisher, the Venetian music magnate Antonio Gardano—supplied was a composite bass line, drawn from all the other parts, that showed the lowest note sounding at any given moment. This new organist's aid was informally called *basso seguente* ("bass that follows"), because it tracked the progress of the vocal parts from start to finish. By using it, the organist could accompany the whole ensemble without even seeing the other parts.

As always, the introduction of a laborsaving device inspired a backlash from those proud of their laborious skills. Adriano Banchieri himself inveighed against his fellow townsman Giacobbi's publication, sneering that "soon we shall have two classes of players: on the one hand Organists, that is to say, those who practice good playing from score and improvisation, and, on the other hand, Bassists who, overcome by sheer laziness, are content with simply playing

FIG. 18-5 Colophon of the Venetian music printer Antonio Gardano.

the Basso Continuo."[7] Behind these petulant words lay a profound and legitimate concern that unwritten ("oral") traditions were about to be lost to literate habits that carried literalism and lessened creativity as their undesirable corollary. And so they were.

But there was no stopping the process. The mandate of the marketplace was more compelling than any musician's strictures, and any music publications that remained in print past the date of Gardano's innovation had to be fitted out with a *basso seguente* to remain viable. Thus the popular Viadana's first publication, a collection of Vespers Psalms in five parts (1588) was reissued in 1609 with a note on the title page, in proper church Latin, that *additus est bassus continuus pro organo*, in reality a *basso seguente*; his first book of four-part Masses, published in 1596, was reissued in 1612 *cum basso generali pro organo*, and so on.

Even older music was renovated in this way. Palestrina's *Missa Papae Marcelli*, the prime embodiment of the earlier, less musically radical phase of the Counter Reformation, and almost from the moment of its creation a revered "classic," was arranged in the early seventeenth century both as a polychoral composition (for two four-part choirs) and as a continuo-accompanied one. Re-outfitting was the price of currency; "authentic" performance practice for music in obsolete styles had to await the advent of Romanticism, which had a strong nostalgic component and which despised the marketplace (at least officially).

THE ART OF ORCHESTRATION IS BORN

Beyond the provision of an organ bass, none of the publications mentioned so far actually specified the instrumentation for concerted compositions — or as perhaps we ought therefore to say, for concerted performances. All the parts were furnished with text, none was "vocal" or "instrumental" to the exclusion of the other possibility, so the assignment of voices and instruments to specific parts had to be made by the director of the performance *ad hoc* ("for the nonce"). The first composer to furnish definite specifications for his concerted works — in other words, the first composer to practice the art of orchestration as we know it — was Andrea Gabrieli's nephew and pupil Giovanni Gabrieli (ca. 1553–1612), who took the post of second organist at St. Mark's during the last year of his uncle's life, and stayed there for the rest of his own. It was Giovanni who edited Andrea's sacred works for publication in 1587 and included a few concerti of his own. It was a genre in which he would surpass his uncle and, through his own pupils, transform church music thoroughly, in the process dealing a body blow to the *ars perfecta*, no less effective for its being unintended.

Besides the eleven concerted motets of his own that he published along with his uncle's *concerti*, the only volume of music Giovanni Gabrieli saw fit to publish during his lifetime was a book of what he called *Sacrae Symphoniae* (Venice: Gardano, 1597) — "Sacred Symphonies," here adapting the new concerto idea of many-different-things-simultaneously-coordinated to an old word (first used, we may recall from chapter 5, in the ninth-century *Scolica Enchiriadis*) with classy Greek roots that meant "things sounding together in harmony," or (to be equally classy in English) "sacred concinnities." This was a collection of double-choir motets plus a few for three or four choirs (and some instrumental pieces to be described later), issued in twelve vocal part books (without even a special organ part; at least none survives), but with a title page that calls for the *concertato* mixture of voices and instruments in performance. So far he was perfecting his uncle's style.

The second book of *Sacrae Symphoniae*, issued posthumously in 1615, was the epoch-maker. Its contents cannot be precisely dated, but all the motets in it were presumably written after the date of the first collection, fixing their *termini* at 1597–1612. The great departure (actually nothing more than making explicit what was formerly implicit, but to spectacular effect) was the exact specification of the performance medium, and the extremely contrastive exploitation of the diverse resources at the composer's disposal.

In ecclesiis benedicite Domino ("Bless the Lord in the congregations," Ex. 18-13), probably composed sometime after 1605, shows the younger Gabrieli at the height of his powers. There are fifteen parts in all, deployed in three choirs plus an organ part that combines the roles of *basso continuo* and *basso seguente* in what was customarily called the *basso generale*, the "general bass." The three choirs are of distinctive, mutually exclusive, composition. There are four parts (SATB) labeled *cappella*, standing for the chorus; there are four parts (SATB) labeled *voce*, standing for vocal soloists; and there are six parts assigned to specific instruments — three cornetti on top, two trombones at the bottom, and a *violino* (then a new instrument, making an early appearance in notated music) in the middle, its range suggesting that it was of a size more like that of a modern viola than what has subsequently been standardized as the violin we now know. The vocal and instrumental parts are distinguished both in style and in function; but so are the choral and solo parts within the vocal contingent. The soloists' parts have a great deal of written out embellishment that again probably reflects what was previously the unwritten ("oral" or "improvisatory") norm. Even in bald verbal description the piece makes a vivia impression; but comparing what follows to a recording or a complete score will help.

In ecclesiis begins more or less like a Viadana solo "concerto," with a single soprano voice supported by an independent organ (*continuo*) line. In the score as given in Ex. 18-13, the right hand of the organ part is "realized" by an editor for the benefit of modern musicians who are even more the victims of their literacy — i.e., wholly dependent on what is fixed in writing — than those in Gabrieli's time, when printed music books had been available for only a century. The chorus enters as if in response at *Alleluia*, its music contrasting in every conceivable way with that of the soloist: in texture, in its homorhythmic relationship with the bass, and (most strikingly of all) in its dancelike triple meter. The soprano soloist, meanwhile, sings in alternation with the chorus, emphasizing the ancient responsorial effect and showing its relationship to the novel *concertato* style.

But even more basic to the *concertato* idea, and its truly subversive aspect from the standpoint of the *ars perfecta*, is its emphasis on short-range contrast rather than long-range continuity (recall old Jacques Buus from chapter 15 and his ten-mile ricercari!). And also indicative of the new style's incompatibility with old ideals is the "general pause" — the rest in all parts — that comes before the choral metric shift and cadence in m. 10. It is not only a rhetorical pause but a pragmatic concession to the reverberent enclosed space that is receiving and reflecting Gabrieli's sonic overload. The grand pauses are there to let the echo clear—an echo that at St. Mark's lasts a good six seconds (as one can learn from "on location" recordings) when the music is on the elephantine scale of a "sacred symphony." Next the bass soloist sings another little "concerto" to the bare organ's support—and now the chorus is back with another *Alleluia* in response. But whereas the bass's music differed from the soprano's, the chorus's responses are both the same. The Alleluias, in other words, are acting as refrains, or, to use the newer word Gabrieli would have used, as *ritornelli*. The use of a ritornello, a recurrent musical strain, is as endemic to the *concertato* style as the use of a basso continuo. Where the one

EX. 18-13   Giovanni Gabrieli, *In ecclesiis* (*Sacrae Symphoniae*, Book II) mm. 1–12

EX. 18-13 *(continued)*

In the congregations, bless ye the Lord, Alleluia.

unifies — or, perhaps better, anchors — the unprecedentedly heterogeneous texture, the other anchors the unprecedentedly heterogeneous sequence of events.

At this point, after two solo verses and two choral refrains, the instruments interrupt the proceedings for a ceremonial proclamation of their own, marked *Sinfonia* to show that they have the stage, so to speak, to themselves. After they have shown off their lips and tongues a bit with dotted rhythms and quick upbeat figures in tiny note values that Gabrieli would have called *semicrome* (and that we call sixteenth-notes — the first we've encountered!), the two remaining vocal soloists, alto and tenor, join them for the next verse. Another aspect of *concertato* writing — the one that has become primary over the years — emerges when the singers begin vying in virtuosity with the cornetti, *semicrome* and all. The verse is capped, by now predictably, with the choral Alleluia ritornello, but now the chorus trades off not with one singer but with two, backed up by the full instrumental choir.

The fourth verse ventures yet another combination, pitting soprano against bass over the continuo in a duel of *semicrome* and smart dotted rhythms. The chorus enters on schedule with its ritornello. And now, with only one verse to go, Gabrieli pulls out all the stops: the full three-choir *tutti* is heard for the first time, and to magnify the sublime effect the composer adds some chromatic "madrigalian" harmony, thus combining both techniques of Counter Reformation church-militant bravura in a single irresistible onslaught, to defeat the reasoning mind by overwhelming the senses. The peak is reached when the vocal soloists pour on the virtuosity atop the massed sonority. The final ritornello, needless to say, maintains the *tutti* to the end, reinforcing the sense of arrival by twice repeating the final cadence, capped by the cornetti at the brilliant high end of their range.

What remains to be said after that? Only this: Like any church composer of his time, Gabrieli, who not only studied with his uncle Andrea but also worked for a time in his twenties alongside Lasso in Munich, would have traced his musical ancestry back to the Netherlands — to Willaert, to Mouton, and ultimately, somewhere in the distance, to Josquin des Prez. And yet what is left of their style in his? To see how far behind he has left the *ars perfecta* we need only take note of one amazing fact: from the beginning of this monster motet to the end, there has been not a single point of imitation. There are motives that pass from voice to voice, all right, especially in the vocal soloists' parts. But never are these motives combined into a continuous interwoven fabric; instead, they are forever being tossed back and forth like sonic projectiles, heightening a sense of agitated contrast rather than one of calm commingling.

Further, and to the same general point, the aspect of virtuosity, of executive skill on display, places a new emphasis on the act of performance and its public, hortatory aspect. In a word, the act of making music has been *dramatized*. And it has been more thoroughly professionalized than ever before. From now on, musical performers — whether in church, in aristocratic chambers, or in theaters (a new venue!) — would be public figures on spectacular display. Anywhere that music was made by virtuosi became, in effect, a theater.

That new dramatic element — music making a spectacle of itself — subsuming all the newfangled expressive resources discovered by the madrigalists, the new mixtures of media contrived by the "concertists," and the new craving for *mimesis* (realistic representation) inspired by the "radical humanists" whose acquaintance we are about to make, was the great conceptual innovation — the "paradigm shift," as historians of science would call it — lurking behind all the shocking stylistic novelties that doomed the *ars perfecta* and gave rise to that aggressively exteriorized sensibility we now call "baroque."

"SONGS" FOR INSTRUMENTS

Even instrumental music was "dramatized" under the new dispensation, and here too the Gabrielis played a decisive role. Ever since the publications of Attaingnant began circulating abroad, and even before, Venetian organists had been fond of arranging racy "Parisian" chansons for their instrument and performing them during services alongside the staider, motetlike ricercari with which we are already familiar. (The first publication to include such pieces was a 1523 volume by Marco Antonio Cavazzoni, an organist active both as player and as singer in several Venetian churches, including St. Mark's.) Andrea Gabrieli issued a whole book of *Canzoni alla francese per sonar sopra stromenti da tasti* ("French-type songs for playing on keyboard instruments") in 1571: it contains arrangements of chansons by Janequin, Lasso, and others (see Ex. 18-14a). By the end of the century, however, the "canzona" (for some reason turned into a feminine noun; the normal Italian word for "song" is *canzone*) had become an independent instrumental genre more or less modeled on the style and structure of the chanson, even taking over its typical "pseudodactylic" opening rhythm as a trademark. The earliest books of independent organ canzonas were published by Claudio Merulo, a now retired organist who had once beaten the elder Gabrieli out for the plum St. Mark's post (see Ex. 18-14b).

EX. 18-14A   Canzona incipit by Andrea Gabrieli

EX. 18-14B   Canzona incipit by Claudio Merulo

Just as in the case of the learned ricercare at mid-century, the entertaining canzona was soon adapted for instrumental ensembles. The earliest examples are found as fillers or bonuses in madrigal books, suggesting that they were meant for home use, to spell the singers or provide some variety at convivial music parties. The earliest book devoted entirely to *canzoni da sonare* was by Florentio Maschera, a pupil of Merulo, who worked as cathedral organist at Brescia, one of the more westerly cities in the republic of Venice. Short, simple four-part works for home use, they were published in Venice in 1584 and went through many editions.

By then, however, the Venice organists had begun adapting the canzona to their wonted theatrical purposes. Andrea Gabrieli and his older colleague Annibale Padovano (1527–75), possibly in friendly competition, had each written a canzona-to-end-all-canzonas for eight-part wind ensemble deployed antiphonally in double choirs, based on the old chanson-to-end-all-chansons, Janequin's *La guerre* (alias "La battaille de Marignan"). Like some other big concerted works of Andrea's, they were probably composed for the Lepanto victory celebrations in 1571. The second half of Andrea's *Aria della battaglia* (Ex. 18-15), corresponding to Janequin's "Fan frere le le lan fan" (see Ex. 17-9), and as idiomatic to the wind instruments as Janequin's mouth-music was to tongues and teeth, is one of the earliest examples of real instrumental concert music in something like the modern sense.

The big band battle-piece became a standard instrumental subgenre in the heyday of the canzona. It even exerted a curious back-influence on vocal liturgical music. The flamboyant nine-part *Missa pro Victoria* by Tomás Luis de Victoria (1548–1611), a Spanish organist and composer who worked for many years in Rome, was published in Madrid in 1600. Often described as a parody Mass on Janequin's *La guerre*, it is really

EX. 18-15   Andrea Gabrieli, *Aria della battaglia, secunda pars, mm. 1–4*

more like a big canzona for voices, very much in the highly sectionalized fanfare-like style of Gabrieli's *Aria della battaglia*. The Benedictus section from the Sanctus (Ex. 18-16) is yet another big blowout on Janequin's immortal "Fan frere le le lan fan."

This was precisely the kind of piece the Council of Trent had tried to ban at an earlier phase of the Counter Reformation: "Let nothing profane be intermingled," so the decree read in 1562, "when Masses are celebrated with singing and with organ."[8] That was then. By the turn of the century the "church militant" had decided it had better pack them in by hook or crook. A church service that included battle-pieces along with "concerted" motets or psalms or Masses was to all intents and purposes a "concert." And indeed, Venetian cathedral services at the height of the Counter Reformation could well be looked upon as the earliest public concerts (for a "mass" audience, so to speak). Huge congregations flocked to them, and their fame was spread abroad so that travelers made special journeys to Venice, already a major tourist spot, to hear the music. Thomas Coryat, an English court jester and travel writer, visited Venice in 1608 and left an unforgettable account of Vespers at St. Mark's.

EX. 18-16   Tomás Luis de Victoria, *Missa pro Victoria*, Benedictus, mm. 7–13

EX. 18-16 *(continued)*

The most spectacular impression was made not by the singers but by the massed instrumentalists:

> Sometimes sixteen played together upon their instruments, ten sackbuts, four cornetts, and two violdegambas of an extraordinary greatness; sometimes ten, six sackbuts and four cornetts; sometimes two, a cornett and a treble viol. Of these treble viols [actually violins, most likely] I heard three several there, whereof each was so good, especially one that I observed above the rest, that I never heard the like before.[9]

For an idea of what these instrumentalists were playing, we can turn either to Giovanni Gabrieli's first book of *Sacrae Symphoniae* (1597), which contains sixteen canzonas, or to his last (posthumous) publication, *Canzoni et sonate a 3.5.6.7.8.10.12.14.15.&22. voci, per sonar con ogni sorte de instrumenti, con il basso per l'organo* ("Canzonas and other instrumental pieces for 3, 5, 6, 7, 8, 10, 12, 14, 15, or 22 parts, to be played on all kinds of instruments, with a basso seguente for the organ"), printed by Gardano in 1615. As

EX. 18-16 *(continued)*

the title already suggests, the contents of the later book cover a wide range of styles, all reflected in Coryat's descriptions.

The ones for larger numbers are of course polychoral, deploying massed instruments — the first orchestras, in a sense (though with only one player per part) — in antiphonal groups that answered one another in the resonant interior space of the basilica. The ones for smaller ensembles are florid studies for cornetto and violin virtuosos. As the title of the 1615 publication also shows, the word *sonata* was gaining currency alongside *canzona* to designate the newly theatricalized instrumental genre. It did not mean anything special as yet; like *canzona*, it was an abbreviation of the full name of the genre, *canzona per sonare*. From *canzona per sonare* ("a song for playing") came *canzona sonata* ("a played song"), and then plain *sonata* — something "played." The word sonata still means "something played," of course, but the thing in question has changed many times since Gabrieli's time.

One of the items in the 1597 collection is called *Sonata pian'e forte* — "the piece played loud and soft" — and has a big, not quite deserved, historical reputation

FIG. 18-6   Venetian musicians in the service of the doge playing "six silver trumpets" in procession.

going back to Carl von Winterfeld's *Johannes Gabrieli und sein Zeitalter* ("Gabrieli and his time"), one of the earliest scholarly biographies of any composer. The book was published in Berlin in 1834, when (despite its title) great composers tended to be viewed in relative isolation from their times, and when their greatness was apt to be viewed in somewhat anachronistic terms emphasizing innovation and originality — in other words, the traits by which a nineteenth-century composer's greatness was measured.

Gabrieli's piece (see Ex. 18-17 for its ending) was touted by Winterfeld as the first sonata, the first work to specify its instrumentation, the first work to use the violin, and the first work to specify dynamics. It was actually none of those things. Contrasting loud and soft passages had been implied for a long time in "echo" pieces, both vocal and instrumental, for which there was such a craze that as early as 1581 Lasso published a famous madrigal for two four-part choirs ("O là o che bon eccho," roughly "O gee, what a nice echo") making fun of it. In 1596, a year before Gabrieli's publication, Adriano Banchieri had published a book of four-part *canzoni alla francese* that included one (no. 11, "La Organistina bella: in echo," roughly "The pretty little lassie at the organ: with echo effects") in which the echoes were obtained not by contrasting choirs but by explicit *forte* and *piano* markings. Gabrieli's piece was thus not innovative but symptomatic. It was a symptom of the sensuous delight listeners had begun to take in sonic effects and displays of all kinds in this early period of music-as-spectacle.

EX. 18-17   Giovanni Gabrieli, *Sonata pian'e forte*, end

EX. 18-17 (continued)

Another highly symptomatic piece, and perhaps a more significant one, is the *Sonata per tre violini* from the collection of 1615 (see Ex. 18-18 for its concluding fireworks). It may very well have been on the program that Thomas Coryat described, where he mentions "these treble viols" of which "I heard three several there," playing so impressively. Since all three solo parts in this sonata are treble parts, the *basso per l'organo* in this case is a true basso continuo, an actual fourth part, not a basso seguente. Such a composition,

EX. 18-18   Giovanni Gabrieli, *Sonata per tre violini*, end

for treble or trebles above an independent bass with a vague harmonic filler to be added in performance, is by standard modern definition a "baroque" sonata. Its inclusion in a book of canzonas testifies conclusively to the genealogy of what has been ever since the seventeenth century the principal genre of soloistic chamber music—instrumental music for "pure" listening enjoyment. After four hundred years, we take such a thing for granted. As we shall see, though, when it was new (and especially when it began to travel beyond the borders of Italy) it raised some knotty esthetic problems. Putting this piece at the end of our chapter on the effects of religious unrest underscores the irony: what would remain for centuries the elite genre of "absolute" secular instrumental music was born in church.

Pressure of Radical Humanism

The "Representational" Style and the Basso
Continuo; Intermedii; Favole in Musica

THE TECHNICAL, THE ESTHETIC, AND THE IDEOLOGICAL

As hinted in previous chapters, the central irony of the "Renaissance," as the term is applied to music, is the way in which the Greek revivalism that motivated the "rebirth" of philosophy and the other arts actually undermined the dominant "Renaissance" musical style, if we take that style to be the *ars perfecta*. It would be even sillier to say that the neoclassical revival produced the musical "Baroque," since that term was never used about art until the middle of the seventeenth century, when it was used to describe Roman architecture, and was only first applied to a musical composition (Jean-Philippe Rameau's opera *Hippolyte et Aricie*, as it happened) nearly a century later, in 1733, as an insult. "Baroque" is a term that musicians do not need. Trying to justify it in any terms that actually relate to the music of the period has never led to anything but quibbling, sophistry, and tergiversation. All it is now is a commercial logo for a kind of "classical music" that record companies and radio stations market as sonic wallpaper. Let's try to forget it.

So what shall we call the music that we used to call "baroque"—the repertory that arose in Italy at the end of the sixteenth century and died out in Germany some time past the middle of the eighteenth, and what shall we call the period of its ascendancy? We could simply call it the Italian age, since almost every musical innovation during that century and a half took place in Italy and radiated out from there to other parts of Europe. (There were pockets of resistance, to be sure, but conscious resistance is an acknowledgement of dominion.)

If we want to emphasize its philosophy we could call it the Galilean period, after Galileo Galilei, the great astronomer (1564–1642), who was the world's first "modern" (that is, empirical or experimental) scientist, and therefore emblematic of what we now call the "Early Modern" period, when for the first time secular thought and secular art reached decisive ascendancy in the West. (That is why the story of Galileo's persecution by the Inquisition has achieved such mythic resonance.)

We might do even better to call it the Cartesian period, after René Descartes (1596–1650), the philosophical founder of empirical science, whose extreme mind–matter dualism made possible the idea of objective knowledge and representation. A great deal of music between 1600 and 1750 seeks to represent objects (including objectified emotions) rationally and systematically and accurately, and to formulate rules for doing so. The principle of "objective" musical representation that could be formulated as "doctrine" was a very important idea at this time. (Still, the idea of musical representation was neither born with this repertory, nor did it die out afterward.)

If we want to emphasize media, we could call it the theatrical age. Music theater as we know it today was born at the turn of the seventeenth century (a great age for drama generally), precisely under the influence of the neoclassical revival, and it was much abetted by the new emphasis on representation, for that is what theater is: represented action. But we could just as well call it the orchestral age. Orchestral music and large "abstract" instrumental forms were also an innovation of the seventeenth century, and it was also a great age of instrumental virtuosity — which is to say instrumental music made theatrical. (Again, though, both music theater and orchestral music — not to mention virtuosity — are with us still).

If we want to keep the emphasis on musical technique, then the obvious name for the period — and perhaps the best one — would be the continuo age: the basso continuo as a virtually obligatory aspect of any musical performance that was not a keyboard solo originated around the turn of the seventeenth century, as we learned in the previous chapter, and it died out before the end of the eighteenth. Clearly the presence of the basso continuo (a bass line "realized" in chordal harmony) as a constant factor throughout this period, and its failure to survive the period, in some sense define the period. And that sense has to do with harmony itself, reconceived and newly emphasized as a driving or shaping force in music. It was the development of harmony as an independent shaping factor, and its deployment over larger and larger temporal spans, that made possible the development of "abstract" musical forms.

But were there no connections between the technical and the esthetic and the ideological? Were there no affinities binding the neoclassical impulse, the theatrical impulse, and the rise of the continuo? There certainly were; and to locate them we must turn our attention to the Florentine academies of the late sixteenth century, and to the writings of a remarkable scholar, Girolamo Mei.

ACADEMIES

The original Academy, a school located in the gardens of Academus (a legendary hero) near Athens, was founded by Plato early in the fourth century BCE and lasted until 529 CE, when, having long since moved to the grounds of Cicero's villa at Tusculum near Rome, it was closed down by the Emperor Justinian as part of an antipagan campaign, an act often associated with the coming of the "Dark Ages." The revival of the term by associations of artists and thinkers — beginning with the Accademia Platonica, an informal circle led by Marsilio Ficino that met at the palace of Lorenzo dei Medici in Florence between 1470 and 1492 — was thus one of the most self-conscious, programmatic acts of the humanist rebirth of learning.

During the sixteenth century *Accademie* — literary and artistic coteries supported by noble patronage — flourished in many Italian cities, but Florence would always be the center. The most prestigious one of all was the Accademia degli Umidi, later the

Accademia Fiorentina, founded in 1540, which commissioned translations of works by Greek and Latin authors and also treatises on Italian (that is, Tuscan) literary style. Mei (1519–94) was at twenty-one the youngest charter member of this academy. His initial academy-sponsored treatises, though devoted to Italian literature, already reveal some knowledge of Greek music theory. Beginning in 1551, he made Greek music his main subject and completed a four-volume treatise on the modes (*De modis musicis antiquorum*, "On the musical modes of the ancients") in 1573, by which time he was living in Rome.

This enormously erudite dissertation, which draws on classical writers from Aristoxenus and Ptolemy to Boethius, and also summarizes "modern" mode theory up to and including Glareanus, deals both with the tuning and structure of the modes and with their expressive and "ethical" effects. The concluding book is a discussion, based mainly on Aristotle, on the uses of the modes in education, in therapy, and, finally, in poetry and drama. In ancient times, Mei asserted, poems and plays were always sung—and always monophonically, whether by soloists or by the chorus, whether unaccompanied or doubled by instruments. Despite the wealth of information it contains, Mei's treatise contains no actual examples of Greek music beyond the late Delphic hymns mentioned and illustrated near the end of the first chapter of this book.

So despite all his expertise and diligence, Mei's treatise contained everything anyone might have wanted to know about Greek music except an idea of what it sounded like. And that, paradoxically enough, is exactly why it became an important influence on the course of contemporary music. There was no musical evidence to contradict his impressive assertions about what Greek music could do and how it did it, and why contemporary music could no longer equal its effects.

Mei did not know what Greek music sounded like, but he knew (or thought he knew) what it did not sound like. It was not full of counterpoint, the invention of conceited sensualists preoccupied with their own technique and with mere aural titillation. Their music was just a lot of sound and fury signifying nothing, because its many simultaneous melodies "convey to the soul of the listener at the same time diverse and contrary affections."[1] It was precisely because their music was monophonic, Mei believed, and because their modes did not all use the same set of pitches, that the Greeks were able to achieve their miracles of ethos, or moral influence through music.

Mei's researches became known to a group of Florentine humanists who in the 1570s and 1580s were meeting at the home of Count Giovanni de' Bardi, a hero of the defense of Malta against the Turks and a favorite courtier of Grand Duke Francesco I of Tuscany, for whom he had the job of organizing court entertainments, including musical spectacles. It was in this latter capacity that Bardi became interested in theatrical or dramatic music. He corresponded with Mei about the music of the Greek tragedies and comedies, and also put Vincenzo Galilei (ca. 1530–91), a lutenist-singer in his employ, in touch with the great scholar.

Galilei, who had studied with Zarlino (and whose son Galileo, as we know, made something of a name for himself in another field), was the best-trained musician in Bardi's inner circle. He had already published a treatise on arranging polyphonic music for solo voice accompanied by lute, and had begun a gloss on Zarlino's *Istitutioni*

FIG. 19-1   Vincenzo Galilei in a nineteenth-century engraving after a contemporary portrait.

harmoniche, supplemented with information on ancient music theory as it was being disseminated among humanists. It was in connection with this project that Galilei began corresponding with Mei, whose research had revealed the differences between the ancient system of modes and tunings and the modern, contradicting Zarlino's assertion that the new had grown directly out of the old. This challenge to the historical legitimacy of the *ars perfecta* estranged Galilei from Zarlino. It became Galilei's mission to effect a true reconciliation of ancient theory and modern practice.

This he never achieved; indeed such a thing was scarcely achievable. But his correspondence with Mei won him over to the view that the *ars perfecta*, far from the ultimate perfection of music, was a frivolous deviation from the true meaning and purpose of music as practiced by the ancients, and that the only way of restoring to music the expressive powers of which the ancients wrote would be to strip away the purely sensuous adornments of counterpoint and return to an art truly founded on the imitation of nature.

Galileo cast this inflammatory thesis into the suitably Platonic form of a dialogue: the *Dialogo della musica antica e della moderna* ("Dialogue on music ancient and modern"), in which the two fictitious interlocutors were named after Count Bardi (to whom the book was dedicated on publication in 1581) and Piero Strozzi, a noble dilettante in Bardi's circle, called the Camerata. Coming from a practicing musician, and couched in bluntly argumentative language, this formulation of principles derived from Mei's purely "academic" research caused controversy (Zarlino himself retorting acidly a few years later in an addendum to his treatise called *Sopplimenti musicali*).

Galilei's strongest invective was reserved for the madrigalists (this despite the fact that he himself had published a book of madrigals seven years earlier and would publish another six years later), because the madrigalists already thought of themselves as the humanist reformers of music. They already claimed to be imitating nature in their work, and they were having an enormous influence even on composers of church music during the Counter Reformation. Galilei, presuming to speak for the Greeks, ridiculed the madrigalists for committing a travesty. "Our practicing contrapuntists," he sneered, will say

> that they have imitated the words, each time they set to music a sonnet, a madrigal, or other poem in which one finds verses that say, for example, "Bitter heart and

fierce, cruel desire," which happens to be the first line of one of Petrarch's sonnets, and they see to it that between the parts that sing it are many sevenths, fourths, seconds, and major sixths, and that by means of these they have made a rough, bitter, grating sound in their listeners' ears. Another time they will say they have imitated the words when among the ideas in the text are some that have the meaning "to flee," or "to fly." These will be declaimed with such speed and so little grace as can hardly be imagined. As for words like "to vanish," "to swoon," "to die," they will make the parts fall silent so abruptly that far from inducing any such effect, they will move their listeners to laughter, or else to indignation, should they feel they are being mocked. . . . Finding words denoting contrasts of color, like "dark" versus "light hair," and the like, they will set them to black and white notes respectively, to express their meaning most astutely and cleverly, they say, never mind that they have altogether subordinated the sense of hearing to accidents of form and color which are properly the domain of vision and touch. Another time, they will have a verse like this: "He descended into Hell, into the lap of Pluto," and they will make one of the parts descend so that the singer sounds to the listener more like someone moaning to frighten and terrify little girls than like someone singing something sensible. And where they find the opposite — "He doth aspire to the stars" — they will have it declaimed in such a high register that no one screaming in pain has ever equaled it.

Unhappy men, they do not realize that if any of the famous orators of old had ever once declaimed two words in such a fashion they would have moved their hearers to laughter and contempt at once, and would have been ridiculed and despised by them as stupid, abject, and worthless men.[2]

We have seen all of these techniques and many more of the same sort practiced with utmost seriousness and effectiveness. Even "Augenmusik" — music for the eye, as in Galileo's example of white and black notes — had a perfectly serious motivation and could produce hair-raising aural effects in the hands a musician like Jacobus Gallus (see his St. John Passion in the previous chapter, Ex. 18-11). But Galilei had a certain point in ridiculing "madrigalisms": they are indirect and artificial imitations, based on analogies — i.e., shared features — rather than homologies, real structural congruities. As such they are like plays on words, or witticisms. Depending on mechanisms of wit, they can be taken as humor — and indeed, we often do react to a madrigalism, even a serious one, the way we do to a joke: we laugh with delight when we "get it."

THE REPRESENTATIONAL STYLE

The question is, are there any homologies at all between music and nature? There is one, Galilei contended, if by nature we mean human nature: and that is speech, or what linguists still call "natural language." Plato himself had accounted for the "ethos" of the modes — their ability to influence the soul — on the basis of this homology. In the *Republic*, Socrates asks that just two modes be allowed for music in his ideal state: the one "that would fittingly imitate the utterances and the accents of a brave man who is engaged in warfare or in any enforced business, and who, when he has failed, either meeting wounds or death or having fallen into some other mishap, in all these conditions confronts fortune with steadfast endurance and repels her strokes"; and the one that imitates the speech of "a man engaged in works of peace, not enforced but voluntary, either trying to persuade somebody of something and imploring him — whether it be a god, through prayer, or a man, by teaching and admonition—or contrariwise yielding himself to another who is petitioning him or teaching him or trying to change his opinions, and in consequence faring according to his wish, and not bearing himself arrogantly, but in all this acting modestly and moderately and acquiescing in the outcome."[3] Glaucon, his interlocutor, informs Socrates that he has described the Dorian and the Phrygian modes, respectively.

So human speech—not just words, but intonation, pitch, tone of voice, and every other "paralexical" aspect of speech that communicates over and above the literal meaning of the words (aspects that, in case of contradiction or irony, are to be trusted over words)—is the true object of musical imitation within Galilei's radical humanism. And notice especially that Plato's Phrygian mode is the *persuasive* mode. That is the purpose of music: it is the great persuader. So Galilei's radical humanism is another, particularly literal manifestation of musical rhetoric: music as an art of persuasion. "Therefore," Galilei concluded,

> when musicians go henceforth for their amusements to the tragedies and comedies played by the actors and clowns in the theaters, let them for a while leave off their immoderate laughing and instead kindly observe in what manner the actors speak, in what range, high or low, how loudly or softly, how rapidly or slowly they enunciate their words, when one gentleman converses quietly with another. Let them pay a little attention to the differences and contrasts that obtain when a gentleman speaks with one of his servants, or one of these with another. Let them consider how the prince converses with one of his subjects or vassals; again, how he speaks to a petitioner seeking a favor; how one speaks when infuriated or excited; how a married woman speaks, how a girl, a simple child, a witty wanton; how a lover speaks to his beloved seeking to persuade her to grant him his wish; how one speaks when lamenting, when crying out, when afraid, and when exulting with joy. From these diverse observations, if they are carried out attentively and considered with care, one can deduce the way that best suits the expression of whatever meanings or emotion may come to hand.[4]

What musicians will gain, in short, will be a true *stile rappresentativo*: a true "representational style." Such a thing was not unknown to the madrigalists: we have already observed some pretty effective and accurate imitation of speech in Cipriano de Rore's *Dalle belle contrade* (Ex. 17-15). But even in the most effective and rigorously representational polyphonic setting, there is a fundamental contradiction between the singleness of the expressive poetic or textual voice and the multiplicity of actual singing voices. The solution Galilei proposed was not a return to literal monophony but to what he called *monodia*, "monody"—namely, a single voice accompanied by the lute (likened in this context to Apollo's lyre). In this way not even expressive harmony need be sacrificed to representation.

He was proposing, in short, a kind of music that he had already long since advocated and exemplified: solo singing to the lute, a variety of continuo practice, one might say. But what had long been one performance option among many (and one rarely committed to writing) now became a high cause. And the vocal style now advocated was new in that, even more than the polyphonic madrigal's, it took its bearings from actual, enacted, enunciated speech rather than from the formal arrangements of verse. Galilei made a setting of some verses from Dante's *Inferno* the next year and performed them for Bardi's Camerata as a demonstration of the monodic style. Neither these nor any other monodic compositions by Galilei have survived, however; the kind of music Galilei imagined on the basis of Mei's research can only be inferred from the work of others.

INTERMEDII

One of the first practical demonstrations, or tests, of the new radical–humanist esthetic came in 1589, when Count Bardi was asked to organize the entertainment for the wedding of the Grand Duke Ferdinando de' Medici of Tuscany, the brother and successor (some said the murderer) of Bardi's original patron Francesco, to the Princess Christine of Lorraine. Seizing the opportunity, he put his friends to work on a colossally extravagant set of *intermedii*, allegorical pageants with music to be performed between the acts of a spoken comedy (*La pellegrina*, "The pilgrim girl," by the court poet Girolamo Bargagli).

Such entr'actes were a North Italian theatrical specialty. Their original purpose was utilitarian and the music correspondingly modest: since the curtain was not lowered between the acts, the musical interludes (often instrumental, played from the wings) merely signaled the divisions of the play. Particularly in Florence, and especially at court celebrations, the *intermedii* became increasingly lavish and costly — a form of conspicuous consumption meant to impress invited guests with their noble host's wealth and liberality. Their height was reached at Medici family weddings, each successive one striving hard to outdo the last.

The first Florentine ruler to glorify himself in this way was Lorenzo de' Medici (not "the Magnificent" but his grandson, the Duke of Urbino), in 1518. The first Medici wedding for which the music survives was that of Cosimo I in 1539. It was composed by the madrigalist Francesco Corteccia, and consists of motets and madrigals for up to 24 voices, doubled by full family choirs of instruments. This was "concerted" music before its time, so to speak; but the instruments did not yet have independent parts. Between the concerted numbers, a singer representing Apollo sang to the "lyre," probably a lute or harp. His music is not notated; presumably it consisted of "arias" improvised over a ground, according to a method that (as we know) went back to the fifteenth century.

FIG. 19-2   Ventura Salimbeni, *Wedding of Ferdinand de' Medici and Christine of Lorraine* (1589). This was the occasion for which members of the Florentine Camerata devised their intermedii.

From then until 1589 no *intermedio* music has survived, but souvenir books contain copious illustrations of the sets, descriptions of the action, and lists of participants, from which one can get an idea of the scale on which the musical entertainments were cast. The souvenir book from the 1565 wedding of Francesco I, Bardi's friend and patron, for example, lists thirty-five instruments, including four double manual harpsichords (suggesting that continuo-style accompaniments were already in practical use decades before such a thing was ever written down) and two *lyre da braccio*, chord-playing bowed string instruments that were used to accompany Apollo's solos.

The 1589 nuptial festivities for Ferdinand were the most lavish of the Medici extravaganzas. Texts for the six *intermedii*—composed by, among others, Ottavio Rinuccini, a famous poet and, like Bardi, a noble "academician"—were a sort of mythological history of music. They represented, respectively: the harmony of the spheres; the song contests of the Muses; Apollo slaying the Dragon; the coming of the Golden Age (this one unrelated to the theme but required by noble-nuptials protocol); the story of Arion, a semilegendary poet who, according to a myth, was saved from drowning by a dolphin responding to his song; and a concluding allegory, "The Descent of Rhythm and Harmony from Heaven to Earth." The staging was by Emilio de' Cavalieri, who had been director of music for Ferdinand during the latter's years as a cardinal in Rome before his accession to the Tuscan ducal throne.

The big concerted numbers—for up to thirty voices in seven choirs, often fitted out with instrumental ritornellos or *sinfonie*—were mainly the work of the great madrigalist Luca Marenzio and of Cristofano Malvezzi, the organist of the Medici chapel and a friend of Bardi, to whom he had dedicated a book of *ricercari*. Cavalieri, as Ferdinand's personal musician, was given pride of place. He composed the opening madrigal (*Dalle più alte sfere*, "I, Harmony, come down to you from highest spheres," words by Bardi), with a fiercely embellished part for the virtuoso singer Vittoria Archilei, his protégée (Ex. 19-1a); and, to close the show, a grand panegyric finale directly addressed to the grand duke and his bride (*O che nuovo miracolo*, "O what newest miracle is this!"), a *ballo* or concerted dance-song for the whole company (Ex. 19-1b is the main ritornello) over a ground bass that would live on for a while in other compositions as the "Aria di Fiorenza" (Air of Florence) or the "Ballo del Gran Duca" (the Grand Duke's Ball) or the "Ballo di Palazzo" (the Palace Ball).

And yet Bardi nevertheless managed to work in a few numbers by his younger friends, the musicians who frequented the meetings of his Camerata and were involved with Galilei's neoclassical experiments. Giulio Caccini (d. 1618), a well established singer at the Medici court, later claimed that he learned more from the "savant speeches" of the poets and philosophers who met at Bardi's "than I had in over thirty years' study of counterpoint."[5] He contributed a solo aria for a sorceress (sung by his wife) to open the fourth intermedio, one of the first original "continuo" compositions ever to be written down (Ex. 19-1c). Jacopo Peri (1561–1633), technically an aristocratic dilettante but a highly accomplished musician, was a pupil of Malvezzi and a self-styled "Orphic singer" who accompanied himself on a specially constructed giant lute (or archlute) that he called the *chitarrone*, after the Greek *kithara* or lyre (Fig. 19-3; more casually, it was known as the *theorbo*, literally "hurdy-gurdy"). He both composed and sang to the *chitarrone* the show-stopper from the fifth intermedio: an aria for Arion, lying at the bottom of the sea, with echo effects to suggest his waterlogged condition (Ex. 19-1d).

EX. 19-1A   From the *intermedii* of 1589, opening aria, mm. 5–9

Quai voi,_____ no - va Mi - ner - va e for -

- - - te Al - ci - de, e_____ for -

te Al - ci - de,

From the highest spheres,
As friendly escort to the heavenly Sirens,
I am Music, and come to you, O mortals,
After rising to Heaven on beating wings
To carry the noble flame:
For never had the sun seen a nobler pair
Than you, the new Minerva and mighty Hercules.
(Only the last line included in the example.)

THE "MONODIC REVOLUTION"

The arias by Caccini and Peri were the only moves toward "monodic insurgency" (in the words of music historian Piero Weiss) in the 1589 *intermedii*.[6] The expression is a witty one, because historians have fallen into the habit of calling what happened scarcely a dozen years later the great "monodic revolution," and because many

EX. 19-1B   From the *intermedii* of 1589, main ritornello of closing *ballo* (*Aria di Fiorenza*)

EX. 19-1B *(continued)*

O what a new miracle!
Descending to the Earth
In a noble, celestial display,
Behold the life-kindling gods!
See Hymen and Venus
Set foot upon the Earth.

EX. 19-1C   From the *intermedii* of 1589, Giulio Caccini, *Io che dal ciel cader*, beginning

EX. 19-1C *(continued)*

(The Sorceress's aria)
I who could make the moon
Fall down from the sky,
Command you
Who sit on high
And see the Heavens entire,
Tell us when the almighty, eternal Jove
Will pour his every grace upon the Earth.

of the same names as took part in the 1589 festivities—Rinuccini, Peri, Caccini, Cavalieri—are to of the same names be found among the turn-of-the-century monodic "revolutionaries." Yet what actually happened around 1600 was no sudden musical revolution, but only the emergence into print of musical practices that had been in the process of formation over the whole preceding century. These practices had been given an additional impetus by the recent humanist revival with all its attendant neoclassical theorizing, and by the backing of prestigious patrons. They emerged into print in four famous books, as follows.

In 1600, the last year of the sixteenth century, Emilio de' Cavalieri published in Rome his *Rappresentatione di Anima, et di Corpo*

FIG. 19-3   Jacopo Peri as Arion, singing his own compositions in the fifth intermedio of 1589 (costume design by Bernardo Buontalenti at the Biblioteca Nazionale Centrale in Florence).

("The [dramatic] representation of soul and body"), a sacred play designed, according to the title page, *per recitar cantando*, "for recitation in singing" (literally, "to recite singingly"). It was meant for performance by a society of Roman lay preachers called the Oratorio del Crocifisso (the Preaching Society of the Crucifix), which met in the assembly rooms of the church of San Marcello where members of the Cavalieri family had overseen the Lenten music for many years, Emilio himself from 1578–1584. (It was actually performed, however, during carnival in the assembly hall of the Church of Santa Maria, the so-called Chiesa Nova or "new church".) In terms of its actual contents, the *rappresentatione* was not all that different from the Florentine *intermedii*, though of course it was more modest by many orders of magnitude. But it was one continuous dramatic whole rather than half a dozen loosely connected episodes.

The solo music consisted of a string of little songs (some strophic, some in florid single stanzas like madrigals, some in dance meters) connected by musicalized prose recitations of the sort that would later be called "*recitativo*." It is notated in score over what was in point of fact (but only fortuitously) the earliest printed "figured bass"—that is to say, a continuo bass line in which the harmonies to be filled in are indicated by little numbers (figures) representing intervals (Fig. 19-4).

EX. 19-1D   From the *intermedii* of 1589, Jacopo Peri, *Dunque fra torbid' onde*, beginning

(Arion's aria)
Then from the murky waves
The last of my sighs will I utter (utter ... utter ...)
There goodness with thine sweet accents (ents ... ents ...)
Redouble my torments (ents ... ents ...).

FIG. 19-4 Dialogue of the body (Corpo) and soul (Anima) over a figured bass (the first to be printed), in Emilio de' Cavalieri's *Rappresentatione di Anima, et di Corpo* (Rome, 1600).

In the late months of 1600 (or, by the calendar now in use, the early months of 1601, the first year of the seventeenth century), two different musical settings of the same mythological play were printed. The authors were Peri and Caccini, who had become jealous rivals. The play was an eclogue or pastoral drama by Rinuccini called *Euridice*, after the story of Orpheus and Eurydice as told by the ancient Roman poet Ovid in his

Metamorphoses. Peri's was the earlier setting: it was performed (with some interpolations by Caccini, at the latter's insistence) on 6 October 1600 as part of the nuptial festivities honoring the marriage of Maria de' Medici to the King of France, Henri IV. (Caccini's hastily composed setting would not be performed complete for two years following publication: doubtless he was trying to "scoop" his competitor.) The music of both plays was similar in design to that of Cavalieri's *Rappresentatione*, except that it had far more *recitativo*. Dramatic continuity was given greater emphasis than spectacle.

Late in 1601 (or early in 1602 by the new-style calendar), Caccini issued a book of solo songs with figured bass, called *Nuove musiche*. That title has been one of the most oversold in all of music history. All it means is "new songs" or "new musical pieces," but it has been invested with a much deeper significance by those who, misunderstanding Italian usage, have seen in it the proclamation of a "new music" or the dawn of a new musical epoch. The din of neoclassical propaganda must partly account for the inflation of the volume's reputation, but surely even more critical was its appearance at the turn of a century. (The influence of the calendar — or just the decimal system, really — on our sense of history should never be underestimated, as anyone who lived through the millennial frenzies of the year 2000 will hardly need reminding.)

Cavalieri's, Peri's, and Caccini's cluster of turn-of century publications — plus Viadana's *Cento concerti ecclesiastichi* of 1602, familiar from the previous chapter, which amounted to "nuove musiche" set to sacred Latin texts — brought the monodic style into the authoritative medium of print. Print spread it far and wide: *that* was what made the difference. And there was also the prestige of high aristocratic patronage behind the publication of the *Euridice* plays, which now have the reputation of being the first operas. Owing to that prestige and that authoritative dissemination, performance practices that had been cooking in Italy for many decades could now become standard *compositional* practices in all the countries of Europe.

And that was a revolution after all. It was not, however, a revolution brought about singlehandedly by a determined composer or band of composers. That is how traditional historiography — bourgeois historiography, lest we forget — represents and celebrates change. Whether in the arts or elsewhere, change is brought about in such narratives by the heroic efforts of superior, visionary ("revolutionary") individuals. In fact, the monodic revolution was the slowly evolving work of performers, arrangers, patrons, churchmen, scholars, teachers, composers, and printers, to put the overlapping personnel in rough (and again overlapping) chronological order. The only sudden role was that of the printers.

MADRIGALS AND ARIAS REDUX

For a closer look at the early printed artifacts of the "revolution," the most expedient way to proceed will be in reverse chronological order, which in this case produces an order of increasing size and complexity of genre. Caccini's *Nuove musiche*, which may contain songs composed (or, possibly, first improvised) decades earlier at meetings of the Camerata, amounts to a sort of showcase displaying the basic elements or raw materials out of which the early continuously musical plays and "representations" were fashioned. Indeed, it contains bits of Caccini's own larger spectacles, including four arias and two choruses from a musical play called *Il rapimento di Cefalo* ("The jealousy of Cephalus," after Ovid), which had furnished the main entertainment for the same Medici wedding pomp as witnessed the unveiling of Peri's *Euridice*.

The larger part of *Nuove musiche* is given over to individual songs and to a treatise that instructs the singer on the properly aristocratic way of tossing them off—with great artfulness, but carelessly. The songs are of two basic types, both familiar to us from previous incarnations. The strophic ones, based on repetition, are the "airs" (*arie*). The others—in single stanzas, or "through-composed," as we now rather gracelessly say in musicologese (a dialect of German)—are the "madrigals." Thus we are reminded (and we should remember!) that a madrigal is not necessarily a part-song. Any setting of a single stanza in a word-sensitive style that employs no formulaic repetitions or refrains could be called a madrigal. And when we do keep this fact in mind, then we have a new way of understanding the importance Caccini attached to his madrigals, the songs in which, egged on by the Camerata, he experimented along neoclassical lines and discovered the *stile recitativo*, the style that, better than any other, could *muovere l'affetto dell'animo*: "move the soul's affection,"[7] or as we might put it now, move the listener emotionally.

So Caccini claimed or boasted in the preface, where he says the great discovery had taken place some fifteen years earlier, in the mid-1580s (as indeed it would have had to in order to be associated with the Camerata). His claim of priority was hotly disputed by Cavalieri, and need not detain us, since Galilei was probably there first anyway. But Caccini's madrigals are indeed the place to look first to see "monody" in action.

Amarilli mia bella (Fig. 19-5 [facsimile]; Ex. 19-2 [transcription of the first couplet]) has for a text a typical love lyric from Guarini's *Pastor Fido*, long a major quarry for madrigal verses. Setting it was a programmatic or polemical act—proof that only monody could really do a madrigal's job. And yet it is a madrigal without "madrigalism." Not a single word is "painted." There is no rapid scale to show the arrow's flight. There is no thumping throb to show the beating heart. There is only speech, delivered at something close to normal speech tempo and restricted to something like normal speech range: the whole vocal part is confined to an ambitus of a ninth but really an octave since the high note is reached only once, near the end—an obvious correlation of range with rhetorical emphasis.

And that rhetorical emphasis is the whole purpose of the song. Everything is correlated with it, including the harmonies specified by the early figured bass. The figures show only what cannot be taken for granted; as time went on, and as habits were established, fewer and fewer figures became necessary, and those that remained became more conventionalized. The first figure, 6 over the bass F♯, denotes what we now call the $^6_3$ position, a term that actually reflects and recalls the old figured bass notation. (We also call such a harmony a triad in "first inversion," but the concept of chord roots and inversions would not enter musicians' vocabulary for another hundred years or more.) Note, however, that by the fourth system an F♯ is allowed to imply the same harmony without a figure, since by then (or so the composer assumed), the reader will have caught on that leading tones (or indeed any sharped note) in the bass normally

FIG. 19-5 Giulio Caccini, *Amarilli mia bella* (*Le nuove musiche*, 1601).

required a sixth rather than a fifth (in addition to the always implicit third) to complete their harmony.

The expressive harmonies occur at cadences, under long drawn-out notes whose delayed resolutions not only represent but actually evoke in the listener the desire that is the main subject matter of any love poem. Thus the ancient Greek ideal of ethos — affective "contagion" — is realized (not that Plato would have approved of spreading this particular affect around!). At this early stage of continuo practice, the figures represent specific pitches fixed in register, rather than generic intervals. The main cadential formula — 11 – #10 – 14 (occurring six times, beginning with the second system) — would later be represented as 4 – #3 – 7, subtracting an octave (= 7 steps) from every figure; it is now recognizable as the familiar "four-three" suspension, another term that we have retained from early "thoroughbass" notation. (Later still, the

EX. 19-2   Giuliu Caccini, *Amarilli mia bella*, first couplet in transcription, mm. 1–10

Amaryllis, my fair one,
do you not believe, o my
heart's sweet delight,
that you aare my love?

cor mio   deh   non langui   re.   gui   re.

Di quello adunque, che poſſa eſſere, con maggiore, ò minor grazia intonato nella maniera detta, ſe ne può fare eſperienza nelle ſopraſcritte note con le parole ſotto, , Cor mio deh non languire , prò che nella prima minima col punto ſi può intonare , Cor mio, , ſcemandola à poco a poco e nel calar della ſimminima creſcere la voce con vn poco più ſpirito, e verrà fatta l'eſclamazione aſai affet-tuoſa per la nota anco, che cala per grado; ma molto più, ſpiritoſa apparirà nella parola, , deh, per la tenuta della nota, che non cala per grado, come anco ſoauiſſima poi la ripreſa della ſeſta mag-giore, che cala per ſalto, ſi che hò voſuto oſſeruare, per moſtrare altrui, non ſolo che coſa è eſclama-zione, & onde naſca, ma che poſſono eſſer ancora di due qualità vna più affettuoſa dell'altra, ſi per la maniera cõ la quale ſono aeſcritte, ò intonate nell'vn modo, ò nell'altro, come per imitazione della parola quãdo però ella hara ſignificato cõ il cõcetto: oltre che l'eſclamazioni in tutte le muſiche affet-tuoſe p vna regola generale ſi poſſono ſempre vſare in tutte le minime, e ſemiminime col punto per diſcẽ-dere, e ſaranno me più affettuoſe p la nota ſuſſeguente, che corre, che non ſaranno nelle ſemibreui, nelle quali harà più luogo, il creſcere, e ſcemare della voce ſenza vſar le eſclamazioni: intendẽdo per conſeguenza, che nelle muſiche arioſe, ò canzonette à ballo in uece di cõ affetti, ſi debba vſar ſolo la viuezza del canto, il quale ſuole eſſere traſportato dall'aria iſteſſa, nella quale benche talora vi hab-bia luogo qualche eſclamazione, ſi deue laſciare l'iſteſſa viuezza, e non porui affetto alcuno, che hab-bia del languido. Il perche noi venghiamo in cognizione quanto ſia neceſſario per il muſico vn certo giudizio, il quale ſuole preualere tal volta all'arte come altreſi poſſiamo ancora conoſcere dalle ſopra ſcritte note quanta maggior grazia habbino le prime quattro crome ſopra la ſeconda ſillaba della pa-rola, , languire, , coſi rattenute dalla ſeconda croma col punto, che le vltime quattro vguali, coſi de-ſcritte per eſempio. Ma però deſcritte molte ſono quelle coſe, che ſi vſano nella buona maniera di cãtare, che per trouarſi in eſſe maggior grazia, deſcritte in vna maniera, fanno cõtrario effetto l'vna dall'al-tra, onde ſi dice altrui cantare con più grazia, ò men grazia mi faranno ora dimoſtrare prima, in che guiſa, e ſtato deſcritto da me il trillo, & il gruppo, e la maniera vſata da me per inſegnarlo à gli n-tereſſati di caſa mia, & in oltre poi tutti gli altri effetti più neceſſarij, accio non reſti ſquiſitezza da me oſſeruata, che non ſi dimoſtri.

Trillo.   Gruppo.

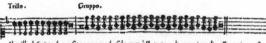

Il trillo deſcritto da me ſopra vna corda ſola, non è ſtato per altra cagione dimoſtrato in queſta guiſa, ſe non perche nello inſegnarlo alla mia prima moglie, & ora all'altra viuente con le mie figli-uole, non ho oſſeruato altra regola, che l'iſteſſa, nella quale è ſcritto, e l'vno, e l'altro, cioè il comin-ciarſi dalla prima ſemiminima, eribattere ciaſcuna nota con la gola ſopra la vocale, à, ſino all'vlti-ma breue, e ſomigliantemente il gruppo, il qual trillo, e gruppo quanto con la ſudetta regola foſſe appreſo in grande eccellenza dalla mia moglie paſſata lo laſcierò giudicare ne' ſuoi tempi i vdi cantare, come altreſi laſcio nel giudizio altrui potendoſi vdire, in quanta ſquiſitezza ſia fatto dall'altra mia viuente, che ſe vero è che l'eſperienza ſia maeſtra di tutte le coſe poſſo con qualche ſicurezza affermare, e dire non ſi poter e vſare miglior mezzo per inſegnarlo, ne miglior forma per deſcriuerlo.

FIG. 19-6   Examples of *gorgia* (*trillo* and *gruppo*) from the preface to Caccini's *Le nuove musiche* (1601).

sharp would by itself come to imply a raised third, and the figures would read 4–#–7. The line cannot come to rest until two dissonances — the suspension fourth and the appoggiatura seventh (not allowed in *ars perfecta* writing) — have been resolved. Such a harmonic intensifier will reinforce any emotion with rhetorical emphasis.

The most obvious rhetorical effect — borrowed from the polyphonic madrigal but vastly augmented — is the textual repetition. Where polyphonic madrigalists liked to repeat the last line or couplet to make the final cadence stick, Caccini repeats the last four lines, amounting to more than half the poem. But what is so rhetorical about literal repetition? Such a thing might sooner pall than enhance expression.

And so it certainly would if it really were literal, but it is not. It just looks literal, and again we have to be on our guard that music cannot be judged by its looks. There is still an oral practice to consider, one to which Caccini devoted a lengthy illustrated discussion in the preface to *Le Nuove musiche* — a preface that is for us a precious document, more famous by far than the actual songs it served to introduce. What it introduces, as far as we are concerned, is not a book of songs but the whole practice of musico-rhetorical embellishment, a constant "oral" factor in almost every musical performance that took place during the seventeenth and eighteenth centuries, but one that left scant visible trace in the musical sources.

In this wonderful preface, Caccini, a virtuoso singer long before he became a "composer" (that is, a writer-down of songs), generously divulges to his readers his whole bag of singerly tricks, called *gorgia* ("throat-music," already a clue to its production), learned in the first instance, he tells us, from his own teacher Scipione del Palla, who guarded them closely as guild secrets. While sternly counseling against their overuse by enthusiastic bumblers, Caccini provides the first systematic survey of the methods by which solo performers (the only kind in monody) were expected to enlarge and dilate rhetorically on written texts. It is a revealing lesson in charisma and a chastening reminder of how much is lost from any performing repertoire that survives only in textual form.

Caccini's rhetorical embellishments included some that multiplied (or, as the analogy then went, divided) the written notes in *pasaggii*,—fast runs and the like. Others were calculated to imitate (or rather, to stylize) various tones of voice or "manners of speaking" that give evidence of strong emotion, and that therefore should be used only when singing "passionate songs," never in "canzonets for dancing." The very word Caccini chose for one of them—*esclamazione* (exclamation), described as "the foundation of passion"—shows the directness with which the emotions were to be physically portrayed.[8] It consists of a gradual loudening of the voice on long notes into an outcry, made more artful by first diminishing the volume before beginning the increase—"reversed hair pins," musicians familiar with modern crescendo/descrescendo marks would say. (Where the harmony permits, an *esclamazione* can also be executed by starting a third lower than the actual pitch and gradually sliding up; this, Caccini warns, is not for beginners.) Clearly, the *esclamazione* is the likeness of a sigh.

Caccini then proceeds to the likenesses of unsteady speech—tremblings and catchings of the throat. The artfully simulated vocal tremble or shake, involving the rapid alternation of contiguous notes of the scale, he calls the *gruppo* or "note-group." We of course would call it a trill. Caccini's *trillo* is something else: it is the rapid, controlled repetition of a single pitch. (For Caccini's examples of *trillo* and *gruppo*, see Fig. 19-6.) What it sounded like, whether (for example) the repetitions were entirely detached or whether the *trillo* was more a kind of amplitude vibrato, his words do not convey. He recognizes this lack, inviting the reader to listen to his wife's singing for a perfect illustration. Modern would-be performers of monodies have had to content themselves with the author's words and their own experiments.

Finally, Caccini lists some "graces," ways of modifying a melodic line to heighten the effect of "speaking in harmony" and "neglecting the music." They mainly involve little rhythmic liberties that put the singer "out of sync" with the bass. In this respect, monody singing seems to have a lot in common with "crooning"—a manner of soft, subtle, highly inflected and embellished singing with intimately expressive intent that was adopted during the 1920s by male nightclub singers in response to the invention of the electric microphone. The word is said to be of Old Scandinavian derivation (*krauna* means "murmur" in modern Icelandic), but the singing style was pioneered and maintained in large part by singers of Italian extraction—Russ Columbo, Frank Sinatra, Perry Como, Tony Bennett (Anthony Benedetto). Imagining how one of these singers would have sung the repeated strain in Caccini's *Amarilli* might give a better idea of how such a song was actually put over than any verbal description of *gorgia*, even Caccini's own.

Beginning in 1602, then, madrigals existed—and were available for purchase—in two forms. Traditional polyphonic madrigals remained popular; they continued to be published and reprinted until the 1630s. Continuo madrigals like Caccini's, and eventually "concerted" madrigals with instrumental parts, gradually gained on the older type, outstripping it in numbers of new publications in the 1620s. (The word *musiche*, incidentally, became standard for continuo songs, further belying the programmatic significance that is often read into the title of Caccini's publication.) The genre produced a line of specialists in Caccini's footsteps. Marco da Gagliano (1582–1643) was perhaps the consummate Florentine musician of the early seventeenth century: a churchman of distinction, he was by 1615 (his thirty-third year) a high official of the church of San Lorenzo, the chief court musician to the Medicis, the *maestro di cappella* of the Florence cathedral, Santa Maria del Fiore (celebrated by Du Fay — see chapter 8), and the founder and focal point of a musical Academy, the Accademia degli Elevati, which comprised "the city's finest composers, instrumentalists and singers," as well as the poets whose verses the musicians set and performed.[9]

Gagliano's most famous monody, *Valli profonde* ("Deep valleys," Ex. 19-3), was published in 1615, the year of his ecclesiastical elevation, in a volume of modern-style *Musiche* that appeared after Gagliano had already published five books of conventional polyphonic madrigals. The poem, a sonnet by the famous sixteenth-century Petrarchist Luigi Tansillo, belongs to the recognized subgenre of "hermit songs" (compare Petrarch's own *Solo e pensoso* as set by Marenzio in Ex. 17-16). Such a song was a natural for monody, because crazed loneliness in the wild was monody's most "natural" subject.

Gagliano's setting shows some reconciliation between the ascetically neoclassical *musica recitativa* proclaimed by the Camerata (and by Caccini) and older madrigalian techniques. A residual interest in counterpoint peeps through almost immediately, when the singer's opening phrase, full of "hard" intervals and harmonies as befits the bleak general mood of the poem, is taken up by the bass in imitation (Ex. 19-3a). Galilei probably would not have approved of Gagliano's "serpentine" melisma on the word *serpenti* ("snakes"): this is old-fashioned madrigalism (Ex. 19-3b). But the unprepared dissonances on *pianto eterno* ("eternal weeping") a few lines later was the kind of thing monody was made for — harmonic effects (apparently) liberated from contrapuntal voice-leading (Ex. 19-3c).

Sigismondo d'India (1582–1629) and Claudio Saracini (1586–ca. 1649) were both noble amateurs. That puts them in Gesualdo's line, and indeed, when writing "passionate" madrigals rather than strophic songs they show the same gift for harmonic

EX. 19-3A   Marco da Gagliano, *Valli profonde*, mm. 1–8

EX. 19-3B   Marco da Gagliano, *Valli profonde*, mm. 38–45

EX. 19-3C   Marco da Gagliano, *Valli profonde*, mm. 51–54

affectation as their polyphonic forebear. The beginning of d'India's *Piange, madonna* ("Weep, O My Lady," to a poem by Giovanni Battista Marino), from d'India's *Primo libro di musiche* of 1609, is a study in what Shakespeare (a contemporary) called "sweet sorrow," and a real slap in the face of "rules." It goes Gesualdo one better in containing a triadic progression in which all three pitches are inflected chromatically—except that one of the chromatic passes is merely implied by the bass (as part of its unnotated but conventional harmonic realization) rather than expressed in counterpoint. The two notated voices, meanwhile, make their chromatic pass in the first measure through the baldest parallel fifths imaginable, the octave displacement in the bass notwithstanding (Ex. 19-4a). The first four lines of the poem are repeated (as Caccini had repeated the last four in *Amarilli*) and d'India writes out the *gorgia* (or at least some of it), putting in writing what Caccini had left to the performer's tasteful discretion (Ex. 19-4b). It

EX. 19-4A   Sigismondo d'India, *Piange, madonna*, mm. 1–4

EX. 19-4B   Sigismondo d'India, *Piange, madonna,* mm. 8–17

Milady cries, and I
enjoy her tears as I enjoy mine,
seeing her cry,
she who laughs at my tears.
O soul accustomed to tears,
have you ever felt sweetness arising out of sorrow?

is likely that d'India transgressed the boundaries of what Caccini would have deemed tasteful (or, in his vocabulary, properly "negligent").

Saracini's *Da te parto* ("I part with thee," Fig. 19-7; Ex. 19-5), from his *Seconde Musiche* (second songbook) of 1620, is another hermit song, spectacular both for its chromaticism and for its gorgia—two "noble" expressive avenues that by 1620 were becoming rather well-trod paths. The opening progressions actually pit major and minor thirds against one another: the bass makes its minor–major inflection in advance of the voice, which, prodded by the changed harmony, is probably meant to slide slowly from natural to sharp on the crest of an *esclamazione* (Ex. 19-5a). The notated effect and the one unnotated are equally necessary to an artful performance of what on the page is crude. The explosion of expressive virtuosity on the final word,

FIG. 19-7 Claudio Saracini, *Da te parto* (*Seconde musiche de madrigali & arie . . . a una voce sola*, 1620).

ardente (ardent, burning), meanwhile, is an ideal illustration of what *gorgia* was all about (Ex. 19-5b). By iconically representing—and of course exaggerating—what happens to the speaking voice when the soul is aflame, the soul's flame is itself by extension "imitated."

The strophic aria Caccini used in the *Nuove musiche* to demonstrate the application of *gorgia* is based on the old Romanesca "tenor" (as they had called it in the sixteenth century), now of course a "basso." Going over an old "ground" like this further demonstrates the continuity that links the monodic "revolution" with earlier unwritten traditions, and provides a link with later written compositions as well, for the Romanesca remained remarkably popular and durable, especially in Florence. In Ex. 19-6 the old tenor is given alongside two composed variants: first Caccini's (compare Fig. 19-8), in which—again, evidently in accord with long-established extemporizing habits—each successive note of the original controls a measure in the fully realized composition; and second, the variant employed by Girolamo Frescobaldi (1583–1643), the greatest organist of the seventeenth century, in one of his *Arie musicale*, published in Florence in 1630. Ex. 19-7 shows the beginnings of its four strophes.

EX. 19-5A   Claudio Saracini, *Da te parto*, mm. 1–4

EX. 19-5B   Claudio Saracini, *Da te parto*, end

FAVOLE IN MUSICA

The style developed by Caccini and the others *in camera* (or in Camerata) did not stay long in private chambers but was immediately returned to the theater whence, in a sense, it came. The monodist's objective was to recapture the emotional and ethical contagion of the Greek poet-musicians—in effect, the idea was to resurrect or reinvent the Greek (sung) drama as reimagined by Girolamo Mei. Galilei had exhorted his musician contemporaries to copy the inflections of actors, which implied from the beginning that the ideal destination of the monody would be the mouths of actors—singing actors, who would add the powers of music to their already highly developed histrionic skills.

EX. 19-6   Romanesca tenor, with Caccini's and Frescobaldi's variants

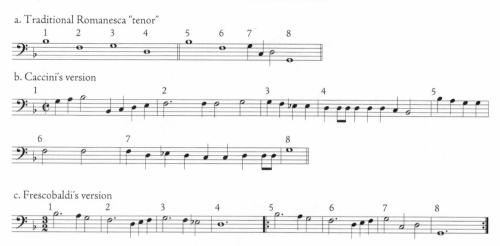

a. Traditional Romanesca "tenor"

b. Caccini's version

c. Frescobaldi's version

The birth of new music out of the spirit of old drama was (like everything else that seems sudden in history) a gradual thing, with phases unrepresented in written sources. The first extant continuo songs that were performed in the course of a stage spectacle were the ones in the 1589 *intermedii*. But they undoubtedly had precedents. As early as the late fifteenth century we hear tell of musicalized dramatic presentations at the northern Italian courts.

FIG. 19-8   Caccini's *Aria di romanesca* from *Le nuove musiche* (1601).

A *Fabula di Orfeo*, a dramatic representation of the same tale from Ovid that would form the basis of the earliest published musical plays, was composed by the Medici court poet Angelo Poliziano and performed, at least partly sung, during the 1480 carnival season in Mantua. Poliziano (or Politian, as humanistically Latinized) also collaborated with Lorenzo de' Medici on a sacred play (*SS. Giovanni e Paolo*) that was performed with music by Henricus Isaac, Lorenzo's Flemish-born music master, in Florence itself, the eventual hotbed of the "monodic revolution." Between the 1589 *intermedii* that he masterminded and his own *Rappresentatione di Anima, et di Corpo* of 1600, Emilio de' Cavalieri produced in Florence a number of sung pastorals of his own composition, with texts by the same poet, Laura Guidiccioni (née Lucchesini), to whose words he had composed the great concluding *ballo* in 1589. According to Jacopo Peri's own generous remark (in the Preface to *Euridice*), these pastorals were the first stage works to put the *stile recitativo* into practice.

EX. 19-7A   Girolamo Frescobaldi, *Dunque dovro (Aria di romanesca)*, mm. 1–6

EX. 19-7B   Girolamo Frescobaldi, *Dunque dovro (Aria di romanesca)*, mm. 19–24

But we do not know these works, just as apart from a few fragments we do not know what is often called the first "true" opera. That distinction belongs to *La Dafne*, after another mythological tale adapted from Ovid's *Metamorphoses*, which recounts—or rather, represents—the story of the nymph Daphne who, pursued by Apollo, is changed by the earth-mother Gaea into a laurel tree. The music is by the same team later responsible for the 1600 *Euridice*. The poem, by Rinuccini, was an

EX. 19-7c   Girolamo Frescobaldi, *Dunque dovro (Aria di romanesca)*, mm. 37–42

EX. 19-7d   Girolamo Frescobaldi, *Dunque dovro (Aria di romanesca)*, mm. 55–60

Thus must I, O cruel one, now be rewarded
for my service with torment and pain?
O betrayed hopes, O vain desire
which keeps my soul buried in anguish.

You, you alone, Love, must I blame,
You who, O tyrant, steal all my joy,
You I must blame, you who made sport of the fact
that the fire of cruelty burns my heart.

adaptation and enlargement of the third *intermedio* of 1589. The music was by Peri, with some assistance (probably unasked for) from Jacopo Corsi, a noble dilettante who after 1592 (when Count Bardi was summoned to Rome to serve as chief of staff to Pope Clement VIII) cast himself as primary supporter and promoter of neoclassical musico-dramatic experimentation. Corsi maintained at his palace what Claude Palisca, the leading historian of the early musical plays, calls "a kind of semi-professional musical and dramatic workshop."[10]

Peri's musical plays were hatched in Corsi's incubator, *La Dafne* possibly as early as 1594. Its first performance took place, possibly at Corsi's residence and with Peri himself in the role of Apollo, during the Florence carnival of 1597 (1598 by the modern calendar), in the presence of the leading nobles of the city including the resident Medici overlord. It was revived several times thereafter, the latest revival taking place in 1604 at the brand new Pitti Palace. The libretto was set again in 1608 by Marco da Gagliano, and Gagliano's preface to the published score of his setting, which survives, is our chief witness to the original *Dafne*. It is Gagliano's insistence on the novelty of Rinuccini's and Peri's spectacle that has led to its being accorded the exalted position it now occupies in history as the first opera, in preference to Cavalieri's pastorals or any previous "musical tale" (*favola in musica*), to use Gagliano's expression.

Calling the work the first opera, of course, puts it in a line that connects it with us; for opera is the first genre encountered since the beginning of this narrative that has persisted in an apparently unbroken tradition all the way to the present. As we shall see, however, the apparent continuity may be somewhat misleading; and so we shall resist the word "opera" for a while and instead go on calling the early spectacles of Peri, Caccini, Gagliano, and (in the next chapter) Monteverdi "musical tales."

"The pleasure and amazement produced in the audience by this novel spectacle cannot be described," Gagliano reports. "Suffice it to say that each of the many times it was performed it generated the same admiration and the same delight." Then comes a significant remark: "This experiment having taught Signor Rinuccini how well singing was suited to the expression of every sort of affection, and that it not only afforded no tediousness (as many might perchance have presumed) but indeed incredible delight, he composed his *Euridice*, dilating somewhat more in the dialogues."[11] So the difference between Rinuccini and Peri's *Euridice*, the first musical tale that does survive, and their previous *Dafne* was the same as the difference between Dafne and earlier musico-scenic spectacles. That difference lies in the greater emphasis on the dialogue-music as opposed to the song-and-dance music, and the greater concomitant emphasis on music that imitated speech as opposed to the music that "imitated" (or simply functioned as) musical entertainment. Accepting the speech-music — the *stile recitativo* or *stile rappresentativo* — as dramatically viable, and accepting as credible the act of speaking from the stage in song (what Cavalieri called *recitar cantando*) required an imaginative leap that not all were prepared (or are even now prepared) to take. Peri himself put the esthetic problem in a nutshell when he wrote in the preface to *Euridice* of his paradoxical aim "to imitate with singing whoever speaks (and without doubt no one ever spoke singing)."[12]

So what made the Florentine (and later Mantuan) musical tales the "first operas" was not the mere fact that they were sung continuously. So were Cavalieri's pastorals, and maybe even Isaac's *SS. Giovanni e Paolo*. And there have since been many types of opera, especially but not only comic opera, that do not use continuous singing but instead alternate singing with spoken dialogue, the very thing that Rinuccini courageously eschewed in his tales. The novelty of the tales was that they maintained and even accentuated the dialogue aspect of the drama (which is to say they did not make formal concessions for the sake of the music) and nevertheless represented all that dialogue through singing. The essential "operatic" move, then, was the insistence that music function on two levels — as representing music and also as representing speech — which meant that some of the music was coded one way for the characters on stage and another way for the audience. There was a music that both the audience and the stage characters "heard" as music (the songs and dances) and another music that the audience heard as music but that was "inaudible" to the characters on stage who were represented (albeit through music, and sometimes very elaborately!) as speaking. (The further complication presented by the instrumental music can wait for now.) It is a dichotomy that every form of opera, and every opera audience, has had to come to terms with, and different types of opera can (and in this book often will) be distinguished on the basis of how they have negotiated this representational crux.

The critic Carolyn Abbate has adopted a useful (and suitably neoclassical) terminology for the "two musics" that have always coexisted in opera. The kind that is "heard" (i.e., interpreted) both on stage and in the house as music she calls "phenomenal music," from the Greek *phenomenon*, meaning not an extraordinary thing or occurrence (as in common colloquial usage) but something whose reality exists on the level of sensory perception. The kind that the audience hears as music but that the stage characters do not "hear" that way she calls "noumenal music" from the Greek *noumenon*, the idealized ("Platonic") essence of a thing — a higher reality that is hidden from the senses and can only be contemplated by the mind.[13]

Of the six scattered fragments that survive from Rinuccini and Peri's *Dafne* in monody collections, only one counts as "noumenal music" of the kind that distinguishes opera esthetically from other kinds of sung spectacle. (The rest are dance-songs and a strophic "aria" over a ground bass sung by Ovid directly to the spectators by way of prologue.) That singular survivor is the recitative "Qual nova meraviglia!" — "What new marvel is this!" — in which a messenger who witnessed it describes the nymph's arboreal transformation (Ex. 19-8).

This is the *stile rappresentativo* at full strength — the earliest surviving example of it that was meant expressly for the stage. The text is madrigalian: a single strophe in irregular meter. The bass line is remarkably static; often whole lines are declaimed over a stationary harmony, and there is no thematic interplay between voice and accompaniment. Since the versification is irregular, the harmonic changes are unpredictable. There is, in short, nothing that can be identified as a "purely musical" pattern or gesture, nothing that aspires to musical wholeness or memorability. Music, far from exulting in its own stylistic perfection, has been ruthlessly subordinated, a

EX. 19-8   Jacopo Peri, *La Dafne*: "Qual' nova meraviglia!"

Messenger (Thyrsis):
What new marvel
have my eyes seen?
O eternal Gods,
who in Heaven make our mortal fate
either sad or happy,
was it punishment or pity
to change that beautiful soul?

music lover might object, to the text. To which a strict neoclassicist might respond, that's just where it belongs.

If the music has to be so minimal why have it at all, both the music lover and the theatergoer might wonder, to which the dramatist might respond that the musicalization accomplishes definitively what the actor accomplishes only haphazardly, depending on his gifts—namely the surefire transmission of the affective content of the words to the listener. The composer, then, functions like a supreme actor or stage director, able by the use of harmony (especially chromatic harmony, as in the fifth measure) and dissonance to magnify the rhetorical effects of vocal inflection and delivery.

The *Dafne* recitative is a tame one; there is no expressive dissonance to speak of. The ones in *Euridice* show a marked advance not only in sheer prevalence over the phenomenal music, but also in expressive confidence. Whole scenes are played *recitar cantando*, and dissonance of a harshness that can still sound impressive abounds in proportion to the intensity of the dramatic situation.

Gravest of all is the moment when Orpheus (sung by Peri) gets the news of Eurydice's death from Daphne, sung by a boy at the first performance while Corsi, on the harpsichord, and three gentlemen on *chitarrone*, on lute, and on the bowed *lira grande*, a sort of bowed lute, churned out the continuo from behind—yes, behind—the scene. Note that all four instruments were "lyres,"—that is, chord-producers, not melody-makers; as a "line," the continuo was a figment of notation, not sound). Some excerpts from the scene are given in Ex. 19-9.

The first thing to notice is the rigor with which the composer has spurned every temptation of the text's imagery, jam-packed though it is with opportunities for word painting—flowing water, murmuring water, light, dark, singing, dancing, to say nothing of the serpent's bite. Not one of these images is painted in tones. There is nothing left of wit, nothing to bring a smile of recognition. Instead, the brutal affective contrast is transmitted through the musical analogues of rhetorical delivery and gesticulation. When, for example, Daphne describes the cold sweat that bespattered Eurydice's face and matted her hair during the death throes (Ex. 19-9a), the music is concerned not with the object described but rather with the emotion of the describer, conveyed in a shocking false relation between the voice and the bass. The moment of Eurydice's death, at the end of Ex. 19-9a, is described with even greater, colder horror: the words *i bei sembianti* ("her beautiful features") are set with hideous irony, using the ugliest harmonies the composer could devise—an augmented triad followed by a blatant harmonic contradiction between voice (on B-flat) and accompaniment (an E-major triad), "resolved" through a descent by a "forbidden" diminished fifth.

Orpheus's lament (Ex. 19-9b) is set with great subtlety, all conveyed by musical "modulations" to match the modulations of his mood. He goes from numb shock ("I neither weep nor sigh. . .") through a sudden outpouring of grief ("O my heart! O my hope. . .") to firm resolve. The first section has a particularly static bass to match Orpheus's initial torpor. The second section, where lethargy gives way to active distress, is introduced by a brusque harmonic disruption: the cadential "Phrygian" E major replaced out of nowhere by "Dorian" G minor. This most anguished section of the lament has the highest dissonance quotient. Orpheus's lines seem altogether uncoordinated with the bass harmonies. He leaves off after "Ohimè!" (Ah, me!) with a gasp, his line dangling on an A over the bass G. The bass having changed to D as if to accommodate the A, Orpheus reenters ("Dove si gita?"/"Where have you gone?") with a new contradiction, on E.

EX. 19-9A   Jacopo Peri, *Euridice*, scene 2, mm. 39–51

EX. 19-9B   Jacopo Peri, *Euridice*, Orfeo's closing monologue

EX. 19-9B (*continued*)

The bass once again moves to accommodate the E, which becomes the cadence harmony. The third section begins with the same disruption as the second: a G-minor chord impinging on the cadential E major. This time, however, the G minor moves through the circle of fifths to a cadence on F, the "Lydian," still the symbol—after eight hundred years!—of mollitude (the primary association by now is not to Plato's resurrected theorizing but to everyone's daily experience in church). At the same time the bass begins to bestir itself iconically, moving rhythmically as one does when animated by determination.

This is no tentative first step like the *Dafne* recitative. By 1600, at least in Peri's hands, the *stile rappresentativo* was artistically mature, a fully viable *seconda prattica*—a "second practice," as Monteverdi would shortly call it in response to its critics—that would eventually consign the "first practice," namely the *ars perfecta,* to the status of a *stile antico.*[14]

Did it immediately cause a revolution? By all accounts it did not even cause an immediate sensation, at least with its audience. At the 1600 royal nuptial celebration very few actually heard it. The main entertainment, as we know, was Caccini's *Rapimento,* more of a song-and-dance affair on the spectacular scale of the traditional Florentine *intermedii.* It was performed before an audience—a real public—of 3,800 in the enormous hall atop the Uffizi gallery. *Euridice* was performed three days later, in a small room in Don Antonio de' Medici's apartment on one of the upper stories of the Pitti Palace, for no more than two hundred specially invited guests selected by Corsi. Many of those who were privileged to hear it were unimpressed: a joke that made the rounds afterward likened the music to the monotonous chanting of the Passion on Good Friday (not such a bad analogy, actually, in view of the original purpose of the chant as a sacralized public oration; but of course that was far from the minds of the jokers).

And yet, clearly, a work performed before those specially invited two hundred (nobles all) inevitably commanded greater prestige than one open to all comers as a token of the celebrants' liberality. And the protocols that applied to *intermedii* and other festive spectacles remained in force in *Euridice*, making a mockery of any claim that the work was a revival of the ancient Greek tragedy. (It is clear from this alone that no such claim could have seriously been made; the idea is a historians' conceit hatched long after the fact.) The tale is furnished with a prologue that has exactly the same function as the prologues to the old *intermedii*: to cajole the audience and laud the nuptial pair. La Tragedia herself appears before the assembled nobles to say that, while her usual role is to draw sighs, shed tears, and "make the faces and expressions of a crowd in an amphitheater pale with pity," just this once she is going to relent in honor of the wedding pair and their friends in attendance: "I thus adorn myself in the realm of Hymen [the marriage god] and tune the strings [of my lyre] to a gayer mode to give delight to the noble heart."

And indeed, the play is made to end happily: Orpheus gets Eurydice back with no strings attached; there is no second death, no second loss. The play remains, as it had to, within the boundaries of the dramatized *favola pastorale*, the pastoral play, a light genre that did not exist in classical times. Not only would a truly tragic representation have been unfit for a festivity of state, but Ovid's mythological romance could never have supported one. In a tragedy a hero falls in consequence of a flaw; an accidental death like Eurydice's is by no classical definition a tragic one (even if Orfeo does lack the ultimate in self-control). The early musical plays did not — could not — aspire to the tragic style. Tragic opera came later, and elsewhere.

ORATORIO

Just a brief word now, in closing, about the genre represented by Cavalieri's *Rappresentatione di Anima, et di Corpo*, the sacred play that happened to scoop all the other early figured-bass publications into print. This work, too, has been claimed for consideration as "the first surviving opera" (to quote the *New Grove Dictionary of Opera*). It was produced in Rome in February 1600, about eight months before Peri's *Euridice* saw the stage. It was set to continuous music, though without much recitative, and fully staged.

The Soul, a soprano, and the Body, a tenor, each with teams of allegorical supporters, advisers, and tempters, struggle against the blandishments of worldly delights, and are finally successful. The work ends with spectacular visions of hell and heaven. This too was a *favola in musica*: the Counter Reformation's answer, perhaps, to the Florentine neoclassical entertainments; and if Peri's pastoral counts as an opera, so does Cavalieri's. They were both musicalizations of existing dramatic genres, neither of

EX. 19-10A   *Anima mia che pensi*, the original lauda (pub. 1577)

Body: My soul, what are you thinking?
     Why are you so sad,
     always bearing grief?

Soul: I would have rest and peace,
     I would have joy and delight,
     but I find sorrow and discontent.

EX. 19-10B   *Anima mia che pensi*, beginning of Emilio de' Cavalieri's dialogue setting

them ancient. But the same reservations proposed above — against calling the Florentine musical plays operas — apply to Cavalieri's Roman one.

The *sacra rappresentazione* or sacred play with music had a long history, even if we do not attempt to trace it all the way back to the medieval liturgical dramas described in chapter 3. In the fifteenth century it had developed out of the singing of *laude* that embodied dialogues. Most of the fifteenth- and sixteenth-century *rappresentazioni* were declaimed, aria-style, to melodic formulas or over ground basses, with frottolas, madrigals, and instrumental pieces interspersed. Some surviving instrumental works by Henricus Isaac, including a wild Moorish dance and a *battaglia*, are thought to be remnants from such plays, possibly from Lorenzo de' Medici's own *SS. Giovanni e Paolo*.

Cavalieri's *Rappresentatione* was very much in the existing tradition, since it was basically an expansion of an old lauda, *Anima mia che pensi*, that took the form of a dialogue between body and soul. It was, however, the first such play to sport continuous music, some of it in the new dramatic style that the composer had pioneered in his pastorals. The first dialogue between the title characters (some of it shown in Fig. 19-3) is actually a setting of the old lauda, of which a polyphonic version had been published in 1577 (Ex. 19-10a). What had merely been two successive strophes in the lauda now becomes a highly contrasted colloquy (Ex. 19-10b): the question, posed by the body in recitative style, is answered by the soul in a dancelike aria.

At its first performance it was a play in the full sense of the word, but since it was performed immediately before Lent in the assembly hall of an Oratory, it prefigures the specifically Lenten genre of Biblical *favole in musica*, scriptural musical tales in dramatic "*recitar cantando*" form but nonstaged. That genre, which came to be called *oratorio* after its performance venue, arose a few decades later in response to the institution of public musical theaters, which had to close during Lent. It will be the subject of a later chapter.

Notes

Introduction

1 Francis Bacon, *Of the Dignity and Advancement of Learning*, trans. James Spedder, in *The Works of Francis Bacon* (15 vols., Boston, 1857–82), Vol. VIII, pp. 419–20.

2 Paris, 1961, trans. Rollo Myers as *40,000 Years of Music* (New York: Farrar, Straus & Giroux, 1964).

3 Robert Walser, "Eruptions: Heavy Metal Appropriations of Classical Virtuosity," *Popular Music*, II (1992): 265. The authority to which Walser appeals is Eric Hobsbawm and Terence Ranger, eds., *The Invention of Tradition* (Cambridge: Cambridge University Press, 1983).

4 Most relevantly for our present purposes in his *Distinction: A Social Critique of the Judgement of Taste*, trans. Richard Nice (Cambridge, Mass.: Harvard University Press, 1987).

5 Pieter C. van den Toorn, *Music, Politics, and the Academy* (Berkeley and Los Angeles: University of California Press, 1995), p. 196.

6 Mark Evan Bonds, *A History of Music in Western Culture* (Upper Saddle River, N.J: Prentice Hall, 2003), pp. 142–43.

7 Carl Dahlhaus, *Foundations of Music History*, trans. J. Bradford Robinson (Cambridge: Cambridge University Press, 1983), p. 19.

8 David Hackett Fischer, *Historians' Fallacies: Toward a Logic of Historical Thought* (New York: Harper Torchbooks, 1970), p. 10.

9 See Anne C. Shreffler, "Berlin Walls: Dahlhaus, Knepler, and Ideologies of Music History," *Journal of Musicology* XX (2003): 498–525.

10 See James M. Hepokoski, "The Dahlhaus Project and Its Extra-Musicological Sources," *Nineteenth-Century Music* XIV (1990–91): 221–46.

11 It was a book review by the British sociologist Peter Martin that put me on to Becker's work: "Over the Rainbow? On the Quest for 'the Social' in Musical Analysis," *Journal of the Royal Musical Association* CXXVII (2002): 130–46.

12 Béla Bartók, "The Influence of Peasant Music on Modern Music," in Piero Weiss and Richard Taruskin, *Music in the Western World: A History in Documents* (New York: Schirmer Books, 1984), p. 448.

13 Howard Becker, *Art Worlds* (Berkeley and Los Angeles: University of California Press, 1982), p. 1.

Chapter 1: The Curtain Goes Up

1 This account follows that of Richard Crocker in R. Crocker and D. Hiley, eds., *The New Oxford History of Music*, Vol. II (2nd ed., Oxford and New York: Oxford University Press, 1990), pp. 121–23.

2 St. Basil, *Exegetic Homilies*, trans. S. Agnes Clare Way, *The Fathers of the Church*, Vol. XLVI (Washington, D.C.: The Catholic University of America Press, 1963), p. 152.

3 Martin Gerbert, ed., *De cantu et musica sacra*, Vol. I, trans. R. Taruskin (St. Blasien, 1774), p. 64.

4 Jacques Paul Migne, ed., *Patrologiae cursus completus, Series Latina*, Vol. XXXVII (Paris, 1853), p. 1953, trans. Gustave Reese in *Music of the Middle Ages* (New York: Norton, 1940), p. 64.

5 Martin Gerbert, ed., *De cantu et musica sacra*, I, trans. R. Taruskin (St. Blasien, 1774), p. 74.

6 For a summary of this controversy and a bibliography, see Kenneth Levy, "On Gregorian Orality," *Journal of the American Musicological Society* XLIII (1990): 185–227. The article, but not the bibliography, is reprinted in K. Levy, *Gregorian Chant and the Carolingians* (Princeton, N.J.: Princeton University Press, 1998), pp. 141–77. See also James McKinnon, *The Advent Project: The Later-Seventh-Century Creation of the Roman Mass Proper* (Berkeley and Los Angeles: University of California Press, 2000).

7 N. Temperley, "The Old Way of Singing: Its Origins and Developments," *Journal of the American Musicological Society* XXXIV (1981) 511–44.

8 W. Berg, "Hymns of the Old Colony Mennonites and the Old Way of Singing," *Musical Quarterly* LXXX (1996): 77–117.

9 Peter Wagner, *Einführung in die gregorianischen Melodien*, Vol. III (Leipzig, 1921), p. 395.

10 They are described and illustrated in Leo Treitler, "Homer and Gregory: The Transmission of Epic Poetry and Plainchant," *Musical Quarterly* LX (1974): 347–53.

11 Anne Draffkorn Kilmer, Richard L. Crocker, and Robert R. Brown, *Sounds from Silence: Recent Discoveries in Ancient Near Eastern Music* (Berkeley: Bit Enki Publications, 1976).

12 All the extant fragments of ancient Greek music have been collected and given new and authoritative transcriptions in Egert Pöhlmann and Martin L. West, *Documents of Ancient Greek Music* (Oxford: Clarendon Press, 2001).

Chapter 2: New Styles and Forms

1 J. M. Hanssens, *Amalarii episcope opera liturgica omnia*, Vol. III (Studi e testi, 140; Vatican City, 1950), p. 54. Translation adapted from that of Daniel J. Sheerin given in Ruth Steiner, "The Gregorian Chant Melismas of Christmas Matins," in J. C. Graue, ed., *Essays on Music in Honor of Charles Warren Fox* (Rochester: Eastman School of Music Press, 1979), p. 250.

2 Hanssens, *Amalarii*, Vol. XVIII, p. 6.

3 The best translation of the preface to Notker's *Liber hymnorum* is Richard Crocker's, in *The Early Medieval Sequence* (Berkeley and Los Angeles: University of California Press, 1977), pp. 1–2. An adaptation of it can be found in Piero Weiss and Richard Taruskin, *Music in the Western World: A History in Documents* (New York: Schirmer Books, 1984), p. 47.

4 The chief questioner is Richard Crocker, in *The Early Medieval Sequence*.

5 It is given a stern "interrogation" in Leo Treitler, "The Politics of Reception: Tailoring the Present as Fulfilment of a Desired Past," *Journal of the Royal Musical Association* CXVI (1991): 280–98.

6 St. Augustine, *Confessions*, trans. R. S. Pine-Coffin (Harmondsworth: Penguin Classics, 1961), p. 238.

CHAPTER 3: RETHEORIZING MUSIC

1 *Scolica enchiriadis*, in Martin Gerbert, ed., *De cantu et musica sacra*, Vol. I (St. Blasien, 1774), p. 196.

2 The informal distinction proposed here between music and Musica follows Hendrik van der Werf's longstanding and useful habit. See, for example, "The Raison d'être of Medieval Music Manuscripts," Appendix to his *The Oldest Extant Part Music and the Origin of Western Polyphony* (Rochester: H. van der Werf, 1993), pp. 181–209.

3 See Richard Crocker, "Hermann's Major Sixth," *Journal of the American Musicological Society* XXV (1972): 19–37.

CHAPTER 4: MUSIC OF FEUDALISM AND *FIN' AMORS*

1 St. Basil, *The Letters*, Vol. IV, trans. Roy J. Deferrari (London: W. Heinemann, 1934), p. 419.

2 James McKinnon, "The Church Fathers and Musical Instruments" (Ph.D. diss., Columbia University, 1965), p. 182.

3 H. J. Chaytor, *The Troubadours* (London, 1912), pp. 38–9.

4 This lovely analogy was suggested in conversation by Imanuel Willheim of the University of Hartford.

CHAPTER 5: POLYPHONY IN PRACTICE AND THEORY

1 Giraldus Cambrensis, *Descriptio Cambriae*, trans. adapted from that of Ernest H. Sanders in F. W. Sternfeld, ed., *A History of Western Music*, Vol. I (New York: Praeger, 1973), p. 264, by comparison with that in Shai Burstyn, "Gerald of Wales and the *Sumer* Canon," *Journal of Musicology* II (1983): 135, where the original Latin may also be found.

2 Haggh wrote up her discovery in "The Celebration of the 'Recollectio Festorum Beatae Mariae Virginis,' 1457–1987," *International Musicological Society Congress Report* XIV (Bologna, 1987), iii, pp. 559–71.

3 Claude Debussy, letter to Igor Stravinsky of 18 August 1913, facsimile and transcription in *Avec Stravinsky*, ed. Robert Craft (Monaco: Éditions du Rocher, 1958), pp. 200–201. The work of Stravinsky's that elicited the comment was *Zvezdoliki* (*Le Roi des Étoiles*).

4 Ring Lardner, *The Young Immigrunts* (1920).

5 Carl Parrish, *The Notation of Medieval Music* (New York: Norton, 1959), p. 65.

6 Leo Treitler, "The Polyphony of St. Martial," *Journal of the American Musicological Society* XVII (1964): 42.

7 Treitler, "The Polyphony of St. Martial," p. 38.

CHAPTER 6: NOTRE DAME DE PARIS

1 In Russian, *vnutrislogovaya raspevnost'*; see Izaly Zemtsovsky, *Russkaya protyazhnaya pesnya: Opït issledovaniya* (Leningrad: Muzïka, 1967), p. 20.

2 Eudes de Sully, *Contra facientes festum fatuorum*, in Jacques Paul Migne, ed., *Patrologiae cursus completus, Series Latina*, CCXII (Paris, 1853), col. 70ff. See Janet Knapp, "Polyphony at Notre Dame of Paris," in R. Crocker and D. Hiley, eds., *The New Oxford History of Music*, Vol. II (2nd ed., Oxford and New York: Oxford University Press, 1990), pp. 561–62.

3 See C. Wright: "Leoninus: Poet and Musician," *JAMS* XXXIX (1986): 1–35.

4 See Anna Maria Busse Berger, "Mnemotechnics and Notre Dame Polyphony," *Journal of Musicology* XIV (1996): 263–98.

5 Wright, "Leoninus: Poet and Musician," p. 19.

6 John of Afflighem (a.k.a. John of Cotton), *De Musica*, trans. Warren Babb, in *Hucbald, Guido and John on Music*, ed. Claude Palisca (New Haven and London: Yale University Press, 1978), p. 105.

7 Alexander de Villa-Dei, *Doctrinale* (1199), trans. Anna Maria Busse Berger in "Mnemotechnics and Notre Dame Polyphony," p. 279.

8 Franco of Cologne, *Ars cantus mensurabilis*, Chap. 11, as translated in Oliver Strunk, *Source Readings in Music History* (New York: Norton, 1950), p. 155.

CHAPTER 7: MUSIC FOR AN INTELLECTUAL AND POLITICAL ELITE

1 An English translation is available: Johannes de Grocheio, *Concerning Music*, trans. Albert Seay (2nd ed., Colorado Springs: Colorado College Music Press, 1974).

2 Grocheio, *Concerning Music*, trans. Seay, p. 16.

3 See Christopher Page, *The Owl and the Nightingale: Musical Life and Ideas in France, 1100–1300* (Berkeley and Los Angeles: University of California Press, 1989), pp. 19–25.

4 Grocheio, *Concerning Music*, trans. Seay, p. 16.

5 Page, *The Owl and the Nightingale*, p. 172.

6 Richard Crocker, "French Polyphony of the Thirteenth Century," in R. Crocker and D. Hiley, eds., *The New Oxford History of Music*, Vol. II (2nd ed., Oxford and New York: Oxford University Press, 1990), p. 639.

7 Grocheio, *Concerning Music*, trans. Seay, p. 26.

8 Peire d'Alvernhe, quoted in H. J. Chaytor, *The Troubadours* (1912; rpt. Port Washington, N.Y.: Kennikat Press, 1970), p. 36.

CHAPTER 8: BUSINESS MATH, POLITICS, AND PARADISE: THE *ARS NOVA*

1 John of Tewkesbury, *Quatuor principlaia musice* (1351); see M. Bent, "Vitry, Phillipe de," in *New Grove Dictionary of Music and Musicians*, Vol. XXVI (2nd ed., New York: Grove, 2001), p. 804.

2 Maistre Nicole Oresme, *Livre de Politiques d'Aristote*, ed. A. D. Menut (Philadelphia: American Philosophical Society, 1970), p. 347; quoted in Julie E. Cumming, "Concord Out of Discord: Occasional Motets of the Eearly Quattrocento" (Ph.D. diss., University of California at Berkeley, 1987), p. 14.

3 See Anna Maria Busse Berger, *Mensuration and Proportion Signs: Origin and Evolution* (Oxford: Clarendon Press, 1993), Chap. 2.

4 Jacobus de Liège, *Speculum musicae*, Book VII, Chap. 43, trans. R. Taruskin.

5 *De musica libellus* (Anonymous 7), in Coussemaker, *Scriptorum de musica medii aevi nova series*, Vol. I (4 vols., Paris, 1864–76), no. 7.

6 Aegidius of Murino, *Tractatus cantus mensurabilis*, in Coussemaker, *Scriptorum de musica medii aevi nova series*, Vol. III, pp. 124–5; trans. R. Taruskin in *Music in the Western World*, pp. 66–67.

7 Aegidius of Murino in Coussemaker, *Scriptorum*, Vol. III, p. 125.

8 Gary Tomlinson, *Music in Renaissance Magic* (Chicago: University of Chicago Press, 1993), p. 46.

9 Peter M. Lefferts, *The Motet in England in the Fourteenth Century* (Ann Arbor: UMI Research Press, 1986), p. 186.

10 Cumming, "Concord Out of Discord," p. 173.

11 C. Wright, "Dufay's *Nuper rosarum flores*, King Solomon's Temple, and the Veneration of the Virgin," *JAMS* XLVII (1994): 395–441.

12 Giannozzo Manetti, quoted in G. Dufay, *Opera omnia*, ed. Heinrich Besseler, Vol. II (Rome: American Institute of Musicology, 1966), xxvii.

13 Cumming, "Concord Out of Discord," pp. 83–4.

CHAPTER 9: MACHAUT AND HIS PROGENY

1 The translation is by H. E. Wooldridge, in *The Oxford History of Music*, Vol. I (Oxford: Oxford University Press, 1901), pp. 294–96.

2 Ann Walters Robertson, "The Mass of Guillaume de Machauit in the Cathedral of Reims," in *Plainsong in the Age of Polyphony*, ed. T. Kelly (Cambridge: Cambridge University Press, 1992), pp. 100–39.

3 See Chistopher Page, "Machaut's 'Pupil' Deschamps on the Performance of Music," *Early Music* V (1977): 484–91.

4 See Ursula Günther, "Die Anwendung der Diminution in der Handschrift Chantilly 1047," *Archiv für Musikwissenschaft* XVII (1960): 1–21.

CHAPTER 10: "PLEASANT PLACE": MUSIC OF THE TRECENTO

1 Michael Long, "Trecento Italy," in *Antiquity and the Middle Ages*, ed. J. McKinnon, *Music and Society*, Vol. I (Englewood Cliffs: Prentice Hall, 1991), p. 241.

2 Kurt von Fischer, "'Portraits' von Piero, Giovanni da Firenze und Jacopo da Bologna in einer Bologneser-Handschrift des 14. Jahrhunderts?" *Musica Disciplina* XXVII (1973): 61–64.

3 *Capitulum de vocibus applicatis verbis* (ca. 1315), quoted in Long, "Trecento Italy," p. 248.

4 Long, "Trecento Italy," p. 253.

5 Michael Long, "Landini's Musical Patrimony: A Reassessment of Some Compositional Conventions in Trecento Polyphony," *JAMS* XL (1987): 31.

6 *The Decameron of Giovanni Boccaccio*, trans. Richard Aldington (Garden City, N.Y.: Garden City Publishing, 1930), p. 329 (Sixth Day, Fifth Tale).

7 Michael Long, "Francesco Landini and the Florentine Cultural Elite," *Early Music History* III (1983): 87.

8 Othmar Luscinius, *Musurgia seu praxis musicae* (Strasbourg, 1536), quoted in Jessie Ann Owens, "Music Historiography and the Definition of 'Renaissance,'" *MLA Notes* XLVII (1990–91): 307.

9 Johannes Tinctoris, *Liber de arte contrapuncti* (1477), as translated in Oliver Strunk, *Source Readings in Music History* (New York: Norton, 1950), p. 199.

10 Cosimo Bartoli, *Ragionamenti Accademici* (1567), quoted in Owens, "Music Historiography," p. 311.

11 Renhard Strohm, *The Rise of European Music 1380–1500* (Cambridge: Cambridge University Press, 1993), p. 541.

CHAPTER 11: ISLAND AND MAINLAND

1 Frank L. Harrison, *Music in Medieval Britain* (2nd ed., London: Routledge and Kegan Paul, 1963), p. 144.

2 Walter Odington, *De speculatione Musicae*, in Coussemaker, *Scriptorum*, Vol. I, p. 245, trans. R. Taruskin.

3 See *New Grove Dictionary of Music and Musicians* (2nd ed., New York: Grove, 2001), s.v. "Pycard."

4 Margaret Bent, "Roy Henry," in *New Grove Dictionary of Music and Musicians* (London: Macmillan, 1980).

5 John Stevens, "Carol," in *New Grove Dictionary of Music and Musicians* (1980).

6 Tinctoris, *Proportionale musices* (ca. 1476), as translated in Oliver Strunk, *Source Readings* (New York: Norton, 1950), p. 195.

7 Manfred Bukofzer, "English Church Music of the Fifteenth Century," *New Oxford History of Music*, Vol. III (London and New York: Oxford University Press, 1960), p. 185.

8 Natalie Zemon Davis, foreword to Christine de Pizan, *The Book of the City of Ladies*, trans. Earl Jeffrey Richards (New York: Persea Books, 1998), p. xi.

9 The strongest exponent of this view, both in scholarship and (with his ensemble, Gothic Voices) in performance, has been Christopher Page. See his *Voices and Instruments of the Middle Ages* (London: Dent, 1986). For a stimulating and wide-ranging critique of the attendant debate, see Daniel Leech-Wilkinson, *The Modern Invention of Medieval Music* (Cambridge: Cambridge University Press, 2002).

Chapter 12: Emblems and Dynasties

1 Manfred F. Bukofzer, *Studies in Medieval and Renaissance Music* (New York: Norton, 1950), p. 217.

2 Michael Long, "Celestial Motion and Musical Structure in the Late Middle Ages," unpublished paper (1995), by kind courtesy of the author.

3 Charles Burney, *A General History of Music*, ed. Frank Mercer (New York: Dover, 1957), Vol. I, p. 731.

4 See Craig Wright, *The Maze and the Warrior: Symbols in Architecture, Theology, and Music* (Cambridge: Harvard University Press, 2001), Chap. 7, "Sounds and Symbols of an Armed Man."

5 Nigel Wilkins, *Music in the Time of Chaucer* (Cambridge: D. S. Brewer), p. 128.

6 See William F. Prizer, "Music and Ceremonial in the Low Countries: Philip the Fair and the Order of the Golden Fleece," *Early Music History* V (1985): 113–53.

7 Bukofzer, *Studies in Medieval and Renaissance Music*, p. 217.

8 Craig Wright, "Dufay at Cambrai: Discoveries and Revisions," *JAMS* XXVIII (1975): 217.

9 Alejandro Planchart, "Fifteenth-Century Masses: Notes on Performance and Chronology," *Studi musicali* X (1981): 17.

Chapter 13: Middle and Low

1 Frank L. Harrison, *Music in Medieval Britain* (2nd ed., London: Routledge and Kegan Paul, 1963), p. 328.

2 Tinctoris, *Proportionale musices*, in Oliver Strunk, *Source Readings in Music History* (New York: Norton, 1950), p. 195.

3 David S. Josephson, *John Taverner: Tudor Composer* (Ann Arbor: UMI Research Press, 1979), p. 124.

4 Franchinus Gaffurius, *Tractatus practicabilium proportionum* (ca. 1482), published as Book IV of *Practica musice* (Milan, 1496).

5 Tinctoris, *De inventione et usu musice* (Naples: Nathias Moravus, ca. 1482), ed. K. Weinmann: *Johannes Tinctoris und sein unbekannter Traktat 'De inventione et usu musicae'* (Regensburg, 1917), p. 31.

6 Bonnie J. Blackburn, "A Lost Guide to Tinctoris's Teachings Recovered," *Early Music History* I (1981): 45.

CHAPTER 14: JOSQUIN AND THE HUMANISTS

1 Charles Burney, *A General History of Music*, Vol. I, ed. Frank Mercer (New York: Dover, 1957), p. 752.

2 Martin Luther, *Table Talk* (1538), quoted in Helmut Osthoff, *Josquin Desprez*, Vol. II (Tutzing: H. Schneider, 1965), p. 9.

3 Sebald Heyden, *Musica, id est Artis canendi* (Nuremberg, 1537), p. 2.

4 Frank Tirro, "Spataro (Spadario), Giovanni," in *New Grove Dictionary of Music and Musicians*, Vol. XVII (London: Macmillan, 1980), p. 819.

5 Trans. Edward E. Lowinsky in "Musical Genius: Evolution and Origins of a Concept," *Musical Quarterly* L (1964): 481.

6 The phrase has been traced back to a seventh-century commentary on Horace's *Ars Poetica* by William Ringler in "*Poeta Nascitur Non Fit*: Some Notes on the History of an Aphorism," *Journal of the History of Ideas* II (1941): 497–504. It became a commonplace in the sixteenth century.

7 Quoted by Burney in *A General History* (ed. Mercer), Vol. I, p. 752.

8 Trans. Edward E. Lowinsky, in E. Lowinsky and Bonnie J. Blackburn, *Josquin des Prez*, trans. Edward E. Lowinsky (London: Oxford University Press, 1976), p. 682.

9 Glareanus, *Dodekachordon* (Basle, 1547), p. 441.

10 Osthoff, *Josquin Desprez*, Vol. II, 39.

11 L. Matthews and P. Merkley, "Iudochus de Picardia and Jossequin Lebloitte dit Desprez: The Names of the Singer(s)," *Journal of Musicology* XVI (1998): 200–226.

12 C. Sartori, "Josquin des Prés, cantore del duomo di Milano (1459–1472)," *Annales Musicologiques* IV (1956): 55–83.

13 See Emond vander Straeten, *La Musique aux Pays-Bas avant le XIXe Siècle*, Vol. VI (Brussels: G.-A. van Trigt, 1882; rpt., New York: Dover, 1969), 79n.

14 Letter from Gian di Artiganova to Hercules of Ferrara, 2 September 1502, in Osthoff, *Josquin Desprez*, Vol. I (Tutzing: H. Schneider, 1962), 211–12. For a translation of the full text of the letter, see Piero Weiss and Richard Taruskin, *Music in the Western World: A History in Documents* (New York: Schirmer, 1984), p. 99.

15 Girolamo da Sestola (alias "il Coglia"), letter to Hercules of Ferrara, 14 August 1502, quoted and translated in Lewis Lockwood, *Music in Renaissance Ferrara, 1400–1505* (Cambridge: Harvard University Press, 1984), p. 203.

16 Lockwood, *Music in Renaissance Ferrara*, p. 204.

17 Gioseffo Zarlino, *Le istitutioni harmoniche*, Vol. III (Venice, 1558), p. 66.

18 Herbert Kellman, "Josquin and the Courts of the Netherlands and France: The Evidence of the Sources," in Lowinsky and Blackburn, *Josquin des Prez*, p. 208.

19 For a study of this in-between genre see J. Peter Burkholder, "Johannes Martini and the Imitation Mass of the Late Fifteenth Century," *JAMS* XXXVIII (1985): 470–523.

20 Edward E. Lowinsky, "The Concept of Physical and Musical Space in the Renaissance," *Papers of the American Musicological Society* (1941): 57–84; rpt. in E. Lowinsky, *Music in the Culture of the Renaissance and Other Essays*, ed. Bonnie J.

Blackburn (Chicago: University of Chicago Press, 1989), pp. 6–18 (quote is on p. 11).

21 E. Lowinsky, "On the Use of Scores by Sixteenth-Century Musicians," *JAMS* I (1948): 21 (rpt. in *Music in the Culture of the Renaissance*, p. 800).

22 T. Noblitt, "Die Datierung der Handschrift Mus. Ms. 3154 der Staatsbibliothek Munchen," *Die Musikforschung* XXVII (1974): 36–56.

23 Jeremy Noble, "Josquin Desprez," in *The New Grove Dictionary of Music and Musicians*, Vol. IX (London: Macmillan, 1980), p. 719.

24 Lowinsky, "The Concept of Physical and Musical Space in the Renaissance," in *Music in the Culture of the Renaissance*, p. 12.

25 The point was made first by T. Elizabeth Cason in an unpublished paper ("The Dating of MS Munich 3154 Revisited") presented at Duke University in 1999, and later elaborated by Joshua Rifkin in "Munich, Milan, and a Marian Motet: Dating Josquin's *Ave Maria . . . virgo serena*," *JAMS* LVI (2003): 239–350.

Chapter 15: A Perfected Art

1 Giovanni Santi, *Cronaca rimata* (1490), l.424–26.

2 *The Columbia Encyclopedia*, s.v. "Raphael" (6th ed., New York: Columbia University Press, 2001).

3 Gioseffo Zarlino, *Istitutione harmoniche* (Venice, 1558), Vol. I, *Proemio*; quoted in Jessie Ann Owens, "Music Historiography and the Definition of 'Renaissance,'" *MLA Notes* XLVII (1990–91): 314.

4 Zarlino, *The Art of Counterpoint* (*Istitutione harmoniche*, Vol. III), trans. G. Marco and C. Palisca (New York: Norton, 1968), p. 289.

5 Zarlino, *On the Modes* (*Istitutione harmoniche*, Vol. IV), trans. V. Cohen (New Haven: Yale University Press), p. 102.

6 Zarlino, *On the Modes*, p. 104.

7 Zarlino, *The Art of Counterpoint*, p. 70.

8 Pierre de Ronsard, *Livre des mélanges*, in Ronsard, *Oeuvres complètes*, ed. P. Laumonier (Paris, 1914–19), Vol. VII, p. 20.

9 Glareanus, *Dodekachordon* (Basel, 1547), p. 450.

10 Hermann Finck, *Practica musica . . . exempla variorum signorum, proportionum et canonum, iudicium de tonis, ac quaedam de arte suaviter et artificiose cantandi continens* (Wittenberg, 1556), quoted in George Nugent with Eric Jas, "Gombert," *The New Grove Dictionary of Music and Musicians* (2nd ed., New York: Grove, 2001), Vol. X, p. 119.

11 Joseph Kerman, "On William Byrd's *Emendemus in melius*," *Musical Quarterly* XLIX (1963): 435.

12 Edward Lowinsky, *Secret Chromatic Art in the Netherlands Motet* (New York: Columbia University Press, 1946).

13 Zarlino, *The Art of Counterpoint*, p. 151.

14 Gary Tomlinson, *Music in Renaissance Magic* (Chicago: University of Chicago Press, 1993), p. 113.

15 Jacques Descartes de Ventemille, quoted in Pontus de Tyard, *Solitaire second ou prose de la musique* (1555), trans. Joel Newman in "Francesco Canova da Milano" (Master's thesis, New York University, 1942), p. 11.

16 Translation adapted from Peter Farrell, "Diego Ortiz's *Tratado de Glosas*," *Journal of the Viola da Gamba Society of America* IV (1967): 9.

CHAPTER 16: THE END OF PERFECTION

1 Raphael Molitor, *Die nach-Tridentinische Choral-Reform zu Rom*, Vol. I (Leipzig: F. E. C. Leukart, 1901), p. 297. The complete document is translated in Piero Weiss and Richard Taruskin, *Music in the Western World* (New York: Schirmer, 1984), p. 139.

2 Cosimo Bartoli, *Ragionamenti accademici* (Venice, 1567), Vol. III, f.35'; trans. Jessie Ann Owens in "Music Historiography and the Definition of 'Renaissance,'" *MLA Notes* XLVII (1990–91): 311.

3 Letter from Cirillo Franco to Ugolino Gualteruzzi, trans. Lewis Lockwood in *The Counter-Reformation and the Masses of Vincenzo Ruffo* (Venice: Fondazione Giorgio Cini, 1970), p. 129.

4 Trans. Lewis Lockwood, in Palestrina, *Pope Marcellus Mass* (Norton Critical Scores; New York: Norton, 1975), p. 26.

5 Trans. Lewis Lockwood, in Palestrina, *Pope Marcellus Mass*, p. 18.

6 Trans. Lewis Lockwood, in Palestrina, *Pope Marcellus Mass*, pp. 22–23.

7 Trans. Gustave Reese, in *Music in the Renaissance* (rev. ed.; New York: Norton, 1959), p. 449.

8 Trans. Lewis Lockwood, in Palestrina, *Pope Marcellus Mass*, p. 21.

9 Trans. Lewis Lockwood, in Palestrina, *Pope Marcellus Mass*, pp. 21–22.

10 Agostino Agazzari, *Del sonare sopra il basso con tutti gli stromenti*, trans. Oliver Strunk, in *Source Readings in Music History* (New York: Norton, 1950), p. 430.

11 Giuseppe Baini, *Memorie storico-critiche della vita e delle opera di Giovanni Pierluigi da Palestrina* (Rome, 1828), p. 216; trans. Lewis Lockwood, in Palestrina, *Pope Marcellus Mass*, p. 35.

12 Luigi Barzini, *The Italians* (New York: Atheneum, 1964), p. 308.

13 Artur Schopenhauer, *Parerga and Paralipomena* (1851), 2:§52.

14 Johann Joseph Fux, *Gradus ad Parnassum, Sive Manuductio ad Compositionem Muscae Regularum, etc.* (Vienna: Typis Joannis Petri van Ghelen, 1725), p. 278.

15 London, British Library, MS Harley 1419; transcribed in F. W. Galpin, *Old English Instruments of Music* (London, 1910), pp. 292–94.

16 Lincoln Cathedral Injunctions, 14 April 1548; quoted in Peter Le Huray, *Music and the Reformation in England, 1549–1660* (New York: Oxford University Press, 1967), p. 9.

17 Richard Charteris, *Alfonso Ferrabosco the Elder (1543–1588): A Thematic Catalogue of His Music with a Biographical Calendar* (New York, 1984), p. 14.

18 Memoir of Elizabeth Hastings, Lady Somerset and Countess of Worcester (http://www.kugelblitz.co.uk/StGeorge/Documents/2002%20biographies.pdf).

19 Ferdinand Richardson, "In Eandem Thomae Tallisii, et Guilielmi Birdi Musicam," *Cantiones, Quae ab Argumento Sacrae Vocantur* (London, 1575), facsimile edition (Leeds: Boethius Press, 1976), n.p.

20 See Joseph Kerman, "Old and New in Byrd's *Cantiones Sacrae*, in *Essays on Opera and English Music in Honour of Sir Jack Westrup*, ed. F. W. Sternfeld, N. Fortune, and E. Olleson (Oxford: Blackwell, 1975), pp. 25–43.

21 Joseph Kerman, *The Masses and Motets of William Byrd* (Berkeley and Los Angeles: University of California Press, 1981), p. 188.

22 Dedication of *Gradualia*, Book I (1605) to King James I, adapted from Oliver Strunk, *Source Readings in Music History* (New York: Norton, 1950), p. 328.

23 See Joseph Kerman, "Byrd's Settings of the Ordinary of the Mass," *JAMS* XXXII (1979): 416–17.

CHAPTER 17: COMMERCIAL AND LITERARY MUSIC

1 Daniel Heartz, *Pierre Attaingnant, Royal Printer of Music* (Berkeley and Los Angeles: University of California Press, 1969), p. 107.

2 Thomas Morley, *A Plain and Easy Introduction to Practical Music*, ed. Alec Harman (New York: Norton, 1973), p. 9.

3 James Haar, *Essays on Italian Poetry and Music in the Renaissance, 1350–1600* (Berkeley and Los Angeles: University of California Press, 1986), p. 32.

4 Baldesar Castiglione, *The Book of the Courtier*, trans. Charles S. Singleton (Garden City, N.Y.: Doubleday [Anchor Books], 1959), p. 60.

5 Haar, *Essays on Italian Poetry and Music*, p. 36.

6 H. M. Brown, *Music in the Renaissance* (Englewood Cliffs, N.J.: Prentice-Hall, 1976), p. 213.

7 Roger Wangermée, *Flemish Music*, trans. R. E. Wolf (New York: F. Praeger, 1968), p. 134.

8 Ronsard, *Livre des mélanges* (2nd ed., 1572), in Oliver Strunk, *Source Readings in Music History* (New York: Norton, 1950), p. 289.

9 Alfons Kurfess, "Christian Sibyllines," in E. Hennecke, *New Testament Apocrypha* (Philadelphia, 1965); quoted in Peter Bergquist, "The Poems of Orlando di Lasso's *Prophetiae Sibyllarum* and Their Sources," *JAMS* XXXII (1979): 521.

10 For the main revisionist account see James Haar and Iain Fenlon, *The Italian Madrigal in the Early Sixteenth Century: Sources and Interpretation* (Cambridge and New York: Cambridge University Press, 1988).

11 Haar, *Essays on Italian Poetry and Music*, p. 74.

12 G. M. Artusi, *L'Artusi, ovvero, Delle imperfezioni della moderna musica* (Venice, 1600), in Strunk, *Source Readings*, p. 394.

13 Alfonso Fontanelli to Duke Alfonso II of Ferrara, 18 February 1594; in Glenn Watkins, *Gesualdo: The Man and His Music* (Chapel Hill: University of North Carolina Press, 1973), pp. 245–46.

14 Haar, *Essays on Italian Poetry and Music*, p. 144.

15 Lorenzo Bianconi, "Gesualdo," *New Grove Dictionary of Music and Musicians* (rev. ed., New York: Grove, 2001), Vol. IX, p. 783.

16 Bianconi, "Gesualdo," p. 781.

17 Morley, *A Plain and Easy Introduction*, ed. Harman, p. 293.

18 Joseph Kerman, *The Elizabethan Madrigal: A Comparative Study* (American Musico-logical Society: Studies and Documents, no. 4, 1962), p. 217.

19 Kerman, *The Elizabethan Madrigal*, p. 220.

CHAPTER 18: REFORMATIONS AND COUNTER REFORMATIONS

1 This remark is reliably attributed to the English Methodist preacher Rowland Hill (1744–1833; see *The Oxford Dictionary of Quotations*, 3rd ed. [New York: Oxford University Press, 1979]), only by tradition to Luther. It is resisted by many modern Lutherans. In the January 1997 issue of *Concordia Theological Journal*, Dr. James L. Brauer offered a $25 reward to any Luther scholar who could find the quote about the devil's tunes in Luther's works (see James Tiefel, "The Devil's Tavern Tunes," Commission on Worship website, www.wels.net/worship/art-104.html).

2 Trans. Ulrich S. Leupold, in *Luther's Works*, LIII (Philadelphia: Fortress Press, 1965), pp. 323–24.

3 *D. Martin Luthers Werke: Tischreden*, ed. E. Kroker (Weimar, 1912–21), no. 968 (table conversation recorded 17 December 1538).

4 Martin Luther, preface to J. Walther, *Geystliches gesangk Buchleyn* (Wittenberg, 1524).

5 *The Spiritual Exercises of Ignatius Loyola*, Article XIII, trans. W. H. Longridge (London: Burns and Oates, 1908), p. 119.

6 St. Teresa of Avila, *Vida* (1565), in René Fülöp-Miller, *Saints That Moved the World* (New York: Grosset and Dunlap, 1945), p. 375.

7 Adriano Banchieri, *Conclusioni nel suono dell'organo* (Bologna, 1609), in Frank T. Arnold, *The Art of Accompaniment from a Thorough-Bass* (London: Oxford University Press, 1931), p. 74.

8 Trans. Gustave Reese, in *Music in the Renaissance* (rev. ed., New York: W. W. Norton, 1959), p. 449.

9 *Coryat's Crudities; hastily gobled up in five moneths travels* (London, 1611), p. 251.

CHAPTER 19: PRESSURE OF RADICAL HUMANISM

1 Girolamo Mei, letter to Vincenzo Galilei (8 May 1572), trans. Claude V. Palisca in *The Florentine Camerata: Documentary Studies and Translations* (New Haven: Yale University Press, 1989), p. 63.

2 Vincenzo Galilei, *Dialogo della musica antica e della moderna*, ed. Favio Fano (Milan: A. Minuziano, 1947), pp. 130–31.

3 Plato, *Republic*, 399a-c, trans. Edith Hamilton and Huntington Cairns, *The Collected Dialogues of Plato Including theLetters* (New York: Pantheon Books, 1961), pp. 643–44.

4 Galilei, *Dialogo*, p. 162.

5 Giulio Caccini, preface to *Le nuove musiche* (1601), ed. Angelo Solerti, in *Le origini del melodrama: Testimonianze dei contemporanei* (Turin: Fratelli Bocca, 1903), p. 56, trans. Piero Weiss in Piero Weiss and Richard Taruskin, *Music in the Western World: A History in Documents* (New York: Schirmer, 1984), p. 170.

6 Piero Weiss, review of W. Kirkendale, *L'Aria di Fiorenza, id est Il Ballo del Gran Duca* (Florence, 1972), *Musical Quarterly* LIX (1973): 474.

7 Caccini, preface to *Le nuove musiche*, trans. Piero Weiss in *Music in the Western World*, p. 170.

8 Caccini, preface to *Le nuove musiche*, trans. John Playford in *A Breefe Introduction to the Skill of Musick* (London, 1654), in Oliver Strunk, *Source Readings in Music History* (New York: Norton, 1950), p. 382.

9 Marco da Gagliano, letter to Prince Ferdinando Gonzaga, 20 August 1607; quoted in Edmond Strainchamps, "New Light on the Accademia degli Elevati of Florence," *Musical Quarterly* LXII (1976): 508.

10 Claude Palisca, "The Alterati of Florence, Pioneers in the Theory of Dramatic Music," in W. Austin, ed., *New Looks at Italian Opera: Essays in Honor of Donald J. Grout* (Ithaca: Cornell University Press, 1968), p. 10.

11 Marco da Gagliano, Preface to *La Dafne*, trans. Piero Weiss, in *Music in the Western World*, p. 176.

12 Peri, Preface to *Euridice*, in Solerti, in *Le origini del melodrama: Testimonianze*, p. 44.

13 See C. Abbate, *Unsung Voices: Opera and Musical Narrative in the Nineteenth Century* (Princeton: Princeton University Press, 1991).

14 Giulio Cesare Monteverdi, "Declaration" (Postface to Claudio Monteverdi, *Scherzi musicali* (Venice, 1607)).

Art Credits

6-7b Firenze, Biblioteca Medicea Laurenziana ms. Plut. 29.1, cc. 415v. Su concessione del Ministero per i Beni e le Attività Culturali. E'vietata ogni ulteriore riproduzione con qualsiasi mezzo.

7-1 Bibliothèque Nationale, Paris, MS fr. 2608, fol. 295v. © Giraudon/Art Resource, NY.

7-2a Wolfenbuttel, Herzog August Bibliothek MS. Guelf 1099, fols. 16v – 17.

7-2b Wolfenbuttel, Herzog August Bibliothek MS. Guelf 1099, fols. 146v – 147.

7-3 Staatsbibliothek Bamberg, Msc. Lit. 115, fols. 15v-16r.

7-4 Wolfenbuttel, Herzog August Bibliothek MS. Guelf 1099, fols. 136 – 136v.

7-5 Staatsbibliothek Bamberg, Msc. Lit. 115, fols. 7r – 7v.

7-6 Staatsbibliothek Bamberg, Msc. Lit. 115, fols. 63v – 64r.

7-7 Staatsbibliothek Bamberg, Msc. Lit. 115, fol. 52v.

7-8 Staatsbibliothek Bamberg, Msc. Lit. 115, fol. 14v.

7-9 Montpellier, Bibliothèque Inter-Universaire, section Médecine, H196, fols. 368v – 69.

7-10 Montpellier, Bibliothèque Inter-Universaire, section Médecine, H196, fol. 273.

8-1 Harmonic proportions according to Jehan des Murs.

8-2 Ars nova notation.

8-3 cliché Bibliothèque nationale de France.

8-4 Ivrea, Biblioteca Capitolare, MS 115, fols. 15v – 16.

8-5 Lorenzo d'Alessandro, S. Maria di Piazza, Sarnano, ©Alinari/Art Resource, NY.

9-1 Bibliothèque Nationale, Fonds Francais 22545 – 22 546, ca. 1390, © Snark/Art Resource, NY.

9-2 Antonio Ronzen, Ste. Madeleine, ca. 1520, Saint Maximin, © Giraudon/Art Resource, NY.

9-3 © Foto Marburg/Art Resource, NY.

9-4 cliché Bibliothèque nationale de France.

9-5 Modena, Biblioteca Estense, MS α.M.5.24, fol. 34v.

9-6 Limbourg Brothers, Musée Condé, Chantilly, 1416, MS 65, fol. 52r, © Réunion des Musées Nationaux/Art Resource, NY.

10-1 Fulda, Landesbibliothek, MS D. 23, fol. 302.

10-2 Firenze, Biblioteca Medicea Laurenziana ms. Med. Palat. 87, c. 1r. Su concessione del Ministero per i Beni e le Attività Culturali. E'vietata ogni ulteriore riproduzione con qualsiasi mezzo.

10-3 Firenze, Biblioteca Medicea Laurenziana ms. Med. Palat. 87, c. 7v. Su concessione del Ministero per i Beni e le Attività Culturali. E'vietata ogni ulteriore riproduzione con qualsiasi mezzo.

10-4   Firenze, Biblioteca Medicea Laurenziana ms. Med. Palat. 87, c. 121v.
       Su concessione del Ministero per i Beni e le Attività Culturali.
       E'vietata ogni ulteriore riproduzione con qualsiasi mezzo.

10-5   Giotto di Bondone, Scrovegni Chapel, Padua, ©
       Cameraphoto/Art Resource, NY.

11-1   British Library, MS Harley 978.

11-2   Universitetsbiblioteket, Uppsala, MS C 233, fols. 19–20.

11-3   Musée de la Tapisserie, Bayeux, © Erich Lessing/Art Resource, NY.

11-4   British Museum, London, © Snark/Art Resource, NY.

11-5   Civico Museo Bibliografico Musicale, Bologna.

11-6   Bibliothèque Nationale, Paris, 1451, MS fr. 12476, fol. 98, ©
       Bridgeman-Giraudon/Art Resource, NY.

11-7   British Library, London, Harley 4431, fol. 4, © Art Resource, NY.

12-1   Valencia, Biblioteca Universitaria.

12-2   cliché Bibliothèque nationale de France.

12-3   © Brussels, Royal Library of Belgium, B-Br 5557, fol. 48v.

12-4   © Biblioteca Apostolica Vaticana.

12-5   Library of Congress.

12-6   Library of Congress.

12-7   Anonymous, Châteaux de Versailles et de Trianon, Versailles, ©
       Réunion des Musées Nationaux/Art Resource, NY.

12-8   Naples, Biblioteca Nazionale, MS VI E.40, fol. 58v.

13-1   Adaption of Du Fay's rebus signature.

13-2   © Alinari/Art Resource, NY.

13-3   Bildarchiv d. ÖNB, Wien.

13-4   Ottavio Vannini, Museo degli Argenti, Palazzo Pitti, Florence, ©
       Scala/Art Resource, NY.

14-1   Jean Perreal, Le Puy, © Réunion des Musées
       Nationaux/Art Resource, NY.

14-2   Kunstmuseum, Basel.

14-3   Bildarchiv d. ÖNB, Wien.

14-4   Hans Schwarz, Kupferstichkabinett, Staatliche Museen zu Berlin,
       Berlin, © Bildarchiv Preussischer Kulturbesitz/Art Resource, NY.

14-5   Andrea Sansovino, 1507–1509, S. Maria del Popolo, Rome, ©
       Alinari/Art Resource, NY.

15-1   Raphael, ca. 1510, *The Alba Madonna*, Andrew W. Mellon
       Collections, Image ©2004 Board of Trustees, National Gallery of
       Art, Washington.

15-2   Civico Museo Bibliografico Musicale, Bologna.

15-3   Civico Museo Bibliografico Musicale, Bologna.

15-4   © Art Resource/Art Resource, NY.

15-5   © Alinari/Art Resource, NY.

15-6   Jacques Buus, *Intabolatura d'Organo di Recercari, Libro primo*, Venice, 1549. Reproduced from *Musik in Geschichte und Gegenwart*. Kassel: Bärenreiter-Verlag, 1949–1986, s.v. "Ricercar."

15-7   Royal College of Physicians, London.

15-8   Loyset Liedet, Ms. 5073, fol.117v, Bibliothèque de l'Arsenal, Paris, © Giraudon/Art Resource, NY.

16-1a   Bayerische Staatsbibliothek München, Musikabteilung.

16-2b   © Biblioteca Apostolica Vaticana.

16-2   Theatermuseum der Universität zu Köln.

16-3   Civico Museo Bibliografico Musicale, Bologna, © Scala/Art Resource, NY.

16-4a   Hans Holbein the Younger, Galleria Nazionale d'Arte Antica, Rome, © Scala/Art Resource, NY.

16-4b   Marcus Gheerhaerts, © Snark/Art Resource, NY.

16-5   Bodleian Library.

16-6   Bibliothèque National, Paris, © Giraudon/Art Resource, NY.

17-1a   By courtesy of the Plaint Museum, Antwerp.

17-1b   Paris, Bibliothèque Mazarine, Rés 30345 A.

17-2   Bildarchiv d. ÖNB, Wien.

17-3   Metropolitan Museum of Art, The Crosby Brown Collection of Musical Instruments. (01.2.527).

17-4   Bayerische Staatsbibliothek München, Musikabteilung, Mielan Codex, D-Mbs Mus. MS. AII, fol. 187.

17-5   Michelangelo, Sistine Chapel, Vatican Palace, Vatican State, © Scala/Art Resource, NY.

17-6   Anonymous, Kunsthistoriches Museum, Wien.

17-7   Museo Civico Medievale, Bologna.

17-8   Paolo Veronese, Louvre, Paris, © Réunion des Musées Nationaux/Art Resource, NY.

18-1   Library of Congress.

18-2   From Joseph Klug, *Geistliche Lieder auffs new gebessert* (Wittenberg, 1533). Stiftung Luthergedenkstätten in Sachsen-Anhalt, Lutherhalle, Wittenberg.

18-3   Library of Congress.

18-4   Gian Lorenzo Bernini, Cornaro Chapel, S. Maria della Vittoria, Rome, © Alinari/Art Resource, NY.

18-5   Reproduced from Jane Bernstein, *Print Culture and Music in Sixteenth-century Venice*. New York: Oxford University Press, 2001.

18-6   Matteo Pagani, after Titian, The Metropolitan Museum of Art, The Elisha Whittelsey Collection, The Elisha Whittelsey Fund, 1949 (49.95.139g).

19-1   cliché Bibliothèque nationale de France.

19-2   Ventura Salimbeni, Archivio di Stato, Siena, ©
        Alinari/Art Resource, NY.

19-3   © By concession of the Ministero per i Beni e le Attivatà Culturali
        della Repubblica Italiana. Firenze. BNCF. Pal C.B.3.53 c.6r.

19-4   Library of Congress.

19-5   Library of Congress.

19-6   Library of Congress.

19-7   Civico Museo Bibliografico Musicale, Bologna.

19-8   Civico Museo Bibliografico Musicale, Bologna.